SUPERVISION

A Collaborative Approach to Instructional Improvement

Kenneth T. Henson

The Citadel

Long Grove, Illinois

For information about this book, contact:
Waveland Press, Inc.
4180 IL Route 83, Suite 101
Long Grove, IL 60047-9580
(847) 634-0081
info@waveland.com
www.waveland.com

Cover: Kenneth A. Henson, *The Object*, 2007. Mixed media on paper.

10-digit ISBN 1-57766-589-9
13-digit ISBN 978-1-57766-589-2

Printed in the United States of America

7 6 5 4 3 2 1

Contents

Preface

> *True leaders are enablers of hope in others, thereby empowering opportunities for best practices.*
>
> —G. Clarke & S. Harris, "Preparing scholar-practitioner leaders"

Instructional improvement occurs under the leadership of many individuals, and it happens in many contexts. Sometimes the school district designates a leader, often provided with a title (e.g., instructional supervisor or assistant superintendent for instruction). Some schools assign this responsibility to a department (or grade-level) head or chair. Some large schools have assistant principals for instruction. In some schools, the principal prefers this leadership to emerge from among the teaching ranks. Whatever the arrangement, the building principal is always accountable for the results. For this reason, with or without the title, in many schools the principal is the instructional supervisor.

Sometimes the help is given on a one-on-one basis (clinical supervision). At other times the help is group based. Regardless of the leadership or the context, whenever teachers receive help with improving the quality of learning in their classrooms, *instructional supervision* occurs. A special thing happens when a group of teachers collaborate to make teaching improvement their top goal. These teachers are energized because they take ownership of the responsibility for their profession.

The title of this book could have been *The Supervisor's Role in Helping Administrators and Teachers Create Understanding in an Unnatural Environment* because, although learning is a natural human behavior, the school environment, as most of us know it, is highly unnatural. Critics say that schools do little to cause learning to occur. Some even say that many characteristics of traditional schools impede and prevent in-depth learning (Wolk, 2004). By building a learning community, teachers can collaborate to change this environment by (1) aligning their school's mission and goals with their state standards and (2) working together to meet these goals. But learning is a complex process, and teachers must not bear this responsibility alone.

The author believes that all educational leaders should encourage and help teachers to form a community that is dedicated to improving teaching in their own classrooms and throughout their schools. The book is designed to help anyone whose goal is to assist others in this endeavor, providing special help for those who choose a collaborative approach.

This text is built on three themes: collaboration, constructivism, and concept learning. Its ultimate goal is to equip supervisors with the tools they need to develop a learning community in which teachers and students *collaborate* to invent knowledge. *Constructivism* is a theory upon which teachers can design an environment that facilitates the invention of knowledge (Armstrong, Henson, & Savage, 2009). A concept is a generalization that enables learners to connect facts to form ideas that can be used in varying contexts. *Concept learning* suggests that the actual learning process consists of recognizing recurring themes and drawing generalizations. Concepts are the building blocks that give each discipline its unique structure. Consider Albert Einstein's explanation of the important role that concepts play in learning:

> What precisely is "thinking"? . . .when, however, a certain (memory) picture turns up in many series, then—precisely through such return—it becomes an ordering element for such series, in that it connects series which in themselves are unconnected. Such an element becomes an instrument, a concept. I think that the transition from free association or "dreaming" to thinking is characterized by the more or less dominating role which the "concept" plays in it. (Einstein & Infield, 1938, p. 8)

Einstein believed that all learning involves seeing recurring patterns (concepts), that individual concepts can be connected to form themes, and that themes can even span across disciplines to form interdisciplinary themes. All three themes of this text complement each other. Through collaboration with their colleagues, teachers can design problems that require students to use hands-on, constructivist practices to discover the major concepts within and across disciplines with the ultimate goal of creating their own knowledge.

> Interstate School Leaders Licensure Consortium (ISLLC) Educational Leadership Policy Standard No. 4 requires today's leaders to garner the support of parents, business leaders, and other community agency leaders, helping these members to become not just contributors to the school, but active agents in learning.

The ISLLC holds leaders accountable for working with family and community members. Supervisors must learn how to promote cooperation and networking throughout the school and in the community at large, empowering teachers and others to create and sustain a learning community. This is backseat driving of the best kind, and it hinges on *collaboration*, a major theme of this book.

The Organization of the Contents

Prior to the current wave of education reform, teachers did not spend much time helping each other improve instruction (Gilbert & Smith, 2003). The purpose of this book is to advise supervisors and administrators on ways to help teachers collaborate and use concept learning and constructivism to develop a learning community. Chapter 1 offers a model for developing such a learning community.

Chapters 2 and 3 examine the history of and need for supervisors in twenty-first-century schools, highlighting the supervisor's changing role.

Teachers are special members of our society who have incredible power to impact children's lives (Williams-Boyd, 2004). The primary purpose of education reform is to improve learning, and teachers are at the center of their school's successes and failures. Chapters 4 and 5 explain how supervisors can help teachers combine the existing knowledge bases on faculty development and change, to cooperatively create and maintain a successful learning community.

The recent expanded arena of teachers and the growing knowledge base on the power of a schoolwide learning community give the supervisor's role with curriculum development unprecedented importance. Chapters 6 and 7 are written to prepare supervisors and administrators to help teachers plan and adjust the school's curriculum so that it focuses on those major concepts that are essential to inventing understanding. Chapters 8, 9, and 10 prepare supervisors to help teachers convert this curriculum into daily lessons that will use contemporary knowledge of how students learn. These chapters also provide a convincing argument for teachers to abandon traditional testing and evaluation practices in favor of assessment practices that promote learning.

Classroom management continues to be a major concern of teachers and citizens at large (Rose & Gallup, 2005), though perhaps for the wrong reason. Many beginning teachers view classroom management only as the ability to control classroom misbehavior. Educators who are committed to improving schools know that this view is shortsighted. Chapter 11 provides supervisors insight for helping teachers put a high priority on students' personal well being and their learning, and offers insight on designing a management program that supports both.

Effective teaching demands daily improvement, which requires teachers to continually reflect on daily events. Because teachers may interact with their students a thousand or more times in a single day (Good & Brophy, 2007), and because each interaction—no matter how brief—is significant (Woolfolk Hoy & Hoy, 2008), teachers may find the speed and complexity of classroom events daunting. Chapter 12 offers a variety of observation instruments to help teachers see and make sense of all these interactions.

Most teachers have not sufficiently emphasized concepts, theories, and research to facilitate the invention of understanding, either among their students or among themselves. Chapters 13 and 14 examine the roles that action research, theories, and models play in learning. These chapters will help supervisors and administrators convince their teachers to involve themselves and their students in the use of theories and action research.

Significant education reform requires money, and a recent poll (McLester, 2005) found that teachers are deeply concerned about the difficulties involved in getting grants funded. Because the development of a learning community is often expensive, and because twenty-first-century budgetary resources for education are increasingly limited, chapter 15 prepares supervisors to help teachers write grants to fund their programs.

Standards

Currently, 49 of the 50 states have established standards for student learning. The themes and content of this book have been selected to help supervisors meet the learning needs of students while meeting the required standards. Special emphasis is placed on the Interstate New Teacher Assessment and Support Consortium (INTASC) Principles, the Interstate School Leaders Licensure Consortium (ISLLC) Standards, and the Educational Leadership Constituents Council (ELCC) Standards. Links between the content and these standards and principles are cited throughout the book.

A *matrix* is provided on the following page, showing which themes and standards are addressed in each chapter. An instructor who is interested in developing the constructivist concept, for example, can quickly select those chapters that address constructivist elements; or instructors who wish to apply INTASC Principle No. 9 in their classrooms can quickly locate the chapters that address this standard.

Technology

Technology has invaded our schools with a speed that has kept teachers scrambling to familiarize themselves with the newest hardware and software. Teachers realize that, by itself, the ability to use these new technological tools will not unleash the potential needed to bring about the required level of improvement in themselves and in their students. Indeed, fewer than 10% of students report using technology to analyze or manipulate new information; most continue using it for word processing and e-mail (Ebert & Culyer, 2008). Perhaps even more disturbing is the finding in a recent study that 97% of administrators were unable to name either a state or national technology standard (Hancock, in press).

There is much reason for hope, however. Teachers in the most progressive schools are creating a seamless integration of technology that will bring a new depth of understanding to their lessons (Pitler, 2006). In many of the following chapters you will find suggestions for using technology to help teachers—first to enrich their own understanding, and then to enrich their classrooms and their entire schools, including technological tools to enhance teacher collaboration and improve their self-concepts. In each chapter, you can use your own imagination and undoubtedly think of additional ways to help teachers use technology to meet the learning mission of their school.

Themes and Standards Matrix

Chapter Number	Collaboration	Concept Development[1]	Constructivism	ISLLC[2] Standard No.	ELCC[3] Standard No.	INTASC[4] Principle No.
1	X	X		1, 2		
2	X	X	X	4		
3	X	X			5	
4	X	X			4	
5	X				1	
6	X	X	X	6		
7		X	X	1	2	
8	X	X	X		1, 2	4
9		X			3	6
10		X	X			8
11	X	X	X	3		
12		X				9
13	X		X			9
14	X	X	X			9
15	X			3		

[1] For in-depth learning
[2] Interstate School Leaders Licensure Consortium
[3] Educational Leadership Constituents Council
[4] Interstate New Teachers Assessment and Support Consortium

Chapter Structure

The full-page graphic organizers that begin each chapter illustrate the major concepts featured, giving an overall view of the chapter and showing how its topics relate to each other. The list of objectives that follow focus on the themes, concepts, and goals central to the content of each chapter.

Vignettes

Each chapter begins with a vignette that offers a "real-world" application of the major concepts presented in the chapter and serves as a frame of reference with which readers can identify. These vignettes provide supervisors with insights about how to use their knowledge of the principles presented. The appropriate supervisory reactions are sometimes contextual, depending on the particular players and the specifics of the immediate situation. The vignettes are a medium through which readers can apply the principles to their own schools. Open discussions of the vignettes can deepen the understanding of the chapter content.

Case Studies

Case studies have the power to cause deep engagement and promote critical thinking (Jacobowitz & Onore, 2004). By doing so, case studies can bridge the gap between theory and practice (Graham & Cannamore, 2006). Case studies and action research provide future administrators with opportunities to confront the complexities of potentially confusing and controversial beliefs about family and community involvement in schools (Shepherd et al., 2008). Each chapter contains a case study that links the chapter with the process of developing a learning community. A prefatory description of each case identifies its relevance and its connection with the book's three themes: constructivism, concept learning, and collaboration. These case studies were written specifically for this book by contemporary educators at universities and elementary, middle, and secondary schools. Their authors share their development of learning communities in a variety of rural, suburban, and inner-city schools located throughout the major geographic regions of the country.

Conclusion, Questions, Suggested Activities, and References

Each chapter ends with a conclusion, followed by a list of questions for discussion and reflection that further tie the chapter to the supervisor's role. Also included is a list of suggested activities, field-based tasks designed to connect the reader with the local community in the context of the chapter's key topics. These activities can be used as individual or group projects or as optional assignments for extra credit. For those who desire a more in-depth treatment of any of the topics covered, the references at the end of the book provide an opportunity for further learning.

Chapter 1

Developing a Learning Community

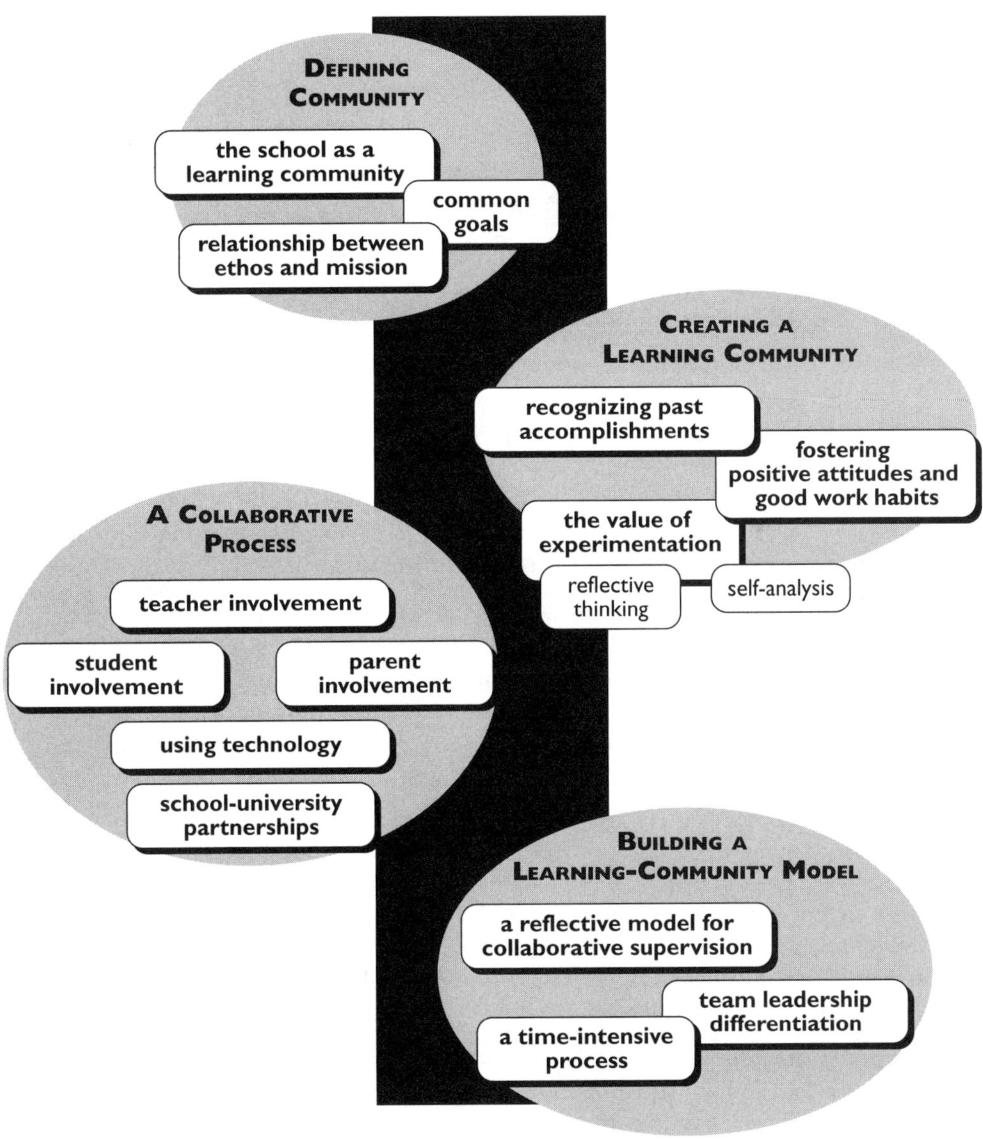

> *Learning communities require teachers to think systematically, become learners, and engage in reflective decision making.*
>
> —V. Doolittle & E. Trombetta, "Defining moments: The transformative potential of professional learning communities"

Objectives

After completion of this chapter, you should be able to

1. Identify the qualities of an effective learning community
2. Realize why the school is the ideal size for a learning community
3. Differentiate between the role of the mission statement and that of the goals in supporting the learning community
4. Develop a commitment to both individual and group goals of your faculty
5. Understand the importance of a learning community's ethos
6. Establish and maintain an appropriate group ethos

In Search of a Community

Frank Clark knew what he was getting into when he left his position as principal at a small suburban elementary school to accept the position of instructional supervisor in the school's district's Jefferson County office. Yet, others questioned his judgment: "Does he really know what he is doing? Does he realize the challenges that this job will offer? Surely, he must not be aware of the political pressures he will face and the educators with whom he must work."

Jefferson County schools epitomized the status quo. Long before the term participatory management *was coined, a "good old boy and girl network" had made the district a participatory management program of the worst kind. The superintendent's office seemed to have an unwritten code that put self-preservation ahead of everything else. This self-preservation code was pervasive. Knowing that without a good support team the supervisor is powerless, Frank began his new assignment by checking out the support system.*

His first visits were to the schools' learning centers. While visiting the director at the first school, Frank noticed that the faculty had access to few journals. When he asked Ruth Hammonds, the director of the resource center, why this was so, she explained that the teachers had once enjoyed several professional journals, but that between the teachers and the students these journals were so popular that they often permanently disappeared from the center. Consequently, over a year ago a decision was made to keep these journals only on microfilm. It had been very effective—the center was no longer losing copies, and all the microfilms are intact. Frank was aghast. This could hardly be described as support.

The visits to the other learning-center directors were about the same. The lack of new programs and materials did not appear to bother the directors, who shared a laid-back sort of satisfaction. Each director reassured Frank that everything was fine. It was difficult to tell whether these directors were purposefully trying to cover up the absence of many curriculum and instructional innovations, or whether they lacked an awareness that their schools were in a rut.

Frank attempted to conceal the many doubts that he was developing about the district because he wanted to stay positive and keep the lines of communications open with everyone. He concluded that a staff whose members had not experienced much change might become uncomfortable if he even hinted that things should be changed.

Frank's next visits were to the counselors' offices. From this round of visits, Frank learned that these counselors saw their roles as mediators between teachers and the parents of troubled students. Occasionally, a counselor would help a student who asked for information about a particular college; yet, in their offices he could see no college applications. It was also apparent that the counselors had not kept any scholarship applications on file. Frank also learned that the district had not attempted to organize a career day in over 10 years, because "the few local students who pursue college do not justify the costs."

Because he wanted to be familiar with the district when he talked to the principals, Frank saved his interviews with the principals until last. The schedule worked; the other interviews had revealed many concerns he could share. He decided to take a conservative position.

Each principal who met with Frank began the meeting with a few pleasantries. Frank appreciated these attempts to make him feel welcome, but he noticed a complete absence of talk about the programs in place at their schools. When faculty members were mentioned, the conversation focused on their personalities.

Frank knew that these administrators, teachers, and support personnel were a collection of good people, individuals who respected and cared for each other. But he also knew that this was exactly what they were, and no more—a collection of individuals. His job would be to transform these individuals into a learning community *with a single mission, and he would have to motivate each member to contribute to that mission.*

Reflection

This vignette provides a brief but accurate description of the dilemma that many of today's supervisors and school administrators face. On one side, they face fierce demands to raise the level of learning in their schools to an unprecedented high. On the other side, they face colleagues in the schools (both administrators and teachers) whose only serious commitment is that of maintaining their comfortable lifestyles by ignoring the world around them. They have found calm in the eye of a hurricane, and they are afraid to leave their safe haven. Though sometimes only a few in number, these reluctant educators can offer powerful resistance to supervisors who want nothing less than the best for their schools.

This book is written to help supervisors (such as Frank) and their school principals change the attitudes of those who would choose to ignore state and national standards and the professional standards of groups such as the ISLLC, the ELCC, and INTASC. It acknowledges that along with its naysayers, each school also has a body of highly dedicated educators who stand ready to work together and do whatever it takes to build an exemplary learning community.

Introduction

> ***Why are learning communities necessary?*** According to Interstate School Leaders Licensure Consortium (ISLLC) Educational Leadership Policy Standard No. 1, "A school administrator is an educational leader who promotes success of all students by facilitating the development, articulation, implementation, and stewardship of a vision of learning that is shared and supported by the school community." Standard No. 2 interprets the role of the administrator as "advocating, nurturing, and sustaining a school culture and instructional program conducive to student learning and staff professional growth."

These standards put student learning first and show that ensuring maximum learning is a collective enterprise. They charge educational leaders with guiding their faculties in building a culture that supports the learning mission of their school. As shown in this case study, the task is not a simple one and it requires finding ways to persuade colleagues to give up the comfortable (but unproductive) position of maintaining the status quo. As you read this chapter, and the rest of this book, think about strategies leaders can use to garner the support of other leaders, including faculty members, in building a learning community.

Developing and maintaining an effective learning community is a way of simultaneously addressing the many needs of today's schools and students (Lunenburg & Irby, 2005). The following chapters provide information to prepare supervisors to help their school faculties develop a highly effective learning community on each school campus. This chapter provides an overview of the job ahead. The process begins with the challenge of providing a vision for the purpose of leading the teachers to shape and support a single mission for the school—a mission that says that "our school puts learning first." In college communities, school–university partnerships are encouraged, with emphasis on collaborating to create knowledge. In many rural communities, teachers must either connect through technology or look to themselves and their colleagues to develop and sustain an effective learning community, one that can give vitality and excitement to all its teachers and students.

Defining Community

A community is more than just a group. It is a group whose members must have a common goal and must direct their specific activity toward meeting the group's mission. Just as members of professions experience growth, professions as a whole also must continuously grow if they are to remain effective.

In their book, *Creating Community Anywhere: Finding Support in a Fragmented World*, Shaffer and Anundsen (1993, p. 10) have provided a list of qualities shared by all communities. Community is a dynamic whole that emerges when a group of people

- participate in common practices;
- make decisions together;
- depend on one another;
- identify themselves as part of something larger than the sum of their individual relationships; and
- commit themselves for the long term to their own, one another's, and the group's well-being.

The first two of these identifying characteristics involve the group members' *behavior;* the last three involve the members' *attitudes*. A distinguishing characteristic that helps define a community is attitude; members of a community think and believe in certain ways. Successful learning communities embody certain attitudes, and these attitudes shape the community behavior. Success depends on the total commitment of each member to the process of building a new learning community and to the community's mission and goals. The energy needed to drive and sustain a learning group is derived from group commitment, from individuals identifying personal goals that they value and are willing to work to achieve, and from the dedication of all members to the goal of generating new knowledge.

Figure 1.1 Defining Community

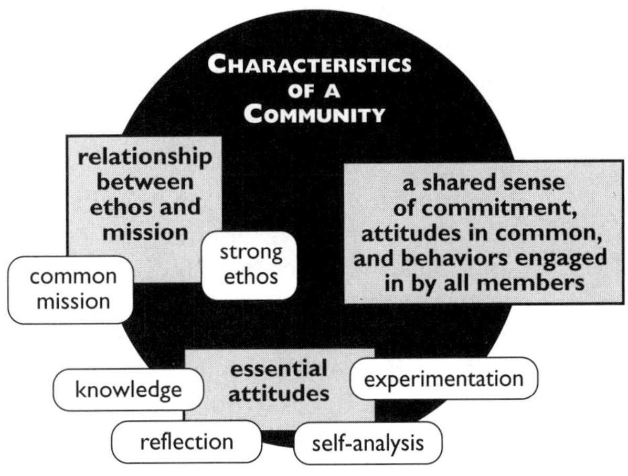

A learning community in this book means at a minimum the students, parents, and all school personnel. Whenever you see the term *learning community* in this book, think about everyone employed in any capacity at the school, joining with students, parents, and other concerned local citizens—working together to improve learning in the school.

The School as an Ideal Learning Community

The school is the ideal size for establishing a learning community. A big error that schools have made in the past is putting teachers in isolated classrooms, disassociating them from other members of the learning community. Furthermore, the self-contained classroom has isolated each age-group of students.

At the other extreme are the attempts that have been made to improve education at the district level. In the past, districtwide programs have brought hundreds of teachers together in annual teachers meetings. But most school districts are so large that the members on any one school's faculty will almost certainly not know all the teachers at another school. Furthermore, the faculties are geographically isolated, eliminating the possibility of all members collaborating and working together on a regular basis, as is required to restructure the school's learning environment. If the classroom is too limited and the district is too vast, perhaps the school is the ideal size. Some educators think this is true, among them Elliott Eisner (1994), who says

> By and large, the "natural" unit in schooling is the school. The school both physically and psychologically defines the environment of teachers and students. It is the school that establishes a territory distinct from the rest of life. The school possesses a physical character that no other aspect of education can achieve: A school district is too large and a classroom is an integrated part of the physical structure of the school. The school stands out as an entity; it is something that secures allegiance and provides students with an identity. (pp. 376–377)

For a case study on developing a learning community, see Stine (2010).

Common Mission and Goals

An effective learning community has a common mission and common goals. Each learning community must develop its own goals, based on the standards they are given and the desires of all members. Those goals should encompass the state and national standards and should be consistent with the philosophies of the school community members. A clear vision of educational outcomes that articulates new standards for student achievement, and for teaching, is required to produce favorable restructuring results for students. As Watkins and McCaw (2007), have noted, "Vision clarifies purpose and gives direction for the future" (p. 434). Collaborative development of a shared vision can garner the commitment of the community's existing members and induct new members into the learning community.

Participation by the entire school community—students, support staff, teachers, administrators, central district office representatives, and parents and other community members—is crucial. Through total participation a school climate is formed. Busch, Johnson, and Robles-Pina (2007) have said, "It is through intentional interaction with the climate of the school that the principal is most able to improve learning" (p. 498). In addition to full participation, total support from the leaders is needed to fire the passions of all members.

The pairing of the two ideas—a new mission and total involvement—will provide a challenge at every school, because some members of the faculty and staff are deeply committed to the existing mission and practices. Most teachers were attracted to teaching because they valued conventional definitions of schooling and teaching. Naturally, they will become uncomfortable with efforts to redefine their roles.

The missions of schools have always been much broader and deeper than portrayed in reform reports. A competitive concern over recent economic gains in other countries has initiated and driven the current reform movement. The critics of public schools attribute the weakening of U.S. economic dominance to the schools' failure to produce world-competitive workers who excel in mathematics. Every time the nation goes to war, schools could also be held accountable for failing to teach world citizenship and the social skills necessary to get along with other nations—for these, indeed, are among the many responsibilities and goals of our schools.

Of these two reform programs' accountability measures, the second pales in the light of the first—that is, the need to excel economically. Put another way, reform programs tend to hold schools more accountable in science and mathematics than in social studies or arts. The nation's long-standing practice of eliminating the arts when times are lean gives credence to this claim; however, according to Reeves (2007), there is evidence that the choice between academics and the arts is a false dichotomy. Reeves cites a recent study (Kennedy, 2006) of a Guggenheim Museum art project that found that students in the program performed better than their peers outside the program in six categories of literacy and critical thinking skills. (See chapter 9 for a more detailed discussion of the importance of the arts in the curriculum.)

As all members of a school's faculty and staff work together to form a learning community, the supervisor's responsibility is to protect the arts, and the multicultural and socialization roles of the curriculum. This responsibility and that of preparing students to compete on mathematics exams are far from mutually exclusive; therefore, one goal should never be chosen at the expense of eliminating the others. These expectations must be woven into the mission of each school and then must be translated into goals, because goals are more action oriented. Goals become stair-steps to reaching the school's mission. Furthermore, good goals can energize the work of group members. To be energizing, goals must be clear and concrete, and they must connect to the mission of the learning community. This can be accomplished by establishing a *mission statement.*

Relationship between Ethos and Mission

Too often, mission statements become an end product in themselves; their whole essence is the physical document, which becomes synonymous with the expression "mission statement." When this happens, the mission statement becomes worthless because the only way any mission statement (the document itself) can have any value is by serving as a guide for the unit's activities (Watkins & McCaw, 2007). This criticism is aimed at the failure of institutions to use their mission statements; it does not question the value that is derived from the joint writing of the statement.

A prerequisite to the full functioning of a mission statement is the presence of a community ethos that supports its mission and parallels the mission statement. *Ethos* is the collective underlying sentiments that guide a group's behavior. Supervisors must discover the faculty's underlying sentiments. A proper ethos for a learning community includes a commitment to learning, inquiry, and experimentation.

Each learning community must view knowledge as temporary, and all members of the community must consider themselves full partners in the ownership of that knowledge. This attitude is possible only through the involvement of all members in generating the new mission and the new knowledge for the learning community.

It Works for Me!

Know Your Faculty

Rodney Davis, Troy University–Dothan Campus

Creating learning communities within the school is rapidly becoming a national trend. The research certainly indicates that when teachers increase their understanding of content and delivery methodologies, student achievement also increases. Preparation is the key ingredient in the successful development of a learning community. Principals should familiarize themselves with their staff in the following ways:

- Know their strengths and weaknesses.
- Know what they need to become better teachers. This could take the form of new strategies, motivation, or encouragement.
- Know their readiness for growth. People cannot be led to places where they are not willing to go.
- Spending a sufficient amount of time in planning and preparation on the front end will increase the likelihood that the learning community at your school will succeed.

The processes called *teaching*, *learning*, and *teacher training* are far more complex than they are frequently presumed and portrayed by legislators. In an attempt to make their efforts appear to have common sense, many legislators tend to oversimplify problems. The reality of the matter is that creating an effective learning community is both complex and challenging. It requires the total involvement of all educators, students, parents, and more—collaboration among *all* members of the learning community. Dialogues should occur not only throughout the school but also in communications outside the school, such as places of worship, community centers, and health centers (Shepherd et al., 2008). Much frequent, continuous, and informed dialogue within and among these groups is essential (Ritchart & Perkins, 2008). This sharing of ideas on proposed change should occur in both formal and informal contexts. As Davies (2002) remarks,

> School success and community success are linked. Public schools are seldom able to be much better than neighborhoods and surrounding communities. Neighborhoods and communities are seldom able to stay healthy and attractive without good schools. (p. 392)

Creating a Learning Community

Creating and maintaining an effective, well-functioning learning community is not something that is quickly accomplished, nor is it ever a "done deal." To keep the learning community working effectively, all members must *continue* to suggest goals and contribute knowledge to the community, and they must constantly ask questions to evaluate the system: "Why are we doing this? How does it lead to achieving our mission? Is there a better way to do it? What did we learn from doing it this way? In what ways do we need to update our mission statement? How must the goals be changed to reflect the new mission statement? What small groups can be formed to best use and hone the talents of all members?"

Recognizing Past Accomplishments

A positive classroom climate that enables teachers to feel good about their work is critical to teaching and learning (Woolfolk Hoy & Hoy, 2009). Creating a new learning community should begin with the realization that through the years American education has been highly successful, and schools should retain those practices that have proven effective. Unfortunately, education reformers may purposefully ignore all pre-reform-era teaching practices in their state as a way of emphasizing the progress made by the current reformers. Unless teachers can feel good about some of their past accomplishments, how can they be expected to be enthusiastic about implementing new practices? Supervisors should compliment their teachers on current successful practices and urge them to use past accomplishments as a foundation on which to build.

If schools are no longer functional (and this depends on the criteria used to measure them), it is not because teachers have become lazy or incompetent but because the world for which the schools were designed has changed (see chapter 4). Acknowledging this condition is an important way to reassure teachers and administrators that they are not being blamed for the many criticisms against today's schools. Feeling guilty for circumstances beyond their control is one thing that teachers do not need and schools cannot afford.

Think of the way our changing laws have impacted special educators, moving at a dizzying pace from general classes for all to special classes for some, to mainstreaming some back into the regular classroom, to inclusion of all in the general classroom. Although some educators may promote such see-

Box 1.1 Recognition of Teacher Accomplishments

The profession of education has had a long struggle. Each time the nation faces a problem, the schools are criticized and scrutinized. As was true of the 1950s, the 1980s and 1990s brought intensive scrutiny. Over many years, our schools have faced an overwhelming multitude of external expectations that keep changing. For example, during the early part of the twentieth century the schools were viewed as a "melting pot" with the intention of distilling perceived "impure foreign elements" and turning them into homogeneous Americans—later to be told that this was all wrong and that we should make salad, not soup. For decades our aim was to provide educational opportunities and ensure that most youths attended school; but now mere attendance is no longer satisfactory: *All children can and will learn*. Although this was a good intention, it didn't stop there. Instead, the authors of NCLB coined the phrase *No Child Left Behind*—a goal that, while admirable in intent, is too idealistic. It ignores differences in abilities and holds teachers accountable for bringing all children to the same achievement level—an impossible expectation. The many criticisms that accompany such waves of reform are painful to educators at all levels.

Inevitably, the instructional supervisor is always in the middle of the discomfort zone, responsible for the reactions of teachers to the many mandates that are sure to follow the often panic-like messages of the critics. One of the most depressing messages that could be sent to professionals is the (either overt or covert) message that their work has been ineffective—or worse yet, incompetent. Yet, this is the implied message that teachers hear with every announcement of a new program, and it isn't true. On the contrary, every school has some faculty members who produce good work. One of the most critical roles of the supervisor is to recognize past accomplishments, to do everything possible to ensure that their teachers view criticism positively, and to work with them to discover ways to use such criticism to improve their own performance and that of the education system.

sawing, most are busy trying to keep up with the latest laws or preparing students for the next round of tests. Ann Lewis (2006) was right when she cautioned, "It makes one wonder about the human costs of the high-stakes testing that consumes the life of schools at the expense of other values" (p. 564).

Because of their isolation from their colleagues, teachers have a special need to have their previous efforts and achievements recognized. The act of coming out of this isolation to collaborate in planning the new learning community can, in itself, be a rewarding experience. Because the traditional system has failed to adequately recognize teachers, today's supervisors have a unique opportunity to help administrators seek out a variety of ways to give rewards and recognition. Finding ways for each member of the learning community to contribute meaningfully to the group learning process is perhaps the best way a supervisor has to reward community members.

Fostering Positive Attitudes and Good Work Habits

You'll recall that Shaffer and Anundsen's (1993) description of the characteristics of a learning community consisted of both attitudes and behaviors. Successful learning communities embody certain attitudes that shape behavior, and repeated behavior develops habits. The new learning community should adopt such attitudes as "The teacher is a lifelong learner," "Knowledge is temporary," and "Wisdom is more valuable than knowledge." Paramount among these attitudes is appreciation for experimentation.

The Value of Experimentation

Some see a scientist who fails to disprove a null hypothesis as a failure—but this is wrong; this scientist has actually contributed to the knowledge base. Similarly, teachers who experiment with new instructional models or with new classroom management models, strategies, and methods are to be commended even though the initial results may appear as failures. School improvement is a problem-rich process. Establishing a climate without fear of failure is a prerequisite for full appreciation of experimental inquiry. Students and teachers alike must learn that failure is to be valued and used, not punished. Problems are to be sought out and pursued, not avoided.

Teachers must harness various ideas, select from a variety of principles, and create different instructional combinations. Like any artist, inspired teachers are intrigued by the challenge of discovering what lies at the end of a series of experimental methods and strategies. What could be more rewarding than knowing that creatively meeting each day's challenge will expand and improve one's talents, understandings, and skills? Such stimulation comes only through experimenting, investigating, and reflecting. Students, too, can discover this stimulation through monitoring their own metacognitive processes and improving their learning skills. Such stimulation is contagious—students may find themselves catching their teachers' enthusiasm for experimentation, discovery, and self-improvement.

The value of experimentation is reflected in the difference between two proverbial teachers who began teaching 20 years ago. One of those teachers analyzed and reflected on each day's teaching and had twenty years of experience. The other teacher repeated the same routines and was left with only one year of experience repeated 19 times.

Self-Analysis. Two prerequisites for the realization of the value of experimentation are self-analysis and reflection (Darling-Hammond & Baratz-Snowden, 2007). These processes must become habits for all teachers. Supervisors are responsible for keeping teachers on track—always seeking connections between their daily actions and the resulting consequences. All members of the new learning community must make self-analysis and reflection integral parts of teaching. No lesson should ever be taught without self-analysis and reflection by the teacher. This analysis and reflection should be guided by the simple question, "How can I improve this lesson the next time I teach it?" Through reflecting on their daily experiences, teachers can improve their prediction of future behavior.

Reflective Thinking. A first step that supervisors can make to lead teachers to become reflective thinkers is ensuring that the teachers have the necessary skills. "Practitioners' reflective narratives can be powerful levers to open and sustain dialogues that promote individual professional growth within the context of overall reform goals, enriching both individuals and systems" (Check, 2002).

A century ago, John Dewey (1910) saw the need for reflective thinking and wrote about it in his book, *How We Think*. According to Dewey, reflective thinking

> involves not simply a sequence of ideas . . . but a consecutive ordering in such a way that each determines the next as its proper outcome while each in turn leans back on its predecessors. . . . Each phase is a step from something to something. . . . Each term leaves a deposit which is utilized in the next term. (pp. 2–3)

Dewey goes on to explain that unlike daydreaming, reflective thought aims at knowledge, at being about facts. "To turn the thing over in your mind, to reflect, means to hunt for additional evidence for new data that will develop the suggestion, and will either, as we say, bear it out or else make evident its absurdity and irrelevance" (p. 13). True thinking occurs only when we encounter a situation that we don't completely understand. Dewey saw the potential for learning in the discomfort we experience when faced with such a situation.

> Recognizing that reflective thinking is as essential to today's teachers as it was in 1910, the Interstate New Teachers Assessment and Support Consortium (INTASC) Principle No. 4 calls for critical thinking, and Standard No. 9 calls for reflective thinking.

> *Critical thinking* involves a wide range of thinking skills leading toward desirable outcomes, and *reflective thinking* focuses on the process of making judgments about what has happened. However, reflective thinking is most important in prompting learning during complex problem-solving situations because it provides . . . [people] an opportunity to step back and think about how they actually solve problems and how a particular set of problem-solving strategies is appropriated for achieving their goal.[1]

Today, reflective thinking is embraced even more than when it was first introduced by John Dewey in 1910. When faced with a statement that we don't clearly understand, we have choices. We can give divided attention to the speaker or writer, which requires little or no thinking, or we can listen carefully, weighing every word (*critical thinking*). Or we can suspend our judgment until we can gather further data to prove or disprove the statement, an evaluative process called *reflective thinking*.

Figure 1.2 offers an exercise to encourage reflective thinking. Although the *Circle, Square, Triangle Reflection Model* was originally created for teachers to use with their students, supervisors can use it with their faculty—or even to promote reflective thinking within themselves. Give your faculty members the following directions:

1. In the circle, write a question about a problem or situation—perhaps the implementation of a new teaching strategy or some other aspect of education reform—that has recently been "going around" in your mind.

2. In the square, capture an idea that "squares" with your thinking about the problem or situation. In other words, based on your prior knowledge and experience, it seems logical.

Figure 1.2 Circle, Square, Triangle Reflection Model*

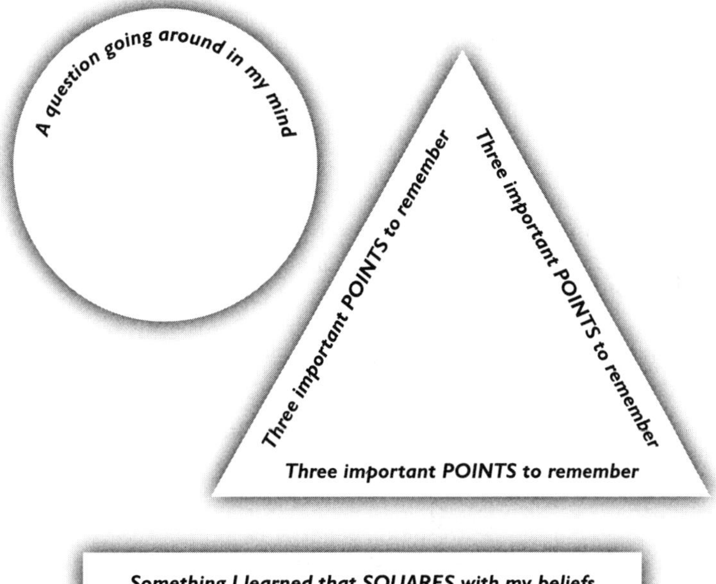

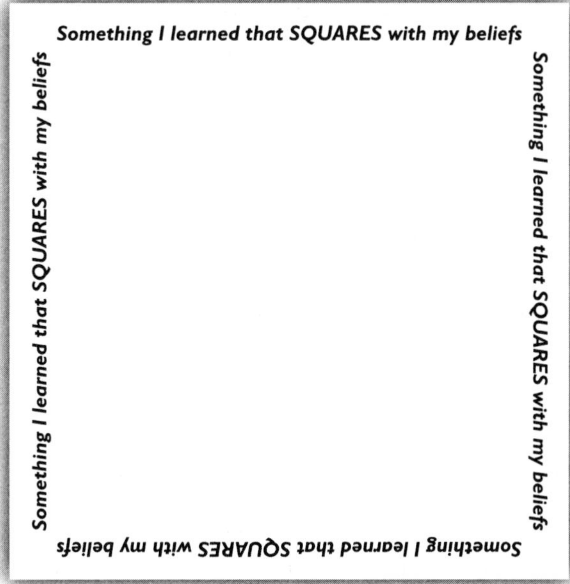

*This model was introduced by Dr. Linda Searby at the 2006 Annual Conference of the National Council of Professors of Educational Administration in Lexington, Kentucky.

3. In the triangle, write what you consider to be the "three most important points" associated with the problem or situation.

Supervisors can use this model to personalize their leadership, building on their teachers' own interests, knowledge, and doubts. This model can be used with groups or with individuals. Try it yourself, and see how it engages your mind in different aspects of problems and new strategies for solving them.

A Collaborative Process

When establishing a learning community, all teachers and administrators must work together. Total involvement promotes a sense of ownership. The community must adopt and foster the idea that learning is valued and practiced by teachers and students alike. Such acknowledgement counters the false attitude that teachers already have all the knowledge required to teach their subjects. Of course, the truth is that no teachers have all the knowledge that their students need to know. The good news is that this isn't a mandatory prerequisite to effectively fulfilling their mission.

Once the learning community is developed, the ultimate goal is that administrators, students, and teachers will learn together—and learn how to work together. Seeing their teachers as partners in learning can empower students and enhance their self-confidence.

Teacher Involvement

It's a well-known fact that traditionally, teachers have had little opportunity to associate with their fellow teachers, but discussing student learning must become central to the collective mission of the school (Bintz & Dillard, 2007). Part of any new learning community must be the structuring of opportunities for teachers to discuss their work with others on a regular, ongoing basis. Such experience is valuable when the discussions focus on such topics as long-term teaching strategies, experimenting with new approaches, and meeting students' needs while meeting state standards.

Research by William R. Penuel and Margaret Riel (2007) provides considerable insight into the social interactions in schools, insight that can be transformed into practical strategies to enhance the collaborative process. For example, each school's faculty has a few members who have more experience than their colleagues in implementing education reform. Administrators should be reminded that these few people have the power to make the biggest difference. Make sure that some members of each of your learning community's subgroups (elementary-grade faculty, or secondary- or middle-level-content faculty members) have regular contacts with these experienced individuals. Having experienced members in such groups encourages those individuals to share their expertise and help others, while at the same time increasing their own self-efficacy. Consider reducing the teaching loads for these experienced education reform teachers to give them time to meet with more colleagues.

It Works for Me!

Teaming Up

Sandra S. Murray, University of Tennessee at Martin

Although there are many opportunities for grade-level/department interactions, there may no opportunity for teachers at different grade levels or departments to network. One way to do this is to establish teams of teachers to provide snacks for staff-development sessions, faculty meetings, and other occasions when teachers have time to meet for fellowship and fun. A random technique that can be used to establish these multi-level/department teams is to place them together based on the color of clothing they wear the first day of school. Once the teams are established, they will function as teams for the entire year, in all activities and training. They must sit together during meetings and are assigned to committees together. This will improve networking opportunities and provide a venue for the formation of a stronger and more cohesive school team.

Several advantages can be derived from collaborative planning. The opportunity to just talk about professional work is especially important to teachers because, traditionally, teachers have had very limited opportunities to share their work experiences with their peers. Discussions with colleagues also cause teachers to reflect on and analyze their own teaching practices.

Penuel and Riel (2007) reported that matrixed formal meeting and committee structures were the most successful. In a *matrixed structure*, individuals participate in a variety of meetings where their school's reform is discussed. For example, at times a seventh-grade English teacher should meet with all seventh-grade teachers to discuss reform; at other times this teacher should attend reform meetings with all other English teachers in the school. The supervisor must ensure that matrixed opportunities occur and provide teachers opportunities to meet with colleagues who share their professional interests (Niesz, 2007).

Tradition has restricted our use of time. As we get desperate for more meeting time, with all members facing crowded calendars, we unnecessarily restrict ourselves with the idea that committee work must be done at a specific time and place. In fact, listservs can free members to collaborate under flexible schedules (asynchronous communication). AirSet (www.airset.com) is a free online tool that can fill this need by allowing members to share calendars and "to do" lists, by invitation only (Brooks-Young, 2006).

Another discovery by Penuel and Riel (2007) was that trust has a heavy influence on network flow. Supervisors can increase trust by ensuring that all members offer their help readily and that all members, especially leaders, follow through on all promises. According to Hoy and Miskel (2008) Trust is the lens through which administrators can effectively examine their school culture and plan for improvement.

Student Involvement

Like their teachers, students must participate in developing a threat-free, inquiry-oriented climate. Total student involvement and student buy-in to the education program are prerequisites for success. William Glasser (2006, p. 13) advised, "The more students have control over their learning, the harder they will work."

Parent Involvement

Involvement of parents is also important. As early as the late eighteenth century, Pestalozzi compared the good school to a good home and the good teacher to a good, caring parent. During the 1960s, studies showed a positive correlation between family income and students' academic performance. Unfortunately, the seemingly obvious, yet incorrect, conclusion was reached—that high income causes good students, and low income produces poor students. Only later did evaluators acknowledge that another factor—the prizing of education—could be causing both high student performance and high family income.

In the 1990s educators rediscovered that maximum learning at school requires a supportive home environment where education is prized. According to an ERIC Clearinghouse study (see Macfarlane, 1995), "Research indicates that parent involvement in children's education, from birth until they leave home, has a major positive impact on children's achievement at school" (p. i). The study reported that parent involvement leads to higher test scores, better grades, better attendance, and better behavior.

Interestingly, greater parent involvement also leads to better school programs and to academic success for children. Even the public acknowledges that parents who actively support their children contribute more to their child's success in school than do those who provide passive support. By 2004, 97% of the public had embraced the idea that parent involvement is essential and should be increased (Rose & Gallup, 2004). Teacher training programs are needed to ensure that teachers will support the involvement of parents (Aldridge & Goldman, 2007). Administrators should "aggressively recruit and engage parents in school activities as early in the school year as possible" (Wherry, 2008, p. 18).

Using Technology to Involve Parents and Other Community Members

This book carries throughout its chapters the theme that schooling occurs best in a collaborative community climate. As Phil Schlecty (2008) has noted, "Good schools require strong communities to support them" (p. 554). This theme is supported by the effective schools research showing that academic success is highest in schools where the learning community expands beyond the classroom walls to include key members from throughout the community. Paramount among these key members are the parents.

According to research published by the Southwest Educational Development Laboratory (Henderson & Mapp, 2002), students with involved parents, no matter what their income or background, are more likely to:

- earn higher grades and test scores, and enroll in higher-level programs;
- be promoted, pass their classes, and earn credits;
- attend school regularly;
- have better social skills, show improved behavior, and adapt well to school; and
- graduate and go on to post-secondary education.

E-mail, classroom Web sites, and online student performance portfolios and grade books are increasingly being used by teachers to keep parents informed of students' academic performance. Schools are turning to the Internet as a vehicle to highlight successful programs, inform parents new to the community, and adhere to state requirements to report school achievement. Internet-based technologies are changing the way educators, parents, and community members exchange information and provide support to families. As educators become more comfortable communicating via technology, and as communication software becomes more robust, technology will play an increased role in supporting community connectedness to schools.

Schools are using technology tools to engage a larger audience in strategic planning efforts by using online surveys, listservs, and e-mail. Involving parents, business partners, and the community in district and school technology planning is key to the success of both the planning process and the actual plan implementation. High-tech instruments such as TeleParent (http://www.teleparent.net), for example, can send individually tailored messages to parents in the language and platform accessible to them.

The use of technology in schools to engage parents in students' education can be a highly effective tool—even with language differences, lower education levels, inflexible work schedules, and socioeconomic disparities (Cearley & Bennett, 2008). Some schools sponsor a Family Technology Event to increase parents' awareness and hands-on experience with the types of technology the school plans to purchase or is already using. For example, the O'Donnell Elementary School in East Boston is using technology training to create a culture of parental involvement. Principal Dr. Robert Martin explains:

> We offer 12 weeks of computer training for students and their parents. . . . What we've discovered is that this powerful learning experience [demystifying computers] also demystifies the school. As parents meet teachers and other parents, they become engaged in other school activities and more willing to take on leadership roles. . . . For many of O'Donnell's parents, English is a second language. At first they were shy about interacting. But as they found that the teachers were actually there to help, shyness gave way to confidence. (Boston Digital Bridge Foundation, 2006)

* * *

The following case study describes how a learning community was established in a community whose once-effective schools had become victims of age. The years had taken their toll on the physical facilities, which no longer reflected the growing population served by the school. Fortunately, unlike the deteriorating buildings, the faculties and administrators of these schools have excellent leadership and refuse to be beaten down by time. While good buildings and facilities are extremely important, the leaders in Greenwood School have triumphed over this adversity, proving that school success is a product of good leadership and highly dedicated teachers with unrelenting positive attitudes.

The Transformation of Greenwood School

Susan Clark and Sharon Kruse • University of Akron

Greenwood Middle School lies tucked away in a small rural community with a population of 5,000. The Middle School has 440 students and 26 teachers. This is the story of its successful transformation from a traditional junior high to an innovative middle school—an evolution from a school in which isolated teachers taught fragmented lessons to one in which teaming, integration, and cooperation were norms.

The School

Housed in an aging building and cramped for space, the old Greenwood Junior High was like most rural junior highs around the country. Good teachers taught good lessons to students who were attentive, interested, and involved with their learning. Yet the school board still felt that the educational opportunity offered to students in grades five through eight could be improved. Specifically, they were interested in providing a balanced curriculum, utilizing varied instructional strategies, offering a full exploratory program of electives, maintaining continuous student progress toward academic goals paired with high expectations for all students, and placing students of the same grade and their teachers in close physical proximity for planning and learning purposes.

A Need for Transformation

The time for change was ripe: both the high school and junior high were in need of new buildings, and the school board was studying a plan that would locate the junior high, high school, and administrative offices in the same new structure. Such a building would serve the community as a hub for activities for students of all ages, providing an unusual opportunity to design a school based on an educational philosophy and student needs rather than trying to restructure in an inadequate setting.

The Faculty

All faculty members were invited to participate in the research effort concerning the new middle school. Word went out that any of these positions would require commitment to the new school and commitment to a new form of teaching and learning; and faculty were selected based on their commitment to the principles by which the new middle school was to operate. Thus, teachers who signed on clearly understood and embraced the assumptions that governed the school. Educating the staff and faculty was only half of the effort. In order to build the new school structure, the community needed to be educated as well.

Involving the Community

Before embracing the new school, the community wanted assurance that tax dollars were well spent and that the proposed changes were necessary. Parental concerns varied and were often in conflict. While the parents of sixth graders wanted assurance that their students would be treated with caring, compassion, and concern, the parents of seventh-grade students expressed anxieties related to high school competition and readiness. A new steering committee established for the creation of the new middle school responded by offering a comprehensive rationale, based on the school's guiding principles and philosophy.

The final agreement affirmed the communities' appeal that the middle school be a positive environment for all students. Fifth graders would remain in a self-contained classroom, while sixth, seventh, and eighth graders would departmentalize. All teachers would teach reading, in addition to a subject-area specialization, ensuring small classes and individualized instruction. Throughout the school, students would see fewer teachers each day, allowing for increased student attention and accountability. Learning at all levels would be integrated and interdisciplinary.

Higher-order thinking skills would be central to all teaching, and efforts would be made to extend learning beyond the classroom. Faculty would receive an hour daily to cooperatively plan and monitor instructional activities and homework. Once the tax referendum was approved and district personnel were assured of both the middle-school concept and the new building, the steering committee got down to the work of developing the staff for the new endeavor.

Believing that discerning, enlightened teachers would make quality decisions about education, curriculum, instruction, and strategy, Principal Jackson led a committee that decided to bring university courses to teachers, on site during the summer. Negotiation with the university ensured that course content would connect philosophically with the new Greenwood Middle School. Consistent communication with the school board throughout the planning process translated into a willingness to pay for both for the classes and the corresponding salary increases that the additional credits would provide the teaching staff.

Collaborating on Curriculum and Instruction

Both the board and the administration spoke volumes with their actions; teachers felt support for their efforts unlike any they had experienced in years. Conservative instructional approaches used in earlier years were abandoned in favor of new, innovative, integrated curriculum and pedagogies. Furthermore, the newly formed teaching teams were given quality time to begin their work together. Three years later, teachers fondly point to the summer institute as the place where the team became cemented, and where they learned to trust and respect each other. Teachers assert that the summer courses were the difference between success and failure.

By simultaneously working on both new curriculum and new techniques with which to teach students, teachers felt that they approached the new school year better equipped to address student needs. Much of the curriculum for the year had been planned, and a process existed for completing the remaining curriculum modules. More importantly, the daily schedule contained an hour for team planning and an hour for individual planning, so teachers understood that time existed during the regular school day to complete ongoing and continuing work.

Team planning time was sacrosanct. Members would gather daily with coffee, calendars, and curriculum, and use the hour to discuss difficulties with lessons, successes with students, or the next interdisciplinary unit. Tasks were often divided between the team members. One member would arrange to have films or speakers, or to gather science and math materials; another would draft an assessment rubric for discussion at the next meeting.

Both content and instructional strategies were discussed with equal regularity—the process of concurrently planning what to teach and how to teach it had become commonplace. Teachers actively reflected upon lessons and activities from the previous days and weeks, searching for cues as to which teaching methods this particular group of kids preferred, where their interests lay, and which teaching techniques were best to get the message across.

Professional communities had begun to grow among the teachers at Greenwood. The time provided for planning paid great dividends in helping teachers feel prepared to enter their classrooms and provide quality instruction. Classroom norms evolved in which students were deeply and continuously engaged in pursuing substantive learning. On-task learning behaviors improved, and lessons were often modified to extend or remediate previous learning.

The Power of Teamwork

Solid planning and extensive preparation could not completely prepare teachers for the radical changes that they had chosen to undertake. Some teachers found the transition a straightforward and simple innovation, enjoying the unconstrained atmosphere and finding the opportunity to explore new curriculum and pedagogy stimulating. Others struggled under the responsibility of teaching reading; it was difficult to address disparate content areas. The formidable goals the staff had set forth seemed insurmountable to some teachers. At this point in time it would have been easy and expected for the principal to step in and order people to get on board.

Instead, Jackson chose to trust the team plan, allowing the teams to mediate their own struggles. Teachers were encouraged to talk through concerns with their teams before taking them to a full staff meeting or to the administration. Through the process of working through conflicts as they arose, the teams built confidence, interdependence, and trust. Jackson would drop by classrooms not to evaluate teachers, but rather to keep abreast on what occurred in classes. This policy provided him with ready topics for informal conferences with students, parents, or teachers interested in discussing the progress at the middle school. Additionally, he could offer ideas and bring together teachers with similar interests. The individual development of a teacher's potential became a shared goal as everyone learned new skills together. Increasingly, the staff felt comfortable with the new structure.

Financial Constraints

Greenwood Middle School was thriving in the following fall as Principal Jackson was promoted to superintendent and Chris Miller became the new principal. The transition occurred with little tension among faculty because they knew that they—not the principal—were the possessors of the skills and knowledge that made their teams and classrooms function. Ongoing rather than first-generation ownership had been established.

At the same time, the district was also attempting to raise considerable funds. Residents of the community had experienced a series of lean years and were reluctant to raise their taxes. Although the district fought a strong battle, the tax referendum failed. Suddenly, efforts to create strong teaching and learning environments for students fell a distant second to efforts designed to help alleviate the budget crisis the school district was facing. Since the middle school was considered Jackson's "baby," rumors held that its budget would be less deeply cut than those of the high school, elementary, or community education programs.

In fact, Jackson and the school board held true to campaign promises that all schools would face equal cuts based on 10% of their budgets. Faculty would be laid off in all buildings and voluntary early retirement would be instituted. One possible solution to the financial problems of the district was to dissolve the middle school and return to a junior high school format. This would save money in two ways. First, staffing of the middle school is expensive and flexibility in scheduling is lost as teachers remain locked into team assignments and are unavailable to teach in other grade levels. Second, teaching assignments could be shared between high school and middle school faculty if the middle school teachers were freed from the team focus.

Preserving the School Philosophy

The middle school faculty governance council banded together to launch a campaign to preserve the middle school philosophy of the building. Although the teachers felt that the philosophy was shared, discussion proved otherwise. A majority of teachers defined the middle school philosophy as including the maintenance of the focus on reading instruction, retaining jointly shared team planning time, and continuing the school policy of single-grade assignments for teachers. The community and school board members' idea of what comprises a middle school was far less focused. Many members felt that as long as the structure of the building and pods of students by grade were maintained, Greenwood had a middle school. For others, parents most notably, maintenance of the middle school meant preservation of the team focus so that their students would have the fewest number of contacts with different adults per day.

The conversation and its disturbing findings quickly filtered out to the full faculty. A meeting was called to discuss the philosophy. Following much conversation, it was decided that reading instruction and team planning were the important defining factors for the faculty. Although many teachers believed that the maintenance of single grade-level assignments for teachers was preferable, in reality the budget probably couldn't sustain such an expensive practice. Miller decided that in the following year the faculty had to work toward a greater shared understanding of the school's policies and practices.

Restructuring Challenges

However, there were the pressing problems of staffing and budget cuts. Like most other schools, teachers to be let go came from the bottom of the seniority list so cuts in the staff roster did not fall evenly across the schools. Many newer teachers, due to certification requirements or licensure restrictions, held their positions while more senior members (in years) were scheduled to be laid off. Involuntary transfers, a practice never used in the district before, were necessary for some teachers to hold a position. Certification became a large problem in this process, because many positions (such as special education teachers and most high school teachers) were licensed in only one area. Those who held two were often transferred to their second choice to make room for single-licensure faculty. Thus, the equity of such decisions was often in question. As Superintendent Jackson stated, "I could offer these people jobs, but sometimes it was way out of their usual placement, so the choice for some staff is a position they would rather not take or no job." The tension around who would stay and who would go was palpable.

One team scheduled to be separated through the cuts and restaffing was the fifth-grade team. A strong team of teachers, known for their capable teaching ability and easy manner, the fifth-grade teachers did not want to be transferred or moved. They felt that they were being punished for working well together and that the proposed transfers had less to do with licensure issues than it did with strengthening weaker teams on the faculty. In part, they were correct. "We had problems with one team and wanted to provide more leadership for them," stated Jackson. He continued, "By transferring some teachers with interchangeable certification we felt we could strengthen a weak team and create a greater sense of schoolwide purpose."

The team fought back. Polly spoke for all the members when she said, "We've worked hard to build the team feeling and working relationship. They cannot then just decide the school is worth more than the team. I understand the problem, but solving it by destroying our situation just isn't fair."

Many tears were shed as the problem continued to fester. Finally, Principal Miller decided to step in and protect the teams. The task was personally difficult. Taking over the building from Jackson had proved a smooth transition in many ways; however, Jackson's move to the superintendent's position permitted a continued hands-on relationship with the operation of the middle school. As Miller stated, "It's as if my parent's been looking over my shoulder. It's time to cut the apron strings."

Miller formally opposed the transfers but, to do so, he required a promise from the closely knit team that it would assume a greater leadership role within the school and begin to share its expertise and skill with other faculty and staff. The team members agreed and held their positions. Important inroads were made in solving the growing problem of team isolation. The fifth-grade team members took their assignment seriously and quickly became visible leaders of districtwide committees designed to study school change and innovation. They worked with Miller to create school meetings focused on the creation of a clear schoolwide communication network and systemic conversation about practice.

The staff of Greenwood Middle School created a mature professional community by looking both backward and forward. A teacher glancing backward could draw on an organizational history rooted in positive memories of support, professionalism, and success. A teacher looking forward saw a clear vision supported by adequate, focused, and available information and the opportunity to reflect, discuss, and study. The Greenwood story points to the importance of social and human relations as a foundation for teachers' learning efforts and to the creation of strong structures as a scaffold on which new relationships can be built.

Issues for Further Reflection

1. Citing specific events and actions in the case study, describe how Greenwood Middle School exemplifies a professional learning community and construct a diagram that illustrates the role of the instructional supervisor in building teachers' professional practice.
2. Compare and contrast the ways in which a professional learning community is sustained under conditions of change and crisis in Greenwood Middle School with the ways your school operates on a day-to-day basis and under those same conditions.
3. From the information you have about the professional learning community, critique its value and usefulness in today's climate of accountability where teachers and instructional supervisors feel the pressures to improve all students' achievement. Weigh your evaluation against other approaches being used to accomplish the goal that no child is left behind.

School–University Partnerships

Supervisors can help their schools extend the collaborative process of building a learning community through school–university partnerships. (Schools that engage in such partnerships are called *professional development schools.*). Partnerships between schools and universities must be forged early and must have a common agenda. According to Noguera (1998), an important starting point for developing a school and university partnership is recognizing that schools and universities have different interests. When the interests of a university-based researcher does not coincide with the interests of the school, there may seem to be no basis for collaboration. However, if time is taken to communicate openly about the interests and needs of the respective parties, mutually beneficial partnerships can be built.

> Universities and schools alike are struggling with the critical issues of teacher quality, student learning, and the gap between research and practice. In order to contend with and address these matters, both entities must collaborate and work together to create learning communities guided by shared beliefs about teaching and student learning, based on mutual trust and respect, and grounded in current evidence-based research and practitioner knowledge. (Lengyel, Vernon-Dotson, & Lane, 2008)

Partnerships enable the school(s) and university to reach multiple goals that are equally important to everyone. For example, by forming a partnership Georgia Southern University's College of Education and the Screven County Schools joined a juvenile minimum-security system to close the achievement gaps between poor and nonpoor students, between minority and mainstream students, and between males and females. For a discussion of this successful program see Parsons, Heaston, and Nettles (2006).

Many university professors are insensitive to the needs of school personnel and school personnel, in turn, are often suspicious of university people. A sensible precaution to ameliorate or overcome these differences in expectations is to forge the partnership early, making sure to address agenda that are important to both groups. Continuously focusing on the ultimate mutual goal of both parties—improving learning opportunities for students—is a positive first step toward bridging this common perceptual gap; however, more is needed. The following generalization extends this building process.

Commitment to common goals requires commitment to individual goals. Many people reject new group goals because they consider them as replacements for their more immediate, individual goals. Professional people often find the idea of needing to adopt group goals much more acceptable than the idea of giving up their highly prized individual goals. One step that can help garner commitment to the group goals is to assure everyone that group goals and individual goals are not mutually exclusive. On the contrary, not only can the two coexist, but keeping some of the members' prized individual goals can make it easier for them to adopt the goals of the group.

The more leadership is spread about, the better the partnership will be. Following World War II, this country entered a building period, unprecedented in magnitude. New homes were built and these grew bigger and better. Businesses, schools, and other institutions expanded. Government agencies became more bureaucratic. Toward the end of the twentieth century, education experienced a backlash against bureaucracy, leaving as a residue some key terms that characterize education of the new millennium—collaborative leadership, decentralization, shared decision making, participatory management, school-based management, teacher empowerment, and even student empowerment. Applying these concepts will enhance the effectiveness of school–university partnerships. (For an example of a successful partnership, see the vignette on Horton's Master-Teacher Development Program in chapter 4.)

In any work environment, suspicion naturally befalls anyone who attempts to introduce change, because those involved know that the change is going to require more work for everyone. When innovations are introduced, before the sound of the drum roll dies, members can be heard giving reasons why (in their opinions) the initiator of the change is willing to spend time and energy on this project. If the change is introduced by an administrator, the immediate suspicion is that the administrator wants personal recognition—another medal. Smart administrators do not introduce innovations; they get faculty members to introduce them, thus freeing themselves to give full support to their faculty members. Even the harshest critics and cynics find it difficult to blame leaders for supporting their subordinates. An even better route to introducing and promoting ideas is by giving several learning-community members shared responsibility for leading, introducing, and promoting the needed changes. This empowers more members and allows for others to share in the leadership and, of course, in the ownership of the innovations.

The school's leaders must play a hands-on role in the development of the learning community. If the product is to be more than empty rhetoric, each administrator must roll up both sleeves and work *hard*. Building a learning community requires a leader and a body of members who are determined to work and get results. The best way to garner teachers' support is by getting the administrator fully involved. Through becoming completely immersed in everyday work, leaders can begin building a unified ethos that puts commitment to learning above all else. As they become fully involved with the new program, leaders can help by providing data on the effectiveness of similar programs. Successful development of a learning community requires that a leader not only provide a vision, but also permit others to share ownership in that vision and sell the new mission to all future members. Building a learning community requires collaboration between the leader and the body of members who are determined to work and get results.

But to succeed, this partnership process must have support. Most improvement also requires considerable financial backing. Because new programs are expensive, and because at most educational institutions money is tight, teachers and professors alike are likely to withhold their support for a change, for fear that the administration will withdraw its support before the new program has a chance to succeed. James Nehring (2007, p. 428) says, "This danger exists everywhere in public education, and it engenders a related tendency on the part of school leaders to assess new programs not by their effectiveness but by the degree to which they fit within the existing system." Before deciding to implement a program, special effort should be made to obtain the necessary human resources and financial support. Because most improvement requires considerable financial support, often the amount of money available is insufficient. Too often, legislated changes either provide too little support or they provide no support at all. Chapter 15 discusses opportunities for garnering financial support through grant proposal writing.

Building a Learning Community Model

The success of the collaborative approach endorsed in this book depends on effective teamwork, behind which is an instructional leader who is supervising and shaping the behavior of the group's members. As Marcellino (2006) has said, "A team does not evolve simply because an instructor places adults into a group and labels them a team" (p. 216). Team goals are not automatically reached when individuals' goals are met. Team success is more than the sum of the successes of its individual members; yet while a team is being formed, individual successes can contribute to team success.

A Reflective Model for Collaborative Supervision

Although the development of each successful learning community is tailored to fit its own unique situation, successful collaborative team building requires an overall plan. A collaborative team can begin as a small, grade-level team in an elementary school, the teachers of a particular subject in high school, or an elementary, middle-level, or high school interdisciplinary team that includes one or several subjects and grade levels. At some point, smaller teams must be brought together by a coordinating committee, and their efforts must be coordinated to meet the school's goals. Team size is important because once a team becomes larger than a half-dozen or so, communication problems and conflicting schedules can become significant challenges. Like a golf team or a bowling team, optimal success from a collaborative planning team requires successes from all its members; therefore, the daily attitudes of members become most important.

In his 1923 book, *The Prophet*, Kahlil Gibran offers the following advice to educators: "If he is indeed wise he does not bid you enter the house of his wisdom, but rather leads you to the threshold of your own mind" (p. 56). The model shown in Figure 1.3 reflects Gibran's advice and is built on the belief that *the supervisor's greatest service is not that of giving information; rather, it is his or her role as facilitator in the creation of a community that invites all its members to share their own knowledge and dispositions*. Such an environment requires a time and place for its members to engage not only in collaborative thinking but also in private, introspective thinking.

This model begins down in the "courtyard" of the figure, with some preliminary "steps" that provide the opportunity to think. For all teachers—those who plan to go it alone and those who plan to team with their colleagues to

Figure 1.3 A Reflective Team-Building Model for Collaborative Supervision

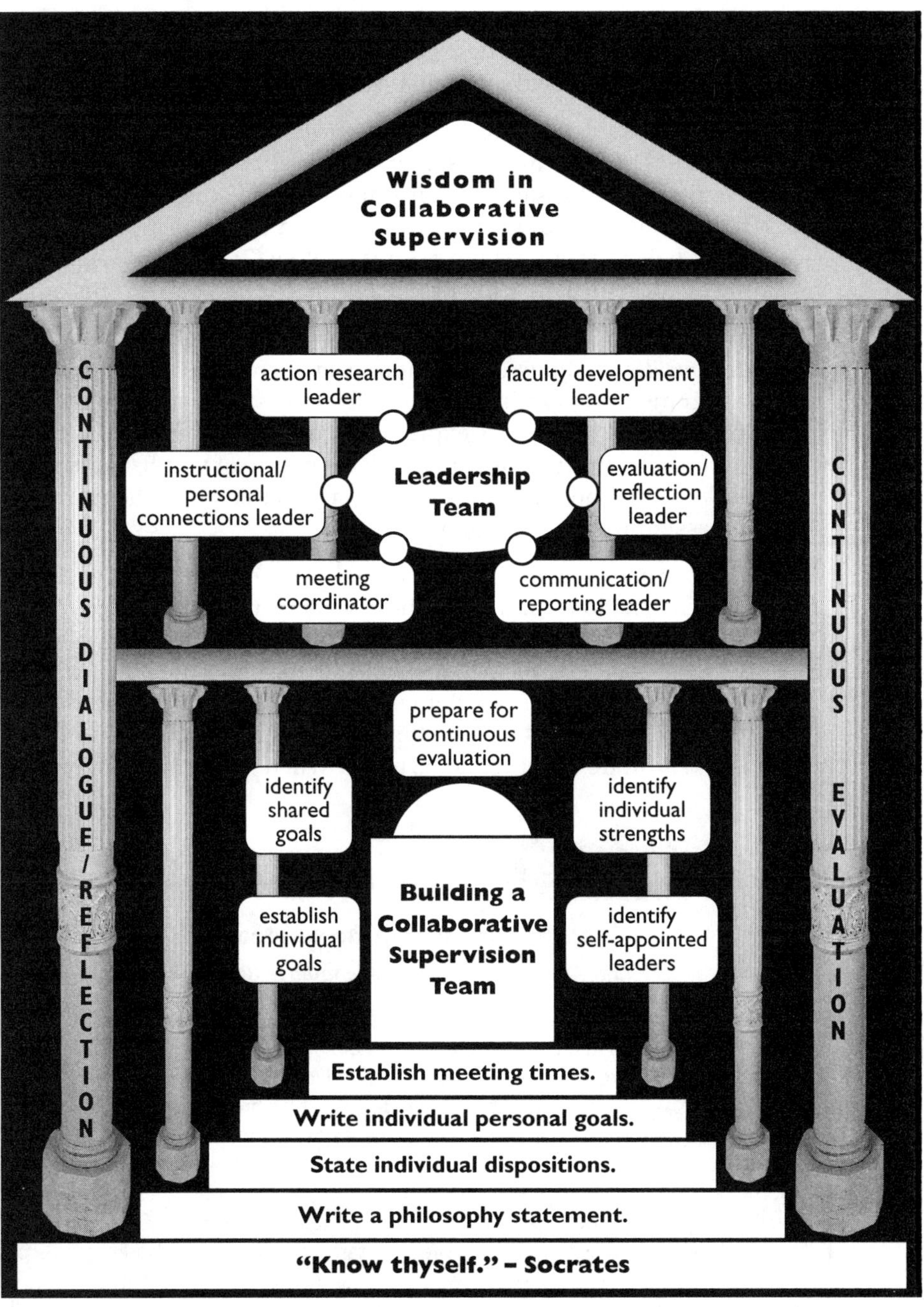

build a learning community—Socrates gave the perfect advice for the first step of the journey: "Know thyself."

The following steps are written from the perspective of the supervisor (who may be a principal, or a designated supervisor or administrator) who will work directly with the faculty to initiate and support the learning community.

Write a philosophy statement. An effective way for a supervisor to achieve the goal of knowing oneself is to request that the team members individually write a short essay on their philosophy of education (Warner, 2010). This reflective piece should contain a minimum of one or two paragraphs on each of their beliefs about: (1) the purpose of life; (2) the purpose of school; (3) the nature of youth (trustworthy or not, curious or not, industrious or lazy, creative or not); and (4) the nature of learning.

State your dispositions. The supervisor then gives the team members a second assignment—to examine their philosophy statements and make a short, bulleted list of brief statements expressing their beliefs and dispositions about the purpose of life, the purpose of school, the nature of youth, and the nature of learning. As a final preliminary step, the supervisor gives the team members their third assignment.

Write your personal goals. Individual team members are encouraged to study their dispositions, and from these write some personal goals that they most wish to achieve with their students. For example, if a member wishes to lead his or her students to the threshold of their minds, that team member might include such goals as developing a passion for learning, becoming a lifelong learner, becoming a reflective thinker or problem solver, and developing the skills and attitudes required to be happy when working in a diverse setting.

It Works for Me!

Using Spreadsheets to Personalize

Linda Searby, University of Alabama at Birmingham

We know that the most effective school principals are those who are visible and in touch with teachers and staff. When I was an elementary principal, I never left my visibility and caring "to chance." Because I valued regularly communicating with and encouraging the teachers and staff, I made myself a spreadsheet with each of their names along the left side and a row of cells beside each name. I would pick five staff members per week to focus on, making sure I made a personal, meaningful visit with them. I also wrote them an encouraging note to place in their mailboxes or on their desks. I would note the date that I did these things next to the person's name on the spreadsheet. On occasions where notes to staff were needed, I also kept a record of them. I carried this spreadsheet in my planner and consulted it monthly to make sure I was not neglecting anyone. My goal was for everybody to receive a personal note of encouragement from me at least three times a year. Many staff members told me how much the notes meant to them.

Those goals for which individuals have a passion can provide strong motivation for reaching both individual and team goals.

Establish meeting times. Find a time that the team can meet on a regular basis. Full schedules often leave teachers and administrators unable to find the time required for in-depth discussions (Hanson & Moir, 2008). Effective teaming is a multi-task process. Meeting times must be reserved so that all team members have the opportunity to collaborate in achieving all the work.

Figure 1.3 features two columns that support the entire temple. The column on the left recognizes the importance of continuous dialogue and reflection, whereby team members get to know each other and develop a commitment to the team. All members get to know their fellow team members' strengths. Because of teachers' fast-paced lives and hectic schedules, providing the team members opportunities to meet together and engage in dialogue is a major supervisory responsibility. The column on the right side of the temple recognizes the importance of continuous evaluation.

Inside the temple, the supervisor can assist the collaborative team members in accomplishing the following tasks that will increase the efficiency of the leadership team and clarify the purposes of its individual members.

Prepare for continuous evaluation. To ensure that the team is making continuous progress, its work must be continually evaluated. Members should ask such questions as, "What mistakes are we making?" and "How can we correct them?" Although adjustments will be needed, it is imperative that the discussions remain positive.

Identify a team of self-appointed leaders. Teaming requires leadership, but unlike traditional governance where leadership is performed by the supervisor alone, building a learning community requires a high level of dedication of all members; therefore, the leadership must first be shared. Second, because team building requires a high level of energy, all members must be committed to the work. Acquiring and sustaining this high level of energy requires that individuals enjoy their assignments. Supervisors need not worry about the supply of good leaders; it is always there. Fortunately, as experienced educators know, each school has latent leaders waiting to emerge. These leaders materialize with each accreditation cycle.

The upper level of the temple in Figure 1.3 represents a round table to symbolize the collaborative leadership of the team members. By being committed to the team goals and by knowing each other's strengths, effective teams can allow leadership to emerge.

Team Leadership Differentiation

Several leaders are required to initiate and sustain the building and operation of a learning community: (1) action research leader, (2) meeting coordinator, (3) faculty development leader, (4) evaluation/reflection leader, (5) instructional/personal connections leader, and (6) a communications/reporting leader. The role of each leader is examined below.

Action Research Leader. For an example of the role of an action research leader, let's visit a school in north Texas. Claudia Whitley (see Mayo & Whitley, 2004), a principal in Nacogdoches, Texas, has discovered a way to keep her teachers apprised of the newest education-reform knowledge and skills available. She lets each teacher select and join an action research team whose members share his or her interests. Those teachers who have expertise and interest in research should be encouraged to join the research team. This team has two purposes: to review and share research found in professional journals and other literature, and to help colleagues develop and conduct their own action research projects.

Meeting Coordinator. This leader schedules and oversees meetings. The meeting coordinator must ensure that each meeting begins by reminding team members of the purposes of the meeting, with either a volunteer or designated member to ensure that the team uses its time effectively by staying on track and pursuing its goals. This leader has responsibility for watching the clock, moving the meetings forward when members stall on particular topics, and ending each meeting on time. Prior to departure, the coordinator must remind the committee of its next steps, including setting a time for the next meeting.

Faculty Development Leader. Faculty development must be continuously aligned with the school's learning mission, and it must be ongoing. The faculty development leader must ensure that these two conditions are met. Meeting these two standards helps increase teachers' sense of upward mobility in the profession (Steel & Craig, 2006).

Evaluation/Reflection Leader. One of the building-high columns in Figure 1.3 focuses on evaluation and reflection. These activities serve two purposes. First, they have a very practical dimension: They prevent the team or teams from heading down the wrong paths, allowing them to make adjustments as they are needed. Second, evaluation and reflection provide feedback to give needed recognition to the faculty. The extent to which teachers can and will use educational ideas depends on (a) the extent to which the teachers are self-actualized, and (b) the learning climate, in particular the type of principal and the degree to which teachers agree on the institutional goals.

The lower level of the temple recognizes that there are two different kinds of goals: individual teachers' goals and team goals. As members gain a clear understanding of, and a commitment to the team goals, the individual goals tend to lose their importance. If the direction of the team becomes unclear or strays from the team goals, the evaluation/reflection leader is responsible for refocusing the team so that all tasks are serving the team goals.

Since community building is a collaborative process requiring everyone to discuss the long-term community goals, the evaluation/reflection leader must ensure that such discussions occur on a regular schedule.

Instructional/Personal Connections Leader. Because the learning community is built and maintained for students, leadership is needed to place and retain the students' welfare in the center of all learning community activities.

The TIMSS Studies (Roth & Garnier, 2006/2007) tell us that the one factor which causes our students to perform at a level below that of their counterparts in several other countries is our teachers' failure to make connections—between subjects, and between class activities and students' lives outside the school. Gleibermann (2007) warns that pressure to meet reform standards is robbing teachers of the opportunity to make the personal connections. A leader is needed to ensure that the personal welfare of students is not being ignored. Strong student representation on several committees can help address this concern. For example, students can make strong contributions to and can derive significant benefits from serving on committees for social justice, technology, homework, and curriculum. Leadership is needed to ensure that connections is a frequently found topic in the dialogues of team members, and to provide examples of how various members make these connections in their classrooms.

Communications/Reporting Leader. Clearly, some of the responsibilities of these leaders overlap. Although some learning communities may find that the evaluation/reflection leader can also maintain communications, other teams will need a separate leader who is responsible for communications within the team and with the community at large. For a case study based on an actual experience, portraying a newly hired administrator who does an exemplary job establishing community relations, see Stine (2010). Regular and accurate communications and reporting are essential for attaining the necessary support for the team.

A Time-Intensive Process

Restructuring and building a new learning environment takes time. Effective restructuring requires that teachers be provided with opportunities to discuss their experiences with their colleagues. A special ongoing faculty development program, as opposed to the traditional piecemeal program for individual teachers, is required for building an effective learning community. The instructional supervisor has a major responsibility to help administrators find time for these meetings.

> Interstate School Leaders Licensure Consortium (ISLLC) Educational Leadership Policy Standard No. 2 recognizes the need for faculty development, holding leaders accountable for "advocating, nurturing and sustaining a school culture and instructional program conducive to student learning and staff development growth."

Many features of this restructuring process require large amounts of time. One of the most time-consuming is faculty development, which must be an ongoing process. Some of the important goals that supervisors can encourage their faculty to accomplish are listed below.

- Teachers should take on responsibility for leadership in all aspects of the curriculum (Lunenburg & Irby, 2005).

- Teachers must involve their students in generating knowledge.
- Teachers must ensure that the climate in which effective learning community development occurs is relatively free of fear and from the urgency to complete assignments by given deadlines.
- Teachers must embrace research and make it a part of their self-images; all teachers should research the institutional goals that they agree are important.

Building a successful learning community requires the support of the school administration. Supervisors can make these tasks easier for the faculty by doing whatever they can to obtain financial support and released time for faculty to work on all aspects of these time-consuming tasks.

The social and human resources needed to build a better learning environment include openness to improvement, trust and respect, a cognitive and skills base (particularly the use of metacognition to enrich teaching), supportive leadership, and socialization (especially consensus-building skills). When these elements are combined within the learning community, its members strengthen their images of themselves and their colleagues, and a more trusting and supportive environment is formed.

Once the restructuring process is underway, school is no longer business as usual. Small teams must have time to embrace the goals of the entire team. The school must become a laboratory for curriculum development and research. Because it is essential to work *together,* teachers and principals must have time to develop collaborative skills. Collaborative investigations take time, but they are necessary to provide continuous renewal of energy and commitment for all members. Because the development of a learning community is a two-step-forward and one-step-backward process, and because changing the learning community requires changing all of its members, this process must occur slowly, if its effect is to be permanent.

Generalizations for Developing a Learning Community

Box 1.2 lists 12 generalizations about developing a learning community. In the constructivist spirit they can be adapted to fit each school and used as a starting point, with the recognition that each learning community must blend the characteristics of the local faculty, administrators, students, and community, and that it must remain fluid and responsive to the changing needs of its students.

Conclusion

The No Child Left Behind legislation demands levels of academic achievement that cannot be reached by traditional methods. Consequently, professional organizations such as ISLLC, ELCC, and INTASC require administrators to lead teachers in the development of a common mission for their school, a

Box 1.2 Generalizations about Building a Learning Community

1. The school is the ideal-size arena for establishing a learning community.
2. Establishing a learning community is a collaborative process.
3. Optimal learning requires participation of all members of the community, including teachers, students, administrators, parents, counselors, and school support personnel.
4. Each learning community must establish an ethos that supports its mission.
5. The processes called teaching, learning, and teacher "training" are far more complex than frequently presumed and portrayed by education reformers.
6. Creating a new learning community should begin with the realization that through the years American education has been highly successful and should build on those practices that have proven effective.
7. Experimentation is cherished: Learning communities must foster certain attitudes, such as the love of inquiry and problem solving.
8. Self-analysis and reflection must become habitual for all teachers.
9. Restructuring and building a new learning environment is an expensive and time-consuming process.
10. The school–university partnership process must have teachers' support.
11. Successful development of a learning community requires a leader who can provide a vision that ties in with the school's ethos and mission.
12. Developing a learning community is an ongoing process that requires continuous faculty development.

mission that puts learning first. Realizing that the implementation of the mission will require the collective efforts of all, supervisors must guide their teachers to help them cooperatively pool their energy to reach this common goal. More specifically, each school must develop a learning community with a clear mission that all teachers, administrators, and other members understand and are willing to work hard to achieve. The development of a new learning community must be paralleled by a strong, continuous, school-based faculty development program. The instructional supervisor is an excellent leader for this type of development.

Because restructuring on this scale is both expensive and time consuming, the supervisor must find ways to garner the needed support. This can be achieved by making each teacher a full partner in community development from the beginning of the planning process, and by ensuring that each teacher remains a full decision-making partner throughout the life of the learning community.

A good place to start when developing a learning community is to recognize the faculty's strengths and prior achievements. From there, a secure, risk-taking, experimentally-based climate must be developed. The following chapters will help prepare supervisors and administrators to provide leadership and support in the development and implementation of this community.

Questions for Discussion and Reflection

1. What excuses have you heard teachers or administrators give for wanting to maintain the status quo?
2. Why should supervisors always be prepared to praise the positive attributes of a school and the accomplishments of a faculty?
3. Why is the school the ideal size for building a learning community?
4. Why is collaboration essential to building a learning community?
5. What are the respective roles of parents and students in building a learning community?
6. Describe the use that your school has made of its mission statement and tell whether this practice must change if, indeed, the school is to have a new learning community.
7. What is one way that a supervisor might strengthen the image that an elementary or secondary school faculty holds of the local college faculty, and vice versa?
8. How does spreading leadership strengthen it?
9. Why shouldn't administrators initiate innovations without first introducing them to the faculty?
10. How can supervisors help teachers secure financial support needed to implement innovations?

Suggested Activities

1. Offer to help a local principal improve the school's ethos. Using a copy of the school's mission statement, ask the department chairs to identify department goals that will help the school reach its mission.
2. Lead a school administrator and a team of teachers in identifying a new reform practice that the faculty would like to implement. Next, meet with the administrator and a guidance counselor and identify the types of faculty development needed to support this change.
3. Ask a local administrator to assist you in interviewing a school counselor to determine the best way to entice teachers to attend faculty development workshops.
4. Ask a school's department chairs to identify the faculty achievements in their departments. Using these achievements in your introduction, prepare a general statement calling for the school to use these achievements to improve the school program.

Note

[1] Anonymously posted on a Web site from the Hawaii Institute of Geophysics & Planetology, Kids as Airborne Mission Scientists (KaAMS) (http://www/higp/Hawaii.edu/kaams/resource/reflection.htm [accessed January 14, 2009]), as part of curriculum support materials for teachers.

Chapter 2

The History of and Need for Supervision

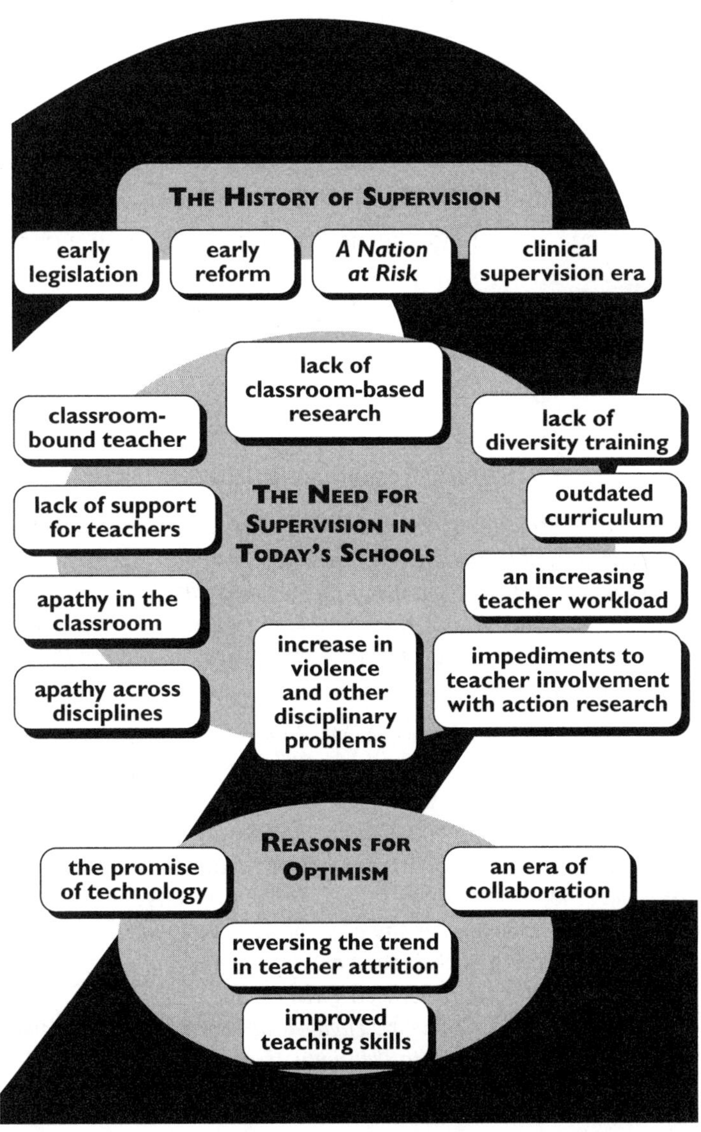

THE HISTORY OF SUPERVISION
early legislation
early reform
A Nation at Risk
clinical supervision era
lack of classroom-based research
classroom-bound teacher
lack of diversity training
lack of support for teachers
THE NEED FOR SUPERVISION IN TODAY'S SCHOOLS
outdated curriculum
an increasing teacher workload
apathy in the classroom
increase in violence and other disciplinary problems
impediments to teacher involvement with action research
apathy across disciplines
REASONS FOR OPTIMISM
the promise of technology
an era of collaboration
reversing the trend in teacher attrition
improved teaching skills

The challenge is to implement a program of study that will meet national standards for leadership preparation by embracing a student-centered approach to learning.

—B. Graham & P. Cannamore,
"Case pedagogy and standards-based teaching"

OBJECTIVES

After completion of this chapter, you should be able to

1. Understand and describe the history of supervision in the United States
2. Identify and discuss several needs for supervision in today's schools
3. Challenge or defend the use of collaborative supervision in today's schools
4. Define constructivism and describe the constructivist teacher's role

Creating an Academic Environment

To an outsider, King Street Elementary is not a very attractive school. The community is in an older part of town. The small houses are on lots that seem even smaller. The steel mills that power this community's economy leave a sulfur odor in the air and a fine residue of grime on the cars parked along both sides of the narrow streets. Just inside the foyer of the 1960s, one-story, flat-roofed building is the office of the principal, Ms. Joyce Myers.

Though in her late fifties or early sixties, Ms. Myers sparkles with enthusiasm. Two activities that she loves are meeting strangers and showing off "her" school. When she speaks of the "school," she doesn't mean the physical facilities or the programs so much as she does the faculty, staff, and students. They are like a family—a good, close family. Ms. Myers' pride in each teacher and her intimate knowledge about each teacher's personal school projects are obvious. Equally obvious are Ms. Myers' appreciation and respect for every teacher and even for the custodians, lunchroom workers, and bus drivers. It is clear that their roles are appreciated and considered indispensable to the overall operation of the school. Furthermore, that respect is reciprocated. Throughout the school, the students are engaged in their assignments; most seem to ignore the many guests that come to see innovative practices. At any time, visitors can see students working on a variety of small-group and individual projects.

A sister school in the district, Crestwood Middle School, has experienced some problems in recent years but seems to be on the mend. Crestwood has received a consider-

able amount of bad publicity over the violence and crime associated with the school. In one way or another, drug abuse is behind most of Crestwood's problems. The principal, Melvin Garner, has one goal: to keep the lid on crime and avoid negative publicity. Some of the criminal activities—perhaps most—are committed by older youths, most of them school dropouts who have found a market for drugs among the Crestwood students. Recent court rulings seem to protect the criminals and permit them to continue their criminal activities at the expense of innocent youths.

The faculty members at Crestwood are cordial and pleasant. Unlike the King Street teachers, who ignore the presence of guests in their classrooms, most Crestwood teachers are willing to put their lessons on hold while their guests visit their rooms. Lectures and in-class assignments seem to be the most popular teaching/learning methods at this school. Almost all classroom assignments involve the use of photocopied worksheets. The Crestwood students seem less than enthusiastic over both the seatwork and the lectures.

In contrast to King Street Elementary and Crestwood Middle School, Jackson High School is more difficult to classify as either traditional or experimental. In fact, both its curriculum and its instruction are a combination of the traditional and the experimental. Although certain Jackson High teachers can easily be identified as traditional and others as experimental, with others it's not so easy. We may tend to think of traditional teachers as dull, rigid, and boring, but some of Jackson High's most traditional teachers are enthusiastic. Their lectures are filled with excitement. Those teachers are skilled in using carefully selected questions to involve their students in each lesson. Other Jackson High teachers are humorous; some are relaxed and comfortable, allowing the students to exercise their sense of humor in all of their lessons. These teachers are able to let the lesson stray long enough for the humor to develop and then draw the lesson back on target without losing the students' attention.

Unfortunately, Jackson High also has its share of dull teachers, and consequently some of the traditional classrooms are less than exciting. Some teachers are boring; the assignments are boring; and the students are bored. In these classrooms, students do not seem to understand the lessons' major concepts, and these are the students who are attempting to follow the lessons. Other students in these traditional classes silently tune out, and some constantly disrupt their classmates.

But Jackson High also has its innovative, experimental teachers. Some of these teachers use case studies; others use simulations, games, and role playing. Cooperative learning is abundant. As they move from room to room, visitors can see the marked contrast at this school. The Jackson High principal could probably get far better results by focusing her attention, energy, and support on the innovative, student-centered classes, but she knows that the teachers and students in the dull classes also need help.

Although these schools are as different as day and night, all are in the same school district and all have a central purpose—to help every student achieve the maximum academic gains possible, and these principals are responsible to ensure that their schools realize this goal.

Reflection

The schools in this case study are different, yet all are compelled by the NCLB legislation, and all share a common mission—to help all their students achieve their potential. Supervisors have responsibility for helping their schools succeed. Administrators can make the difference between faculties that just try to get by and faculties that are working hard to raise their student achievement levels. Consider the supervisor's role in helping the administrators improve their levels of commitment to converting a status-quo faculty into a faculty that works hard to improve learning in their school.

Teachers can and should have a major impact on the levels of success experienced in their classrooms (Shechtman & Leichtentritt, 2005). But to have the potential to become catalysts for changing their classrooms into active, academically productive environments, the teachers themselves must be empowered with the freedom and ability to make judicious decisions about their workplace. Supervisors must help schools create such an environment, and the job is never done. As Clarke and Harris (2006) have said, we must hold "a continuous dialogue between ourselves and our practice that is never finished" (p. 53).

Teachers' ability to create academically productive classrooms also requires a sound knowledge base about student learning and behavior, and about such factors as the environmental and cultural influences on the learner, the cognitive functioning of students, managing the classroom, how students learn, and how all these variables relate to teaching. Such knowledge can help teachers make the many decisions that are required of them daily. Supervisors must help teachers use the current knowledge base on teaching to develop their own knowledge base so they will be able to analyze their classrooms, design and evaluate appropriate curricula and instruction, test these in the classroom, reflect on their implementation, and revise their plans and actions accordingly.

Creating and maintaining a school climate that promotes academic achievement requires the caring and respect shown by the principal at King Street Elementary, the motivation and instructional leadership missing at Crestwood Middle School, and the experimental climate found in some of the classrooms at Jackson. The three schools in this case illustrate two factors about schools: First, the quality of learning occurring in schools varies among schools, and among classrooms within the same school. Second, the teacher makes the difference, and this makes the roles of supervisors and principals profoundly important. While it is true that supervisors can work with teachers exclusively on an individual basis, the results are likely to be scattered at best, as exemplified by Jackson High with its stimulating teachers and its boring teachers. By developing a schoolwide learning community, the supervisor and principal can influence learning throughout the school.

Introduction

This chapter provides a brief history of supervision. Special attention is given to clinical supervision because in just two decades, this type of supervision has advanced as far as supervision had advanced over the two previous centuries. The chapter also reviews education reform and the conditions and concerns that characterize today's schools and challenge the work of supervisors. The chapter ends on a positive note, sharing some good news about teaching, news that supervisors can share with teachers.

The ability of supervisors to function successfully requires a sound knowledge base, including an understanding of the history and purposes of supervision. Thomas Jefferson is credited with saying that those who are ignorant of history are doomed to repeat its mistakes. Although an understanding of the history of supervision will not guarantee success, it will certainly point out some errors that supervisors have made in the past. Paramount among these is how supervision is perceived.

The roles of the supervisor have changed so much and in so many ways that the work of a supervisor whose practices were effective ten years ago would be totally inadequate today, had that supervisor failed to make continuous changes. Following is a brief discussion of the development of instructional supervision. As you read it, consider the many changes that have occurred in your life in the past few years and the demands that some of those changes might have made on schools. The schools' responses to demands for change are often greatly influenced and sometimes are totally determined by the work of the supervisor. As mentioned earlier, this makes the supervisor's instructional role profoundly important.

The History of Supervision

The need for supervisors has been recognized since formal schooling first began in this country. The Old Deluder Satan Act of 1647 required that when each new community grew to 100 families or households, the community had no alternative; it must erect a school building and hire a teacher. Because the country was sparsely populated at that time, and highways as we know them were nonexistent, an instructional supervisor was needed to travel on horseback from school to school to ensure that quality education was being provided in all schools.

Even today, three centuries later, research links the school's leadership to the school's success (Campbell & Porter, 2006; Hunt, 2007; Morford, 2007).

Early Legislation

Since the days of the dame schools (early seventeenth century), Americans have always passed laws concerning the individuals charged with overseeing the education of their children. Soon after the initial settling of this country, laws were enacted to ensure that the children received not just an education but a quality education. In 1647, the Massachusetts Bay Colony passed a law that said,

> Every grammar-school master [is] to be approved by the minister of the town, and the ministers of the two next adjacent towns, and be it further

> enacted, that no minister of any town shall be deemed, held or accepted to be the schoolmaster of such town within the intent of the law. (Holmes, 2005, p. 470)

This was both the nation's first certification law and also the first law that designated individuals as responsible for the "approval" of teachers. Inspectors, who were the forerunners of today's supervisors, were hired to oversee the early public schools. They operated for over two centuries before supervision became professional.

Eventually, the local school boards got involved with examining the qualifications of prospective teachers, but as late as the twentieth century the criteria for evaluating teachers were poorly developed. Huggest and Stinnett (1958, p. 416) describe the evaluation of a new teacher:

> Grandfather was on the school board in the little rural community in which he lived. He and another board member had in mind a young man named Matthew as a teacher of their school. Matthew had little "book larnin." He attended church regularly and his character seemed to be quite satisfactory. So far as was known he did not use intoxicating beverages. . . . But he had only attended and finished the local one-room school. The certification law at the time stated that all candidates must be examined in respect to character, ability to teach, and soundness of knowledge of subject to be taught. . . . Matthew was examined by Grandfather—who commanded him to open his mouth. . . . Grandfather peered inside the tobacco stained cavity and then ran his fingers over the blackened teeth. Grandfather said to the other member of the Board present (the two of them made a legal majority of the three-member board), "Write Matthew out a certificate to teach. . . . I find him sound in every way."

Early Reform

As a profession, supervision began just after the end of the Civil War. Within 50 years, the national population more than tripled and had become much more diversified. No longer was the high school a college preparatory school for the privileged. The curriculum had to be altered to meet the needs of an increasingly multicultural population. More and better prepared teachers were needed; yet, the rapid growth in population had created a severe teacher shortage.

This paradox—the increasing demands on teachers and a general teacher shortage—created extreme concern over the lack of qualified teachers. The current teacher force was limited in both number and skills, and the critics were not reluctant to express their concerns. Lowery (1908, p. 4) said that many of the newer teachers were "immature" and "unevenly prepared." The critics were also concerned over the variation in content that the early twentieth-century teachers were covering. (Through the years, failure to teach the "right" content has been and continues to be the number-one complaint of the critics.) At that time there was no established curriculum; individual teachers made up their own curricula. Although we might think of national standards as a new idea, as early as 1918 one of the earliest curriculum writers, Franklin Bobbitt, called for a standardized curriculum and for trained supervisors to ensure proper use of the designated curriculum. Bolin and Panaritis (1992, p. 34) addressed the supervisor's responsibility for ensuring quality instruction when they said, "The supervisor, a curriculum specialist, was to develop curriculums based on activity analysis and direct the teacher in its proper execution." Because superintendents were usually considered to be the best trained curriculum developers, they were often designated the responsibility for making sure that their districts had quality teaching.

Between the turn of the century and 1920, two movements shaped the superintendent's supervisory role. In the industrial world, Frederick Taylor's management theory, known as *scientific management* and often referred to as Taylorism, dominated. The process consisted of breaking down each worker's role into small parts so that these parts or steps could be closely monitored by a supervisor. Simultaneously, the field of educational psychology was developing its own scientific methodology. As a result of these two parallel forces, it was only natural that the perceived need for educational supervisors grew.

The need for some type of control over teaching methodology was paralleled by a need to ensure that the content being taught was adequate. Curriculum development, thus, began as a field of study whose growth was to parallel supervision as a field of study. In fact, by the time formal studies were being conducted and supervisors were being hired, educators had begun to realize that there was an inherent problem in viewing supervisors as either inspectors or administrators. Supervisors could not work effectively to help teachers who perceived supervisors as inspectors or administrators, because the ultimate goal of the supervisor is to help teachers with their self-improvement—something that cannot occur easily or readily in an environment of fear (Clarke & Harris, 2006), in a hierarchical climate, or in situations where the main concern is pleasing a superior. To be successful, the self-improvement of teachers must occur in a climate that permits teachers to focus their attention on improving their skills to better serve their students. Consequently, the formal study of supervision quickly aligned with the new field of study called *curriculum development*.

By the 1920s, textbooks began shaping the curriculum and were also used in programs to train superintendents. A. S. Barr and William H. Burton's new textbook (1926),*The Supervision of Instruction*, had the biggest impact on shaping supervision for the next several decades. Since 1930, supervisors have been careful to distinguish between supervision and administration. Supervisors have also, at least in part, acknowledged the complexity of teaching, rejected the scientific management view of supervision, and proclaimed that to be effective both supervisors and teachers must be creative. The role of the teacher as one that demanded considerable autonomy was far different than the popular view held in industry at that time, for it was firmly believed that workers needed close scrutiny and lock-step supervision to keep them on task and on target.

The very act of assigning a supervisor suggests that others doubt teachers' ability and willingness to improve on their own. In fact, according to the definition of "professionalism," the presence of supervisors seems to suggest that teachers are considered to be something less than professional. A characteristic associated with the concept of professionalism is autonomy; it is widely known that professionals have more autonomy than nonprofessionals. It is assumed that professionals are capable and trustworthy of regulating the quality of their own work. If, indeed, this autonomous professional concept could be applied to all teachers, an argument could be made that there would be no need for supervisors.

Another problem that has bedeviled supervision through the years is the association that it has had with management. From the early days of formal supervision, supervisory responsibility has been assigned to superintendents, magnifying the perception that the supervisor is *above* the teachers in the overall hierarchy. Although members of other professions have superiors to whom they must answer regarding organizational and administrative concerns, shouldn't teachers be the experts on teaching? Does the superintendent have more expertise in teaching than teachers? If not, then why should the superintendent be supervising instruction? Through the years, these questions have perplexed some teachers. Recent emphasis on teacher empowerment has rekindled and intensified this concern.

There have always been individuals and groups in society who have attempted to shape the schools. These early attempts to control the quality of instruction were paralleled by attempts to regulate the curriculum. Franklin Bobbitt's call for the standardization of the curriculum has never subsided, and the echoes of his plea ring louder today than they have in the past 50 years, bringing American education closer than ever to a national curriculum.

A *Nation at Risk*

In a democratic country such as the United States, there are recurring periods of expressed malcontent. Often during these periods, criticism is aimed at the public schools. There appears to be no off season for these attacks on the tax-supported bulwarks of a democratic society. When public anxiety is aroused by war, threat of war, inflation, depression—whatever shocks people into action—discontent and fault finding are almost certain to follow, and all too often the first suspected cause is the schools. Almost as a reflex action, the populace focuses on tax-supported public schools as the cause célèbre of social, economic, and political problems.

The USSR's 1957 launch of the earth's first artificial satellite, *Sputnik I,* is a good example of the national exercise of fault finding. Frightened that the USSR was winning the space race, in a state of panic Americans turned their basements and storm cellars into bomb shelters. Attributing the Soviet Union's space victory to the failure of American schools to adequately prepare students to compete with the Russians in preparing scientists, Americans moved quickly to correct the problem. Thirty-five of the nation's top businessmen, scientists, and educators were assembled in Woods Hole, Massachusetts, to determine what had gone wrong with U.S. schools and what was needed to fix them.

Although the Woods Hole Conference was stimulated by what today might be seen as a state of unfounded panic, several excellent landmark curriculum improvements resulted. These changes are discussed in later chapters. Now, more than half a century later, the schools find themselves responding to another national panic. This time the alleged failure results from an economic recession. Other countries have developed the ability to produce better automobiles and comparable or better electronics at competitive prices. The general conclusion of some of the critics has been that our schools have totally failed to produce workers who are competitive in the world market. However, schools are only one of several factors that have influenced the economy, and treating them as the sole influence is unwise.

In the words of the reform report *A Nation at Risk* (National Commission on Excellence in Education, 1983, p. 5), "If an unfriendly foreign power had attempted to impose on America the mediocre educational performance that exists today, we might well have viewed it as an act of war." As in many other education reform reports, this inflammatory language suggests an attempt to incite alarm and stir the public's emotions. To say the least, as with earlier reform movements, the impetus for the current reform has been a climate of dissatisfaction with the schools. Too often, education reform amounts to no more than school bashing. Some of the blame can be traced back to *A Nation at Risk*. By urging reformers to address these *symptoms* of educational failure instead searching for its true *causes*, the report pointed our national reform effort in the wrong direction.

During periods of national crisis of any type, the significance of the supervisor's role has been accentuated because the schools have been the targets of blame for the country's failure. Supervisors must help teachers remain positive in a nation that has a history of criticizing its schools. At best, the practice of criticizing demonstrates a level of concern and a desire for quality education. The role of supervisors must transcend the practice of criticizing the schools, and the goal must be nothing short of improving instruction to the maximum degree possible.

The Clinical Supervision Era

By the early 1960s a new term began appearing in educational supervision literature: *clinical supervision*. The term described several trends in the practices of supervisors. Foremost among these was a trend toward working with teachers on an individual basis. The term *clinical* implies the common practices of medicine—analysis, diagnosis, and prescription. Because the term clinical has medical overtone, it gave status to teaching. For example, I once worked with a dean of a nursing college who wore a white coat and a stethoscope. Although many educators continue to embrace this connotation to enhance their professionalism, most realize that the level of improvement demanded can be reached only by collaboration. Incidentally, the last of these clinical/medical practices (prescription, usually from so-called "experts") has drawn a lot of resentment in recent years, unlike the role of colonial-era inspectors who were expected to be prescriptive.

An important quality associated with the term "clinical supervision" is *classroom-based*. This quality has several advantages that cause many educators to embrace clinical supervision. Perhaps the most appealing quality of classroom-based supervision is that it offers a refreshing change from the traditional districtwide staff development which, itself, was never very effective because over the years few districts have taken staff development seriously.

Yet another quality of clinical supervision that is much appreciated by most contemporary educators is the involvement of teachers in improving their own teaching. The districtwide workshops that were predominant prior to the advent of clinical supervision were not workshops at all, but rather opportunities for teachers to come together to listen to "experts" give advice. Boyer (1997, p. 44) explains: "All too often these 'in-service sessions' are little more than lectures offered by 'experts,' who are 'long on process and short on substance.'"

At its onset, clinical supervision symbolized the work of the so-called "expert" sent to help teachers. Over the years teachers' own expertise has come to be recognized, and supervision as we know it today is a process designed to use that expertise to solve problems and create and maintain a positive learning climate.

There is disagreement in the profession as to whether supervision should be a one-to-one practice or a group practice. The pros and cons of this argument will be discussed in chapter 4. A couple of salient points to remember as you pursue the study of teacher development are that good, ongoing faculty development programs are critical to the effective functioning of all schools. As shown in the vignette at the beginning of this chapter, there is much variance among schools because most schools have considerable latitude in designing their own programs.

A half-century after its recognition as a formalized process, clinical supervision continues to be widely accepted. Perhaps its longevity can be attributed largely to the fact that it has been flexible enough to meet the ever-changing demands made on the supervisor.

Supervision has changed:

- from a heavy-handed, dictatorial process to a cooperative partnership process whereby the supervisor and the teacher seek improvements together
- from a process where one "expert" dictated to a subordinate to a process that involves two experts working together
- from a process with ready solutions known in advance to a problem-solving process
- from a process where the supervisor identified needed changes to a process in which the supervisor and the teachers all work together to choose areas for improvement
- from a process where change meant that something was identified as wrong and needed correction to a process where change is viewed as a way to make effective processes even better.

These changes are summarized in Table 2.1.

Teachers tend to view as most useful those professional improvement activities based on their own identified needs and problems. Faculty meetings planned by teachers or by both teachers and administrators are judged by faculty to be more useful than meetings planned by administrators alone.

Table 2.1 The Changing Nature of Clinical Supervision

From	To
• Dictatorial leadership • Ready solutions known in advance • Supervisor-identified areas of needed improvement • Change viewed as a signal that something is wrong	• A voluntary process • A problem-solving process • Teacher/supervisor-identified areas for improvement • Change viewed as a constant need to make good practices better

The Need for Supervision in Today's Schools

The 1980s and 1990s reform reports and the No Child Left Behind legislation have made two important positive contributions: They have rekindled earlier concerns with American education, and they have identified additional legitimate weaknesses in the schools. The impact of NCLB is so great that it has become the symbol of all that is good and bad in education (McColl, 2005). Whether the messages about our schools have been authentic or contrived, their power to affect teachers and schools has been substantial. To help teachers and other school personnel get the facts straight, supervisors must be familiar with the current educational issues that concern teachers and other citizens. Following is a discussion of some of the more pronounced concerns, including: (1) classroom-bound teachers, (2) lack of teacher support, (3) lack of induction programs for novice teachers, (4) apathy in the classroom, (5) apathy across disciplines, (6) a lack of diversity training, (7) an increase in violence, (8) lack of classroom research, (9) outdated curriculum, (10) an increasing teacher workload, (11) exclusion of teachers from the school-reform process, and (12) problems resulting from reform efforts.

Classroom-Bound Teachers

Unlike most professions that permit and even encourage their members to associate daily with each other, and through no fault of their own, for well over two centuries our teachers have spent most of their teaching lives within the boundaries of their own classrooms, separated from other teachers, unable to benefit from the psychological support that can come from associating with professional peers. At many schools this handicapping practice still continues in the twenty-first century. Isolated from their colleagues, administrators, and other school personnel, teachers cannot benefit from the insights of other teachers, and the opportunity to refine their own perceptions and skills by having discussions with their peers is lost.

Confinement to their classrooms limits faculty planning in both breadth and depth. Without the ability to associate with other teachers, most of them are left out of the planning process for the rest of the school's curriculum. This means that teachers are prohibited from connecting their classes with those of others—unable to take advantage of integrating their curriculum, providing continuity through the grades and articulation across the disciplines at the same grade level. In contrast, the power of teacher collaboration teams to improve learning has become so obvious that it is recognized as the engine that drives student achievement (Marshall, 2005).

Lack of Support for Teachers

Economic retrenchment resulting from the goal of balancing the national budget is placing demands on teachers that, if not unfair, are at least restricting teachers' effectiveness in the classroom. For example, many teachers' classrooms lack essential equipment and supplies. In nonunion districts, teachers are often encouraged to hold bake sales or other fund-raisers to purchase equipment or even supplies. Paradoxically, although NCLB has increased the funds for schools tremendously, many schools have fewer funds than ever before. Supervisors can help by recommending inexpensive demonstrations and student activities that require minimum use of expensive equipment; and by helping teachers locate inexpensive software applications that provide realistic simulations, enabling students to develop the same generalizations that would be developed by more expensive laboratory experiments. Supervisors can also encourage their faculty to apply for grants to fund specific (and often costly) projects (see chapter 15).

Art and music teachers are especially vulnerable to economic recessions, and in many districts these positions are considered less than essential. Yet, the fine arts have been proved to contribute to the development of critical thinking. (See chapter 9 for a more detailed discussion of the importance of the arts in the curriculum.) Eric Jensen (2008a) has reminded us that a school cannot remove the arts from its curriculum and at the same time claim to be doing what's best for the minds of its students. Most education reform reports reinforce this perception by stressing mathematics and science and ignoring the arts.

During the 1960s, the fear stimulated by *Sputnik* introduced doubt in teachers' ability to teach effectively. Consequently, "teacher proof" curricula with carefully specified instructions and hands-on materials were developed. The idea behind this approach was to give lock-step instructions for learners so that their success would not depend solely on the ability of their teachers to guide their learning. Clearly, teachers were not trusted to lead the learning of their students. Later, Secretary of Education Terrel Bell (1993), who commissioned the damning report, *A Nation at Risk*, admitted that attempting to develop teacher-proof curricula to bypass teachers was a mistake:

> We have foolishly concluded that any problems with the levels of academic achievement have been caused by faulty schools staffed by inept teachers and [that] by fixing the schools we can attain the levels of success we so desperately need in this decade. . . .We also know that teacher leadership of and involvement in school improvement must become a more integral part of our plans. (pp. 595, 597)

Unfortunately, by the time this retraction was issued, the American public had been given a decade to think about their schools and teachers as mediocre (meaning terribly poor), which was the label this national committee had given them.

However, in addition to brewing needless worry about the condition of teachers and schools, the reform reports also identified legitimate weaknesses, some of which are characteristics of the schools; others are characteristics of the communities outside the schools. The following sections address some of these concerns.

Lack of Induction Programs for Novice Teachers

Traditionally, teachers have abruptly moved from the status of student teacher to a position of total responsibility—the professional teacher. As a result, many novice teachers have found the demands during their first year of teaching to be overwhelming and, for many, their first year of teaching has been their last. Forced to learn through trial and error, many of those teachers who do survive their first year are left with a set of behaviors that can be described more accurately as survival skills than effective teaching skills. According to Turley, Powers, and Nakai (2006, p. 27), "Almost all teachers experience reality shock and some level of discouragement or frustration during their induction years." Rather than this trial-and-error approach, teachers need an encouraging environment with a carefully planned, differentiated, professional development program to meet their needs during each phase of their careers (Gray & Smith, 2005). The importance of such a program is so great that it should be entrusted only to a dedicated support team (Normore & Floyd, 2005).

Aware of the importance of this formative first year, many states have initiated internship programs to provide first-year teachers with special supervision. Although the roles and responsibilities that all supervisors share in

It Works for Me!

Supporting the Novice Teacher

Sandra S. Murray, University of Tennessee at Martin

I have found that an effective method of supporting the novice teacher is to have a veteran teacher provide monthly tea parties for all the new teachers in the school, including not only teachers new to the profession but also those new to the building. During the initial tea party the teachers introduce themselves, take a tour of the school, learn some of the history of the school from a peer rather than from an administrator, and establish dates and topics for future tea parties. Subsequent tea parties can feature guest speakers or articles for discussion—or can just be an occasion when teachers can speak their minds.

The administrator is deliberately eliminated from attendance at the tea parties to provide a safe venue for novice teachers to discuss problems, share successes and failures, and obtain help. The veteran teacher must establish the tea parties as a safe place for open discussion and must not share discussions with the administrator or other teachers.

working with first-year interns vary from state to state, these teachers are part of the teaching staff in almost every district, making teacher interns a concern of all supervisors. Further discussion of this topic appears in chapter 4.

Apathy in the Classroom

Through the years, teachers have faced the growing challenge of trying to teach youths who display an increasing amount of apathy, students on drugs, and students whose only goal in life is to reach the legal age for dropping out. At many schools, as many as 90% of all students are at high risk of dropping out prior to graduation.

The challenge is clear: Teachers must discover ways to motivate these students, and supervisors must help by ensuring that every teacher has a repertoire of alternatives to the lecture. Chapters 8 and 9 provide a variety of strategies that have proven to be much stronger motivators than the lecture. Supervisors can also help by preparing teachers to involve their students in action research projects, the subject of chapter 13.

Apathy across Disciplines

The Woods Hole Conference recommended redesigning curricula and creating interdisciplinary themes. National research and development laboratories located in each geographic section of the country led the development of a variety of prepackaged interdisciplinary programs that were rather short-lived, and the majority of schools soon reverted to self-contained classrooms.

Perennially, teachers have disagreed on the issue of responsibility. Common among these disagreements have been arguments over whether teachers have responsibilities for teaching content, skills, behaviors, and attitudes in areas outside their teaching field—for example, whether teachers of subjects other than English have responsibility for correcting spelling and grammar errors and whether they have the right to deduct academic credit for these errors. The emphasis on integrated themes, common to many reform programs, gives reason for optimism; hopefully teachers will no longer feel that these responsibilities belong only to those who teach language-arts disciplines.

A Lack of Diversity Training

Although teachers should view classrooms with culturally diverse student bodies as positive opportunities to learn about other cultures, many teachers feel threatened by the challenge of working productively with members of other cultures. The problem is magnified by the fact that the vast majority of today's teaching force is Caucasian and the size of the non-Caucasian student population is rapidly growing. A recent study showed that although 76% of new teachers said that teaching an ethnically diverse student body was covered in their training, only 39% say that their training in this area helps them a lot now that they are in the classroom (Public Agenda, 2008).

Historically, textbooks (with inadequate or inaccurate coverage of minorities) have been a major contributor to this problem. Fortunately, in recent years publishers and professional associations have become more responsible. Over the years the Association for Supervision and Curriculum Development has taken a strong, positive position toward promoting appreciation for diverse cultures. The national teaching associations have embraced multicultural education, and supervisors have a responsibility for helping teachers meet this goal.

Clearly, a meaningful and highly effective diversity-trained teacher workforce should start with quality preparation, bolstered with good induction and mentoring programs for new teachers (see chapter 3). Supervisors should stay current on the most recent diversity-training techniques and make sure that they are available to their faculty.

* * *

In some way or another, almost every chapter in this book addresses the effects of poverty and changing demographics on education. The following case study shows that even in the poorest and most diverse schools, high expectations can be met by a collaborative faculty who is not satisfied with the status quo.

Pacific Cove School

Gary Hoban • National University

This case is about a school district that is being forced to change in order to meet a rapid ethnographic shift in the community. Like many communities throughout the country, the number and percent of non-mainstream students is growing rapidly and creating the need for a once stable and peaceful faculty to make swift changes in programs and practices.

Supervisors have always served as change agents. Recent changes in society have intensified this role. Twenty-first century supervisors must be highly skilled engineers who are able to guide both their faculty members and parents in their often volatile and illogical responses to societal changes.

This case study is particularly appropriate because it reflects the heavy impact poverty has on schools throughout the country, and particularly pertinent because the school accomplishes its objectives through collaboration.

The School

Pacific Cove Elementary School (not its real name) is located in a large urban school district in southern California. The district began changing in the 1970s and ultimately was placed under a court-ordered desegregation mandate. Today that court order has been lifted, but many of the issues remain.

Over the years the district in which the case takes place has clearly become diverse, with over 70% of the student population being classified as being non-Anglo. Approximately 40% of the students in the district are Hispanic, with other ethnic groups accounting for the remaining 30% of non-Anglo students.

Pacific Cove School had an enrollment of 466 students when its new principal, Ben Sanchez, arrived. Its student body was representative of the changing demographics in the district, with more than 50% of its enrollment being Hispanic. The number of students classified as non-English proficient (NEP) or limited-English proficient (LEP) was 173 or 37% of the student body. The number of NEP/LEP students was nearly three times the number it was three years before Ben Sanchez took on the school's principalship. Approximately 50% of the students came from homes where Spanish was the spoken language. Twenty-five percent of the students were bussed to the school from other areas of the district.

Eighty-three percent of the children were from families believed to be in poverty, with this percentage being based on those children receiving AFDC and/or receiving a free lunch. Only five families from among the student population owned their own homes. All of the others were renters, many living in military housing.

The school is located close to a major recreational area within the city, and it is not far from the most affluent area of the district. It is close to a high school that ultimately receives its students after they complete middle school nearby. A major factor in the school's demographic picture has been its mobility rate. Many of the students come from military housing, and the transience rate is extremely high. There are virtually no wealthy families with children in the school, even though the school is in a popular area of the city and is quite close to a highly affluent area of the city.

For the most part, the faculty and support staff seemed content with the status quo and were not motivated to make changes, even though many had been there for a number of years and had seen the school change from a predominately white school with a strong majority of native-English speakers from the lower-middle and middle class to the type of school described above. One long-time observer of the school noted that many of the teachers had grown quite comfortable with the status quo, knowing that the school was not all that visible to the district; that the community was relatively complacent; and that, because so many children moved during the school year, it was not easy or perhaps not even desirable to be held all that accountable for student learning.

The Case

Ben Sanchez arrived at Pacific Cove Elementary School by coming up through the ranks of a large, bureaucratic school system that still puts pressures on its administrators to meet the needs of a rapidly changing student body. Ben was the first Hispanic to be appointed principal of Pacific Cove; in fact, he was the first member of a minority group to hold a leadership position in the school. One of the first challenges Ben faced was a belief on the part of the white parents that he would favor the Hispanic children. The Hispanic parents, on the other hand, feared he would not do enough for their children. He clearly was caught in the middle of the conflicting perceptions of these two groups and had to finesse the issue. It was important that he enhance his credibility by being totally objective, not only toward both groups but also toward the other racial/ethnic groups.

Ben also noted that up until the time he arrived at Pacific Cove, principals did not appear to stay long at the school. The teachers and the staff had come to expect that they would outlast the principal. Ben's immediate predecessor stayed as principal for one year. The principal before his predecessor stayed two years. Pacific Cove was not a school conducive to change.

Perhaps the most pressing academic problem in the school was in the primary grades. Parents approached Ben to complain that the instructional program in the first grade was weak, that their children were not being prepared for advancement to higher grades, and that they did not think that present first-grade teachers were up to the task.

Ben noted that he had some creative, risk-taking teachers at other grade levels. He consulted with two of them. One was willing to take on a first-grade assignment to try to improve the program; the other was reluctant to move. It quickly became apparent to Ben that ordering the teacher to move wouldn't work and that the first-grade program would remain the same. Gradually, Ben began using a different strategy. Instead of coldly analyzing the problem, he began working directly with the reluctant teacher and the other first-grade teachers as well. His involvement stressed human relations activities—trust-building activities such as luncheons and appreciative messages for work well done, to name but a few. This approach worked. Gradually the reluctant teacher was won over and took on the first-grade assignment with her colleague. The curriculum was revised, with an emphasis on setting high expectations.

The issue of trust was of equal concern to members of the community. The school was seen as a formal, aloof institution. While Ben was a good listener, as he had to be in situations such as the need for first-grade changes, he also needed to be more accessible. Parents were not always comfortable in the school setting. To meet this need, Ben began a series of coffee klatches at the homes of parents, most often in Spanish. He traded acceptable gossip, shared information, and most important, he learned directly that parents' input was needed to revitalize the school. Ben outlasted his predecessors, and much was accomplished at Pacific Cove School.

What Did Happen at Pacific Cove Elementary School?

- Two teachers saw a need for children at the kindergarten level to have a readiness program before the start of school that would stress skills as well as learning-readiness activities. As a result of Ben's leadership, the school began Project Jump Start, which for three weeks offered a three-hour daily session for children at the school before kindergarten started. A related problem was that many parents felt uncomfortable or alienated from school personnel. Project Jump Start offered a six-hour program for the parents of kindergarten students before the start of school. The parent program oriented them to what was expected of them once their child entered school.
  - Since many of the parents did not speak English, ESL classes were offered to them at Pacific Cove.
  - Parent education classes became routinely offered whereas, in the past, parent involvement in the schools was low.
  - In one year there were 3000 parent volunteer hours.
  - The first-grade instructional program was changed to benefit children who needed special help before beginning grade one.
  - First-grade standardized test scores went up dramatically.
  - Pacific Cove became a summer-school hub for the elementary schools in its region of the city, with a special emphasis on reading.
- Children from Pacific Cove routinely began to compete in scholastic competitions against children from more affluent schools and districts. At the beginning they were not winning, but they achieved a sense of confidence in their abilities and a more competitive drive to succeed academically.
- Partnerships with the local newspaper, a regional restaurant, and a major car lubrication franchise were established to help support the school.

Did Pacific Cove become the perfect school? Ben Sanchez would hardly say so. He knows that a quiet, inconspicuous beginning was made; that faculty, staff, and parents began talking; that projects got underway; that there were some small victories. More importantly, he noted that Pacific Cove became a place that "no longer wallows in poverty. It is a happy place to be."

Issues for Further Reflection

1. Are the changing demographics noted in this district and in this school consistent with what you have seen happening in your school or district?
2. Has the curriculum in your school kept up with the kinds of demographic shifts described above?
3. Are most teachers comfortable in a school without high expectations? Should they be?
4. Do you think that most teachers are resistant to change or are they mainly victims of their teaching environment?
5. Why do you think the principals who were at Pacific Cove before Ben Sanchez did not survive?
6. If you had been in Ben Sanchez's position, how would you have begun your first principalship?
7. What do you see as the weaknesses of Ben Sanchez's approaches to change? Were they too fast or too slow?
8. What do you see as the strengths of Ben Sanchez's approaches to change?
9. Although Ben Sanchez started out by being directive, he changed to a strategy of cultivating teachers through personal rewards. Was this a sound way to proceed?
10. Ben Sanchez started the movement toward change at the first-grade level and moved slowly. Should he have been more aggressive?
11. There are different kinds of leadership styles that can be used in a change situation. Among them are authoritarian, charismatic, transformational, situational, and participatory. Which styles of leadership do you think Ben Sanchez used, and which styles do you think would be most effective in a situation like the one which existed at Pacific Cove?
12. Some observers have concluded that the sweeping demographic changes such as those that have occurred at Pacific Cove make it impossible to provide quality education for all children. Now, with No Child

Left Behind, many believe that it is a thankless and maybe impossible task. They argue that schools like Pacific Cove should be closed and that parents should be given vouchers to secure private education for their children. What do you think?

Increase in Violence and Other Disciplinary Problems

For several years, discipline problems at school have escalated in number and severity. A decade of Gallup Polls of the public's attitudes toward the public schools have reported "lack of discipline" as the number-one concern, and the problem has worsened. By the mid-1990s, for the first time fighting, violence, and gangs shared the number-one position with lack of discipline (Elam, Rose, & Gallup, 1996, p. 41). Discipline topped the problem list over the first 16 years of this poll, replaced by use of drugs and, later, lack of financial support. In the 2005 poll, lack of discipline followed only lack of financial support and overcrowded schools (Rose & Gallup, 2005). A recent study showed that nearly 9 in 10 high school teachers (88%) say that the most pressing problems facing high schools come from "social problems and kids who misbehave" rather than academic issues (Public Agenda, 2007). Novice teachers report discipline as their number-one concern.

Clearly, the old clichés that once shaped classroom behavior will no longer work. The "sage" advice, "Don't smile until Christmas," is one example. The common use of threat (which, incidentally, never worked in the past) still does not work. The lavish use of corporal punishment that was once unanimously supported by parents is now effective only for getting teachers and administrators into court. Corporal punishment threatens the welfare of all children and can be especially damaging today in a society where many children are neglected or abused.

Because of changing demographics and a busier lifestyle, the family support that characterized communities throughout the first half of the twentieth century virtually disappeared, often leaving teachers to control the behavior in their classrooms without the help of parents. Fortunately, the final years in the twentieth century experienced a resurgence in strong parental involvement in schools. Supervisors have a vital role in helping teachers learn how to involve parents productively. Supervisors must help schools build learning communities that expand beyond the teachers' immediate classrooms and include parents and other members of the community at large.

For more on parental involvement, and on discipline as it relates to classroom management, see chapter 11.

Lack of Classroom-Based Research

As mentioned earlier, prior to the No Child Left Behind Act most American elementary and secondary classrooms essentially had been devoid of research. Teachers have considered research and teaching as either unrelated or as opposites, making research and teaching mutually exclusive. This slighting of research raises two concerns: the failure of teachers to benefit from the research findings of other researchers, and the failure of teachers to conduct their own action research in their classrooms.

Since the beginning of the current wave of education reform (in the early 1980s), the literature documents educators' concern over teachers' failure to use research studies in their classrooms (Miech, Nave, & Mosteller, 2005). Although teachers are commonly acknowledged as having had experience, they are credited with little knowledge gained from that experience. Teachers' failure to conduct their own research has several negative effects on American public education. Obviously, teachers who are not involved with conducting research miss the benefits of having the steady inflow of fresh data for content in their classes, but there are many additional losses. Teachers who shun research miss the opportunity to develop energy and confidence, elements that are natural products of involvement with research. These teachers also miss a major force that leads teachers to become reflective and critical, two important qualities shared by scientists. Some of the reasons for the lack of research in the classroom are discussed later in this chapter.

Outdated Curriculum

Contemporary educators certainly realize that the expectations on all educators are great and that the accountability level is at an unprecedented high. This makes the curriculum-improvement role of the supervisor more vital than ever before. In many ways our schools truly have not made the improvements of which they are capable. For example, the curriculum has not kept pace with the times. Today's curriculum is largely Victorian—a late nineteenth-century expression of the Industrial Revolution as applied to the education industry.

The first teachers in this country made the total curricula for their classes like they made their biscuits: from scratch. This practice gave teachers a high level of expertise in applying curricula to the students' needs. Over a half-century ago, Hilda Taba called for curriculum development that started by developing teaching or learning units. The approach was so different from the norm that it quickly became known as Taba's Inverted Curriculum Model, whose practices still dominate classrooms throughout the country.

Many of today's teachers find themselves unprepared to construct the excellent curricula that are required to enable students to achieve at mandated levels. For example, many American teachers suffer from a lack of appreciation for philosophy, without which it is impossible to design curricula that are compatible with their values—curricula that capitalize on the teachers' strengths, enabling them to use their creative, artistic talents—curricula which, in turn, enable their students to unleash their own talents and develop their creative abilities—curricula which prepare students to skillfully weld ideas and shape them as master artisans use their tools, always in control and always with a purpose. Nel Noddings (2008) offers a look into the future at the types of requirements that will be made of our students: "Occupational success will require flexibility, a willingness to continue learning, an ability to work in teams, patience and skill in problem solving, intellectual and personal honesty, and a well-developed capacity to think" (p. 13). Our curricula must reflect our students' twenty-first-century needs, and the supervisor has a responsibility to work with teachers and administrators toward this end.

Students need the insights required to recognize their own creative potential, and they need the power to develop and cultivate these latent talents. Teachers will not find the curricula needed to equip their students with this power in their state or district curriculum guides, in state or national standards, or in textbooks—and yet, teachers who lack the skills required to develop their own excellent curricula must depend on the textbook and other ready-made curricula sources (e.g., photocopied handouts) for their students. Students rarely find such sources either helpful or interesting.

An Increasing Teacher Workload

Many teachers are overwhelmed with the demands being placed on them. When faced with seemingly impossible demands, a common reaction is to seek shelter. Many of today's schools are hostile and confusing places where teachers, principals, and students try to create islands of safety and sanity for themselves and are reluctant to leave those safe shores for parts unknown. Supervisors must help teachers discover ways to redistribute the load of responsibilities. Prior to the No Child Left Behind legislation, teacher collaboration was (and in many schools throughout the nation still is) countercultural and rarely happens without leadership from the supervisor (Marshall, 2005). However, team teaching in integrated disciplines now is increasingly important for all schools. Supervisors can help by providing the faculty with development opportunities that will increase their comfort levels with such programs by helping teachers lessen their reliance on the content in their textbooks. Instead of just covering information, the goal of teachers should be involving students in activities that enable them to discover and create major understandings.

Exclusion of Teachers from the School-Reform Process

> How come almost everyone who writes about school reform works someplace other than a school? . . . In our ongoing national dialogue on school reform, there are few voices from "the bottom" that matter. We are missing the unmediated voice of practitioners who are actually attempting reform, achieving it, failing at it, or partially achieving it and wondering why they haven't done better. (J. Dowd, quoted by J. Check in Peterson, 2002)

In some communities education reform is discussed without input from teachers, principals, and superintendents, yet these educators are experts who are capable of providing important input. Ironically, these are the professionals who will be charged with the responsibility of implementing the externally developed programs and making them work.

As indicated earlier, the reform of the 1960s produced some significant curriculum and instruction improvements. Unfortunately, some of these important changes have been gradually discarded. If supervisors are to lead today's teachers and administrators to the levels of excellence to which they are being held accountable, both supervisors and teachers will need to make maximum use of existing knowledge of the learning process. Helping teachers reach this goal may be the most important role of current and future instructional supervisors.

Joe Check, director of the Boston Writing Project, says that a key component of school reform is that teachers must write about their classrooms if positive educational change is to take hold (Peterson, 2002). Supervisors must encourage teachers to participate in action research, write about their findings, and collaborate to share their results with their peers. However, many factors are currently working against this process, the most important of which are discussed in the following section.

Impediments to Teacher Involvement with Action Research

Teachers who conduct action research experience a renewed desire to stay current. *Action research* (i.e., short-term investigations that teachers themselves initiate and conduct to improve their own practices) also serves to sharpen perceptions, stimulate discussion, and energize questioning. Involvement in research makes teachers more critical of both university-based research and standard school practices. Teachers who conduct research challenge taken-for-granted assumptions about theory and practice. Involvement with research seems to improve teachers' attitudes in general.

Action research can be either interpretive (i.e., teachers attempting to understand a situation or occurrence within their own schools and determine what meaning participants make from it) or critical (i.e., teachers examining and challenging established ways that things are done at their schools) (Glickman, 2007). More on action research appears in chapter 13.

Supervisors can assist by making sure that teachers are prepared with the knowledge to gather and analyze data, and to analyze and summarize it. Make sure that your faculty has established ethical guidelines prior to conducting any action research. Action research is especially effective when it is collaborative in nature and is especially suited to teamwork (described in chapter 1). Later in this chapter, we discuss the importance of collaboration in research.

Constructivists are concerned about teachers who don't conduct research, because they fail to create knowledge for themselves and therefore cannot involve their students in this creation. The results, according to constructivist theory, are that both teachers and students are dealing with used, secondhand knowledge that they can never fully understand. Several day-to-day pressures impact teachers' ability and willingness to perform research. Among them are an increased work pace, increased accountability, negative education-reform reports, and unrealistic or unattainable goals.

An Increased Pace. Today's "microwave lifestyle" has swept through the schools. A combination of elements—most introduced and/or intensified by NCLB—has increased the pace of teachers, administrators, and other school personnel, a situation that greatly reduces discretionary time that might be used for action research. The knowledge explosion is partially responsible for this urgent need for speed. Teachers of every discipline rush to cover the topics that next year's teachers will expect this year's students to bring to their classes (Noddings, 2008). The personal computer has pushed many teachers to compete technologically with some students who spend most of their time in front of a computer screen. The problem is intensified by the rapid development of new computer technology (both hardware and software). How can teachers ever keep up with technology and also keep up with new developments in their teaching fields, much less keep up with research on pedagogy? Supervisors can help by sharing current information with their faculty, encouraging them to collaborate (as with the reflective model for collaborative supervision in chapter 1), and offering time-saving suggestions. Throughout this book suggestions appear about ways that technology can decrease teacher workload and increase the relevancy and effectiveness of instruction.

Increased Accountability. Another source of pressure on teachers that takes away from potential action research time is their responsibility for the improvement of their students' test scores. Reform programs in some states threaten to take over those schools whose students do not score well on standardized tests, bringing covert and sometimes even overt pressures on teachers to ensure that their students excel. Making matters worse, the nation has a recent history of setting impossible goals for its schools. For example, *Goals 2000* made the unrealistic claims that by the year 2000 all children would start school ready to learn; American students would be first in the world in mathematics and science achievement; and every school in America would be free of drugs and violence and would offer a disciplined environment conducive to learning. The subsequent No Child Left Behind legislation required all students to score at or above proficiency levels on standardized state tests by 2014. Evaluation expert James Popham (2007) has labeled its unrealistic achievement targets for schools as "the most salient shortcoming of NCLB" (p. 83).

Negative Reports. Teachers are also under pressure because of messages from many education-reform reports that label the teachers as inept and the schools as an embarrassment. Although some of the education-reform reports have identified areas of true concern, many reflect the biases and narrow-mindedness of their authors.

In contrast, some would argue that ours has been, and continues to be, one of the best education systems in the world. They offer as evidence the fact that for decades more immigrants have chosen to pursue higher education in this country than in any other country in the world. They point out that far more Nobel Prizes have been awarded in America than in any other country. A comparison of number of Nobel Prizes awarded since 1901 shows the United States with 270, compared to Great Britain with 101 and the other 45 countries with an average of 9 awards each. Further evidence of the success of American schools is seen in the percentage of youths who complete high school. For centuries, our school system was the only one in the world that attempted to educate all of its youths. The American Dream that each generation will have a higher standard of living than its parents is founded in the nation's long-standing belief in the right of all youths to a quality education.

Contemporary educators, and especially supervisors, need positive outlooks to offer teachers who may be misguided by the critics' exaggerations. Supervisors should arm themselves with facts that can be used to help today's teachers feel good about themselves and their chosen profession. For example, the current wave of reform reports and reform movements underway throughout the country reaffirm the message that "American schools are important!"

Unattainable Goals. Even prior to NCLB, most reform reports held teachers accountable for the success of all students. For example, the Goals 2000 seemed at face value to be an admirable set of goals for any teacher, but they were also a formidable piece of rhetoric for education critics to wield. The Goals 2000 were never actually feasible, nor were they ever expected to be fully met; rather, they were political tools. A review of this list (see Box 2.1) will confirm this conclusion. Unfortunately, such political fodder sidetracks teachers and prevents them from getting on with the real business of teaching.

Reviewing the goals in Box 2.1 is enough to remind any educator that some of society's expectations for today's teachers are beyond their reach. After all, society does not always produce students who are physically, emotionally, and mentally healthy and eager to learn. On the contrary, no matter how much they change, schools will always be challenged to cope with all the ills its clients bring to their doors each day. The No Child Left Behind legislation is just the latest result of the history of flawed reform reports, public-school bashing, teacher bashing, and increased workloads—all of which have left many teachers feeling confused, unappreciated, discouraged, threatened, and even angry.

The variety and nature of the groups of problems facing future teachers call for a new approach. Teachers can no longer continue to remain in their isolated

Box 2.1 Goals 2000

- By the year 2000, all children in America will start school ready to learn (i.e., in good health, having been read to and otherwise prepared by parents, etc.).
- By the year 2000, the high school graduation rate will increase to at least 90% (from the current rate of 74%).
- By the year 2000, American students will leave grades 4, 8, and 12 having demonstrated competency in challenging subject matter, including English, Mathematics, Science, History, and Geography. In addition, every school in America will insure that all students learn to use their minds, in order to prepare them for responsible citizenship, further learning, and productive employment in a modern economy.
- By the year 2000, American students will be first in the world in mathematics and science achievement.
- By the year 2000, every adult American will be literate and will possess the skills necessary to compete in a global economy and to exercise the rights and responsibilities of citizenship.
- By the year 2000, every school in America will be free of drugs and violence and will offer a disciplined environment conducive to learning.

classrooms, solving their own problems without the help of their colleagues. Principals can no longer remain in their offices, controlling the budgets and the physical plant at the expense of the curriculum and instructional programs. Teachers and principals must participate in all types of decision making designed to enhance the academic and social development of students. Most teachers have not been prepared for these new roles, having little to no training in collaborative decision making. Tomorrow's supervisors must provide help for teachers and administrators as they prepare for these new roles.

Reasons for Optimism

In reporting the shortcomings of the schools, the mass media provide both a blessing and a curse: a blessing because identifying problems is often the first step in their removal, and a curse because the improvements seldom get the attention that is given the problems. Nevertheless, much good news has occurred since the early 1980s reports were released. Following is an account of some of these improvements.

An Era of Collaboration

> Interstate School Leaders Licensure Consortium (ISLLC) Educational Leadership Policy Standard No. 4 requires leaders to collaborate with faculty and other community members.

Today's teachers are being encouraged to work collaboratively with university professors, their local school principals, and other teachers to develop a new schoolwide learning environment (Teitel, 2006). Such collaborative approaches are not new. As early as the last quarter of the nineteenth century, teachers were being encouraged to work collaboratively in the development of curriculum and instruction. For example, Colonel Francis Parker, superintendent of the Quincy (Massachusetts) schools, held a special type of teachers meeting designed not to lecture or tell the teachers how to teach, but rather to demonstrate teaching methods and cooperatively plan curricula. By the 1920s, in many school districts throughout the nation, supervisors were available to work with teachers to develop courses of study. Jesse Newton, superintendent of the Denver schools, encouraged collaborative development of courses of study by teachers and supervisors.

Although there has been a long-standing precedent for the practice of teachers collaborating with their peers, the teacher's role in this collaboration has changed considerably. The minimal role formerly played by the teacher would not and should not be accepted today. Although established early on, this precedence for collaboration is just now being used in its fullest sense to empower teachers as full professionals.

This change can be seen clearly by reviewing the history of teachers' involvement with research in early school–university "partnerships." Early involvement consisted of teachers simply helping the university researcher by offering their students and classrooms for study, and by collecting data. Often, teachers were merely responsible for delivering the data to senior partners in the research, without ever finding out the outcomes of the studies. However, for a school–university alliance to really work, the principal and teachers must be full partners in defining the collaborative agenda. (For more on school–university partnerships, see chapters 1 and 4.)

In the past, teachers were assigned only minor roles in the process, yet the practice of collaboration holds significant potential for teachers. Teachers need opportunities to interact with other teachers. When they are assigned roles that parallel the roles of their partners, collaboration provides excellent professional growth opportunities (Rallis et al., 2006). Collaboration with other teachers may revolve around joint work (e.g., team teaching and mentoring) and teacher networks (e.g., school-to-school and school–university partnerships). Among several other benefits, collaborating on research can lead to a deeper understanding of the act of teaching.

This book places a strong emphasis on collaboration—a collaboration that includes all members of the learning community. Experience has proven repeatedly that teachers are more productive when they work together as opposed to working in isolation, and their level of productivity rises sharply when the principal rolls up both sleeves and participates. However, Steve Lapan and Patricia Hays (2010) have reminded us that, "More often than not, teachers perform their daily teaching duties in the isolation of a self-contained classroom." Supervisors should spend most of their time working with groups as opposed to helping individuals (allowing, of course, for exceptions when a particular situation requires one-on-one help). Unfortunately, most have not yet made the transition from individually based supervision to collaborative supervision.

Group supervision must be linked with continuous school improvement and experimentation and must be viewed as an activity whose primary aim is learning about and improving teaching. Sometimes teachers are uncomfortable when they are asked tough questions about their own teaching. Collaboration and mutual support from colleagues can be vehicles for enabling teachers to risk facing those tough questions. However, there is a danger that teachers might misinterpret collaboration as a means of supporting one another without rocking the boat or causing any discomfort. When this happens, collaboration can degenerate into a mechanism for skirting tough questions and giving unwarranted assurances that things are just fine. To avoid this degeneration, all participants must understand that learning about the instructional process and improving student learning are the primary goals of group supervision. Collaboration is a means to an end, not an end in itself. It is a mechanism for providing support as teachers engage in the sometimes disquieting, uncomfortable process of learning.

Given the research on cooperative learning and teacher collegiality, if supervision were carried out as a group process in which the supervisors and

It Works for Me!

Finding Common Ground

Sandra Harris, Lamar University

When working with teacher leaders, I use the following activity to demonstrate that no matter what the conflict situation, it is necessary and possible to find common ground.

I begin by asking that all participants partner with the person to their right. At this time I point out that partners are responsible for each other—that it will be each partner's responsibility to make certain that his or her partner follows the instructions correctly. Then I instruct each participant to choose a number. Since no one can have the same number, as participants call out their numbers I write them on chart paper. (If someone has picked a number that was already chosen, they must make another choice.) Then I give the group specific instructions concerning what they are to do with their numbers.

1. Take your number and *double* it. (Everyone should tell their partner what their "problem" will be—for example, 2 + 2 = 4).
2. Add the number 8 to your answer: (e.g., 4 + 8 = 12).
3. Divide your new answer by 2 (e.g., 12 ÷ 2 = 6).
4. Take your new answer and subtract the number you started with: (e.g., 6 – 2 = 4).

After each step, I remind partners to check each other's work.

After step 4 has been completed, I ask each participant to share his or her final solution. *Everyone's solution should be 4!* Explain that although each individual started with different "problems," by working together everyone came up with a common answer. This demonstrates that while common ground always exists, sometimes we must actively seek it out.

Finally, I write *Barriers to Finding Common Ground* on one side of a white board or chalkboard and *Advantages of Finding Common Ground* on the second. Collaboratively, we take turns writing the barriers and advantages. Identifying the barriers leads to an in-depth conversation about our differences that sometimes lead to perceived conflict, and how these perceptions are often inaccurate. The conversation concludes with a discussion of the many advantages of finding common ground.

teachers worked interdependently in achieving both group and individual goals, the supervision process would more effectively help teachers to learn about and improve their teaching. In addition, if those teachers who may be less committed to growth can work together with colleagues who are more committed, they may create shared norms that complement the supervisory process. Supervision is a tool of teacher empowerment and professional enhancement, bringing colleagues and their expertise together to generate critical yet also practically grounded reflection on what they do as a basis for more skilled action.

In the past, when research was conducted to enhance the effectiveness of teamwork, most of the studies focused on the team leader. Now we know that action research (see chapter 13) must focus on sharing leadership among team members (Marcellino, 2006), a process that Glickman et al. (2007) call *shared governance.* Success with group supervision, then, is contingent on having: (1) clear group goals and individual goals, (2) junior faculty members belonging to groups that also have productive senior teachers, and (3) a format that allows those teachers to discuss their varying views.

The Promise of Technology

Perhaps the greatest promise for the future of our schools—and, indeed, the future of our nation—lies in technology. New and better computer hardware and software are evolving at an amazing pace, and this rapid growth rate should continue. Equally dramatic are the ways our abilities to use technology are changing. A major goal of many educators and technologists is a seamless integration of technology in the schools (Veronikas & Shaughnessy, 2004). As you read this book, you will discover many ways that supervisors can use technology and also myriad suggestions for helping teachers use technology—to benefit both their students and themselves. The examples in this book are just a small sample of the potential opportunities that technology offers for improving schools.

> Fortunately, there are newly available computer technologies that . . . in addition to allowing easier accountability reporting . . . allow user-friendly data access at all educational levels, meaning that teachers can use these tools to engage in the informed reflection necessary to improve classroom practice. (Wayman, 2005, p. 295)

As a supervisor you can work collaboratively with your faculty to think of ways to employ the use of technology at your school to achieve this goal.

Reversing the Trend in Teacher Attrition

For decades we have suffered an ongoing need for more teachers in almost every discipline, especially science and mathematics. Historically our states and school districts have responded to the shortage by issuing emergency certificates. During the past two decades, an increasing number of states have created alternative programs to fill the need, but some of these programs have produced ill-prepared teachers, many who have fled the profession at an unprecedented rate (see Figure 2.1 on the following page).

In response to the political critics who said our students' low test scores resulted from teachers' lack of knowledge in their disciplines, many programs were created that required little or no more than a bachelor's degree in science or mathematics. Illustrating just how wrong-headed this thinking was, two-thirds of science and mathematics teachers prepared by these short-term programs have left the teaching profession within three years.

The results in Figure 2.2 (on the following page) show that in our response to the continuous teacher shortage, we should have paid more attention to the quality of our new teachers and to the attrition rates, which have been high in all disciplines, especially high in science and mathematics. Fortunately, the quality of teacher education has been improving. Findings from a 2000 survey

Figure 2.1 Increased Number of Teachers and Increased Attrition Rates from 1987 to 2000

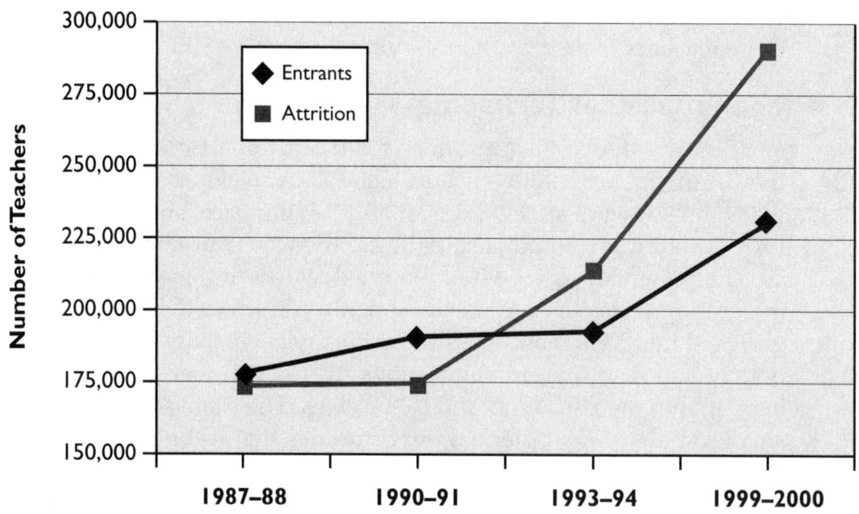

From D. R. Sterling (2004), The Teacher Shortage: National Trends for Science and Mathematics Teachers. *The Journal of Mathematics and Science: Collaborative Explorations*, Vol. 7, p. 86.

Figure 2.2 Average Retention Rates for Teachers Who Remain in Teaching after Three Years

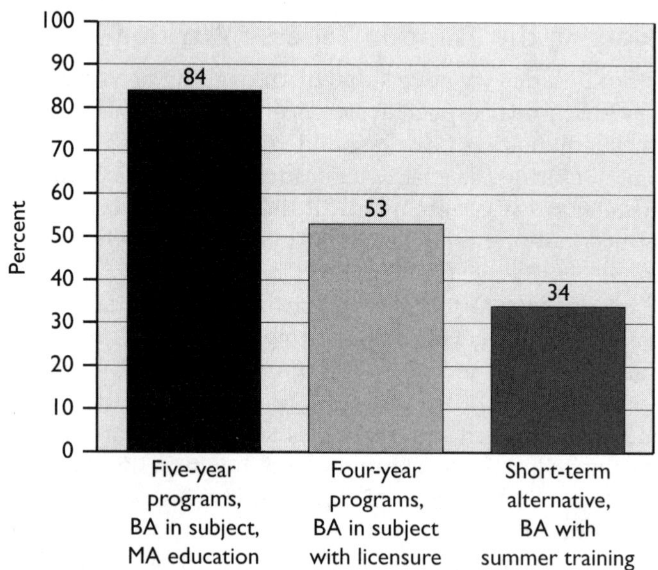

From D. R. Sterling (2004), The Teacher Shortage: National Trends for Science and Mathematics Teachers. *The Journal of Mathematics and Science: Collaborative Explorations*, Vol. 7, p. 91.

(NCES, 2001) indicate that virtually all public school teachers held a bachelor's degree and 45% held a master's degree, with 1% holding a doctorate. The ongoing problem, then, is how to keep these qualified teachers from leaving.

Following closely behind the main reason teachers give for leaving (poor salaries) is lack of administrative support. This is especially true of science and mathematics teachers, who, more than their counterparts in other disciplines, give lack of administrative support as their reason for leaving teaching (see Figure 2.3).

Throughout the disciplines, the highest teacher attrition rates are among two groups: retiring teachers and beginning teachers. Since, obviously, little can be done to retain retiring teachers, it seems prudent that energy and resources should be spent on retaining beginning teachers.

Figure 2.3 Various Reasons for Dissatisfaction-Related Turnover

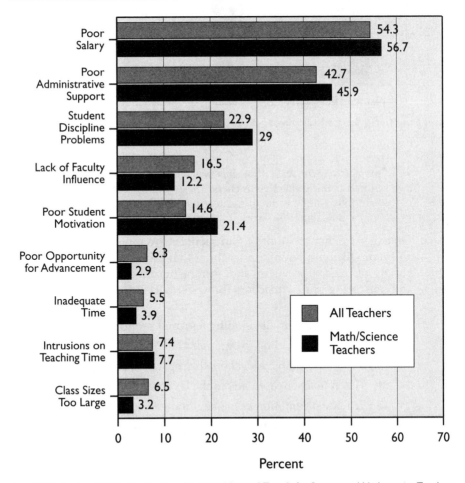

From D. R. Sterling (2004), The Teacher Shortage: National Trends for Science and Mathematics Teachers. *The Journal of Mathematics and Science: Collaborative Explanations*, Vol. 7, p. 94.

Figure 2.4 Teacher Involvement in Mentoring, Peer Observation, or Coaching

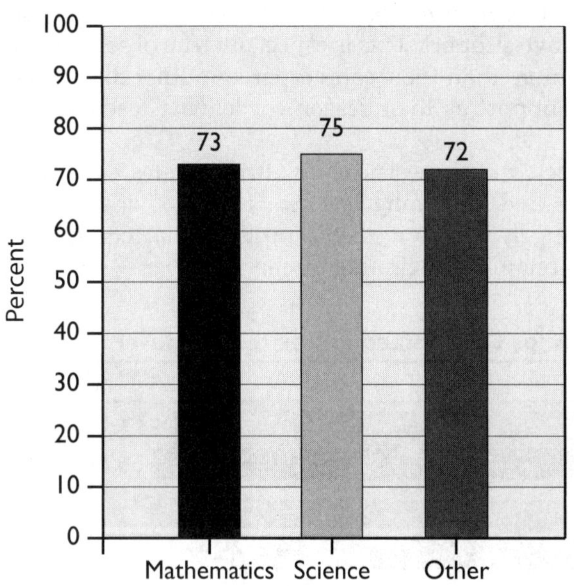

Adapted from National Science Foundation, *Science and Engineering Indicators 2008.*

The good news is that instead of the twentieth-century practice of showing new teachers to their classrooms and leaving them to "sink or swim," an increasing number of twenty-first-century beginning teachers are being assigned mentors to give them much-needed support. The number of mentored new teachers has doubled in the past decade (Kopkowski, 2008). A national NCES survey (SEI, 2008) reported that almost three-fourths of all middle and high school teachers had participated in mentoring activities during the past twelve months (see Figure 2.4).

> Mentoring programs are crucial . . . because without them, novice teachers often develop "coping" strategies and defenses to help them survive in the classroom. However, these strategies may be the very ones . . . that prevent them from becoming effective teachers. These coping strategies can then "crystallize" into a non-productive, career-long teaching style. (Mentoring Leadership and Resource Network, 1998–1999)

First-year teachers who have had mentors are more likely to "feel supported" and more likely to remain in teaching that those without mentors. There are a variety of roles supervisors and administrators can take to support induction and mentoring of new teachers (Brewster & Railsback [2001], quoted in Dexter et al., 2005):

1. Take the lead in developing a formal program.
2. Commit to funding programs.
3. Do not assign new teachers the most challenging classes.
4. Match teacher caseloads to the level which they student taught.
5. Provide orientation at the beginning of each school year.
6. Provide as much information as possible on the students they will teach.
7. Provide the new teachers with the resources they need.
8. Clearly communicate expectations.
9. Be sincere with your support of their success.

10. Be in their classrooms on a weekly basis.
11. Find ways to integrate the new teacher into the school community.
12. Support their participation in staff development.

More on induction and mentoring of new teachers can be found in chapters 3 and 4.

Lower Attrition for Minority Teachers. Another reason for optimism in reversing the attrition trend concerns minority teachers. Disaggregating the data by ethnicity shows that the attrition rate for minority teachers is less than for the combined teaching force (Guarino et al., 2004). Further studies are needed to investigate the causes of this disparity. Some researchers believe that minority teachers provide minority students with a positive sense of cultural identity (Payne & Washington, 2008). Minority teachers' own experiences with discrimination help them understand their students' experiences (Torres, Santos, Peck, & Cortes, 2004). One might further speculate that minority teachers experience more job satisfaction and success in today's increasingly diverse classrooms because of this minority teacher-student rapport.

According to Torres et al. (2004), the major reasons for the underrepresentation of minority teachers today are unsupportive working conditions and a lack of social and cultural support groups—two areas in which the supervisor has the potential to make a difference.

Improved Teaching Skills

An equally strong reason for optimism is the shift that is currently occurring in teacher preparation programs. Twenty-first century teachers are being taught to use learner/student-centered teaching methods (shifting the focus of activity from the teacher to the learners). When teachers use such methods, student achievement increases (Sterling, 2004).[1] After our schools had suffered for three decades at the hands of political pressure groups (including governors, legislators, and education reform commissions) who told us that our schools' main weakness was the lack of teachers' subject-matter knowledge, a 2000 study by Wenglinsky (see Sterling, 2004) dispelled this myth. Although the reform critics downplayed the importance of pedagogy and the possibility that improved pedagogy could influence student achievement, Wenglinsky found that when teachers received professional development of higher-order thinking skills their students' performance increased 44% of a grade level. When mathematics teachers received professional development focused on ways of working with different student populations, student performance increased 107% of a grade level. When mathematics teachers frequently gave specific tests on student understanding, student achievement increased by 44% and science students' achievement increased by 92%.

Supervisors should familiarize themselves with constructivist (learner-centered) education methods, including active learning (or "learning by doing"), cooperative learning, and inductive teaching and learning (learning by problem solving), and they should encourage their faculty to adopt these principles in their classrooms.

Conclusion

This chapter has given a brief history of instructional supervision, which began in colonial days as inspecting, later to be conducted by superintendents and then disassociated with administrators. During the 1970s and 1980s, supervision was characterized by a clinical approach. Currently, promise is found in a collaborative effort in which the school principal or a designated supervisor leads the faculty to work together and form a common vision or mission.

The reform reports have identified several weaknesses in our current schools and have also created several new problems in the schools. Common problems include poor economic support, overemphasis on test scores, isolation of teachers in their classrooms, inability to adjust to an increasingly diverse student population, increased violence, outdated curriculum, heavy workload for teachers, failure to conduct and use research, exclusion of teachers from reform efforts, and impossible goals that divert teachers' attention from the business of teaching.

Yet there are reasons for optimism. Teachers are happier with their career choice today than were their predecessors. Today's teachers are better prepared than ever before. By redirecting their teachers to adopt a mission and work collaboratively to attain it, principals can lead their schools in creating a vastly improved learning community. The remainder of this text will be directed to helping the principal and other supervisors reach this important goal.

All these changes give educators reason to feel good about contemporary education. By keeping abreast of these twenty-first-century developments, supervisors can create new opportunities to help their faculty implement truly meaningful education reform at their schools.

Questions for Discussion and Reflection

1. In an era of daily criticism against schools and teachers, how can the supervisor make adjustments to show support for teachers who may feel overworked and underappreciated?
2. What significant improvements in curriculum and instruction were introduced at the Woods Hole Conference and later forgotten?
3. Criticize the concept of *teacher-proof curriculum*.
4. What is your opinion about today's role of constructivism in learning?
5. What is your knowledge about the current education reform practices in your state? Which of these practices offer the most hope for improving education in your state?
6. What is the supervisor's responsibility for helping local education reform efforts succeed?
7. What, if any, responsibility does the supervisor have for making teachers aware of the flaws in education reform reports?

8. Throughout the nation, teachers are being pressured to increase students' test scores. What should be the supervisor's role in helping faculties improve students' standardized test scores?
9. What responsibility does the supervisor have in ensuring that increasing test scores is not the sole purpose of schools?
10. Why must teachers expand their working arenas beyond the walls of their classrooms?
11. What do you consider the main purpose of elementary and secondary schools?

Suggested Activities

1. Interview three teachers, asking each to describe one collaborative effort and the benefits gained from participation in the project. Make a combined list.
2. Visit the local district office and ask an official to identify an exemplary interdisciplinary program in the district. Interview one of the teachers that led the implementation of this program. Note any strategies or incentives used to solicit the cooperation of teachers in each representative discipline.
3. Ask a school administrator to identify examples of constructivist programs currently in the school's curriculum. Interview some teachers working in these programs, and make a list of student activities that require students to connect new information to previously acquired understandings.
4. Interview a counselor. Ask about programs and practices at the school that help all students feel positive about their school experiences. Interview 10 students, asking each to identify the best features of this school. Compare the summaries of the two lists.
5. Ask a local principal to identify ongoing group research projects. Interview a group leader and make a brief report on the incentives that encourage teachers to participate in research groups. Ask the leader for suggestions you can use to encourage teachers at other schools to begin collaborative research projects.

Note

[1] For a thorough review of the development of learner-centered education, see K. T. Henson (Fall, 2003), Foundations for learner-centered education: A knowledge base. *Education, 124*(1), 5–16.

Chapter 3

The Supervisor's Role

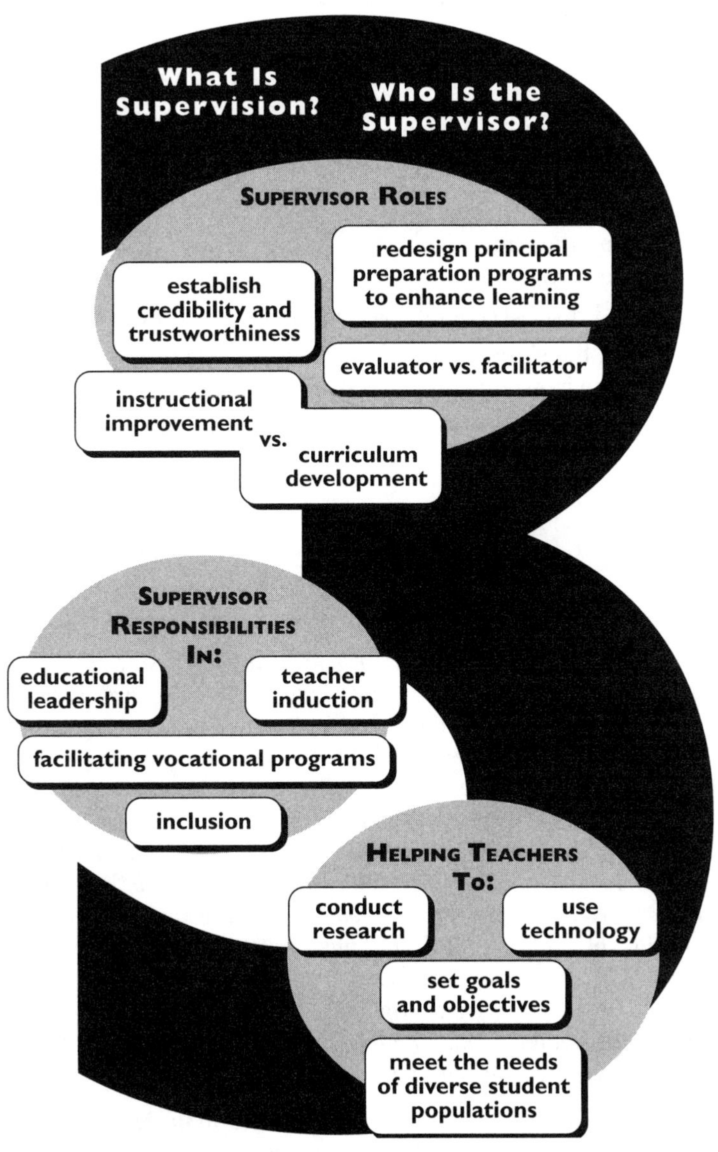

It is important to help beginning principals understand those areas that will be strengths and find ways to cope with the areas that will create stress.

—S. Johnson & S. Busch,
"Understanding leadership behaviors of principals"

Objectives

After completion of this chapter, you should be able to

1. Define supervision and give several benefits of supervision conducted by principals
2. Describe the supervisor's role in curriculum development and instructional improvement
3. List and discuss several roles and responsibilities of the supervisor
4. Explain the significance of a common sense of mission and the supervisor's role in establishing this mission
5. Discuss the supervisor's role in teacher induction

My First Day of Teaching

I will always remember my first day on the job. That was one of the busiest and most exhausting days of my life. My biggest surprise during my first-year internship program came at the end of my first day of teaching. I was exhausted. I knew that my condition was more emotional than physical. Although I was tired, I was also highly motivated, so I stayed an hour late, working hard to pull some things together, reflecting on the day and planning for tomorrow. I remember leaving the school building that first day. As I walked down the hall, I remember how dedicated and professional I felt. I was excited about being a teacher. I was also very pleased with myself. Without being asked, I had decided to give a full extra hour to my job. But when I left the building and entered the parking lot, I could hardly believe my eyes. The faculty parking lot was full! Not one teacher had left. I immediately realized that I wasn't staying late. On the contrary, I was the first teacher to go home that day. I got a clear message that first day, to say the least; I knew right away that I had chosen a demanding profession. Although I had been with a multitude of youths throughout the day, I felt a type of loneliness because I had hardly made any contact with the other teachers.

Later, after dinner, my sense of weariness was replaced with the realization that my first day of teaching was loaded with situations that required me to make decisions that were forced and instantaneous and for which I had no definite, surefire correct answers. On the contrary, I was compelled to use my judgment, and I didn't always feel completely confident in my response.

Reflection

This vignette gives a view of the hectic world in which contemporary teachers live and work, a world with a surplus of stress and a shortage of time. Supervisors can help by keeping teachers focused on their mission, by helping teachers collaborate to help one another, and especially by helping new teachers. By keeping a central focus on learning, teachers can help each other meet their daily challenges while working together to meet the state and national standards. Some questions that emerge include: What is supervision? Who is the supervisor? Should supervisors' roles be limited to the improvement of instruction, or should the supervisor also be involved with curriculum development? What is the supervisor's role in teacher induction? What should the supervisor do regarding research? What is the supervisor's role in helping teachers use technology? What should be the vocational role of the supervisor? What is the proper role concerning goals and objectives? What is the supervisor's role regarding inclusion? What should be the supervisor's role in accommodating and promoting diversity?

Introduction

These questions and many others represent issues that supervisors face today. An *issue* is a topic of disagreement which, if left unattended, can erupt in divisive arguments; but when carefully addressed, issues can provide the stimulus for informative and insightful discussions. Though important, many of these questions do not have clear-cut answers. The purpose of this chapter is to introduce the supervisor's role and several issues the supervisor faces, providing enough information to stimulate discussion of the issues. The answers for some of these questions will depend on the context surrounding the issue, that is: the supervisor, the school, the community, the teachers, and the students.

Supervision: 14 Issues Involving Definitions, Roles, and Responsibilities

As you study these issues, relate each one to a school that you know well, perhaps one where you now work or have worked, or even a school that you attended. Consider how you would answer each question as you keep that particular school, community, teachers, and students in mind. Consider also how each of the supervisory roles discussed in this chapter can contribute to education reform and to meeting multicultural and constructivist goals.

Issue #1: What is supervision?

Over time, this definition has changed. Currently, *supervision* refers mainly to helping teachers create a classroom climate and a schoolwide climate that promote learning. In one way or another, all supervisor responsibilities are connected to this goal. Current emphasis on education reform has forced school personnel to be accountable for the amount of academic achievement that occurs in the classroom. Increased accountability as measured on achievement tests has made instruction an important criterion in the definition of supervision.

We must also remember that school has other important purposes including (1) the social development of each student, (2) helping all students reach their maximum potential, and (3) acculturating each student into our democratic way of life.

Issue #2: Who is the supervisor?

Until recently, most supervisors worked out of school district offices. Some large school districts still have positions designed to help teachers throughout the district improve learning. But, today, by and large, the role of instructional supervision has been given to principals. This new shift makes the principal more than a manager; today's principal must be a leader of curriculum development and instructional improvement (Woolfolk Hoy & Hoy, 2009). At the center of this leadership are curriculum and instruction; for indeed, the principal must help teachers discover ways to make the school's curriculum and instruction more effective. Even more basic, today's principals must influence the thinking of their teachers. Of paramount significance is the way teachers view their mission and that of their school, and the principal must help the teachers shape and constantly update a general mission for the school. Then the supervisor must help teachers discover ways to use their individual talents to contribute to the attainment of that mission.

Issue #3: What is the main issue that supervisors face?

The supervisor must be aware of the continuous flow of emerging issues that affect educational leadership. The national cry for more principals with the capacity to improve learning in their schools exacerbates the importance of the role of supervision in twenty-first-century schools. According to a report issued by the Southern Regional Education Board (Frye, Bottoms, & O'Neil, 2005), the most important and pressing issue facing educational administrators is redesigning their programs to prepare principals to enhance learning in their schools: "Given the urgency for increased student achievement, it would seem that redesigning principal preparation programs around leadership practices that have a high impact on students' learning would be a high priority at every university" (p. 2). The successful development of such a program must involve partnerships between universities and K–12 schools.

Issue #4: How can supervisors establish trust?

Trust is essential to providing maximum leadership. (See the tip by Robert Kladifko in chapter 4.) Teachers need the assurance that the supervisor's main concern is with helping them improve. They also need to know that the supervisor has the expertise to succeed in this role. It is important to realize that trust cannot be demanded, nor can it be bought with favors. A good place to begin earning trust is by being honest in all matters.

> Educational Leadership Constituents Council (ELCC) Standard No. 5 requires leaders to act "with integrity, fairly, and in an ethical manner."

Trust must be earned and then modeled by educational leaders (Barth, 2006: Irons & Aller, 2007). For example, although compliments are essential, when overused or given without being earned they can raise doubt and suspicion. Trust demands credibility, and credibility can be enhanced by clarifying your role and adhering to it. For example, from the outset you should advise teachers of the extent to which they will be informed about forthcoming visits.

Once you clarify your approach to supervision, keeping true to that style is essential. For instance, suppose you tell teachers that you do not make unannounced visits, but later you find that some other business has brought you to the school. You could save a trip, and valuable time, by dropping in on a lesson while you are there on campus, but you would be defaulting on your agreement to make only announced evaluation visits. Just one breach of agreement can quickly introduce distrust into your relationship with teachers.

Another important area of trust is confidentiality. The supervisor/teacher relationship is similar to that of counselor/patient. Discussions with teachers must be protected. Supervisors should be prepared to respond to criticisms and questions about other teachers in ways that do not break this trust.

Issue #5: How can supervisors handle the conflicting role of evaluator and facilitator of instructional improvement?

Supervisors cannot choose between these paradoxical responsibilities; they must do both. The challenge appears to be that of finding a way to perform the evaluator role to ensure schoolwide accountability for quality education without creating unnecessary stress on the teachers. Three suggestions come to mind.

First, take the time to provide all the necessary information, including holding a preliminary discussion about why evaluation is necessary, the nature of evaluation and how it will be conducted, and the nature of both the supervisor's and the teacher's role. We fear the unknown, and reducing the unknown reduces the level of fear.

Second, be positive. Savannah principal Lucy Phillip (2005) posts her "Lucy Premise" on her office door: "Our students can learn more than they are currently learning, and we can do more to help them." But being positive doesn't mean you can or should ignore weaknesses. When addressing areas of weakness, choose your words carefully. For example, such sensitive areas can be referred to as "challenges" and "opportunities to improve." Being told that you need to improve, without being shown *how* to improve, can stimulate feelings of insecurity and can promote unnecessary levels of concern; yet informing teachers about areas of needed improvement is an important responsibility of all supervisors. When told that they need to improve, many teachers react by feeling that all that they have been doing is totally wrong—that they are total failures. The damage can be minimized by balancing each suggestion for improvement with some recognition of achievement (see chapter 1). We never outgrow the need to have our achievements recognized, and the supervisor's responsibility for recognizing teachers' achievements is just as important as identifying areas of needed improvement.

Third, involve the faculty in using formative assessment daily to improve learning. In doing so, assessment gradually becomes viewed as a tool and not a weapon. Clarify the connection between assessment and learning. Make continuous evaluation aimed at learning improvement a badge of pride, promoting the idea that "it's the way we do things around here."

Issue #6: Should supervisors' responsibilities be limited to the improvement of instruction, or should they also include involvement with curriculum development?

Continuous improvement of instruction requires effective curriculum planning. The key word here is *continuous.* Historically, supervisors have been supervisors of instruction. Their role has been limited to making classroom visits, observing lessons, and giving feedback to teachers. Often, teachers received glowing feedback that ignored areas in need of improvement, or the feedback given was so general that it failed to help teachers reshape their instruction.

The No Child Left Behind legislation, and required national and state standards, make the supervisor's focus on daily lesson plans alone totally inadequate. Rallis and colleagues (2006) have noted that teachers are inclined to work with a set of issues one at a time, continuously dropping the current issue as new and more urgent issues emerge "without the notion that they are working on a sustained problem" (p. 545). In Rallis's words, "Principals overmanage the occasional lesson and undermanage the bigger picture of whether teachers are truly making a difference in student learning" (p. 730).

However, this practice is gradually changing. As Wineburg (2006) has said, "Brave principals and teachers are taking matters into their own hands and changing the curriculum themselves" (p. 402). The actual job of improving the curriculum and instruction belongs to supervisors and teachers, and any attempts to improve instruction while ignoring the curriculum are like giving directions without the use of a road map. Supervisors can do better by encouraging teams of teachers to examine the standards for which they and their students are being held accountable, and by holding open discussions and collectively choosing one or more areas of weaknesses (standards) where teachers believe they need to improve most.

The next step is to develop a curriculum conducive to meeting these standards. Marshall (2005) offers some excellent advice.

> The best way to ensure that teaching is done right the first time (versus having to provide corrective instruction for substantial numbers of students after the fact) is to have teachers work in teams to plan each curriculum unit with the end in sight. Before they dive into teaching, teacher teams should

> work backwards from the state standards to identify clear learning objectives, decide on the big ideas and essential questions of the unit, draft assessments they will use to determine whether students have learned what was taught, create a game plan and calendar for instruction, and run the plan by the principal for feedback. . . . The three- to six-week curriculum unit is an ideal chunk of instruction for principals to supervise, far better than an individual lesson. (p. 733)

When leading a team in the planning of curriculum units, the supervisor's role should make some clear shifts. Early in the development of the units, the supervisor should ensure that each unit's objectives are aligned with the standards for which its team designed it to achieve. Some successful principals require benchmarks in each subject of state-mandated objectives (Aguirre, 2005). An option that some supervisors find attractive is to require the team members to give their students formative weekly tests to measure the unit's success and then hold follow-up meetings to discuss the outcomes. The ultimate goal is to make evaluations an ongoing way of life, never the ultimate concern. Learning must remain the most important concern, and evaluations should be considered merely a tool to support learning.

Like their students, all teachers need to experience success along the way. The supervisor can help by sharing each team's successes with the rest of the school. This approach gives ownership to faculties, eventually building a culture that makes learning the focus and mission of the faculty. Lucy Phillip (2005) calls this leadership style *leading from behind.*

It Works for Me!

Encouraging Teacher/Supervisor Interaction

Sandra S. Murray, University of Tennessee at Martin

One way to draw teachers into the principal's office is with candy, especially chocolate. First, place a candy dish just inside the door to the office and invite teachers to partake of the treat whenever they want. Then, as they become more comfortable with entering the office, move the dish closer to your desk and a chair. Eventually move the candy dish to a corner of your desk, strategically placed near a comfortable chair. Soon the teachers will be coming into the office, sitting down, and having a pleasant chat or discussing concerns.

Issue #7: What is the status of educational leadership, and how does this affect the supervisor's role?

To say that the status of leadership for learning by educational institutions (K–graduate levels) is dismal is probably not an exaggeration (Kowalski, 2006). Few attempts have been made to identify the behaviors of instructional leaders (Daresh, 2007). But Carol Mullen (2006) says that today's education system is not beyond hope: "The chronic depiction of the state of scholarship in our profession as impoverished, then, is not a completely accurate assessment" (p. 107). Mullen supports this conclusion by saying that educational administration programs throughout the country are experimenting with a vast variety of constructivist strategies "including writing/inquiry, scaffolds, assisted and reciprocal strategies; problem-based learning, case method (and) administrative simulation teaching" (p. 107). Supervisors' educational leadership responsibilities include promoting staff development, helping teachers to meet school goals and objectives, and many other topics that are discussed throughout this book.

It Works for Me!

Animal Crackers

Janice M. Walker, Drake University

After my students have spent a number of weeks discussing supervision and evaluation and have completed their work on clinical supervision cycles and peer coaching, they are ready for a change of pace. Here is an activity that is easy and fun.

Each student receives an animal cracker and a piece of paper with the statement,

"When I think about supervising teachers, it reminds me of a(n) ____________ because ____________."

Ask the students to complete the statement, using the animal they have been given and their own ideas regarding supervision. Students share their statements and the relevance of their statement to the practice of good supervision. This is a fast and fun way to review and reinforce some important concepts of supervision.

Issue #8: What is the supervisor's role in teacher induction?

The first year of teaching impacts heavily on the rest of a teacher's career. Each year, over 32,000 new teachers begin their careers. Like the teacher intern who shared his first day of teaching at the beginning of this chapter, most beginning teachers will be shocked to learn about the many and varied requirements made on today's teachers. As Newcom et al. (2006, p. 64), have said, "Teaching is undeniably a difficult job for anyone, especially for today's beginning teachers who are called upon to face numerous challenges, including demands for increased and better assessment, greater academic rigor, and infusing technology across the curriculum."

Excessive expectations and demands on teachers take their toll; within five years, half of the new teachers will have dropped out of teaching. This high rate of new-teacher attrition leaves little doubt that beginning teachers need some sort of help that they are not getting, help that is needed to avoid later problems. Although some states have developed some type of program to help beginning teachers, many schools still do not have any system for helping new teachers. Furthermore, they continue to treat first-year teachers the same way they treat experienced teachers. Lack of time is a major concern. Teachers need more time to reflect on the major concepts in each unit, time to deepen their own understanding, and time to reflect on how they approach each unit.

One approach to helping new teachers succeed in high-challenge environments is mentoring. Educators across the disciplines are embracing mentoring, which helps the mentors (experienced teachers) while supporting new teachers' needs (Hanson & Moir, 2008). Resta et al. (2006) report success from an urban school in Austin, Texas, where veteran classroom teachers were given released time to serve as full-time mentors for beginning teachers. Released time enables the mentors to do a good job while sending the message to other teachers throughout the school that supporting new teachers is an important responsibility. Saffold (2003) states that those who stepped out of their classrooms for three years [to be a mentor]

> increased their knowledge of the performance-based standards and strengthened their teaching and leadership skills. Mentors described four specific benefits of participating in the program: improved reflective practices, a higher level of professional responsibilities, a broadened view of the profession, and a renewed appreciation for the education field.

See chapter 4 for information about using technology to mentor new teachers.

Issue #9: What should be the supervisor's vocational role?

A review of early American schools indicates that public schools have a major responsibility for preparing youths for vocations. This need was so strong that the early Latin Grammar School, with its curriculum heavily steeped in the classics, was totally replaced by the Franklin Academy with its vocational curriculum. The vocational role of the public school was reaffirmed in 1918 by the Seven Cardinal Principles of Secondary Education (see chapter 8), containing the principle titled "vocational efficiency."

The emphasis on vocationalism in secondary education has experienced a resurgence, and many schools are experimenting with a wide variety of vocational and technological programs, often under the label of integration. Growth in vocationalism in secondary schools can be attributed to the concern of

It Works for Me!

Helping Teachers Become Reflective

Anthony J. Colella, Seton Hall University

All significant and lasting change begins from within. The ability to effect change requires an awareness of the power that one has within. This awareness comes through internal dialogue or self-talk. As a means of raising your teachers' levels of consciousness and helping them become more reflective, ask that they silently address the following questions when involved in group activities:

What am I *feeling*? What am I *thinking*? How am I *acting*?

employers over the lack of skills needed for employment in today's world (Gordon, 2008). The vitality and success of these programs demand strong leadership, increasing the importance of the supervisor's role.

Issue #10: What is the supervisor's role regarding inclusion?

Inclusion involves meeting the needs of special students in the regular classroom as opposed to providing separate classes for these children. The No Child Left Behind mandate—which calls for more inclusion and also requires that all students, including those with disabilities, must achieve academically—has left many teachers perplexed (Owens, 2006). The supervisor can assist by helping teachers understand why this approach is being used. The research shows that learners with disabilities who are taught in regular classes perform better on standardized tests and develop better social skills, while the learners without disabilities learn to value individual differences and develop higher self-esteem (Armstrong et al., 2009).

When the Individuals with Disabilities Education Improvement Act (IDEA) was reauthorized in 2004, it contained many references to NCLB, including the participation of children with disabilities in state and district assessment systems, goals for children with disabilities that reflected goals for all children, the flexible use of funds to carry out schoolwide programs under the NCLB, and a mandate that all personnel be adequately prepared to work with children, subject to the NCLB provisions. Supervisors should familiarize themselves with the strengths and weaknesses of such reforms and help their faculty address these reform issues. This may include coordinating teams of parents and educators to formulate individualized education programs (IEPs) and including special-education students in the assessment process at their schools (Weishaar et al., 2007).

* * *

Responding to the No Child Left Behind legislation, schools everywhere are developing better ways to meet state standards by increasing the amount of learning throughout their school. Although this is happening in many different ways, behind each successful transformation are effective leadership and supervision. The following case study shows that this transformation usually requires challenging traditions. It requires both the forming a new vision and the serious raising of expectations. Once the administration gets a firm grasp on the job at hand, the next step is to begin weaving it into the minds of faculty, who can then sew it into the fabric of the school's curriculum.

The Emerging Nature of Instructional Supervision

Diane Ricciardi • Clemson University

With state and national legislation calling for equitable education for all students, educators are even more accountable for student learning outcomes. Many scholars report that high-quality teaching and leadership significantly impact student achievement. The role of principal continues to shift from traditional management to instructional leadership that supports collaborative supervision with teachers.

Role transition is evident not only in the principalship, but also in the aging workforce as large numbers of principals retire. District superintendents struggle to hire new principals who bring high levels of instructional expertise to the job. Role transition and the changing principal workforce have created challenges for district leaders, novice principals, and teachers experiencing these transitions.

This case study portrays typical experiences of entry-year principals in schools where effective instructional leadership was not in place. In the past, supervision was a task owned by formal leaders. As a result, great variety exists in principals' approaches to supervision—either to the benefit or detriment of teachers. It is noteworthy that no single action addresses the complexity of successful supervision; instead it is a deliberate, collaborative blend of the efforts of many.

The Community: It's All About Context

Located on the coast, Tyler is a community in transition. In five years, the town and rural extremities have experienced rapid population growth, from 40,000 to 70,000 citizens. School enrollment has doubled. With this growth, construction and service-oriented jobs have increased, attracting varied socioeconomic and ethnic groups to Tyler. The influx of affluent parents has resulted in demand for more college preparatory offerings in Tyler schools. Likewise, the influx of lower socioeconomic families has increased needs for more bilingual and special services.

The School: Shaking Boundaries of Tradition

Tyler High School is one of the district's three secondary schools. With 1,800 students, enrollment is 80% white, 7% black, and 13% Hispanic. About 35% of students qualify for free lunch. Principal Franklin Bryant recently retired after 20 years of service. Beloved by many, he built his reputation on keeping tradition alive at Tyler High. His efforts were spent on supporting extracurricular activities, networking with alumni groups, and using his assistant principals to "run a tight ship"—keeping the budget and facility in order, ensuring that student misbehaviors were minimal, and providing absolute autonomy to teachers to make curriculum and instructional decisions as they saw fit.

The school's reputation was now on the line, and teachers were feeling the pressure. Educating all students was now more difficult than ever. Recently released student achievement scores showed that Tyler High was not meeting accountability goals. Although scores at the other two high schools in the district were improving, this was not so at Tyler High, and the local newspaper headline read, "Tyler High Not Keeping Pace."

The New Principal: Considering Professional Suitability to Job Roles

Relocating from a state in the northwest, Alexis Ford has been hired as the new principal at Tyler High. During the past fifteen years Alexis served as a math teacher, a department chair, an instructional coach, and most recently as an assistant principal. She understands issues of high school transition; has built a solid reputation as a fair, consistent leader; and has used her strong instructional and leadership skills to help a team of teachers at her last school in implementing a successful ninth-grade academy. Even though Tyler had been home to Alexis in the 1980s, she realized that she was now an outsider hired into the most challenging and visible job in the Tyler district. Alexis wanted a job where she could use her instructional leadership skills and passion. Her initial experiences as an applicant convinced her that she may have found the right fit in Tyler.

Laying a Solid Foundation— Hiring for Instructional Expertise

Alexis found the hiring process in Tyler was unique. The grueling multistep process gave her insight into the academic culture and professional expectations set by Tyler's visionary leader, Superintendent Andrew Hodges. Hired two years ago, Dr. Hodges understood accountability demands. As an ethical leader, through words and actions he showed that every child in the district could be well educated in spite of family income levels or student learning difficulties. He believed his job was to ensure that they did.

Of the district's twenty-two principals, over 50% were retirement eligible. Dr. Hodges saw both a challenge and an opportunity. This was his time to get principal hiring and leader development right, and he invested time and resources to do both. Principals needed stronger instructional roles, and Dr. Hodges was willing to hire for instructional expertise. No longer believing that internal candidates have job entitlement, the superintendent pledged to hire the strongest candidate for each vacancy and convinced the board to support his decisions.

To achieve his vision, Dr. Hodges crafted a screening process that included performance-based exercises, using work samples and simulations to measure applicant knowledge of instruction and collaborative leadership. Alexis participated in screening simulations and presentations of her own work samples to demonstrate her skills in teacher conferencing, conducting professional development, analyzing lessons, and assessing student work quality. She faced some management-related interview questions, but clearly the selection process targeted her instructional expertise. Dr. Hodges and his hiring committee used multiple tools to screen for principal candidates who demonstrated both passion and skills for leading instructional improvement. The process sent a resounding message to Alexis. Clearly, her vision of instructional supervision aligned with the superintendent's—that great schools cannot exist in the absence of a competent and instructionally focused principal.

After successfully completing the selection process, Alexis was offered the position at Tyler High and given her charge by her superintendent.

First Things First: Testing the Waters and Building Shared Focus

Dr. Hodges told Alexis in their first meeting, "Tyler High is a good school that used to be better. I need you to reconceptualize the role of principal as instructional leader and supervisor. Through no fault of their own, teachers haven't stayed current. In the past, instructional supervision was neglected. I need you to assess the situation and tell me when you need support. I want you to build an academic culture at Tyler High where your decisions and actions leverage teaching quality and student learning." Alexis had been given her orders and realized that her task could be massive.

Understanding that principal transition can bring anxiety and concern to teachers, Alexis knew she must listen, observe, and learn before implementing a new vision for instructional supervision. She had the courage and knowledge to lead change but wanted to avoid trivial quick-fixes. Alexis wanted to work with teachers using adaptive change strategies to create new ways to improve instruction at Tyler High.

Her first order of business was to learn key issues identified by teachers and to build rapport, a foundation for trust, and a culture of high expectations for professional performance. Alexis wanted others to know that she would sustain her focus on instruction, but to begin this effort she had to be the primary learner! Drafting her first letter, Alexis invited each teacher in to meet privately with her before school started, and asked the secretary to schedule half-hour appointments for interested and available teachers. Alexis made immediate contact with teachers, issuing an invitation to partner with them and hear about their goals and challenges.

About 70% of the faculty scheduled appointments. Some were nervous, but all were interested in knowing more about Alexis and her approach as principal. Establishing herself as a collaborative yet task-focused leader, Alexis wanted to meet teachers, listen to their ideas and goals, and share her emerging vision as instructional supervisor. Alexis prepared a few prompts to elicit discussion, including: "What are the strengths and areas of improvement for Tyler High?" "What challenges do you face as a teacher working here?" "What should the administrators and teachers be doing to help more Tyler students achieve?" and finally, "Please talk about your goals as a professional and how I might help you be successful." After brief but genuine pleasantries to open the conferences, Alexis used each conversation to lay a foundation for collegial respect and to learn priorities held by teachers. Logging many hours during her first few weeks, Alexis found the time spent to be invaluable. She took notes after each conference and began formulating initial priorities for herself as instructional supervisor.

Using Data to Confirm Perceptions and Identify Early Steps

Alexis' next step was to mine school data documents to verify impressions she had heard from teachers and to create questions for future conversations. Through her conferences, Alexis had discovered that teachers were data-starved. Although somewhat knowledgeable, most teachers had only partial truths. They had never examined raw data, had never wrestled with its interpretation, and had rarely talked about implications for their own classroom practices.

Fundamentally, teachers had not owned the data. They knew scores were flat and blamed changing student demographics—a partially valid but shallow view of student performance.

Looking at the data herself, Alexis noted learning disparities in ethnic and gender categories. She had heard teacher confusion about curriculum standards, frustration over not knowing how individual students performed, and resentment about meaningless workshops and failed attempts at clinical supervision that had focused more on compliance than teacher improvement.

Alexis' general impression was that most teachers were looking for leadership and for someone to work with them on curricular and instructional issues. Although teachers considered the teaching faculty as a strength at Tyler, when questioned further they revealed that few teachers had opportunity to develop expertise as trainers or coaches—skills that would be very helpful in supporting both new and experienced teachers. Although teachers didn't complain about the laissez-faire approach of the last principal, Tyler was now being spotlighted as an underperforming school. Clearly, they felt instruction should be a higher priority for administrators and should not fall solely on the shoulders of teachers.

Teachers said that they had little opportunity to learn from one another. Classroom doors, literally and figuratively, closed at each bell, and peer observations had never been supported with time and resources. Alexis heard teachers' discomfort about heat coming from parents who wanted more acceleration for their children. They struggled ethically with giving priority to students of affluent, vocal parents while shortchanging students whose parents were not involved.

In only a few of her interactions with teachers did Alexis detect apathy, satisfaction with the status quo, or unwillingness to improve. Her knowledge of the cost of teacher burnout and dissatisfaction helped her remember the need to differentiate her supervision strategies and styles according to teacher needs. Being cautiously optimistic and knowing that she still hadn't spoken with all teachers, Alexis reminded the secretary to schedule those conferences once everyone had returned in September.

From her conversations, Alexis realized that teachers had operated in survival mode. Her task was to work with them to change the paradigm of supervision from one of clinical observation and teacher evaluation to one utilizing a variety of supervision processes that addressed faculty needs.

Finally, Alexis met with her three assistant principals and counselors. Like Alexis, all were early-career administrators, but unlike Alexis instructional responsibilities were never a part of their jobs. Assistant principals had managed student discipline, bus routing, facility issues, and the yearly teacher evaluations. Counselors made sure that teacher grades, master scheduling, and student graduation requirements were met. Fundamentally, the assistant principals and counselors had worked in isolation and had not connected their work responsibilities to instructional improvement with classroom teachers. The lack of communication and collaboration between administrators and teachers was alarming. This did not fit Alexis' leadership vision or hands-on, collaborative approach.

Alexis identified an important goal for herself—to create an instructional supervision process that would engage teachers and others in ongoing, collaborative problem solving around instructional issues. She drafted a brief plan that she would discuss with department chairs prior to the start of school. She needed multiple ways to engage teachers and to distribute leadership to them. Creating an instructional leadership team (ILT) of teachers and administrators would be an early order of business once school started.

Likewise, she found that several professional development days had not been planned for August. She could think of no better way to begin the year than to have teachers work in mixed teams to examine data, chart focus areas, and begin mapping a new direction. The ideas generated by the faculty on those workdays would set the agenda for the ILT. She knew that teacher ownership in identifying issues would be important in developing collective action.

In her first month Alexis was even more convinced that she was in the right job. She gave her administrators and teachers near-total autonomy to define instructional supervision processes in order to elevate teaching quality at Tyler. She felt fortunate to be working with a faculty that, on first impression, appeared ready for the challenges of instructional improvement.

Reflecting on Year One and Anticipating the Future

As the year progressed and the ILT worked with Alexis, they saw that they were playing a key role in implementing an instructional monitoring and supervision process that could improve the teacher skills. One teacher team member worked with an assistant principal to draft a proposal for a new teacher mentoring program, including a well-designed mentor training component. Several teachers worked with issues of professional development (PD) for experienced teachers. They researched delivery models that offered job-embedded approaches and studied a book on PD evaluation that they discussed with the faculty and ILT.

Alexis won Dr. Hodges' support for flexible funding to give two teachers an extra release period per day. With this, classes were covered for all teachers to participate in a peer observation process where teachers requested targeted instructional feedback and had a peer volunteer to observe and debrief with helpful feedback. Dr. Hodges also offered an extra four-hour part-time position known as a school manager who assumed tasks like textbooks, report preparation, and facilities issues. With the assistance, Alexis and her assistant principals created an administrative peer rotation process among themselves for classroom visits. Administrators conducted bi-monthly walk-through observations with each teacher and used personal data devices to record and compile data for schoolwide analysis.

Alexis was trained in the mandated district teacher evaluation system and worked with her assistant principals to strengthen the formal supervision process at Tyler. Once each month, she and an assistant would observe a teacher, script the lesson, and coplan the teacher conference. Either Alexis or the assistant principal would lead the conference with the teacher, while the other administrator observed the skills of the instructional supervisor. Following the conference, Alexis and the assistant principal explored ways to improve their own planning and conferencing techniques. As a bonus, they created a growing wish list of instructional materials and equipment needed by teachers to address pertinent content standards.

By year-end, the closed classroom doors at Tyler High were beginning to swing open as a majority of teachers opted to participate in the peer observation process. Also, an assistant principal and teacher team visited a local elementary school that had been charting individual student data progress for the purpose of teachers making mid-year instructional adjustments. The group shared the strategy with the ILT and drafted a modified process that would work for a pilot study at Tyler High. The math department voted to use the process the following year and built an action research activity around the process to measure possible impact. The ILT analyzed results collected by the Professional Development Subcommittee and began planning for more job-embedded PD the following year.

As with most new principals, Alexis struggled to adjust to some demands of the job. She needed better balance between work and family life, she needed to improve her delegation skills, and she still had more to learn about staffing and budgeting. In retrospect, she had made significant progress. She kept her focus on student learning, used her instructional expertise as a strength, and made significant strides in building teacher capacity for leadership. As an instructional supervisor, she was beginning to weave the processes of supervision into the fabric of her school's culture and mode of operation.

Summary

The emerging nature of instructional supervision and improvement at Tyler was not the result of one action, but rather a blend of intentional, focused actions that started prior to principal hiring. The case story shows that with principal turnover, districts need to fill positions with leaders who possess both passion and expertise to lead collaborative instructional improvement with teachers. Next, during the entry year, principals need to help teachers identify on- and off-target assumptions about teacher efficacy. With teachers, principals should prioritize the few but focused instructional changes and plan the supervision methods that would be most effective.

Since numerous supervision processes need not be "owned" by any one job group, effective principals use instructional leadership teams to connect all professionals to the important task of student learning. Great principals are always ready to learn more about instructional supervision and model powerful convictions about ongoing professional learning and improvement.

This case study serves as a springboard for cases that follow. Other stories focus more in depth on specific forms of instructional supervision dealing with issues of change, effective lesson planning, and using research and professional development to improve instruction.

Issues for Further Reflection

- What essential skills and prior work experiences should new principals have to lead schools where student performance appears to be "stuck" or has not made progress over time?
- What strategies can districts use to hire and retain principals who are strong instructional leaders and supervisors?
- How do principals assess the effectiveness and impact of instructional supervision in their own schools, and how do they work with others to strengthen narrowly defined supervision models?
- How do principals work with teachers to clarify and align teacher evaluation with other processes of instructional supervision?
- How do principals maintain focus on instructional supervision while balancing job demands, pacing themselves and teachers so that instructional improvement is sustained over time?

Issue #11: What is the supervisor's role in helping teachers conduct research?

Because learning requires the creation of new understanding by tying newly acquired information to previously developed understandings (or to old knowledge), the supervisor must help teachers learn how to create new knowledge. A major way to create knowledge is through conducting research. Supervisors can begin by first helping teachers learn to be reflective and assisting them in conducting their own action research studies (Lindahl, 2007). This might include developing research proposals and advising teachers on the appropriate use of research methodology (Pawlas & Oliva, 2008). The supervisor's role is to help teachers develop their own research skills, which they need to solve their own problems. Establishing an environment where teachers and researchers are continuously learning and helping others is a primary responsibility of today's supervisors. This topic (teacher-researchers) is pursued in depth in chapter 13.

Issue #12: What is the supervisor's role in helping teachers use technology?

Technology is changing the way teachers teach and students learn. No matter how much training teachers receive in preparation for integrating technology into their teaching, their attempts will fail unless they have the leadership and encouragement of their principal. Without strong support, teachers are likely to feel frustrated and give up on using technology. The rapid growth of technology in recent years has naturally brought massive change to the supervisor's role. Some of the ways that technology has impacted the role of supervisors have been through direct changes; others have been indirect.

Is the supervisor responsible for providing encouragement and opportunities to develop basic computer skills? The answer must be a resounding *yes.* Since many schools can neither afford the cost of substitute teachers nor the travel cost involved to send teachers to technology workshops, most supervisors are preparing to bring the workshops to the teachers. The supervisor must be aware of the types of workshops teachers need, and of the availability and accessibility of these workshops to their faculty. Not only are there workshops to improve teachers' use of technology, there are also some technology-based staff development programs that supervisors might recommend to (or implement with) teachers.

Some of the newer technologies seem to be almost tailor-made to promote collaboration and constructivism. For example, Blackboard is a family of software applications designed to help teachers build courses online and engage with students in an integrative manner to meet class learning goals. The Blackboard Academic Suite is designed to encourage student interaction, small-group work, and peer knowledge sharing; promote reflective thinking among groups, and enhance collaboration. For a more detailed description of Blackboard, visit the Web site (http:/www.blackboard.com). See chapter 4 for more on the use of technology in staff development.

Another major technology requirement of supervisors is the ability to help teachers discover ways to blend technology into their curricula. Restructuring the curriculum to incorporate technology is no longer a trend but has become a requirement.

Box 3.1 International Society for Technology in Education

Supervisors can turn their faculty on to Web sites such as The International Society for Technology in Education (ISTE), which defines itself as

> The trusted source for professional development, knowledge generation, advocacy, and leadership for innovation. A nonprofit membership organization, ISTE provides leadership and service to improve teaching, learning and school leadership by advancing the effective use of technology in K–12 and teacher education. (ISTE, 2008)

The ISTE Web site (http://www.iste.org) contains useful ideas and resources, including an online bookstore filled with great ideas about technology for use by supervisors and faculty alike. An interesting ISTE project is their Emerging Technologies Database to "increase the educational community's knowledge and understanding of effective infusion of new and emerging technologies to support teaching and learning" (ISTE, 2008).

In recognition of the rapid advances in technology that continually put new demands on educators, in 2008 ISTE launched its latest version of National Educational Technology Standards (NETS), providing a framework for educators to use as they transition schools from Industrial Age to Digital Age places of learning. In addition to standards for teachers, ISTE offers standards for administrators. According to Don Knezek, ISTE's chief executive officer,

> Administrators play a pivotal role in determining how well technology is used in our schools. The NETS for Administrators enable us to define what administrators need to know and be able to do in order to discharge their responsibility as leaders in the effective use of technology in our schools. Integrating technology throughout a school system is, in itself, significant systemic reform. We have a wealth of evidence attesting to the importance of leadership in implementing and sustaining systemic reform in schools. It is critical, therefore, that we attend seriously to leadership for technology in schools. (NETS, 2008)

Supervisors must be prepared to help teachers familiarize themselves with and become proficient at offering distance education and eLearning to students. Fifty-six percent of 2- and 4-year colleges offer distance education (U.S. Department of Education, 2005a) and at least 15 states provide some form of virtual schooling to supplement regular classes or provide for special needs (U.S. Department of Education, 2005b). A full one-fourth of all K–12 public schools offer some form of eLearning or virtual school instruction (U.S. Department of Education, 2005b).

For useful information, tools, and resources, check out the Web sites of such organizations as Distance-Educator.com or the Distance Education and Training Council (http://www.detc.org/about.html).

Issue #13: What is the supervisor's proper role regarding goals and objectives?

Because goals and objectives have a profound effect on what students learn, the supervisor's responsibility for helping teachers learn how to use goals and objectives effectively is undeniable. Supervisors should be familiar with the various taxonomies of instructional objectives and share this information with their faculty (Pawlas & Oliva, 2008). Students who know the goals their teachers have set for them are more likely to become involved in class activities and feel capable of achieving and assessing their achievements. Students are more likely to experience success in attaining goals and objectives when they are meaningful, clearly stated, and challenging yet attainable. The use of objectives prevents unexpected or surprise results, since both parties have agreed on the end product.

Supervisors often ponder over the extent to which they should require their teachers to use goals and objectives. A common question teachers ask is, "Must I have objectives written for *all* class activities, even for learning units that do not require mastery—activities whose purpose is just to broaden the students' "awareness?" Perhaps the best answer is, "Yes, if the desired behavior requires new knowledge, attitudes, or skills."

Issue #14: What is the supervisor's role regarding diversity?

By the year 2020 half of the nation's public school students will be minorities, but only about 5% of the teachers will be minorities (Gordon, 2008; Meyer & Rhodes, 2006). Currently, most prospective teachers are white females, in sharp contrast to the backgrounds of the students they will teach. American teachers are concerned over this imbalance. Most of our citizens, regardless of where they stand on the political spectrum, agree that although meeting the needs of all students is a monumental challenge, it is, nevertheless, an important responsibility of all teachers (Rose & Gallup, 2005). Jean Haar and Jerry Robicheau (2007) have referred to this responsibility as doing what is "right and just" (p. 196). Today's teachers have an obligation to provide their students an open forum for members of all cultures, and to provide a safe environment for students to reflect on their own opinions and the opinions of others.

For several decades, Americans have realized that school curricula needed adjustments to meet the needs of the many cultures represented among American children. Yet for several decades, knowing that these needs exist, teachers have been reluctant to make the adjustments required to meet the needs of all children. Perhaps the greatest cause for this failure is teachers' fear to change. Therefore, an important role of the supervisor is to help teachers learn to accept change, the topic of chapter 5.

The 37th Annual Phi Delta Kappa/Gallup Poll (Rose & Gallup, 2005) found that 90% of the respondents think that closing the achievement gap between mainstream and majority students should be a goal for all schools. The 38th Annual Phi Delta Kappa/Gallup Poll (Rose & Gallup, 2006) found that 88% of the public considers this goal important, and 82% believe that it is possible while at the same time maintaining high standards for all students. Tom Good and Jere Brophy (2007) have reported that progress is being made on this important goal. Highlights from the TIMSS 2007 report on mathematics and science achievement of U.S. fourth- and eighth-grade students in an international context (Gonzales, 2009) reported that "over time, U.S. white, black, Hispanic, and Asian students in both fourth and eighth grades have generally shown overall improvement in mathematics" (p. 23). In science, U.S. black and Asian fourth graders and U.S. black, Hispanic, and Asian eighth graders had an overall pattern of improvement (p. 48).

How should curricula be changed to meet the needs of a diverse student population? It should provide all children opportunities to express themselves. Encourage your faculty to learn more about the students, a good way to begin planning for teaching multicultural classes. If your teachers can assign activities that require students to work together toward common goals, they will improve both their self-concepts and their social skills. According to Daresh (2007),

> For school leaders, this has enormous implications. . . . Now, the educational leader is faced with the challenge of bringing about true unification with an eye toward maintenance and appreciation of diversity. . . . Diversity now must include appreciation of linguistic differences, lifestyle differences, and differences in terms of learning abilities and needs. . . .The issue will not simply be one of reactively avoiding discriminatory practice, but rather in how to proactively include differences in the improvement of practice and learning for all. (p. 368)

Supervisors can begin by encouraging teachers to use the research that is available and by involving teachers in schoolwide curriculum development. Saffold (2003) believes that the best place to begin is by tapping into community resources.

> All communities have funds of knowledge and resources that teachers can use to create curricula and educational environments that are inclusive of students' backgrounds and provide students greater access to new knowledge. . . . Learning to teach culturally diverse students involves classroom practices that respect and take advantage of students' cultural knowledge and experiences.

The most frequent incentives that motivate teachers are intrinsic rewards, such as increased self-confidence or the opportunity to develop new skills. Faculty development programs that encourage teachers to set high standards and become involved in changing the curriculum can be effective. Supervisors must find ways to provide teachers the time they require to develop multicultural schoolwide curricula, an opportunity which teachers have been denied in the past (see chapter 12).

Most schools with heavy minority student populations have high rates of poverty, leaving many of these schools without the materials and equipment needed to offer top-quality experiences to the students and often creating a feeling of hopelessness. But Sara Nelson, the principal of an elementary school in Austin, Texas, has proved that the situation can be reversed. By forming partnerships with Texas State University professors and other community institutions, the faculty of Sara's school has turned it into a model, high-performing school with innovative programs, national board-certified teachers, and low teacher turnover rates. To read a case study on this school, see Resta et al. (2006).

Another supervisory role, that of partnership facilitator, is discussed in chapter 4.

Conclusion

Supervision means helping teachers create a classroom and schoolwide climate that promote learning. The principal is usually the school's instructional supervisor. The dual, conflicting role of evaluator and helper presents a major challenge to supervisors: how to develop and maintain a trusting relationship. Trust can be earned through communicating the supervisor's and teacher's roles and through behaving consistently within the agreed-upon roles. Confidence at all times is essential.

Supervisors must go beyond focusing their attention on daily instruction and help teachers develop curricula. Beginning teachers need special help, because they don't yet have the knowledge of teachers with years of experience. Supervisors should also help teachers learn how to conduct research, because learning requires creating knowledge.

Today's teachers must be able to use technology to improve learning in their classes. Teachers need to learn how to work computer assignments into their curricula. Objectives can give direction to planning. Students with special needs require help so they can learn in the regular classroom. Supervisors need the skills necessary to help teachers adjust curricula to meet all of these needs.

Maximum gains are realized when teachers use team-based curriculum development. Supervisors must assist their teachers in interpreting and upholding those standards that are most difficult for teachers to reach. By helping them align curriculum unit objectives and the evaluation of curriculum units with these standards, the supervisor can empower teachers and enable their school to comply with state and national standards by making the maximization of learning the main priority, and a way of life in their school. Further gains can be realized by reaching out to the local community for support and leadership.

Questions for Discussion and Reflection

1. Why is the supervisor's help so important during the induction year?
2. How can supervisors reduce the barrier caused by their role as evaluator?
3. Examine each of the supervisory roles introduced in this chapter. How can technology be used to enhance the effectiveness in each role?
4. One challenge that supervisors face repeatedly is the need to get teachers to unlearn many of their adopted attitudes. What are some of the attitudes that teachers must unlearn?
5. The supervisor's effectiveness can be enhanced by soliciting parents' support. Who are some other key members in the community whose support will benefit the supervisor?

Suggested Activities

1. The annual Phi Delta Kappa/Gallup Poll of the Public's Attitudes toward the Public Schools always appears in the September issue of the *Phi Delta Kappan* journal. Study the poll in the most recent September issue for data that you can use to help your school meet its statewide standards.
2. Interview a special educator and ask for a list of suggestions or tips for helping special-needs students when they are in a regular classroom.
3. Attend an interdisciplinary teaching team's meeting. Note the leader's strategies for encouraging members to focus on learning as opposed to just raising test scores.

Chapter 4

Staff Development

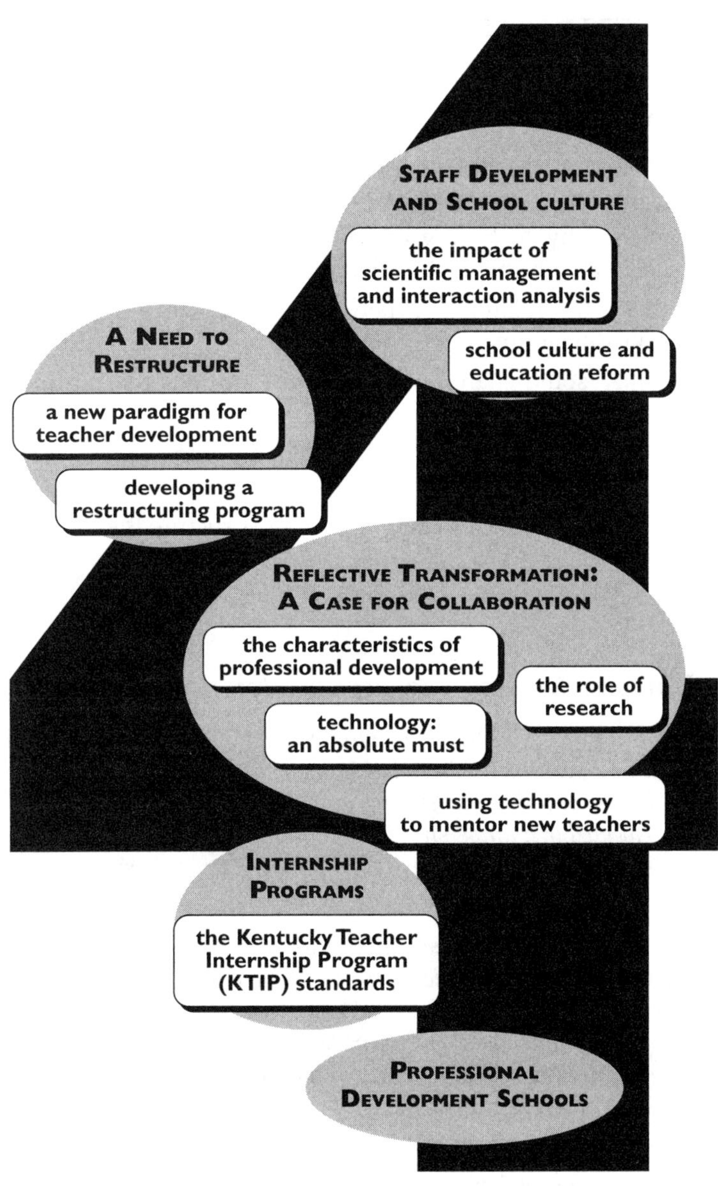

Staff Development and School culture
the impact of scientific management and interaction analysis
school culture and education reform
A Need to Restructure
a new paradigm for teacher development
developing a restructuring program
Reflective Transformation: A Case for Collaboration
the characteristics of professional development
the role of research
technology: an absolute must
using technology to mentor new teachers
Internship Programs
the Kentucky Teacher Internship Program (KTIP) standards
Professional Development Schools

Competent future school leaders must attend first to their own learning needs.

—J. S. Tripses,
Best practices: Statewide collaborations to strengthen school leadership

Objectives

After completion of this chapter, you should be able to

1. Identify weaknesses in traditional teacher development programs and explain why such programs will no longer work to effectively prepare teachers to promote education reform
2. Explain the relationship between teacher development programs and school development programs
3. Identify some changes in teachers' attitudes that are prerequisite for restructuring schools
4. Discuss some ways in which contemporary school cultures must be changed
5. Develop a program to help teachers restructure their school

Horton's Master-Teacher Development Program

Horton school is a K–12 school with an enrollment of 700 to 750 students. In many ways Horton is a typical small school, but in some ways its culture resembles that of a university. This university atmosphere can be attributed to a combination of factors. Horton is located in a university town. Many of the students actually take university courses for credit while still in high school. In fact, at Horton this practice is so common that by graduation, most students have earned several college credits.

Another contributing factor to the university- or college-like climate in Horton School is the experimental attitude at Horton. The administrators, teachers, students, and parents embrace the concept of experimentation, inquiry, and research. These open attitudes have made Horton School a natural environment for implementing new education reform practices, and the realization of this potential has led to the development of a powerful partnership program between Horton and the local Southcentral University.

Education reform is a major focus of Southcentral's mission statement. Like other universities, Southcentral faces increasing economic challenges. So far, the administra-

tion's attempts to keep the institution financially solvent have succeeded. In fact, often called "Campus Beautiful," the university has never lost this appearance. Despite its shrinking budgets, the university has remained a strong leader in education reform, and this, too, can be attributed to the creativity of its faculty and administration.

Five years ago, Horton's principal and Southcentral's education dean began to envision a partnership program aimed at increasing the school's involvement in education reform and strengthening the university's leadership position in education reform. The idea is simple, and the cost is actually nothing—on the contrary, the program saves money.

Original plans were to hire the two best, brightest new teachers in the state. The beginning teachers would teach their first three years at Horton. During this time, they would naturally be immersed in education reform because all teachers at Horton are already working with education reform practices. Special efforts would be made to involve these teachers in as many new education reform practices as possible.

The idea was solid, but the partners needed a special drawing card to lure these exceptional new teachers. The university held the key to this problem in its faculty scholarship program, a program that permits each professor to take a free university course each semester so long as the course directly relates to the faculty member's teaching assignment. Given this opportunity, by taking advantage of summer school the new teachers could earn a free master's degree in three years.

In addition to the advantage of a free master's degree, each teacher would be provided with a rich opportunity to develop expertise in the state's education reform program. The advantage for the university was increased leadership in education through a strong partnership with a local school. The advantage for the school was the program's ability to draw extremely bright, energetic novice teachers. All three parties benefited from the positive publicity given to this program and the reputation everyone earned from being part of it.

Five years later, the program has excelled above and beyond all expectations. The number of master-teacher development program participants has been increased to six. The school also benefits from having hired several of these participants, placing them in tenure-track positions. This unexpected event has proven a great advantage to these new teachers and to the school, enriching an already strong "experimental" ethos at Horton school.

Reflection

The value in schools forming partnerships with universities has been documented in recent literature (Stine, 2010) and was introduced in chapter 1. Such participatory partnerships have been advocated by many educators (Tubbs, Terry, & Chan, 2006). Some of the positive outcomes from such collaborative efforts are common to all school/university partnerships—for example, hermeneutics (the idea that individuals bring to each meeting questions and interpretations of events that are common to their own culture and experiences). Other advantages of school/university partnerships are specific to individual partnerships and are planned into the partnership. The

Horton/Southcentral Program shows that with careful planning the possibilities from university/school partnerships are unlimited. To protect the program's continuity at Horton school, current plans are to limit the maximum number of participants to six. What began as an experimental program is now considered a permanent fixture at these schools. The school/university partnership model was a deliberate attempt to increase the university's leadership and the school's participation in education reform.

An innovative program such as this Horton/Southcentral partnership program can be a win-win situation for all parties. Similar partnerships can be found all over the country, but such partnerships don't just happen. Each is the result of someone's initiative. Traditionally, the individual change agents involved have been members of university faculties, but an increasing number of partnerships are now being initiated by public school supervisors. This is yet another example of many new roles that supervisors are playing. As you reflect on the many new roles of supervisors (many of which are described in chapter 3), remember that each one was initiated by an individual. Sometimes all that is required to create a new partnership is a supervisor's encouragement.

Introduction

Two major purposes of schools are to nurture social development and help students learn; yet, according to Comer (2005), "Generations of teachers, administrators, and policy makers have been prepared in ways that do not enable them to create a school culture that can support student development and learning" (p. 763). In contrast to the isolated programs of the past, the arrangement described in Horton's Master Teacher Development Program is a collaborative model that involves a university and a school. This is just one of several types of collaborative programs being used to bring substantive improvement to schools' instructional programs. The case studies embedded in chapters throughout this book show other collaborative efforts.

Reports from the literature indicate that principals are being pressured to narrow their staff-development opportunities to meet science and mathematics expectations (Hunt, 2007). On the other hand, they are being pressured to improve the overall academic performance of the entire school, and that type of substantial improvement requires transforming the entire school. In turn, transformation requires new and innovative faculty development initiatives. Prior to deciding how to transform the school's culture, educators need to examine the current culture to identify needed changes.

Staff Development and School Culture

Several characteristics of the culture in today's schools have led to undesirable school practices that must be changed if meaningful and permanent progress in learning is to be made. Most of these essential changes involve teacher attitudes. Among the most seriously needed changes are: (1) the teacher's classroom-bound operating arena, (2) the institution's self-surviving nature, (3) teachers' attitudes toward research, (4) teachers' attitudes toward their own leadership skills and those of their fellow teachers, and (5) all teachers' attitudes toward the knowledge base of teaching.

The physical isolation of teachers was discussed in chapter 2, but the particular problem we discuss here refers to a different mind-set—teachers' *psychological* isolation, which has resulted from their having had little involvement in shaping the school's curriculum and culture outside their own classrooms. Throughout the history of our formal education system, and through no choice of their own, teachers have been trained to work in the confines of a classroom. Having first become comfortable and secure within these boundaries during their student teaching program, most teachers have elected to continue restricting their environment to the classroom. The very idea of a teacher's homeroom gives new meaning to "ownership." Here, they are at home. Here, they understand the rules because they themselves set them. Seldom have teachers ever questioned the idea that they belong in their classrooms. The classroom is the focal point of the comfort zone. Thus, a teacher's classroom becomes an extension of the teacher's self. Experienced teachers and administrators know just how difficult it can be to convince certain other teachers to change in this regard.

A detrimental effect resulting from their isolation has been a general restriction on teachers' power. Because of their limited working arena, teachers are perceived by others (and by themselves) as having little power (Irons & Aller, 2007). Traditional staff-development programs have reinforced this "powerless teacher" image by bringing in outside "experts" to give teachers the word. These so-called "experts" are usually around for only a day or two, far too brief a time to affect changes that are either substantive or lasting. Ironically, although teachers often find these alleged experts motivational, they may secretly question their benefit. Some refer to consultants as those "experts" who "blow in, blow off, and blow out." Others joke about the definition of *expert*, saying that an *ex* is a has-been and a *spurt* is a drip—so an expert is both a has-been and a drip.

These negative side effects (a sense of psychological isolation, a perception of teacher powerlessness, and a cynical view of teacher-development programs) at least partially result from the teacher's inactive role. Teachers are often viewed as passive recipients of someone else's knowledge. These persistent negative images reinforce the need for constructivism, where teachers can create their own understanding rather than depending on someone else to lead them.

A second problem with the culture in many contemporary schools is the institutions' need for self-survival, which leads them to hold on to the familiar and strive to maintain the status quo. A felt need to "keep to the tried and proven" can filter into the classroom and often amounts to nothing short of teachers staying in a comfortable rut. Perhaps the greatest cause for this shortcoming is teachers' fear of change. Supervisors can play a critical role in helping teachers learn to accept change (see chapter 5).

Ironically, even some of the programs designed to change the schools often end up preserving existing practices. Teachers' seeming inability to shape their environments may result, at least in part, from their failure to recognize their own power (Normore & Floyd, 2005). Many teachers also have difficulty in recognizing a fellow teacher as a leader. This attitude is unfortunate for a profession with a wealth of current literature on the importance of efficacy, with studies showing that high expectations and self-confidence are prerequisites to success.

Another limitation that some teachers place on themselves is their lack of faith in the knowledge base on teaching strategies. Although expert teachers know their content and pedagogy (Berry, 2005), many of these same teachers deny the existence of a true knowledge base on teaching. Faculty development programs may have actually contributed to teachers' feelings of incompetence. This type of faculty development, commonly called in-service education, has been popular for many years and continues to be popular in the twenty-first century. Supervisors must help teachers understand the need for a comprehensive, systematic faculty development program that focuses on the goals and needs of the entire school as opposed to the historically piecemeal, one-day workshops that deliver quick-fix tricks of the trade aimed at helping teachers with their individual problems.

According to Deal and Peterson (2009), schools with a negative or toxic culture lack a clear sense of purpose, have norms that reinforce inertia, blame students for lack of progress, discourage collaboration, and often have actively hostile relations among the staff. "Supervisors must work with teachers to assess the underlying norms and values of the culture and then as a group activity, work to change them to have a more positive, supportive culture" (Cromwell, 2008).

The Impact of Scientific Management and Interaction Analysis

Historically, the development of school cultures has paralleled the development of cultures of business. During the first two decades of the twentieth century, Fredrick Taylor's influence on business was so powerful that he shaped not only the practices of business and industry but also the nation's mind-set toward workers. Taylor's approach, known as *scientific management*, was to break each job down into many small parts and closely supervise each worker to ensure that each part is done correctly. Critics of scientific management theory say that such an approach probably grew out of, and undoubtedly promoted, the idea that each worker should be told exactly what to do and how to do it. The critics also say that this oversimplification and exaggerated overseeing left no room for workers to use their creative abilities to provide input; their ideas were not solicited for a purpose; they were unappreciated; they were unwanted.

The critics also say that another underlying premise supporting scientific management theory is a belief that workers need close supervision, because people are naturally lazy and are not trustworthy. This premise leads to the conclusion that if left alone, individuals will do only the minimal amount of work possible. These popular general assumptions about human nature and human behavior carried over into the schools. The implication was that since teachers are human and, therefore, are subject to those weaknesses, teachers could not be trusted to improve education. The idea ignored the possibility that people could be self-motivated.

Unfortunately, mistrust of teachers has continued through the years. In fact, at one point the mistrust was so extensive that attempts were made to completely remove teachers from the decision-making process. By the late 1950s and early 1960s, efforts were being made at regional research and development centers to develop *teacher-proof* curricula.

As discussed in chapter 2, the effects of scientific management theory overflowed into the schools and right on into supervision. Proponents of scientific management are quick to point out that it increases productivity. The bottom line, they say, is that it works. It seemed only natural that sooner or later scientific management would come to the schools. *Interaction analysis*, like scientific management, was a system designed to break down the act of teaching into many small, single parts. Interaction analysis was adopted as a system to be used to analyze the instructional process. Instruments were designed to help supervisors record, categorize, and analyze specific teacher behaviors. Interaction analysis became commonplace in the preparation of teachers.

In teacher education programs, interaction analysis and competency-based teaching were blended to form the counterpart to scientific management's system of breaking the job down into small pieces. One major university identified over 2,500 teacher competencies. Clinical supervision, a team approach, began dominating the supervisory process. Supervisory teams were formed to check all teachers in the state to ensure that they had mastered these competencies. What at first appeared to be a refreshing breeze turned into a powerful tornado that eventually disappeared after running its course.

Although seriously flawed, many of the reform practices of the 1980s and 1990s have had some positive effects. Ironically, many have stimulated the introduction of positive reform. One beneficial result is an awareness that the current system of elementary, middle level, and secondary schools truly does have significant weaknesses that cannot be fixed or removed from the current system by tampering with the present educational system's individual parts. Rather, it has become increasingly apparent that the entire system must undergo major, systemwide or "systemic" changes. One of the biggest mistakes we could make would be to try to prepare teachers to do the usual things better. Clearly, though, the situation requires more than just destroying the current school systems.

School Culture and Education Reform

Finnian (2000, p. 9) identified five underlying assumptions that influence the success or failure of reform implementation:

1. assumptions the adults in the school (i.e., teachers, administrators) hold for students,
2. assumptions regarding leadership and decision making,

3. assumptions about faculty and administration roles and responsibilities,
4. assumptions about best practices and structures for educating students, and
5. assumptions about the value of change.

Supervisors should collaborate with their faculty to explore these assumptions about their school's culture and how they impact reform efforts at their school.

School culture is not a static entity. It is constantly being constructed and shaped through interactions with others and through reflections on life and the world in general (Finnian, 2000). School culture is of such importance that it requires constant monitoring.

School culture develops as staff members interact with each other, the students, and the community (Hinde, 2004). "In a school with a positive culture, staff and administrators believe they have the ability to achieve their ambitions. Their counterparts operating in a negative school environment lack faith in the possibility of realizing their visions" (Cromwell, 2008).

It may be difficult to determine the nature of a school's culture because the faculty's own personal experiences, values, and cultural influences may cause them to unconsciously filter their view of the status quo and influence their ideas of what needs evaluation and change. Finnian (2000) concludes that in order for reforms to be accepted by schools, the assumptions of the chosen reform model and those of the school must be compatible. This requires the culture of the school to be analyzed and brought to the conscious level of staff and administrators. Before engaging in an elaborate and extensive analysis of your school's culture, supervisors can share the School Culture Triage Survey with their faculty. The survey (Box 4.1), created by Christopher R. Wagner, provides a quick method of assessing the current cultural status of your school and can assist in determining the wise allocation of valuable time and resources.

Ideally, all full-time teachers, administrators, counselors, and teacher assistants should participate in the survey. The survey can be administered at a faculty meeting, without providing the scoring sheet to the participants. To ensure truthful and accurate feedback from the participants, prior to administering the survey there must be an ironclad guarantee of anonymity. Ask participants to complete the survey with a minimum of explanation. To enforce the anonymity of the survey takers, have someone other than a secretary or administrator collect the completed surveys.

To tabulate the responses and make an item-by-item analysis, a *school culture task force* (consisting, for example, of three teachers and one administrator) may be formed. The task force can use EXCEL or some other spreadsheet application to make charts and graphs of the results for presentation at an upcoming faculty meeting, where everyone can brainstorm about any areas that need improvement. Many schools use the survey three times per year to monitor progress.

Box 4.1 School Culture Triage Survey

Directions: Please circle the number to the right of each statement that most closely characterizes the practice in your school.

Rating: 1 = Never, 2 = Rarely, 3 = Sometimes, 4 = Often, 5 = Always or Almost Always

Professional Collaboration

1. Teachers and staff discuss instructional strategies and curriculum issues.	1	2	3	4	5
2. Teachers and staff work together to develop the school schedule.	1	2	3	4	5
3. Teachers and staff are involved in the decision-making process with regard to materials and resources.	1	2	3	4	5
4. The student behavior code is a result of collaboration and consensus among staff.	1	2	3	4	5
5. The planning and organizational time allotted to teachers and staff is used to plan as collective units/teams rather than as separate individuals.	1	2	3	4	5

Affiliative Collegiality

1. Teachers and staff tell stories of celebrations that support the school's values.	1	2	3	4	5
2. Teachers and staff visit/talk/meet outside of the school to enjoy each other's company.	1	2	3	4	5
3. Our school reflects a true "sense" of community.	1	2	3	4	5
4. Our school schedule reflects frequent communication opportunities for teachers and staff.	1	2	3	4	5
5. Our school supports and appreciates the sharing of new ideas by members of our school.	1	2	3	4	5
6. At our school there is a rich and robust tradition of rituals and celebrations including holidays, special events, and recognition of goal attainment.	1	2	3	4	5

Self-Determination/Efficacy

1. When something is not working in our school, the faculty and staff predict and prevent rather than react and repair.	1	2	3	4	5
2. School members are interdependent and value each other.	1	2	3	4	5
3. Members of our school community seek alternatives to problems/issues rather than repeating what we have always done.	1	2	3	4	5
4. Members of our school community seek to define the problem/issue rather than blame others.	1	2	3	4	5
5. The school staff is empowered to make instructional decisions rather than waiting for supervisors to tell them what to do.	1	2	3	4	5
6. People work here because they enjoy and choose to be here.	1	2	3	4	5

(continued)

Scoring the Triage Survey

To determine the value of each rating, tally the number of respondents for each. For example, in a group of 33 survey participants, let's say that a question was ranked in the following way:

Rating 1 (Never) had 2 responses;
Rating 2 (Rarely) had 8 responses;
Rating 3 (Sometimes) had 3 responses;
Rating 4 (Often) had 13 responses; and
Rating 5 (Always or Almost Always) had 7 responses.

To find the value for each group of responses, take the number of responses for each and multiply it by the value of the rating. In this case:

- Rating 1, with 2 responses multiplied by a value of 1, yields a total value of 2.
- Rating 2, with 7 responses multiplied by 2, yields a value of 14.
- Rating 3, with 3 responses multiplied by 3, yields a value of 9.
- Rating 4, with 13 responses multiplied by 4, yields a value of 52.
- Rating 5, with 7 responses multiplied by 5, yields a value of 35.

Then add all the values: 2 + 16 + 3 + 9 + 52 + 35 = 114

Since there were 33 responses, we divide the 114 by 33 for the mean score of 3.56.

The lowest triage score is 17 and the highest score is 85. After utilizing the triage questions in several program evaluations, Dr. Wagner's data suggest the following:

17 – 40 Critical and immediate attention is necessary. Conduct a full-scale assessment of your school's culture and invest all available resources to repair and heal the culture.
41 – 59 Modifications and improvements are necessary. Begin with a more intense assessment of your school's culture to determine which areas are most in need of improvement.
60 – 75 Monitor and maintain, making positive adjustments.
76 – 85 Amazing! A score of 75 was the highest ever recorded.

A Need to Restructure

Over the years, although most public and private school teachers have participated in the aforementioned workshops and in-service education, the impact of such endeavors unfortunately has been minimal at best—and negative at worst. Supervisors must realize that the level of school improvement demanded by the NCLB-based standards can never be achieved by occasional, random, piecemeal workshops that are divorced from the school's mission and goals. Teacher improvement and school improvement must be integrated. The word *integrate* implies a tight connection between the school development program and the teacher development program. Just as schools need total restructuring, teachers also need more than sporadic opportunities to improve. Effective teacher development can occur when teachers become involved in ongoing, systematic goal setting and problem solving with their administrators and fellow teachers. Furthermore, to make significant improvement, teachers must believe in the efficacy of this process.

Supervisors must convince teachers that curriculum, instruction, and social climate affect student learning and that academic achievement is not determined by factors that lie largely *outside* the school, in the genes and social backgrounds of the students. Fortunately, ample research is available to explain how learning occurs. The current knowledge base on teaching is substantial enough that teachers can design educational climates that will bring about the needed learning improvement. Lieberman and Miller (1992) testify to this progress:

> We are fortunate that at the present moment in education we can point to several practices, developing separately and simultaneously, which challenge conventional assumptions about instruction. These approaches share a common belief that the learner is at the center of the educational enterprise... The implications of research on cognition and of the approach are nothing short of revolutionary. They direct us to reconceptualize teaching, to see it as being woven of the same cloth as learning. Teaching and learning are interdependent, not separate functions. Under this view, teachers are primary learners. They are problem posers and problem solvers; they are researchers, and they are intellectuals engaged in unraveling the learning process both for themselves and for the young people in their charge. Learning is not consumption; it is knowledge production. Teaching is not performance; it is facilitative leadership. Curriculum is not given; it is constructed empirically, based on the emergent needs and interests of learners. Assessment is not judgment; it documents programs over time. Instruction is not technocratic; it is invented, craft-like, and, above all, an imperfect human enterprise. (pp. 166–167)

Like instruction, restructuring is an imperfect human enterprise. We do not know everything about restructuring, but we do know that successful restructuring

- is a long-term process,
- is a collaborative process,
- is a schoolwide process,
- occurs best in a risk-taking environment,
- requires changing the school culture,
- occurs slowly,
- requires people—both teachers and students—to change,
- may require making deep social changes,
- involves the community, and
- empowers teachers and students.

It involves learning which

- is student-generated,
- involves major concepts,

- ties new information to existing knowledge,
- involves generalizing, and
- involves examples and nonexamples.

A New Paradigm for Teacher Development

> Educational Constituents Council (ELCC) Standard No. 4 holds educational leadership candidates responsible for helping teachers design professional growth plans.

Restructuring schools requires changing the roles of all personnel to such a degree that the type of teacher behavior required is almost the opposite of traditional teacher behavior. Because the task at hand is so comprehensive, and since it will require major changes of both teachers and students, a much different type of teacher development program is needed. The type of teachers in demand are those who are competent in problem solving, experimenting, and knowledge generating. Faculty development programs must engage teachers in a continuous flow of questions about student learning and best practice (Scheetz, Waters, Smeaton, & Lare, 2005).

The new paradigm for teacher development will change teachers' ways of thinking and behaving. Instead of having so-called experts deliver the truth to teachers by way of a one- or two-day dog-and-pony show, today's world demands that teachers *become experts themselves*—not in memorizing information or in implementing whatever knowledge can be gained through workshops, but rather in *generating* knowledge. Teacher development means continually transforming theory into practice; it is both teacher renewal and renewal of schools, and it is culture building. Such development programs can and will increase student achievement (Wenglinsky & Silverstein, 2006/2007).

In an article in *Forum* magazine, National Staff Development Director Dennis Sparks (1994) spoke of a paradigm shift in staff development

- from solely individual development to individual *and* organization development;
- from fragmented, piecemeal improvement efforts to staff development driven by a clear, coherent strategic plan for the school district, each school, and the departments that serve schools;
- from district-focused to school-focused staff-development approaches;
- from training attended away from the job as the primary staff-development delivery system to multiple forms of job-embedded learning;
- from staff developers who function primarily as trainers to those who provide consultation, planning, and facilitation services as well as training;
- from staff development provided by one or two departments to staff development as a critical function and major responsibility performed by all administrators and teacher leaders;

- from teachers as the primary recipients of staff development to continuous improvement in performance for *everyone* who affects student learning; and
- from staff development as a "frill" that can be cut during difficult financial times to staff development as an essential and indispensable process, without which schools cannot hope to prepare young people for citizenship and productive employment.

* * *

We have already seen that to meet current expectations, schools need more than the traditional piecemeal workshops where experts tell teachers what they must do and how to do it. This chapter explains that total restructuring of the school is a must. Put simply, it requires changing everything, which can be accomplished only by involving everyone. Furthermore, it cannot begin in the middle. The principal can share a vision to fire the interest of the teachers, but the teachers themselves must shape their mission.

The following case study shows a principal bringing forth a vision and then orchestrating total faculty involvement in shaping that vision into a mission. The mission this faculty chose is lifelong learning. As you read the case, notice how this principal enables the faculty to develop this mission, giving ownership to every teacher in the school. Ownership leads to the enormous amount of energy and enthusiasm needed to build and sustain a professional learning community.

Getting the Job Done: Taking Care of the Students

Jane B. Huffman • University of North Texas
Anita M. Pankake • University of Texas–Pan American

Leaders are continually challenged to address accountability issues by facilitating shared decision making, implementing collaborative best practices, and focusing on continuous learning for all. Developing professional learning communities provides one of the best strategies to build personal and organizational capacity for systemic reform. Mitchell and Sackney (2001) state:

> A learning community is a place where there are communities of leaders, where students, teachers, noninstructional staff, parents, and administrators share the opportunities and responsibilities for decision making. (p.133)

This case study describes a middle school dedicated to meeting student needs by providing a supportive environment and strong instructional program amidst multiple challenges. The story also provides an account over 10 years, offering a longitudinal view of both progress and problems.

The Community

Whitney Lake Community School District (WLCSD) is located in the southwest and includes the community of Whitney Lake and segments of land within a large, highly industrialized city of which Whitney Lake is a suburb. In 2003, WLCSD reported a student enrollment of 20,000 housed at 22 campuses (3 high schools, 4 middle schools, 13 elementary schools, a sixth-grade campus, and an educational center). Currently, the district claims an increased student population of 21,180 and the addition of two campuses.

The community has a population of approximately 10,500 comprised of 69.3% Hispanic, 22.2% White, 7.6% African American, 1.4% Native American, and 3.7% from two or more races. *(The total can be greater than 100% because Hispanics could be counted in other races.)* The median household income in the community was $31, 660 with nearly one quarter of the population below the poverty line.

The district's mission is to *prepare students to become productive citizens and lifelong learners*. Based on the state's rating system, WLCSD was labeled as "exemplary" in 2002, "recognized" in 2004, and "academically acceptable" every year since.

The School

Whitney Lake Middle School's (WLMS) parental community is composed primarily of first-generation immigrants who look to the school to provide the American Dream for their children. The school's mission is "making students successful lifelong learners." WLMS enrolls more than 900 students in grades 6, 7 and 8. Seventy-nine teachers, 1 principal, 3 assistant principals, 3 counselors, 1 librarian, and 8 instructional specialists serve the school.

The ethnic breakdown of the student population has changed slightly over the past four years. The percent of African American students has dropped from 7.7 to 5.2; Hispanic students now make up 89.4% of the enrollment, up from 86.6% in 2003; the percentage of White students has generally remained steady, with 5.7% in 2003 and 5.2% in 2006–2007. The percent of Limited English Proficient population has nearly doubled from 11.1% to 20.8%. The school remains a schoolwide Title I campus; the economically disadvantaged percentage was 75.1% in 2003 but has since increased to 85.7%. The per-pupil expenditure was $6,186 and has increased very little during this time; for 2006–2007 at WLMS it was $6,302.

The percentage of students meeting the state standard on mandated tests increased each year from 1996 through 2001 (Table 1). While percentages varied slightly, the rating for the school, as a whole, moved from "academically acceptable" in 1999 to "recognized" status in 2000 and remained so through 2002. When the state test changed in 2002–2003, the school moved to academically acceptable status until 2006–2007, when it improved to recognized status (Table 2).

The Case

Much of the literature regarding professional learning communities (PLCs) offers a snapshot

Table 1 Whitney Lake Middle School: SAAS Test Scores and State Ratings

Whitney Lake Middle School	1996 Acceptable	1997 Acceptable	1998 Acceptable	1999 Recognized	2000 Recognized	2001 Recognized	2002 Recognized
Reading	62.5%	79.6%	78.9%	87.8%	86.3%	89.8%	89.4%
Writing	64.0%	76.3%	75.0%	92%	91.6%	89.7%	91.9%
Math	57.1%	72.5%	80.8%	90.9%	93.1%	96.3%	95%
Social Studies	Not tested	Not tested	Not tested	Not tested	Not tested	68.9%	87.3%
All Tests	47.3%	64.1%	70.4%	83.5%	83.5%	86.8%	85.9%

Table 2 Whitney Lake Middle School: SAKS Test Scores & State Ratings

Whitney Lake Middle School: Met Standard (Sum of All Grades Tested)	2002–03 No rating—1st year of new test	2003–04 Academically Acceptable	2004--05 Academically Acceptable	2005–06 Academically Acceptable	2006–07 Recognized
Reading	74.8%	81%	73%	76%	83%
Writing	77.8%	89%	85%	89%	92%
Math	52.0%	63%	59%	66%	75%
Social Studies	76.1%	86%	85%	71%	81%
Science	Not tested	Not tested	Not tested	35%	42%

of a school or district at a particular point in time. This case, however, presents information about a PLC over nearly a decade, allowing the reader to see the overall direction of development. This case demonstrates the powerful influence the central office can have on the development of a PLC at a campus. As you read about Whitney Lake Middle School, watch for information to help you address the following questions:

- What causes the interruptions in continuous improvement in the school?
- What actions were taken to redirect the process?
- How would WLMS be different if the district had not been so supportive?

Researchers have studied transitions at WLMS for nine years. They have visited WLMS repeatedly to conduct surveys and group and individual interviews with campus personnel, and to review documents. In 2005, interviews were also conducted with central office administrators. Initial interviews at WLMS revealed four themes in the school's culture: leadership, focus, relationships, and the involvement of central office administrators. The 2005 interview transcripts revealed that all four themes had continued to develop, although at some points the development stalled or even regressed.

Leadership

In 2003 an assistant principal acknowledged that leadership is shared at many levels: "The team leaders and department chairs are quasi-administrators. . . in charge of academics, grades and disciplining the students." The librarian noted, "Teachers have good ideas and aren't hesitant to speak up. They provide suggestions, make decisions, ask others' opinions and adjust accordingly." In 2005, shared leadership in the school continued. A WLMS department chair talked about leadership in the school:

> We have a leadership team that is made up of department chairs. . . . The principal and the assistant principals are also meeting in there. . . . A lot of decisions are made in there. . . . Our faculty meetings are exactly the same way. So, it's once a month . . . team leaders are in there too. . . . Department chairs and team leaders.

The process for identifying a new principal for the school was described by the department chair for social studies:

> We were given a questionnaire asking each teacher . . . what qualities are you looking for in a new principal . . . then they're [District Chief of Staff and the Human Resources Director] coming out Thursday . . . so he kind of said ok. It's not somebody in the administration building that's going to decide for you; it's your leadership committee here that's going to. . . .

Leadership succession has been important in sustaining efforts to function as a PLC by keeping stability in vision and mission, leadership style, and focus on student learning. Two succession issues were of primary concern in the district in 2005. First, a new superintendent was making his leadership style known to the school community. He began work in the 2004–2005 academic year and initiated various changes in leadership at the central office and the schools. An assistant principal described these leadership changes as disruptive to "everything." After nine years of the same superintendent, a new person was bringing changes in both personnel and practices throughout the district.

The second issue was the retirement of the WLMS principal. In 2005, all teachers were asked for their ideas and opinions on a profile for this new leader and several would serve on the search committee. Key central office administrators visited to hear what teachers had to say and to conduct a written survey about preferred characteristics for the new leader. This provided teachers a strong voice in the selection process.

Focus

In 1998, the principal commented: "What we want to do is be a team, we're a family, but we have a job to do . . ." She referenced the efforts underway to help all of the teachers and administrators help all of the kids. P.E. and art teachers were helping with reading; administrators were teaching math. The focus was "on trying to make recognized status on our campus reading, 80% on all levels." The lead teacher in 1998 stated: "The goal is to produce a lifelong commitment to learning, success in both academic . . . and other fields . . . basically every decision that we make focuses on student learning."

Clearly, from 1998 to 2003 the principal and team leaders were focused on helping teachers reach the student learning goal. In 2003 the new principal said her priority was *students first,* as was the previous principal's. The staff knew better than to bother her with something if it didn't focus on or help the kids.

Teachers, in spring of 2000, verified that student achievement was the focus and that expectations had changed over time. One teacher noted that in years past, what percentage of kids did well on the state test wasn't a big deal, but now, "We want to do well on the SAAS test every year. That's kind of like the main goal that everybody is aiming at right now." In 2003 interviews garnered the following responses to the question, "What is most important in your school?": "Our students are first priority"; "We're interested in our students' learning"; "Learners, everything we do is learner-centered"; "Creating successful students."

An assistant principal said that department chairs were responsible for monitoring the school improvement process by going back through the action plan, checking on whether or not various tasks in the plan were completed and, if not, determine if they should be modified, deleted, or postponed. The principal added, "We have little binders in the teacher's planning room that they actually go through and look at their action plan constantly." She stated that the school's action plan could be considered a *living document,* continuously guiding the work in the school.

The 2005 interviews gathered information on the process that made the school and district so successful over the decade. The Total Quality Management tool of *benchmarking* was used to identify practices in other districts that might be employed in WLSD. A central office administrator, instrumental in initiating the process, stated:

> At WLMS, the focus on students as a priority appears to have begun in 1998. Throughout that time, the mantra regarding the priority/focus of the school remained the same. The depth and breadth of its adoption have increased over the years so that in 2003 it was not an administrative platitude, but rather a genuine believed and behaved value embedded in the school culture.

According to him, this focus pervaded the district as well as the school:

> . . . saying every child can learn is like saying every child can breathe. . . . It's not a question whether they learn or don't learn. They're going to learn one way or another. . . . Question is, are they going to learn what you're supposed to be teaching them?

Relationships

The idea of *team* is woven through the WLMS story, from the beginning through 2005. *Team* at WLMS refers to the individual instructional units, the formal administrative organization, the faculty efforts to help students, and the decision-making processes. Early on, individuals expressed pleasure at being able to work at WLMS. Either they liked it at WLMS and/or they were skeptical about finding anything similar to it at other campuses. Positive feelings among staff toward the formal leadership progressed from sporadic to pervasive. In the spring of 2000 one teacher stated:

> Well, I think since [the principal] has been here, it's been like that . . . she says if you have a problem, you come to me. Don't let it fester . . . and get larger than it should be. . . .

By 2003 interviewees described the culture of the school with terms such as: "family," "dedicated or committed," "everyone involved with student learning," "don't give up on kids—keep on striving for the best results," "everyone wants to help out," and "hard working". While student achievement was almost always identified as the priority for the school, thoughts went beyond the cognitive dimension—"lifelong learning, successful students," "creating successful students," "academics and life," and "we're interested in our students' learning—students are everything."

Commitment to children in this school was amazing. If a strategy didn't work, another strategy would be tried. If one person couldn't get through to a child, others were sought for assistance. Tests were important, but life success was the real goal.

Based on the most recent interviews, the collaborative culture was still in place. WLMS has some obvious but unspoken expectations, and anyone unable to accept and meet them needs to find another place to work. No animosity toward those who *don't fit* was detected, just an acknowledgement that working at WLMS is not for everyone.

Central Office

In 1998 the perceived impact of the central office was minimal. In the 2003, however, the principal and assistant principal commented about a new and positive direction for Whitney Lake. The central office was being viewed as a support for rather than a barrier to the school's work. Many people spoke positively about all levels of the central office. An assistant principal stated:

> Central Office is very supportive. This is what sets us apart from other districts. Our administration gets us what we need. This is the message passed down from our superintendent.

Instructional specialist was the most often mentioned position when someone from WLMS was asked about supports for the campus. Many individuals from WLMS have moved to leadership positions at the central office or in other schools. These existing relationships appear to have contributed to the strong central-office-to-campus and campus-to-campus links. These strong positive relationships were echoed in the 2005 interviews.

In recounting the district's improvement process, a central office administrator, instrumental in this effort, spoke about the major steps taken to get things moving:

> We trimmed our budgets at Central Office by 30%, put that money out on campuses. We provided instructional specialists for each campus . . . we developed . . . district assessments . . . to inform instruction . . . so you know where kids are, at any given time. . . .

He described the overall philosophy used in developing the central office/campus relationship in this long-term districtwide improvement process:

> You build accountability and then you provide support for the accountability . . . if we're going to hold them accountable . . . we have to provide the support that they need to do it . . . whatever it takes. . . .

Issues for Further Reflection and Application

The themes of focus, leadership, relationships, and central office emerged in the earliest data and continued to be evidenced in the 2005 interviews. Over this decade the themes remained constant, though none of them developed smoothly.

Consider the following tasks as reflective processes.

1. Huffman and Hipp (2003) describe Hord's five dimensions of PLCs (1997) and include external factors as important to implementing and sustaining strong instructional cultures. Locate evidence from the story that is related to the following PLC dimensions:

   Shared and supportive leadership
   What internal and external events, helped build leadership capacity at WLMS?

   Shared values and vision
   Does WLMS have a vision? What is it? How was it created? Has it changed at all from 1998 to 2005? On what do you base your answers?

   Collective learning and application
   Do teachers at WLMS engage in collective learning and application of that learning? Has this changed from 1998 to 2005? If so, how?

   Supportive conditions (structures)
   What structures were created to support WLMS's development as a PLC?

   Supportive conditions (relationships)
   Describe the continuum of relationships from classroom teacher to superintendent as supportive conditions in WLMS and the district.

2. Identify examples from the story that
   - explain how high expectations for students are reflected in teacher actions.
   - explain teacher feelings of satisfaction.
   - illustrate how leadership succession impacted PLC development in the school.
   - describe the role central office had in the development of WLMS as a PLC.

3. Relate this case story to your own school, regarding
   - *Leadership succession*—Is leadership succession important at your school? Why?
   - *Vision development*—How was the vision developed in your school? What words would best describe your school's focus?
   - *Collective learning*—Does collective learning occur in your school? If so, how does it align with your school's mission and improvement plans?

- *Involved central office*—Does the central office impact student learning in your school? Why or why not?
- *Strong relationships*—Offer suggestions on how you would create and maintain these positive feelings in your school.

Developing a Restructuring Program

The proposed type of development program that is generally labeled *restructuring* differs from traditional teacher development programs in several ways. A major difference is that proponents of this type of program recognize that there are many unanswered questions; much is to be learned about helping teachers become researchers, successful problem solvers, and self-actualized human beings who feel good about themselves, professionally and personally.

Paradoxically, education reform programs are providing both opportunities for and barriers to this type of teacher development. For example, school restructuring is, itself, recognized as a practice in many reform programs; yet the pressure to increase student test scores, a quality that characterizes many of these programs, is often so excessive that it becomes counterproductive to teachers' self-development.

Traditional teacher training workshops are insufficient for the job of developing a teacher-researcher, which involves much more than merely helping teachers develop the techniques used by researchers. The goal is to imbue these skills, *and attitudes that support their use*, into teachers so that they become part of each teacher's natural behavior. Much is heard today about the importance of teacher dispositions. Embracing research, for example, is touted as an indispensable disposition for all teachers. It follows that teachers must become good consumers of research, become skilled in research techniques, and become practicing researchers.

Because, as youths, most teachers were taught to think sequentially and to learn by themselves, preparing teachers to work and grow cooperatively and to become knowledge generators will require time. From the onset, to prevent discouragement from developing later in the program, teachers should be advised that becoming a teacher-researcher and knowledge generator is a time-consuming process. It does not happen all at once—rather, it occurs in incremental steps.

To be effective, a teacher development program requires that teachers reach a state of *self-actualization*—becoming the type of person that one can be happy to be—and it is the long-term product of repeated success. Teacher development programs should provide ample opportunities for success and the encouragement needed to succeed. Teachers can develop self-confidence and self-esteem (and, as a result, self-actualization) with the knowledge they create through their own research, and by sharing the results of their research with their colleagues. Collaboration has several positive effects on teacher development: (1) It forces teachers to expose their teaching practices to others; (2) it gives teachers a willingness to experiment at the cost of risking failure; (3) it develops the ability to self-analyze; and (4) it develops the ability to discuss.

Rather than happening automatically, successful collaboration requires the following conditions:

- adequate professional development, including a sufficient knowledge base and enough time;
- a credible leadership team;
- support from the school administration—philosophically and materially;
- continuing support by those who understand the new practice(s);
- regular opportunities for reflection and problem solving;
- relief from the constraints of traditional evaluation and testing while new ways are learned; and
- hope that those structural changes that teachers begin to find necessary to sustain their efforts can indeed happen.

Another precaution that supervisor can take to increase the probability of a new program's success is to garner overwhelming support from all members of the learning community for the project before it is adopted. A southern California principal who was hired to improve the test scores at his new school said, "The first step (in restructuring a school) is to determine the most important challenge" (Stine, 2010). He spent the first few weeks holding discussions at school, in the homes of parents, and at civic organizations, asking two questions: "What are we doing right?" and "What needs changing?" Obviously, the more support for any new program has, the better. A highly successful accelerated school in Sacramento required 90% support for program adoption.

Although critical of the schools they read and hear about in the media, Americans are quick to embrace their local schools (Rose & Gallup, 2005). Many community members, including non-parents, are eager to help improve the local schools but do not know how (Lefkowits & Miller, 2006). The principle here is straightforward: When participants in a program feel ownership, they are bound to give more support; when they don't, they will be inclined to perceive the program as a pet project of the principal or of a particular group of colleagues. If it is perceived as someone else's project, then those outside the "in group" will always suspect that anything they are asked to do will be an attempt to use them to benefit others. Another way of saying this is that to be successful in getting the support of others, those others must know how the project will help them meet some of their own individual goals. Further discussion on goals appears in chapter 8.

Successful restructuring also requires the support of the community. As seen in the example of the southern California principal, the program can be strengthened even further by garnering the support of nonschool community leaders. Education reform increasingly focuses on staff development at the local level, both in schools and in local communities. Site-based governance and a felt need to involve parents have brought an increased emphasis on school-based improvement. According to Lefkowits and Miller (2006), "Increased parent involvement continues to top the list of priorities for school improvement" (p. 406).

No innovation can be successful without an adequate power supply, and the support bases represented by teachers, students, administrators, and the public can be thought of as power sources. Successful change requires both internal and external power sources. Certainly, the 1980s and 1990s education reform programs and the No Child Left Behind legislation have given further testimony to the effects of power groups outside the school. The twenty-first century will reveal new ways of energizing internal sources—teachers, administrators, and other school personnel—but only if all groups within the learning community increase their levels of involvement in generating knowledge.

Even after all of these precautions are taken, changes of the magnitude required for restructuring will have opposition, and rightfully so. Opposition must be allowed and, when appropriately accommodated, can actually be healthy. Special meetings should be arranged to provide a forum for resisters to the restructuring process.

Reflective Transformation: A Case for Collaboration

A prominent theme of this book is collaboration, an essential practice for all teachers if they are to succeed in today's demanding schools. Yet, because of their toxic school cultures, only two-thirds of our teachers engage in regularly scheduled collaboration that focuses on instructional issues (Science and Engineering Indicators, 2008), as shown in Figure 4.1.

Figure 4.1 Regularly Scheduled Collaboration with Other Teachers on Issues of Instruction

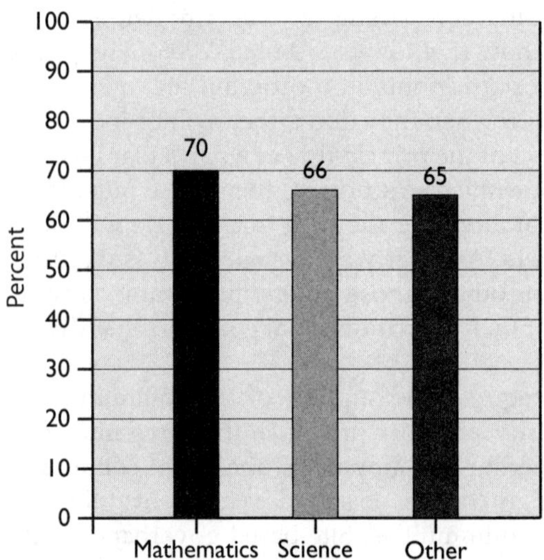

From Figure 1-15, Collaborative Professional Development of Public Middle and High School Teachers: Academic Year 2003–04. National Science Foundation, *Science and Engineering Indicators 2008.*

The alternative to isolated, ineffective, classroom-bound teachers is the involvement of every teacher in all types of activities aimed at improving learning at the school. Collaboration with other members of the school's learning community can transform the school into a richer learning environment for all students (Tripses, 2006). "But," the skeptics might say, "we have always shared our experiences. It happens daily in the teachers' lounge. We often talk over lunch. Hardly an hour of a day passes without teachers sharing their concerns over all types of issues. So why hasn't transformation already occurred?"

The simple discussion of problems may never go beyond criticizing the students, administrators, or even other teachers. Transformation requires true reflective thinking, and the supervisor is responsible for ensuring that the discussions are means to positive ends—improving learning opportunities at the school. Topics that are of significant concern to teachers is a good place to start. With each issue, the goal should be to involve other teachers who consider the issue important, and they should play an important part in solving the problem. The supervisor's role is to help teachers discover areas of common concern and encourage the formation of collaborative groups to discuss the issues. Once formed, the supervisor should actively join in the discussions of such groups, becoming an equal partner in the process.

Reflective transformation is essential in professional development, the aspects of which are detailed below. Technology and research also play a crucial part. More information on the supervisor's collaborative role in staff development appears in the section on the Kentucky Teacher Internship Program later in this chapter.

It Works for Me!

Assisting the Struggling Teacher

Sandra S. Murray, University of Tennessee at Martin

One of the less pleasant responsibilities of a supervisor is to assist the struggling teacher. This can be accomplished in a positive manner by using a structured method of support. One method of assistance is the N-E-A-T process.* The administrator and teacher work to develop a plan that is intended to lead to remediation of the identified deficiencies. The plan consists of ***Notice*** to the teacher that a deficiency exists and that the deficiency could lead to disciplinary action. The administrator thoroughly ***Explains*** the deficiencies and suggests ways to improve. The administrator then works with the educator to determine what ***Assistance*** is needed and can be practically afforded. This can be in the form of staff development, visits to other classrooms, etc. ***Time*** is provided for improvement and a realistic timeline is established. Opportunities for observations and discussion of progress are arranged within this timeline. By providing Notice, Explanation, Assistance, and Time, the teacher is given the opportunity to improve with the assistance of the supervising administrator.

*The Code of Ethics of the Education Profession in Florida. (n.d.). State Board of Education Rule 6B-4.08. Retrieved December 2, 2008, from http://www.advancedlearningenvironment.org/lms/Portals/1/Content/33/docs/TeacherHandout.doc

The Characteristics of Professional Development

Michelli (1995, pp. 146–147) offers the following characteristics of professional development.

1. *Professional development must be coherent*. It must be based on a particular set of standards and beliefs, including a clear sense of what an excellent teacher knows and is able to do.

2. *Professional development must take place over time.* It cannot occur in one afternoon. It must allow time for reflection, thoughtfulness, and growth.
3. *Professional development must link research and practices.* We have made great progress in understanding what works in education and what doesn't. Professional development must take into account the relationship between theory and practice.
4. *Professional development must be based on input from professionals, interfacing their practical knowledge with the research-based standards.* It must be planned collaboratively, and when possible, involve close working relationships between universities and schools. It cannot be imposed, but must reflect the real needs of practicing teachers.
5. *Professional development must be accountable.* In the long run, the vision of education that formed the basis for professional development must be translated into expectations for students in classrooms of teachers who are beneficiaries of professional development. This process must be carefully documented.

Technology: An Absolute Must

Today's professional teacher development programs must include technology, and it must not be done as an add-on that, at best, distantly relates to the school's plans for meeting the district's standards. Accountability mandates such as No Child Left Behind have drawn attention to the practical use of student data for school improvement. However, student data are often stored in forms that are difficult to access, manipulate, and interpret, precluding their use at the classroom level to inform and impact instruction. Wayman (2005) notes that there are newly available computer technologies that promote efficient organization and access to student data, allowing easier accountability reporting and user-friendly data access at all education levels. Teachers can use these tools to engage in the informed reflection necessary to improve classroom practice.

Prensky (2005) has noted that since technology offers a way to lead students "to teach themselves in profoundly deep and engaging ways" (p. 12), supervisors and administrators should want and settle for nothing less for teachers. To reach this goal, supervisors should make every effort to ensure that programs aimed both at teachers and at students must be personalized. The need to personalize technologically based programs is especially critical with online programs (Bogle et al., 2007). For example, immediate feedback on assignments and quick responses to phone calls and e-mails can make personal connections with distance learners. When such efforts are made, the program completion rate among online students is comparable to that of students attending campus-based programs.

Tuttle (2006) suggests a way to personalize the use of technology in the faculty development program by encouraging teachers to make technology-based presentations showing how they are leading their students to higher levels of thinking. This goal can become a way for teachers to meet the required standards. To show teachers how others are linking their state standards and how they are collecting and analyzing data in their classrooms, check out the following Web sites:

Mid-continental Research for Education and Learning (McRel) educational laboratory
www.mcrel.org/standards.benchmarks
This Web site lists a compendium of content standards and benchmarks covering all disciplines for K–12 education in both searchable and browseable formats. Here, your teachers can find the major concepts at each grade level, and ways to help students develop these concepts. Also available are quick links to teaching materials developed by McRel.

Learning Point Associates
www.ncrel.org/toolbelt
Today's teachers are often overwhelmed by large amounts of data given them by their school district or their local administrative office. The big question is how they can best use these data to improve learning most in their classes. This Web site explains how educators can create data reports that are easily understood by learning teams. It also provides guidance in initiating conversations around constructive use of data through professional development. For further information, contact Gaye Zarazinski at 1-800-356-2735 or gaye.zarazinski@learningpt.org

Teacher Magazine's Teacher Professional Sourcebook 2008 (Woods, 2008) provides valuable online professional-development resources for teachers looking to deepen their practice and extend their reach:

PBS TeacherLine
www.pbs.org/teacherline
This Web site offers an extensive selection of professional development resources, featuring a TeacherLine Peer Connection that allows a search-and-save resource and research function and enables educators to collaborate online. It also gives educators access to a variety of educator-friendly multimedia tools, some of which coincide with PBS broadcasted programs.

TeachAde
www.teachade.com
An interactive Web site for finding, creating, and sharing teaching resources such as lesson plans, related Web sites and search engines. Here, teachers can join discussion threads on any education-related topic and can also build professional networks by forming subject-based groups around their specific needs.

PD 360
www.schoolimprovement.com
This online professional development tool from the School Improvement Network allows educators to access hundreds of indexed and searchable video segments on topical issues such as improving minority achievement, differentiated instruction, and classroom management. These videos, presented by experts in the field, provide examples of best practices from more than 1,000 schools. Appropriate for mentors, coaches, administrators, and content specialists, they can be tailored to meet the needs of any state or school system's standards.

Inspiring Teachers
www.inspiringteachers.com
This site provides professional development resources for teachers, mentors, and administrators, such as book recommendations, classroom resources, Web sites, blogs, and an "Ask a Mentor" feature. Courses can be customized for interactive school and district staff development workshops, and "Webinars" provide practical strategies for improving student classroom learning.

4Teachers
www.4teachers.org
Also available in Spanish, this Web site specializes in the development of instructional Web-based and professional development resources addressing issues such as ELL and at-risk or special-needs students. The site provides ready-made virtual resources such as Web lessons, quizzes, rubrics, and classroom calendars for educators to integrate into their classrooms. Here teachers can create quizzes in foreign languages, compile online lessons, and study classroom teaching techniques to enable a more productive learning environment.

UTeach
https://uteach.utexas.edu/go/wings/Home
The University of Texas at Austin created UTeach as a valuable online database for their students and novice teachers, but it is useful professional-support resource for any educators at any stage of their career. The Web site features multiple links to lesson plans, collaboration resources, classroom management advice, counsel on school culture, tips for mentors, federal guidelines for student discipline and even inspiration and humor pages. Discussion on career stages may be of interest to mentors and novices.

Using Technology to Mentor Teachers. John Franklin (2005) suggests using blogs to mentor new teachers. Perhaps one of the greatest benefits of blogging is the potential for support that it offers new teachers who are struggling through that difficult first year. According to the National Center for Education Statistics, close to 30% of new teachers leave teaching or switch schools by the end of their first three years. In heavily urban areas, the number jumps to nearly half within five years. Educators say that sharing advice and experiences online can go a long way toward lowering these statistics.

"It's hard to believe that someone who never met you, who is not in your district, will come to you and say that without your support they would have quit teaching because they were drowning," says John Norton, moderator of the Teacher Leaders Network and a blogger himself. "A lot of districts have a sink-or-swim culture. People think, 'That's how it was for me, so that's how it should be for you.'" With blogs, he says, teachers can share lesson plans, strategies, and ideas to help one another survive the rough patches that accompany being in the front of the classroom. Many of the blogs that he sees narrate the experience of teaching for the first year, and he says they're a great way of accumulating and organizing information. The virtual nature of blogs is what makes them so effective. A student-teacher might post a question about a par-

It Works for Me!

Using DVDs and CDs

Beverly Findley, Eastern Illinois University

Not enough released time for staff development? If it is provided only on designated days, you are correct. However, anything that helps staff grow as professionals, as individuals, or as team members is staff development. Therefore, it can occur every day. Here is a tip for providing staff development on a daily, weekly, or ongoing basis.

When attending conferences where presentations are recorded, buy several of the DVDs and CDs, keeping in mind the times when staff discussed what they would like to know more about. If the content is of interest to the staff, they will check them out of the professional library on an as-desired basis. Staff can listen to the CDs and watch the DVDs during their "free" time. Staff may find it convenient to listen to presentations as they are commuting, or watch a presentation at home. This eliminates conference registration fees, travel expenses, and costs of substitutes. Most importantly, it allows the teachers to be in their classrooms during the school day.

ticular issue, and the post generates discussion on the subject that, in turn, generates reflection and further discussion that helps formulate ideas and strategies for the classroom (Franklin, 2005).

Traditionally, mentoring has meant a system that uses highly accomplished teachers to assist less accomplished teachers. Harry Tuttle (2006) suggests developing a technology mentoring program that uses technologically competent students to mentor teachers. Such a program frees teachers to focus their attention toward developing technology-infused learning. For example, a teacher might call on a mentoring team to create visual explanation of a math problem.

The Role of Research

Earlier in the chapter, Michelli (1995) identified one of the characteristics of professional development as the linking of research and practices. One of the Principles of High-Quality Professional Development that came into being as a result of the Goals 2000 states that professional development "reflects best available research and practice" (National Awards Program for Model Professional Development, 2002). Research has at least two major implications for teachers. First, teachers should be wise consumers of research. Experiences can be educative, but only when we reconstruct or reorganize the experience, giving it meaning. While experience provides opportunities to learn, experience in and of itself is a highly inefficient trial-and-error approach to learning. Supervisors must ensure that teachers guard against the temptation to limit their knowledge to their own direct experiences. A combination of research and experience is a far better approach. The supervisor can help teachers achieve a balance by getting teachers to read research literature regularly, and to apply these research findings to their own teaching. Although this sounds logical and simple, interpreting data and using those data to improve practices often requires both time and assistance. Fortunately, the needed help can also come through colleagues. Collaboration can provide an easy avenue for increasing and improving teachers' analytical practices and can encourage teachers to change when change is warranted.

A second way that research can contribute to professional development is through teachers' direct involvement with research studies (Stine, 2010). Teachers who conduct research become more analytic and critical of their own behaviors, and they develop clearer understanding about their content areas and about how each of these is learned. Perhaps most important of all, involvement with research leads teachers to an improved self-confidence as professionals, an essential personality trait for working with and through others (Pinnick, 2006). Additional benefits from conducting research will be seen in chapter 13.

When teachers use action research, they may engage in *reflective transformation*. Sharing their individual classroom experiences in a collaborative manner can raise teachers' aspirations and confidence in their achievement beyond their current levels. This comes about when they realize the importance of putting group goals above their own and subsequently meeting higher-order needs, thus contributing to self-actualization (Lunenburg & Irby, 2005).

Teacher learning communities provide opportunities for individual teachers to interact collaboratively in the process of inquiry and experimentation, resulting in a shared culture. Reflective transformation is initiated when teachers inquire into their classroom practices as a group, in response to individual issues and concerns:

> When experienced teachers had opportunities for collaborative inquiry and its associated learning, the result was a body of wisdom about teaching that could be widely shared. When teachers engage in the process of generating knowledge about their own teaching, their teaching is transformed in important ways. These teachers become theorists articulating their intentions, testing their assumptions, and finding connections and contradictions in their teaching practices. . . . Such reflective transformations lead to improved daily classroom practices and consequently, student achievement. (Gimbert, 2000, pp. 2, 4)

A summary of the supervisor's role in helping teachers engage in reflective transformation appears in Box 4.2.

Internship Programs

The category of teachers who may arguably stand to gain the most from professional development efforts is the novices, or interns. Recognizing that the first year may be the most important year in molding the teacher's behavior (Newcom et al., 2006)—and, indeed, the *only* year for some teachers who become frustrated with their inability to manage the classroom—a few states use all the research available to make this year a positive, controlled, and fully evaluated year of experiences. The Kentucky State Department of Education,

Box 4.2 A Summary of the Supervisor's Roles in Reflective Transformation

- Help teachers identify common problems.
- Encourage the formation of discussion groups.
- Keep the membership to discussion open for others to join.
- Ensure that all group members enjoy equal leadership status.
- Join faculty research teams and discussion groups regularly, and participate enthusiastically.
- Encourage the reading of professional literature.
- Introduce research findings into group discussions.
- Help individuals transform group-discussed solutions to apply to their particular classrooms.
- Encourage teachers to conduct research.
- Keep the students' welfare as the focus of all activities.

for example, has developed and continued to improve one of the nation's best internship programs for teachers. Kentucky also has a parallel program for administrators. Following is a discussion of Kentucky's programs for teacher interns and the important roles various educators play in it.

The Kentucky Teacher Internship Program

Contemporary educators acknowledge that teachers progress through a sequence of growth levels from the time they begin teaching until they reach a level of mastery (Armstrong et al., 2009). The first year is a key year in the developmental process because it is a time when many lifelong behaviors are formed. For example, during the first year of teaching, every teacher should develop desirable skills in classroom management, planning, and testing. During this year, each teacher should learn to cooperate with fellow teachers, administrators, and other school personnel. During the first year of teaching, teachers should develop behaviors that show respect and appreciation for administrators, other teachers, and students. During this year, teachers should learn to be good conductors and consumers of research.

Recognizing the importance of this initial growth period, several states now blend theory and practice (Tripses, 2006) and provide structured supervision and leadership for their first-year teachers. Over the past two decades, the state of Kentucky has developed and refined a program to provide its first-year teachers the support and regulation needed to develop the skills and habits required to become successful teachers. The Beginning (New) Teacher Standards were first adopted in 1993. After revisions in 1994 and 1999 they were replaced in 2008 with the Kentucky Teacher Standards that appear in boxes 4.3 through 4.12 with the permission of the Kentucky Education Professional Standards Board.

KTIP Standard 1. The teacher demonstrates applied content knowledge. Standard 1 (Box 4.3) can help by requiring all interns to know their content area(s) and to know how to lead their students to understanding this content. Standard 1 parallels another theme of this book, that of constructivism. Recall that in chapter 1 Kahlil Gibran recognized that, as much as we might like it to be otherwise, teachers cannot pass their understandings along to their students. But, as standard 1 requires, we must help our students grasp their own understanding of the content by helping them connect each lesson to their own lives and to other disciplines by using authentic (lifelike) activities. In chapter 1, we noted that the TIMSS international studies—the same studies that found our students trailing their counterparts in a dozen other countries in mathematics and science—found the cause of this poor performance to be our teachers' failure to spend time helping their students make these important connections.

Box 4.3 Standard 1: The Teacher Demonstrates Applied Content Knowledge

The teacher demonstrates a current and sufficient academic knowledge of certified content areas to develop student knowledge and performance in those areas.

Initial-Level Performance	***Advanced-Level Performance***
1.1 Communicates concepts, processes, and knowledge.	
Accurately and effectively communicates concepts, processes, and/or knowledge and uses vocabulary that is clear, correct, and appropriate for students.	Accurately and effectively communicates an in-depth understanding of concepts, processes, and/or knowledge in ways that contribute to the learning of all students.
1.2 Connects content to life experiences of students.	
Effectively connects most content, procedures, and activities with relevant life experiences of students.	Effectively connects content to students' life experiences including, when appropriate, prior learning in the content area or other content areas.
1.3 Demonstrates instructional strategies that are appropriate for content and contribute to student learning.	
Uses instructional strategies that are clearly appropriate for the content and processes of the lesson and make a clear contribution to student learning.	Consistently uses instructional strategies that are appropriate for content and contribute to the learning of all students.
1.4 Guides students to understand content from various perspectives.	
Provides opportunities and guidance for students to consider lesson content from different perspectives to extend their understanding.	Regularly guides students to understand content from appropriate diverse, multicultural, or global perspectives.
1.5 Identifies and addresses students' misconceptions of content.	
Identifies misconceptions related to content and addresses them during planning and instruction.	Consistently anticipates misconceptions related to content and addresses them by using appropriate instructional practices.

KTIP Standard 2. The teacher designs and plans instruction. As evidenced by standard 2 (Box 4.4), it is obvious that Kentucky wants its teachers to set learning objectives for mastery of major concepts in each lesson and to use a variety of authentic, learner-centered activities that require students to engage in higher-order thinking.

Box 4.4 Standard 2: The Teacher Designs and Plans Instruction

The teacher designs/plans instruction that develops student abilities to use communication skills, apply core concepts, become self-sufficient individuals, become responsible team members, think and solve problems, and integrate knowledge.

Initial-Level Performance	***Advanced-Level Performance***
2.1 Develops significant objectives aligned with standards.	
States learning objectives that reflect key concepts of the discipline and are aligned with local or state standards.	Develops challenging and appropriate learning objectives that are aligned with local/state/national standards and are based on students' needs, interests, and abilities.
2.2 Uses contextual data to design instruction relevant to students.	
Plans and designs instruction based on contextual (i.e., student, community, and/or cultural) and pre-assessment data.	Plans and designs instruction that is based on significant contextual and pre-assessment data.
2.3 Plans assessments to guide instruction and measure learning objectives.	
Prepares assessments that measure student performance on each objective and help guide teaching.	Develops well-designed assessments that align with learning objectives, guide instruction, and measure learning results.
2.4 Plans instructional strategies and activities that address learning objectives for all students.	
Aligns instructional strategies and activities with learning objectives for all students.	Plans a learning sequence using instructional strategies and activities that build on students' prior knowledge and address learning objectives.
2.5 Plans instructional strategies and activities that facilitate multiple levels of learning.	
Plans instructional strategies that include several levels of learning that require higher-order thinking.	Plans a learning sequence using strategies and activities that foster the development of higher-order thinking.

KTIP Standard 3. The teacher creates and maintains a learning climate. Research findings have shown that high expectations correlate with high academic achievement. These interns are expected to hold and communicate high expectations. Standard 3 (Box 4.5) also requires interns to use creative instructional time and materials to help all class members reach these high expectations while working in a safe, creative, and flexible climate with respect for everyone.

Box 4.5 Standard 3: The Teacher Creates and Maintains Learning Climate

The teacher creates a learning climate that supports the development of student abilities to use communication skills, apply core concepts, become self-sufficient individuals, become responsible team members, think and solve problems, and integrate knowledge.

Initial-Level Performance	*Advanced-Level Performance*
3.1 Communicates high expectations.	
Sets significant and challenging objectives for students and verbally/nonverbally communicates confidence in students' ability to achieve these objectives.	Consistently sets significant and challenging behavioral and learning expectations for all students and communicates confidence in their ability to achieve those expectations.
3.2 Establishes a positive learning environment.	
Establishes clear standards of conduct, shows awareness of student behavior, and responds in ways that are both appropriate and respectful of students.	Maintains a fair, respectful, and productive classroom environment conducive to learning.
3.3 Values and supports student diversity and addresses individual needs.	
Uses a variety of strategies and methods to supports student diversity by addressing individual needs.	Consistently uses appropriate and responsive instructional strategies that address the needs of all students.
3.4 Fosters mutual respect between teacher and students and among students.	
Treats all students with respect and concern and monitors student interactions to encourage students to treat each other with respect and concern.	Consistently treats all students with respect and concern and actively encourages students to treat each other with respect and concern.
3.5 Provides a safe environment for learning.	
Creates a classroom environment that is both emotionally and physically safe for all students.	Maintains a classroom environment that is both emotionally and physically safe for all students.

KTIP Standard 4. The teacher implements/manages instruction. The heart of the supervisor's role is teaching, and Standard 4 (Box 4.6) focuses on the development of good methods of instruction. Recognizing that individual students respond differently to different teaching styles and that individuals have their own preferred learning styles, this standard ensures the effective use of time, space, materials, and multiple methods and activities to meet these diverse needs, which is essential if students are to reach higher levels of thinking.

KTIP Standard 5. The teacher assesses and communicates learning results. The power of both formative and summative assessment, administered at short intervals and followed by giving students feedback on their test scores, was mentioned in chapter 3. Standard 5 (Box 4.7 on p. 118) requires this same practice. Two

Box 4.6 Standard 4: The Teacher Implements and Manages Instruction

The teacher introduces/implements/manages instruction that develops student abilities to use communication skills, apply core concepts, become self-sufficient individuals, become responsible team members, think and solve problems, and integrate knowledge.

Initial-Level Performance	*Advanced-Level Performance*
4.1 Uses a variety of instructional strategies that align with learning objectives and actively engage students.	
Uses a variety of instructional strategies that engage students throughout the lesson on tasks aligned with learning objectives.	Consistently provides a well-planned sequence of appropriate instructional strategies that actively engage students in meeting learning objectives.
4.2 Implements instruction based on diverse student needs and assessment data.	
Implements instruction based on contextual information and assessment data.	Implements instruction based on contextual information and assessment data, adapting instruction to unanticipated circumstances.
4.3 Uses time effectively.	
Establishes efficient procedures for performing non-instructional tasks, handling materials and supplies, managing transitions, and organizing and monitoring group work so that there is minimal loss of instructional time.	Makes thoughtful choices about the organization and implementation of both instructional and non-instructional tasks to maximize time for student learning.
4.4 Uses space and materials effectively.	
Uses classroom space and materials effectively to facilitate student learning.	Makes optimal use of classroom space and uses a variety of instructional resources and technologies to enhance student learning.
4.5 Implements and manages instruction in ways that facilitate higher-order thinking.	
Instruction provides opportunity to promote higher-order thinking.	Consistently uses a variety of appropriate strategies to facilitate higher-order thinking.

very important qualities of standard 5 are that: (1) it requires the intern to conduct evaluations of both individual and group work, including self-assessment; and (2) it emphasizes the need to give students ongoing feedback on their performance. More than ever before, today's teachers realize the power of formative assessment to promote learning. To meet the requirements of Standard 5, Kentucky interns are required to use both formative and summative assessment to guide instruction. The goal is no longer the memorization of content. Today's students must reach a much deeper understanding of the content by engaging in higher-level thinking, which requires the blending of instructional media and technology in problem-based assignments. Standard 5 also ensures that students and parents are made full partners in learning by engaging students in self-assessment and by giving students and parents continuing feedback on student progress.

Box 4.7 Standard 5: The Teacher Assesses and Communicates Learning Results

The teacher assesses learning and communicates results to students and others with respect to student abilities to use communication skills, apply core concepts, become self-sufficient individuals, become responsible team members, think and solve problems, and integrate knowledge.

Initial-Level Performance	***Advanced-Level Performance***
5.1 Uses pre-assessments.	
Uses a variety of pre-assessments to establish baseline knowledge and skills for all students.	Consistently uses student baseline data from appropriate pre-assessments to promote the learning of all students.
5.2 Uses formative assessments.	
Uses a variety of formative assessments to determine each student's progress and guide instruction.	Consistently uses appropriate formative assessments to determine student progress, guide instruction, and provide feedback to students.
5.3 Uses summative assessments.	
Uses a variety of summative assessments to measure student achievement.	Consistently uses appropriate summative assessments aligned with the learning objectives to measure student achievement.
5.4 Describes, analyzes, and evaluates student performance data.	
Describes, analyzes, and evaluates student performance data to determine progress of individuals and identify differences in progress among student groups.	Consistently describes, analyzes, and evaluates student performance data to determine student progress, identify differences among student groups, and inform instructional practice.
5.5 Communicates learning results to students and parents.	
Communicates learning results to students and parents that provide a clear and timely understanding of learning progress relative to objectives.	Clearly communicates to students and parents in a timely manner the evidence of student performance and recommends future actions.
5.6 Allows opportunity for student self-assessment.	
Promotes opportunities for students to engage in accurate self-assessment of learning.	Provides on-going opportunities for students to assess and reflect on their own performance in order to identify strengths and areas for future learning.

KTIP Standard 6. The teacher demonstrates the implementation of technology. Standard 6 (Box 4.8) focuses on technology. Like the mission of the International Society for Technology in Education (ISTE), this standard seeks to ensure that our teachers are able to use technology in many varied ways to enhance instruction and learning. Standard 6 requires the ability to select and use multiple applications of technology to promote learning.

Box 4.8 Standard 6: The Teacher Demonstrates the Implementation of Technology

The teacher uses technology to support instruction; access and manipulate data; enhance professional growth and productivity; communicate and collaborate with colleagues, parents, and the community; and conduct research.

Initial-Level Performance	*Advanced-Level Performance*
6.1 Uses available technology to design and plan instruction.	
Uses technology to design and plan instruction.	Uses appropriate technology to design and plan instruction that supports and extends learning of all students.
6.2 Uses available technology to implement instruction that facilitates student learning.	
Uses technology to implement instruction that facilitates student learning.	Designs and implements research-based, technology-infused instructional strategies to support learning of all students.
6.3 Integrates student use of available technology into instruction.	
Integrates student use of technology into instruction to enhance learning outcomes and meet diverse student needs.	Provides varied and authentic opportunities for all students to use appropriate technology to further their learning.
6.4 Uses available technology to assess and communicate student learning.	
Uses technology to assess and communicate student learning.	Uses technology to assess student learning, manage assessment data, and communicate results to appropriate stakeholders.
6.5 Demonstrates ethical and legal use of technology.	
Ensures that personal use and student use of technology are ethical and legal.	Provides and maintains a safe, secure, and equitable classroom environment that consistently promotes discerning and ethical use of technology.

KTIP Standard 7. The teacher reflects on and evaluates teaching and learning. Effective teaching requires ongoing data gathering on the effectiveness of classroom strategies, reflecting on those data, and using them to improve the quality of instruction and learning. Rather than focusing only on teachers gathering data on student performance only for purposes of *improving student learning*, Standard 7 (Box 4.9 on the following page) also requires teachers to use data on their students' performance *to improve their own instructional practices*.

KTIP Standard 8. The teacher collaborates with colleagues/parents/others. As mentioned in chapter 2, the twenty-first century has marked an era of collaboration. Both KTIP Standard 8 (Box 4.10 on the following page) and ELCC standard No. 4 require teachers to collaborate with each other and with parents. However, it's important to remember that professional collaboration is not the same as casual meetings where teachers talk about anything that comes to mind.

Box 4.9 Standard 7: Reflects On and Evaluates Teaching and Learning

The teacher reflects on and evaluates specific teaching/learning situations and/or programs.

Initial-Level Performance	*Advanced-Level Performance*
7.1 Uses data to reflect on and evaluate student learning.	
Reflects on and accurately evaluates student learning using appropriate data.	Uses formative and summative performance data to determine the learning needs of all students.
7.2 Uses data to reflect on and evaluate instructional practice.	
Reflects on and accurately evaluates instructional practice using appropriate data.	Uses performance data to conduct an in-depth analysis and evaluation of instructional practices to inform future teaching.
7.3 Uses data to reflect on and identify areas for professional growth.	
Identifies areas for professional growth using appropriate data.	Reflects on the evaluations of student learning and instructional practices to identify and develop plans for professional growth.

Box 4.10 Standard 8: Collaborates with Colleagues/Parents/Others

The teacher collaborates with colleagues, parents, and other agencies to design, implement, and support learning programs that develop student abilities to use communication skills, apply core concepts, become self-sufficient individuals, become responsible team members, think and solve problems, and integrate knowledge.

Initial-Level Performance	*Advanced-Level Performance*
8.1 Identifies students whose learning could be enhanced by collaboration.	
Identifies one or more students whose learning could be enhanced by collaboration and provides an appropriate rationale.	Describes an on-going process for identifying situations in which student learning could be enhanced by collaboration.
8.2 Designs a plan to enhance student learning that includes all parties in the collaborative effort.	
Designs a plan to enhance student learning that includes all parties in the collaborative effort.	Designs a plan that involves parents, colleagues, and others in a collaborative effort to enhance student learning.
8.3 Implements planned activities that enhance student learning and engage all parties.	
Implements planned activities that enhance student learning and engage all parties.	Explains how the collaboration to enhance student learning has been implemented.
8.4 Analyzes data to evaluate the outcomes of collaborative efforts.	
Analyzes student learning data to evaluate the outcomes of collaboration and identify next steps.	Uses appropriate student performance data to describe, analyze, and evaluate the impact of the collaborative activities on student learning and to identify next steps.

For this reason, the KTIP standard requires more, saying that interns must plan purposeful collaboration, and each discussion must be designed to enhance learning. Following each discussion, interns are required to reflect on the discussion to identify areas that might enhance learning. (Effective collaboration requires excellent communication skills. Because most teacher education programs do not require coursework in communications, chapter 9 contains a section designed to help you and your faculty improve your communication skills.)

KTIP Standard 9. The teacher evaluates teaching and implements professional development. With far too little time to meet both the needs of their students and the demands of state and national standards, today's teachers must learn to set priorities. Standard 9 (Box 4.11) requires interns to assess their own performance; identify the areas in which their need for improvement is the greatest; and then produce evidence that they are, indeed, growing in these areas.

Box 4.11 Standard 9: Evaluates Teaching and Implements Professional Development

The teacher evaluates his/her overall performance with respect to modeling and teaching Kentucky's learning goals, refines the skills and processes necessary, and implements a professional development plan.

Initial-Level Performance	*Advanced-Level Performance*
9.1 Self assesses performance relative to Kentucky's Teacher Standards.	
Identifies priority growth areas and strengths by thoroughly and accurately assessing current performance on all the Kentucky Teacher Standards.	Thoroughly and accurately assesses current performance related to the Kentucky Teacher Standards and any school/district professional development initiatives.
9.2 Identifies priorities for professional development based on data from self-assessment, student performance and feedback from colleagues.	
Identifies priorities for professional development based on data from self-assessment, student performance and feedback from colleagues.	Reflects on data from multiple sources (i.e., self-assessment, student performance, feedback from colleagues, school/district initiatives) and identifies priority areas for growth.
9.3 Designs a professional growth plan that addresses identified priorities.	
Designs a clear, logical professional growth plan that addresses all priority areas.	Designs a clear, logical professional growth plan that addresses all priority areas.
9.4 Shows evidence of professional growth and reflection on the identified priority areas and impact on instructional effectiveness and student learning.	
Shows clear evidence of professional growth and reflection relative to the identified priority areas and impact on instructional effectiveness and student learning.	Shows clear evidence of the impact of professional growth activities on instructional effectiveness and student learning.

KTIP Standard 10. The teacher provides leadership within school/community/profession. As mentioned in chapter 1, maximum learning requires teachers to go beyond the boundaries of their classrooms and engage the entire school and the community. Standard 10 (Box 4.12) holds each intern responsible for discovering ways to involve the community and the profession, providing leadership opportunities and an organized plan for using this leadership to improve learning. Interns must provide a detailed description of those members of the community and the profession who will be involved and the purpose, scope, and timeline of events for this involvement. Interns must also design a way to assess the impact of community and professional involvement on learning.

Box 4.12 Standard 10: Provides Leadership within School/Community/Profession

The teacher provides professional leadership within the school, community, and education profession to improve student learning and well-being.

Initial-Level Performance	*Advanced-Level Performance*
10.1 Identifies leadership opportunities that enhance student learning and/or professional environment of the school.	
Identifies leadership opportunities in the school, community, or professional organizations and selects one with the potential for positive impact on learning or the professional environment and is realistic in terms of knowledge, skill, and time required.	Identifies leadership opportunities within the school, community, or professional organizations to advance learning, improve instructional practice, facilitate professional development of colleagues, or advocate positive policy change; and selects an opportunity to demonstrate initiative, planning, organization, and professional judgment.
10.2 Develops a plan for engaging in leadership activities.	
Develops a leadership work plan that describes the purpose, scope, and participants involved and how the impact on student learning and/or the professional environment will be assessed.	Develops a leadership work plan that clearly describes the purpose, scope, participants involved, timeline of events/actions, and plan for assessing progress and impact.
10.3 Implements a plan for engaging in leadership activities.	
Implements the approved leadership work plan that has a clear timeline of events/actions and a clear description of how impact will be assessed.	Effectively implements the leadership work plan.
10.4 Analyzes data to evaluate the results of planned and executed leadership efforts.	
Analyzes student learning and/or other data appropriately to evaluate the results of planned and executed leadership efforts.	Uses data from the leadership effort to describe, analyze, and evaluate the impact on student learning.

Note how closely these standards align with the current research database on teaching and learning, and with the ISLLC, ELCC, and ISTE standards. Supervisors will find the KTIP standards extremely useful in helping both interns and experienced teachers.

Professional Development Schools

It bears repeating that the type of teacher development demanded in today's schools cannot occur in an isolated environment, independent of school improvement. If good schools remain functional in a rapidly changing community, the community must grow and develop just as individuals grow and develop (Pawlas & Oliva, 2008). Indeed, not only must schools change, they must change at the rate that their communities are changing (Bassett, 2005). As discussed earlier in the chapter, the task at hand is to develop schools with a particular culture. Schools where teachers, students, and professors work together to build a culture that promotes cooperative learning are called *professional development schools* (PDSs).

We first discussed professional development schools in terms of school/university partnerships in chapter 1. The National Council for Accreditation of Teacher Education (NCATE) (2008) defines professional development schools as innovative institutions formed through partnerships between professional education programs and P–12 schools. PDS partnerships have a fourfold mission: (1) the preparation of new teachers, (2) faculty development, (3) inquiry directed at the improvement of practice, and (4) enhanced student achievement. Such partnerships "blur the boundaries that have traditionally existed between preservice, induction, and inservice teacher education and connect teacher education to school reform" (Zeichner, 2005, p. 1).

Lieberman and Miller (1992) identify several examples of teacher-development activities that are common to professional development schools (sometimes known as professional practice schools)—activities that involve collaboration, experimentation, and reflection.

- *informal teacher study groups* that meet regularly to discuss an agreed upon topic
- *curriculum writing* to produce a common instructional writing project that meets particular needs of the teachers
- *teacher research projects,* simply designed and focusing on collecting data
- *peer observations* of each other's teaching to look for predetermined behaviors
- *case conferences* where one group member writes a case and the others raise questions and solve problems
- *program evaluation* of a curriculum or instructional practice agreed upon by all members, whereby the group collects data and turns it over to the larger faculty to decide the action to be taken

- *experimenting with or trying new practices* and meeting regularly to discuss their results
- *using teacher resource centers* to hold informal but professional discussions and read books and journals
- *participation in outside events and organizations,* such as visiting other schools that are experiencing program restructuring

Conclusion

The education reform reports of the 1980s and 1990s place demands on schools and teachers that cannot be met by the types of schools that exist today, even if parts of the schools are changed. Meeting these professional development demands will require all teachers to become collaborative researchers or problem solvers. But this will never happen in schools with traditional cultures where teachers stay in their classrooms, avoid working with other faculty members, and shun involvement with research in order to avoid possible criticism. Teachers need to engage in the process of reflective transformation in order to reach their full potential, and only then can they pass on the benefits to their students.

Traditional teacher development programs are piecemeal; they offer quick-fix type workshops which rely on expert presenters to bring hands-on tricks to teachers, or they require teachers to leave school to attend such workshops. This type of in-service teacher development program will not bring the changes that are currently being demanded of schools and teachers. Instead, the type of teacher development being demanded is long-term, continuous, collaborative programs located in the schools, programs aimed at making teachers lifelong researchers and problem-solvers.

Successful development of this type of teacher development program will require choosing problems that the teachers and students find important and getting support for the program by a strong majority of those teachers who will be involved in the program. Successful participation in such programs will require some major changes in teachers' attitudes. For example, teachers will have to learn to appreciate the value of research and cultivate their abilities to conduct research. Teachers will also have to expand their work arena and begin working with schoolwide curriculum, instructional, and research projects.

Programs that require changes in attitudes will occur slowly. Preparing teachers to accept their new roles as constructivist, knowledge-generating teachers will take time. In fact, this type of faculty development is never complete; it becomes a way of life for teachers, and a new culture that tolerates mistakes and supports experimentation is essential to continue encouraging teachers to use constructivist practices.

Questions for Discussion and Reflection

1. What should be the relationship between the development of a learning community and faculty development?

2. In what ways has faculty development changed?
3. What responsibility has a teacher to the group goals and what responsibility has the teacher to serve his or her individual goals?
4. What are the most important skills that supervisors can help teachers develop?
5. In what ways can/should a supervisor help change a school's culture?
6. What are three or four of the most undesirable qualities of schools' cultures?
7. In what ways do American schools suppress the development of minority students?
8. What changes in schools would help minority students most?
9. How can supervisors encourage teachers to conduct action research?
10. What are some effective methods to garner teachers' support for a perceived needed change?
11. Should a supervisor ever be asked to evaluate teachers?
12. Should all states require their teachers to complete an internship program?
13. How can supervisors encourage teachers to use reflection?
14. Why is involving teachers and students in the selection of teacher research project topics essential?
15. How can supervisors encourage the administration to support teacher research projects?
16. What is the connection (relationship) between school restructuring and faculty development?
17. Changing school cultures and teacher attitudes takes time. How can supervisors help sustain teacher interest in improving over long periods of time?
18. How can supervisors help with the task of reducing teacher risk and establishing a climate that tolerates mistakes?
19. Frequently, resistance to improvement stems from a poor self-image. How can faculty development programs contribute to the development of self-esteem?
20. How should yesterday's practices affect tomorrow's practices and what is the supervisor's role in connecting the two?

Suggested Activities

1. Interview a local school administrator. Ask what noticeable changes are occurring in the school's in-service programs. Ask whether there has been an increase in the number of programs that have required return visits.
2. Interview three teachers. Ask what in-service education has provided that they have found helpful.
3. Interview a local school counselor. Ask about the availability of staff development opportunities for counselors in your state. Write a brief summary on the importance of development programs to counselors.

4. Visit the local district office. Ask for a list of topics of recent faculty development programs. Separate these into two lists: Instructional and Other.
5. Survey three classmates, asking them how many in-service faculty development programs they have been involved in during the past two years. Ask how many of these restricted memberships to their discipline and how many involved the total faculty.

Chapter 5

Helping Teachers, Administrators, and Schools Change

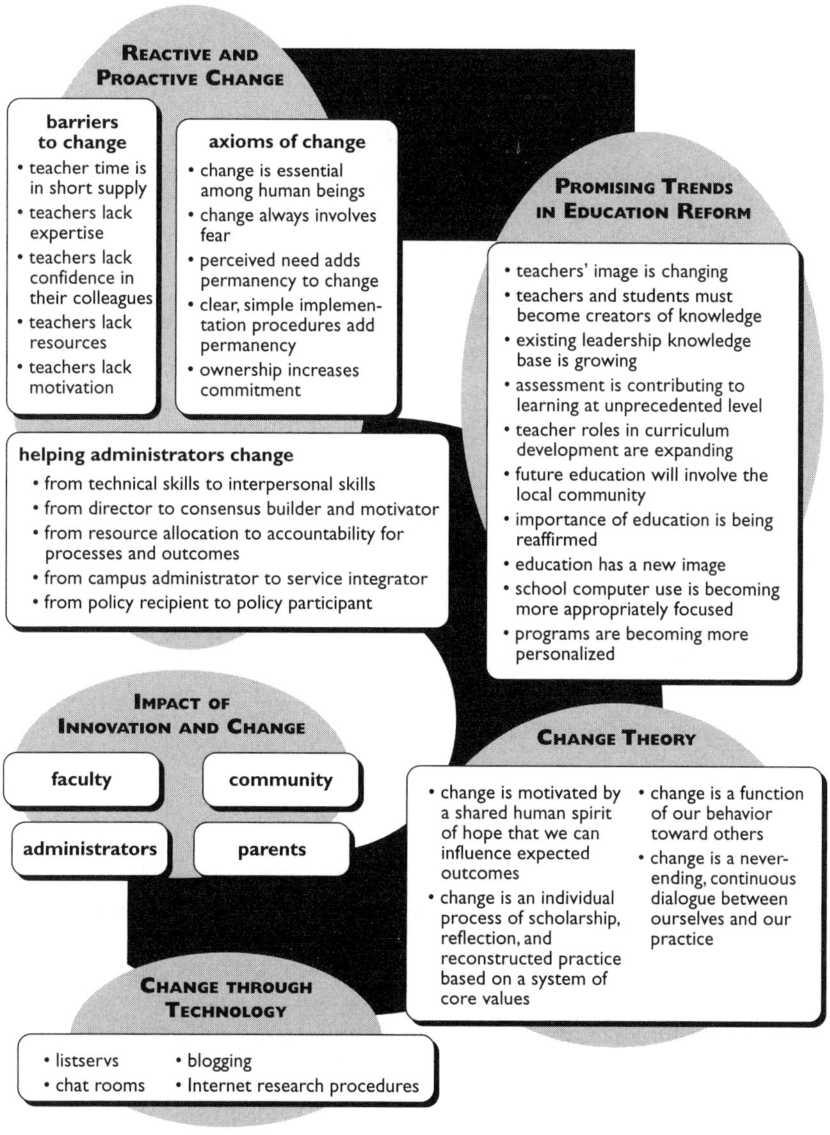

Reactive and Proactive Change

barriers to change

- teacher time is in short supply
- teachers lack expertise
- teachers lack confidence in their colleagues
- teachers lack resources
- teachers lack motivation

axioms of change

- change is essential among human beings
- change always involves fear
- perceived need adds permanency to change
- clear, simple implementation procedures add permanency
- ownership increases commitment

helping administrators change

- from technical skills to interpersonal skills
- from director to consensus builder and motivator
- from resource allocation to accountability for processes and outcomes
- from campus administrator to service integrator
- from policy recipient to policy participant

Promising Trends in Education Reform

- teachers' image is changing
- teachers and students must become creators of knowledge
- existing leadership knowledge base is growing
- assessment is contributing to learning at unprecedented level
- teacher roles in curriculum development are expanding
- future education will involve the local community
- importance of education is being reaffirmed
- education has a new image
- school computer use is becoming more appropriately focused
- programs are becoming more personalized

Impact of Innovation and Change

- faculty
- community
- administrators
- parents

Change Theory

- change is motivated by a shared human spirit of hope that we can influence expected outcomes
- change is an individual process of scholarship, reflection, and reconstructed practice based on a system of core values
- change is a function of our behavior toward others
- change is a never-ending, continuous dialogue between ourselves and our practice

Change through Technology

- listservs
- chat rooms
- blogging
- Internet research procedures

> *If you always do what you always did, you will always get what you always got.*
>
> —C. Brown, J. Combs, & S. Jackson, "Using student feedback to improve faculty effectiveness"

Objectives

This chapter will prepare you to

1. Name five change axioms and explain how supervisors can use each
2. List several barriers to education reform and discuss the supervisor's reactionary role
3. Identify several actions supervisors can take to cause teachers to embrace education reform
4. Name major shifts in the roles of school leaders, and discuss how these shifts affect the role of the instructional supervisor

A New Principal Is Challenged by Traditional Teachers

Peggy Miller is beginning the new year with a blend of optimism and concern. She thinks she made the right decision in agreeing to accept the superintendent's personal request for her to apply for the recent elementary principal vacancy in the Carroll County Public School District. Peggy thought that the Carroll County District had responded favorably to NCLB. She was confident that she could help the school make a difference. But she was a little worried because she knew that the superintendent, Mr. Tony Graham, wanted one thing: He wanted the Carroll County standardized test scores to go up. This made Peggy a little nervous.

Over the past three summers Peggy had attended summer institutes on cooperative learning. There she learned that teachers can use cooperative learning to develop social skills and reach learning goals. Because each cooperative learning group gets a group grade, each member is encouraged to take responsibility for helping other group members. Because cooperative learning classes are student centered, the level of motivation in cooperative learning classes is high. Peggy guessed that her involvement with the cooperative learning institutes was the reason that Mr. Graham had asked her to apply for the elementary school principalship.

But cooperative learning was just one of Peggy Miller's strengths. Since she began teaching almost 20 years ago, Peggy had displayed an extra high level of commitment to learning about each new development in curriculum and instruction. She had enjoyed teaching in the Carroll County District because of the freedom she had been given to try new instructional approaches. For example, she had become interested in the research on matching teaching styles and learning styles, had read all the literature she could find on the topic, and had set up her classroom to accommodate a variety of preferred learning styles. Although she had drawn some suspicion and criticism from some of her more traditional colleagues, her students seemed to appreciate her efforts and especially enjoyed the variety of learning activities available in her classes.

After a visit to several British Infant Schools, Peggy developed an open classroom with several student workstations. During any week, students were rotated so that over a week's curriculum they benefited from all the different types of activities given at each station. But one thing worried this innovative teacher. She knew that several of her teachers did not share her enthusiasm for experimenting. Although they were not pleased with their classes, they continued using the same traditional textbook, lecture, and worksheet approach; and in the teachers' lounge they continued to complain about their disinterested students. Peggy was not sure how many teachers belonged to this group, but she knew there were too many to be ignored. On the other hand, Peggy wondered how much time she should invest in this group. Perhaps her time and energy would be more productively spent focusing on those teachers who shared her love of experimentation. To decide which reform issues to deal with first, she reviewed a list of recent state initiatives.

While pondering this challenge, Peggy remembered several reform reports that recommended total restructuring and developing a learning community, studies saying that the traditional piecemeal approach to school improvement wouldn't work. These reports spoke of the need for a new vision held by all members of the faculty and staff, emphasizing the need to empower teachers. These ideas seemed to make sense, and Peggy found herself silently agreeing with them.

But remembering the teachers with whom she would be working, Peggy also remembered studying the nature of change in an educational leadership course. One thing that stood out in her mind was the natural resistance to change. She knew that a faculty that spent much of its time in the faculty lounge complaining about the system was a long way from being empowered by a vision for its school. She wondered what type of power would work best with this faculty.

Peggy also reflected on the types of professional development workshops that she had attended over the past 20 years. She remembered several workshops with dynamic speakers who had stirred her emotions and left her wanting to hurry back and try some of the techniques that sounded so exciting. But she worried because she couldn't think of many lasting effects of these workshops. In fact, whenever she returned to the classroom, her many students, her daily routines, and her hectic schedule seemed to wash away her newly found ideas and enthusiasm. Peggy knew that this job would require a very different type of professional development.

Then there was the district office. Her superintendent was supportive but his office was not progressive. No steps had been taken to correct a stagnated system. Would the superintendent support a new principal who wanted to radically change the sys-

tem? She feared that the principal expected the impossible—significant improvement in test scores without major, systemic changes.

Reflection

It appears that lack of proper vision is a major barrier that Peggy Miller faces. She must find ways to pass on to her new faculty her enthusiasm for cooperative learning, in particular, and her love for experimenting in general. She knows that persuading her traditional faculty to embrace experimentation and change is a monumental challenge. Indeed, it will require the faculty to develop a new vision and mission. Only then could they have the ownership and drive to embrace her experimental approach.

Introduction

> Educational Leadership Constituents Council (ELCC) Standard No. 1 for Advanced Programs in Educational Leadership says that candidates who complete educational leadership programs will promote the success of all students by facilitating the development, articulation, and implementation of a vision of learning supported by the school community.

In spite of the U.S./Russian competitiveness in the 1960s that began with the launch of *Sputnik* and ended with putting a man on the moon (see chapter 2), the American public still experienced lingering doubts about the quality of U.S. schools. A gradual decline in S.A.T. scores over the next dozen years—gradual indeed when the increase of the schools' holding power is considered—was enough to keep the public skeptical toward its schools. Then, in 1983 the National Commission on Excellence in Education released its scathing report, *A Nation at Risk*. As mentioned in chapter 2, although the authors of this report would later retract the serious accusations leveled at the schools, the damage had been done and the message was tantamount to a judge's ordering a jury to disregard an emotionally charged accusation.

A Nation at Risk may have been the result of malicious writers who were determined to deliver a devastating blow to the schools, or it may have been the work of dedicated, public-minded servants whose intentions were honorable but whose efforts were misguided. In all likelihood, it was a combination of the two. Whatever the motivation, this document was carefully crafted to incite public panic over the state of U.S. education and its schools. Its authors, like most of the authors of the reform reports it inspired, failed to understand that genuine reform is not about repairing the dilapidated structure of traditional schooling. Instead, it is about discerning a new vision of what it means to educate and be educated in a world that is fundamentally different from the one our schools still believe themselves to inhabit. To fulfill this vision and be able to function in a changing world, *our schools must also change.*

A major criticism of our schools over the last decade has been their reluctance to change, yet as Lapan and Hays (2010) have noted, "Change is an issue every teacher must face from the day they enter a teaching training program until the day of their retirement" (p. 263). This chapter is about change: teachers' attitudes toward change, helping teachers change, changing learning communities, and the nature of change in general. Change begins by examining the existing knowledge base. In addition to the nature of change, the chapter focuses on the specifics of changing teachers and changing learning environments.

Leadership theory has always embraced studies of change because the role of leaders is to effect change. By knowing more about the nature of change and the way that change affects people, leaders can improve their abilities to effect change. First, leaders must recognize that not all change is good. Change for the sake of change is likely to be a mistake, because change involves taking risks and expending time, energy, and money. However, purposeful change is worth investing time and energy (and when available, money), and it is worth taking some risks. Making decisions about whether to keep conditions stable or whether to change them, and then making these changes, are the essence of leadership and supervision.

Reactive and Proactive Change

When change occurs in many schools, it is solely reactive—that is, changes are made as a direct response or reaction to immediate problems. It is commendable and, indeed, necessary to respond promptly and creatively to the current problems in your school. Effective leaders understand that both the organizations and the individuals for whom they are responsible have qualities that are worth maintaining. An important role of all supervisors is to recognize and protect these qualities. Conversely, all organizations and individuals have qualities that impede their effectiveness or their ability to realize the institution's mission. Supervisors are also responsible for helping rid the institution and its members of these negative qualities.

A negative side effect of schools that experience only reactive change is that educators always feel that they are trying to "catch up" or "keep up" with the changes occurring in their school.

Schools that ride the crest of the wave of change—schools that step up to meet twenty-first-century educational challenges with confidence, creativity, and innovation—are schools that are forward thinking. The key is in thinking *proactively*—to take what one has learned in the past and apply it in anticipation of future changes. An important role of the supervisor is recognizing qualities that the institution and its members will need in the future. This responsibility is often overlooked. When this happens, sooner or later it leads to mediocrity and obsolescence. There is a danger that both the institution as a whole and its members as individuals become dysfunctional. This type of leadership has been described as status-quo leadership, which is an oxymoron since it eventually leads the institution or individual to failure. Following are some of the obstacles that the supervisor and his or her faculty must collaborate to overcome.

Barriers to Change

Barriers to change present challenges to both teachers and supervisors. Because changing schools requires changing the people who work in schools, and because such change requires overcoming such barriers, supervisors should be familiar with them. The state of the art of supervision is such that we know how to circumvent or overcome some of the common barriers to change; other barriers have yet to be overcome. Some of the most common barriers are a short supply of teacher time (and supervisors should heed Michael Simkins' [2005] reminder that teachers are prisoners of time), a lack of teacher expertise in reform practices, a lack of teacher confidence in the expertise of fellow teachers, a lack of resources needed to implement the many reform laws, and a lack of teacher commitment to reforming the schools. All supervisors should give some thought on how to best to cope with the challenges presented by these barriers. A summary of them appears in Table 5.1. Each of them is discussed in detail below.

Table 5.1 Some Barriers to Change and Proposed Strategies to Overcome Them

Barrier	Suggested Strategies to Overcome Barrier
Lack of teacher time	Encourage teachers to examine their calendars and give up some less important responsibilities.
Lack of teacher expertise to fulfill new reform responsibilities	Arrange for needed faculty programs to be taken simultaneously while reforming the schools.
Lack of teacher confidence in their colleagues	Place teachers in leadership roles, and make risk taking and mistakes accepted practices.
Lack of resources necessary to implement reform	Encourage and assist teachers in writing grant proposals to procure needed financial and human resources.
Unmotivated faculty	Learn and accept the nature of change, and share this knowledge with your faculty. Channel your energy toward those faculty members who are leaders.

Teacher time is in short supply. Of all the complaints that teachers lodge against education reform, perhaps the most common complaint heard is, "I don't have the time required to give to this practice or that." The No Child Left Behind legislation has further diminished teachers' supply of time. Although this may sound like a contrived excuse, the fact is that, through the years, in most schools many additional responsibilities have been assigned to teachers.

Gradually, these responsibilities have stripped away teachers' time until most contemporary teachers are busy all the time (Simkins, 2005). This means that in order to take on new responsibilities teachers must give up some of their existing responsibilities.

As teachers increase their time and energy commitment to changing their learning community, they need their principal to ensure that they get released from some of their other responsibilities, and to help them identify current practices that they should give up to provide time for new responsibilities. Most of all, teachers and administrators need time and opportunities to brainstorm about drivers of change, periodically collecting information about indicators of change and then, periodically, reviewing the data and discussing implications (Lefkowits & Miller, 2007).

Teachers lack the expertise required to adequately fulfill reform-initiated responsibilities. Only a small percentage of teachers have expertise in problem solving, constructivist teaching, or conducting research, yet these skills are required to restructure schools. Fortunately, teachers do not have to be experts in these areas to contribute to reform. Education reform is often referred to as a process of building a plane while flying it. Teachers can be developing necessary skills while they are contributing to reform. The supervisor can help by working to ensure that the school provides teacher leaders with opportunities to develop needed skills and by giving these teachers recognition for making gains in those and other areas of development.

Teachers lack confidence in their colleagues. In the past, teachers have resisted reform because they were left out of the decision-making loop. Accustomed only to reviewing directives from administrators, some of these teachers will be reluctant to respond favorably to requests from their peers.

Fortunately, this stereotype will gradually diminish as an increasing number of faculties place teachers in reform leadership positions. In the meanwhile, supervisors can help by providing encouragement to all teachers, by working to create a risk-taking climate, and by seeking out and hiring only empathetic teachers who are committed to meeting group goals and meeting the needs of students (Prensky, 2005).

Teachers lack resources. By mid-2008 a steady economic decline over several years had caused teachers throughout the country to struggle without the supplies needed to promote maximum achievement. The No Child Left Behind legislation had taken its "do more with less" approach about as far as it seemed it could go when the economy collapsed into an outright recession. Through the years, the only teachers with the materials and supplies needed to help their students reach maximum levels of achievement had been those teachers who taught in private schools and those who used their own time and energy—and, in many cases, their own money—to equip their classrooms.

Ironically, the rapid growth in popularity of computers, which many had hoped would greatly improve the education world for teachers and learners, actually worsened it for teachers who lacked the money to buy the constantly upgraded hardware and software. To compensate, by the new millennium an increasing number of teachers had begun writing grants. In many schools, groups of grant-writing teams were formed.

Having never had any training in this area, many teachers choose not to write grants because they don't know how to begin. Many feel lost because they don't even know the key elements that are common to most grant proposals.

Supervisors can help by providing encouragement and familiarizing their teachers with the process. Some supervisors already possess grant-writing skills. Those who don't can locate community members with such skills in other schools and in businesses, and they can arrange in-service workshops on grant writing. Many contemporary professional journals have articles aimed at helping teachers and administrators write grants. Supervisors can arrange to have such articles available and visible at all times in the offices of department chairs, articles that describe successful collaborative grant-writing projects. Chapter 15 describes such programs, identifying the unique qualities of each grant that enabled it to win out over its competition.

Teachers lack motivation. Many teachers began their careers with high levels of confidence and determination to make a difference, only to discover that each problem they solve leads to additional barriers. Overburdened by more and more nonteaching responsibilities, many of these teachers eventually give up, concluding that the odds they face make all their efforts hopeless.

Yet, when teachers work together to improve learning in their departments and grade levels and throughout their schools, they quickly learn that they can become energized, confident, and excited over their work. Many of the case studies found throughout this book provide examples of successful learning communities. Some resulted from careful planning while others were the products of a few teachers putting their heads together with only one purpose: to improve learning in their classes. You can help your teachers by introducing these success stories and by challenging them to locate examples of similar developments in their own school district. Consider inviting a successful team to your school to share its story.

Once teachers begin sharing their own successes, a psychological state called collective efficacy develops (Protheroe, 2008). Increased levels of confidence and energy spread throughout the faculty and students, and in many cases to the community (Brinson & Steiner, 2007).

Axioms of Change

Following are five change axioms which are, at least for the time being, considered truths about the nature of change. Supervisors can use these beliefs to enhance the levels of effectiveness of the schools and school personnel with whom they work.

1. *Change is essential among human beings*. Psychological studies conducted in hospitals have found that the human body and mind require stimulation. In a sterile environment free of sound, sight, odors, and touch, humans quickly begin hallucinating; the mind creates its own stimuli. There is,

It Works for Me!

Jump-Starting Teachers

JoAnn Susko, Rider University

Most teachers will jump at the chance to differentiate instruction, but some wonder where and how to begin doing this. These teachers need a jump-start. Encouraging teachers to provide students with some choice regarding assignments may be the perfect place to begin. Since most teachers already provide their students with a choice of activities at the end of a curriculum unit, teachers would likely be more comfortable with this familiar practice than with something new. Suggest that your teachers provide students with a choice of writing prompts, or even a choice of questions to complete for homework. Increasing choice provides students with an opportunity to pursue their interests, thereby increasing their motivation to complete a given task.

then, within all of us an impulse to change. Creativity is a natural drive that individuals share (some to larger degrees than others, of course). As with other natural impulses, fulfilling this need can bring satisfaction.

Supervisors frequently become challenged to discover the creative drive in some individuals; yet, fortunately other individuals seem to have more than their fair share of this urge to change things. Supervisors must develop insight into the personalities with whom they work. Once the motivators in individuals are discovered, supervisors can use them to change or guide individual behaviors in directions that serve the institution's mission.

2. *Change always involves fear.* Paradoxically, although people are internally attracted to change, they are also afraid of it (Oliva & Pawlas, 2008). Initially, this fear may be a minor concern, yet if left unaddressed it can become destructive. A good example of how fear can disrupt and even destroy institutions is seen in houses of worship when a congregation's membership physically outgrows a church, temple, or tabernacle and the congregation is forced to move to a new building. Some members often resist this need to change—even to the point that they discontinue their membership in the institution. Yet, fear of change is often worse than the change itself.

   Schools are not isolated from this natural fear that accompanies change. A school's math teachers may ban together to resist a new program; the entire elementary faculty may resist trying a new reading curriculum; or a primary faculty may resist trying a nongraded program. Such behavior might reflect an arbitrary resistance to change. Of course, the decision to reject a proposed change may also be reached sensibly rather than arbitrarily; these same teachers may review the current research and literature and, based on their findings, decide against using one of these programs. This type of behavior is a professional decision made by responsible teachers. The difference in the behaviors of the two groups may also be a reflection of the behaviors of their supervisors.

3. *Perceived need adds permanency to change.* Members of an institution are more willing to give their support to changes when they perceive the changes as necessary (Glickman, Gordon, & Ross-Gordon, 2007). Most changes in school programs result either from external funding or from being initiated internally. Interestingly, the availability of money can stimulate change, but in the absence of continuing funding those changes seldom last. The substantial change studies funded by the Rand Corporation found that changes resulting from availability of grant monies did not last as long as changes that were initiated by perceived needs at the organization.

   As early as the beginning of the twentieth century, some teachers were developing their own curricula. By the middle of the century, Hilda Taba stressed the need for teacher-made curricula, the advantages of which are that teachers (1) see a need for those changes that they introduce; (2) understand how to implement those changes; and (3) have ownership and commitment to making the new programs work.

4. *Permanency is added when the procedures for implementation are clear and simple.* Innovators can increase the life of an innovation by making the procedures for implementation simple and by giving clear and simple instruction. This principle is especially applicable to schools because the teacher's day is made complex with the many responsibilities involved in teaching—research has shown that in a typical day each teacher makes a thousand or more decisions (Good & Brophy, 2007). This level of complexity forces teachers to make many daily activities routine.

   Teachers' evenings are equally complex. Time and energy are needed for lesson planning. This means that teachers simply do not have the time (and many lack the necessary energy) to master new programs if those new programs are highly complex.

5. *Ownership increases commitment.* Whether or not teachers and administrators view themselves as innovators and implementers of change can significantly affect their level of commitment to the success of a change. Acceptance and support at the classroom and building levels come more easily when the change agents are classroom teachers (Lapan & Hays, 2009). Some types of schools are viewed as leaders for change. Laboratory schools, professional development schools, and partnership schools all are variations of a type of school that focuses on change. In states where education reform is strong, these schools are often first to implement reform practices. Long before the reform reports insisted on changing, the faculties and administrators in many of these schools, like good administrators in other innovative schools everywhere, were implementing new practices—not because they were being pressured

by reformers to do so but because they wanted to discover new ways to improve learning opportunities for students.

The currently popular practice of restructuring schools and building new learning communities makes this an excellent time and opportunity for establishing a culture that enables teachers and other members of the learning community to perceive themselves as innovators. Partnerships between schools and universities (see chapters 1 and 4) can motivate faculties from both institutions to experiment with innovative practices.

Helping Administrators Change

The importance of the building principal's role in creating a new learning environment must not be overlooked. Indeed, any major change in any part of a school is likely to occur faster and last longer if the principal is involved in the implementation of that change. Although the fact that principals play an important role in shaping the environment of a school has remained constant, this is about the only thing at schools that has remained unchanged. The National Policy Board of Educational Administration (NPBEA) (2008)—a board with representatives from ten professional administration associations—has been so cognizant of the fact that the instructional role of administrators is changing that it has identified five broad shifts in the knowledge and skills required of educational leaders today. These were enumerated in recently created ISLLC 2008 guidelines to prepare teachers for educational leadership, middle school/junior high principal, secondary principal, supervisory and curriculum personnel and superintendent/assistant superintendent. These shifts are:

1. *From technical skills to interpersonal skills.* Working with people, rather than financial or administrative expertise, defines the contemporary leader. Gaining a common vision, generating a school culture for learning, working with staff to improve instruction, developing collaborative action, identifying and solving problems, and responding to ethnic or gender differences all require strong interpersonal skills. Leadership is achieving goals through others.
2. *From director to consensus builder and motivator.* Common goals rather than edicts optimize results. Leaders will continue to be responsible for decisions, but the path to determining those decisions is being broadened to include significant numbers of persons affected by the decision. This inclusive process ordinarily improves the quality of the decision as well as the motivation of stakeholders to achieve the goal. Thus, principals and superintendents may "lead from the middle" as well as from other points on the organizational compass to gain agreement for action. Consensus building requires effective communication, motivation, problem analysis, delegation, implementation, and oversight skills. One example of this shift would be the principal's role, from that of sole instructional leader to that of instructional team leader (Martin, 2006).

3. *From resource allocation to becoming accountable for learning processes and outcomes.* Leaders can no longer allocate resources independent of outcomes. With the current national and state emphasis on improving student achievement, principals and superintendents must focus on outcomes. Administrators who haven't already done so will, therefore, become involved in the design and management of instruction, in analyses of program results, and in the redesign of programs based on results. These actions require familiarity with curriculum planning, instructional methodologies and technologies, and measurement and evaluation, and the capacity to build a school culture for learning.
4. *From campus administrator to integrator of school and community services.* The expanding needs of students, caused by family and social problems and by the growing heterogeneity of the student body, require that community resources be added to traditional school resources on behalf of students. These resources include health services, family counseling services, ethnic organizations, youth agencies, religious bodies, and special-interest groups, among others. To utilize these resources educational leaders need planning and interpersonal skills, multicultural and political sophistication, an awareness of value systems, and a clear understanding of the role of schools in American society.
5. *From policy recipient to policy participant.* A chorus of disagreement about purposes and priorities for schools can lead to policy turmoil, making successful operations difficult. School leaders, therefore, must be involved in policy development to ensure that policy guidelines reflect consensus or compromise rather than contradiction. In a society of competing interests and values, educators require clear policy direction to pursue their work. The outcome is less conflict at the school site, improving the learning environment for students. Policy development requires a broad understanding of social and political issues, familiarity with legal and administrative codes, strong communication and consensus-building skills, analytical abilities, and a value system grounded in the welfare of students.

A review of these major shifts in the roles of these leaders gives administrators an idea of the increased significance of their responsibilities for promoting change. These shifts involve more than just learning new cognitive skills; they require many administrators to change the way they think and to consider ways to help fellow administrators participate in developing policies that reflect current social and political issues.

* * *

To say that today's supervisor is a change agent would be an understatement. Changing the school requires changing its faculty. The following case study explains how one supervisor brought her school and community together to create a collaborative learning community that learned to welcome change.

Initial Strategies for Helping Teachers and Schools Change

Jerry Lowe • University of Texas–Pan American

This case study concerns a new school leader who accepted the challenge of transforming a low-achieving public school in a poor southern Texas rural community. It is a story that focuses on this educator's understanding that "the people side of school" is the most important. It highlights her initial efforts to change the perceptions of teachers, students, parents, and the community toward the school and its work.

The Community

This story originates in Guajolote (Turkey) Springs, a poor, rural, mostly Hispanic community of about 900 people situated on the banks of the Rio Grande River in deep South Texas. While several large ranches located across the area employ much of the community workforce, many families follow the "migrant trail" and spend several months each year working as field hands throughout the country. Since Spanish is the dominant language, many local adults and preschool-aged children have little or no English-speaking skills.

The School

The Guajolote Independent School District (ISD) has one elementary campus which houses 200 students in grades Pre-K–6 and a secondary campus serving 145 students in grades 7–12. Current total enrollment stands at 345 students, of which over 95% are Hispanic. The district employees an elementary principal and a secondary principal, who also serves as the superintendent. The district office is located in the high school building. There are 34 professional employees and 14 auxiliary personnel. Based on yearly student achievement scores, the school had been designated as "low-performing" by the state education agency. The school was plagued by an apathetic faculty and staff, students, parents, and community.

The Principal

Yolanda Cortez has been the principal/superintendent of Guajolote ISD for one year. She came to the community from a large urban school system in the lower Rio Grande Valley of Texas, where she was employed for several years as an instructional supervisor. Having grown up in a rural South Texas town, she felt a need to reconnect with her roots and believed her past experience in education could benefit this small, low-performing school. She knew that serving in this district would be a challenge and was excited about the work ahead.

The Story

During the three-month interim between the time Yolanda accepted the position and her first day on the job, she received almost no communication from the school. A major project she was directing in her home school district left little time for visits to her new community. She did, however, subscribe to the regional newspaper and was able to find a place to live. On one of her rare visits she was able to obtain copies of the school-board policy manual and the student-teacher handbook. She also spent some time going over minutes from previous board meetings and was able to visit with several teachers, students, and community members. Following her visits, Yolanda realized her new school was plagued with poor student attendance, low teacher morale, and almost no parental involvement. Throughout the community there appeared to be considerable apathy toward the school; however, there was some indication that positive change would be welcomed.

Yolanda gave the situation at Guajolote much consideration and when she arrived to begin her new job she had developed a short-range plan which she hoped would "jump-start" the transformation of this school and community.

Address Critical Issues First. Yolanda knew that she had to bring this school and community together. She believed her first task must be to create a shared vision for the school. In order to ensure that the vision was going to be truly "shared" she asked the faculty to nominate a teacher from each of the elementary, junior high, and the high school grades to serve on a committee to develop the vision statement for the school district. She also asked the auxiliary staff to nominate a committee member. She was able to include two students from the newly formed student council, two parents, the postmaster and the director of the local migrant council. With the establishment of this group, Yolanda had taken the first important step in her plan to transform the school. Committee members were initially apprehensive about serving, but after Yolanda shared her ideas with them they became more receptive. The more they worked on the statement and collaborated with each other, the more enthusiastic they became.

As they began to enjoy the task at hand and their meeting time together, a vision statement was soon developed that focused on student achievement and overall school improvement. The vision statement was approved by the faculty and staff and then communicated to local media outlets. It soon appeared on all school district letterhead, and beautiful posters containing the mission statement were made for every classroom. Yolanda made sure that all school employees understood the meaning of the mission statement and could relate its significance to their individual work efforts. The more time this committee spent together, the more they bonded as a group, and soon they became excited about helping plan other activities and programs to enhance the teaching and learning environment of the school.

Yolanda was also convinced that building authentic trust serves as the foundation of leadership and that it must be developed before any significant change could occur in the school. Under her leadership, the committee began to make suggestions and help initiate measures that would serve to develop a trusting atmosphere in the school. An authentic school-based decision-making committee was established which included the principal, three teachers, two parents, and one member of the business community. Yolanda helped committee members develop their ability to reach consensus on issues and made sure that decisions were implemented.

The student council was reactivated after many years of dormancy. Officers and homeroom representatives were elected at the beginning of the year and two teachers volunteered to serve as sponsors. Activities for student participation and representation were initiated, and the student body soon found itself in a new and exciting environment.

The general perception of the school was less than positive. Many students, teachers, parents and other community members felt that the school was just not very good. Many believed that it would probably stay that way. In order to combat these negative perceptions, Yolanda knew the school must do a better job of telling its story.

For the first teacher workday in September, Yolanda did something that had never been done in the district before: She scheduled a day-long retreat for all employees. The meeting took place at a conference center in a city about 35 miles away, and she provided school buses for those who did not want to drive. The retreat was a great success. Employees began the day with a series of enjoyable, team-building activities that established a relaxed and happy tone for the meeting. Participants were allowed to become members of several groups that would brainstorm and develop solutions to a variety of critical issues facing the school, such as curriculum alignment and sequencing, student assessment, personnel evaluation and supervision, and public relations. By day's end, the employees were working very well together and each group had developed a sound list of strategies for school improvement.

The retreat accomplished several important things other than addressing critical issues of the school. It brought the entire faculty and staff closer together and helped lay the foundation for a more trusting and collegial work environment within the entire school community. Employees became more friendly and supportive of each other and of the mission of the school. They also gained a greater appreciation for the important contributions of each employee in support of student achievement. They returned home from the retreat feeling better about themselves, their jobs, and the school. Yolanda was especially pleased to learn that when they returned to school most, if not all, group members wanted to remain in their groups and continue working on the issues they had addressed during the retreat. As part of a strategic planning process, she encouraged this continued involvement and soon the groups were meeting regularly. For the first time in a long time, employees appeared to be excited about their work. Word soon began to spread throughout the community that good things were happening at the school.

A public relations program was developed that included new and positive contacts with the local media, and this led to a significant increase in positive news about student activities and accomplishments. Students from both the elementary and secondary campuses became very much involved in the design of a bright, interactive Web page for the school district that not only provided up-to-date information about district and campus operation but also included information about the history and culture of the school and its vision for teaching and learning. The Web page helped communicate the story of the school to the community and public in general. It also helped build community within the school as teachers, students, and other employees shared their efforts and ideas. In addition, the Web site contained current information for parents such as schedules, calendars, homework assignments, and student accomplishments. It also served to highlight school traditions and values and contained information about student, faculty, and staff accomplishments.

In order to help develop school and community pride, the search for historical information about the school and community became an ongoing project for a newly organized student history club. One of their early projects consisted of gathering information about the U.S. Cavalry and the role it played during the early days of Guajolote Springs. Located a few miles south of town were the dilapidated buildings and grounds of old Fort Rio, which was established by the U.S. Army in 1848 and served as a "frontier fort" to provide protection for the people who settled in this remote area and to ensure the Rio Grande as the U.S. border with Mexico. The fort remained in service until 1933 when the Army abandoned it and deeded it to the county. The student investigation revealed that several notable military personalities had served tours of duty at the fort including Robert E. Lee, John J. Pershing, and George Patton.

The search further revealed that the house of Colonel Robert E. Lee still stood on the grounds of the old fort. Several local families had descendants who were in the army and served at Fort Rio as well. As an ongoing project, the history club wanted to preserve the Lee house and turn it into a museum. Permission was obtained from the county and the project got underway. Yolanda, with help from the history club members and several teachers, was instrumental in obtaining grants from the National Historical Society and the Texas Historical Society. These funds provided enough money to completely renovate the residence of the famous soldier. Community and business members became involved in the project and provided free labor and materials. Parents organized work groups, and soon the project turned into a community effort that has now evolved into other community revitalization projects. Membership in the history club has continued to grow, and several of the historical accounts they produced have been published in book form by The University of Texas Press.

Located just inside the front entrance to the high school was an empty classroom that had been used at one time as the board room. Yolanda had the room renovated and placed several large glass panels in the wall located along the inside way of the school. She asked a dedicated and highly energetic teacher if she would be willing to move her classroom into this space. The idea was that when visitors came to the school, the first thing they would see when they got inside was teaching and learning taking place. A beautiful sign placed under the windows read, "Welcome to Guajolote ISD. . . . Where Teaching and Learning Rule." The teacher and her students were excited about the opportunity and most people who came into the building stopped for a short time and observed this class in action. Members of the news media came to the school and interviewed the teacher and some of the students. The story appeared in several regional newspapers and was the focus of a short TV segment on the stations throughout South Texas. Each campus began a monthly "celebration" assembly that acknowledged the accomplishments of students, faculty, and staff members. These assemblies, which were attended by parents and community members as well as students and teachers, were held during the day and became a very important and anticipated part of the school program.

On several occasions, Yolanda was heard to say that "if the community won't come to the school, we should take the school to the community." She encouraged the band and music teachers at both the elementary and secondary levels to provide several concerts each year at various community locations such as the nursing home, the local bank, and the town square. These concerts were provided during the day at times when Guajolote Springs was the busiest. Crowds gathered to watch the students perform. Students distributed information about the school and its accomplishments to each audience. This was an opportunity for people who rarely, if ever, came to the school to connect with it in a very positive way.

Yolanda's short-range planning efforts soon began to show results. Teachers appeared to be happier with the school environment. Conversations in the teacher's lounges gradually turned from the traditional gripe sessions to discussions about teaching innovations and other efforts to raise the achievement level of their students. A great part of this transformation in teacher attitudes was due to the fact that Yolanda had provided many opportunities for faculty and staff to attend professional development workshops, seminars, and other professional meetings. This was something new to this school, and it became a very exciting component of this district's evolution.

Yolanda knew that "the people side of school" is the most important and that when faculty and staff members are happy at work, better teaching and learning occur. The few important changes Yolanda made during the first several weeks of school helped develop the overall trusting foundation she knew must be in place before major change could take place.

Examine the Culture. Based on common sense and on her past experience, Yolanda felt that one critical component necessary for positive and lasting change to occur in the school must be addressed immediately. She realized that she must understand the historical/cultural evolution that had taken place in the school and community throughout the years. She must find out what events had occurred during the past that led to this apathetic attitude and low performance in the school. Soon after she moved to her new community, Yolanda began looking into Guajolote's past. She became familiar with the local culture and was able to identify a number of significant historical events that had occurred and would impact her decision making as well as her plans for implementing positive change in the future. She was able to identify the power structure in the community and became familiar with their past involvement in school and community issues.

At the end of her first year in Guajolote Springs, Yolanda was able to see much improvement in the environment of the school. Teachers were happier and spent much more time in collaboration with their colleagues. Student achievement was on the increase, and more school spirit and pride was evident throughout the school. Parents were visiting the school more often and showing their growing support for the school in a variety of ways. All in all, Yolanda felt she had done a pretty good job.

Issues for Further Reflection

1. What are some additional strategies Yolanda might have initiated at the beginning of the year?
2. Should she have spent more time addressing curriculum and instruction as part of her short-range planning?
3. What would be the most important changes that should be considered as part of the long-range planning process?

Promising Trends in Education Reform

Because the shortcomings of the schools involve such basic issues as school culture and teachers' attitudes toward themselves and their fellow teachers, the schools' needs cannot be met by "fixing" one or two parts of the schools. Restructuring means having everybody involved in changing everything. At a minimum, restructuring involves changing three or more of the twelve practices shown in Table 5.2 (Lee & Smith, 1994).

The restructuring of high schools throughout the nation has been extensive, as evidenced by professional development. According to Science and Engineering Indicators (National Science Foundation, 2008, see Figure 5.1), during the 2003–2004 school year, across the disciplines (including science and mathemat-

Table 5.2 Restructuring Practices

Structural Practice	Probability
Students keeping same homeroom throughout high school	.30
Emphasis on staff solving school problems	.29
Parents volunteer in the school	.28
Interdisciplinary teaching teams	.24
Independent study, English/social studies	.23
Mixed-ability classes in math/science	.21
Cooperative learning focus	.21
Student evaluation of teachers important	.20
Independent study in math/science	.18
School-within-a-school	.15
Teacher teams have common planning time	.11
Flexible time for classes	.09

From "High school restructuring and student achievement: A new study finds strong links" by V. Lee & J. B. Smith (1994, Fall), *Issues in restructuring schools, 7*, p. 3. Used with permission of the Center on Organization and Restructuring of Schools.

ics) over 90% of all middle level and high school teachers said they had been involved in workshops, conferences, or training sessions during the previous 12 months. Although 12% of the 320 high schools surveyed have none of those characteristics, a full 42% meet this definition of "restructured" schools. Table 5.2 shows structured practices that have been occurring in the schools and the probability of each practice occurring. Notice that staff problem solving through collaboration and constructivist practices (two of the themes of this book) are highly probable in restructured schools.

Figure 5.1 Teacher Participation in Workshops, Conferences, and Training Sessions

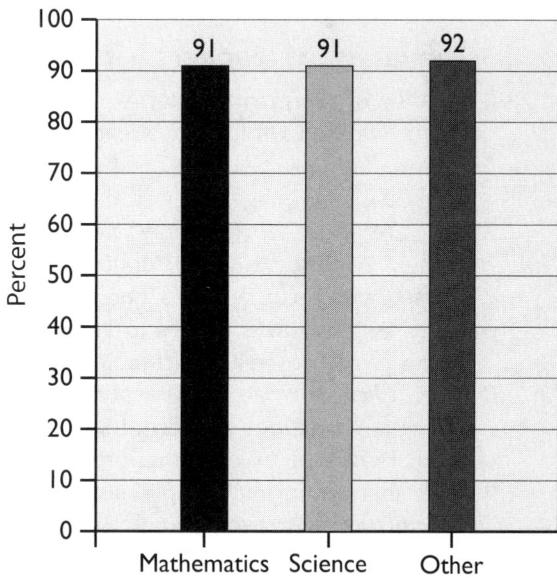

From Figure 1-14, Professional Development of Public Middle and High School Teachers during the Past 12 Months by Format: Academic Year 2003–04. National Science Foundation, *Science and Engineering Indicators 2008.*

Other promising observations have been made. Although finding fault without feeling any responsibility for offering suggestions to improve appears to be human nature, occasionally positive suggestions are made. Supervisors should take heed of every one of these suggestions, because each suggestion can become an indispensable tool to improve schools.

Some of the many important observations in contemporary literature involve a changing teacher image—from teachers who can't teach to an image of empowered teachers; from classroom-bound teachers to schoolwide leaders. Current trends indicate a new responsibility of teachers and students for creating knowledge, a growing knowledge base on instructional leadership, a growing realization of untapped potential in the use of assessment to promote learning, and an expanding role of teachers in schoolwide curriculum development. Other observations include a recognition that future education must involve the community (acknowledged and required by the No Child Left Behind law), a reaffirmation that education is important to Americans, an emerging image of education as an ends-driven engagement of learners with information rather than a process that teachers impose on students, and a shift from technologically literate students to technologically competent students.

In the past, as Bunting (2006, p. 76) has said, "Each day typically progresses in such a skill-jammed, test-locked, other-directed format that teachers have little room for experiencing satisfaction or for having constructive thoughts about their work." But reflection is a prerequisite for improvement, and today, reflection on these observations gives much cause for hope. Following is a discussion of some of these positive observations.

The image of teachers is changing.

One of the great mysteries that characterize the American people is their determination to hold on to a teacher image that does nothing but harm the profession. Perhaps the blame can be traced to Washington Irving, who created the Ichabod Crane image of the clumsy teacher, steeped in book learning but totally unaware of the world around him. A decade of Gallup Polls of the American Public's Attitudes toward Public Schools has found that the public is generally pleased with its own local schools and teachers, and yet the same public consistently assigns lower grades to American schools and teachers in general than they give their own local schools and teachers (Rose & Gallup, 2008).

Teacher empowerment is a popular term in current education reform literature. To an outsider, the term may sound like much of the empty rhetoric that characterizes many of the reports, but this concept of empowering teachers is more than rhetoric; it is an absolute requirement for the magnitude of education reform that is mandated. Even former U.S. Secretary of Education Terrel Bell (who fathered the report *A Nation At Risk*) admits that serious reform cannot be achieved without the work of teachers. Fortunately, many current reform efforts are empowering teachers. For example, site-based decision-making councils usually comprised of teachers, parents, and administrators, now feature teachers as the majority of members.

For site-based decision making to empower teachers, three conditions must occur. First, teachers must realize that their appointment to these councils is an acknowledgment that others are willing to entrust them with the leadership of the school. This means that in the professional judgment of their colleagues they have the capability required to move the school to an improved level of performance. Under conditions of increased accountability for student performance, such confidence is not placed lightly. Second, to succeed in this assignment, individual team members must recognize their own strengths. Empowerment is not a commodity that is given by one person to another; rather, it is earned through performance. Third, the power cannot reside within a few individual team members—it must be spread about to all members of the education team and, indeed, to all fellow teachers, parents, and students. Supervisors can help by learning their teachers' dreams and finding ways to help those dreams become a reality (Bunting, 2006).

Teachers and students must become creators of knowledge.

Historically, schools have been thought of as repositories where teachers and students meet to have information passed on from the former to the latter. But educators now know that when information is merely passed on from one person to another it remains just that—information. Raw information, like crude oil, has little value in its natural form. To become useful, both must be refined. Today's schools must be converted into refineries where teachers lead student workers to provide the necessary treatments to transform this information into meaningful knowledge. In essence, schools must be knowledge factories where teachers and students work together to manufacture understanding.

Fortunately, contemporary educators know how to convert raw information into understanding. Effective schools help students develop understanding by tying newly acquired information to what they already know. Constructivist learning theory provides suggestions for teachers to use to help students tie new information to previously acquired knowledge. Supervisors can help by encouraging and helping teachers conduct action research projects aimed at improving learning in their classrooms and school.

A growing knowledge base on leadership already exists.

The knowledge base on leadership and theory has been accumulating for almost a century, and this accumulated research links school principal leadership to student achievement (Campbell & Porter, 2006). Although this body of knowledge and theory is not complete and never will be, the existing knowledge is substantial. The knowledge base suggests that leaders must

- help provide a vision for their schools;
- help communicate the school's mission;
- help teachers develop enthusiasm toward their membership on learning teams;
- be team members;

- help secure financing (the subject of chapter 15);
- help teachers become lifelong learners;
- earn trust;
- remain open-minded; and
- recognize the contributions of others.

In many school districts the pressure to meet education reform requirements seems to militate against some of these leadership responsibilities (Bunting, 2006). For example, many education reports and commissions are designed to meet one goal and one alone—to raise the level of student performance on standardized tests. But effective supervisors know that although this is a valid goal, the mission at every school should be much broader. In some schools, reform requirements keep teachers and administrators too busy to think much about helping faculties acquire a clear vision of the school's mission and goals; yet the hard labor that characterizes most contemporary teaching facilities is unlikely to achieve beyond the level of vision of the school's faculty. Supervisors can help by ensuring that such professional journals as *Educational Leadership* and *Phi Delta Kappan* are present and readily accessible. Reading articles in these and similar professional journals will expand teachers' visions as it expands their knowledge base.

Assessment is contributing to learning at an unprecedented level.

Traditionally, the concept of assessment in education has been synonymous with grading and, as Levin (2005) has observed, "Most large-scale assessment is shockingly disconnected from the processes of instructional improvement" (p. 12). Yet in many schools throughout the country, assessment has taken on a much broader meaning. In these schools, assessment programs are being designed to promote learning, and some of the best instruments for this purpose are teacher-made tests. Portfolios (both traditional and electronic/digital) are being used to encourage continuous self-assessment by students. Performance tests are being developed to ensure that students are learning to solve problems. Authentic assessment instruments are being created to ensure that school learning prepares students for life beyond school. The progress being made in the assessment area may be the single greatest contribution to education reform in America. These and other assessment topics are discussed in further detail in chapter 10.

Teachers' roles in curriculum development are expanding.

One of the most exciting occurrences associated with education reform is the expanding roles of teachers. History has shown that the type of reform required for schools to meet the challenges of the reform reports cannot be met at the national, state, or district levels. Since each reform requires restructuring (changing the ethos of the school), successful education reform must occur at the individual school level. Furthermore, any successful, permanent reform has always required the involvement of those who are charged with the task of implementing the new programs; therefore, teachers—*all* teachers—must be involved with schoolwide curriculum development.

A long-standing axiom of curriculum development is that it is a continuous, ongoing process. In contradiction to this wisdom, because teachers are often under duress as they work tenaciously to meet state and national mandates, they have shunned schoolwide curriculum development, restricting their planning to instruction and using curricula developed by others. Historically, teachers' primary interest was in translating curriculum into instruction. Today's teachers can no longer afford to continue this practice within the safe harbor and narrow viewpoint of their classroom walls; they must be equally at home outside the classroom, collaborating with others to bring about continuous, schoolwide curricular improvement.

It Works for Me!

Sharing Best Practices

Karen Hayes, University of Nebraska at Omaha

Faculty, department, and grade-level meetings provide opportunities for promoting job-embedded professional learning. A growing number of schools have changed their faculty meetings by including time for teachers to share best practices. At these meetings, teachers can present new instructional procedures that they have found to be successful. In department and grade-level meetings, teachers use some of their time "sharing" best practices: They talk about curriculum, help colleagues solve instructional problems, discuss alternative approaches to meeting the needs of diverse learners, and analyze assessment in making data-driven decisions.

Future education will involve the local community.

As mentioned by Tubbs, Terry, and Chan (2006), "Educators are advocating a participatory planning approach to involve teachers, administrators, parents, and community members" (p. 190), and the No Child Left Behind legislation provides financial support for schools that seek to increase the level of community involvement.

Educational Leadership Constituents Council (ELCC) Standard No. 4 requires educational leadership candidates to "promote the success of all students by collaborating with families and other community members."

As illustrated in the vignette at the beginning of this chapter, some schools are getting more support than others for making needed changes. A national survey (Rose & Gallup, 2004) showed that 97% of the public believes there should be more parent involvement in schools. Parents and other concerned citizens in many communities are exerting pressure in local districts to become involved in improving their schools. This increase in community awareness and involvement will give support to many teachers who work in schools that are reluctant to change.

South Carolina, a leading state in education reform, has made significant strides in involving its entire communities. Some of its innovations so far include opinion polls to determine what practices the public is willing to support, education forums scheduled in the evenings to permit working people to discuss education, a toll-free hotline to receive reform suggestions, a speaker bureau with 25 speakers prepared to give proactive speeches to support legislation, and bumper stickers and newspaper ads to support reform efforts.

The importance of education is being reaffirmed.

Of all the messages communicated through the education reports and through the legislation these reports have provoked, perhaps the greatest contribution has been the resounding message that *in America, education is important*. Elementary, middle, and secondary schools are important; teachers are important. Furthermore, it has been established that education is a necessity that must be supported, financially and otherwise, by the public.

Supervisors will do well to acquaint themselves with their state and federal legislators and familiarize themselves with these politicians' positions on education reform. Although some legislators work continuously to support education, others unfortunately are eager to lend empty rhetoric to the need for school improvement but are reluctant to press for the financial support essential to achieve this goal. Although some legislators work hard throughout the year to get support for schools, some pass education laws without input from administrators, teachers, and teacher educators. Such omissions become highly visible when the implementation process begins. Effective reform requires the involvement of these partners at all stages, including the planning stage.

Education has a new image.

In this country education traditionally has been considered to be a rather simple, straightforward process. Many people believe that if you understand a topic or process, then you should be able to teach it. Some ongoing, simple-minded certification processes perpetuate this myth by basing certification standards exclusively on work experience (and in some cases granting certificates to retirees who have never had a course in pedagogy or a course in their major discipline in a quarter of a century). Supervisors can help parents realize the complexity that teachers face daily by encouraging teachers and principals to start programs that increase parent involvement with instructional responsibilities. For example, teacher-for-a-day programs and parent-substitute teacher programs can give parents firsthand experience and increased understanding of teaching. For further information about such programs, see a case study written by David Stine (2010).

The use of computers in schools is becoming more appropriately focused.

The promise that computers offer to offer to the improvement of education is staggering. It's difficult to believe that computers once were no more than a topic in high school and college curricula. Initially, schools taught about computers rather than making them part of the instructional process, with the aim of helping students become *technologically literate*. This goal is no longer adequate: Today's curricula must provide students the opportunity to become *technologically competent*. Today's schools increasingly use computers as instructional tools to deliver the curriculum (Ebert & Culyer, 2008). In addition, more and more teachers and students rely on the Internet for knowledge-building research purposes. Teachers and administrators are discovering new uses of technology as a time-saving tool to simplify their daily tasks and responsibilities. According to Matthews and Brown (2007), "The principal is the key to making the technology clear and useful." (p. 61). As long as restructuring and technology are twisted to fit the Industrial Age of the past, they will not affect educational practices. When restructuring and technology are driven by challenging goals for students and supported by long-term commitment to change and investment in human resources, they will increase the productivity of our schools—and ultimately of our society. A way for supervisors to increase the technological competency of their faculty is discussed later in this chapter.

Programs are becoming more personalized.

Paradoxically, as schools become more technologically oriented, they must also become more personalized (Prensky, 2005). In spite of high-stakes testing and the national standards movement, several compelling realities demand that schools become more personal (Wildman, 2006a). The need to personalize the schools is reinforced by constructivist theory. By personalizing programs, we ensure that students become involved in choosing problems to solve and in selecting their own methods to seek solutions (Butler, 2010). These problems include (but are not limited to) changes in the workplace, society, and the nature of the learner and learning. Personalized programs will enable students to teach themselves in profoundly deep and analytical ways (Prensky, 2005).

Demographic changes, such as the population's increased mobility, intensify the need to personalize school programs. According to Ohler (2005),

> Tomorrow's workers will not work alone but rather in groups with others of many varied cultural backgrounds. The demand on workers for technological competency will be met with an even greater challenge: the ability to work closely—even collaboratively—with workers of different cultures, perceptions, behaviors, and values. Today's and tomorrow's workers require high levels of communication, collaboration, interpersonal, and leadership skills. A personalized learning environment is needed to prepare future students for this new work environment. (p. 5)

Another factor that calls for more personalized schools is the decline of the traditional nuclear family (two parents, with one parent at home during the day). Today, this image describes only 3% of American families. The degree of this shift and the swiftness of this change are typical of many other changes experienced in twenty-first century society. A personalized school community is needed to provide students with stability, a solid base from which they can cope with a rapidly changing world.

As a theory to guide instruction, constructivism plays a leading role. Although constructivism focuses on learning as a cognitive process, it also stresses the learner's need for personalized schooling. The constructivist approach, which many consider essential and indispensable to school restructuring, involves helping students relate new information to knowledge gained from prior experiences and to helping individuals understand their own cognitive strategies. Since prior experiences differ for each student, constructivist teaching requires personalizing the learning process. For example, constructivist teachers inquire about students' individual understanding of concepts before sharing their own understandings.

Supervisors should help teachers to recognize that social discourse is a powerful way to develop and transfer meaning, and they should encourage teachers to engage students in dialogue—with both the teacher and fellow classmates. These teachers will encourage student inquiry, and when students respond, the teachers will follow with probing questions to cause students to think more deeply about the issues. Because constructivist teachers value the depth of understanding a concept over breadth of knowledge, their students will spend more time investigating and explaining content. All of these activities are personalizing.

It Works for Me!

On Target

Donald Wise, California State University, Fresno

To help schools understand the need for change and how to use it, I have downloaded the best practices rubric from the National Center for Educational Achievement.* In a work session, administrators and teachers together select one of the five areas of the rubric and, in small groups, assess their own school practices against the rubric (Missing the Mark or On Target). Each group reports its findings while a recorder writes essential points from each report. The leader (usually the school principal) asks if all are in agreement with the summarized findings of the faculty. Then, the group selects an area for growth and develops a plan. The Web site contains examples of successful implementation of each best practice. More than one work session is needed to develop a plan and a monitoring system for change.

*http://www.just4kids.org/en/research_policy/best_practices/framework.cfm (retrieved January 9, 2009)

Innovation and Change

Without change, there could be no education reform, no improvement. This makes all of the aforementioned observations tantamount to promises of good things to come. Each observation promises to make a substantial improvement in elementary, middle, and secondary education, but the results are never guaranteed. Therefore, it is important for supervisors to make these positive reform features part of their toolkits and use them to encourage those teachers who tend to see the disadvantages of education reform more clearly than the advantages. These observations are indicative of the need to change and mark ongoing initiatives in particular areas. Table 5.3 shows examples of some pre-reform assumptions and the related changes already happening in teachers' lives.

Table 5.3 Reform-Based Changes in Today's Schools

Pre-Reform Assumptions	Reform-Based Changes
Teacher stereotypes as clumsy, inept figures with no capacity for leadership	Teachers recognized as professionals with the expertise and judgment skills required for effective leadership, capable of making all types of decisions needed to lead a school
The teacher's instructional role as the transferer of knowledge	The teacher's instructional role as a cocreator of knowledge
The learner's role as a passive receiver of information	The learner's role as an active creator of knowledge
Assessment to assign grades	Assessment to promote learning
The classroom as the teacher's arena	The whole school as the teacher's arena
Limited or prohibited community involvement in instruction	An ongoing series of activities to inform and involve the community
Education perceived as relatively unimportant	Education perceived as essential and worthy of the public's full support
Making students technologically *literate*	Making students technologically *competent*

Notice the number of these changes that contribute to the empowerment of teachers (e.g., enhanced leadership role, expanded work arena, and creation of knowledge).

Given the nature of the school and its relationship to the community, educational innovations affect many groups including the learners, administrators, teachers, parents, and the community at large. Most school innovations seek to improve the conditions under which young people learn and relate to such things as organization of materials, emphases on particular subjects, social organization of schools and classrooms, utilization of new technologies, and consideration of individual learning styles.

Faculty Attitudes toward Change

Most substantive changes are met with resistance, regardless of how sound the proposal or how long overdue the need for the proposed change. Change always requires some adjustment. Some may initially feel resentment when confronted with new and unfamiliar approaches. To expect every faculty member to immediately buy into a proposed change is unrealistic. According to Rogers (1983), of those who do adopt, only 3% of the adopters will give their immediate support to a proposed change. These are the risk takers who have a flair for the new. Unfortunately, this group cannot be depended on to garner the support of others—they're in it for themselves. Many may actually consider them a little strange and would likely not follow their lead. But each faculty has its movers and shakers who stand ready to lead their colleagues. On the average this group constitutes about 13% of all adopters. Members of this group are perceived as leaders. They are highly influential, and they enjoy garnering the support of their colleagues.

Rogers (1983) says that about a third (34%) of all adopters wait to see what the early adopters do. They listen to Ben Franklin's advice: "Be not first on whom the new is tried or the last to lay the old aside." An equal number of adopters (34%) are reluctant, giving in only after social or peer pressure is applied. Rogers calls the remaining 16% of adopters laggards. Not only are they very late to adopt, but they also remain skeptical and unhappy, always believing that they would be better off without the change.

Impact on Administrators

Many changes affect decisions that are the responsibility of principals and other school administrators. For example, innovations changing traditional attendance boundaries or rearranging the school day so that not all learners follow the same schedule might require changes in arrival and departure times of buses. Certain kinds of mandated learning resources might require diversion of funds from one account to another. Maintenance schedules could be affected. Principals could even find increasing demands on their time, as community groups and parents ask them to make presentations explaining changes.

Innovations may require teachers to work in unfamiliar ways. In making efforts to integrate content from several disciplines, they may be confronted with massive course-development responsibilities. They could be called upon to plan and implement cooperative learning activities and other content-delivery techniques with which they have had little prior experience. A few teachers may have to adjust psychologically to the suggestion that what they have been doing previously has not been effective enough.

Teachers may have to learn how to customize their lessons to fit the needs of each learner (McLester, 2005); they may have to learn how to empower their students (Levin, 2005); they may have to make their curriculum more standards-based (Francis, 2005); or they may be required to support their choices of curriculum and instructional methods by citing research or by conducting their own action research (see chapter 13), a requirement of the No Child Left

Behind law. These are only a few examples of the types of innovation and change faced by teachers today.

Impact on Parents

Innovations may affect parents in several ways. Some parents may be unsettled by innovations that seem to mark a significant departure from the kinds of practices they remember form their own school days. A lack of familiarity may breed some suspicions about "what the schools are up to." Changes involving attendance patterns and school schedules can influence family life, particularly when school schedules and parents' schedules conflict because of their own employment schedules. The types of choices confronting parents, regarding the schools their children attend and the kinds of programs they follow, may be choices that they have never previously had to make (Armstrong et al., 2009). In some instances, they may be asked to play substantive roles in making decisions about school curricula.

Impact on the Larger Community

Influences of innovations on the larger community represent both indirect and direct effects of changes in school practices. For example, a change in school schedules that would allow some high school students to go to school from 1:00 p.m. to 8:00 p.m. rather than from 8:00 a.m. to 3:00 (or 4:00) p.m. might result in swarms of students descending upon local shopping centers in the morning hours. Innovations featuring emphases on new technologies might result in tax increases to support equipment purchases. Outreach programs might require local businesses and government offices to set up more internship programs designed to give learners a feel for the professional workplace.

When discussing proposed changes with community members, supervisors and teachers should remember that the audience is likely to be suspicious and can easily become defensive. Therefore, it is important that change agents avoid negative words as much as possible.

Change Theory

A 2006 study by the American Management Association (*Secrets to Making Change Happen*) reported that surveyed human resource professionals cited change management as their top challenge. Although to many it may seem as if the call for change in our schools is a relatively recent phenomenon, today's study of the change process can be traced back to the mid-twentieth century.

Early Change Theory

In the early 1950s, psychologist Kurt Lewin developed a three-step model that began with a first step called *unfreezing*, during which traditional practices were abandoned to make room for more promising practices that offered hope for improvement. The second step was called *molding*. During this step the new practices were implemented and the change agents watched to see the reactions to the innovations. The last step, *refreezing*, involved soliciting constructive input from those who were affected by the change (Kreitner, 2007).

Although designed for businesses, Lewin's model is enlightening to educators. Edgar Schein (2006) expanded Lewin's theory and evolved it for teachers, moving it from *planned change* to *managed learning*.

A Contemporary Model for Change

Concerned that most leadership doctoral programs throughout the country are not adequately preparing their students for the responsibilities to establish a culture of social justice, Sandra Harris (Clarke & Harris, 2006) led a class of 16 doctoral students at Lamar University in a project that outlines an effective model for change. The project began by asking the students to write individual essays that reflected their changing identities, enabling them to articulate their views on the following personal practices in their lives:

- This is what I believed.
- This is what my practice looked like then.
- This is what I believe now.
- This is what I want to become.
- This is what I envision my practice looking like in the future.

Through examining their essays and describing critical life issues (both professional and social), the group identified four change dimensions (see Figure 5.2):

1. Change is motivated by a shared human spirituality of hope that we can influence expected outcomes.
2. Change is an individual process of scholarship, reflection, and reconstructed practice based on a system of core values.
3. Change is a function of our behavior towards others.
4. Change is a continuous dialogue between ourselves and our practice that is never finished.

Figure 5.2 Dimensions of Cyclical Change in a Scholar-Practitioner Leadership Program

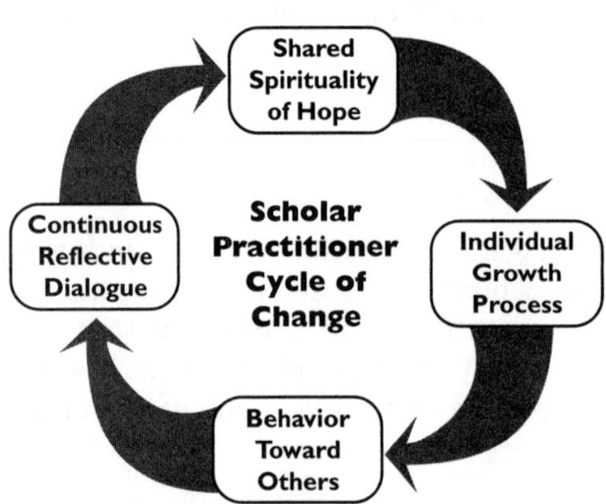

From Clarke, G. & Harris, S. (2006), Preparing Scholar-Practitioner Leaders: A suggested model for change. In F. Dembowski & L. Lemasters (Eds.), *NCPEA Yearbook 2006*. Adapted with permission of the authors.

These changes led to a second order of changes that included change as a shared spirituality of hope, change as an individual process, change as behavior toward others, and change as continuous, unfinished dialogue.

This introspective written exercise, followed by reflective discussions, can make teachers aware that improving schools involves changing others—that although they may find it necessary to change policies, what really has to happen first is changing their own behavior in order to change others' behaviors. Perhaps the most important realization that can emerge from this exercise is the awareness that continuous change is necessary and that, through dialogue, each member has the potential to rise to the challenge. This project resulted in the model shown in Figure 5.3. In their own words, Clarke and Harris (2006, p. 55) describe this model:

> The struggle for increased personal capacity for shared human spirituality, individual, our behavior toward others, and this unfinished dialogue resulted in a deeper dialogue or dialogic model, if you will, of a changing dynamic understanding of a student's own potential capacity to learn more and do more as a change leader. This model of change dimensions was broadly categorized as (1) conceptual-motivational, (2) applied-methodological, and (3) personal-renewal. These three themes contribute to the uniquely personal framework that learning can and does alter the learner and has the capacity to influence the leadership outcomes of the community or culture.

Just as the physical exercise of leaders/students writing their leadership philosophies on paper leads to deeper understandings of how they really believe and feel toward their leadership roles, the combined writing of individual essays followed by the reflective discussions about how their attitudes had changed energized these students and fired a passion that can remain throughout their careers. This hope, and the power to instill it in others, gives everyone a hope for the future.

Figure 5.3 A Model for Emergent Dialogical Change Themes in a Scholar-Practitioner Program

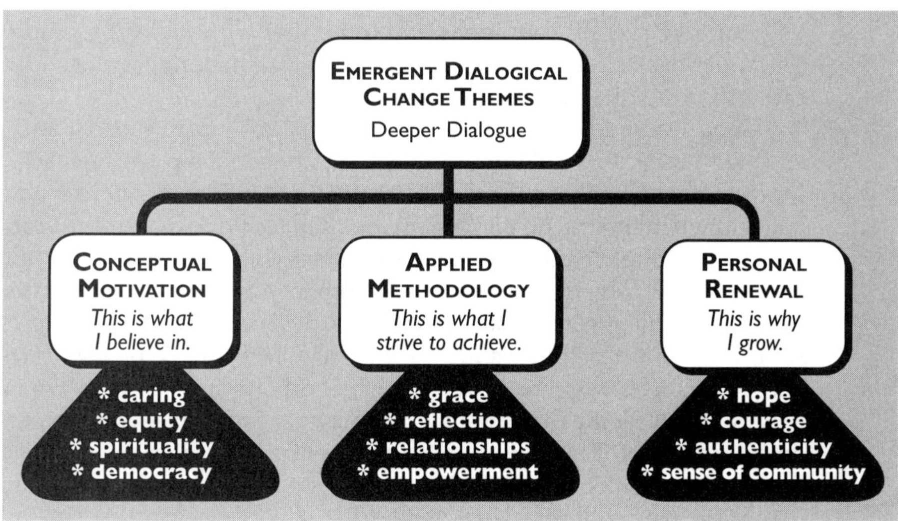

From Clarke, G. & Harris, S. (2006), Preparing Scholar-Practitioner Leaders: A suggested model for change. In F. Dembowski & L. Lemasters (Eds.), *NCPEA Yearbook 2006*. Adapted with permission of the authors.

Change through Technology

Some teachers may be reluctant to embrace their new role in reform because they are technologically challenged. When individuals begin lagging in one area, it is easy to fall behind in another until eventually they cease to be a valued team player. One approach supervisors can use to help teachers make technological changes is to create a technical support group staffed by the more technically competent teachers, whose sole responsibility will be to help their less technically oriented colleagues. Initially, schedule adjustments and time allotments will be required to permit members of the support group to meet regularly with their colleagues to provide assistance and encouragement.

During the initial meetings, members of the support group can introduce technically challenged teachers to such useful technological tools as listservs, chat rooms, blogging, and research procedures on the Internet. Gradually, the assistance of the technical group can be shifted from group meetings to blogging online. As teachers gain technical skills, they will be empowered to use these tools in their classrooms.

To see how the Mid-Continent Research for Education and Learning (McREL) is predicting the future of technology and other factors that affect schools will change, visit their Web site (www.mcrel.org).

Conclusion

Leadership theory has always embraced studies of change, because effective leadership involves persuading and helping people change. True leadership involves helping people learn how to discriminate between changes that will improve present conditions and those that will not lead to improvement. The supervisor's role includes responsibility for helping faculties identify and preserve those qualities that are worth keeping.

Good leaders help teachers abandon unsuccessful practices and preserve effective practices. Furthermore, these supervisors help teachers see the need for changing. Changes are more permanent when they are perceived as essential, and when those who implement the changes understand a clear and simple process for implementing them. Through early involvement at the decision stage, teachers develop ownership of the change and commitment to its success.

The old image of teachers as someone who cannot do anything especially well, including teaching, is giving way to a new image of highly competent decision makers who create knowledge and help their students create knowledge. Paralleling the development of a new teacher image is a currently developing image of learning as a rather complex process. New technological developments must be part of learning and must be used to personalize learning for each individual.

Effective instructional supervision requires skills in identifying and dealing effectively with those segments of the population who support change and those who resist change. The supervisor must realize how proposed changes will impact learners, administrators, teachers, parents, and the community at large and must learn how to help each cope with those changes.

Teacher reform must occur simultaneously with school reform. Successful education reform will require total restructuring of schools to change the schools' cultures, which will also require changing teachers, as a result making them more confident in themselves and in their fellow teachers.

Questions for Discussion and Reflection

1. How is education reform empowering teachers?
2. Why must teacher reform and school reform occur simultaneously?
3. How have education reform reports shaped public attitudes toward teachers?
4. How can the supervisor help teachers whose technological skills lag behind their peers?
5. Why do so many people resist change?

Suggested Activities

1. Visit a local school's computer laboratory. Interview the computer laboratory director and ask the director to describe one of the most interesting and effective projects that teachers are using the computers to implement. Write a summary description of this project.
2. Interview an elementary school department chair and a secondary school department chair. Referring to the right-hand column in Table 5.1, ask these chairs how they overcome each of these barriers.
3. Interview an elementary, middle or secondary school administrator asking this person to identify a highly successful program at the school. Ask what alterations the administration had to make to accommodate this program. Ask a student, teacher, and parent what types of hardships the program had on each of them. Make a chart showing these results.
4. Interview the chairperson of a site-based school council and ask this person to describe how the council has handled a controversial issue. Ask what was learned from the experience. Write a summary report titled "Using a Site-based Council to Resolve Controversial Issues: Some Precautions and Suggestions."

Chapter 6

Helping Teachers Plan the Curriculum

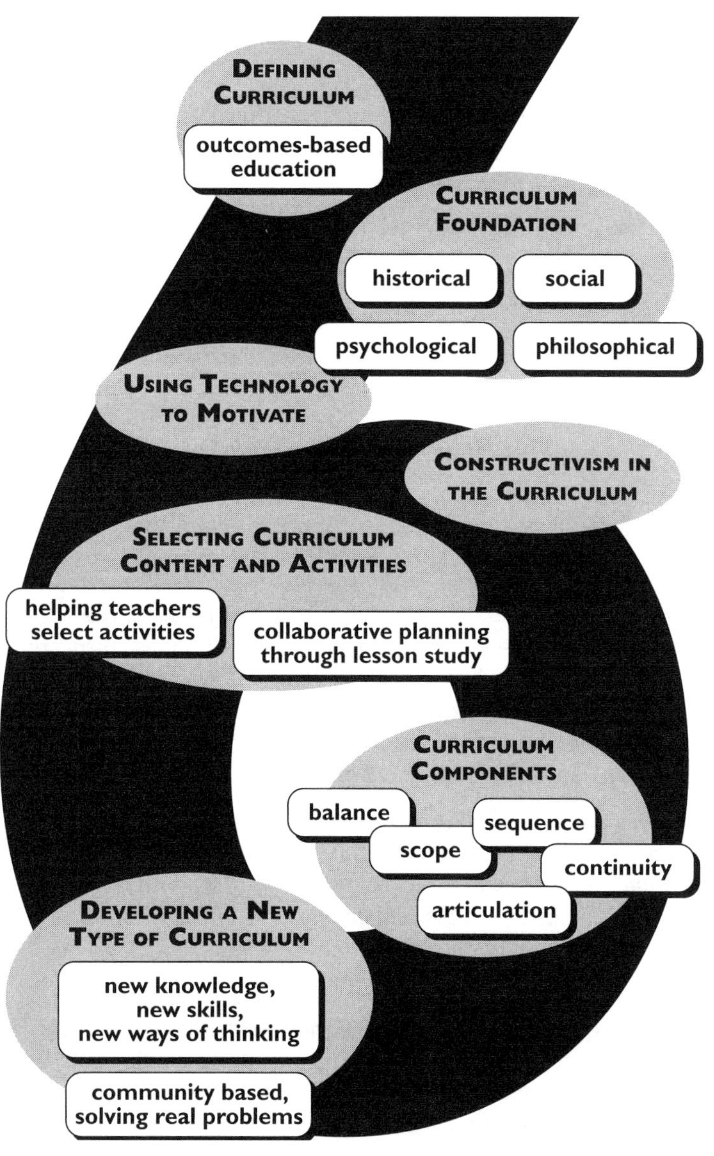

> *Brave principals and teachers are taking matters into their own hands and changing the curriculum, themselves.*
>
> —S. Wineburg, "A sobering big idea"

Objectives

After completion of this chapter, you should be able to

1. Formulate your own philosophy of education and assist others in doing so
2. Describe the way curriculum is usually developed and how it should be developed
3. Name and discuss several bases for selecting curriculum content
4. Apply knowledge of curriculum components to curriculum development
5. Describe several ways to balance a curriculum

Block Scheduling: A Losing Decision

The chatter in the hallway at Northside Middle gradually got louder and louder. At ten minutes until 6 p.m., the buzzing noise had become a loud roar.

Among the crowd were the members of the school's site-based council, several other faculty members, and parents. Several weeks ago, the site-based council announced that the school would possibly adopt a block schedule. Since then, much debate ensued over the pros and cons of block scheduling. It seemed that each party to be affected by the new program (teachers, students, and parents) had its own unique set of concerns. Tonight, the final decision would be announced, and the school would either keep its traditional curriculum or adopt block scheduling.

The council had announced an open hearing for the first hour to permit interested parties to share their concerns. A designated spokesperson from any party who had gotten its name on the agenda would be given up to 10 minutes to present its concerns to the council. At 7 p.m. the council would break for 15 minutes and then go into closed session to make the decision.

Fred Hodges was the first to be called upon to speak. Fred, a parent of two Northside honor students, expressed concern that the new block schedule might not provide the structure needed by some children, especially those who were on the college preparatory track. He said that he understood that the large blocks of time would provide more time for certain topics of interest, but he also said that to him, providing time for interest groups did not justify robbing college-bound students of the subjects that are required for college entrance.

The next speaker was Sally Moore, an eighth-grade earth science teacher at Northside. Sally spoke in support of block scheduling, saying that for the past eleven years she had always found the schedule impossible: "I am responsible for teaching geology, physical geography, mineralogy, oceanography, paleontology, and space science. I'll be frank with you. Our students are being cheated out of opportunities to learn some important content. There has never been enough time in the year to cover all of these topics. Since the block schedule would permit me to offer some of these topics that we never have time to cover, I'm in favor of the block schedule."

Bobby Wallace, an English teacher, was the next to speak. "Thank you for the opportunity to speak on behalf of the English Department. As department chair I have recently become aware of some new opportunities for the department to make significant improvements in our overall approach to teaching. Last summer, the faculty in our department and the social studies teachers got together and voted to bring in a specialist to conduct a workshop on integrating the disciplines. We have since decided to use our in-service days next summer to begin planning a merger between these two departments.

"All of you will remember that our last schoolwide in-service program speaker emphasized that 'less is more.' At first, some of us found the idea a little strange, but then we seemed to agree that it is better to cover less content and have the students understand it at a greater depth. Our speaker said that a recent national study found that only a third of the nation's secondary students could find a given country on the map. That really got the attention of the social studies teachers. You also know the trouble that many of our students have with grammar. I'm embarrassed for the whole English department when I think about the quality of the written papers submitted to the non-English teachers. We English teachers have had to choose between teaching grammar, literature, or poetry.

"The block schedule would provide more time for us to teach all three. But, more importantly, the block schedule would give these two departments an opportunity to really integrate their disciplines. It would also serve all the other subjects. Ms. Moore just expressed a need for time to cover more of the sciences. The block schedule would provide that time, and it would also provide time for field trips and more experiential studies. We've been moving toward such curriculum changes as using electronic portfolios and performance evaluation. I think an experientially based curriculum would support these new practices; it would give students time to really get involved with the types of activities being required in the electronic portfolios and it would familiarize students with the types of activities expected of them on the new performance tests. Our teachers vote a definite 'yes' on the proposal change. Thank you."

The next speaker was a parent who said that block scheduling was too confusing to middle-level students. "My daughter, Brenda, is not a good organizer. I'm afraid she would find the proposed block schedule too confusing." A couple of other parents spoke against the proposal and one parent in support of it. Most speakers held strong opinions, and emotions ran high. When the meeting broke to clear the room of nonmembers, it was clear that whatever decision the council would make, several parties would be very displeased.

Reflection

The "less is more" position addressed in this vignette reflects the constructivist attitude toward the importance of placing the goal of understanding above that of covering content. Today's teachers are suffering as they are being pulled in two directions, trying to meet the demands of both their administrators and their students. The need to prepare their students for standardized tests has replaced the important goals of personalizing teaching and promoting student creativity and self-esteem. Supervisors have a responsibility for keeping the goal of depth in understanding alive in a climate which often appears inhospitable to such a goal.

Introduction

The opening vignette reflects a moment in the history of schools when some parents have become quite vocal regarding their expectations for their schools, a time when the entire management of many schools is entrusted to a council that involves noneducators. Many teachers find themselves frustrated because they do not know how to respond to evaluations of their schools, evaluations that many consider educationally unsound and based on highly scripted curriculum materials (Steel & Craig, 2006). Instead, teachers want more involvement in curriculum development (Dagenhart et al., 2005). Many educational leaders are telling us that to make the necessary changes in our curricula, teachers must be *empowered*. This means that "they must be connected between a sense of personal competence and a desire for and willingness to take action in the public domain" (Steel & Craig, 2006, p. 680).

> Interstate School Leaders Licensure Consortium (ISLLC) Educational Leadership Policy Standard No. 2 requires advocating, nurturing, and sustaining a school culture and instructional program conducive to student learning.

It is imperative that teachers understand curriculum development, especially the foundations that undergird well-developed curricula. Exacerbating the need for sound curriculum development are the many hands-on curricula, some which are excellent activities but, in the absence of a good working knowledge of curriculum development, are likely to have only temporary effects. A badly crafted curriculum can cripple learning, and an overly rigid curriculum can increase teacher turnover (Chan, 2009).

This chapter begins by involving the readers in the process of developing working definitions of curriculum and proceeds to explain how supervisors can help teachers base their selections of content and activities on sound principles. The chapter also shows the supervisor how to make teachers aware of the important curriculum components.

Defining Curriculum

The meaning of curriculum development has changed over the years. Today, it has many definitions. This chapter reviews the history of curriculum development, discusses several definitions, and documents the historical, social, psychological, and philosophical foundations that undergird it. The chapter focuses on ways supervisors can help teachers use foundations and knowledge of curriculum development to select content and activities. Curriculum components—including articulation, continuity, balance, scope, and sequence—are described, along with their implications for developing a new type of curriculum designed to prepare students for future society.

Curriculum has its origin in the Latin word meaning *racecourse*. Traditionally, in this country "curriculum" has referred to a series of courses. By the 1920s, American education had borrowed from European curricula the activities-centered design. By the 1940s, Ralph Tyler had introduced his ends-means curriculum model, starting the curriculum development process by identifying the desired outcomes and then designing the curriculum accordingly. Tyler's model paved the way for the early 1960s development of objectives-writing systems. As was seen in chapter 2, the 1959 Woods Hole Conference report recommended designing the curriculum around carefully chosen student activities coupled with major concepts or content generalizations. Together, these developments gave a balance of emphasis on objectives, content, and activities. The *curriculum*, then, could be defined as the objectives, content, and activities planned by the school to enable students to achieve the school's broader mission and goals.

When defining curriculum, however, each individual brings an array of personal experiences into the definition. In a way, this is good because many educators work with curriculum in many different ways. The cumulative result is that there are about as many different definitions as there are people who work with curricula. Box 6.1 is a list of definitions of curriculum taken from the literature (Henson, 2006). Though few in number, notice how much these definitions vary. A casual review of these definitions gives the reader a

Box 6.1 Definitions of Curriculum

Curriculum is:	As viewed by:
• A series of courses	The typical layperson
• Planned actions for instruction	Macdonald
• All learning activities provided by the school	Saylor & Alexander
• All the experiences that children have under the guidance of teachers	Campbell & Campbell
• A sequence of potential experiences set up by the school for the purpose of disciplining children and youth in group ways of thinking and acting	Smith, Stanley, & Shore

(continued)

Curriculum is:	As viewed by:
• All the experiences that learners have under the auspices of the school	Doll
• [The] learning experiences and intended outcomes formulated through systematic reconstruction of knowledge and experience, under the auspices of the school, for the learner's continuous and willful growth in personal-social competence	Tanner & Tanner
• All the planned learning outcomes for which the school is responsible	Popham & Baker
• The entire culture of the school	Gay
• A plan for learning	Taba

sense of variety in the ways educators view curriculum. Yet, a closer look shows some recurring patterns. For example, Figure 6.1 shows such recurring patterns as means vs. ends, content vs. experiences, and process vs. product (or plan). As is seen in the figure, there are several ways of viewing curriculum. Each perspective can affect the supervisor's role regarding the curriculum. Some supervisors view their role as improving instruction, yet "the curriculum serves as the heart of the teaching and learning environment" (Pultorak et al., 2006, p. 103). If quality instruction is to endure, the curriculum must be designed to give permanence to instruction. While the curriculum produces ongoing quality instruction, the supervisor has responsibility for working to improve both. This interrelationship has intensified with the expansion of teachers' arenas beyond the classroom, as required by the school restructuring movement.

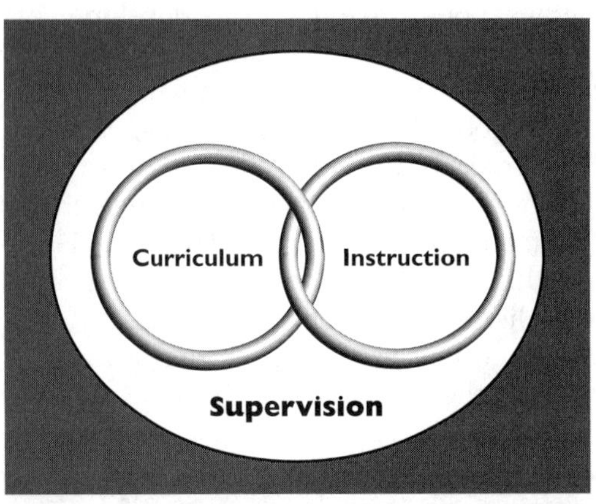

Several definitions of curriculum also refer to objectives. Obviously, many educators view the curriculum as something that is created in order to reach certain specified objectives. Because so many definitions of curriculum include objectives, perhaps a discussion of objectives-based curricula (also known as *outcomes-based education*) is appropriate at this time.

Outcomes-Based Education

Outcomes-based education means clearly focusing on and organizing everything in an educational system around expected student competencies (after graduation). This requires a clear picture of the tasks that students should be able to perform, and then aligning curriculum, instruction, and

Figure 6.1 Categorizing Definitions of Curriculum

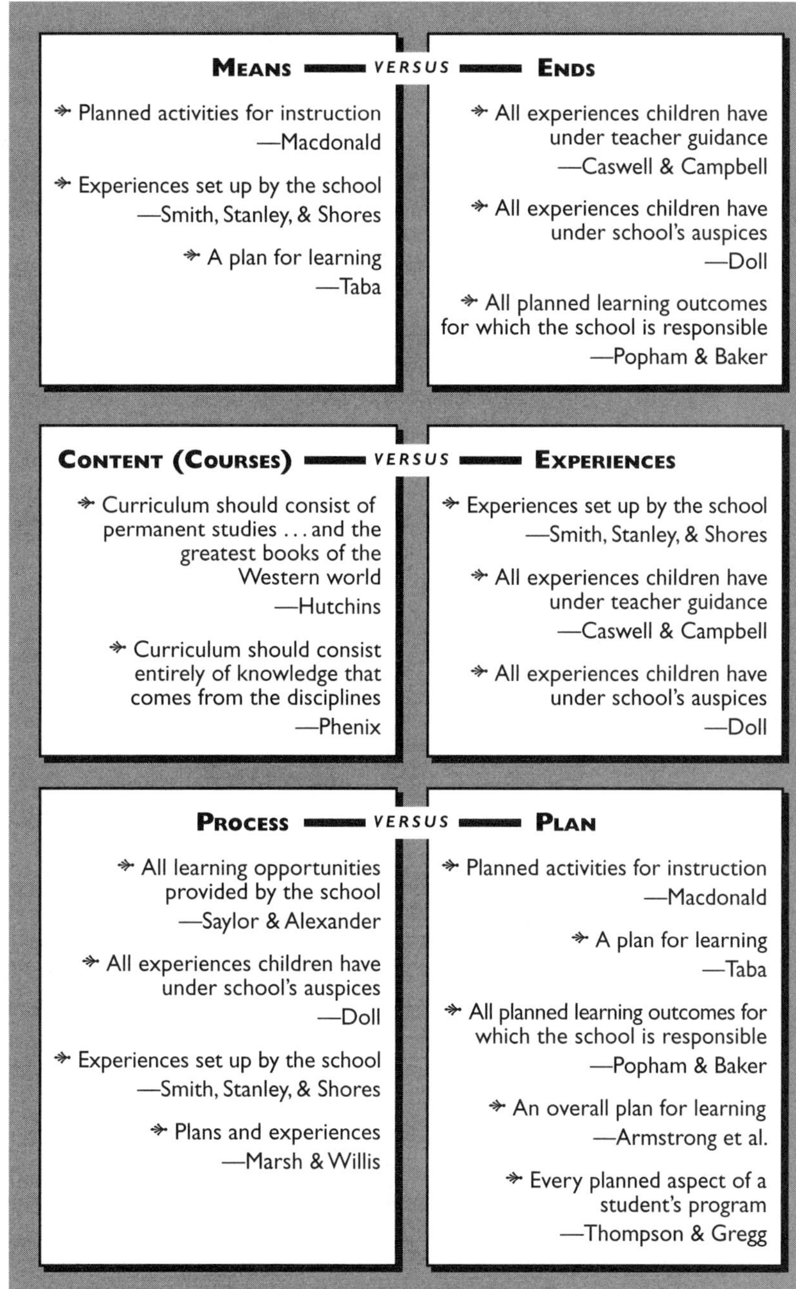
MEANS VERSUS ENDS
Planned activities for instruction —Macdonald
Experiences set up by the school —Smith, Stanley, & Shores
A plan for learning —Taba
All experiences children have under teacher guidance —Caswell & Campbell
All experiences children have under school's auspices —Doll
All planned learning outcomes for which the school is responsible —Popham & Baker
CONTENT (COURSES) VERSUS EXPERIENCES
Curriculum should consist of permanent studies . . . and the greatest books of the Western world —Hutchins
Curriculum should consist entirely of knowledge that comes from the disciplines —Phenix
Experiences set up by the school —Smith, Stanley, & Shores
All experiences children have under teacher guidance —Caswell & Campbell
All experiences children have under school's auspices —Doll
PROCESS VERSUS PLAN
All learning opportunities provided by the school —Saylor & Alexander
All experiences children have under school's auspices —Doll
Experiences set up by the school —Smith, Stanley, & Shores
Plans and experiences —Marsh & Willis
Planned activities for instruction —Macdonald
A plan for learning —Taba
All planned learning outcomes for which the school is responsible —Popham & Baker
An overall plan for learning —Armstrong et al.
Every planned aspect of a student's program —Thompson & Gregg

assessment to make sure this learning ultimately occurs. The keys to having an outcomes-based system are: (1) developing a clear set of learning outcomes around which all of the system's components can be focused, and (2) establishing the conditions or opportunities within the system that enable and encourage all students to achieve those essential outcomes. Today's curricula must experience substantial change if future students are to meet reform goals.

In response to the No Child Left Behind legislation, many states have written statements of desired outcomes for high school graduates, and several states are currently raising the level of these expected outcomes. Supervisors can help teachers by constantly talking to them about the purposes of their classes, so teachers will begin each curriculum development project by explaining the intended outcomes. Supervisors can also help teachers align the objectives of their classes with their state's intended outcomes. Failure to meet annual yearly progress (AYP) expectations for two consecutive years indicates schools in need of improvement, and schools that don't improve their AYP expectations in three years can lose their curriculum and their teachers. Some states purposefully set low expectations to avoid failing to meet their AYP expectations (Woolfolk Hoy & Hoy, 2009). Because students are unlikely to achieve beyond the expectations that are set for them, supervisors should encourage educators to set high expectations (Good & Brophy, 2007). (Outcomes-based education is discussed in conjunction with performance objectives in chapter 8.)

Curriculum Foundations

Good curriculum development is based on solid historical, social, philosophical, and psychological foundations (Ferrero, 2005). In other words, curriculum development should use the knowledge that educators have gained over the years through philosophy; the knowledge gained throughout our previous experiences (historical foundations); knowledge of the nature of behavior, in particular, learning (psychological foundations); and knowledge about society (social foundations). Now, each of these sources of knowledge will be examined to determine what it can offer to the curriculum development process.

Historical Foundations

The first public schools in this country, the Latin Grammar Schools, were developed to prepare young men for the Harvard College of Ministry. As the name suggests, the Latin Grammar Schools had curricula steeped in the classics. Because such subjects as Latin and Greek seemed highly inappropriate in a rapidly developing nation, these schools were soon replaced by the Franklin Academy schools, whose curricula were highly practical, including such subjects as astronomy, mathematics, bookkeeping, navigation, and surveying.

The Franklin Academy had one major weakness: It was too expensive for most families to afford. In the following century Thomas Jefferson pressed for education for all citizens, proposing three years of free public schools to all citizens of Virginia. A century later, Horace Mann started the first normal school to ensure the availability of quality teachers for public schools. These two leaders spent much of their lives shaping American education into a system that has continued to carry a unique quality, distinguishing American education from all other education systems in the world, a system designed to be free to all youths. This national commitment to free education was reconfirmed by the Northwest Ordinance of 1787, which reserved one-sixteenth of every township to finance the public schools. By 1860, half of the nation's children were in school.

In 1918 the National Education Association issued its enduring list of seven expectations for American schools. Known as the Cardinal Principles of Secondary Education, these were (1) health, (2) command of fundamental processes, (3) worthy home membership, (4) vocational efficiency, (5) citizenship, (6) worthy use of leisure time, and (7) ethical character. These aims are a good overview of the American people's expectations of their schools.

Social Foundations

The influence of the community on the schools was strong when most schools were located in rural areas (Clabaugh, 2004), and the school was the hub of many community activities. Originally, the major support for the schools came from the local communities. The first schools (the Dame Schools) were located in the homes of individual families, and the mothers gave their time to serve as teachers. As recently as the mid–twentieth century, fish fries, cake walks, and local festivals were held to raise money for the local schools. Since then, however, the majority of the nation's communities have become urban. Small schools that were originally located in the center of their communities have been consolidated into much larger schools, often located in another part of the city. Mandated busing has further removed many students from their communities. The cumulative result of these changes has been a reduction in the level of involvement of American citizens with their schools.

Although most schools no longer serve as the hub of their community, administrators and teachers continue to feel the pressures of several community forces aimed at reshaping the schools. Debates over what should be included in school curricula fire passion, grab headlines, and lead off the evening news. Many educators consider such influence as interference because some pressure groups want to make changes that should require the expertise of educators. However, communities will probably continue to effect changes in the schools. In a way, society has every right to be demanding of its schools—after all, the public schools belong to society; they were created by society and for society, and through public taxes they continue to be supported by society. Throughout the last century, each state contributed heavily to support its schools. Over the decades, the percentage of total support for schools has increased at the state level while decreasing at the federal level. Of course, the constitution gives the states the right to control their schools. This, too, is a unique characteristic of American education.

The point is that school curricula must be responsible to society in general, and specifically to the local communities. Most education reform programs are statewide and, through them, most states are reshaping their schools. Supervisors frequently find themselves caught between the state legislators and state department of education officers who take one side of an issue, and the teachers and other local school personnel who take the other. The fact that the schools are being largely supported by state and local taxes should be considered when supervisors attempt to define their position on school reform.

A democracy cannot exist without an educated populace (Mathews, 2008). Democracy requires citizens who participate broadly in informal public decision making with an eye toward a common goal. Democratic society's mere existence relies on good schools that prepare all students to participate in public decision making. A democracy also requires of its members a particular type of values and an ongoing sense of community, an obligation to the common good.

Citizens should see themselves as members of the community that makes their individuality possible, and they should value and nurture that community. As seen in the vignette at the beginning of this chapter, many citizens are quick to speak out regarding the activities at their schools. These parents are to be applauded for their involvement with their schools. Throughout the country, parents and other citizens are volunteering many hours each week to serve on site-based councils.

But correct answers are seldom clear. As we shall soon see, supervisors also are accountable to students; they must do right by them. This means that supervisors must use their knowledge of the nature of development and the nature of learning. This often creates a problem because some state reform laws are contrary to and militate against our knowledge of behavior, development, and learning.

Psychological Foundations

The psychological foundations of curriculum are given a cursory review here, with particular focus on their proper role in curriculum planning. Students succeed in school only to the degree that they perceive education as important, and to the degree to which they perceive themselves capable of succeeding. Self-efficacy is a great motivator. Thus, the curriculum must nurture the development of strong self-concepts and self-confidence among all students. Supervisors can help build an environment where teachers are encouraged to use praise and avoid sarcasm, and by making these elements the subject of classroom observations. Help is provided in chapter 12 (see Box 12.1).

Philosophical Foundations

Philosophy helps us make sense of our world (Ferrero, 2005), never by telling us what we should or should not do but by shaping our thinking, causing us to ask important questions. For example, philosophy helps guide curriculum decisions by asking important questions such as: What is the purpose of school? What is the purpose of life? What is the nature of learning? What is truth, and how do we come to know it? What is wisdom, and how do we lead others to become wise? What is good and valuable?

Philosophy has fields of study (or philosophical constructs) that focus on such questions. A working knowledge of different schools of educational philosophy can be extremely useful in moving groups of people through the curriculum planning process (Warner, 2010). Some of the most important philosophical constructs include metaphysics, epistemology, axiology, idealism, realism, pragmatism, existentialism, essentialism, perennialism, and reconstructionism. Let's look briefly at each of these constructs.

Metaphysics. Metaphysicists recognize that some of our knowledge and understanding comes from sources other than the empirical. In other words, we know some things that we did not learn through the use of our five major senses. For example, if you ask deeply religious people how they know that they have a personal relationship with their God, they might be hard pressed to give a response that could be verified empirically. In fact, not all of our knowledge comes through our five senses.

How does this fact pertain to curriculum development? How would a supervisor, teacher, or other curriculum worker who understands that not all knowledge is empirically derived design curricula differently than someone who is not aware of this fact? How would a supervisor who understands this construct react differently than a supervisor who does not understand it? Supervisors who understand that not all knowledge is empirically derived would encourage their faculty to consider their instincts and feelings when making decisions, and they would not always demand each decision to be research driven.

Epistemology. Epistemologists are concerned with the nature of knowledge. How do we learn best? Through observation and inquiry? Through logic? Through debating issues with others? Through insight? Through reflection? Through tactile (hands-on) activities? Through working alone? Through group work? Does a first grader learn in the same way that a high school chemistry student learns? Does each discipline have its own unique best way to be learned? Supervisors who have taken time to search out answers to questions such as these are likely to lead teachers to design curricula that will capitalize on this knowledge.

Axiology. This philosophical construct is concerned with values and ethics. What is good? What is really valuable? What is right? What is wrong? Toward what kinds of goals should our schools aspire? Is beauty one of these goals? Is inner peace? A love of knowledge? A curious attitude? An appreciation for other cultures? A spirit of competition? Of cooperation?

To maximize learning in their classes, some teachers purposefully attempt to conceal their own values from their students. These teachers will admit that they do not believe they have a right to try to teach these values to their students. Yet, through their own actions, either purposefully or unwittingly, all teachers teach values. Some contemporary educators are quick to point out that our nation was built on strong moral values and that our citizenry has since lost much of its concern for morals and values.

John Lounsbury (1991, p. 5) said, "We need classrooms in which beauty is savored, truth honored, compassion practiced, and fellowship honored." For society's sake, teachers need to foster the development of certain values. Through the arts we learn how to appreciate beauty and how to express our insights and feelings in creative ways (Eisner, 2005). We help ourselves and others understand who we are through the arts. Yet, the arts have always been and continue to be neglected in elementary and secondary schools. (See chapter 9 for a more detailed discussion of the importance of the arts in the curriculum.)

All educators who have responsibility for influencing the curricula should search their own minds and hearts for their beliefs and feelings toward the role of the curriculum in promoting morals and values. Information about right and wrong can lead students to understand the difference and how to behave accordingly. Useful and sensitive confrontation about conduct can help lead a student to an understanding of restraint and of action and to know when each is appropriate. The whole question of character education is within the boundaries of axiology.

Value-laden questions represent axiology. For example, over the decades the use and role of technology to educate has been a topic that waxes and wanes. A concern that has reoccurred with each rebirth of technology is whether technology will dehumanize students. Proponents of technology often claim just the opposite: They say that technology can be used to make the curriculum more humane. If so, how can this happen and what is the supervisor's role in causing it to happen? Can more humane curricula reduce the growing crime rates?

Idealism. Idealists believe that there are universal truths and that God is the supreme source of absolute truth. Plato is considered the father of idealism. Webster's Collegiate Dictionary defines idealism as a theory that the essential nature of reality lies in consciousness or reason. Perhaps at no other time in history has society had more need to stop and think. Some say that in today's world of computers and microwaves there is no time to think, which is ironic because these machines were developed to give us more time. According to a study conducted by the Mid-Continent Research for Education and Learning (Lefkowits & Miller, 2006),

> The public no longer questions the wisdom of standards, assessments, and accountability per se, but it is not only academic success that is on the minds of the public, and especially parents. Participants in the dialogues acknowledged the importance of test scores but expressed equal or greater concern about students' civic-mindedness, sense of caring for others, flexibility and adaptability, work ethic, and creativity. (p. 407)

Some graduate classes (particularly seminars) provide time to think; yet because today's society is so accustomed to living in the fast lane, when people are given time to stop and think it makes them uncomfortable. It just doesn't seem right to sit with others unless someone is talking. We wonder what is wrong when we see someone who is quietly contemplating.

As educators plan curricula, idealists would encourage the planning of thinking time into the curricula. Discussions and debates are excellent vehicles for encouraging thinking. In recent years, schools have been severely criticized for failing to challenge students to think at higher levels. In his reform report, *A Place Called School*, Goodlad (1984) reported,

> Only rarely did we find evidence to suggest instruction likely to go much beyond mere possession of information to a level of understanding its implications and either applying it or exploring its possible applications. Nor did we see activities likely to arouse students' curiosity or to involve them in seeking a solution to some problems not already laid bare by teachers or textbook. (p. 236)

By channeling attention toward memorizing facts and figures, the No Child Left Behind law has perpetuated this focus of attention at lower levels (Gross, 2005).

Higher-level thinking cannot be demanded. We must acquire it by nurturing a series of successfully more advanced learning tasks until the student researches the desired level of performance. Perhaps the nature of the American culture itself militates against idealism. Perhaps because our schools have never placed much emphasis on time to think, we feel guilty when we are caught just sitting and thinking. Instructional supervisors can encourage teachers to address this issue as a concern for the ethos in their schools and classrooms.

* * *

Teachers everywhere are feeling pressured to select the best content for meeting their state standards. The following case study shows how a faculty can be taught how to select, prioritize, and align curriculum content with their state's mandated standards.

Baby Steps . . . Giant Gains

James L. Stone • Western Kentucky University

The curriculum question, "Of all that we ***might*** teach, what ***must*** we teach?" is even more problematic in a reform state with high-stakes accountability. The norm-referenced summative assessment can easily take priority over all else. Standards, core content for assessment, academic expectations, and the program of studies give a composite view of the demands placed upon students and staff.

The Kentucky Education Reform Act established school-based decision-making councils and identified their primary function as providing an instructional program resulting in student academic achievement. Curricular decisions are ultimately the responsibility of the local school, specifically the council.

The role of the principal has made a dramatic shift, from manager to instructional leader. Principal preparation programs are being redesigned to reflect that change in emphasis. Principal candidates are expected to demonstrate proficiency in the areas of curriculum, instruction, and assessment.

It is within the above-described context that difficult decisions are being made as to what ***must*** be taught. Correspondingly, perhaps even more difficult decisions are being made as to what is *not* taught. The following case describes the process of prioritizing the curriculum and the vital role of the principal in that process.

The Community

The school in this case is located in a small rural town in south-central Kentucky. The community takes pride in its natural and cultural resources. Also, residents have easy access to a regional comprehensive university which has earned an enviable reputation in the areas of teacher education and school administration. In fact, the department of educational administration is well into the implementation of a newly redesigned principal preparation program with the guidance of the Southern Regional Education Board.

The School

The school is one of only three in this independent school district. Its annual test scores have been increasing, but not at a rate that will meet state mandated goals. The middle school under study contains grades 6 through 8 with a student enrollment of approximately 200 and some 13 certified full-time teachers.

The Principal

The principal has earned the respect of his teachers through his leadership and his evident passion for student success. While a strong advocate for students and staff, he holds himself and others accountable. He has consistently shown his openness to change and has indeed provided the lead in adapting various cutting-edge instructional interventions to the school. The large volume of programs has, however, resulted in a lack of focus. He speaks strongly of commitment versus compliance. However, he, like many of his colleagues, is realistically concerned with job security and is reluctant to deviate from the state mandated curriculum. His attention to test scores reflects the political realities of the environment in which he works.

The Teachers

The faculty can be described as competent, caring, compassionate, collegial, and committed. In this small, intimate environment teachers know each other, their students, and the community well enough to personalize learning. The small size of the faculty and the student body is both a strength and a challenge. There is a definite positive aspect when it comes to communication and collaboration. A negative aspect of the small size is the tremendous impact that the poor performance of a few students on the accountability test can have on the school's rating and the resulting impact on perceptions in the community.

The faculty was overwhelmed by the sheer volume of subject-matter content they were expected to teach. They conscientiously attempted to meet the challenge but found the goal unattainable. A survey of teachers indicated that the majority thought the school's curriculum was too big and the percentage of mastery of standards too small. It became clear that mere coverage of material would not result in student learning, nor would it raise test scores.

After a review of the research-based literature on curriculum, teachers and administrators came to the realization that "what you teach and how you teach it" really are the major factors affecting student achievement. With the strong support of teacher leaders and the principal, a curriculum prioritization process was implemented.

In an environment of collegiality, tough decisions were made as to what not to teach as well as what to teach. All faculty, across grade levels and subject areas, were involved in the decision-making process. Standards were categorized as "essential, important, or condensed." The "essential" or "power" standards were identified as those that are enduring, applicable to a wide range of subjects, prerequisite for the next grade level, and/or likely to be assessed on the state accountability test.

Part of the prioritization process required teachers to "unpack" or "unwrap" each standard, which caused them to closely examine the standard to determine what knowledge and skills were being required of the student. Teachers used the technique of converting standards into essential questions to further determine their relative worth.

Professional development was provided for and by teachers, including research supportive of prioritization, writing essential questions, categorizing the standards, and consensus decision making. Emphasis was placed on adaptation as opposed to adoption of strategies.

While there were many areas of agreement in the prioritization process, there also were areas of disagreement. Having established a culture of mutual trust and respect for each other's professional expertise, teachers were able to reach consensus on those standards they would not focus on in a given subject or grade level. There were struggles along the way to keep certain standards they "'liked' to teach, not really 'needed' to teach." In summary, the prioritization process proved beneficial not only in identifying and clarifying standards to be taught, but also in producing strong support for the revised curriculum. In addition, it provided the basis for the next step in curriculum development, mapping the prioritized curriculum.

Reflection on the process in the form of individual interviews revealed the following perceptions of those involved:

1. The reduction in the number of standards to be taught made their job doable and, therefore, less stressful.
2. Teachers no longer felt alone in making decisions as to what to teach and not teach in their classrooms.
3. Teachers now have adequate time to teach for mastery rather than simply for coverage.
4. However, teachers remain anxious because of accountability testing, which may include material not specifically taught.

Issues for Further Reflection

1. Given the description of the principal in this case study, what would you see as his role in the prioritization process?
2. How might the school-district supervisory staff support these efforts?
3. Describe what you would anticipate if you were to lead the prioritization process at your school.
4. List the benefits of a prioritized curriculum at your school.
5. Identify the challenges you would anticipate as a result of prioritizing the curriculum at your school.
6. Prioritizing the curriculum has little if any impact on the taught and tested curriculum unless it is mapped and monitored. Develop a plan of action to implement these next two vital steps.

Realism. Realists, too, seek the truth but don't place any confidence in the methods used by the idealists—namely, just thinking things through. Instead, realists believe in the scientific method of English philosopher Sir Francis Bacon that originated in the sixteenth and seventeenth centuries. As an educator, you will recognize the steps in this method:

1. Define the problem.
2. Formulate a hypothesis.
3. Gather data.
4. Interpret the data.
5. Use reason to draw a conclusion.
6. Test your conclusion.

Realists depend on the five senses for gathering information. They would build problems into the curriculum and require students to use their five senses and the scientific method to solve them. The many programs that resulted from the Woods Hole Conference in 1959 make full use of the construct of realism. As a profession, teacher education has a history of valuing realism. Most graduate programs require students to take one or more courses in research methodology that stress empirical research. In the education profession, only recently has qualitative research received serious attention, but this practice is now growing rapidly. A review of a decade of copies of *The Journal of Educational Research* (Shank & Villella, 2004) found that during the first seven years an average of one qualitative article appeared in each year, but over the next three years the number of qualitative articles averaged one article per issue.

Pragmatism. Although Americans Charles Pierce and William James contributed so much to this construct that it is often considered to be American, pragmatism originated in Europe. German philosopher Immanuel Kant and English philosopher Sir Francis Bacon were major contributors to this theory. The term pragmatism, coined by Immanuel Kant, means practicality. Pragmatists believe in learner-centered curricula. They view the world as ever-changing and the role of the schools to prepare students for this changing world. The student-centered progressive curriculum of the 1920s, 1930s, and 1940s reflected pragmatism.

Existentialism. Existentialists do not believe in life after death, nor do they believe in a Supreme Being. Therefore, existentialists espouse the idea that we should live for today: Enjoy life because when it's over, it's over. They also believe that every individual is responsible for the choices he or she makes in life; there is no such thing as fate for an existentialist.

Curricula reflecting the existentialist perspective are permissive. French philosopher Jean Jacques Rousseau exhibited many existentialist qualities. Rousseau considered himself wild and free; he even gave away his own children so he could be free to roam the countryside. Rousseau was fired from one job after another. After holding the job of tutor of a small boy and girl for a year, Rousseau wrote a book to serve as a guide for educating children. For two centuries, this was the most widely read book on education. The book was titled *Émile*, after the boy's name. Existentialists believe that curricula should offer freedom and that education should be natural. The schools should ensure that society does not corrupt children.

Essentialism. Essentialists believe the curriculum should contain the content needed to prepare students for life. Essentialists are much more concerned with content than with how the content is taught or learned. The Progressive Education Movement, a highly learner-centered program, was lauded by those who supported it, and yet it was vigorously condemned by its critics, many of whom mistakenly labeled it as a permissive program. The critics said that the curriculum had become soft. Reacting critically to the Progressive Education Movement, critic William Bagley started a curriculum to make sure that the schools' curricula contained those subjects that are essential for life. Later, these subjects became known as the basics. They included history and the Three Rs (reading, writing, and arithmetic).

Perennialism. Perennialists would argue that some subjects never cease to be important. These perennial subjects include the classics. Perennialists believe that by reading the classics, students will learn how to think. Mortimer Adler, author of one of the education reform reports of the 1980s (The Paideia Proposal), is considered a teacher in this field of philosophy. American education is rooted in perennialism. Its first curricula were steeped in the classics. Latin has doggedly held its place in the curriculum over the years and is still an important part of the curriculum in many secondary schools.

Reconstructionism. Reconstructionists believe that society has lost its way and that the schools are responsible for producing leaders who will correct the undesirable conditions of society. Reconstructionists believe that the schools should empower students to change society. One of the better known reconstructionists is George S. Counts (1932), who wrote a book titled *Dare the Schools Build a New Social Order?*. Unlike revolutionists, who believe that the only way to improve society is to destroy the existing society, the reconstructionists do not recommend such destruction as a solution. On the other hand, they were very intolerant of the Progressive Education Movement because they thought it lacked rigor.

Contemporary educators' reactions to education reform efforts—influenced by their philosophical constructs—will be determined to a large extent by their degree of commitment to improving society. Some teachers embrace reform, seeing it as an unprecedented opportunity to improve the learning opportunities for students; others view education reform as the efforts of legislators and state department officers to make a positive showing to their constituents.

A comparison of these philosophical constructs is shown in Table 6.1 on the following page.

Most educators can see positive features in several of these philosophical schools of thought. Often teachers become eclectics and selectively agree with all or many of them; however, by forcing themselves to choose one or two of these positions over the others, educators can clarify their beliefs. By more clearly understanding their own philosophical beliefs, educators improve their ability to construct sound curricula that will lead all students toward fulfillment of the school's mission. Supervisors can help teachers by involving them in discussions of their own philosophical beliefs and by encouraging them to write a philosophical statement about their beliefs. The process of actually writing an individual philosophy statement can bring clarity to educators' beliefs, attitudes, and feelings. You can use Table 6.1 to help teachers identify their positions by asking them to limit their choices to only one or two philosophical constructs.

Using Technology to Motivate

One way to offset the effect of narrow standards is to use technology to create a more visual classroom. Following are some suggestions for helping teachers create a visual classroom.

- *To help your teachers create a visual classroom, share the following example with your faculty.*

  When teaching a unit on democracy, John Harris downloaded and prominently displayed in his classroom a close-up photo of a big, fat turkey. This alone was enough to pique his students' interest, but John carried things a step further. Pointing at the photo of the "gobbler," he asked his class if anyone knew the derivation of the word "gobbledygook" and who might have nominated the turkey to serve as a symbol in our nation.

Table 6.1 A Comparison of Philosophical Constructs

Philosophical Construct	Essence	Implication
Metaphysics	The belief that all understanding comes through the five senses	Actual experiences to enable students to acquire new understandings
Epistemology	The study of the nature of knowledge	Activities tied to the ways in which most learning occurs
Axiology	The study of values	Opportunities to discuss such questions as What is good? What is right? What is valuable?
Idealism	The study of ideas	Allows students time to think, ponder, debate; promotes higher-level thinking
Realism	The belief that all understanding comes through the five senses	Problem-centered curricula
Pragmatism	The study of the practical	Problem-centered curricula
Existentialism	The belief that the present is all there is to life and that we are responsible for our life choices	Natural experiences; encouraging individual creativity, discovery, inventiveness
Essentialism	The belief that purpose of school is to prepare students for life	Teaching through experiences essential for life (basics)
Perennialism	The belief that some subjects will always be important (i.e., those subjects that prepare students to think)	Making the classics a prominent part of all curricula
Reconstructionism	The belief that the purpose of schools is to prepare students to change society	Teaching about social issues and change strategies

The nominator of the symbol, John said with a grin, is Benjamin Franklin. A Texas senator names Maury Maverick coined the term *gobbledygook* to describe Washington politicians who strutted around all puffed up, with their heads thrown back and their chests out, spouting a lot of wordy and generally unintelligible jargon—a lot like the gobbling turkey!

- *Help your faculty use visual-image-only presentations to review the major concepts in a unit of study, as in the example below.*

Keisha Thomas gave her classroom the assignment to prepare a PowerPoint visual summary presenting the current unit of study. Keisha told the class that the purpose of the exercise was to highlight the three most

> important concepts in the unit. Then Keisha separated her students into small groups. The first step was for the groups to identify the major concepts and agree among themselves about which three were most important. Each group was to go online to download images to represent its chosen concepts. Each group selected ten of the best images it retrieved to represent each concept it had chosen as most important, incorporating them into a PowerPoint presentation—with no words, only the images. Then each group presented its PowerPoint visual summary to the class, remaining speechless while the classmates identified the concepts represented by the symbolic images displayed in the group presentations.

Most teachers already know about the versatility and potential of PowerPoint Presentations, and in chapter 3 we discussed the popular Blackboard software. Recommend the use of Inspiration software or an online tool such as Gliffy to diagram concepts or storyboard (www.gliffy.com). A large variety of presentation media is offered at www.thumbtacks.com.

Another use of technology that your teachers will find motivating is in *lesson study* (discussed later in the chapter).

Constructivism in the Curriculum

As mentioned previously, constructivists believe that understanding results from relating newly acquired information with previously developed understandings. It is both a theory of how students learn and how teachers should arrange learning experiences. By now you should be aware that constructivists believe that developing understanding requires creating new knowledge and that it occurs best in a threat-free climate where students discover new insights through solving problems.

The roots of constructivism run deep in the history of education and curriculum. As early as the seventeenth century, British philosopher and educator John Locke urged teachers to acknowledge the role that experience plays in learning. According to Locke, at birth the mind is a *tabula rasa,* or blank slate, that is filled solely through experience. By the mid-to-late nineteenth century, several European educators including Froebel, Pestalozzi, and Herbart began developing school curricula that reflected Locke's call for experience-based or activities-centered curricula.

Near the turn of the twentieth century, Col. Francis Parker returned from visiting European schools and began developing programs to implement many activities-centered (or experiential) curricula. John Dewey endorsed this type of curriculum and used the concept as a basis for the Progressive Education Movement from the 1920s to the 1940s. Dewey furthered this philosophy by saying that *we learn by doing*.

Cognitive studies have supported the involvement of the learner in learning. Albert Einstein's identification of the concept as the most important variable in learning (see chapter 8) gave additional credence to learner-centered education. By mid-century, cognitive psychologists believed that understanding any discipline requires the learner to identify and understand the major concepts in that discipline. Let's consider the logic behind this history of support for learner-involved education.

First, consider that the world is full of information. The particular portion of that information that is *chosen* for inclusion into the curriculum is called *content*. The intent of educators is that students will come to understand this content; therefore, teachers plan the types of activities that they hope will enable their students to interpret meaning from the lesson content.

As all teachers know, in a typical class some students will master practically all of the content included in the curriculum, while others will master little or none of the content. Stimulus-response psychologists of the early 1900s attributed learning and failure to learn largely to the learner's innate cognitive ability (i.e., the learner's level of intelligence). But studies of the late 1900s have revealed that earlier understandings of intelligence were much too narrow (Gardner, 2003). We now know that by identifying additional variables that affect learning, teachers can improve the design of classroom instruction.

One major variable that affects learning is *attention*. Noticing, being aware of, or attending to content is a prerequisite to learning that content. The awareness of the role that attention plays in learning has led to designing methodology to gain students' attention and help them focus on the content selected for studying. An example of this improved methodology is the study and use of advance organizers (discussed in chapter 9).

A variable that highly influences attention is *perception*, and individuals vary in the degree to which they perceive events worthy of their attention. The idea of a perceptual screen can be used to help others understand why some people consider an event worth remembering while others seem to ignore it. Figure 6.2 represents two individuals' varying perceptions. Notice that, at least

It Works for Me!

Breaking Logjams

Douglas M. DeWitt, Salisbury University

As a high school principal, a number of years ago I was charged with planning and implementing a major state-mandated curriculum change. There was considerable opposition and resistance by much of the faculty. We ended up in a site curriculum council, going around and around in our arguments about whether or not the state should be mandating these changes. We were going nowhere and getting there fast.

To break the logjam, I posed the question regarding whether the essence of the changes would be good for our students. After much discussion, we came to a consensus that yes, in fact, most of these changes would be beneficial for our students. At that point, it was a whole new ball game. We began problem solving and discussing *how* we would make the changes and not *if* we would make the changes. It all started with finding common ground and building a consensus that was agreeable to everyone. Once we accomplished that, the planning became the focus and we got the job done.

for the moment, the individual shown in Figure 6.2b is more open to learning than the individual shown in Figure 6.2a.

Figure 6.2 Perceptions Affecting Individuals' Acceptance of New Information

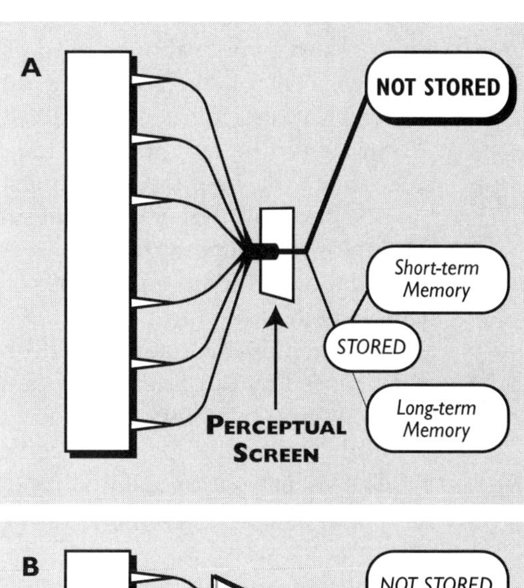

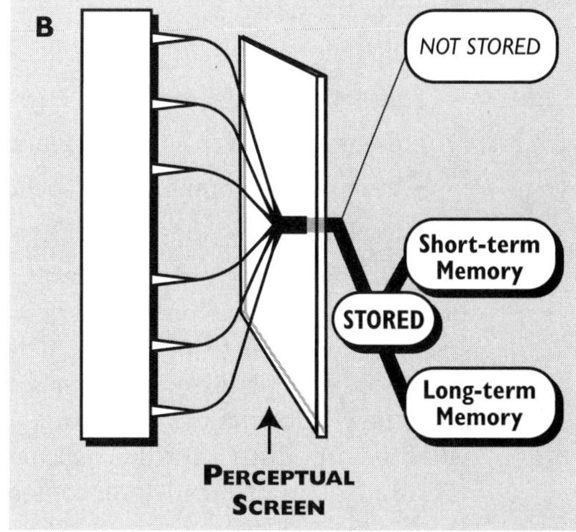

Some individuals' perceptual screens are more open than others'. Individual A is not at all open to receiving this content at this time. Individual B is slightly open to focusing on this content. The more narrow opening for individual A may result from a lack of previously acquired knowledge, without which this individual cannot relate this new information. This limitation is obvious, for example, when two individuals are watching the world news and the name of a foreign country or city is mentioned. Suppose that one individual has traveled to and perhaps even lived there for a few weeks, months, or years. This previous experience makes that individual aware of and receptive to this new information. In contrast, the other individual who has never visited the area may completely ignore this segment of the news. This idea of *selective perception* is widely accepted.

In addition to prior knowledge, emotional attachments also can have an impact on attention. Phenomenologists tell us that how much and how well we attend to information are affected by our emotional attachment to the information. To continue the televised news example above, suppose this news involves a serious train or plane accident. If someone has a close relative in this geographic area, the individual may give undivided attention to this news.

Selecting Curriculum Content and Activities

Each teacher has responsibility for curriculum content selection. Most states require teachers to cover some particular topics. When responding to a national survey only about a third (36%) of the teachers reported that they have complete control over selecting the content and topics they teach in their classes (National Center for Education Statistics, 1995, p. 14). The question, "What should be taught?" and the even more relevant question, "What must be learned?" deserve top priority in every school.

The curriculum development process in American schools is much like the settling of sediment in the oceans, resulting in a gradual buildup of accretion. A similar accumulative process works on textbooks, which through the years have remained the most powerful curriculum determiners. As new standards and requirements are added, all curricula periodically need to be reevaluated and cleansed by purging or stripping away the buildup of "nice" but unnecessary content. The ability to rid curricula of unnecessary content is as valuable as the ability to select pertinent content.

The supervisor frequently has opportunities to affect teachers' selection of content. At the very least, the supervisor should appeal to teachers to consider

- the known information or the knowledge pool from which the teacher can choose;
- society's needs, including current trends and perceived future needs;
- the needs and interests of learners;
- human development, the social worth of education; and
- the major concepts in each lesson.

The knowledge pool available to teachers continues to grow. Teachers should work to develop two types of knowledge pools: one in their content area and the other in pedagogy. The content-knowledge pool should include the major concepts in the teacher's discipline. To encourage students to internalize new information, constructivist teachers do not share this information with students until after their students have expressed their own conceptualizations. You will recall that constructivist teachers share their own understandings of concepts only after they inquire about students' understandings of those concepts. For example, an English teacher (or for that matter, a history, science, or social studies teacher) who has given a written assignment may find it difficult to refrain from correcting spelling, punctuation, or subject-verb agreement errors. But the constructivist knows that the student should be encouraged to express the major concepts in the lesson before being distracted by grammatical errors.

When selecting content for their curriculum, teachers should always consider society's needs. For example, consider the science instructor who is teaching Newton's laws of motion. This part of the curriculum provides an excellent opportunity to teach the danger that speed introduces to driving. Several years ago, when the national speed limit was lowered to save gasoline, some people

It Works for Me!

A Time to Play

Beverly Findley, Eastern Illinois University

Give staff time to "play" together. Have pitch-in lunches or other activities in the staff lounge. When staff can play together, they work together much more easily. The idea of sharing ideas and brainstorming with those whose company they enjoy becomes a natural progression of the fun event.

were shocked to learn that this legislation reduced the number of automobile accident fatalities by half. Had the curriculum been functioning correctly, this news would have come as no surprise. Anyone who lives near or travels on an interstate highway can see that our curricula are shortchanging today's youth. Those who read the statistics on lung cancer and cancer of the mouth and throat can identify another area in which our curricula are failing to meet the needs of society. Teachers should always consider students' interests as well as their needs when selecting content for their curricula. Some content should be included just because students find it interesting.

Helping Teachers Select Activities

Supervisors can help teachers by arranging workshops in which teachers can collaborate to identify social conditions and student characteristics that they consider important enough to use in selecting content. A good place to begin is with the course objectives. Many teachers will benefit from help in identifying the broad content generalizations that must be mastered in order to achieve the objectives in each course. Then they can select activities that will help their students meet these objectives. When selecting content, constructivist teachers know that the degree to which students come to understand a topic depends on the opportunities they have to tie the new information to previously developed understandings.

Generally, contemporary teachers are more aware of the value of using learner activities than were their predecessors; however, this awareness may result from their contact with "hands-on" curricula through one-day workshops. This means that many teachers may fail to see the relationships between the activities and the concepts. Thus, the supervisor's role may focus on helping teachers learn to select activities that identify these relationships for their students. Chapters 8 and 9 introduce several teaching/learning strategies ranging from direct instruction (which is heavily teacher dominated and textbook based) to inquiry learning and simulation gaming (which are heavily student oriented). As former teachers, most supervisors know that all students enjoy hands-on activities and that many low-achieving students can learn only from such activities.

Using Tyler's Ends-Means Model, curriculum planning should begin with identifying desired outcomes or valued outcomes. Box 6.2 is a list of valued outcomes for one state. Note that this state has six broad goals and that in order to be brief only three valued outcomes are listed for each goal. Note, also, that each stated valued outcome connotes action or student performance.

Box 6.2 A List of Valued Outcomes for Six Learning Goals

Goal 1—Basic Communication and Math Skills

1. **Accessing Sources of Information and Ideas:** Students use research tools to locate the source of information and ideas relevant to a specific need or problem.
2. **Reading:** Students construct meaning from a variety of print materials for a variety of purposes through reading.
3. **Observing:** Students construct meaning from messages communicated in a variety of ways for a variety of purposes through observing.

Goal 2—Core Concepts and Principles

1. **Nature of Scientific Activity:** Students use appropriate and relevant scientific skills to solve specific problems in real-life situations.
2. **Mathematical Procedures:** Students demonstrate understanding of concepts related to mathematical procedures.
3. **Aesthetics:** Students appreciate creativity and the values of the arts and the humanities.

Goal 3—Self-Sufficiency

1. **Positive Self-Concept:** Students demonstrate positive growth in self-concept through appropriate tasks or projects.
2. **Healthy Lifestyle:** Students demonstrate the ability to maintain a healthy lifestyle.
3. **Adaptability and Flexibility:** Students demonstrate the ability to be adaptable and flexible through appropriate tasks or projects.

Goal 4—Responsible Group Membership

1. **Interpersonal Skills:** Students effectively use interpersonal skills.
2. **Productive Team Membership:** Students use productive team members skills.
3. **Consistent, Responsive, and Caring Behavior:** Students individually demonstrate consistent, responsive, and caring behavior.

Goal 5—Thinking and Problem-Solving

1. **Critical Thinking:** Students use critical thinking skills in a variety of situations that will be encountered in life.
2. **Creative Thinking:** Students use creative thinking skills to develop or invent novel, constructive ideas or products.
3. **Conceptualizing:** Students create and modify their understanding of a concept through organizing information.

The sample list of valued outcomes in Box 6.2 includes creative thinking. Louis Wildman (2006a) gives this goal high priority when he emphasizes that schools have a responsibility for developing the unique talents and abilities of each student. Whatever the valued learner outcomes a teacher and students select for the class, a corresponding learner activity should be planned. As explained later in chapter 8, a one-to-one relationship between objective and learner activities is not necessary. The use of some *multipurpose activities* (activities that lead to the attainment of several objectives) is preferred. Supervisors might choose to ask their teachers to peruse the valued outcomes listed in Box 6.2 and, for each outcome, see if they can think of an activity that would lead students to reach the outcome—preferably including some multipurpose activities.

Collaborative Planning through Lesson Study

For many years elementary teachers in Japan have used a process called lesson study to combine lesson planning and cooperative development (Marble, 2006). *Lesson study* is a theoretically based approach to improving teaching through careful observation of each other's lessons and reflection on the lessons' successes and shortcomings (Shimahra, 2002). Wiburg and Brown (2006) define lesson planning as "a collaborative process in which teachers devise a research lesson, teach and observe the lesson, and then revise and reteach the lesson in an interactive cycle of professional learning" (pp. 1–2). Murata, Lewis, & Perry (2004) describe lesson study as "an interactive process of resource development and professional capacity development" (p. 7). Lewis (2000) offers five suggestions for using lesson study: (1) ask others to observe the lessons, (2) plan the lessons over a long period of time, (3) design each lesson to bring a "vision of life" into it, (4), record each lesson, and (5) discuss the lessons.

Technology makes lesson study possible even across geographically diverse areas. For example, in the Math Star project teachers throughout the state of New Mexico received a grant that provided them with 100 laptop computers. They used these computers to collaborate about lesson study. These teachers participated in two lesson study cycles ("through Web chats, e-mail, and VideoCapture software to communicate what students were learning in their classrooms") and presented their findings at an annual lesson study conference (Wiburg & Brown, 2006, p. 7)

Curriculum Components

Curriculum components are qualities and parts of a curriculum that can be used to plan, evaluate, and implement the curriculum. Supervisors can work with their faculty to adjust the curriculum by using the curriculum components of balance, scope, sequence, continuity, and articulation. Below we discuss ways in which each component can be used to improve a school's curriculum.

Balance

Placing somewhat equal emphasis on different aspects of a school's offerings is known as *curriculum balance*. It can be viewed from several perspectives. For example, the school's curriculum should offer an array of tracks, including vocational, technical, business, and college preparatory. If the curriculum is predominately business, or vocational, or college preparatory, it lacks balance. Similarly, if a school's curriculum offerings are composed almost entirely of science courses or practically all arts courses, it is said to lack balance. A curriculum should maintain a balance between curricular and cocurricular activities.

The concept of curriculum balance can also be applied to an individual student's program. Each program should maintain a balance among several disciplines including language arts, physical sciences, social sciences, mathematics, and fine arts. A major criticism made toward several of the education reform reports is their overemphasis on science and mathematics. Supervisors can alert teachers to imbalances in their curricula.

Curriculum balance can also be viewed from the perspective of options or electives. At times, curricula have become too liberal in letting students choose their courses. At other times, curricula have been designed without any electives. Although offering students choices helps uphold the level of motivation, giving too may choices weakens the program. Curricula that offer students too many electives or leave little or no room for the students to select courses suffer from a lack of balance.

In recent years, American schools have received considerable criticism for failing to promote higher-order thinking and for failing to prepare students to apply information learned in their classes to solve practical problems. Certainly, contemporary curriculum planners should make a special effort to ensure that curriculum objectives, activities, and evaluations maintain a balance among the various levels of the cognitive domain. As mentioned earlier, another criticism aimed at the schools is failure to instill morals and values. Each learning/teaching unit and perhaps even each lesson should contain a balance of objectives among the three domains of the taxonomies: affective, cognitive, and psychomotor (see chapter 8).

Pawlas and Oliva (2008, p. 289) list some important aspects of a curriculum that require balancing:

- There must be a balance between general education and specialized education.
- There must be a balance between the academic and the vocational aspects of the curriculum.
- There must be a balance between content aimed at the immediate and long-range needs of learners.
- There must be a balance between the child-centered approach and the subject-centered approach to curriculum.

Scope

Because of pressures inside the school, pressure outside the school, or the teacher's own preferences, the *scope* (or breadth) of curriculum becomes very narrow at times. Currently, several education reform reports call for more sciences and mathematics (at the expense of eliminating the fine arts). Should educators yield to these demands, the curriculum would lose its breadth.

Scope can also be used to describe an individual student's curriculum. Given the choice, most students would eliminate some subjects from their curriculum. Counselors and advisors guard to ensure that both the school's curriculum and each student's curriculum maintain adequate scope.

Sequence

The order in which various objectives, content, and activities are taken is referred to as *curriculum sequence*. Cognitive psychologists are sensitive to curriculum sequence because they know that certain content must be understood before the student can comprehend more advanced ideas.

Two guidelines can be used to sequence the curriculum. First, the curriculum planner can examine the content to see if there is a natural process involved (e.g., rainfall produces runoff, which in turn produces evaporation and later condensation.) A second guideline involves the relative complexity of the material (e.g., the memorization of multiplication facilitates solving complicated division problems; elementary students must learn their ABCs before learning to spell words or write letters.)

Margaret Hammer and Barbara Polnick (2007) suggest having students create their own scope-and-sequence document, assigning each student a grade level. When it is completed, each student will explain the document to the rest of the class. The presentations will be ordered from lowest to highest grade so that students can see that each grade level builds on the others and that their contributions are important preparation for the grade levels that follow.

Continuity

The absence of disruptions, when the curriculum is viewed vertically, is called *curriculum continuity.* For example, fourth-grade teachers depend on the third-grade teachers to have covered certain "third-grade" topics that are needed to progress in the fourth grade. A break in continuity can lead to misunderstanding, confusion, and frustration. McNamee and Chen (2005) say that teachers can improve the continuity in their classes by using assessments *for* learning (as opposed to assessments *of* learning, which provide little or no help in curriculum development). Assessments for learning help by listing the important concepts in a unit, and by letting students track their own progress in mastering these concepts.

Articulation

The horizontal dimension of curricula (or the smoothness across the curriculum) is called *curriculum articulation*. Constructivists encourage the use of broad themes that run across the curriculum and, indeed, even across individual subjects. These themes provide for smooth articulation among the disciplines. The curriculum and understanding are both enriched when students can apply concepts learned in one class to increase their understanding in another. *Block scheduling,* or the use of long class periods (such as double periods), is being used to tie subjects together and improve articulation.

Developing a New Type of Curriculum

This cursory view of curriculum development has taken a look at practices of the past, some of which continue to exist in many schools. But the future demands new types of curricula, and the future begins now.

In preparing teachers to develop new types of curricula, teacher education colleges must provide a role model for curriculum development. The nature of future pre-K–12 curricula and teacher-education college curricula has yet to be determined. Yet, much is known about the type of curriculum that is needed in the twenty-first century. According to James Comer (2005), "Generations of teachers, administrators, and policymakers have been prepared in ways that do not enable them to create a school culture that can support student development and learning, to say nothing of their own learning and that of a school's other stakeholders" (p. 763). Many educators agree with this author's perception—in fact, some question that a curriculum that meets the needs of the future can even be developed, at least not without a new type of believing.

Curriculum development must be radical. It must prepare teachers and students to do different kinds of things that require different knowledge and skills. Perhaps an even greater challenge is the need for a curriculum that prepares people to think in different ways. The emphasis here is on the uniqueness of each student.

The twenty-first century curriculum must be developed cooperatively by all members of the learning community and should address real, community-based problems. Your teachers should prepare students to cooperate with others. Small-group instruction and cooperative learning methods are needed as part of the curriculum. Problem solving, defined as "what you do when you don't know what to do (Martinez, 2006, p. 697), must also play a part (Stine, 2010). Simulations and the case-study method are ways to prepare students for making decisions and solving problems that will impact them both in the classroom and in the greater community. Supervisors can help teachers develop the skills they need to prepare students for problem solving by arranging opportunities for teachers to collaborate on problem solving themselves.

Demographic changes intensify the need for skills to teach ESL (English as a second language) students and students with special challenges. What once were specialized professional skills are now core professional skills. Supervisors should work with teachers to effectively integrate individual education programs (IEPs) for students with special needs with the regular education curriculum (Weishaar et al., 2007).

To ensure commitment to all these goals and aspirations, supervisors should begin by leading groups of teachers to identify improvements that they would like to see in their school's curriculum. Initially, these groups could be content or discipline specific, but eventually they should be integrated groups—where math teachers work with English or history teachers, and so on. Working together, teachers should address problems in all of the curriculum components previously discussed.

Glickman et al. (2007) offer some final words of wisdom:

> Large-scale teacher-driven changes in curriculum content, organization, and format will not take place unless teachers change their curriculum orientations or beliefs about the purpose of curriculum. Yet, teachers are not likely to change their orientations unless their levels of understanding of and involvement in curriculum development gradually increase. Supervisor openness and trust building, staff development in curriculum design, and time, support, and rewards for teacher involvement can all foster teacher *and* curriculum development. (p. 394)

Conclusion

Curriculum is a term with many meanings, depending on who is defining it. Through the years, the meaning of curriculum has changed from that of a racecourse to that of a program (or content, plus activities, objectives, and evaluation). Some major differences in definitions of curriculum include means versus ends, content versus experiences, and process versus document (plan). Understanding curriculum foundations is essential for effective curriculum development. By writing their own educational philosophies, teachers can clarify and improve their understanding of their own views about such issues as the purpose of schools, the nature of learning, and the nature of youth. Teachers can build the curriculum by knowing about the history of education, By understanding social foundations, teachers design curricula to improve the community and society at large.

Understanding several philosophical constructs can enable teachers and supervisors to improve their curriculum planning, including metaphysics, epistemology, idealism, realism, existentialism, essentialism, perennialism, reconstructionism, and axiology.

Curriculum components such as articulation, balance, scope, and sequence can be used to improve either the school's curriculum or an individual student's personal curriculum. *Articulation* is the flow or absence of disruptions across the curriculum. *Sequence* is the flow or absence of disruptions through the vertical curriculum or through time. *Balance* refers to curriculum tracks, subjects, disciplines, curricular vs. cocurricular activities and a variety of other qualities. *Scope* is the breadth or horizontal dimension of the curriculum.

Supervisors can help by arranging work sessions where teachers identify areas in their curriculum that they want to change, by keeping the objectives of the projects before the teachers, and by arranging for the various disciplines to merge their work. Once the disciplines are merged, the supervisor can help teachers check for weaknesses in the many components discussed in this chapter.

Questions for Discussion and Reflection

1. Can a curriculum have good continuity without good sequence and vice versa? Why or why not?
2. In what ways is education reform affecting curriculum balance? Articulation?
3. Why are teachers encouraged to write their educational philosophies?
4. What advantages and disadvantages can you see in block scheduling?
5. What is the most important characteristics in your personal definition of curriculum? Explain your answer.
6. How can you use your most important curriculum characteristic to improve curricula?
7. How can you help a school save its arts program?
8. What are your thoughts about constructivism? How would you respond to a teacher who says that all teachers are constructivists?
9. Which two philosophical constructs do you consider to be the most important, and why?
10. How can you use your selected philosophical constructs to improve curricula?
11. In what ways have you seen curricula get out of balance?
12. What arguments can you give in support of electives? In challenging the offering of electives?
13. What are some major responsibilities of first-year teachers for which teacher education programs fail to prepare them?
14. How can you help community members accept the concept and use of valued outcomes?
15. What is the greatest strength that you bring to curriculum development?

Suggested Activities

1. Interview a local school counselor. Ask this counselor to identify and discuss two or three features in the school's curriculum that affect students positively and two or three features that affect students negatively.
2. With the permission of the principal of a local elementary or secondary school, ask the counselor to assist you in evaluating the school's curriculum to determine whether it has proper: (a) articulation, (b) balance, and (c) scope. Write a paragraph or two about each.
3. With the help of a local school counselor, design a plan to make the school's curriculum more humane to students.
4. Interview a local art teacher. Ask this teacher to help you develop a rationale statement to be used to support the retention of the arts program during times of financial cutbacks.
5. Interview a district curriculum director or assistant or associate superintendent for curriculum. Ask this person to identify major current concerns and to discuss how each is being addressed. Try to identify philosophical constructs represented in these actions.

Chapter 7

Evaluating the Curriculum

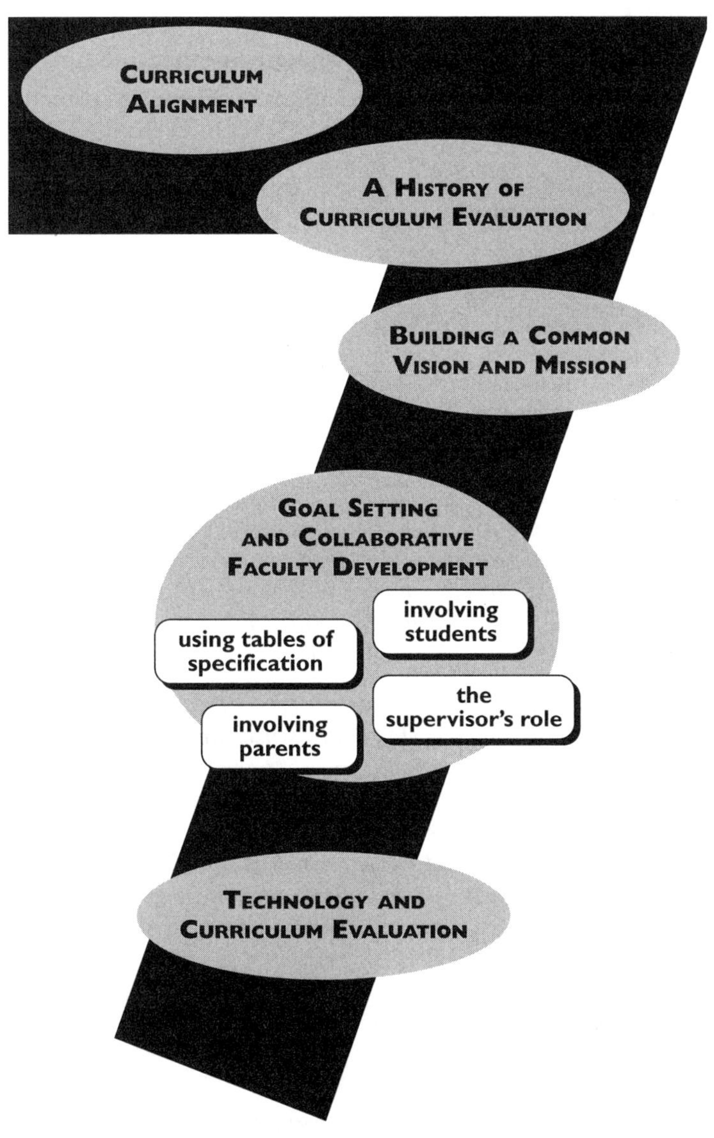

> *To change the curriculum is to fiddle with important matters in American culture.*
>
> —L. Cuban, *Teachers and machines*

Objectives

After completion of this chapter, you should be able to

1. Name some purposes of curriculum evaluation and identify those you consider most important
2. Discuss the supervisor's role in curriculum evaluation
3. Explain the inextricable connection between curriculum evaluation and faculty development
4. Describe your school's curriculum evaluation program

*The Team-Teaching Family**

Model School is a nursery-through-grade-12 laboratory school located on the campus of a large state university. Model received its name from its mission, which includes modeling new instruction and methodology that reflects the state's education reform program. Each time the state reform program introduces a new practice, Model School immediately implements the practice, serving as a model to other schools that may wish to send representatives to see the practices in action.

Three qualities make Model School unique and special: the administrators, the teachers, and the parents. The faculty and staff at this school are constantly reading professional literature, attending professional meetings, giving professional presentations, and writing professional journal articles and books. Through these activities they stay abreast of the most current state, national, and international developments. Somehow these administrators and faculty members also find time to write grant proposals. These proposals make possible the development and implementation of new programs that otherwise would not be available to the students who attend this school. This high level of professional involvement of the Model administrators and faculty members has brought many changes to the school's curriculum. An example of the uniqueness of this curriculum is the school's "alternative curriculum."

*Appreciation is given to Dr. Bruce Bonar and Ms. Jackie Vance, former director and assistant director of Model Laboratory School (respectively), for the time and expertise they contributed to this case study in particular, and to this chapter in general.

The high levels of involvement in professional activities have also resulted in major changes in the faculty and staff that are not so obvious to the outsider. But those who work closely with this school see changes in the thinking and behavior of this faculty and staff that are equal to if not greater in magnitude than the changes brought to the curriculum. Perhaps a visit inside this school would reveal the depth of changes that are occurring daily. Today, we are going to review only one of the many innovative programs at this school, a program that has developed as a direct result of a schoolwide evaluation of the school's curriculum. The teachers we will visit are part of the middle-level faculty.

Two and a half years ago, when the entire school was in the middle of a curriculum evaluation process, a couple of the middle-level teachers let this discussion stray off on a tangent to the planned topic for the meeting. Each of these teachers learned that the others were interested in "team teaching." The teachers became excited, and they infected their peers with their enthusiasm as they discussed the values of teaming. Sensing the level of energy that was being generated over this discussion, the administrators made a conscious decision not to even try to bring the conversation back on target. In a discussion two years later, one of the administrators made these comments:

> *Too often, faculty development has been conducted by the local administration or at the district or state level. Too often, attempts at faculty development have treated teachers as though they are at the awareness stage when in fact the teachers are at the refinement stage. It occurred to us that these teachers had advanced to the refinement stage, so we decided to give them a lot of support and a minimum of direction. The leadership we would give would be a collegial support for the ideas being generated.*
>
> *New curriculum, or for that matter any new practices, cannot be integrated into an existing curriculum until the philosophies of the faculty have melded with the philosophies of the administrators. We knew that we had to have faith in these teachers if we were to give the level of support that was required; yet, at that time they had not asked for any support at all.*

The merging of individual philosophies cannot be forced, but it can be encouraged by recognizing individuals' strengths and accomplishments. Once this blending occurs, a type of generator is formed and the administrators can step back and let the teachers take charge. In fact, once the faculty members realize that they have gained the confidence and respect of their administrators, faculty members who are professionally involved at a high level will unconsciously take charge.

At this point, something highly predictable and very important occurs: The faculty members begin to examine and understand their own strengths. This realization is a prerequisite for the forming of an effective curriculum development team, a restructuring team, or a learning community. As this discussion progressed, it became obvious that these middle-level teachers were becoming increasingly committed to the concept of team teaching. During this meeting some decisions were made, and some teams were formed. Two and a half years later, these teachers are still teaming.

Since that initial meeting, news of the success of these teams has spread and, without being recruited, a few high school teachers have joined the group, each teaming with a middle-level teacher. When asked about the longevity of this group, an administrator replied,

> *I think that the success of the team teaching group can be attributed, at least in part, to the group's tight organization. This team has always met regularly. It still meets every Wednesday afternoon at 3:15. There is an agenda for almost every meeting. The agenda is specific. For example, "Today, Mr. Rhodes will. . . ."*
>
> *Even if there is no topic set for a meeting, an announcement is sent before the meeting that says that there is no preset agenda for the coming meeting. So there are four vital parts to the structure of these meetings: (1) A reminder sent every Tuesday, (2) an agenda statement for every meeting, (3) a meeting held every Wednesday at 3:15, and (4) a report of minutes sent every Friday.*
>
> *The meetings serve two major purposes: They provide a forum for individuals to share their opinions and they deal with curriculum issues, student issues, and day-to-day operational issues. The only way that I can describe this group is to say that it has become a middle-school family.*

Reflection

Getting a glimpse of the inside of this school changes observers, causing them to ask many questions. Sometimes these questions are literally raised by the observers, and at other times they surface in the observers' minds. Why has this team-teaching project been successful when in other schools attempts to innovate frequently fail? How should consideration for teachers' levels of development affect the degree and type of supervision they need? Do teachers eventually reach a level of professionalism that doesn't require any supervision? Under what conditions does the "more is less" rule apply to supervision of the curriculum evaluation process? What factors should determine teachers' levels of involvement in schoolwide curriculum evaluation? Should all teachers be involved? Why must supervisors support teachers' individual projects and goals? Let's explore the answers to some of these questions.

Introduction

The school curriculum purports to affect society. As all twenty-first-century educators know, society also shapes the curriculum. Hall (2006), who has used the term *treacherous terrain of politics*, reminds educators that "Politics is always a major factor in key decisions at every level of the school system; for most of us, political maneuvering can be a make-or-break game" (p. 525). Society is always changing and, as seen in chapter 6, the curriculum must change accordingly. It is this quality of curriculum that necessitates continuous evaluation.

Another cause for curriculum change is the constantly evolving nature of curriculum goals and objectives, because as these goals and objectives change, other elements of the curriculum must be adjusted or realigned to correspond to these purposes (Warner, 2010).

Alignment has been called the linchpin of standards-based reform (Herman & Baker, 2005). This chapter explains to supervisors how tables of specifications can be used to align and evaluate the sequence of the many parts of the curriculum. A *table of specifications* (discussed in more detail later in the chapter) is a chart designed to ensure coverage of varying levels of desired objectives, knowledge, and skills. It is a useful tool for aligning the curriculum objectives and evaluations with state and national standards. As explained by Guskey (2005a), a table of specification serves two important functions:

> First, it adds precision and clarity to teaching (by helping teachers break down standards into meaningful components). Second, a table of specifications serves as a guide for consistency among standards, the steps needed to help students attain them, and procedures for checking on students' learning progress. (p. 34)

Education reform has focused educators' attention on the mission and goals of the school. This chapter offers supervisors tips on including faculty members in the goal-setting process and, in turn, fulfilling the school's mission through collaborative faculty development. Staying current, and serving the school's ever-changing mission and the state and nation's changing standards and goals, requires continuous curriculum evaluation. Hanushek (1994) explains,

> That schools should regularly evaluate the achievements of school programs seems obvious. Yet, schools have seldom made any serious effort to assess the performance of either existing programs or major innovations. This failure poses fundamental problems for performance improvements in general. How can schools hope to improve systematically without ascertaining what is and not currently working? (p. 125)

Curriculum evaluation is certainly one of the most misunderstood concepts in education. A confusing factor about curriculum evaluation is its relationship to instructional evaluation. Though often used interchangeably, these terms have different meanings. Yet, the two terms are intertwined because the purpose of instruction is to deliver the curriculum. Measuring the effects of instruction is one part or subset of curriculum evaluation. The relationship between curriculum evaluation and instructional evaluation is shown in Figure 7.1.

Figure 7.1 The Relationship between Curriculum Evaluation and Instructional Evaluation

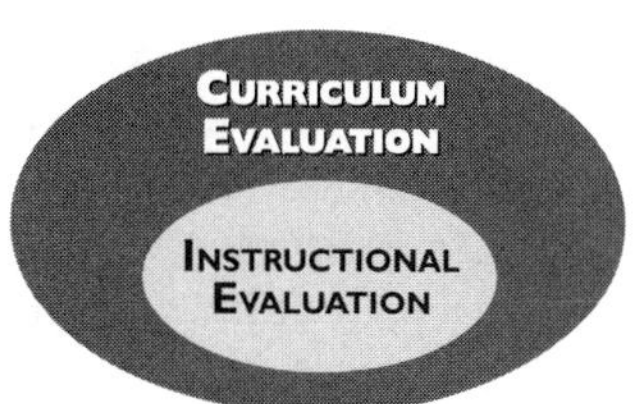

As shown in the Venn Diagram, instructional evaluation is a part of curriculum evaluation because it is an evaluation of the performance of the engine that drives the curriculum. But evaluating instruction is only one of many ways to evaluate the curriculum. One type of curriculum evaluation is *product evaluation* (i.e., evaluating the end results, or product, of the curriculum). An example of product

It Works for Me!

Curriculum Evaluation Walkthroughs

Dean Halverson, Western Illinois University

Incorporating required walkthroughs for students in your supervision classes greatly enhances their awareness of varied teaching styles and procedures. Most teachers are unaware of what is happening in other classes and come to class "amazed" at the variations they observe in others' classrooms. I have them begin with three- to five-minute observations in at least eight classrooms, with no note taking during the observations. Afterwards they write a one-page reflection on what they learned in the process.

As the semester progresses, the students select from a variety of formats for their walkthroughs. We then discuss the role of walkthroughs as a tool for use in teacher supervision. Student evaluations of the class indicate that this is one of the best learning experiences in the entire educational leadership program.

evaluation is the standardized tests commonly used by education reformers to determine the effectiveness of both the school's curriculum and its instruction.

Another way to evaluate the curriculum is by analyzing the ongoing work or process of the curriculum. Such evaluation is called *process evaluation*. The vignette at the beginning of this chapter gives a good example of this type of evaluation. At the school depicted in this case, the entire faculty collaborated in examining the total school curriculum, and parents were sent questionnaires to prompt them to critique various qualities of the curriculum at their school. As shown in the vignette, curriculum development occurs best when teachers are free to identify and address weaknesses that interest them.

Curriculum Alignment

Interstate School Leaders Licensure Consortium (ISLLC) Educational Leadership Policy Standard No. 1 requires leaders to facilitate the development, articulation, implementation, and stewardship of a vision of learning that is shared and supported by the school community.

One good way of examining a curriculum is to begin with the school's mission statement. The *mission statement* spells out the purposes of the school. Since the function of the curriculum is to achieve the school's purposes, an excellent way to begin evaluating any curriculum is by reviewing the school's mission statement to see whether the curriculum is aligned with the school's mission. Because all states now require schools to meet standards, aligning the curriculum with the school's mission statement also involves aligning it with state and national standards.

Schools are not unique in spelling out their missions. Corporations, industries, churches, and professional societies all have mission statements. Preventing the extinction of rare animals might be an important part of a wildlife society's mission, for example. Most businesses have annual and quarterly evaluations to determine how successfully they have operated. Dividends and bonuses are frequently given as rewards when these institutions make good progress in achieving their mission. Profit is an essential part of every business corporation's mission, for without it a business cannot survive. Membership or service may be part of a church's or a professional society's mission. The "dividends" and "profits" of a school mission statement, of course, will be measured by other than monetary means.

Allen Warner (2010) says that curriculum alignment deals with the degree to which the formal curriculum (what we want to be learned) is actually implemented in the classroom (instruction) and is formally assessed. That is, do curriculum, instruction, and evaluation have some reasonably linear relationship with one another?

All schools have at least four types of curricula: (1) the written curriculum, (2) the taught curriculum, (3) the evaluated curriculum, and (4) the silent (or hidden) curriculum. By aligning all of these curricula to the school's mission, the planned curriculum becomes functional, the taught curriculum becomes a manifestation of the planned curriculum, and all four curricula become more realistic.

Another type of curriculum alignment is among the objectives, content, and activities. Such evaluation seeks to answer two questions: Is the content that is purposefully selected and taught the same content that is needed to meet the objectives? Do the activities planned for this lesson help achieve the lesson objectives? One way to check is to use a table of specifications (discussed later in the chapter).

Because the curriculum is the heartbeat of the school (the mechanism that enables the school to reach its goals) and because the curriculum is influenced daily by events that occur nationally, statewide, and locally, the curriculum is like a carburetor on a car; it must be periodically checked and fine-tuned, even when it is working well. Unfortunately, curriculum is also like a carburetor in that it can become dysfunctional, and when this happens the whole school becomes dysfunctional. Increasing the effectiveness of an existing curriculum requires a basic understanding of the way a curriculum operates. Since this book is concerned with taking the role of the instructional supervisor beyond the traditional role, the type of evaluation explored here also will go beyond the traditional, sporadic evaluations that have become synonymous with the concept of curriculum evaluation. The type of evaluation discussed in this chapter is needed to restructure a school and build an effective learning community.

A History of Curriculum Evaluation

Traditionally, the evaluation of school's curricula has been initiated by the district office or by the state department. More often than not, curriculum evaluation has lain dormant except during those times when schools prepared for accreditation-team visits. Because curriculum evaluation has not been a continuous process, and because most teachers have not played a major role in it, teachers have been neither knowledgeable about nor committed to curriculum evaluation. Perhaps it might be more accurate to say that many teachers have not given much thought to curriculum evaluation because they have been left out of the process. Consequently, when decisions have been made to change a curriculum, the teachers have not felt motivated to implement the revision. A worse, yet common, scenario has been districtwide discussions to implement a new type of curriculum without input from the teachers. Obviously, this leaves teachers feeling unable or even unwilling to implement the new programs. So, the way that curriculum evaluation has been practiced has been flawed, often starting at the wrong place, involving teachers at the wrong time or not at all, and occurring sporadically.

Curriculum evaluation should begin in the minds of the administrators and teachers. With the school's mission in mind, the administrators must lead teachers to examine their personal philosophies about the purposes of school, the nature of learning, and the respective roles that teachers, students, and administrators should play in learning.

Administrators must realize that they set the tone for curriculum evaluation. Unless the school faculty is extremely progressive (and, to be sure, some faculties are), significant curriculum evaluation is unlikely to occur. Someone (or a designated group) must be in charge of initiating and managing the curriculum evaluation process. Administrators are usually the ones in charge, and, in fact, administrator involvement is essential to show the faculty that the administration supports the process. Involvement of administrators is essential also because it is a key to understanding the faculty's needs, and administrators must understand these needs before they can support the process. Administrators simply cannot provide an atmosphere to support curriculum evaluation unless they understand the process, and there is no better route to understanding than hands-on involvement.

Immediately, administrators must analyze their beliefs about such concepts as decentralized or participatory leadership. Do they believe that curriculum evaluation is important? Do they believe that systematic, ongoing curriculum evaluation is needed? Do they believe that by working together teachers can guide the analysis and reshaping of a curriculum? Do they believe that both administrators and faculty must play a significant role in this revision? If administrators can answer yes to these questions, they must then prepare themselves to trust their faculty to conduct major parts of the ongoing curriculum evaluation process.

Once administrators have analyzed their philosophies, they must begin setting the conditions that are needed for the change to occur. This can be done by sharing their beliefs. Administrators are not likely to secure unanimous support from the faculty. One case study in this book reports on a school that has adopted a policy requiring 90% faculty agreement before any changes are made; another case reports on a school that requires 80% agreement. Unanimous support is not required, but a consensus is needed. Minor disagreements between administrators and teachers can inhibit and sometimes prevent meaningful curriculum evaluation. A common mistake made by administrators is failure to give the faculty the latitude it needs to succeed.

* * *

Since the development of NCLB, concerns have been voiced in teacher lounges and teachers' meetings throughout the nation that the government has taken over curriculum evaluation. But effective school reform requires teacher control, and this case study shows how teachers can take charge of evaluation and, in doing so, can reclaim ownership of their schools.

Aligning the Stars to Dazzle

Joyce A. Piveral, Carole Edmonds, and Jennee Barnes • Northwest Missouri State University

Through reform and accountability measures, educational stakeholders have created a culture ripe for new learning. Part of this new learning is achieved through collaboration and examination of school data—more specifically, of student performance measures. Many schools have found an effective way to examine these data by creating professional learning communities (Dufour, Eaker, & Dufour, 2002). This case study tells the story of one elementary school principal who collaboratively worked with her staff and empowered them to set and achieve high educational goals. She coached her staff in the development of whole-faculty study groups (or professional learning communities) and charged these study groups to examine data in order to more effectively help evaluate curriculum. The collaborative approach has led to the adoption of a shared vision and goals to address the needs of the students, faculty and staff, parents, and the community at large. In this case, the coach has formed a learning team to bring together many change forces, and the outcome has been a win–win situation for all.

The Community

King City R-I School District is in a rural community. The district consists of one building that houses the district administrative staff, the P–6 elementary school, and the 7–12 middle and high school. The school is the center of this farming community and is a great source of pride, providing the main source of social activity for school families and community patrons.

The School

The King City R-I School District has approximately 338 students in grades K–12. The elementary school has 175 students. Forty-nine percent are enrolled in the free and reduced lunch program. The elementary school has eleven full-time faculty with one special education teacher. Seven percent of the elementary students are in special education. Twenty-six percent of the elementary students receive Title I services for reading and/or math. The elementary school has traditionally not scored well on state standardized tests. However, in the last few years the students have shown great gains.

The Principal

Ms. Barnes has been the principal and instructional coach for the King City R-I Elementary School for six years. She had a vision for change and a will to institute a culture rich with learning in her school. Also, the time was right for this school to strive for improved achievement. Her challenge was to unite the staff, students, parents, and community in supporting this change.

The Case

This case story illustrates Ms. Barnes' guidance and support in "coaching a learning team" for improved student achievement. The vertical-teaming, whole-faculty study groups meet regularly to identify research-based instructional strategies and examine student work. The groups use a cross-analysis approach of student work. As a result of this examination and rich discussion, the faculty then evaluates progress and short-term goal achievement and creates an action plan to effectively progress toward the yearly teacher, building, and district goals. The work of this school has resulted in a high-performing learning team with a culture of shared learning, which includes shared vision, mission, collaboration, and ongoing evaluation.

Now the rest of the story, from Ms. Barnes:

"I think we do a lot of curriculum evaluation through our SMART goal process where teachers set goals at the beginning of the year, tied to active learning strategies used specifically in the reading and writing curriculum. Then the teachers collect the data at progress-monitoring points throughout the year. The SMART-goal analysis (the acronym stands for goals that are **S**trategic, **M**easurable, **A**ttainable, **R**esults-oriented, and **T**ime-bound) is definitively evaluating their curriculum and the instructional strategies used to deliver their curriculum. But I can use the SMART goals from staff development as a supervisor, because it's a main piece of information about how teachers are able to develop and use their curriculum evaluation skills.

"Another thing I can share is the evaluation of the curriculum—we do that monthly through our staff development design. Each book-study group delves into current research, and based on that research the teachers implement the newly learned instructional strategies they have researched in their own classrooms. The teachers are doing a lot of collaboration through the staff development design of the monthly whole-faculty study groups. They also bring examples of student work and examine the results of instructional delivery and curriculum material.

"We begin planning for each successive school year at the end of the year by establishing overall district and building goals based on data from the previous year. An instructional leadership team (ILT) was formed by recruiting from the "superstar teachers" for this team. We wanted to utilize those individuals because they have good networks within the culture of the building. To be nominated to be a member of this team is very much a professional compliment. We now have teachers striving to achieve this goal so they too can be recommended by their peers to be a member of the ILT.

"This team sets the coming year's goals, not only by looking at building and district data but also by examining the building needs assessment that is given each spring to the faculty and students. Because of the whole-faculty study groups and SMART goal development, we are also constantly collecting data based on student performance from our classroom teachers. For instance, the teachers' SMART goal analysis—whether they did or did not meet their goal and then the teachers' level of reflection based on their goal attainment—provides a great deal of information for evaluating student performance and curricula. The SMART-goal data inform the ILT continuously throughout the year.

"The teachers have goals developed at three levels, the district level, the building level and the classroom level. The classroom level is the most powerful. This year the building goal was to increase the amount of active learning that was being applied in daily instruction. Therefore, each teacher developed a goal in this area. Because we are now in our third year of implementation, we also focused on literacy, so each of my teachers have a goal stated in the area of reading instruction and writing development.

"So at the onset of the year, the district goals and the building goals are communicated. The first full month of the school year is when the teachers begin determining what their goals are going to be for the school year. The reason they have the full month of preparation is because we do not want them establishing goals just with what they feel they want to achieve—we want the goals based on the examination of existing data. So within that month, depending on what our focus is, the students are given a pre-assessment. The data from these pre-assessments are analyzed, and from that data then they establish a realistic goal about the progress they want their students to achieve by the end of the school year.

"It is a learning curve for teachers to be able to set realistic goals. This was something that had to be modeled. I have learned that modeling is very important, and that you must make your expectations clear and specific and must demonstrate processes for them. If teachers understand what is clearly expected of them, they are more apt to implement the practice and believe in it. In fact, the first year was a learning process just in establishing the goals and realizing what was expected and what was realistic, and what the indicators should be for that goal to be achieved. My expectation as a building leader and coach was that my staff should learn how to write goals. Of course you want them to meet the goals they set—but not necessarily that first year, because just establishing the goals is a learning curve. A high percentage of my staff in year one did not meet their SMART goal, and that was because a lot of the goals were not realistic and obtainable; but at the end of year two we established a celebration meeting for sharing results.

"All staff members in the building come together for a celebration of goal achievement. We come to the library, and each teacher will lead in sharing a report about their SMART goals. They plot on charts those goals that were met and those that were not. If you compared the year-one report to year two, it is truly amazing. Eighty-five to ninety percent of my teachers met their goals for year two."

Ms. Barnes believes that her teachers in year two had high expectations and were also more skilled in developing and achieving their goals. She said, "I feel they stretched them." The reason: "I had some teachers who were allowed to modify their goals if they realized, at the first progress monitoring (three progress-monitoring points are set per year), or in winter when we do benchmark testing, that they did not set their goal realistically enough; or, if they have already obtained their goal, it obviously was not set high enough. They can go ahead and amend the goal to make it higher (they can only set it higher, not lower) for the end of the year. The teachers can only set the goal higher because if they have not achieved it after the first assessment, then obviously they are going to continue to work on that goal."

One overall observation shared by Ms. Barnes was that she has witnessed engagement, focus, and success as a result of implementing the SMART-goal process and vertical teaming of whole-faculty study groups. She stated, "When you are sitting in this seat and you are interacting with multiple teachers daily, you realize that the common language and the discourse in the building are so instructionally focused now, whereas before they were not. The capacity of my staff has grown, based on the many teachers who are becoming leaders. In the beginning of this process, we were learning just by being involved."

Issues for Further Reflection

1. This program had two means of gathering data for assessing the curriculum. Together, these covered the faculty's goals and the state's goals.
2. Three levels of goals were covered: classroom, building, and district.

Building a Common Vision and Mission

Suspecting that the education reform reports, the deliberations of national commissions on education, and the media were giving a biased report on the status of American schools, George Wood (2002) spent several years traveling to schools; interviewing administrators, teachers, counselors, and students; and recording those interviews. Wood wanted to know whether there were some excellent schools in this country and if so, what characteristics were common among these schools. He found the answer to his first question to be a resounding *yes*—there are some schools that are excellent, when measured by almost any standard. And yes, these schools share some common attributes. Paramount among these is a strong vision. Supervisors can help teachers develop a broad-based, community-wide vision by carefully coplanning, with parents and other members of the learning community, opportunities to gather all community members' opinions and suggestions on an ongoing basis. "Establishing a school vision is an important and challenging task; however, the vision needs to be revisited often to ensure that its underlying premises continue to resonate among school and community members" (Shephard et al., 2008, p. 149).

Meaningful evaluation proceeds to the faculty. Administrators can "share the vision" of the school's mission and philosophy with the faculty. When sharing the school's existing philosophy statement, administrators must communicate to the faculty its always fluid nature. At every school the philosophy statement should be reviewed regularly and, when necessary, revised by all members of the learning community to reflect changes in the school and community and changes in the faculty's perception.

The curriculum evaluation process should provide for and require a periodic examination of the school's philosophy. Each teacher will have opportunities to modify this statement. Teacher involvement should first be increased by inviting the faculty to write belief statements. These statements should not be composed in flamboyant or pedantic language but instead with simple, straightforward language that is clear and easy to understand. For example, teachers may believe that "all children can learn," or that "children learn more when they are actually involved." These are simple, yet elegant and functional statements but, when standing alone, they may appear to be little more than empty rhetoric. Actually they are more than that, simply because they have caused the teachers to think about their actions—and inevitably, thoughts turn into action.

Without a system to streamline its many facets and make the transition from thoughts to action, curriculum development can be a sloppy undertaking. This streamlining process should begin at the evaluation stage of curriculum development. To serve the purpose of improving the curriculum, the teachers must move beyond their belief statements to create a different kind of statements to describe student action, sometimes called *generic demonstrators,* that must be translated from thought into action. Box 7.1 lists several generic demonstrators that were generated by K–5 teachers and are currently being used at the author's laboratory school. Are the demonstrators in Box 7.1 realistic expectations for fifth graders? The demonstrators use verbs that are commonly considered desirable in writing objectives, but some of them represent lower-order activities. Although it is acceptable for teachers to use these types of activities, supervisors should make sure that curricula also contain higher-order activities.

Perhaps you have noticed that some of these statements use verbs that are generally considered too broad for use in behavioral objectives. This is acceptable because at this stage the intent is to move from passive, inert belief statements (like "all children can learn") to statements that express student activity. It is important that teachers have adequate time to develop an understanding of these demonstrators. Shared leadership is time consuming, and time is required for participants to digest the information that is to be considered. Additional time is required for discussing these ideas with colleagues. Time must be found for formal teachers' meetings, yet teachers' schedules are tight. Therefore, meetings to discuss pertinent issues must be planned in advance so that teachers can free their calendars at the scheduled times. Although the

Box 7.1 Generic Demonstrators for Levels K–5

1. Read and understand a set of instructions with multiple points at an appropriate level.
2. Work individually, as well as cooperatively in a group, to solve a problem in a timed situation.
3. Plan for an event by presenting a set of sequenced steps clearly enough to be understood.
4. Justify decisions made as a group by supplying supporting evidence and reporting as an individual.
5. Select appropriate measurement materials to solve a problem.
6. Produce a variety of functional and creative writings for varying audiences.
7. Collect, record, and interpret data in order to draw conclusions and/or perform tasks.
8. Design and conduct research or an experiment.
9. Manipulate materials to perform a task.
10. Choose from several presented alternatives a workable solution to a problem.
11. Given a set of research tools, a choice will be made on the appropriate tool needed to respond to a question.
12. Report on a chosen topic by using various media in a final product.
13. Observe, classify, predict, and sequence in the process of addressing a solution to a problem.
14. Identify and communicate a problem to be solved.
15. Use reference materials.
16. Demonstrate an open mind to differing opinions and viewpoints.

rather brief and simple list of generic demonstrators shown in Box 7.1 may look like the work of one teacher's scribbled notes taken during a faculty meeting, it is actually the result of several hours of meetings among many teachers and spread over a few weeks.

To avoid the possibility that demonstrators might become restrictive and enslaving, curriculum evaluation leaders must be flexible. Consider that some fiction writers, for example, describe instances in which the characters they have created take over the plot and determine the direction of the story. This is understandable. But other authors begin their stories by fully developing their cast of characters. Because these characters are so fully described, they can only behave in ways that reflect their "character." When the characters are fully developed at the outset, the author loses much of the freedom to choose or dictate their behaviors, resulting in loss of control of the direction of the story. To prevent the writing process from stalling, successful fiction writers learn to step back and let the plot evolve.

Much like fiction writers, curriculum evaluation leaders often learn that the faculty decides to move in unanticipated directions that the leader might have never chosen. But, if efforts to build a learning community are to succeed, the leader must permit this takeover. Effective participatory leadership requires the empowerment of *all* participants. The event described in the vignette at the beginning of this chapter is a report of an actual faculty's experiences evaluating and redesigning their school's curriculum—which led them in a direction they would not have anticipated. The payoff for allowing this situation to evolve is the high level of energy that occurs within each participant and ultimately within the group.

It is imperative for administrators to remember that curriculum building cannot occur in the absence of professional growth. Administrator responsibilities include both overseeing the improvement of the curriculum and, of course, the rest of the learning environment while simultaneously supporting the empowerment of the faculty. In essence, the administrator's role must move from directive leadership to supportive leadership.

Goal Setting and Collaborative Faculty Development

A somewhat magical relationship exists between curriculum improvement and faculty growth. As faculty members are empowered to contribute to the development of their curricula, their contributions change the faculty members themselves as well as the curriculum. Because curriculum evaluation is part of the early stage of curriculum improvement and runs throughout the process, it seems logical that faculty development should be planned to parallel curriculum evaluation. In fact, the faculty evaluation stage of faculty development should parallel the school's curriculum evaluation process.

One effective way to evaluate faculty performance is by using a pre-conference at the beginning of the year and a post-conference at the end of the year. Some schools require their teachers to provide a written document, or a packet of documents, early in the year. Box 7.2 shows an example of a questionnaire taken from a packet of materials that each faculty member of the Model School (featured in this chapter's opening vignette) is required to submit each year in early autumn. The administrator, or whoever is in charge of curriculum evaluation, can shape the direction of this process by carefully choosing the questions for this instrument. For example, note that part of this questionnaire is devoted to curriculum goals, per se, giving the administrator an opportunity to use an evaluation of the teacher's plans.

The second part of this instrument focuses on innovations, reflecting this school's expectations for all faculty members to experiment with new programs. This is to be expected, since this questionnaire belongs in an evaluation packet developed and used by a laboratory school, and experimentation is at the very heart of the nature and purposes of laboratory schools. Since all of these teachers are already involved with innovations, the form gives teachers an opportunity to list those innovative programs in which they are already involved and indicate their preference for continuing this involvement. The school does not assume that the teachers should continue their involvement with all innovations. On the contrary, it is expected that some programs will not merit continuation and that their abandonment will provide room for introducing other innovations. Like the unplanned growth of textbooks, which are more often than not a compendium of topics, curricula can easily become

Box 7.2 Faculty Professional Development Plan Questionnaire

Model Laboratory School
Faculty Professional Development Plan

Complete the information requested below by the end of August, and return to Bruce Bonar. Individual conferences will be scheduled to discuss these goals.

I. *Curriculum Goals*
List any objectives or statements that include your plans to improve, maintain, or evaluate teaching/learning goals in your particular subject/grade level.

II. *Innovations*
List any statements that reflect new and/or experimental programs you wish to develop or continue using. Include new approaches and trends you may be interested in pursuing.

III. *Professional Development*
List areas in which you wish to develop professionally.

IV. *School Goals*
Mention overall school objectives/goals that you feel need attention either in your area or schoolwide.

V. *"Wish-List"*
If there were unlimited funds, what would you need to facilitate your goals in the above areas?

VI. What can the administration do to facilitate your job and the goals above?

crowded with nonessential content and activities unless they are regularly pruned of their unnecessary programs.

Educational Leadership Constituents Council's (ELCC's) Standard No. 2 requires educational leaders to design comprehensive professional growth plans for staff.

The third part of this instrument is open ended, giving faculty members opportunities to list any directions in which they choose to grow professionally. A strange phenomenon can occur when a school faculty or even a small group of teachers is given total freedom in deciding the direction in which its members want to grow. Rooney (2007) reported on a faculty that was encouraged to determine areas of needed curriculum improvement. Although the leader and faculty had no intention of building a learning community, this is in fact what occurred. Many paths for evaluating the curriculum and identifying needed changes can be taken. These opportunities may include taking workshops in chosen interest areas. If so, these workshops will not replace the series of workshops that will be held at the school for a particular teacher's area. Or the teacher may indicate a desire to take a three-credit-hour university course. The particular school discussed by Rooney encourages the faculty to take courses; its faculty development program allows each faculty member to take one free approved course per

It Works for Me!

E-Walks

William L. Phillips, Eastern Kentucky University

Administrators at our P–12 Model Laboratory School conduct monthly supervision of instruction by recording classroom activities on a handheld electronic device. We call it E-Walks to describe these electronic walks through every classroom every month. Administrators are able to record the number of students off task, any evidence of a clear learning objective, bell-to-bell instruction, evidence-based teaching strategies, higher-order critical thinking, student-generated on-task discussion, teacher lecturing, worksheets, and noninstructional activities. These data are then organized in a simple chart and presented to grade-level teams of teachers for their comments, discussion, and action.

One chart might list the number of classes working from bell to bell. Another chart might indicate the percentage of lessons that had a clear learning objective. These charts enable teachers to immediately visualize and grasp a grade-level problem that needs to be addressed. The administrator does not need to tell the teachers how to address the problem; teachers are in control of the solutions. Each month the cycle repeats. The school is becoming a learning community by using this system of E-Walks to improve instruction.

term. Approval is contingent on available funds and on the administrator's verification that the requested course is directly related to the teacher's teaching assignment or to another area of the teacher's responsibilities.

The distinct advantages of this type of evaluation are that it is criterion-referenced and that the form is completed early in the year. This combination results in the teachers knowing exactly what is expected of them (or what criteria will be used to evaluate their performance for the year), and it permits teachers to know these expectations early in the year so they can guide their activities accordingly. Chapter 5 says that the best (perhaps the only) way to get individuals to commit to group goals is to help them connect their individual goals to those of the group so that the two grow to become parts of the same whole. Perhaps the most important advantage of this system is the latitude it provides teachers to design or personalize their own professional development program. The individual goals will quickly lose their identity as they are replaced by group goals. Perhaps more accurately, the combination of all faculty members' personal goals will blend to form the total faculty's group goals.

An individual conference is held at the beginning of the year to provide each teacher with an opportunity to explain his or her plan to the principal and to get the principal's suggestions and approval. A post-evaluation conference is held at the end of the year to assess the teacher's effectiveness in the area of professional growth. At the Model Laboratory School, this evaluation system is not absolute or rigid. If unexpected opportunities become available during the year, teachers can request to add these to the plan. In some instances when the opportunities for other growth experiences mirror parts of the plan, the teacher may even request to substitute these activities.

As indicated earlier, major improvement in a learning community requires setting and reaching group goals and individual goals, and these activities must occur simultaneously. Furthermore, some of the individual goals should be directly related to the group goals so that individual goal attainment will help the group reach its goals.

This means that in addition to having an individualized professional development plan, each teacher must also participate in the development and revision of the school's development program.

Through involvement in the formulation of the school's mission and in setting school goals, all teachers are ensured ownership in their school community. Some teachers will be involved in actually writing these documents; all will be involved in contributing their ideas to the process. For example, the school may provide the teachers with a list of the current school goals and ask them to identify those goals that they think should be retained.

Box 7.3 shows a goal-setting instrument currently being used to provide all faculty members with the opportunity for involvement in the annual revision of the school's goals.

Teachers are also given the opportunity to add new goals that they wish their peers to consider. When those forms are returned, the results will be compiled and a new list of "revised" goals will be made and submitted to the site-based council for final approval.

Box 7.3 Goal Setting Instrument

Name: ______________________________

Listed below are goals listed for Model Laboratory School in the University's current plan. Please review these goals and rank order the top three.

____ Replace/purchase classroom/office equipment.

____ Conduct research in a controlled environment.

____ Create a strong academic program for students.

____ Develop a diverse student/faculty population.

____ Create an optimum site for student teaching.

____ Provide preservice/in-service experience with exceptional children.

____ Provide experiences for students that facilitate student career choices.

____ Replace school furniture.

____ Provide a quality pre-student teaching experience.

____ Provide a high-quality instructional faculty.

____ Provide a setting for staff development by school districts.

Add other goals you consider important.

Involving Students

Ironically, sometimes the most overlooked group in planning school goals is the group that the goals are intended to benefit—students. There are at least two reasons for involving students. First, students have commonly been perceived as too young and immature to possibly contribute anything worthwhile to a discussion on school goals (a topic believed to be better left to the experts). The truth is that students can—and when given the opportunity, often do—provide a valuable perspective and thus a valuable dimension to the process. Put succinctly, students often provide good ideas that can lead to good educational experiences.

A second reason for involving students in planning schoolwide goals is the status to which students are elevated by their involvement. When students are given a voice in the planning process, their sense of ownership in the curriculum and, indeed, in the adopted goals increases, making the school goals the students' goals. Along with increased ownership comes an increase in learner responsibility to achieve the goals. For other suggestions on ways to involve students, see the instructables.com Web site produced by Squid Labs.

Using Tables of Specifications

To ensure that students are directly involved with all of the school's goals or the state's standards, a table of specifications (such as the one in Table 7.1) can be designed to evaluate the curriculum in each class.

Table 7.1 Table of Specifications for the Cognitive Domain

Activities	Knowledge	Comprehension	Application	Analysis	Synthesis	Evaluation
Constructs 3-D objects						
Stores materials						
Shares with instructor						
Shares with group						
Shares with the class						
Displays, classroom						
Displays, other						
Prepares display						
Selects group						
Shows followership						
Shows leadership						
Accepts others' work						
Evaluates products						
Works alone, cooperates						
Cooperates in groups						
Adapts techniques						

Use this type of table to list the standards or goals in the left-hand column, and match them up with the concepts that are to be addressed during each lesson (the column headings). Administrators and instructional supervisors can use this type of table during walk-through observations to ensure that the standards and goals are being addressed, and to talk to students about the concepts currently being studied. Walk-through observations can create a focused dialogue with teachers about best practices. Lunenburg and Irby (2005) take this process a step further, suggesting that time can be saved for discussion on teaching and learning issues noted during the walk-throughs by performing the administrative tasks (which usually consume time during faculty meetings) via memos or e-mails.

Recall the generic demonstrators in Box 7.1. How would each of these demonstrators rate if put on a table of specifications such as the one for the cognitive domain in Table 7.1?

The Supervisor's Role

The supervisor's role in involving students, parents, and other key community members in goal setting can begin with urging curriculum committees to involve everyone. This role and this responsibility do not end here; the principal can help plan events that facilitate such involvement. Good communication is yet another area for which supervisors have much responsibility. Parents and students who are on planning committees are not the only ones who should be informed of the ongoing changes; make certain that *all* students, parents, and other interested community members are informed of the planning on a weekly basis.

Involving Parents

For almost two centuries American parents were purposefully kept from "interfering" with decisions related to curriculum and instruction, but this tendency to keep parents at arms length changed in the late twentieth century when the effective schools research discovered that involving parents in academic matters can produce remarkable levels of student achievement. American schools might take a cue from Argyle Primary School in London, where teachers initiate a two-way dialogue with parents about the curriculum and experience some exciting results.

> Teachers invite parents into the school for a meeting twice a year. They explain the topics coming up and ask the parents for any useful information and input. The parents work in small groups to make a concept map of each topic, brainstorming ideas around the central theme, thinking about what their children already know and what they would be interested in knowing, and suggesting different activities. A teacher commented, "The concept maps help to demonstrate to parents how we teach thinking to pupils, rather than just facts."
>
> By taking on parents' suggestions, the school now offers a curriculum that truly reflects the needs and interests of the children. The dynamics of the school have also changed. Parents no longer feel that teachers are supe-

rior, and the teachers talk positively about empowering parents to make an effective contribution. School now has a place in family life for both parents and children. Parents are engaged and interested in what their children are learning and leave the planning sessions buzzing with excitement. The ideas they suggest tend to be hands-on and interactive, often involving objects that their children bring in from home. As a result, the children feel represented and valued, and levels of engagement in lessons have improved considerably. The teachers have noticed a difference in their own work as well. Their discussions with parents are inspiring them to leave behind traditional topics and lessons and to focus on things that are more relevant to the children. (Qualifications and Curriculum Authority, n.d.)

Technology and Curriculum Evaluation

Although still in its infancy, technology is being developed to facilitate and enhance continuous improvement of curricula through systems that allow continuous monitoring and feedback, a process that promotes collaborative faculty development. For example, Schweiker, Moore, and Voltmer (2002) have designed a software package called the Enhanced Curricular Evaluation + Portfolio (ECE+P) system. The school administrator is responsible for implementation of the software, which promotes participation and interaction among instructors, administrators, external reviewers, and students. As we move further into the twenty-first century, it is likely that more such software systems will be created to facilitate the process of meaningful curriculum evaluation in our schools.

Conclusion

One factor that makes periodic curriculum evaluation essential is the relentless pressure on schools exerted by the nation, state, and local community. This pressure is continuously growing. In recent years, the need for periodic curriculum evaluation has been greatly intensified by education reform programs.

Periodic curriculum evaluation provides schools the opportunity to take advantage of innovations as they develop. It also provides schools a way to smooth the implementation of new programs. For example, schools that evaluate their curricula annually have an excellent opportunity to introduce new programs each year. Conversely, schools that rarely or never formally evaluate their curricula are likely to hold on to "proven practices" for security.

Curriculum evaluation should begin with the administrators, who must ask themselves and other members of the learning community what they believe about the purpose of schools, the nature of youth, the nature of learning, and the ability of faculty members to self-govern. Those administrators who believe in and are committed to participatory management must be willing to show confidence in their teachers by giving them the latitude to make important decisions about the operation of the schools. In those schools that have site-based councils, these committees play a natural part in evaluating the schools' curricula.

Full faculty participation by all members of the learning community in the curriculum evaluation process is essential to secure the necessary commitment to new directions for the school. Because faculty development, curriculum development, and curriculum evaluation are inseparable and because faculty development supports curriculum development, faculty evaluation and development must occur concurrently with the evaluation and development of the school's curriculum. Individual teachers initially must be permitted to set some of their own professional development goals, but some of these goals should be directly related to, and should contribute to, achieving the school's goals.

As teachers become more involved in the more global schoolwide goals, they become energized and empowered. This empowerment does not result from their determination to take over control of the school but rather is a natural result of the acquisition of new knowledge that the faculty has generated. This knowledge fuels a growing desire to improve learning throughout the school. Parents and students can participate in this process as well.

All schools must contribute to the national, state, and district guidelines for improving their curricula. However, healthy schools do not merely respond to these outside forces. The entire faculty and staff in those schools are generating their own internal forces. Although schools should serve the education reform forces, they should be more than servants—they should, and indeed *must* become navigators who plot their own course. This is the powerful role and responsibility of curriculum evaluation in today's schools.

Questions for Discussion and Reflection

1. Which should have the most influence on shaping the school's curriculum: external forces (such as the national, state, and district guidelines and exams), or internal forces such as annual curriculum evaluations?
2. What is the curriculum evaluator's role?
3. How are faculty development and curriculum development related?
4. How are curriculum evaluation and faculty development related?
5. How does the empowerment that results from curriculum evaluation help a school?
6. What is a supervisor's role in helping the school meet national, state, and district guidelines?
7. How does current faculty development for curriculum improvement differ from traditional faculty development?
8. How much freedom should teachers have in shaping their own faculty development programs?
9. What are some essentials of successful curriculum evaluation programs?
10. Why should all faculty members be involved in curriculum evaluation?
11. Should curriculum evaluation begin with the administrator's philosophy? Why or Why not?
12. How is curriculum revision energizing?

13. In what ways has the administrator's role in curriculum evaluation been diminished, and in what ways has it become more important?
14. Why is regular, periodic curriculum evaluation essential?
15. How are curriculum evaluation and instructional evaluation similar? How do they differ?
16. What is the role of the school's mission statement in curriculum evaluation?
17. What are some curriculum elements that should be aligned?
18. Why is the principal's total involvement in curriculum evaluation essential?
19. How can a school's mission statement be made more functional?
20. What is the function of generic demonstrators in curriculum evaluation?

Suggested Activities

1. At the library, read five articles about the role that mission statements play in an organization and five articles about school ethos or school culture. Write a brief report titled "Using the Mission Statement to Develop or Enrich a School Ethos or Vision."
2. Ask a counselor from each school to accompany you as you visit the teacher lounges at two schools. Observe the behavior there, and write a brief paper contrasting the different types of cultures in these rooms. Include one or more paragraphs about each of the following: (a) relative extent of the use of these rooms, (b) approximate percent of users who are nonteachers (include their titles), (c) average size of discussion parties in each lounge, (d) percentage of time spent discussing academic topics, and (e) percentage of academic topic discussions that focus on a particular discipline. Write a generalizing paragraph or two about the cultures in these schools.
3. Interview a school administrator, and ask how and when the school's curriculum is evaluated. In particular, ask how all teachers provide input into the process. Ask for examples of changes that resulted form earlier evaluations.
4. Ask a school administrator to share a copy of the school's curriculum evaluation plan. If no written plan is available, arrange an interview with the administrator. Investigate the school's evaluation program to learn whether it includes evaluating the faculty. Write a brief description of this part of the plan, noting the regularity and variety used in the evaluations.
5. Interview a principal or chair of a curriculum evaluation committee. Ask for examples of instances in which individual teacher goals became part of the process of reaching group goals.

Chapter 8

Helping Teachers Plan Instruction

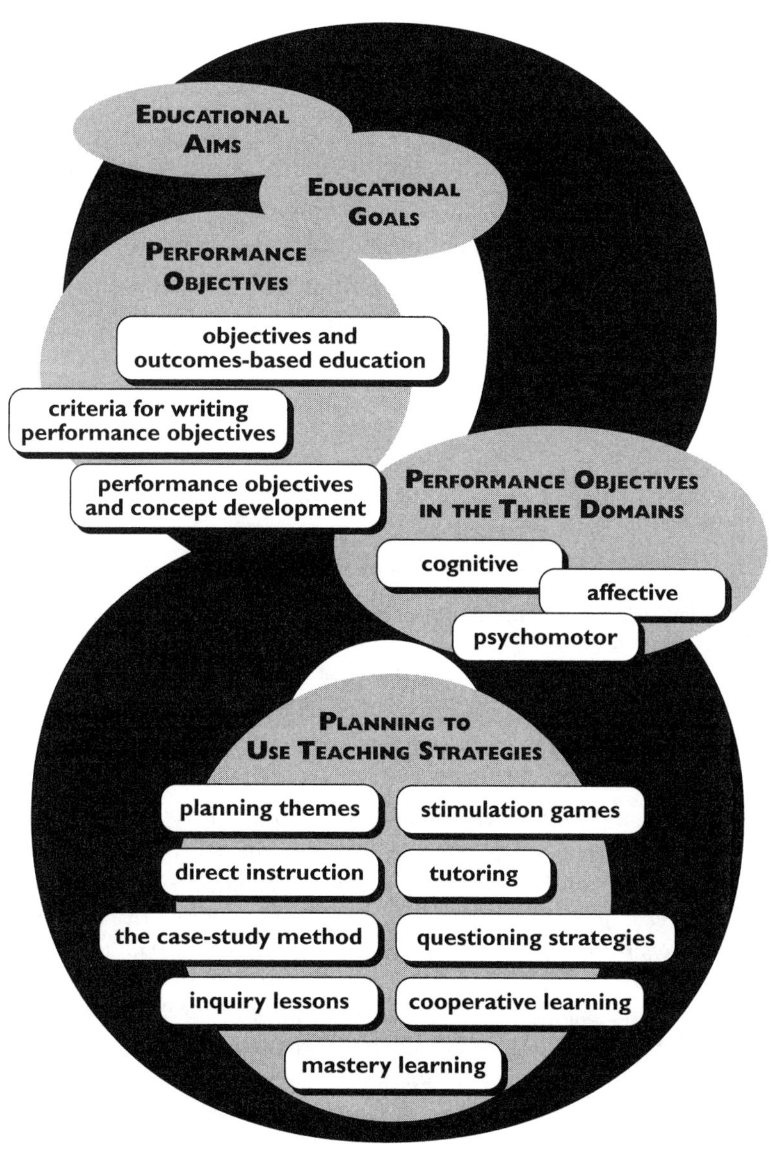

> *The current forces of the No Child Left Behind Act place teachers directly at the center of the student learning equation so that teacher behavior becomes important and leadership for teachers becomes significant.*
>
> —N. Carlson & J. Irons, "Implementing best practices in the classroom"

Objectives

After completion of this chapter, you should be able to help your faculty to

1. Write objectives in each of the three domains
2. Write upper-level (higher-order) objectives
3. Select appropriate instructional strategies to meet particular goals
4. Identify strengths, limitations, and effective application of various teaching strategies
5. Plan daily lessons around various teaching strategies

The New Supervisor

Jan Hubble had been a middle- and secondary-level teacher for ten years when a principalship became vacant six years ago. Although she had been interested in this position, her husband was teaching in the high school at the time, and the state's strong nepotism law prohibited her from working as a principal while her spouse was teaching in the school. Now the position has once again become vacant, and Jan's husband has left teaching to take a management position with a local business firm.

This time Jan was one of the first to submit an application. Within a few days, she was called to the district's central office and given the job. During her interview, Jan had been savvy enough to focus most of her questions on critical issues that depended on her doing a good job. One question that she asked her prospective employer was, "If I should be offered this post and if I should accept it, what would you want most from my service?" The interviewer responded without hesitation, "We would want you to help raise the standardized test scores of the students in Eastwood Middle School. Last year these scores dropped to an all-time low, just two points above the probationary level. They have reached unprecedented lows for the past three consecutive years. We want you to liven up the instruction in this school and turn this trend

This chapter is based on a chapter in the author's book, *Constructivist teaching strategies for diverse middle-level classrooms.*

around before we lose control of this school." Jan felt a little regret over having asked this question, but overall she knew that she had done right in asking. "It is always best to know what your employer wants," she thought. At the conclusion of the interview, Jan was offered the position, and she enthusiastically accepted.

During her first day on the job, Jan called a faculty meeting at Eastwood. In her curriculum course she had learned that teachers have more support for new programs when the decision to adopt the program is partially theirs. Jan resolved that whatever course the school would take in the future would be decided on by the majority of the Eastwood faculty.

Jan did her homework, researching the state's new reform laws. She even procured documents that were still being considered in the state senate, and she talked with officers in the curriculum division and in the certification division of the state department of education, hoping to learn future trends in the state. Jan shared this information at the initial Eastwood faculty meeting. Included was a list of state-approved valued outcomes. A few faculty members questioned the concept of state-adopted outcomes. Jan heard individual, semiprivate comments such as, "Now the state is dictating our curriculum," and "Uh-oh! Now we're letting the testing program drive the curriculum."

By the end of the meeting, however, the faculty had agreed on a strategy to reach the state-approved outcomes. A teacher mentioned having read an article about a nationally known outcomes-based program at Alverno College and agreed to bring copies of the article to the next meeting. Another teacher had attended a panel presentation at a national professional association conference by a group of teachers from the Wichita, Kansas, schools. A representative from each of the faculties of several schools in the Wichita system explained how his or her school was using a learning/teaching styles matching-inventory instrument to improve the instruction in the school. This teacher also agreed to bring the materials gathered at that conference to the next meeting.

Jan distributed a one-page survey designed to discover the types of methods that were currently being used at Eastwood. The responses indicated that almost 90% of the instruction at Eastwood was lecture, followed by seatwork (usually photocopied worksheets), followed by homework assignments, and then tests. The faculty was using almost no problem solving, inquiry lessons, simulations, games, or case studies. Students were not being involved in planning and, for the most part, they remained passive in their classes. For most classes, the textbook was the sole curriculum determiner.

Mr. Mark (Marty) Martin, assistant principal at Eastwood, discussed a curriculum course that he was currently taking. This course was focused on the constructivist method. He agreed to make a five- to ten-minute presentation on constructivist theory and practices. At Eastwood's next meeting Mr. Martin gave a rather moving presentation on the need for constructivism in today's schools. He began his presentation by sharing some rather dismal data on the general status of U.S. education. His report found that in an alarming number of classrooms at all levels, a majority of students are not paying attention and are not learning because they don't want to learn. He also reported that many teachers, perhaps most, do not begin their planning by identifying desired changes for their students to experience or by identifying objectives to be attained. Rather, most teachers began planning by selecting content to be covered. It seemed that their idea of successful teaching was "covering" content.

Mr. Martin also reported a lack of awareness in many classes of the important concepts in the discipline, and a lack of attempts to discover these concepts. Instead, the lessons dealt with seemingly unrelated facts, and the objective appeared to be memorizing these small pieces of information without tying them to previously learned knowledge.

Jan watched as Marty reported one discouraging set of data after another. The teachers responded with silence. Some seemed to be ducking their heads in shame or at least looking downward in hopes that their fellow teachers did not realize that any of Mr. Martin's disappointing comments could be referring to any one of their own classes.

Following the meeting, Jan realized that she had a tough job ahead. "At least," she chuckled to herself, "it won't be boring."

Reflection

Should all classes begin with objectives? Why shouldn't textbooks determine curricula? Should all objectives be written at higher levels? Should teachers try to match learning types, or should they purposefully introduce students to unfamiliar types?

This vignette raises a familiar concern of today's teachers. Many state departments of education are purposefully using assessment to drive the curriculum. Facing the threat of having the schools taken over and operated by "distinguished educators," "master teachers," or private enterprise, schools are forced to respond to the demand for higher test scores. As you read this chapter, consider the dilemma this demand places on the supervisor. Linda Morford (2007) has reminded us that the ISSLC standards are "just the first step in the development of a leader" (p. 4). We must go beyond meeting the goals provided for us by our professional societies and those developed by state and federal bodies outside the schools. What additional goals should schools be meeting, and how can supervisors help teachers meet these goals? How can the school's mission, daily lesson objectives, and state goals be aligned so that all can be reached through the same planned instruction? Some schools try to meet all three goals separately, but teachers and students seldom have the time and energy to do so.

Introduction

> The first two standards of the Educational Leadership Constituents Council (ELCC) call for leadership in creating a "vision of learning supported by the school community' (Standard No. 1) and, realizing that a vision can go nowhere by itself, "providing an effective instructional program, applying best practice to learning" (Standard No. 2).

Too often, teachers let rituals rather than purposeful thinking and planning guide their classroom behaviors (Trowbridge, 2007). Such purposeful thinking and planning, or *vision*, is essential to motivate teachers, elicit their cooperation, and focus them on the goal of improving learning. The school's vision produces general directions called *aims*. Like vision, aims will also go nowhere without goals and objectives. The first half of this chapter focuses on writing aims, goals, and objectives. The second half examines several teaching strategies that supervisors can recommend for teachers to help students reach the school's goals. Because all teachers need to master a variety of teaching methods to meet the variety of learning styles (Lovelace, 2005), this chapter provides supervisors with guidance in developing such teaching strategies as direct instruction, case studies, inquiry, simulation games, tutoring, questioning, cooperative learning, and mastery learning lessons.

Educational Aims

Educational aims are broad statements of schools' purposes. Perhaps the best examples of these are the Cardinal Principles of Secondary Education: health, command of fundamental processes (development of basic skills), worthy home membership, vocational efficiency, civic education/citizenship, worthy use of leisure time, and ethical character. Notice that each aim is so broad and far-reaching that it cannot possibly be attained, not even in a lifetime. Another, newly-emerging aim supported by many contemporary educators is happiness (Noddings, 2005). These statements are useful because they give general direction to curriculum planning.

Educational Goals

Because they are more immediate and more precise than educational aims, *educational goals* are possible to achieve. An example of an educational goal might be to have all students reading at grade level by their senior year. There are two major types of educational goals: performance and mastery. *Performance goals* require competition among groups of students. Such are the goals of high-stakes testing. Failure to outperform often leads to punishment; therefore, performance goals introduce fear into the learning process. In contrast, *mastery goals* are noncompetitive goals that students pursue to gain mastery over the content they are studying. Mastery goals contribute positively to the development of desirable patterns of learning (Shih, 2005).

Performance Objectives

Statements of expectation that require students to perform at specific levels under specified conditions are called *performance objectives*. Unlike educational aims and educational goals, both of which are written for groups of students, performance objectives are written for individual students. They are more specific than aims and goals in that they describe the conditions under which each student is expected to perform, and they list the minimum acceptable level of behavior. Because performance objectives are more immediate and more exact, they have the power to hold students accountable for learning.

This chapter will prepare the supervisor to help teachers write objectives at varying levels in all educational domains. Particular attention is given to three criteria (audience, behavior, and conditions) and to the selection of verbs that denote action.

The No Child Left Behind legislation mandates that teachers use methods that are supported by research. Consequently, in many states new education reform policy is beginning to require teachers to select and use particular types of teaching methods—for example, matching teacher styles to learner styles, cooperative learning, mastery learning, and hands-on activities. Yet, teachers continue to have much autonomy in determining their teaching methods; and with this autonomy comes responsibility: Unless teachers plan lessons effectively, all students are placed at risk.

The knowledge base in education continues to grow, giving teachers an expanding opportunity to improve their teaching strategies. Variety is essential because each learner's needs are different (Lovelace, 2005). It is only when several strategies are carefully and systematically integrated that substantial improvements in learning become possible. Unfortunately, teachers seldom base their planning on factors that improve instruction. Many ignore the research and continue the same teaching practices from year to year. When asked why they continue to use traditional approaches, their response is that it's the way they were taught, or the way they've always taught. Such a response is natural, and blaming teachers or teacher educators for this state of affairs is counterproductive. A better response would be to help teachers strengthen their understanding of their content area(s) and of pedagogy.

Effective teaching requires long-range planning—stepping back from the daily teaching routine and visualizing what expectations are being held for students over the entire year, such as the curriculum planning discussed in chapter 6. Such planning is absolutely necessary. However, each goal must be reached through daily behaviors of teachers and students, if the goal is to bridge the gap between the long-range planning and the daily classroom activities. Constant day-to-day progress on the long-range goals requires solid daily planning, and it can have an impact on the way that class time is used. This is important, because the amount of time students spend engaged in activities that use the lesson's major concepts is directly correlated with the amount of learning that results.

Experienced teachers often do not begin the planning process by determining objectives. Teachers work with one set of issues at a time as opposed to working on an ongoing problem or theme (Rallis et al., 2006). Yet, the effective-schools research has clearly shown that the probability for high achievement increases when clear academic expectations are set.

Objectives and Outcomes-Based Education

Over a half-century ago, Ralph Tyler introduced the idea of determining expected outcomes prior to designing educational activities to reach those expectations. This approach is known as Tyler's Ends-Means Model. A popular contemporary term that reflects the essence of the Tyler model is *outcomes-based education*—a student-centered, results-oriented design based on the belief that all individuals can learn. The basis that underlies outcomes-based education is straightforward and clear. Once students understand what they are expected to achieve, they are motivated to become more involved with their assignment.

Not everyone endorses outcomes-based education; on the contrary, some educators vigorously oppose the use of objectives in any form. Some of these critics fear that using objectives may hinder the education of some of the students, especially the better ones. Others say that behavioral objectives should be replaced with cognitive objectives, because only a cognitive perspective allows us to understand and develop learning (Martin, 2006).

Criteria for Writing Performance Objectives

Depending on the use of the objectives and the content involved, each supervisor should help each teacher develop the skills needed to write objectives in the teacher's own unique ways. Most authorities seem to agree that all performance-objectives statements must meet at least three criteria.

1. They must be stated in terms of expected student behavior (not teacher behavior).
2. They must specify the conditions under which the students are expected to perform.
3. They must specify the minimum acceptable level of performance.

Stating objectives in terms of expected student behavior is important because all teaching is directed toward the students. The success of the lesson will depend on what happens to the students. To be more precise, the school exists to change the behavior of students—psychologically, physically, socially, emotionally, and even morally. When all objectives are stated in terms of desired student performance and specifics are used that are observable and measurable, the teacher and students will better understand what is expected and the degree to which these expectations are being met. The use of active, measurable verbs is essential.

The first column of terms in Table 8.1 (on the following page) shows verbs describing specific behavior that can be accurately observed and measured. The second column lists verbs that are ineffective because of their vagueness and lack of measurability. Objectives should always be written in terms of measurable desired student behavior, stating the conditions under which the students are expected to perform. Verbs that cannot be observed or measured, such as *learn*, *know*, and *understand*, should be replaced by specific, action-oriented verbs such as *identify*, *list*, *explain*, *name*, *describe*, and *compare*.

Table 8.1 Performance Terms

Specific and Measurable	Vague and Unmeasurable
build	appreciate
classify	consider
contrast	desire
demonstrate	feel
distinguish	find interesting
evaluate	have insight into
identify	know
interpret	learn
label	like to
list	love to
match	really enjoy
measure	recognize
name	remember
remove	see that
select	think
state	understand
write	want to

Performance Objectives and Concept Development

Concept development relates directly to performance objectives. Because students can grasp only a limited number of major ideas in a 45- or 50-minute period, the daily lesson plan should contain only four or five major concepts. For example, a teacher teaching composition writing could select four or five of the most important concepts about capturing and holding the readers' attention. These would become the content for the first day's lesson in a unit titled "Composition Writing." Suppose five ideas are essential to capturing the reader's attention and that, once captured, four ideas are essential for holding it. One lesson could focus on strategies for capturing the reader's attention and a subsequent lesson could be designed to teach students how to hold the readers' attention. This teacher's performance objectives should realistically reflect the students' ability to grasp these concepts.

Performance Objectives in the Three Domains

Some of the aims and goals of education deal with thinking (e.g., command of the fundamental processes), others involve attitudes (e.g., development of moral character), and still others focus on physical skills (e.g., physical education). Teachers should be capable of establishing performance objectives in each of these domains (cognitive, affective, and psychomotor). Following are guidelines for writing objectives at varying levels of difficulty in each of the three domains, which are illustrated in Figure 8.1.

The Cognitive Domain

Creating the first real systematic approach to writing objectives at specified levels, in 1956 Benjamin S. Bloom and a group of students at the University of Chicago developed a taxonomy of educational objectives in the cognitive domain that includes six levels (Bloom, 1956). The ability to involve students in tasks that engage them at these different levels requires teachers to be able to write objectives for each level.

Level 1: Knowledge. The simplest and least demanding objectives are those that require only the memorization of facts. The ability to progress to more advanced task levels requires knowledge and certain basic facts. For

Figure 8.1 Writing Performance Objectives

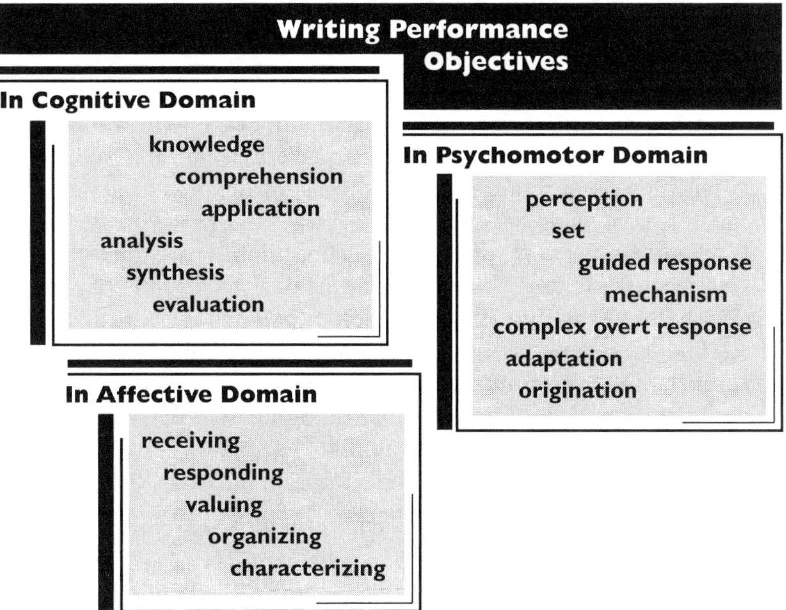

example, effective fiction and nonfiction writing requires knowing correct grammar and spelling; therefore, spelling and grammar rules must be taught. Yet good fiction and nonfiction writing requires more than just correct spelling and proper grammar. Unfortunately, many elementary and secondary classes fail to go beyond this most rudimentary level. There is nothing dishonorable about introducing assignments or tasks at the knowledge level, as long as such assignments have a purpose and do not dominate the curriculum.

An example of an objective written at the knowledge level would be, "When given a list of 10 word definitions, students will be able to correctly spell 8 of the 10 words." Another example is, "When given a paragraph containing 10 misspelled words, the student will identify and correct 8 of the 10 words." Notice that both objectives begin with a statement of the conditions under which students are expected to perform the task ("When given . . .") and are written in terms of desired student performance ("the student will . . ."). In addition, both objectives contain action-oriented verbs that can be observed and measured ("spell," "correct") and end with a statement of the minimum acceptable level of performance ("8 of the 10").

Level 2: Comprehension. Objectives written at the comprehension level ask more of students than mere memorization. Objectives at this level require students to translate, interpret, or predict a continuation of trends.

For example, an English teacher who wants students to know the differences between phrases and clauses may set the following objective: "When given a paragraph containing two clauses and three phrases, the student will correctly underscore the phrases with a single line, and will underscore the clauses with double lines." Because this statement does not mention an acceptable level, it must be assumed that the students are expected to perform with 100% accuracy.

Level 3: Application. Many contemporary education reform programs call for students to apply newly learned information. Objectives written at the application level require students to use principles or generalizations to solve concrete problems.

For example, a mathematics teacher might write the following objective for geometry students: "Given the lengths of both legs of a right triangle, the student will use the Pythagorean theorem to solve the length of the hypotenuse." An English teacher's objective might look like this: "Given the beats and measures in iambic pentameter, the student will write a five-verse poem in iambic pentameter without missing more than one beat per verse." The advantage of writing objectives at this level is that the skill is generalizable; once students learn to apply a principle to one situation, they can apply it to multiple situations to solve many other problems.

Level 4: Analysis. The strong concept-development theme in this book supports the idea that to fully understand a discipline, students must learn the major principles and concepts that hold the discipline together. Like the application-level objectives, analysis-level objectives require students to work with principles, concepts, and broad generalizations—but the students must do so themselves. Students are required to break down the concepts and principles in order to understand them better, and to do this they must understand both the content and its structural form.

For example, a government teacher might write the following objective for a lesson on how a bill becomes a law: "Given a particular law, students will trace its development from the time it was first introduced as a bill, listing every major step without missing any." A teacher of auto mechanics might write the following objectives for a group of students who have been studying the automobile's electrical system: "Starting with the positive battery terminal, the student will trace the current throughout the automobile until it returns to the negative battery terminal, stating what happens in the coil, alternator, distributor, and condenser, without getting more than two of these steps out of sequence." A biology teacher might ask students to trace the human body's circulatory system in a similar manner, designating one of the heart's chambers as a beginning point, with an objective that will enable students to understand the sequence in which the blood travels throughout the body.

Level 5: Synthesis. This book maintains that American schools do an excellent job in preparing students to use their creative talents, and it has emphasized this important responsibility of our schools. Our teachers have excelled in creating environments that promote the development of the creative potential that lives in all our students, and we must not let NCLB or any other federal or state legislation diminish this quality of our schools. Louis Wildman (2007, p. 13) has pointed to the fact that China, Singapore, South Korea, and Japan have all started reforms aimed at fostering more creativity and innovative thinking among their citizens. Creative environments demand a high level of student involvement in designing problems and activities that require the use of creative abilities. In order to make students more capable, proficient, and ready for the employment world, they should be encouraged to get more actively involved in their own educational pursuits. Synthesis-level objectives can be used to reach this goal.

In a way, the synthesis-level objective is the opposite of the analysis-level objective because it requires the student to take several parts. But the synthesis-level objective is more demanding because it requires students to reassemble the parts to form a new whole. The student's attitude is especially important at the synthesis level. Synthesis requires experimentation—investigating the new. Furthermore, the student must understand that the teacher does not have in mind a preconceived notion or a definite solution for the student to reach.

Unlike the analysis-level objectives, synthesis-level objectives require students to use divergent thinking and creativity. For example, a history teacher who wants students to understand the problems faced by the settlers of this country might preface the unit with an assignment involving the following objective: "Suppose you are a member of a team of explorers that is going to another inhabited planet to start a new colony. List at least 10 rules you would propose to guide the new nationals, making sure that at least five of the rules would serve to protect the interests of all the native inhabitants."

Because of their divergent and creative nature, synthesis-level questions are difficult to write. Teachers may need practice before they feel comfortable and competent writing objectives at this level.

Suppose you are helping an art teacher whose students have studied such concepts as cubism (using cubes to form visual objects) and pointillism (using points to form shapes). You might request the teacher to write an objective at the synthesis level. The teacher could begin by identifying a particular effect that he or she would like the students to achieve through the use of cubism and pointillism; this might be a specific feeling or mood. One example of such an objective might be: "After studying some examples of cubism in Picasso's paintings and examples of pointillism in some of Renoir's paintings, the student will combine these two techniques into a new technique to communicate at least three of the following feelings: happiness, surprise, sadness, anger, love." When writing objectives at the synthesis level, teachers should provide enough structure to make the assignment meaningful and yet allow students enough freedom to put themselves into the work. Richards (2006) stresses the importance of involving students in planning their curriculum activities.

Level 6: Evaluation. The highest level in Bloom's cognitive domain is the evaluation level. Here, the student is required to make judgments—not just any judgments, but judgments based on definite criteria. Evaluation-level objectives contain various combinations of elements in the first five levels.

A speech teacher might use the following objective with students who are studying diplomatic and persuasive techniques: "While viewing a video recording of a president's two most recent public addresses, each student will rate the speeches in terms of tact and persuasion, pinpointing in each address at least three areas of strength and three areas of weakness." A physical education teacher who is teaching bowling may want to write an objective that involves the starting position, delivery, and follow-through. You can help this teacher by ensuring that the objective requires the judgment to be based on supportive data or on internal or external standards.

Helping Teachers Write Cognitive Objectives

When helping teachers write cognitive objectives, the supervisor should always check to ensure that each objective includes the three designated criteria. After ensuring that the objective is written in terms of expected student performance, the supervisor might ask the teacher to underscore the part of the objective that identifies both the performer and the performance. The verb used should express action and should be observable or measurable. To make sure that the statement of conditions under which the students are expected to perform this task is present in the objective, the teacher might be asked to circle it. Does it accurately describe the conditions under which the teacher expects students to perform? Does the objective begin with a statement like "Given . . ." or "When given . . ."? This is an easy way to be sure that a statement of conditions is included in each objective. If the statement is very general, such as "When given a test . . ." or "Following a lesson . . .", the teacher should realize that it must be made more specific. The teacher should be challenged to think of a way to alter the task, making it easier to perform by simply changing the conditions.

Finally, to be certain that each objective includes a statement of minimum acceptable level of performance, ask the teacher to draw a box around this statement. Does it tell the student exactly how accurately the task must be performed for performance to be acceptable? Does it contain a percentage or fraction, such as "with 80% accuracy" or "four out of five times?" Can you think of other ways to help the teacher express the concept of minimum acceptable level of performance without using percentages or fractions?

The ability to write objectives at each cognitive level is crucial, since this is the only way teachers can be certain that their students will learn to develop intellectual skills at each level. Because stimulation of learning is the most important work teachers do, and because teachers are an indispensable part of the learning process, they must be able to state objectives clearly.

From his study of several thousands of classrooms, John Goodlad (1984) reported,

> Only rarely did we find evidence to suggest instruction (in reading and math) likely to go much beyond merely possession of information to a level of understanding its implications and either applying it or exploring its possible applications. Nor did we see activities likely to arouse students' curiosity or to involve them in seeking a solution to some problem not

> already laid bare by teachers or textbook. . . . And it appears that this preoccupation with the lower intellectual processes pervades social studies and science as well. An analysis of topics studied and materials used gives not an impression of students studying human adaptations and exploration, but of facts to be learned. (p. 236)

One of the first challenges beginning teachers face is to raise the thinking levels of all students. Paradoxically, if students are to reach the upper levels of the taxonomy it will be the result of purposeful planning by the teacher, yet teachers often hold expectations that are beyond students' levels of development.

It Works for Me!

Using Magic to Build Vision

Victoria Robinson, University of Northern Iowa

I bring homemade "magic wands" to class and give a wand to each student. I tell them this magic wand can be waved and one education reform wish will be granted. I ask the class to have blank sheets of paper on their desks. Excluding unlimited funding as their wish, students are asked to write on the top of their papers the education reform they would seek with their magic wands. The education reform must result in improved student learning.

Students exchange papers with one another, read the magic-wand reform, and then identify (writing on the paper) one reason why this reform would benefit students. Students exchange papers again (with someone other than the persons they exchanged with the first time), read what has been written, and then identify (again, writing on the paper) one barrier other than funding that prevents the implementation of the suggested reform. On the next exchange of papers, students are asked to write suggestions on how this barrier could be overcome. Students then find their original paper, read the other students' comments, and share with the class the reform they wished for and the comments from the paper exchanges. This activity engages all students and also results in an excellent discussion about school reform.

The Affective Domain

In addition to the greatest accusation currently aimed at the schools, their failure to teach students basic skills (cognitive domain), a rapidly growing concern is the schools' failure to discipline today's youth (affective domain). Factors such as student attitudes, motivation, perceptions, and values fall under the heading of the affective domain. Educators are increasingly concerned about the effect of schooling on the *attitudes* of students, stimulated in part by the students' own acknowledgment of the difference between their attitudes and values and those of "the system." Such differences began to show up in the 1950s with the beatniks, who rebelled against the material wealth syndrome that was sweeping the nation (when everyone seemed determined to "keep up with the Joneses" by building a larger house and owning a larger car or boat).

Rebellion against these material values carried over to the youth of the 1960s, who also expressed their dissatisfaction about U.S. involvement in Vietnam by burning draft cards and holding moratoriums and demonstrations. Many students expressed dissent against racial intolerance in civil rights marches.

In more recent years the community at large has sometimes blamed the schools for such *value*-laden social ills as environmental pollution, exhaustion of natural resources, and economic recession. Teachers often question whether they have a right to purposely try to influence the values of students. It must be noted that teachers cannot avoid affecting students' values. All teachers should attempt to promote such values as honesty, fairness, and good citizenship. On the other hand, teachers should avoid trying to impose their own religious, political, and cultural or ethnic values on their students.

Another important role of the school and the teacher in the realm of values is to help students become aware of their own values, to question these values, and to discover the basis for these values: are they factual and logical, or prejudiced and illogical? David R. Krathwohl and his colleagues (1964) led in the development of a system to categorize values. The outcome was a hierarchy of objectives in the affective domain, emphasizing a feeling tone, an emotion, or a degree of acceptance or rejection. Following are observations that supervisors can share with teachers for writing objectives in the affective domain (see Figure 8.1).

Level 1: Receiving. This level refers to the students' being aware or alert to new information or experiences. Students receive information in varying degrees. In a single class, some may not receive the information at all, while others attend or receive at a low level of awareness. Still others may be very selective, attending only to the things that are most meaningful to them. Students can be encouraged and taught to develop attention skills.

All teachers want their students to listen carefully to their lessons and to be aware of the feelings of their peers. You might encourage teachers to write an objective that would enable them to measure the degree to which students pay attention to a lesson. This objective is especially important now that many laptop-equipped students are surfing the Web throughout their lessons. The objective should include a statement of the conditions under which the teachers want their students to perform. Does each objective specify a minimum acceptable level of performance? Is it observable and measurable? An example might be: "When participating in a group discussion, the student will ask every other student at least one question." Teachers should be able to write an objective at the receiving level for their class to take a field trip to a local art museum.

Level 2: Responding. At the responding level, students react to whatever has attracted their attention. This requires physical, active behavior. Some responses may be overt or purposeful behaviors as contrasted to simple, automatic responses. A student who becomes involved at the responding level might—at the teacher's instruction, or even voluntarily—go to the library and research an issue further. Or the student may begin obeying the rules set forth in the class.

Teachers should be able to write an objective at the responding level—for example, an objective for a homework assignment. This objective should involve active student participation and reflect the student's attitude(s). Specifically, performance of this objective should show a commitment to the homework assignment—commitment that a student who does not complete the objective might not have.

Level 3: Valuing. A value is demonstrated when someone prizes a behavior enough to be willing to perform it even in the face of alternatives. A value is not necessarily reflected when a person reacts without having had time to think. In other words, if people really value a behavior, they are likely to perform it even though they know the results it may bring, and they will do so repeatedly.

For example, a mathematics teacher whose students are learning to use simulation games might write the following valuing objective: "When given free time next week at the end of each period to read, play simulation games, talk to friends, or sleep, each student will choose to play simulation games at least two out of the five days." Note that the objective asks students to choose individually of their own free will and to repeat that choice. Also notice that there are other alternatives from which to choose.

Level 4: Organization. The organization level of behavior in the affective domain requires individuals to bring together different values to build a value system. Whenever there is conflict in two or more of their values, they must resolve the conflict. For example, students constantly encounter conflicting expectations of friends and parents. As students mature, it is hoped that they will not always react according to the expectations of the people they are with at the moment, but will learn to combine the two different sets of values with their own existing beliefs and knowledge about themselves. They will respond to the orderly composite of the combined values, developing their own value systems. At this level students may change their behavior or defend it.

For example, a teacher might assign students to defend opposing positions on a controversial issue. By defending both sides, each student will, in effect, compare the two points of view and may even learn to compromise between the two extremes. A teacher of a class in U.S. government might introduce a hypothetical bill and have students form two teams, one composed of those who favor the bill and one of those who oppose it. The objective might read, "After having had the opportunity to support the bill, and the opportunity to try to defeat it, the students will combine all the information and write a statement that expresses their feelings for and against the bill. Given the opportunity, the students will choose to modify the bill to make it fit better with their own value systems."

Level 5: Characterization by a Value or a Value Complex. At the characterization level, students have already developed their own value systems. They are so consistent in the way they behave that they are predictable. At this level, students also demonstrate a degree of individuality and self-reliance.

An example of an objective written at the characterization level is, "Each student will bring one newspaper article or news report to class and explain at

It Works for Me!

Teaching and Learning: Methodology Review

Marjorie C. Ringler, Eastern Carolina University

In our definition of curriculum we discuss that it is a design *plan* for learning that requires the purposeful and proactive organization, sequencing, and management of the interactions among the teacher, the students, and the content knowledge we want students to acquire. Therefore, much of the curriculum that is taught and learned depends on the instruction that occurs in the classroom and the instructional leadership one provides to continually improve student learning. Teaching and learning strategies are discussed in depth to refresh the methodology courses each teacher took sometime during their teacher preparation program. To do so, the teaching strategies I used are intended to model active learning in the classroom.

I first begin by grouping students creatively in order to encourage interactions among students. I ask each student to pair with someone (who is not their neighbor) with whom they have something in common (glasses, same color shirt, like sports, etc.). This provides an ice breaker and the opportunity to work with a student that they have not worked with before. Next, each pair is asked to list in a t-chart on large chart paper examples of teaching strategies that are teacher-centered on one side and learner-centered on the other side. After creating their lists, each pair is then asked to find another pair with which they have something in common (using the same criteria as above). Then, in groups of four, they share their lists and discuss any strategies that they may not be familiar with. The benefits of the grouping and t-chart information is that students learn from each other about teaching practices unfamiliar to them, and also from sharing their own practices with others.

least two ways in which the article caused the student to change his or her mind from a previously held position on a controversial issue." Does this objective prove that the student has really changed values? What if the student just *says* that the change has occurred? At the moment the student may believe that a change has occurred, but what about a week from now or a year from now? Teachers should be encouraged to rewrite this objective so that this doubt will be removed or reduced.

The Psychomotor Domain

The psychomotor domain involves development of physical skills that require coordination of mind and body. It is especially relevant to such courses as physical education, art, drama, music, and vocational courses, but all subjects provide many opportunities for developing psychomotor skills.

Although this domain was the last to have a taxonomy developed for it, at least two scales have now been developed. The following taxonomy of the psychomotor domain is based on a scale developed by E. J. Simpson (1972).

Level 1: Perception. Purposeful motor activity begins in the brain, where phenomena received act as guides to motor activity. The performer must first become aware of a stimulus, pick up on cues for action, and then act upon these cues. For example, a writer discovers that she is separating her subjects and verbs, thus diluting the impact of her themes. Or a baseball batter notices herself flinching and taking short steps away from the plate when striking, causing her to miss the ball. Or a piano student perceives that he is failing to reduce the interval between double notes.

A sample objective at the perception level would be, "Following a demonstration, a geometry student who has been confusing *x* and *y* axes in plotting graphs will notice that the *x* axis always runs horizontally and the *y* axis always runs vertically."

Level 2: Set. In the psychomotor domain, "set" refers to an individual's readiness to act. It includes mental, physical, and emotional readiness. For example, a high diver is always seen pausing before a dive to get a psychological, emotional, and physical set. Emotionally, the diver must feel confident in her ability to make a safe and accurate dive. Psychologically, although she may have performed the same dive hundreds of times, still she takes the time to think through the sequence of steps before each dive. Physically, she must ready her muscles in order to respond quickly and accurately. On a less dramatic scale, a student preparing to take notes or do a writing assignment may be seen flexing his fingers or rubbing his eyes—in short, getting set to perform at his best.

An example of a psychomotor objective at this level for piano students is, "Upon the signal, 'ready,' each student will assume proper posture and place all fingers in correct keyboard position." Since no minimum level of performance is specified in this objective, the reader may wish to rewrite this objective to assign a more meaningful type of behavior. Take a moment to think about this objective, and list two ways you could establish minimum levels of performance. Does either of your objectives explain what is meant by "correct posture" or "correct keyboard position?" Do both of your suggested changes help to make the act measurable?

Level 3: Guided Response. Once the students see the need to act and ready themselves to act, they may find that whenever the act involves skills, they will need guidance through their first few responses. For example, students in the photography club may need oral guidance as they process their first negatives.

An example of an objective to enhance the development of these skills would be: "Given step-by-step directions about darkroom procedures, each student will open the film cylinder, remove the film, and, without touching the surface of the film, wind it on the spool so that the surface of each round does not touch previous rounds."

Level 4: Mechanism. This level involves performing an act somewhat automatically without having to pause to think through each separate step. For example, the photography teacher eventually might want students to be able to perform the entire sequence of development operations while simultaneously counting the number of seconds required to wait between each step. A chemistry teacher might write the following objective at the mechanism level: "Given a series of compounds to analyze, the student will operate the electron microscope, without having to pause even once to think about the sequence involved in mounting the slide, focusing the projector, and changing the lens size."

Level 5: Complex Overt Response. This level is an extension of the previous level, but it involves more complicated tasks. For example, at this level a driver-education teacher may write an objective such as, "When given an unexpected and abrupt command to stop, the student will immediately respond by applying the correct amount of pressure to the brakes, giving the correct signal, and gradually pulling off the road."

Level 6: Adaptation. At this level the student is required to adjust performance as different situations dictate. For example, to allow for an icy surface a driver would adjust her brake pressure and swerve. A cook would adjust the timing when changing from an electric stove to a gas stove. A batter would alter her stance to adjust for a left-handed pitcher.

An example of a psychomotor objective at the adaptation level is, "When planning a budget vacation, the student (without being reminded of the gas cost increase) will eliminate unnecessary automobile travel and substitute gas-saving strategies."

Level 7: Origination. At the origination level, the highest level of the psychomotor domain, the student creates new movement patterns to fit the particular situation. For example, the cook adds his own touch of genius, and the pianist alters her style or perhaps even the music itself. An art teacher might write the following objective: "Given a mixture of powders and compounds of varying textures, the student will use them to accentuate the feeling he is trying to communicate in an oil painting."

As seen in this chapter, clear objectives are essential in all classes to clarify teacher expectations. With practice, you will learn how to lead teachers in the process of writing objectives at all levels in all domains.

Planning to Use Teaching Strategies

Interstate New Teachers Assessment and Support Consortium (INTASC) Principle No. 4 mandates that "The teacher understands and uses a variety of instructionals to encourage students' development of critical thinking, problem solving, and performance skills."

Paramount in teachers' pedagogical needs is an awareness of a variety of teaching strategies. The choice of strategies teachers should use depends on the content being studied and on the teacher and students. To be prepared to meet students' needs, teachers should include in their pedagogical knowledge base the following strategies at a minimum: direct instruction, case-study method, inquiry learning, simulation games, tutoring, questioning, cooperative learning, and mastery learning. A prerequisite to effectively planning to use each strategy is understanding its purposes, appropriateness, strengths, and weaknesses, and ways the strategy can be improved. A list of these methods and their characteristics is shown in Table 8.2.

Table 8.2 Characteristics of Teaching Methods

Method	Characteristic(s)
Direct instruction	Economical, good for building a framework and summarizing
Case study	Slow, student-centered, builds judgment and problem-solving skills
Simulation games	Slow, student-centered, highly motivating, high-retention
Tutoring	Highly personalized
Inquiry	Slow, student-centered, develops problem-solving skills
Questioning	Involves students, can be used to raise thinking levels
Cooperative learning	Develops social skills, encourages cooperation, uses group rewards
Mastery learning	Uses criterion-reformed evaluation and formative evaluation, uses remediation without penalty

Themes

When planning to use any of these strategies, teachers should be reminded of the need to focus on themes as opposed to isolated concepts. "Current U.S. textbooks are strong on presenting information and vocabulary and short on putting concepts and activities together to coherently develop big ideas" (Roth & Garnier, 2006/2007, p. 22). Keeping this in mind—and based on the TIMSS studies (2003) and the fact that each lesson should be built around a strong story line—Kathleen Roth and Helen Garnier (2006/2007) say that supervisors can help teachers plan by ensuring that they (the teachers) clearly understand how the major concepts of each lesson's theme or story line will tie into the learning cycle.

Direct Instruction

In direct instruction the teacher provides new information to the class; carefully monitors student behavior; gives assignments for students to perform at the board, in their seats, or at learning stations; and then reteaches the material if necessary.

Strengths and Weaknesses of Direct Instruction. Direct instruction has several advantages. The lecture, the most common form of direct instruction, is a good method for building a mental framework. Therefore, it is an effective method for introducing and summarizing a topic. It is also an effective approach for clarifying misunderstandings. In addition, when using direct instruction, students stay on task (i.e., focus on the lesson for a greater proportion of class time than when studying under most other methods). The number of minutes actually spent learning is the time measure most frequently found to contribute to learning.

Direct instruction also has some limitations, being appropriate only for lessons that are concerned with learning information (i.e., lessons whose primary objectives are in the cognitive domain). Direct instruction is not an effective means for developing attitudes, social skills, or problem-solving skills.

Remember that teachers usually choose those methods that their own former teachers used most. The single method most favored by teachers—the lecture—is also the method that offers teachers the most security, because it is the most familiar and because it is tied closely to the textbook. However, an inherent weakness of the lecture is that its success depends on the ability of students to take notes, and most students are notoriously poor note takers. When taking notes from lectures, students usually record bits and pieces rather than major ideas.

Another weakness of the lecture is that its success depends on self-motivated students. A more direct and frank way of expressing this is to simply say that the lecture is a poor motivator. This quality can be attributed to the fact that the lecture seldom involves students at a high level of thinking (Ebert & Culyer, 2008). The implication here is that teachers need to involve students more in their education, even in its planning.

Still another weakness of the lecture is the failure of the audience to focus on the lesson's major concepts. To understand a topic or discipline, students must come to know those major concepts that give the topic or discipline meaning. A *concept* is a content generalization. Albert Einstein recognized the concept as the basis of all thinking: "I think the transition from free association or 'dreaming' to thinking is characterized by the more or less dominating role which the 'concept' plays in it" (1951, p. 7). Yet, as important as the role of concept is in learning, most American students fail to understand the major concepts in the disciplines they study, and this is true in all disciplines. The message is clear: Teachers need help in lesson planning so that students will master the important concepts found in each lesson.

Effective planning for any strategy involves finding ways of avoiding the strategy's weaknesses and taking advantage if its strengths. Since the lecture is a very poor motivator, it is appropriate for elective classes, but its use in required classes (such as remedial classes) should be limited. More specifically, it should be used predominately in classes of capable students and students who are highly motivated.

Helping Teachers Plan Direct Instruction. When helping teachers plan instruction, perhaps the most important role of the supervisor is to encourage teachers to use the lecture *only* for those purposes for which it is most suited. To compensate for the inability of the lecture to motivate, supervisors should advise their faculty that these lessons should have brief introductions followed by a variety of stimulants, including audiovisuals and student activities. Furthermore, the lecture itself should be planned so that only a few major concepts are introduced, and those concepts should be accentuated and clarified.

Ironically, although effort must be made to clarify concepts, lessons should also provide contradictions that will promote the state of disequilibrium recommended by Piaget (see chapter 14). *Disequilibrium* is needed to enable students to realize their limitations and misunderstandings. Each lesson should have planned into it both examples and nonexamples of each concept.

The teacher's philosophy should guide each decision that shapes each lesson. For example, the teacher's view of the purposes of school and the nature of youth and learning should guide objective setting and the selection of content and activities. The most successful lessons taught by direct instruction are those in which it is blended with indirect instruction (Ryder et al., 2006).

The Case-Study Method

This method of instruction refers to the use of cases as educational vehicles to give students an opportunity to put themselves in the decision maker's or problem solver's shoes. Case studies enable individuals to consider a variety of perspectives when addressing complex issues (Larson et al., 2007). In some ways, the case-study method is the opposite of the lecture: It is an excellent motivator; it puts students in an active rather than a passive role, and it prepares students to make judicious decisions. Unlike the lecture, which is a highly economic method in the sense that it allows the expedient coverage of much material, the case study-method is much slower to implement. Therefore, teachers who feel obligated to cover a large amount of content (e.g., the entire textbook) should not use the case-study method.

Throughout the years, the case-study method has been widely used in schools of business and law. In particular, the Harvard University School of Business has made extensive use of this method throughout most of the twentieth century.

Helping Teachers Plan Case Studies. To be effective, the teacher who uses the case-study method must have good cases. Actual experiences provide an excellent basis for developing cases, although they need not be based on real events to be of high quality. Contrived cases (also called armchair cases) can be equally effective if they have the necessary qualities, one of which is the right information. Good cases contain both relevant and irrelevant information, forcing the reader to sift through the material and cull the irrelevant information. Good cases also end with a problem, and the solution process will enhance knowledge of the topic at hand. Teachers should be encouraged to write their own case studies and to include both relevant and irrelevant information.

Inquiry Lessons

Inquiry learning (or problem solving) is a student-centered approach. Students take charge in determining what they will study and in leading the investigations (Aldridge & Goldman, 2007). Inquiry learning derives its support from the fact that it is student centered, activities centered, and problem centered. The inquiry method became popular in the late 1950s and throughout the 1960s because of the report of the Woods Hole Project (see chapter 2). The group recommended a concept-based, theme-centered, interdisciplinary, problem-solving, inquiry-based curriculum.

Paradoxically, although inquiry learning is concerned with solving problems, its success does not require finding solutions to those problems. In fact, as Albert Einstein said, the formation of a problem is often more essential than its solution because it requires creative imagination and marks a real advance in science (Einstein & Infield, 1938). Even at an early age, students can use their powers of imagination and creativity. They can be taught to identify and solve problems, and they will work harder to reach their own goals.

Inquiry learning has two types (convergent and divergent), and the advantages of inquiry learning depend on the type. Of the two, convergent inquiry lessons have been the most popular through the years. Most mathematics problem solving is done through convergent inquiry. Here, a specific answer is sought—a single, "correct" answer. In contrast, divergent thinking begins with certainties and proceeds to explore uncertainties. Most good inquiry lessons include both convergent and divergent thinking.

Examining the skills needed in the workplace of the future can give us a good idea of the skills needed in all parts of life. Problem solving is certainly going to be one of the most important skills demanded for successful living. The labor market has always had a place for problem solvers, and it always will. Twenty-first-century workers also will be expected to be creative, to discover new and better ways to do their jobs, to collaborate in diverse settings, and to have the capacity to set up procedures to test and evaluate alternative ideas. Supervisors must help teachers prepare their students to think in both divergent and convergent directions.

Helping Teachers Plan Inquiry Lessons. In inquiry learning, students are given a problem and assigned the task of discovering the answer. This process of problem solving is an effective way of engaging students in deep learning (Johnson, 2007). Although some inquiry learning starts by giving students a specific problem to solve, other inquiry lessons may have very loosely defined problems. Unlike strict problem solving, the emphasis of inquiry is on the *process*, not on *solutions*. In fact, a successful inquiry lesson may not have a solution at all!

The amount of supervision given the students determines the type of discovery. Closely supervised programs, known as *guided discovery learning*, require a highly skilled teacher (Aldridge & Goldman, 2007). Loosely supervised programs are called *inductive discovery learning*. There are even categories that represent degrees between these extremes.

When considering the use of inquiry, supervisors should remind teachers that it is a very uneconomical strategy in the sense that material is covered slowly. For example, a teacher who feels pressured to cover the textbook so that students won't leave the class at the end of the year with severe gaps in their knowledge, unprepared or poorly prepared for entering their class next year, probably should forego planning inquiry lessons. For teachers who have a strong compulsion to feed information to their students, the inquiry process may be a poor choice. Inquiry learning may be the wrong choice for teachers who teach only for cognitive gains, because of the high potential of inquiry learning for the development of creativity. These issues should be considered before planning an inquiry curriculum; otherwise, the inquiry process can lead to frustration on the part of both teachers and students.

* * *

The traditional practice of teachers working alone to plan instruction is insufficient to meet twenty-first-century state and national expectations. The following case study outlines some of the problems that must be overcome in employing a collaborative strategy for leading teachers to plan their curriculum collectively to meet the state mandated goals.

The Bumpy Road to Instructional Improvement: Leadership that Builds Capacity to Close the Achievement Gap in Reading

Judith Jackson May • Bowling Green University
Kathleen Topolka Jorissen • Western Carolina University

Because school change is a factor in collective change, the role of the principal must also change to that of a resource provider, modeling and encouraging reflective practice. This case study chronicles one principal's path as she coalesces her faculty around one focused goal: improved student achievement in reading.

The Community

St. Lucie is a small semi-rural university town with a population of 30,000. The St. Lucie School District enrolls 3,000 students in six elementary schools, one middle school and one high school. Parents have high expectations for student success, and they want their children to keep pace with the students in a more affluent neighboring community. The economic and academic achievement disparity between the haves and the have-nots, however, is large.

The School

Lincoln Elementary School is a K–6 building situated in the heart of the most socioeconomically depressed area in the town. The student body of 175 has an average class size of 23. Grades K–3 and the primary intervention specialist are located on the first floor, and grades 4–6 and intermediate intervention specialist are on the second floor. Additional full-time staff includes a Title I Reading Teacher. Part-time staff includes a counselor, speech/hearing/language pathologist, art, music, and PE teachers.

The District Initiative

Returning from her meeting with the superintendent, Principal Denise Rigby was tempted to use the ticket to Timbuktu that she always kept in her desk. The superintendent's imperative rang vividly over and over in her head: *"Reading and math test scores in every grade must be raised by an average of six points consistently over the next two years."* However, having already worked as a principal in two much larger buildings, she considered this task manageable. This was her second year at Lincoln Elementary School, and she felt she had done a pretty good job.

The principals could "do their own thing" as long as the goal was accomplished without delay. Denise's school had performed fairly well last year on the state proficiency tests, given the fact that nearly 40% of the student body was economically disadvantaged and 14% of the students were classified as disabled—the highest of all six elementary schools on both counts! While the district had met 17 of 23 state indicators and was designated as an "effective district" during the previous school year, Lincoln was a "continuous improvement" school, having met the six indicators (third-grade math and reading, fourth-grade reading and writing, sixth-grade writing, and attendance) required to make adequate yearly progress (AYP). As shown in Table 1, the fourth-grade scores were on the low average for the district, but the third grade outperformed the district and the state.

Much work was required. Denise would let the full-time staff know of the superintendent's mandate and invite them to make suggestions as to the path to follow. But first, she spent the evening researching strategies for improving student performance on state assessments. She concluded that the key to success was effective readers. Denise decided to copy and distribute two articles to the staff that discussed recent research on improving academic achievement in socioeconomically depressed areas by focusing on reading improvement.

The Players

On her way to the library for the staff meeting early Wednesday morning, Denise reviewed the personalities of her 11 full-time teachers and what each of them brought to the table.

- On the first floor is Mrs. Macon, a 22-year veteran kindergarten teacher who has strong opinions but is flexible, amicable, and excellent at preparing the kindergartners for first grade. The first-grade teacher has been reasonably pleased with kindergarten students' readiness for first grade.
- Mrs. Diels teaches second grade and is not overly engaged in the classroom. She is very pleasant and quickly acquiesces to group wishes. Her lessons are meticulously constructed. She often uses an overhead projector and relies on worksheets for concept reinforcement. Her assessment scores have been declining over the last two years. The third-grade teacher feels that Mrs. Diels does not sufficiently prepare students for third grade.
- Mrs. Block is an excellent third-grade teacher with an unbending routine. She has been teaching for 23 years, is quite rigid, and always produces great assessment scores. Mrs. Block has little patience with less effective teachers and becomes very stressed during the first few weeks of the year, which she claims are spent reteaching skills from second grade. Her anxiety is eased by administrative praise and attention.
- Primary intervention specialist Mr. Jones, a 12-year teacher, has a big heart and loves kids but is largely ineffective. His instructional strategies rely heavily on pencil-and-paper tasks. While Mr. Jones feels like he is providing invaluable intervention to students, the primary teachers do not consider him an asset to the staff.
- Mrs. Jackson is an outstanding 25-year first-grade teacher. She became a National Board Certified teacher a year ago, is not known for adaptability, and is very outspoken. Her students are actively engaged in learning most of the day, and they always excel on annual assessments. Mrs. Jackson is leader on the first floor.
- On the second floor is Mrs. Shaner, one of two fourth-grade teachers. She has taught for eight years and welcomes new instructional techniques, is flexible, well liked, and is not afraid to speak her mind. Because she is teaching one of the "traveling" classes this year, she has an enviable 18 students whom she expects to perform extremely well on the fourth-grade profi-

Table 1 Previous Year Annual Assessment Results

Teacher	Grade Level	Lincoln School			District		
		Reading	Math	Writing	Reading	Math	Writing
Mrs. Block	3rd	84.2	94.7		82.1	83.6	
Mrs. Shaner	4th–1	81.3	50	81.3	85.2	66	82.8
Mrs. Connor	4th–2	73.2	43	75	85.2	66	82.8
Mr. Detmer	5th	50			83.2		
Mrs. Peters	6th	55	60	95	78.5	68.6	95.3

ciency test. Last year's scores were "so-so" in her opinion, and she does not want to be disappointed again.

- Miss Connor, a fifth-year teacher, has been the looping teacher with the traveling classroom for the past five years. Currently, she is the second fourth-grade teacher. The students are randomly assigned each year, and the class size is always less than 20. Apparently, she never has a class with the ability to achieve, maintains low expectations, and demonstrates little motivation. Past evaluations include suggestions for instructional improvement, but there is no documentation of administrative follow-up.
- Mr. Detmer, a fifth-grade teacher, has been teaching for 15 years and is largely ineffective. He relies on the intervention specialist who chooses to team teach in his room. While he appears to be "tolerated" by the staff, he has enjoyed satisfactory evaluations over his teaching career—yet his students consistently perform poorly on annual assessments.
- Mrs. Rose, a 20-year intermediate intervention specialist, is very effective teaching in all situations, whether in small groups, one-on-one, or in the classroom. She has overhauled Mr. Detmer's class (with his permission) in an effort to "get him organized." She sets the goals and prepares all plans when team teaching in his room.
- Mrs. Peters, a sixth-grade teacher of 27 years,. carries herself with great class and is flexible as long as it does not necessitate additional time at school. She attempts but fails to connect with students from lower social classes. Mrs. Peters is not a fan of change and would prefer to spend her last remaining years just as she has been doing. Her lesson plans and room are organized, and she helps students on manners and the social graces.
- Mrs. Wiley is a two-year, Title I teacher who works well with all teachers, has high expectations, keeps excellent documentation, and aspires to great heights. She rolls with the program, is very dependable and gracious, and is very highly valued among all teachers.

As Denise strode the last few steps to the library she came face to face with her staff, waiting patiently for her to dispel or confirm the rumors that had run rampant since Monday's meeting with the superintendent.

The Search for a Curriculum Plan

Denise spoke honestly to the staff and reiterated the district goal of raising math and reading scores six points over the next two years. The teachers seemed puzzled because they had received high praise for their performance on last year's assessment test, as Lincoln had made AYP and had remained in continuous improvement. Nonetheless, the teachers accepted the principal's direction to brainstorm on what course should be taken. The teachers formed two groups, with kindergarten, first, second, third, fourth-1, and Title I teachers in one group. In another group sat fourth-2, fifth, sixth, and both intervention specialists. During the open brainstorm and discussion, Denise noticed immediately that Mr. Detmer (fifth grade), Miss Connor (one of two fourth-grade teachers), and Mrs. Peters (sixth grade), were seated toward the back of the room, creating a group-within-a-group, and were not actively involved in the discussion, even though it was clear they were listening intently.

After a thirty-minute period, the teachers quieted and Mrs. Jackson, the first-grade teacher spoke, apparently for the group. She said, "We feel that the recommendations in the articles you handed us, and the research I have done on my own, makes great sense. If we improve our overall reading skills, then other subjects should follow. So we propose a new reading program, one that will be used by all teachers, and one that has a proven track record of success with all students. We propose investigating the adoption of the Four Blocks Reading Program."

As Mrs. Jackson spoke, both Mrs. Shaner (fourth-1) on her right and Mrs. Diels (second grade) on her left nodded in supportive agreement. Quickly scanning the teachers, Denise noticed that the kindergarten teacher, Mrs. Macon; the third-grade teacher, Mrs. Block; the intermediate intervention specialist, Mrs. Rose; and the Title I teacher, Mrs. Wiley, appeared enthused as well. It was apparent that Mr. Detmer, Mrs. Peters, and Miss Connor were less than pleased. They were leaning suspiciously in their chairs, exchanging glances, with hands folded across their chests.

Mrs. Peters poked her finger up and asked, "Do we really need a whole new program to improve scores?" Mr. Detmer added, "Yeah, seems like our test scores from last year were pretty good." Mrs. Shaner turned around, faced Mr. Detmer, and retorted, "Well, I think some scores were good, but I guess pretty good isn't good enough. Besides, I have heard about this program for two years and teachers who use it rave about it."

Mrs. Jackson weighed in with, "It is one of the more successful data-driven programs that address all the discreet skills relevant to the teaching of reading." Mrs. Jackson, on a roll, took the opportunity to explain a bit about the program. "Four Blocks," she continued, "is a program that was created for students in grades 1–3 by incorporating four different approaches to reading on a daily basis. Obviously, it will not affect all of us in the same way, but since we have so many students not reading on grade level, the actual instructional techniques may be useful in the upper grades as well. It can't hurt to have continuity from the downstairs to the upstairs."

Denise believed that a new reading program would be a great and invigorating way to begin, but that it would also require much time, energy, cooperation, and patience on everyone's part. After calling for volunteers for a research committee, it surprised no one when Mrs. Jackson, Mrs. Shaner, and Mrs. Block volunteered. Denise thought it best to have a committee of four, so she asked Mr. Detmer to join them. He said he probably could serve, as long they did not meet before school. Denise could feel a knot developing in the pit of her stomach.

Before leaving the library, Denise suggested the committee meet with her at 10:30 a.m. the following Wednesday to share information they had gathered and establish a time line. As the teachers left the library, lines were clearly drawn in the sand: Mrs. Jackson, Mrs. Shaner, and Mrs. Block strolled excitedly through the door, chattering about what they needed to do. Mrs. Wiley, Mrs. Diels, and Mrs. Macon followed contentedly after. Mrs. Rose and Mr. Jones followed, discussing the scheduling of upcoming multi-factored evaluations; and finally Mr. Detmer, Miss Connor, and Mrs. Peters stayed behind to share.

Changes on the Horizon

During the ensuing week, the committee was clearly hard at work and there was much discussion around the school about Four Blocks and the impending changes. The program would necessitate first-order and second-order changes. Mr. Detmer missed one morning meeting and was quite late to the other one. When he was there, he used the pronoun "you" more often than he used "we," and questioned why the changes to the primary classrooms had to affect the intermediate teachers.

The kindergarten teacher, Mrs. Macon, second-grade teacher, Mrs. Diels, and the Title I teacher, Mrs. Wiley, shared hallway and lunch discussions of how they thought the program would allow them to reach more students, and Miss Connor and Mrs. Peters shared trepidation that perhaps this was not the best time for a whole-school change. Mr. Jones seemed oblivious to the hallway hubbub.

When Denise met with the committee a week later, they were excited to share their news. Mrs. Jackson said that she felt that implementation for the entire school would cost about $35,000. This included ongoing professional development for all teachers, materials for K–3 teachers, and release time for teachers to visit schools currently using Four Blocks. Denise told the committee that the state was offering grants of up to $50,000 for school reading and/or math initiatives, but the funds were very competitive and the staff would have to begin work immediately on submitting a grant proposal for review. Mrs. Shaner and Mrs. Jackson enthusiastically offered to work on writing the grant. With a mixed sense of accomplishment and anxiety, Denise announced that the new curricular initiative was a "go."

In a rather solemn yet upbeat speech, Denise affirmed that a schoolwide curricular instructional change would require a strong commitment from all, and that grant awards were based on proposals that include comprehensive evaluative procedures. She further stressed that subsequent approval of the grant would require observable, measurable benchmarks for teachers as well as students. Denise slowly and methodically scanned the faces of her 11 teachers. She realized that the small group had an incredibly diverse array of talent, ability, and most importantly, motivation and commitment.

Once the grant was completed and ready to submit, its approval would be an exciting and positive event. Teachers would receive extensive professional development and training, new leveled reading books, and other classroom materials. University students would be utilized as interns to assist with weekly reading evaluation and classroom intervention. Schedules would be modified to accommodate common planning times, and a professional trainer/coach would be employed for six months, with one visit to each classroom monthly. Finally, and perhaps most exciting, teachers would receive stipends to purchase materials of their choice to enhance their classroom reading efforts. On the day of submission, the entire staff was on hand for the celebration. Whether the grant was approved or denied, all agreed that incredible strides had been made in four short weeks.

Conflict Emerges

Upon notification of the grant approval, Denise felt pride beyond belief and enjoyed the buildingwide celebration with the teachers. Training was scheduled to include three full in-service days and three half in-service days, followed by one day a week of after-school sessions for three weeks and six months of visits from a trainer/coach. The coach would also serve as an evaluator and report ongoing progress to the principal.

Initial full and half in-service days were reasonably positive and enjoyed 100% attendance. Most teachers showed high energy through most sessions, although three of the upstairs teachers required encouragement to contribute. The after-school sessions proved to be a different story; Miss Connor and Mr. Jones missed Week One, Mr. Detmer and Mrs. Peters missed Session Two. The third and final after-school session was poorly attended, with most absent teachers reporting legitimate personal and family obligations. Mrs. Wiley, Mrs. Shaner, Mrs. Jackson, and Mrs. Block were present for the session.

The first month of implementation experienced some bumps and bruises. Arranging the morning reading block required schedule changes to accommodate art, PE, Music, Title I, and speech. Everyone seemed agreeable until it was *their* schedule that was altered. Mrs. Jackson was not happy because her class had always gone to lunch at 10:50, and she said that was best for first graders. Mr. Detmer was up in arms, as his planning time had always occurred at 9:30 a.m. and he needed his morning planning time. Mrs. Wiley wanted to choose the classes in which she assisted. Denise also heard some grumblings about the one-day-per-week common planning time. The downstairs was feeling a bit dominated by Mrs. Jackson. She was very knowledgeable and offered to assist Miss Connor, who complained that her students just "weren't into it." Mr. Detmer and Mrs. Peters seemed less than focused and did not have much to share. But for all the issues the new instructional plan was in full force.

After the first eight-week period the trainer/coach spent a solid week in the building, moving from room to room. On Friday at 2:00 p.m. the trainer/coach entered Denise's office quietly, shut the door, and sat down. The look on her face told Denise that she should have boarded that plane for Timbuktu some time ago.

Issues for Further Reflection

As you reflect on the experience of building instructional capacity at Lincoln Elementary, you might use the guiding questions below.

1. What were the most effective instructional leadership strategies Denise Rigby used to initiate instructional improvement? To implement the new plan? To monitor the plan? To reward and celebrate improvements?
2. What additional strategies would you employ?
3. What evidence is there that this school reflected the common concerns of implementing a new program? How did Denise leverage an understanding of teacher concerns to keep the momentum going?
4. Critique Denise's response to the conflict and the uneven implementation of the staff development component of the plan. What leadership strategies are most effective in achieving consistency among staff members?
5. What criteria should be used to evaluate the success of the program?

Simulation Games

A *simulation* is a technique that teaches some aspect of the world or environment by imitation or replication. A *game* has the element of competition, a quality that makes simulations highly motivating. A *simulation game* offers students the opportunity to safely learn about the real world. The advantages of simulation games are that they:

- are highly motivating
- are highly interactive
- involve communication
- involve social interaction
- make the abstract more concrete
- provide immediate feedback
- invite experimentation
- invite risk taking
- allow for mistakes
- provide opportunities for reflection
- provide self-evaluation

Consider using this list to lead a discussion with your faculty. By making teachers aware of these advantages and, hopefully, collaborating with teachers from other schools to share their ideas for using them, you can encourage your faculty to use these strategies. Using simulation games can be as simple as creating classroom versions of *Jeopardy!* or *Wheel of Fortune*, or as complex as computer simulations in areas such as sociology/anthropology, languages, astronomy, psychology, and many other areas of learning. Computerized simulation in the classroom is increasingly popular, with some students even designing games and simulations for other students to use. One exceptional example is a class of inner-city fourth graders who programmed games to teach fractions to third graders (Seay, 1997). Supervisors could recommend *Simulation & Gaming: An Interdisciplinary Journal of Theory, Practice and Research* as a valuable professional publication for interested faculty members. Many software companies such as Gamespot offer simulation games to enhance learning. Visit the Web site (www.gamespot.com) and search "education" to see the variety of simulation games available.

Tutoring

Tutoring has a place in education's history that dates back at least as far as the lecture. In many countries it remains the dominant teaching method. In some British colleges and universities tutoring is such a key teaching strategy that instead of having offices, professors have tutorials, which are more personal than offices.

In a way, tutoring is the ultimate form of individualizing instruction. It provides the student with undivided attention. The results are increased motivation and increased learning. Because tutoring is so time consuming, only those students who have a commitment to helping others will volunteer to serve as tutors. In addition to its motivational power, tutoring can help fill gaps in students' learning and can level the playing field between minorities and mainstream students.

Helping Teachers Plan Tutoring Lessons. When developing tutorial lessons, supervisors should remind teachers to focus on major concepts. The fewer the number of concepts pursued in a lesson the better, since depth of learning should take precedence over the desire to cover more information. The tutor helps the learner become familiar with the major content. Deep understanding occurs when the presence of new information prompts the emergence or enhancement of cognitive structures that enable the learner to rethink prior ideas (Aldridge & Goldman, 2007).

Because the use of tutoring does not guarantee increased learning, help tutors to design each lesson to capitalize on tutoring's advantages. For example, at-risk students often need individual help and socialization. Tutoring can be combined with follow-up, small-group discussions, providing tutors and learners opportunities to discuss their views.

Questioning Strategies

As with other teaching strategies, planning to use questions should begin by examining the purposes for which this strategy is to be used. Like other strategies, questioning has both strengths and limitations. A major advantage of using questions in class is the capacity that questioning has, when correctly used, for helping students move from simple recall thinking to higher levels of thinking (Ebert & Culyer, 2008).

Teachers should be aware that some questions are productive and others are reproductive. *Productive questions* require students to produce their own information; *reproductive questions* only require students to reproduce information given by the teacher, textbooks, or another source. If a teacher's purpose for using questions is to raise the level of students' thinking, then productive questions (rather than reproductive questions) should be planned into the lesson.

You can help your teachers use questions that stimulate higher-order thinking by reminding them to ask, "Why?" and "What if . . . ?" Asking such questions can cause students to internalize the material they study—for example:

- "Why is that important?"
- "How does that affect your life?"
- "What would you do if . . . ?"
- "How do you feel about that?"

Helping Teachers Plan Empirical Questions. Empirical questions provide students with opportunities to express their views or perceptions. These questions include the act of generalizing. Providing students an opportunity to share their perceptions enables the teacher to know when their perceptions are wrong. Only then can the teacher help students correct for their misconceptions. Therefore, when planning questions to help students increase their understanding of content, teachers should use questions that focus on the main concepts in the subject. These are not always easy questions. We must realize that in education, and in the arts, the questions with easy-to-measure answers are seldom the most important ones. To avoid confusion, questions to students should be kept simple as opposed to using questions that have several parts.

Questions can also be used to engage students in conversation and integrate them into the socialization process. All students have their own ways of viewing the world; some students need encouragement to share their views. When selecting questions for this purpose, the focus of content is less relevant than the comfort (or discomfort) level surrounding the question. To govern the use of questioning, ground rules should include an absolute ban on sarcasm and ridicule by other students. Following are a few questioning strategies that supervisors can share with their faculty.

Helping Teachers Plan the Socratic Method. The Socratic Method consists of making a series of statements and questioning your subject with the goal of getting him/her to agree with each statement as it is presented in turn. To help his students become aware of their faulty thinking, Socrates very skillfully aligned his questions so that his students would, without realizing what was happening, eventually agree with a statement that was exactly opposite or contradictory to an earlier statement.

Planning for Student-Generated Questions. When questions are asked in classrooms across the country, most of them are asked by the teacher. Yet, students, too, ask questions, and these questions can be invaluable to teachers, who can use them to shape instruction to fit students' needs.

An effective way to plan for student-generated questions is a strategy called *reciprocal peer questioning*. This method sharpens students' questioning skills while improving their understanding of the content being taught. Students are given a set of generic questions and trained to use those questions as a guide for generating their own specific questions on the lecture content. During the self-questioning step of the procedure, students usually make up two or three thought-provoking questions. Those questions may or may not be ones that they, themselves, are able to answer. Following the self-questioning, they engage in peer questioning. Working in groups of three or four, students pose their questions to their group and then take turns answering each other's questions.

A study on reciprocal peer questioning (Johnson, 2006) documented 160 students in an educational psychology course of used WebCT discussions to satisfy one of two virtual online study-group conditions: reciprocal peer questioning or mnemonic devices. Students made postings according to their assigned study strategy in order to facilitate the learning in their group. Students in the reciprocal peer-questioning condition made more postings and read more articles than students in the mnemonics group, and the reciprocal peer-questioning group reported higher levels of satisfaction with the virtual study experience.

Cooperative Learning

Because our nation is a young and successful country, and because it was settled by aggressive, competitive individuals who were willing to risk their lives, it seems natural that our population would remain competitive and our schools would stress the value of competition. Through the use of a norm-referenced evaluation system, our schools have forced students to compete with their classmates for good grades. The result has often been "winners" and "losers," and this labeling as a result of competition can produce negative qualities, among them a sense of inferiority in "losers" and even outright hostility among learners.

An alternative to teaching competition is the strategy known as cooperative education or *cooperative learning*, which encourages all members to help other members of their group. It has been shown that some student ethnic groups, particularly African Americans, prefer cooperative group assignments over assignments that force individual students to compete with their classmates (Armstrong et al., 2009). Group success actually depends on the success of any and all members of the group. When planning cooperative learning, teachers don't have to worry about whether the intended group of students is right for cooperative learning, or vice versa. Research has shown that cooperative learning techniques

- promote student learning and academic achievement,
- increase student retention,
- enhance student satisfaction with their learning experience,
- help students develop skills in oral communication,
- develop students' social skills,
- promote student self-esteem, and
- help to promote positive intercultural relations.

Helping Teachers Plan to Use Cooperative Learning. Some of the tips found throughout this book (under the heading *It Works for Me!*) are effective vehicles for creating cooperative learning. Sandra Murray's tip, "Teaming Up" (see chapter 1) is an excellent example because it requires individual teachers to become part of a team. Experiencing this exercise only once is sufficient to convince some teachers to try other group projects. As experienced with these activities, cooperative learning is usually motivating because it is free of individual competition. Always arrange for a relaxed atmosphere and enjoy the humor with your teachers.

Mastery Learning

Since the first quarter of the twentieth century, when E. L. Thorndike created and perfected the first tests to measure humans' intelligence quotients, Americans assumed that the normal curve (or bell curve) represented the intellectual capacity of the population. Thorndike himself did not suggest that this model represented small groups of people, but professors began using it freely with classes of all sizes. Many professors took considerable pride in the fact that they based their grading on the bell curve.

Although most public school teachers were not so bold as to admit that they forced their student grades to fit the bell curve, the belief that only a few should be bright enough to receive As and a few should be dull enough to get Fs has indirectly caused elementary and secondary school teachers to limit the number of As and spread the rest of the scores across the continuum in a distribution similar to the bell curve.

Up until the middle of the twentieth century, unquestioned application of the bell curve was the norm. In the early 1960s a professor at Harvard University, John B. Carroll (1963), wrote an article in the journal *Teachers College Record,* in which he openly challenged this practice. Carroll believed that the bell curve distribution represents the distribution of large populations—assuming that all students are equally motivated and equally challenged by teachers of equal commitment and ability. Carroll considered such assumptions ridiculous—the whole idea of a formal education system is to provide a better-than-normal education. On the contrary, thought Carroll, in a country with a history of providing education to the masses, if we believe that the purpose of school is to help all students reach their maximum potential, then the schools should be working to reshape this random learning curve.

In this article, Carroll went further than questioning past practices; he suggested changes that should help all students in all classrooms across America reach their potential. The idea behind this proposed system was to help each student, regardless of innate ability, to master the content and objective in each class. Carroll even went so far as to predict that if the conditions he stipulated in his model were met, at least 90 to 95% of all high school students could master all class objectives. The variables that Carroll believed must be controlled or manipulated to take students to the desired level of mastery include: providing a variety of teaching approaches to increase the students' level of motivation; providing students all the time they need to master the content, recognizing that the amount of time required will vary from one student to the next; and providing those students who fail to reach the desired level of mastery with opportunities to remediate, without penalty, as many times as needed to succeed.

Throughout the history of our schools, practically all evaluation systems have used norm-referenced and summative tests. In contrast, mastery learning programs make extensive use of formative or *criterion-referenced evaluation,* which measures success by the attainment of established levels of performance; individual success is based wholly on performance of the individual, without regard for the performance of others. Criterion-referenced testing contrasts sharply with the traditionally used *norm-referenced evaluation,* which compares the individual's performance to the performance of classmates. The difference between criterion-referenced and norm-referenced exams is discussed in further detail in chapter 10.

Mastery learning uses *formative evaluation,* which occurs before or during instruction and is aimed at improving teaching and learning, as compared to the traditionally used *summative evaluation,* which occurs after instruction ends and is used to determine grades. Criterion-referenced tests can be strong clarifiers of teacher expectations, thereby guiding students toward expected outcomes. Proponents of mastery learning believe that assessment should be used to promote further learning and should be a positive experience.

Helping Teachers Plan Mastery Learning Programs. Because of the varying goals and characteristics of different communities, teachers, and students, supervisors should be aware that each mastery learning program is unique in some way. However, all mastery programs can be grouped into two types: (1) teacher paced and group based, and (2) individually paced and individually based. In teacher-paced and group-based programs, the teacher lectures and assigns student activities to groups of students; therefore controlling the rate at which learning occurs for all students in the class. In individually-paced and individually-based programs, individuals pursue lessons at their own chosen rate, independent of their classmates. Your faculty should be encouraged to use the programs that best fit their students, as well as their own individual teaching styles.

The Effectiveness of Mastery Learning. Since its origin, mastery learning has been criticized from time to time. But the advocates of this learning strategy say that when enough schools are studied, the evidence is clear: Mastery learning is exceedingly successful. A review of the meta-analyses in almost forty areas of educational research (Kulick & Kulick, 1989) found that few teaching strategies were consistently associated with achievement effects as large as those produced by mastery learning. The benefits of mastery learning are not limited to academic achievement. After conducting an extensive review of the research on teaching/learning strategies, Thomas Guskey (2005a) reported that mastery learning also improves students' confidence, school attendance, and student attitudes toward learning.

Conclusion

Daily use of objectives is required to reach the goals of any curriculum. By using objectives in all domains of the educational taxonomies (affective, cognitive, and psychomotor), teachers can ensure the attainment of a variety of goals, leading to the development of the whole individual.

Throughout history, the textbook has been the number-one curriculum determiner, yet textbooks engage students in only the lowest level of thinking and learning. When correctly used, performance objectives can raise the levels of thinking in the classroom.

Unfortunately, in the past teachers have seldom begun their planning by considering what objectives they most want the lesson to attain. Good objectives share some common qualities: They use action verbs, are written in terms of student performance, set minimum levels of expectations, and describe the conditions under which students are expected to perform.

Effective schools research has shown that students achieve more when the expectations are clear and when instruction and learning occur in a variety of ways. Some of the most effective learning/teaching strategies include direct instruction, the case-study method, tutoring, inquiry learning, questioning, simulation games, cooperative learning, and mastery learning. Each strategy has strengths and limitations; therefore, supervisors should encourage teachers to use a variety of strategies. Prior to using each strategy, teachers should learn its strengths and limitations and should adjust learning conditions so that the advantages of each strategy are reached and the limitations are minimized or avoided.

Questions for Discussion and Reflection

1. Should teachers be encouraged to use more student-centered learning strategies? Explain your answer.
2. Some teachers insist that they do not need objectives and that, indeed, objectives restrict their creativity. How should supervisors react to this claim?
3. The literature cited in this chapter says that teachers generally do not use research when selecting teaching strategies. How can supervisors encourage teachers to use the literature and research?
4. Most classroom experiences have centered on low-level thinking. What can a supervisor do to help teachers raise the level of thinking in their classrooms?
5. According to the literature, students are seldom aware of those concepts that are essential to understanding the discipline they are studying. How can supervisors help teachers to make their students more aware of the important concepts in their disciplines?
6. Traditionally, our schools have not involved students in planning their educational experiences. How can teachers be encouraged to increase the level of student involvement in planning?
7. All learning/teaching strategies have both strengths and weaknesses or limitations. Should the supervisor stress the weaknesses as well as the strengths of each strategy? Why or why not?
8. One reason that teachers stick with the lecture method is because they feel safer with this method. How can the supervisor help create a safer ethos where teachers will feel comfortable experimenting with other strategies?
9. Table 8.2 gives a quick review of the characteristics of all teaching methods discussed in this chapter. Which methods would be best for introducing a topic? Developing social skills? Motivating student interest? Raising thinking levels? Summarizing a topic?

Suggested Activities

1. Interview five students, asking them to describe their best teachers. Write a brief report on these teachers' strengths. Make a summary chart to show their characteristics.
2. Ask a local teacher who teaches a subject other than your teaching field(s) to coplan a team-teaching lesson with you.
3. Ask a local principal to identify an outstanding teacher. Review this teacher's lesson plans and ask the teacher to identify planning skills that lead to good lessons.

Chapter 9

Helping Teachers Execute Lessons

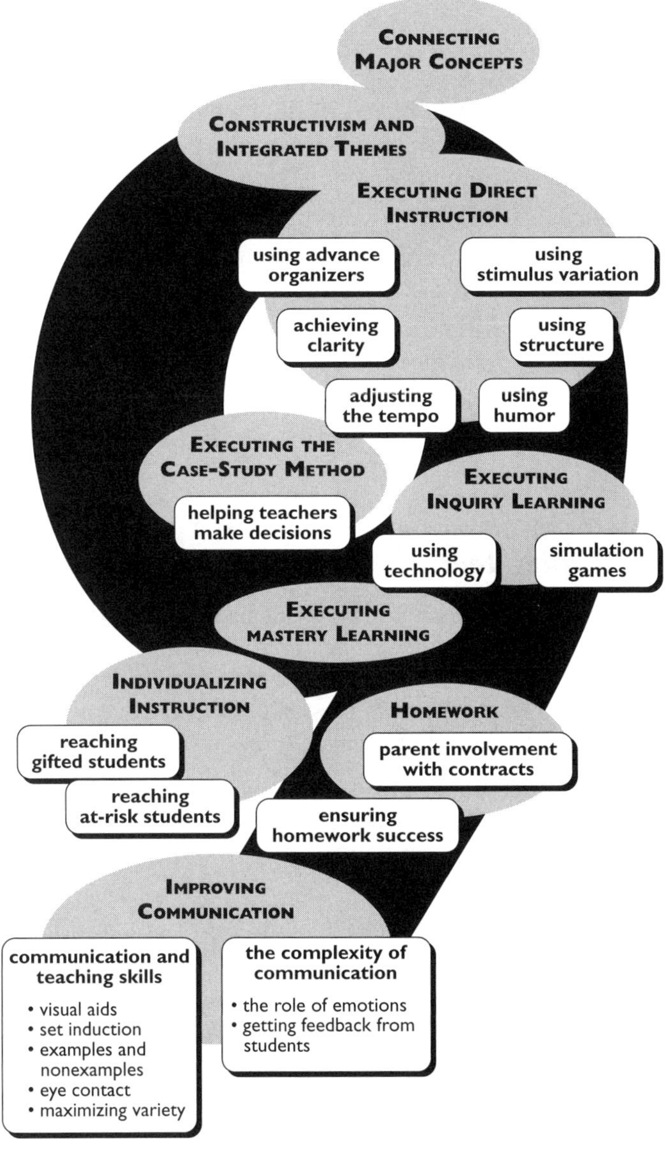

Connecting Major Concepts
Constructivism and Integrated Themes
Executing Direct Instruction
using advance organizers
using stimulus variation
achieving clarity
using structure
adjusting the tempo
using humor
Executing the Case-Study Method
helping teachers make decisions
Executing Inquiry Learning
using technology
simulation games
Executing Mastery Learning
Individualizing Instruction
reaching gifted students
reaching at-risk students
Homework
parent involvement with contracts
ensuring homework success
Improving Communication
communication and teaching skills
• visual aids
• set induction
• examples and nonexamples
• eye contact
• maximizing variety
the complexity of communication
• the role of emotions
• getting feedback from students

> *Knowing how to communicate different patterns and perceptions expands the interaction effectiveness most educators seek.*
>
> —M. B. Gilbert,
> "Are you talking too much? Considerations for best practice"

Objectives

This chapter will assist you in preparing to help teachers

1. Improve their execution of direct instruction, case study, inquiry, and simulation/gaming lessons
2. Use the latest research to improve their classroom communications
3. Use advance organizers and set induction in preparing students to focus on key concepts for each lesson
4. Identify appropriate and inappropriate uses of homework and describe ways of making it more effective
5. Involve parents in their children's academic work

Helping Teachers Improve Their Teaching

Reba Arnold was excited to begin her first principalship. Although the competition for the position had been keen, her teaching expertise made her the best choice to provide true instructional leadership. Reba knew that keeping her position required improving student scores on the state's test of basic skills. She also knew that the public expected improvement to occur much more quickly than was feasible.

Quickly, Reba began constructing a plan to improve schoolwide academic performance. The first step would be to begin visiting classes, making sure that she visited every teacher's classroom. Her first visit would be to the classroom of Renee Calee, a second-year social studies teacher.

Renee entered the room, called the roll, and started the lesson by asking volunteers to give definitions of several key words found in a list at the beginning of the textbook chapter on elections. Each student who gave a definition read it verbatim from the text without making any errors. To avoid disrupting this lesson or distracting the students, Reba stood outside the door and listened until the lesson was well under way, and then she quietly entered and took a seat at the back of the room.

Reba waited for the definitions to end so the students could get into the heart of the lesson. While waiting, she noticed that Renee was using her "teaching voice" to drown out the several small chit-chat discussions occurring throughout the room. Reba found the force and volume of Renee's voice strident and unpleasant; it almost seemed that she was angry at her students.

The second part of the lesson consisted of a review of several dates that had been introduced in the previous lesson. Reba noticed that the same students who had volunteered to give the definitions were now volunteering to give dates. As the teacher acknowledged a student and received a response, she immediately asked for another date without discussing the significance of the date just given. Reba realized that this was the same pattern she had witnessed with the definitions—no discussion there, either.

Reba knew that a large number of this school's students were at risk of dropping out; most were just waiting to reach the legal dropout age. The at-risk students in this classroom were pleased to be left alone to watch passively while their more adept classmates dominated each lesson. She wondered why Renee didn't at least give some examples from their world to try to personalize and clarify the concepts for them. And that was another problem: Where were the major concepts? What *were the major concepts? Those underdeveloped, scattered definitions and dates could hardly be considered as such. Renee knew that she had much work to do to help this teacher improve her lessons.*

Reflection

How should teachers introduce lessons? How can teachers lead students to develop the major concepts in their lessons? How can the teacher reach the wide diversity of students in classes where students' abilities range from gifted to intellectually challenged? How can teachers personalize a lesson for thirty or more students simultaneously? What can supervisors do to help teachers reach these goals? Was Reba's one-on-one approach the best approach to improving instruction throughout the school?

Introduction

Effective teaching and instruction exist in a variety of forms. Students have preferences about how they receive information (Gilbert, 2006). Chapter 8 gave supervisors advice on ways to encourage teachers to expand their teaching-methods repertoire. This chapter will focus on the deliveries of those strategies. To become and remain effective, teachers must become lifelong learners (Phelps, 2006). Understanding how to implement strategies effectively requires continuous investigation into each strategy. The pros and cons of several teaching strategies are discussed in this chapter, including the case-study method, direct instruction, and simulations and games. Because successful teaching requires effective communication, this chapter investigates the nature of communication. Other important topics include the execution of tutoring, questioning, and homework strategies.

Connecting Major Concepts

As noted in chapter 3, if students are to be able to make sense of the content they study, they must see how it relates to what they already know (TIMSS Video Mathematics Research Group, 2003). Chapter 6 addressed the indispensable role that the concept plays in teaching and expressed concern that most students fail to understand those concepts that are essential to understanding the disciplines. An even greater worry is that teachers seldom understand what students do and do not know. Too often, those concepts that are in the curriculum are not clearly understood because they are taught only by definition (Bybee & Scotter, 2006/2007).

Regardless of which teaching and learning strategies teachers select, they must be reminded that students learn most when they recognize the lesson's main concepts, the connections between the concepts they study, and the lesson's activities (Roth & Garnier, 2006/2007). Kathleen Roth and Helen Garnier (2006/2007) emphasize the TIMSS video study[1] finding that high-achieving countries link science learning activities to strong concept development. This is what teachers in high-achieving countries do exceedingly well and, unfortunately, it is what most U.S. teachers do poorly or not at all. The responsibility of all teachers to help students discover major concepts and connect other information and classroom activities to these concepts is reflected in Figure 9.1,

Figure 9.1 To What Degrees do Science Lessons Focus on Concepts?

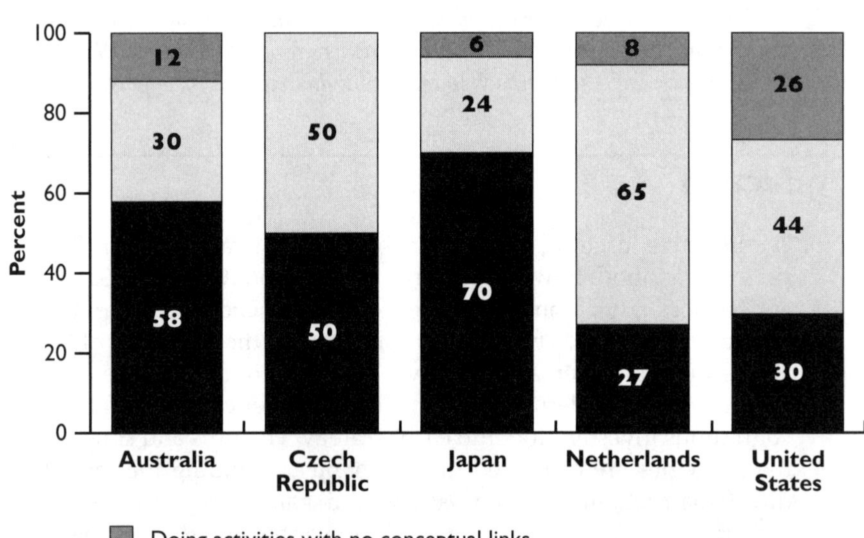

From K. Roth & H. Garnier (2006/2007), What science teaching looks like: An international perspective. *Educational Leadership*, *64*(4), p. 21. Reprinted with permission of the authors.

which shows a comparison of the percentage of time spent focusing on concepts in U.S. science classrooms with the percentage of time spent by students in high-scoring science and mathematics countries. This figure shows that U.S. students spend over one-fourth of their time on activities that do not connect at all to the major concepts in the lesson. U.S. students spend almost half of the remaining time learning content with weak or no conceptual connections, leaving only 30% of the time for learning content with strong conceptual links.

The supervisor can help teachers correct this imbalance in focus by encouraging them to

- identify one main learning goal,
- communicate the purpose with goal statements and focus questions,
- select content representations that are matched to the learning goal,
- select activities that are matched to the learning goal,
- sequence the content story line,
- link content ideas and activities,
- highlight for students important ideas and links among them, and
- summarize and synthesize important ideas.

Helping teachers realize the important role that concepts play in learning is a good first step in reaching the goal of in-depth learning. Each discipline has a unique structure, which is the key to unlocking its understanding. The supervisor can direct teachers to the Internet to identify and clarify their understanding of the major concepts in their disciplines, through special professional associations such as

- International Reading Association (IRA)
- National Council for the Teaching of English (NCTE)
- National Association of Young Children (NAYEC)
- National Middle School Association (NMSA)
- National Science Teachers Association (NTSA)
- National Social Studies Education (NSSE)

By emphasizing concepts, your teachers can ensure coverage of the most important ideas in their subjects. It bears repeating that concepts also raise the level of thinking. Focusing on concepts offers another major benefit. When students ask the perpetual question, "Why do we have to learn this?", a focus on concepts is much easier to justify than the teaching of mere facts. For an example of how one elementary science teacher used concepts to answer this question, direct your teachers to the Sheppard's Science Resources Web site (http://www.can-do.com/uci/lessons99/concepts.html).

Recall from chapter 8 that teachers need to build a repertoire of several teaching strategies. For each strategy, teachers should ensure that students confront the major concepts in each lesson. A list of those methods that have appropriate teacher roles with each appears in Table 9.1 (on the following page).

Table 9.1 Teaching Methods and Teachers' Roles

Teaching/Learning Method	Appropriate Teacher Behavior
Direct instruction	Use advance organizers. Keep it simple. Maintain a brisk but reasonable pace. Use stimulus variation, and permit humor.
Case study	Stay out of students' way; do not interfere. Be available to answer student questions. Provide encouragement and praise. Use computers.
Simulation games	Use few rules; don't interfere.
Peer tutoring	Spend time with slow learners.
Mastery learning	Give short, formative tests at least once or twice a week. Always go over the answers until all students understand them.
Inquiry learning	Give only enough information to enable students to make the discoveries.
Questioning	Always include "why" questions.
Cooperative learning	Include hands-on group projects with group-based grades to ensure that more capable members help their less capable peers.

Constructivism and Integrated Themes

Constructivist learning makes full use of integrated themes (Woolfolk Hoy & Hoy, 2009). C. Beck and C. Kosnick (2006) make the following observation:

> A social constructivist preservice program faces the challenge of finding time to explore integrated themes, especially given the current pressure from government agencies to "cover" a wide range of topics. In a sense this provides argument *for* integration, since discrete coverage of all the required topics is clearly impossible. (p. 51)

Supervisors should work with administrators to ensure that teachers have enough time to use this effective instructional tool with their students. According to V. N. Morphew (2000),

> The relevancy of connections becomes apparent to learners when themes and concepts are integrated holistically. For example, the learner who constructs meaning about the lifestyle of colonists during the American Revolution at the same time she learns about the science of that time and place has a better chance of building connections than if she were taught these concepts in isolation. Elementary instructors more often teach integrated thematic units than secondary instructors. Unfortunately, the traditional isolation of secondary teaching faculty doesn't allow for integrated planning and thus, presentation to learners. (p.1)

Beyond the obvious role of integrated themes (minimizing faculty isolation), supervisors should remind teachers to focus on themes as opposed to isolated facts. Roth and Garnier (2006/2007) say that based on the TIMSS studies (coupled with the fact that current U.S. textbooks are strong on presenting information and vocabulary and weak on putting concepts and activities together to coherently develop big ideas), each lesson should be built around a strong story line. Supervisors can help teachers plan by ensuring that they (teachers) clearly understand how the major concepts of each lesson's theme or story line will tie into the learning cycle (Robertson, 2006–2007).

Helping Teachers Execute Direct Instruction

Effective use of direct instruction must start with the onset of the lesson and continue throughout the lesson. Everything the teacher does impacts the academic outcomes of each lesson. Supervisors should work with their faculty to perfect the following techniques of direct instruction.

Advance Organizers

To be effective, teachers must separate unimportant information and salient information and find ways to simplify the important concepts in each lesson. In direct instruction, a constructivist method for separating and emphasizing the major concepts in each lesson is the use of the *advance organizer*—an initial statement about a subject to be learned that provides a structure for the new information and relates it to information students already possess. Advance organizers help students sort out fragmented pieces of information, enabling them to better understand the purposes of the lesson. For example, when introducing a lesson on weather, a teacher might begin by showing a film. When introducing the film, the teacher might ask the students to be alert to such general terms as *warm front*, *cold front*, and *occluded front*. Another lesson might focus on such terms as *sea breeze* and *land breeze*, and ask that students try to understand the process that each term represents.

Chapter 6 noted the advantage of having students themselves discover the major concepts rather than the teacher simply writing the concepts on the board or verbalizing them to the students. The time that the concepts are introduced affects the resulting learning. For example, when given concepts to look for at the *beginning* of the lesson, students tend to have a better understanding of those concepts. Yet the common practice in many classrooms is to point out the concepts *after* the lesson is taught, the film is seen, or the seatwork or homework is completed. When concepts are identified at the end of the lesson, students tend to spread their attention among more concepts, attaining a lower-level of mastery of each.

Some advance organizers are introduced orally—for example, at the start of class the teacher tells students what will be covered that day, or at the beginning of the lesson someone sings a song or reads a story to make a point, raise curiosity, or stir emotions. When introducing a unit on patriotism, a social studies teacher might play Samuel Francis Smith's "My Country 'Tis of Thee" or Francis Scott Key's "The Star-Spangled Banner" (the national anthem). Other advance organizers are introduced through activities. For example, a group of students might perform a skit, or two students might begin a lesson or unit by debating the topic. Others—graphic organizers—are visual. The teacher might show a film to give an overview of the lesson or unit. The visual that prefaces this chapter, often called a *chapter organizer*, is an example of a visual graphic organizer. It is located so that, before reading the chapter, the reader can see the major forthcoming concepts and how they are ordered in the chapter.

Achieving Clarity

Many teachers use direct instruction day after day. Unfortunately, some teachers seem to equate pedantry and jargon with scholarship; yet lecturing above the cognitive level of the students leads to failure. The problem of pedantry has been worsened by many of the reform reports calling for more "rigor" in the curriculum. The supervisor's appropriate role with direct instruction and with other teaching methods is not to dissuade teachers from using any particular method, but rather to help teachers learn how to use each method more effectively. We don't have to choose between using direct instruction and student-centered inquiry methods or between meeting pre-determined standards and promoting creativity. Louis Wildman (2006b) advised supervisors to insist that education achieve a balance between what we want to pass on to the next generation and education that allows students to investigate and pursue their own ideas.

Adjusting the Tempo

Students prefer a quick pace. When students lag behind the lesson they become discouraged, yet when the lesson drags, students become bored. The result of either error is a state of physical, program-related fatigue known as the *pall level*. Teachers can avoid this condition by planning thoroughly and moving the lesson along at a brisk but reasonable pace.

Using Stimulus Variation

To reduce boredom and increase the level of motivation, smart educators encourage the use of variety during direct instruction. This variety comes in many forms, such as voice inflection, nonverbal gestures, pausing, and moving about the classroom. Although such activities correlate positively with student recall of lecture content, students of different ages react differently to such variants. At the primary level, students often find them disruptive, and consequently they impact negatively on lecture test performance. In contrast, middle-level and high school students often find these variations refreshing. Your teachers will quickly be able to determine what works best for them.

Using Structure

Direct instruction seems to work best when the events within a lesson have a specific sequence. Because most lessons have so many topics that they clutter the students' minds, most teachers can improve their lessons by: (1) restricting the number of major concepts to a maximum of three or four, (2) ordering the concepts in a logical or natural sequence, (3) limiting the introduction (lecture) to 10 to 15 minutes, (4) providing tasks to enhance the understanding of each concept, and (5) summarizing the lesson. When structuring lessons, teachers must learn to listen to themselves. This means they must *think reflectively*, which enables them to make rational and ethical choices about what and how to teach, and to assume responsibility for those choices.

Using Humor

Humor is both stimulating and relaxing, and it works best when it is not forced. Some of your teachers may find it difficult to relax enough to let the students' humor emerge. A learning community where teachers are encouraged to experiment and where mistakes are accepted as part of the learning environment can release tension between students and teachers. Another common goal in most classes, particularly in multicultural groups, is promoting socialization. Humor can act as the glue that binds an assorted group of individuals into a community.

Helping Teachers Execute the Case-Study Method

The case-study method holds a lot of potential for classes at all levels, and yet it has been grossly underused in schools. The overriding benefits of the case-study method are its power to motivate and its ability to provide opportunities for students to improve their decision-making skills. Case studies also enable students to strengthen their critical thinking skills and become more deeply engaged in learning (Jacobowitz & Onore, 2004).

Students and teachers alike enjoy the case-study method. Success with this method requires much student interaction and must allow students the freedom to make decisions. As is true with some other strategies, one of the best roles a teacher can play when using the case-study method is to withdraw from the lesson and give the students opportunities to discuss the cases and make their own decisions.

Initially, letting the students lead the lesson is difficult for some teachers, yet most teachers who do try the case-study method in their classes never return to using more didactic methods. One approach that can add even more interest to the application of the case-study method is to video record the case. An equally stimulating variation is for students to role-play the case. Through the art of acting, students can use their imagination and creative skills to show their interpretations of the case.

Another alternative worth communicating to your faculty is to encourage students to write their own cases, as either an individual or a group assignment. Such open-ended, divergent writing assignments are also invitations for students to be creative, and students who develop cases should be awarded credit for this work.

Whatever methods they choose to present the cases, teachers should follow some precautions. Invariably, students seem to seek the *correct* solution when actually, well-written cases have no single correct solution. The teacher is responsible for getting this message across to the students. Often, some particular pertinent information that students seek is not provided in the case. Although some students feel cheated upon discovering that essential information is missing, the teacher's role is to help them understand that this condition, itself, is true to life. Good teachers spend part of their time and energy trying to *anticipate* and *circumvent* problems and additional time trying to *solve* problems. Seldom, if ever, do teachers have all the information they desire; therefore, they must make decisions under imperfect circumstances.

Making Decisions

A major advantage of using the case-study method is the opportunity it offers to help students learn how to make decisions. This is important because teachers virtually spend their working lives making decisions. When faced with an opportunity or responsibility to make a decision, teachers have several options. They can ignore the situation, hoping that their failure to make a decision will not have serious repercussions. They can use common sense and do what seems best, or they can take the advice of others. Or they can use best practices, evaluate the outcomes, and fine-tune their response. You can help by encouraging teachers to learn and use best-practices research. A good reference for your teachers is the Best Practices section of Dembowski and Lemasters (2006).

It Works for Me!

Prioritizing and Decision Making

Janice M. Walker, Drake University

I have used the following technique with my students to demonstrate prioritizing and decision making in our curriculum. Students are provided five note cards. On each of the cards, the students are asked to write one idea identifying what they want to know or be able to do at the end of their program. They place their cards on a large, flat surface or the floor, writing side up. They work together, sorting the cards into columns or categories so that all the cards within a category fit together. They select a title for the card category and indicate the number of cards in each category. The number of cards decides the priority of ideas in the curriculum for this group of students. The prioritized categories are listed on poster paper and displayed. This prompts much discussion about the program and about their desired outcomes, and about how the students can take this activity and apply it to their own work in a curriculum committee, faculty group, parent group, or with their students.

Helping Teachers Execute Inquiry Learning

In executing inquiry learning, the proper teacher role is that of a catalyst. In inquiry lessons, students must have considerable freedom to ask their own questions, set their own problems, choose their own paths of inquiry, and make their own mistakes. Students who frame questions and issues and then go about answering and analyzing them take responsibility for their own learning, becoming problem solvers and—perhaps more important—problem finders.

The teacher's role in inquiry lessons is to step back from the common information-giving role and give students these freedoms, including time to solve problems (Richards, 2006). The teacher can provide direction and support by being available to answer students' questions and by giving cues and feedback when the group bogs down. For teachers who are accustomed to dominating their classes, it may be prudent for supervisors to warn against interrupting students pursuing inquiry lessons.

Teachers of inquiry lessons must also provide much encouragement and occasional praise. Even when students take their investigations down dead-end paths, their teachers should compliment their efforts. Feedback can be both motivational and informative if it focuses on performance. Most students have been taught, either overtly or covertly, that they can succeed only by getting the correct answer. Because in inquiry lessons they have no correct answer by which they can gauge their work, students may not recognize that they are making progress. Supervisors should emphasize the importance of teacher encouragement and rewards.

Using Technology in Inquiry Learning

Computers offer new ways of helping students learn how to inquire. Storytelling provides opportunities to record the past and shape the future (Trowbridge, 2007). Furthermore, open-ended stories are an excellent way to prompt divergent inquiry. A teacher in any discipline at any grade level can begin telling a story and abruptly stop, leaving the rest of the story for the students to write. The students continue to write the stories using word processing, and after a designated time period teachers can again call a halt to the writing process so students can change computers and add to the stories that their peers had continued. When the stories are concluded, students can share the different versions that resulted from their collaboration. In this manner, teachers can help their students expand their creative abilities while simultaneously increasing their sense of efficacy or self-confidence.

Technological tools such as Whiteboards can engage all students simultaneously in creative writing projects and myriad other applications. Not to be confused with "dry erase" boards, the electronic Whiteboard can be used in several kinds of writeable presentation display for classrooms or videoconferences. The most sophisticated option, the interactive board, is like a large touchscreen monitor that can be synchronized to an attached computer. Users can interact with the display, visit Web sites, and access databases directly from the board.

Carol Brown (2005) suggests that when students create their own projects they should be encouraged to use presentation software, such as Microsoft PowerPoint, to present their findings. In addition to honing their IT skills, this culminating activity will require students to explore new and original ideas by discussing, collaborating on, and expanding their knowledge.

Computers offer today's teachers many other opportunities to involve students in active learning and can be used to empower students of all ages. Although initially used primarily in distance learning, educators are beginning to acknowledge this learning tool as a legitimate mainline curriculum approach. Interactive videos now offer teachers a way to involve all students with inquiry. Open-ended assignments allowing students to choose their topics can empower students of all ages. Teachers should encourage students to put their writings on blogs, inviting feedback from readers. Students can then revise these writings and submit the revisions for possible publication in newspapers, magazines, and journals. Those who do so experience a considerable increase in self-concept. These examples are no longer exceptions but are standard procedures in elementary and secondary classrooms throughout the country.

The computer can be a window through which students can enter many academic realities. Brown (2005) helps teachers select from among several genres of software that help students think at higher levels. One particularly useful genre to recommend to your teachers is *generative software* that includes computer resources to help students generate or construct understanding of a subject. Examples of generative software include computerized simulations and inquiry-learning-based applications. Elementary and middle-level teachers can benefit from accessing WebQuest projects (http://webquest.sdsu.edu). A WebQuest is an inquiry-oriented lesson format in which most or all of the information that learners work with comes from the Web. Secondary and middle-level teachers and students can also design and develop their own WebQuests. Another simulation-based inquiry learning application, SimQuest (http://www.simquest.nl/), allows learners to be in control of their own learning process. Students create and observe a simulation model, manipulating input variables and observing output variables to acquire deeper understanding of real-life situations.

* * *

The ability to read well is a prerequisite for success in any discipline. In one or more ways, most of the teaching strategies discussed in this chapter involve reading, yet almost every classroom has some students whose learning is limited by their poor reading skills. The following case study shows how a teacher can involve families in creating a community-based reading program.

Collaborative Supervision of Reading Programs

Isreal Eady • Jacksonville State University

Several years ago, *The Goals 2000: Educate America Act* influenced school reform by emphasizing high achievement for students of all ability levels. Goals 2000 supported state efforts to develop clear and rigorous standards for what every child should know and be able to do. The general belief was that improvement in reading was needed to improve overall academic achievement. For this study, a collaborative approach to supervising reading programs involved staff, students of all ability levels, and their families, working in special ways to promote school achievement.

The Community

Students in this school community came from low-income families that lacked the enrichment resources needed for reading enhancement. The lack of books in the homes often prevented adequate reading practice. Many families could not afford to take their children on educational trips. Most of the families depended on the school for reading enrichment in addition to basic teaching in reading.

The School

Located in a small southern city, Blue Mountain School is a public elementary school with 30 teachers, serving about 450 students. This school was organized as a result of a merger between a primary school and an elementary school in the same community. Special-needs students made up a significant portion of the school's population. The principal and support staff (such as the learning resource specialist, counselor, psychologist, and teacher leaders) comprised the administrative team of the school.

Support Staff

Some teachers served as counselors as well as instructional staff, which also placed them in the category of support staff. These teachers used their special skills in relating to learners of all ability levels. The learning resources teacher used her particular skills in relating to learners of all ability levels, and she also modeled instructional effectiveness. The psychologist used her skills in relating and promoting school programs. Because the support staff possessed these special skills, the stage was set for involvement in interviews and study sessions for reading-program effectiveness at Blue Mountain School.

The Principal

Dr. E, an experienced school supervisor, had served as a band director and principal at all school levels. These experiences prepared him to be a collaborator and a promoter of a creative climate for learning. Dr. E had been involved in statewide training for technology-connected lessons. He was able to jointly plan and coteach technology-connected lessons, especially incorporating music into language arts lessons. Dr. E involved supervisors of support staff in interviews and literature reviews regarding reading programs. He also involved the teaching staff in a survey about reading programs. This collaborative involvement helped to build a creative climate at Blue Mountain School. In this case, the collaborative involvement of the principal, support staff, and teaching staff provided a strong foundation for the expansion of reading programs at Blue Mountain School.

The Case

As principal of Blue Mountain School, several years ago Dr. E. used a collaborative approach to supervise reading programs and they were successfully expanded. He collaborated with and involved support staff, teaching staff, and supervisors in interviews and study sessions to increase the effectiveness of the school's reading programs. The following questions were used to interview support staff at the school: How can teacher-counselors enhance student achievement? How can teacher-leaders and psychologists model relationship building for learning? Can all students learn if motivated to do so?

Data Obtained from Interviews

Mrs. R. believed that motivation is a collaborative problem-solving tool in the school. This teacher also believed in working with the psychologist to promote caring relationships and reading skills for student achievement. The learning resources teacher, Dr. J., related to students as a dancer and academic resource specialist. She believed motivation involves building caring relationships with students by using the arts to challenge and reward reading success. Reading is acknowledged as a foundational skill for learning in other subject areas. A teacher-leader, Mrs. L. believed in reading-skill improvement for students; the psychologist should be involved to promote caring and student learning by celebrating academic success. Support staff, especially psychologists, can reinforce academic focus. They should be involved with teachers as teams in academic celebrations to help communicate that learning is highly valued in the school, which is important as a hidden curriculum. Dr. E. involved Dr. W., the head district psychologist, in recognizing and honoring Mrs. R. for her success in counseling and motivating her class to achieve the Most Improved Scores on the ITBS for 1999–2000.

Dr. E.'s experience had taught him that collaboration does not just happen; the school leader must set a collaborative tone by orchestrating a creative climate in which mutual trust, respect, and commitment exist. The leader must also involve support staff, teaching staff, and supervisors to continuously communicate high expectations for learning. The school community must communicate high expectations for successful implementation of learning programs.

Recently, Blue Mountain School had implemented reading programs (*Accelerated Reader* and *Reading First*) on a limited basis. The programs provided instruction and strategies to address problems dealing with reading practice, sight words and phonics, including Saxon Phonics. In an effort to expand the reading programs schoolwide, more buy-in was needed from support staff and teachers. A collaborative study was conducted by the principal and support staff.

The purpose of the study was to assess the perceptions of Blue Mountain School staff about the effectiveness of a collaborative approach to reading programs on student achievement. Staff members who had supervised and taught the existing programs were interviewed. Plans were made to expand the collaborative approach to reading programs by implementing a schoolwide project. The main question to be addressed in the collaborative study was: How do teaching-staff members feel about the existing collaborative approach to reading programs? After the principal collaborated with the support staff in reviewing related literature, the following survey was compiled for use in conducting surveys with the teaching staff.

Attitude Survey for Teaching Staff about Reading Programs

Dear Teaching Staff:

Your reaction to this survey to determine the effectiveness of a collaborative approach to reading programs at Blue Mountain School is solicited. The purpose is to enhance focus on reading for student achievement nationally, statewide, and locally. Please circle the letter code at the end of each statement which best describes your reaction to the statement.

CODE: SA = Strongly Agree; A = Agree;
D = Disagree; SD = Strongly Disagree

1. Family reading activities can bring families together.
   SA A D SD
2. Reading can enable families to share quality time.
   SA A D SD
3. Reading aloud can promote lifelong appetites for family reading.
   SA A D SD
4. Reading programs can enhance attention on classroom teaching.
   SA A D SD
5. Reading practice can improve under Reading Renaissance.
   SA A D SD
6. Phonics achievement can improve under Reading First.
   SA A D SD
7. Sight word achievement can improve under Reading First.
   SA A D SD
8. Saxon phonics resources can enhance learning to read.
   SA A D SD
9. Learning to read is important to success in school and life.
   SA A D SD
10. Teachers are key planners of instructional strategies in reading.
    SA A D SD

Thank You,
Dr. E and Support Staff

The results of the survey, compiled by the principal and staff, were used to compose questions for interviews of teachers. Overall, the teachers' responses indicated strong beliefs that collaborative approaches to reading programs are effective for improving student achievement. Their beliefs coincided with favorable perceptions in the literature regarding the effectiveness of collaborative approaches to reading programs on student achievement, particularly at Blue Mountain School. As a result, the following project was implemented.

In the Schoolwide Reading Project, the goal was to build communities within classrooms and the school to work toward a common goal—a love of reading. The vision and motto, "Readers are leaders and leaders are readers," aimed to provide a foundation for success in all academic areas and performance on standardized tests. The Reading Renaissance model was followed: Daily DEAR (Drop Everything and Read) sessions, weekly read-in sessions, monthly reading assemblies, and monthly reading challenges were held. As an incentive, students earned points for reading books. These incentives provided recognition and rewards that encouraged reading practice. Several classrooms earned the status "Model Classroom for Reading Renaissance," which led to a significant schoolwide outcome.

After several months with the schoolwide project, the school earned the status of "Model School for Reading Renaissance," receiving national recognition for this honor. The local school board recognized the entire school community for the achievement. The local newspaper printed success stories about the school's reading achievement, which further encouraged excellence in reading at the school.

Issues for Further Reflection

How might this study

- influence the development of family literacy programs?
- influence an emphasis of reading for lifelong learning?
- enhance student attitudes about books and reading?
- influence interdisciplinary teaching of subjects such as music and reading?
- promote teacher leadership with respect to planning for instructional strategies in reading?

Today's teachers must be technologically *confident* and technologically *competent*, at a level far beyond mere technological literacy (Armstrong et al., 2009). Supervisors who keep abreast of the latest in educational technology can provide their faculty with valuable information and advice on improving their own as well as their students' knowledge. Powell and Lee (2003/2004) found that preservice early childhood teachers who were exposed to a computerized simulation about teaching techniques before field experience tended to have a more positive perception relative to choice of appropriate techniques within actual classroom settings. These teachers used the computer simulation to change their self-perceptions, and to make appropriate decisions about potential techniques to employ in their future teaching practice.

Executing Simulation Games

Of special importance is the power of simulation games to motivate. Because today's students have grown up on video games, we must not overlook the stimulation power of such games (Curts, 2004). Basic to their stimulating nature are the simulation game's high level of actively involving students and the opportunity that many of these games provide students to socialize. Above all, the teacher should ensure that students enjoy these learning experiences. Even if educators think that the chance element in some games lacks scholarship, this element should never be removed because it is precisely this element that raises the level of motivation.

Simulations are a good option for gifted students because they involve both group-based and individually based problem solving. Most students enjoy independently gathering information for problem solving (Good & Brophy, 2007). Gifted students enjoy the flexibility that simulations offer, in contrast to more traditional rigid, lockstep problem solving.

The teacher's role regarding simulation games is to help ensure that the potentials of both simulations and games are reached. When using games, teachers should (1) say no more than necessary; (2) run the simulation—not the students; (3) run the game (don't teach); and (4) avoid telling the students how to behave. Games run more smoothly when the rules are few and simple.

Helping Teachers Execute Mastery Learning

Because mastery learning is particularly suited to promoting higher levels of thinking (Guskey, 2005b), supervisors should remind teachers to take time to give corrective feedback and give students the time they need to remedy their learning problems. To help students engage in higher levels of thinking, teachers should give assignments that require making inferences, problem solving, synthesizing, evaluating, deductive reasoning, and using creative skills.

Effective use of mastery learning requires curriculum alignment (discussed in chapter 7). Three elements that must always be aligned are learning goals and standards, instruction, and evaluation. The concept development theme emphasized in this book is especially critical to mastery learning. This method requires heavy use of formative assessment, and every time teachers administer a test they should emphasize the major concepts being tested.

The mastery learning model stresses the use of variety. One feature of this model, for example, is that it provides students who do not master content at the desired level with some opportunities to remediate. Special emphasis is placed on the types of remediation experiences students are offered, recommending that they vary from the students' original experiences.

Helping Teachers Individualize Instruction

In any classroom, the range of abilities and the variety of ways students learn will vary considerably. Trying to reach all students and finding ways to motivate them can challenge any teacher. Some differences among students can be attributed to different cultural backgrounds, yet, more differences exist within the same cultures than among cultures. The need to reach each student is a responsibility belonging to all teachers. The essence of education is the tender concern that no talent be lost. This is a powerful challenge to each teacher. With it comes the responsibility of knowing that for some young students, a teacher will be the most influential person in their lives. Regardless of economic background, ethnic background, or possession or lack of innate ability, every youngster deserves to have one person who will demonstrate concern and confidence in his or her success. Encourage your teachers to strive to be that special person.

Reaching Underachieving and Gifted Students

Gifted students are often trapped in a conflict of expectations. Their peers pressure them to do less while their teachers do just the opposite, demanding perfection (Armstrong et al., 2009). Gifted students prefer different types of learning experiences than those predominately offered in the classroom, and they prefer different types of lessons than those their teachers think they prefer. Although gifted students have the ability to learn through audio and visual presentations, most prefer hands-on, tactile, and active learning. Underachieving students also prefer such active, hands-on activities but, unlike gifted students, many underachievers are unable to learn auditorially and visually. One of the most important challenges teachers face is teaching so that their lessons are simple enough for even the slowest students and yet substantive enough to challenge the brightest students. Hands-on, tactile curricula offer a solution to this instructional dilemma.

Perhaps the most important advice you can give to your teachers is frequent reminders that gifted students do not want or need "more of the same." They need new and challenging assignments that will flex their creative abilities. Ironically, gifted students are perhaps the richest source of help when they are involved in planning their own activities.

Curricula for the gifted fall into two categories: enrichment programs and accelerated programs. *Enrichment programs* kept students at the same grade level as their peers but offer them more creative challenges. Enrichment programs are the overall favorite of parents. In contrast to enrichment programs, *accelerated programs* allow gifted students to advance academically, either by promoting them to a higher grade level or by allowing them to move faster and cover more objectives at their current grade level.

Reaching At-Risk Students

At-risk students are those millions of students who are at risk of dropping out of school. The plight of these students has been worsened by NCLB, which has replaced concern for at-risk students with increased competition aimed at serving high achievers (Hess & Rotherham, 2007). Educators and researchers should spend more time with these marginal students, encouraging them and helping them to believe in their own potential.

Unfortunately, many of our schools have inadvertently taught students that mistakes are signs of failure. The simple, straightforward deduction that students often make is that the best way to avoid failure is to avoid all risks. In practical terms, this means avoiding failure by not trying. Of course, this perception is counterproductive. We need more highly personalized classrooms where students can take risks and fail, knowing that this is acceptable so long as the experience is used to grow. Teachers can model this behavior by sharing their failures with students and by providing encouragement and reassurance.

Most at-risk programs are designed to be highly personalized, stressing one-on-one attention. Many at-risk students may benefit more from receiving their teacher's personal attention than from the teacher's cognitive assistance. In fact, because many at-risk students have developed counterproductive behaviors, they cannot make cognitive gains until their behavior has been reshaped. Supervisors should encourage teachers to develop innovative ways of "unteaching "counterproductive behavior. The goal is to be tolerant of these students' slower rates of progress and to gradually lead them to attain the same level of mastery as their peers.

Importance of the Arts. Since artists take risks and learn from their mistakes, the arts are a natural environment for providing the support that at-risk students need. Learning through the arts allows teachers to reach out to at-risk students by using various instructional strategies. Vanessa Camilleri (2007), a social and emotional learning specialist, believes educators can use the arts to help at-risk children improve their social skills and academic performance:

> The creative arts therapies (music, dance, art, drama, poetry) provide unique avenues for working with children. Participation in the arts is fun, playful, and intrinsically gratifying—which increases motivation, investment, and participation. . . . The arts provide an "aesthetic context" in which to support, connect, and heal. (p. 66)

Prevention and Education through the Arts for Kids (PEAK) is one program that can benefit at-risk youth. William Adkins (n.d.), creator of the program, researched the role of the arts in working with at-risk children and discovered that

> The most startling findings . . . revealed the age at which young people are making decisions that will ultimately dictate their life's path. Shockingly, that "at-risk" age is 10–14. . . . [T]he most effective use of both our time and money for the social development of our youth is art. . . . The arts are essential, and the lack of self-awareness through aesthetics has been more detrimental to both the individual and society than a lack of understanding in any other subject. . . . To me it was clear that simply telling our youth to not do drugs, don't join gangs or don't have sex was not effective. I wanted to maintain the integrity of my students' natural artistic expression while creating an opportunity for an honest dialogue about important issues and ideas that will better equip my students to make positive life choices. Therefore, I decided that . . . 20–25% [of the curriculum] would be an art activity that specifically addressed relevant issues such as peer pressure, leisure time, conflict resolution, and media influences. . . .

The ArtSmarts program is another program that is often recommended for at-risk students. The program operates on the assumption that integrating arts into the curriculum and into the classroom will improve the school experience for students, resulting in greater engagement of students in school. Arts educators often contend that the arts and cross-curricular learning help students develop a positive attitude toward school and others, resulting in less behavior problems, more participation, and improved attendance. Other positive impacts of the program are an increased sense of community and belonging, improved thinking skills (including improved comprehension, interpretation, and problem-solving abilities), and a better self-concept as a result of achievement in the arts, as well as a strong work ethic (persevering in the face of difficulties). "For some at-risk students this program may be the first time they receive positive reinforcement in a school atmosphere, which may deter negative behavior and increase their engagement in learning" (PsycholARTSical, n.d.).

Helping Teachers Reach English-Language Learners

Today's teachers have a responsibility and an opportunity to serve the fastest-growing population of students—those who need special help with the English language. Because this challenge and opportunity is faced by teachers everywhere, in 2007 Dr. Christopher Frances, an expert on this subject, wrote the study in Box 9.1 to help educational supervisors assist teachers who have an influx of students whose native language is not English.

Box 9.1 Improving Instruction of Mainstream Teachers of English Language Learners

Educators in the United States are very aware of the major demographic changes that have occurred in public schools over the past few decades. According to the Office of English Language Acquisition (OELA), **5,119,561** Limited English Proficient (LEP) students were enrolled in public schools (Pre-K through Grade 12) for the 2004–2005 school year—approximately **10.45%** of the national public school student enrollment. This represents a **60.76%** increase over the reported 1994–95 public school English language learner (ELL) enrollment (National Clearinghouse for English Language Acquisition, 2006).

The growth in the number of ELLs in public schools has forced districts to recognize language-related issues over and above statutes, regulations, and legal mandates. Districts are required to maintain specialized instructional support programs that ensure equitable student access to comprehensible instruction. Not only is comprehensible instruction required by law (*Lau v. Nichols*, 1974), but the federally mandated No Child Left Behind Act of 2001 (NCLB) does not exempt ELLs from showing improvement in order for schools to achieve adequate yearly progress (AYP). ELLs are one of 11 subgroups measured under the terms of NCLB.

As the LEP population has grown exponentially, school districts nationwide have been hard-pressed to keep up with the demand for English for Speakers of Other Languages (ESOL) certified or endorsed personnel. Currently, 41% of U.S. teachers have taught ELLs, while less than 13% have received any training or professional development on teaching these students (National Center for Education Statistics [NCES], 2002). Consequently, ELLs spend most of their school day in classes with teachers who have little or no training in ESOL methods.

Continuing professional development is considered necessary and often mandated for teachers as the population of school-aged children becomes more heterogeneous. Initial teacher education cannot contain all of the propositional knowledge that is needed. Guskey's (2003) recent analysis of lists of effective professional development showed that individual characteristics vary widely in their frequency of inclusion and that no characteristic is consistently named in all the lists.

(continued)

The most frequently mentioned characteristic of effective professional development is enhancement of teachers' content and pedagogic knowledge; teachers need not only to update their content knowledge but also to understand the ways their students learn. Content knowledge and methodology are both vital dimensions of effective professional development. For mainstream teachers of ELLs, effective professional development should include strategies and methods for teaching these students.

Professional development can be provided in a variety of ways, including graduate-level courses, peer coaching, after school or in-service workshops, and conferences at the district, state or national level. Additionally, many districts are turning to computer-mediated instruction (CMI) as another avenue to provide professional development because of the flexibility, increased access, and reduction in costs these opportunities offer (Keller, 2005). CMI includes a wide variety of technologies, including online instruction.

In a recent research project, methods for delivering professional development in strategies and accommodations for mainstream teachers of ELLs were compared to determine if CMI can be effective. The primary goal of the study was to determine if teachers change the frequency of accommodations and strategies for ELLs when provided with a lesson-plan addendum that informs them of strategies and accommodations that have been proven useful and effective in teaching ELLs. Further, this study sought to determine if there was a significant change in the frequency of strategies and accommodations that teachers use when provided with different versions of the lesson-plan addendum. One group received the addendum on a CD with embedded links to further resources on the Internet; the other group received the lesson-plan addendum with further resources in paper format.

The results of the two-way mixed factor ANOVA supported the hypothesis that providing teachers with a lesson-plan addendum designed to include strategies and accommodations for ELLs would change the frequency of their use of strategies. As shown in Table 1 and illustrated in Figure 1, the mean of total strategies for both the CMI and the paper groups ($n = 7$) increased after receiving the lesson-plan addendum.

Table 1 Marginal Means Total Strategies Pre- and Post-Lesson Plan Addendum ($n = 7$)

Variable	*M* pre-	*M* post	*M* mar
CMI-Total	66.143	96.571	81.357
Paper-Total	47.571	62.286	54.929
Marginal *M*	56.587	79.429	68.143

Note: M-Mean; n-Number in group

After determining that there was, in fact, an increase in both groups after receiving the lesson-plan addendum, the researcher sought to identify the significance of this increase. Table 2 reveals the significance within and between groups for total strategy use.

The significance value for overall strategy use before and after receiving the lesson-plan addendum was $p < .01$. Overall, teachers increased the use of total strategies known to be helpful to ELLs when provided with a lesson-plan addendum. The between-subjects tests revealed that the increase for total strategies with the CMI version was approaching levels of significance with an outcome of $p = .076$. Although this study was attempting to measure a difference in strategy use between those teachers receiving the lesson-plan addendum with Internet-linked resources and those teachers receiving the addendum with paper-based

Figure 1 Estimated Marginal Means for Total Strategies Pre- and Post-Treatment

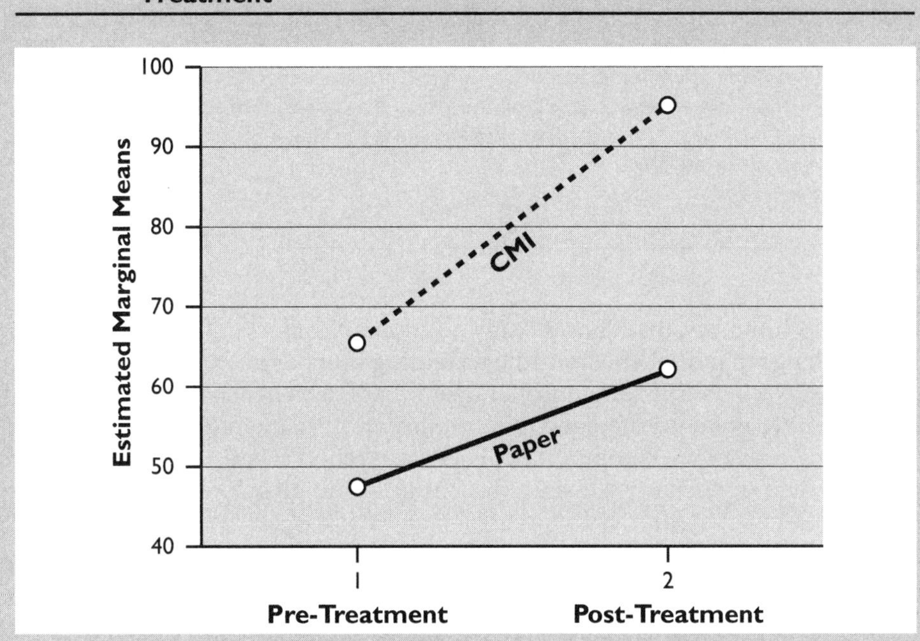

Table 2 Analysis of Variance for Total Strategies within and between Subjects ($n = 14$)

Source of Variance	SS	df	MS	F	Sig.
Total Strategies (Within-Subjects)	3566.286	1	3566.286	22.600	.000[1]
Version: CMI vs. Paper (Between-Subjects)	4889.286	1	4889.286	3.760	.076[2]
Interaction: Version by Strategies	432.143	1	432.143	2.739	.124[3]
Error (Within-Subjects)	1893.571	12	157.798		

Note: SS-Sum of Square; df-degree of freedom; MS-Mean of Square; Total number of cases n = 14
[1]Significant at $p < .01$; [2]Approaching significance at $p = .076$; [3]Not significant at $p = .124$

resources located in the Media Center at the school, none of teachers in the paper-based resources group reported looking at the notebooks containing the resources. Therefore, what was actually measured was the difference between the group that had a list of strategies and accommodations for ELLs with Internet-linked resources and the group that had a list of strategies and accommodations with no additional resources. While both groups showed a significant increase in strategy use after receiving the lesson-plan addendum, the paper-based group increased their use of strategies without additional resources.

(continued)

The findings in this study have several important pedagogical implications for school administrators and supervisors who find themselves with increasing numbers of ELLs and teachers who are not trained in ESOL methods. The results of this study showed that most of the teachers increased their use of strategies and accommodations for ELLs when they were given a lesson-plan addendum. Supervisors should consider encouraging teachers who have ELLs in their content area classes to submit the lesson-plan addendum along with their regular lesson plans so that they will consider implementing the strategies that have been shown to be helpful to these students.

In summary, the Frances study addresses the most critical communications challenge that teachers face—the increasing number of English language learners who will be spending most of their school days in classrooms with teachers who have not been prepared to communicate with them. This study found that giving teachers of computer-mediated instruction classes a lesson-plan addendum will significantly enhance the learning of English language learners.

Assigning Homework

A major strategy that teachers can use to supplement and enhance the effectiveness of lessons is homework. Most teachers have complete freedom to set the amount required in their classes. Throughout the history of our schools, homework has been an accepted practice. Fifty-seven percent of the public would like to see elementary students have more homework assignments, and 73% would like more homework for high school students (Rose & Gallup, 2006). Unfortunately, through the years educators have known little about its effectiveness. As more is learned about homework, educators now realize that some of the commonly held beliefs about it are not true—for example, beliefs such as "it is good for everybody" and "the more the better."

In fact, homework is not good for all purposes. Although it is frequently assigned as a way to have students practice new procedures learned in the classroom, it is not a good method for learning new material or introducing new processes. Teachers should not assign problems for homework until after students have had an opportunity to work similar problems in class under the tutelage of the teacher (Trowbridge, 2007). Many students are incapable of working problems at home without the aid of the teacher unless they have first worked similar problems in the classroom.

Contrary to popular belief, homework is not good for all students. Although it has a positive effect on achievement, the effect varies dramatically with grade level. For high school students, homework has substantial positive effects. Middle-level students also benefit from homework, but only about half as much. For elementary school students, the effect of homework on achievement is negligible.

Precautions to Ensure Homework Success

Beyond using homework for appropriate goals, teachers can take other precautions to ensure homework success. Since some students are poor readers, homework instructions should be kept simple and clear. Other highly capable students—gifted students—are easily bored with mundane assignments. What gifted students do *not* need is boring homework; what they *do* need is assignments that challenge their creativity.

To help teachers judge the amount of homework to assign, supervisors might suggest application of the *ten-minute rule*. Developed by Cooper (2007), this rule states that all daily homework assignments combined should take about as long as 10 minutes multiplied by the student's grade level. Supervisors can share the following guidelines with their teachers about using homework to its greatest advantage.

- Use the 10-minute rule.
- Make assignments that integrate or tie into the ongoing themes and story lines in your class.
- Make assignments that you consider meaningful.
- Explain the importance of each assignment.
- When choosing topics for homework assignments, use your knowledge about your students' abilities and interests.
- Assign problems that students are able to work.
- To ensure that students are capable of completing homework assignments, under your guidance in the classroom have them work at least one problem similar to those assigned as homework.
- Always follow up on homework assignments, using each as a tool to reteach.

Another precaution that teachers can take to avoid giving boring assignments is to limit the number of similar problems. Two or three problems may be better than one to reinforce a particular concept or process, but twenty problems may not be better than four or five.

Effective use of homework requires prompt follow-up on assignments, including asking for assignments when they are due and promptly returning the graded homework. Regular follow-ups bring improvement: When students are held responsible for assigned work, they are more likely to do the work than when their efforts go unnoticed.

Parent Involvement through the Use of Contracts

Educational Leadership Constituents Council (ELCC) Standard No. 4 specifically requires preparing administrators to "collaborate with families."

American schools have a long history of involving parents in school decisions. One approach that the supervisor may wish to suggest is a contract such as the one in Box 9.2.

Box 9.2 Learning Contract

This contract is entered into on the ___ day of __________, 20___ by the following parties whose signatures attest to their full agreement to comply with all of their respective responsibilities.

I ______________________________ (teacher) agree to help by providing special supervision and by explaining each concept until all questions are answered.

I ______________________________ (parent) agree to provide a quiet study area each evening and check on my child's progress periodically during the hours of ___ to ____. I further agree to protect this study time against disruptions by others or by me.

I ______________________________ (student) realize that the final responsibility for my performance belongs to me. I will give my full attention to my homework during this daily study period. I will also ask questions about any concepts that I do not understand.

The contract should be an agreement among the teacher, student, and parent. It should describe the exact role of each party and should provide places for all parties to sign. A major advantage of contracts is their ability to empower students, making them equal partners in learning and shifting learning responsibility to students.

Helping Teachers Improve Communication

> Interstate New Teacher Assessment and Support Consortium (INTASC) Principle No. 6 states, "The teacher uses knowledge of effective verbal, nonverbal, and media communication techniques to foster active inquiry, collaboration, and supportive interaction in the classroom."

The teacher's communication skills in the classroom affect students' thinking. The importance of good communication skills for teachers should be rather obvious, yet few may realize how much they affect learning in each lesson. Your teachers must learn to listen to each student and ensure that others do the same. They should occasionally repeat what their students say, and when paraphrasing they should ask if their interpretation is correct. They

It Works for Me!

Get Personal

Robert Kladifko, California State University, Northridge

Following are some ideas that I experienced and/or tried to practice during my many years as a school administrator in the Los Angeles Unified School District.

- To be an effective communicator, a leader must be an *active listener*.
- A leader must be available, approachable, and able to listen intelligently and carefully to others, conveying the feeling that he or she is as concerned about them as about the situation that is being addressed.
- A leader must be attentive to both the content of the message and the feelings of the sender. The feedback to the sender must make clear that the message was appreciated in terms of its meaning and the feelings with which it was conveyed.
- The school administrator must view communication as a *people process* rather than a language process.
- Understand that communication is a two-way street. It involves giving information and getting feedback from people. It isn't finished when information is given.
- Put more emphasis on face-to-face communication. Don't rely mainly on e-mail, listservs, and other written communication.
- A leader doesn't just talk open-door policy. He or she practices it by walking around and talking to the staff, allowing them to disagree and to come up with new ideas.
- A leader prepares publications and newsletters frequently. Emphasis is placed on current issues that staff care about, and up-to-date information is a must.
- Each time leaders give an instruction, they must ask themselves if the message is clear. Most vagueness is caused by failure to be specific. For example, don't just tell an employee to "show more interest" in his or her work. If an employee spends too much time chatting with others, be specific about it.
- A leader concentrates on building credibility with his or her staff. Leaders who lack credibility and fail to create a climate of trust and openness aren't believed—no matter how hard they try to communicate.

should give examples often and ask others to do the same, and they should provide a safe climate where no one is allowed to ridicule or otherwise embarrass others. The same communication skills that are so critical in effective teaching apply to supervisors interacting with faculty and administrators.

The Complexity of Communication

Traditionally we have been taught that communication is a three-part process involving a sender, a message, and a receiver. But today we know that this model is grossly oversimplified. Communication never occurs in a vacuum, and the context in which it occurs always influences the degree and the ways in which the messages are received. Communications influence the environment in which they occur, and all individual behavior is a part of a system. Each student is immersed in and inseparable from a larger ecological framework of systems. Every student in every class is part of the ecology of the entire classroom.

The Role of Emotions. We have also been taught that communication is a simple, straightforward process, but if we stop and think about it, communication seldom (if ever) occurs in the absence of emotions. In the classroom, good teachers work hard to stir the emotions of their students. This process is called *motivation*. The absence of emotion results in pure boredom, and when boredom rules, communication either is severely retarded or ceases completely.

Emotions affect communication in other ways, too. Sometimes a communication breakdown can occur outside our cognitive selves and within our emotional selves. For example, when hearing tragic news, if the news is bad enough (e.g., the loss of a close relative or friend, or the doctor's announcement to a patient that he or she is terminally ill), individuals can set up a protective screen and refuse to hear the message, openly denying it. When reaching a long-term goal, an individual may selectively filter out any comments suggesting that the reward is not forthcoming. Sometimes we choose not to process information.

Values also seriously affect communications in multicultural classrooms. Members of various cultures may fail to understand or receive messages, not because they lack the necessary cognitive skills but because of *cognitive dissonance* (their homes may harbor value systems that set them apart from the teacher and perhaps even from their fellow classmates).

Getting Feedback from Students. In all types of activities, individuals get feedback from their performance and adjust their future behavior accordingly. Some of this feedback gathering and adjustment making is purposeful; some is done semiconsciously. An example of such conscious gathering and use of feedback is an angler who tries various types of bait, varying depths, and varying reeling speeds and making deliberate mental notes of the results of each change. An example of a less deliberate use of feedback is the office worker who is new on the job and knows little about the effects to expect from certain comments. If this individual is accustomed to telling risqué jokes or using four-letter words, he may gradually cease this behavior if his coworkers do not respond enthusiastically, and this may be done without the new worker being totally aware of the change in behavior. Getting feedback requires the ability to listen, and although listening is a predominant learning mode, supervisors will find that most teachers have had little formal instruction in the art of listening.

Traditionally, when giving feedback teachers have perceived it their responsibility to judge student performance. Too often this leads students to become defensive. The effect is much better received when the teacher arranges for students to judge their own performance. According to Mark Windschitl (2006), teachers need to draw students into classroom discourse and "should use formative feedback to help students understand where their thinking is breaking down" (p. 351). This book emphasizes the teacher's need to help students draw important concepts from each lesson. Feedback can be used to help students learn how to generalize and discriminate.

Feedback is motivational, and the traditional weekly or bi-weekly tests are inadequate to solicit and sustain maximum learning efforts. Nevertheless, supervisors should emphasize the importance and the obligation that teachers have to give immediate and thorough feedback on all examinations. Although today's teachers are burdened with heavy schedules, nothing on the teacher's agenda is more important than promptly returning written assignments and examinations. Although the percentage of objective exams being used is declining (in favor of performance assessment), most teachers will continue to use some multiple-choice exams. When these are used, students deserve more feedback than just the number or percent of items scored correctly. Students need to know why their incorrect answers are wrong and why their correct answers are correct. On essay exams, teachers should explain why some responses received no credit and others received only partial credit. This is an excellent opportunity to reemphasize the important concepts that are being evaluated by assigning more value to those items that test for major concepts.

Communication and Teaching Skills

Effective classroom communication involves a high level of teaching skills. Unfortunately, teaching experience alone will not improve them but, fortunately, teachers who are aware of these skills can improve and perfect their use over time. A list of some of these skills and suggested teacher behaviors is shown in Table 9.2.

Using Visual Aids. Although the overhead projector has been in classrooms for over a half-century, it remains one of the most useful, and one of the most misused, technological inventions. You can help improve the execution of many types of lessons by asking a teacher to demonstrate its proper use.

Table 9.2 Teaching Skills to Enhance Classroom Communication

Skill	Suggested Actions
Visual aids	Make proper and effective use of the overhead projector, PowerPoint presentations, and other visual communication aids.
Set induction	Share clear objectives, use advance organizers, involve students, and use multimedia.
Examples and nonexamples	Give clear examples and nonexamples of the lesson's major concepts.
Repetition and review	Repeat only the major concepts, varying the presentation of these concepts.
Eye contact	Make eye contact with students, even when using the overhead projector or computerized presentations such as PowerPoint. When using the board, always turn to face students before talking.
Variety	Use several strategies; vary group size.

The image should cover most of the screen without spilling over any of the edges. This can be achieved by moving the projector the proper distance from the screen. Next, it should be focused so the image is clear. The room should be darkened, leaving enough light for students to take notes. Finally, the teacher should demonstrate proper use by standing so as not to block the image. Ironically, many critics of pedagogy would scoff at these simple instructions, yet these same people, without realizing their faults, might provide excellent non-examples of how this machine should be used. Teachers at all levels should be reminded that depth of understanding demands clear communication.

Other technology-based instructional tools that visually enhance classroom communication (e.g., PowerPoint presentations) are discussed earlier in this and other chapters.

Set Induction. Effective teachers understand that the success of every lesson depends on the teacher's ability to capture all students' attention at the beginning of the lesson. Less effective teachers may believe (or hope) that they can gain the students' attention later after the lesson is underway. In fact, this seldom occurs, because students who do not give their immediate attention to the lesson often miss instructions or necessary background needed to understand the rest of the lesson.

Consequently, supervisors should encourage their teachers to learn communication strategies to capture all students' attention at the beginning of the lesson. Collectively, these strategies are known as *set induction*, *cognitive set*, or *anticipatory set*. Since the value of involving students in planning has been well established, one way to develop set induction is to let students plan their own strategies for attaining the lesson's objectives. In other words, teachers need to establish among all students a mind-set of anticipation of the lesson's major concepts. Techniques for establishing set induction or anticipatory set include advance organizers, curiosity-provoking questions, and demonstrations.

Early elementary-grade teachers may flip the lights on and off a couple of times to get students' attention. Teachers of higher grades may begin a lesson by talking very softly, with the expectation that students may influence each other to become quiet. A good overhead transparency or PowerPoint projection that focuses on a major concept in the coming lesson is often effective for establishing set induction. Some teachers are able to capture students' attention with a quick joke. The effectiveness of all of these methods is situational or *contextual*—that is, the result varies from one group to another and from one time to another (Davis, 2007).

One teacher uses a method called *lesson agreement*, which involves outlining a sequence of events and asking the students to agree to it. The intent is not to expect all to agree, but to use a moment or two to demonstrate respect for student intelligence, invite collaboration, and request suggestions, so the class moves ahead with maximum cooperation. The lesson-agreement strategy has two goals: to gain the students' attention and to create an opportunity to use an advance organizer to focus attention on the day's lesson.

Using Examples and Nonexamples. When introducing important concepts, an effective communication method for clarifying misconceptions is the use of examples and nonexamples. To avoid confusion, examples should be given *before* sharing nonexamples. For instance, when introducing the concept *equilaterals*, a mathematics teacher might begin the lesson by showing a picture of a variety of equilaterals and asking the students to identify the properties these figures have in common. Once the students point out that all the sides are equal, the definition can then be written. Then a group of equilaterals and one figure that is not an equilateral could be shown, asking the students to identify the exception. Noting the contrast in the figures will help sharpen students' conceptions of *equilateral*.

It Works for Me!

Innovation Configuration

Robert J. Monson, Teachers College, Columbia University

If leaders want teachers to improve their practice, we must be specific about what that improvement looks like. In the 1980s ASCD published a monograph titled *Taking Charge of Change*. In it was a little tool—an innovation configuration—that proved invaluable to me as a superintendent working with teachers. An *innovation configuration* is a one-page "road map" that communicates to teachers the stages of development in their practice as they move from their current practice to the desired practice.

What does an innovation configuration look like? Take a standard-size piece of paper, turn it in the "landscape" position, and draw a straight line across the page (leaving a margin on both sides). Place four marks proportionately along this line: one at each end, then two at the one-quarter and three-quarters points. Under each mark, list the pedagogical strategies that reflect that level of development of practice for the innovation that the teachers are expected to practice. For example, for teaching spelling in balanced literacy, "spelling workbooks" would be under the leftmost mark, and under the rightmost mark "spelling in context" would appear, reflecting the desired classroom practices.

Many teachers' practices do not match their students' learning preferences (Gilbert, 2006). Effective teachers spend more time than less effective teachers in introducing new material and giving guided practice. Much of this time is spent giving examples. Often, the most important variable that makes lessons clear and understandable is the use of examples by the teacher and the act of asking students to give examples.

Using Repetition and Review. An old cliché says that a good teacher tells students what she is going to tell them, then she tells them, and then she tells them what she told them. According to the effective schools research, this old formula is right on target. Your teachers' students learn more when they know what the lesson is going to be about, and when the major concepts are reviewed at the end of the lesson.

A common practice (but a very questionable one) is asking students if they have any further questions. When you already understand something, listening to repeated explanations can be frustrating. A better alternative is to identify students at random and ask for examples. If students can give examples, the teacher should proceed with the lesson; if not, the concept needs further explanation.

It should be noted that good teachers do not attempt to review all of the content covered in a lesson. Students will remember the major concepts better if the teacher reviews only the most important ones.

Using Eye Contact. One of the most common communication mistakes made by beginning teachers is failure to keep eye contact with students. Anyone who has gone through elementary and secondary school can remember teachers who read to students at length, seldom looking up to make eye contact. Or they remember teachers who talked while writing on the board, making their voice difficult to hear and adding boredom to the lesson. Use of the overhead projector and computerized presentations like PowerPoint have tempered this malpractice, because they provide teachers a means of looking at the students while attending to the lesson at hand.

Maximizing Variety. Your teachers should vary their instructional practices and their student activities to make their lessons more stimulating. The need to have a repertoire of teaching strategies has already been stressed. Another way they can add interest throughout the week is to vary the group size within the class. One model, the Trump Plan, suggests that students should spend 40% of their time working in large groups, 20% working in small groups, and 40% on individual assignments. Although these percentages can be argued, the value in the variety offered by this plan is clearly acknowledged. Because this plan is one of the best personalized models ever developed, Keefe and Amenta (2005) predict that it may eventually be recognized as "the pivotal school reform of the second half of the twentieth century" (p. 538).

Conclusion

The body of research on effective teaching supports teachers' development of repertoires of teaching strategies. Each teaching strategy has unique strengths and limitations, and its implementation requires appropriate execution.

Direct instruction has been found to be associated with learner attainment. Although the lecture is a very poor motivator, it is an effective means for building a framework (introducing a unit or lesson) and for summarizing lessons. Most effective when kept simple, it is a highly economic teaching strategy in that it allows much content to be covered quickly.

The case-study method provides a way for teachers to help students make judicious decisions. Good cases may be real or improvised but must contain plenty of relevant and irrelevant information and must end in a problem.

Although case studies are good motivators, they are a slow method for covering content because they require giving students ample time and freedom to discuss the material. Inquiry learning, like the case-study method, is a very slow way to cover content, but it is an excellent strategy for teaching problem solving.

Computers offer new ways to promote inquiring skills. Simulation games are excellent motivators. Content learned through simulation games is retained longer than understandings gained through other methods. Tutoring offers an opportunity for teachers to individualize and personalize teaching to help all students reach their potential.

Effective teaching requires good communications skills. Once thought to be a simple process, communication is seldom simple. The environment in which communication occurs affects the message received. Emotions, too, play an important role in both communication and learning. Good classroom instruction requires the use of several teaching skills, including set induction, examples and nonexamples, repetition, eye contact, and variety.

Teachers are beginning to use the computer and the arts to enhance creativity and self-confidence. Homework, too, can be used to promote student interest and student creativity. When giving homework assignments, teachers must first decide the goals for each assignment and then communicate these goals to students. Tactile activities can stimulate interest and ensure that homework assignments are within range of the students' abilities.

Effective direct instruction requires helping students identify important concepts before lessons begin. If a few major concepts are identified prior to the lesson, students remember them better when tested weeks later. Effective delivery of direct-instruction lessons requires finding ways to simplify the lesson so that all students can understand the major concepts. This requires adjusting the tempo to a crisp, yet manageable pace, varying the use of stimuli, sequencing the content to facilitate its understanding, and using humor to promote socialization among classmates.

Supervisors should make sure that each teaching method is chosen according to its strengths and should be delivered to reach its potential. The case-study method, inquiry method, and simulation/gaming method are highly motivating. Teachers find that a most difficult challenge when using these methods is to resist the temptation to interrupt student activities.

Classroom communications are highly complex and can be improved by controlling classroom climate. When used to communicate effectively, such skills as set induction, examples, repetition, eye contact, and variety can be used to enhance all types of lessons.

As many as half of all students may be at risk of dropping out of school. Meeting the needs of these students presents a challenge. Gifted students also present a challenge. The arts can be used to meet the unique needs of all students. Computers can also be used to personalize lessons to meet individual needs.

Sometimes homework is inappropriately used to teach new concepts or as a second effort to get across concepts that students failed to understand in class. If they cannot understand the topic with the teacher's help, they are far less likely to understand it in the teacher's absence. Homework is an effective method for practicing skills that have already been introduced.

Parents are an often-overlooked asset that teachers can and should use more effectively. Contracts can be drawn up to ensure that parents understand their roles in helping their children succeed in their schoolwork at school and at home.

Questions for Discussion and Reflection

1. How can supervisors help teachers create a classroom environment that is conducive to good communication?
2. Many teachers continue to use the lecture method almost exclusively. How can supervisors persuade teachers to use other instructional methods?
3. When using nondirect teaching methods, teachers' greatest challenge is to resist the temptation to interfere with student activities. How can supervisors help teachers learn to "stay out of the way?"
4. How can supervisors prepare teachers to help marginal students increase their levels of self-esteem?
5. With a multiplicity of events occurring most of the time, how can supervisors help teachers influence the immediate environment to enhance communications?
6. How can instruction be used to achieve appreciation for ethnic and gender diversity? Which instructional methods would be most effective in achieving this goal? Explain your answer.
7. How can supervisors best use the talents and skills of teachers to help other teachers expand their teaching strategies?
8. Should supervisors have a portfolio that includes a variety of sample teaching strategies and, if so, what are some ways to acquire these?

Suggested Activities

1. Ask a local school principal for permission to visit some classrooms. Pay close attention to the teachers' instructional methods. After class, randomly select two students from each classroom and ask each to tell you what is being studied at the moment. Follow up with other questions until you can tell how well the students understand the concepts.
2. Ask a local school principal to identify a teacher who has worked with students to develop an effective simulation game. Interview this teacher and make a set of guidelines that teachers can follow when developing a simulation with their students.
3. Interview three teachers, asking them what they do prior to the beginning of a lesson to capture all students' attention and what they do to focus the attention on the major lesson content. Make a list of these advance organizers.

4. Ask a local school principal to identify a teacher who uses case studies. With this teacher's permission, make a recorded (audio or video) interview, asking the teacher what values are derived from this method. Keep this video to use to encourage teachers to try a case-study lesson.

NOTE

[1] The full TIMSS Video Study science report can be retrieved at http://nces.ed.gov/timss. A public release 5-CD set with five full lesson videos from each country, along with commentaries by the teachers and researchers, is available for purchase from LessonLab at www.lessonlab.com/bkstore (click on the Videos tab and type TIMSS in the Search Videos box).

Chapter 10

Helping Teachers Test and Evaluate Lessons

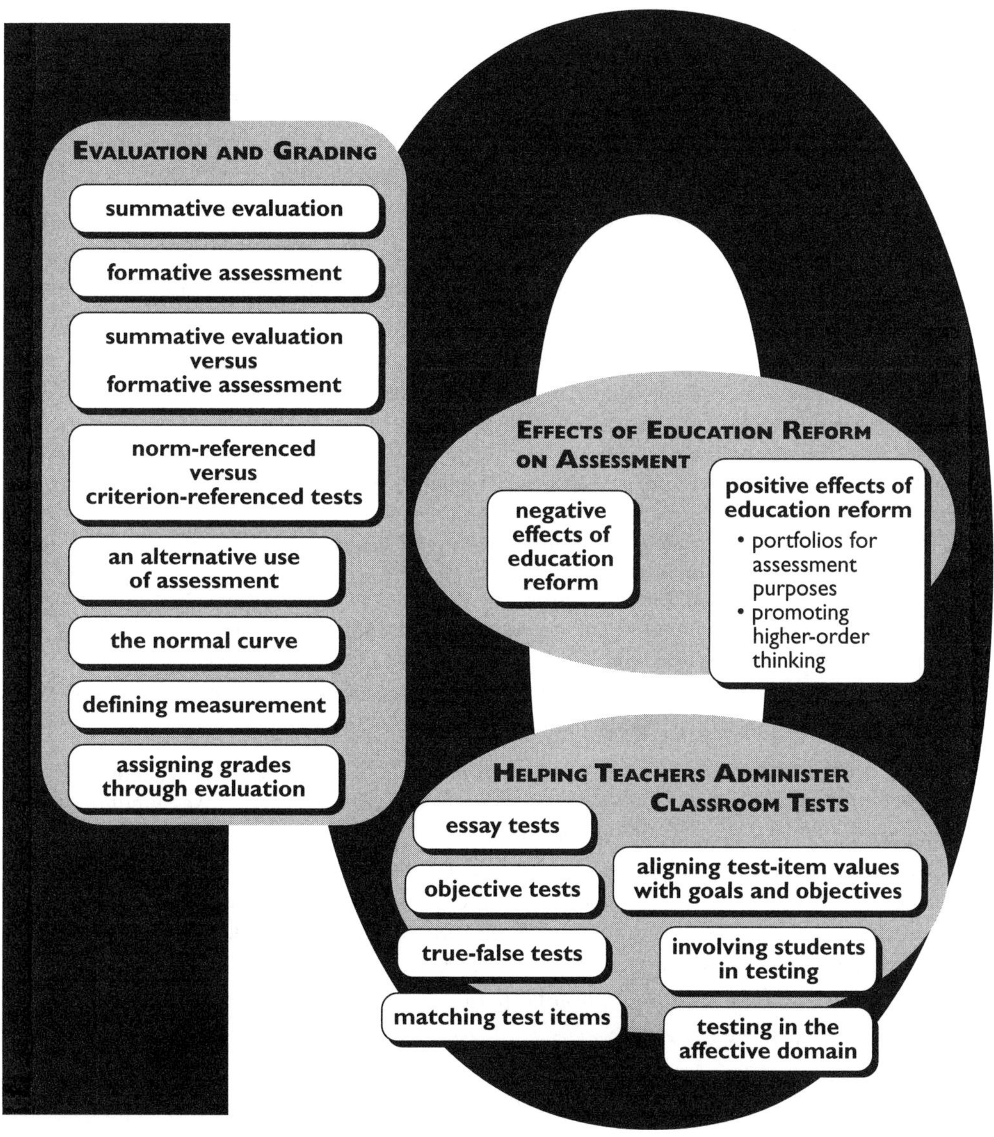
EVALUATION AND GRADING
summative evaluation
formative assessment
summative evaluation versus formative assessment
norm-referenced versus criterion-referenced tests
an alternative use of assessment
the normal curve
defining measurement
assigning grades through evaluation
EFFECTS OF EDUCATION REFORM ON ASSESSMENT
negative effects of education reform
positive effects of education reform
• portfolios for assessment purposes
• promoting higher-order thinking
HELPING TEACHERS ADMINISTER CLASSROOM TESTS
essay tests
objective tests
true-false tests
matching test items
aligning test-item values with goals and objectives
involving students in testing
testing in the affective domain

> *Not everything worth measuring can be measured, and not everything measured is worth measuring.*
>
> —Albert Einstein

Objectives

After completion of this chapter, you should be able to

1. Help teachers differentiate between criterion-referenced and norm-referenced evaluation
2. Persuade teachers to use formative assessment to strengthen the academic program at their school
3. Dissuade teachers from misusing evaluation (in particular, the bell curve)
4. Help teachers establish a continuous, performance-based self-assessment program
5. Help teachers develop a grading system that sets the weight of each part in proportion to the amount of time spent studying it

A Different Type of Course

Alex Demetrius was in the last course in his principalship program at Elmworth College. The course, Philosophy of Assessment, was team taught by professors from two departments. Dr. Raymond Warren, who holds a distinguished chair in the Philosophy Department, designed this course and invited Sarah Bigley from the Department of Education to join him in teaching this graduate-level experimental course.

Alex had heard good reports from former students in this class, who liked its debate format. The curriculum for this course consisted of a series of paradoxes including assessment, the driver of instruction versus instruction, the driver of assessment; measurement versus evaluation; norm-referenced versus criterion-referenced evaluation; formative versus summative evaluation; objective versus subjective assessment; competitive testing: a positive or negative practice; assessment: a cognitive practice or an affective practice; the advantages versus the disadvantages of involving parents; and the pros and cons of portfolios.

At the end of the first lesson, Alex studied the course syllabus and contemplated these paradoxes. These were important issues at a time when assessment was being used to measure schools' success rates. This was going to be an interesting course.

Reflection

Consider the following questions and return to them after reading this chapter. What role should portfolios play in assessment? What are some limits of the use of the normal curve? What, if any, is the proper role of competition in assessment? How can the supervisor persuade teachers to update their assessment practices (e.g., use more criterion-referenced evaluation and increase the variety and number of criteria for determining grades)?

Introduction

> Interstate New Teacher Assessment and Support Consortium (INTASC) Principle No. 8 says, "The teacher understands and uses formal and informal assessment strategies to evaluate and ensure the continuous intellectual, social, and physical development of the learner."

Testing has always been a fixed part of elementary and secondary schools, but in recent years educators have learned that many popular testing practices are educationally unsound (Allen, 2004). Education reform programs have identified many testing malpractices and have made testing-program reform the center of education reform. This chapter reviews several common testing malpractices and suggests ways to help teachers improve testing programs.

Testing and evaluation are among the most important tools your teachers can have to improve learning in their classrooms, yet teachers are seldom prepared to make full use of these tools. Unfortunately, the litany of our knowledge about classroom evaluation does not match our usual practices. The gap between the potential of testing as a teaching–learning tool and the reality of current teaching is wide.

Moreover, not only have most teachers failed to use testing and evaluation in ways that systematically increase learning, of even greater concern is the fact that many teachers have misused testing and evaluation in ways that have actually suppressed learning. Much of the misuse has resulted from teachers attempting to reach goals that tests and evaluation were never designed to reach. Since the advent of the No Child Left Behind program, increased pressure on teachers and students to produce higher test scores has often led to cheating (Lederman & Burnstein, 2006).

Teachers have also used testing and evaluation to enforce and maintain discipline. In this practice they frequently have parents as allies. It is assumed that students with poor grades will naturally work harder to achieve more. Good marks become the objective of learning. Grades become the currency which students, teachers, and parents may use for different purposes. Ask your teachers to consider the effect that poor grades can have on the self-esteem of poor performers when threats are used and when test results are made public.

Evaluation and Grading

When the cook tastes the soup, that's formative assessment; when the guests taste it, that's summative evaluation.

—M. Scriven, *Beyond formative and summative evaluation*

Summative Evaluation

For many years, American students have associated all tests and evaluations with grading. The unfortunate result has been a student mind-set that puts grades above learning (Shepard, 2005). The use of tests and evaluation to determine grades is called *summative evaluation*. Since the early 1990s, another use of summative evaluation has become popular: *accountability*—not only of the students, but also of the school and the teachers. Summative evaluation is used to decide if the school and the teachers meet minimal accountability standards.

Couple this increased level of accountability imposed on schools and teachers by recent reform movements with reform rhetoric such as *All students can and will learn*, and it seems only natural that many teachers dislike and try to avoid their role in testing and evaluation. Some teachers are responding by actually preparing students for the test. The practice of helping students increase their performance on standardized exams is not limited to a few isolated incidents or even to just a few states. On the contrary, the practice is pervasive throughout the nation, resulting in the criticism that teachers are "teaching to the test." Although some individuals within the profession and some outside the profession question this practice, others defend it. Actually, the teacher's only choice is either to align instruction with the tests, or to ignore the tests and risk teaching students one curriculum and testing them against another. The latter just doesn't make sense.

This discussion is not meant to be an indictment on all summative evaluation. On the contrary, when your teachers use it properly, summative evaluation is an important practice in education. Many parents insist on getting letter grades on the performance of their children, and rightfully so. They say they need these evaluations to determine whether adequate progress is being made by their children. Summative evaluation is also needed to measure the success on a learning unit or over a grading period. At the time summative tests are administered, work is completed for that unit or grading period. Summative evaluation occurs after the instruction is over. Used appropriately, summative evaluation gives feedback on the success of a unit.

Formative Assessment

In recent years a newer type of testing called formative assessment has been replacing summative testing (Stiggins, 2005). *Formative assessment* is concerned with improving learning and teaching (by improving curriculum design and teaching methods). Formative assessment has been described as "the arrows students shoot along the way in the learning process" (Christopher 2007/2008, p. 75). Research shows that formative assessment is a key factor in raising student achievement (Sato & Atkin, 2006/2007). Your teachers should be aware that weekly formative assessment has the power to raise student performance by almost a full grade level (Wenglinsky & Silverstein, 2006/2007) and double the rate of student learning (Clymer & William, 2006/2007).

Summative Evaluation versus Formative Assessment

In many ways, formative assessment seems to be the opposite of summative evaluation. For example, summative evaluation occurs at the *end* of the unit or grading period, but formative assessment occurs *during* this time. Summative evaluation is used to issue grades, but formative assessment is never used to assign grades. On the contrary, the purpose of formative assessment is to improve both the curriculum and instruction. Summative evaluation covers long periods of learning, but formative assessment covers short periods. Summative evaluation uses major exams but formative assessment uses short, often daily, quizzes. Stated generally, the purpose of formative assessment is to produce learning and, according to the research, it does this very well (Sato & Atkin, 2006/2007). Summative evaluation is a one-time event; formative assessment is an ongoing process. Formative assessment is designed to improve the teacher's performance. Used formatively, tests can also become strong clarifiers of teachers' expectations. To perform at its maximum, assessment must be a continuous process (Woolfolk Hoy & Hoy, 2009).

Because teachers historically have made little use of formative tests, and because formative assessment has the power to improve curriculum and instruction, supervisors should encourage teachers to use more formative assessment. Perhaps because the vast majority of their evaluation is used to determine grades, students seldom associate testing with learning. Although summative test results can be used to improve learning, when teachers do attempt to use test outcomes for this purpose, students often fail to see the benefit. After a test is finished, students consider it time to shut down the schema. Teachers are sometimes frustrated because students do not exhibit any interest in reviewing their tests.

When helping teachers plan and use formative assessment, supervisors should encourage their faculty to give small tests frequently. By doing so, and then correcting students' tests and giving them feedback on the corrections, teachers can clear up any misunderstandings of the content being tested. The key to using tests to improve learning is giving feedback, and teachers should always cite strengths and errors (Brookhart, 2007/2008). "The best grading practices provide accurate feedback designed to improve student performance" (Reeves, 2008, p. 85). If any student cannot learn well from the original instruction, the student can do so from one or more correctives.

Table 10.1 (on the following page) summarizes the differences between summative evaluation and formative assessment. Supervisors should ensure that their teachers are familiar with the appropriate uses of both processes. Note the sharp contrast between these two types of evaluation. Even the purposes for which they were designed are totally different. Why would it be considered essential to always hold a follow-up session after giving a formative

Table 10.1 A Comparison of Summative Evaluation and Formative Assessment

	Summative Evaluation	Formative Assessment
Purpose	to issue grades	to improve teaching
Time given	following instruction	prior to and during instruction
Basis	norm referenced	criterion referenced
Follow-up	seldom	frequent

test? Because the only purpose of this type of test is to improve teaching and learning. Without feedback, neither the teacher nor the students could use the results to improve their roles in teaching and learning.

Norm-Referenced versus Criterion-Referenced Tests

Historically, parents have insisted on knowing how well their children are performing, as compared to their classmates. Such evaluation is determined by *norm-referenced tests.* This knowledge remains important to parents, especially those who believe that competition is necessary to produce maximum learning. Many parents endorse the use of competition in classes because it was used when they were in school. Yet contemporary educators are equally clear in their message that the need for competition among classmates has been exaggerated. The result of this overemphasis on competition is often detrimental to the education process. Because testing has tremendous potential to promote learning, it should be a positive, supportive experience. But over and over again, in homes and in schools, we set up situations that guarantee that there will be "winners" and "losers," and that some children will feel defeated and inept.

To place students in a more reasonable climate, your teachers may choose to inform students of expectations before they take their tests, setting the standard for success in advance. Tests that spell out the level of performance needed for success before the tests are administered are called *criterion-referenced tests.* Rubrics can be used to further clarify the teacher's expectations (Sato & Atkin, 2006/2007). A comparison of norm-referenced and criterion-referenced tests is shown in Table 10.2. Make sure your teachers know the difference between the two types of tests and the appropriate use of each.

An Alternative Use of Assessment

In some ways educators have made significant progress in the use of evaluation. As discussed in chapter 3, many educators are finding alternatives to norm-referenced tests, which have forced students to compete with their classmates. One alternative is to use tests to cause students to compete with their *own* previous levels of performance by setting minimal levels required to reach particular grades *before* the test is given. Tests used to measure a student's performance with reference to specified criteria or to the student's previous level

Table 10.2 Norm-Referenced versus Criterion-Referenced Tests

Norm-Referenced	Criterion-Referenced
Students might not know what content to expect on a test.	Students always know what content to expect on a test.
Students may not know what type of performance is expected until seeing the test.	Prior to taking a test, students know what type of performance will be demanded.
Student success may depend on how well others score on the test.	Student success depends only on how well the individual student scores on the test.
Student must compete with classmates.	Students only compete with the course expectations.

of performance are a form of criterion-referenced tests. A distinct advantage that criterion-referenced testing has over norm-referenced testing is that all students have a reasonable opportunity to perform as well as or above their own previous levels of performance, whereas some students could never perform at levels that equal or exceed the performance of their classmates.

The Normal Curve

You will recall from chapter 8 that in the 1920s, educational psychologist E. L. Thorndike discovered that the normal distribution of intelligence-test scores formed a bell-shaped pattern. Figure 10.1 illustrates this so-called *bell curve,* also known as the *normal curve* or the *probability curve,* which is derived from graphically plotting the distribution of hundreds of thousands of intelligence-test scores. The same picture can be derived from plotting the distribution of any number of natural phenomena, from the size of an oak leaf to the variation in height or weight of human beings. In other words, the normal curve is no more than a picture of the results of chance happenings.

Figure 10.1 The Normal Curve

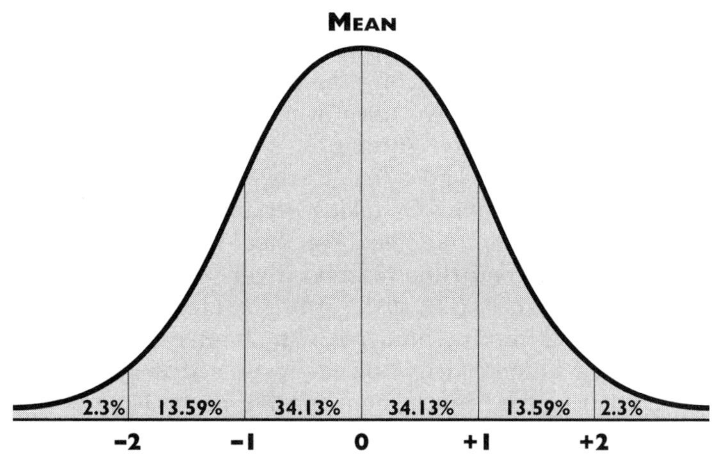

The bell curve in Figure 10.1 shows that nature has a way of distributing many of its tangible and intangible items so that the farther individual items deviate from the average (or mean), the fewer of those items there are. More accurately, about 34% will deviate one standard unit above the mean, and about 34% will deviate one standard unit below the mean. About 13.5% of the population will vary two standard units above the mean, and the same percent will vary two units below the mean. Just less than 2.5% of the population will vary three units away (above or below) from the mean.

Because it was noticed that hundreds of thousands of intelligence-test scores were distributed in this way, educators assumed that the performance of students in elementary, secondary, and college classrooms should follow this pattern. But after using this pattern nationwide to distribute test scores and grades of millions of students over a half-century, educators discovered that the practice is seriously flawed. Because hundreds of thousands of test scores form this pattern when put together, it was assumed that the ability of students in a classroom of, say, 20 to 40 students should vary similarly. This is no truer than the assumption that the deviation of 20 oak leaves chosen at random would follow the larger pattern. Further examination has shown that a minimum of a hundred or more individuals is needed to produce this pattern of variation of ability.

Even with a population of a hundred or more, the normal curve distribution occurs only when the population is randomly selected. For example, the common use of the normal curve to assign grades in graduate school is highly inappropriate, since that population is highly selective. A further error was made in assuming that students' performance on tests and assignments correlates closely with their ability. Such an assumption ignores the role that motivation (or lack of motivation) plays in classroom performance.

Another error is made in assuming that schools should strive for natural or random performance. On the contrary, schools should be dedicated to the task of applying treatment that will cause students to perform beyond the levels at which they would perform without this treatment. For example, schools should be dedicated to motivating students beyond their "natural" levels and should make continuous efforts toward their success when they are not in school. Some students have special learning disabilities, and schools should be dedicated to helping them overcome these disabilities or to succeed in spite of them.

For a half century we have overemphasized the role that innate ability plays in learning while ignoring or seriously underestimating the effect of motivation. We know now that teachers can increase the level of academic gains in their classrooms by taking certain measures to influence the level of motivation and other variables that affect learner success. Although there are instances where competition can positively affect motivation, when used as it has been in the past (i.e., disregarding student differences) it generally produces negative results. Students with limited abilities to perform well on exams often become demoralized by tests that measure their performance against that of their much more capable peers. Help your teachers discover ways to motivate their students and de-emphasize competitiveness.

Defining Measurement

Two terms that many educators find confusing are *measurement* and *evaluation.* Although sometimes they are used interchangeably, their meanings are quite different. Measurement is the act of gathering data: For example, you measure the ingredients called for in a recipe, or you measure the time needed to drive to a particular destination, or you step on the scales to measure your weight. The act of measuring is simply the act of gathering information; therefore, measurement is neither good nor bad.

Teachers assign tests, classwork, homework, and unit projects as a means of gathering information about the amount of understanding students have gained. That is the sole purpose of a test. When the teacher scores the test and learns that Sharon answered 95% of the questions correctly, that, too, is part of the measurement process. Note that neither the gathering of information nor the scoring of the results is value laden.

Assigning Grades through Evaluation

Once the test scores are determined, the teacher must decide what to do with them. If the decision is to assign letter grades to the test scores, the process is no longer that of objectively gathering information. By assigning letter grades, the teacher is giving the process a *value.* The process of measuring should be kept objective and has no room for the teacher's opinions, whereas the process that we call *evaluation* does allow for the opinions of the teacher. Table 10.3 compares the characteristics of measurement and evaluation.

Table 10.3 Measurement versus Evaluation

Measurement	Evaluation
Does not require the teacher's judgment	Requires the teacher's judgment
Is used primarily to score tests and other student products	Is used primarily to change tests scores and other feedback into letter grades
Should be completely objective	Must involve some subjectivity
Results reported in numbers	Results usually reported in letter grades

Notice that measurement is simply the results teachers get when they take a quantitative reading in student performance. The results are reported in numbers—never in terms of grades and never in value-laden terms such as high or low, good or poor. Measurement is always objective and is usually a rather simple task.

In contrast, evaluation—the process of making judgment about something—is a teaching responsibility that many teachers find difficult. Whether attempting to evaluate test scores, seatwork, or unit projects, most teachers always seem to find the process challenging. Following is an easy and effective system for helping your teachers evaluate scores and convert them into term grades.

First, it's important to remember that several separate scores should go into the assignment of a grade for any testing period (Popham, 2005). No test reveals all there is to know about the learner, and no single test should be used as an exclusive measure of any student's capacity. Second, term grades should always reflect a variety of student performances. Third, the individual scores from the variety of performances should be weighted to reflect the relative importance of all scores. One approach worth considering is to have the weighting reflect the relative amount of emphasis given each activity by the teacher; another is the relative time spent in and outside class in these areas—for example, a list of performance activities that might be given during a grading period as in Table 10.4. However, the time spent working on this class totals 51 hours. To simplify the mathematics, the teacher might wish to reduce another activity (say, the homework) by one hour. By assigning 2% (or 2 points) to each hour of activities, this teacher could distribute the weights given each activity. Assigning 2% of the final grade to each hour of activities, the resulting grade distribution of weighing is shown below.

Table 10.4 Approximate Time Spent on Each Activity

Activities	Number of Hours
homework	15
classwork	10
portfolio	10
group project	5
oral presentation	5
weekly tests	5
final exam	1
Total number of hours	51

homework = 28% group project = 10%
classwork = 20% oral presentation = 10%
portfolio = 20% weekly tests = 10%
final exam = 2%

Of course, some teachers may want the exams to count more; others will assign more credit to the portfolios, seatwork, or homework. The portfolio and seatwork credits could be combined, placing all of these credits on the portfolio work.

An advantage of this grading system is that it uses a variety of activities to determine the final grade. The more diverse and imaginative the evaluation activities used by the teacher, the more all-encompassing and valid the evaluation is likely to be. Paradoxically, some teachers need encouragement to use a variety of activities to determine term grades, yet even these teachers need latitude to choose these activities and assign relative weights to their importance. Another advantage is that among the various activities counted in this system, several are informal in nature. Good grading often substitutes direct conferences for formal grading. Conferences could easily be used to evaluate the portfolio work.

Effects of Education Reform on Assessment

Education reform has had many effects on assessment—some good, some bad. This section presents a review of both the concerns that education reform has brought to assessment and some of the positive effects.

Negative Effects of Education Reform

Education reform efforts in all states have increasingly focused on assessment (Popham, 2005). The reason for this special attention has been an increase in accountability. The reform reports proclaimed the schools so poor as to have thrust the country into a state of crisis. It was determined that a new type of assessment was needed to assure the public that the schools were making continuous improvements, and in most states the leaders would settle for only one type of evidence of improvement: higher student scores on standardized tests.

Many educators question the wisdom of aiming the schools toward this one narrow goal of increasing test scores. Overemphasis on test scores tells students that being creative has no rewards: What pays is being able to jump through somebody else's hoops (Lerner, 2006; Hunt, 2007). In several states, school administrators and teachers are feeling strapped with impossible demands. To be able to fare well with their new reward program, their students will have to make high scores in comparison to the scores of last year's class. But educators know that some classes are strong and others are weak. In fact, teachers and administrators know that the difference between two senior classes is often so great that it would be unrealistic to even hope that the performance level of a very poor class will equal or exceed that of a stronger senior class from the previous year. Even those schools that succeed in raising their test scores year after year will soon peak out or reach a level so high that future classes will not be able to top it.

Positive Effects of Education Reform

Recent reform practices have caused several positive changes in the way(s) assessment is used. One of the most welcome developments is the emphasis that has been placed on authenticity. *Authentic assessment* is the use of tests designed and administered throughout the year to cause students to develop valued skills, using real-life activities that require problem solving. Another way to express this concept is to say that the content in the testing program is based on valued outcomes.

Using authentic assessment doesn't require a major curriculum overhaul. For example, a few New Hampshire school districts decided to reduce some of their required Carnegie units to provide more instructional time for authentic assessment. One aspect of valued outcomes is the mere identification of outcomes, or *outcomes-based education* (OBE). Unfortunately, some people read more into the term than was originally intended, which is causing considerable controversy. In some states, emotions run high when the terms "outcomes-based education" or "valued outcomes" are discussed. The disagreements are not over the process of looking ahead and setting outcomes for students to reach; rather, the problem lies in disagreement on what outcomes to strive toward. The role of the supervisor is not to "sell" teachers and parents on OBE but rather to clarify any misunderstandings, especially those that provoke controversy.

From a curriculum alignment and instruction perspective, a good quality embedded in OBE is *application;* these tests require the students to apply the content they learn to some realistic problem or situation. Such tests are commonly called performance tests. *Performance-based assessment* (or performance evaluation) has been embraced by the education community. Few innovations in education have caught on as quickly, giving new life to improvement of curriculum and instruction. The current enthusiasm for performance assessment reflects a hope that it can drive school reform and result in improvements in student performance, particularly in the area of complex thinking skills.

Although it has acquired some new definitions along the way, performance assessment really is not a new idea. Often, when hearing new terms associated with school reform, educators and noneducators alike think these terms represent brand new ideas—educational approaches that are completely unique and have never before been tried. Actually, most new terms in reform programs are variations of ideas that have been tried years earlier. For example, performance assessment/evaluation can refer to verbal performance (such as the old, traditional spelling bee) or it can refer to written performance (e.g., answering word problems such as "If car A leaves traveling west at 60 mph, . . ."). In a computer or music class, performance evaluation can refer to applying skills in keyboarding, playing an instrument, performing voice exercises, and a number of other performance-type activities. The fine arts can be tied to all other subjects, enlivening an otherwise lackluster curriculum. Since performance-based evaluation places students in an active role, it is a good motivator.

* * *

Perhaps the ideal arena for building a learning community is the school building. As shown in the following case study, successful collaboration and community building can be achieved with as few as two teachers who have the drive and determination to improve their school.

Using Collaboration to Help Teachers Evaluate Lessons

Anita Varrati • Kent State University

This story details a collaborative approach in developmental supervision between two classroom teachers and demonstrates the use of critical reflection as a means to evaluate a lesson. Kathy the supervisor, an experienced third-grade teacher, conducted a peer observation of a kindergarten teacher, Mr. Hope, using the clinical supervision model. Kathy was selected by her principal to conduct this peer observation because of her knowledge of the particular instructional strategy being observed. Unlike traditional clinical supervision that primarily focuses on specific teacher behaviors, Kathy was directed to use a more developmental approach that focuses on the impact on student learning. The focus of this observation related to an area of professional growth collaboratively identified by the supervisor and teacher.

To carry out this formative process, Kathy conducted a pre-observation conference, a classroom observation, and a post-observation conference where both she and the teacher collaboratively analyzed and evaluated the data (Glickman, Gordon, & Ross-Gordon, 2007). Throughout this process, Kathy's goal was to promote the teacher's critical reflection and evaluation of how his teaching practices positively affect student learning. In order to set the stage for critical reflection, Kathy organized the supervisory process around Danielson's Components of Professional Practice (1996). The domains of planning and preparation, classroom environment, and instruction provided a framework for collaborative planning of the lesson to be observed and established the criteria that Kathy and Mr. Hope used to analyze and evaluate the success of the lesson.

The Pre-Observation Conference

In a collaborative pre-conference, the supervisor and teacher coplan what will be the focus of the lesson to be observed. When Kathy met with Mr. Hope, she set the conference tone by using some guiding questions. Kathy's initially asked Mr. Hope to describe his students, including those with special needs. Of the 16 students (eight boys and eight girls), one is gifted, three are reading at a first/second-grade level, one has a hearing deficit, and one student is cognitively autistic. Kathy next inquired about what Mr. Hope wanted the students to learn and the characteristics of the lesson to be observed. Mr. Hope wanted students to learn several key language arts and mathematics concepts. He wanted to try the learning-center approach as a means to accomplish that goal.

The following objectives were created: At the seatwork center, students will review their addition facts by adding numbers to ten. They will then fill in the numbers to make an addition sentence. At the reading center, students will read and sound out words in the decodable book and draw a picture inspired by the book. At the math center, students will work in pairs to learn about subtraction using manipulatives. Finally, students will choose one of the following activities: Draw a picture of their favorite community helper, make a ladybug, complete the letter Zz in their picture dictionary, or listen for words that begin with the "Z" sound on a cassette tape.

Next, Kathy asked how these instructional goals would meet the state standards and the district curriculum. Mr. Hope explained that each activity comes directly from the Kindergarten Pacing Guide that has been aligned with the state standards and the district's curriculum. Standards addressed in language arts involve the use of a book, reading from left to right, reading consonant/vowel/consonant words, and reading comprehension. Math standards include adding single digits, using manipulatives to understand a concept, and subtracting single digits.

When Kathy asked how these learning targets were suitable for this particular group of students, Mr. Hope explained that his instructional approach (learning centers) would address the vastly diverse developmental and experiential needs of all students by providing differentiation in the types of learning activities engaged in by the students. The other aspect of differentiation would be the evaluation of students' work, which is based on their individual needs and abilities.

Since Kathy knew that Mr. Hope planned to focus on learning centers as the main instructional strategy, she asked him to provide a more descriptive picture of what the students would do. Mr. Hope explained that he had just begun to incorporate daily independent learning centers for approximately 80 minutes. Within that time, he wanted every student to rotate between four different stations, spending 20 minutes at each one. Center One consisted of seatwork with two worksheets, one math and one language arts, to be done independently. Center Two involved a reading group instructed by Mr. Hope. Center Three was a math group activity that involved solving problems using manipulatives. Center Four was an interdisciplinary center where students could do a language arts activity by choosing to do artwork, complete a listening or phonemic awareness activity, or complete a writing assignment.

When Kathy asked why Mr. Hope chose learning centers as a way to engage students in the content, he explained that he wanted to provide a way for students to experience a variety of learning activities in a short amount of time. As an elementary teacher, Mr. Hope was responsible for student mastery of academic standards in core content areas including language arts, math, science, and social studies. He saw learning centers as a way that he could manage to do this in a more interdisciplinary fashion. Mr. Hope planned to engage the students by involving them in group, paired, and individual reading, collaborating on their work, and presenting their work to the class. He believed that the collaborative and positive nature of the learning centers would help students who normally have trouble sounding out words or blending words into sounds and using math manipulatives to add or subtract.

Kathy's final question involved the lesson focus. What did Mr. Hope want Kathy to look for during the observation? In general, Mr. Hope wanted Kathy's feedback on how the learning-center approach could function as a means to incorporate several key learning concepts. He wanted feedback on whether students could remain on task at each center throughout the learning-center time frame. Since he was using ability grouping, were his grouping strategies for the centers successful? Together, Kathy and Mr. Hope decided how the data would be collected. It was agreed that Kathy would use a focused, open-ended observation (Gordon, Butters, Maxey & Ciccarelli, 2002). The foci for the observation would include the level of participation of students at each learning center. She planned to take some open-ended notes and do a categorical frequency chart, which is a quantitative method for depicting student on/off task behavior (Glickman et al., 2007). Kathy would pay particular attention to the centers where Mr. Hope was conducting student assessments. They would then evaluate the learning of key concepts by looking at student work completed at each center.

The Post-Observation Conference

Three days later, Kathy and Mr. Hope met to discuss the classroom observation. Kathy spent the 75 minutes observing in order to give each group equal time for the data collection. While Kathy had collected the data, she reserved the analysis and interpretation for the post conference. Table 1 shows the completed Categorical Frequency Chart for On/Off Task Learning Center Behaviors that Kathy completed during the observation. Kathy referenced Danielson's Components of Professional Practice as a means to guide the dialogue during the conference. She opened the conference by asking Mr. Hope how he thought the lesson had gone. Mr. Hope hesitated a moment before saying that he thought his educational goals were met, although there were

Table 1 Categorical Frequency Chart for On/Off Task Learning Center Behaviors

Groups	Center 1: Language Arts & Math Worksheets (writing)	Center 2: Reading Groups	Center 3: Math Manipulatives	Center 4: Interdisciplinary (listening, reading, writing, drawing)
Group 1	**Time: 9:00**	**Time: 10:05**	**Time: 9:50**	**Time: 9:35**
Annie	B	C	D	A
David	B	A	D	B
Maria	B	A	D	E
Steve	F	H	D	E
Group 2	**Time: 9:20**	**Time: 9:05**	**Time: 10:10**	**Time: 9:55**
Miguel	F	C	D	E
Angie	H	C	H	A
James	B	F	D	E
Rachel	B	F	D	B
Group 3	**Time: 9:40**	**Time: 9:25**	**Time: 9:10**	**Time: 10:15**
Jack	B	A	D	C
Lamont	B	A	D	B
Michelle	H	C	D	A
Mark	B	A	D	E
Group 4	**Time: 10:00**	**Time: 9:45**	**Time: 9:30**	**Time: 9:15**
Jenny	F	A	D	E
Tia	B	A	D	A
Keisha	B	A	F	E
Austin	B	C	D	E

Key: A = On task, listening, watching
B = On task, writing
C = On task, reading
D = On task, hands-on activity
E = On task, drawing
F = Off task, passive
G = Off task, disturbing others
H = Off task, playing (actively engaged for much of the time)

a few behavioral problems. He was pleased, however, that he had only needed to issue a few verbal reminders to students.

Kathy gave Mr. Hope a copy of the Categorical Frequency Chart for On/Off Task Behavior. She explained that she used their pre-conference discussion to design this quantitative method of data collection on how students were attending to the learning-center tasks by groups and individual students. The key for the chart was created to address the specific tasks required by each center. Kathy asked Mr. Hope to look at the chart to reflect on students' productive engagement. As Mr. Hope studied the data, two patterns emerged. First, he was able to see how individual students and groups attended to tasks required at all learning centers. The second pattern that emerged was the overall student engagement per learning center. The Collaborative Interpretation of the Data (Table 2) represents the patterns that emerged.

Mr. Hope was excited about the data because it gave him valuable information on how individual students and groups responded to each learning center and their respective tasks. It was especially useful for the information pertaining to Steve, his autistic student, and Angie, who is hearing impaired. Mr. Hope was able to see which tasks in which they were or were not engaged. He will use this information to further investigate the reasons for the off-task behavior. This will assist him as he designs future tasks based on student interests, needs, and abilities.

While still looking at the chart, Kathy asked Mr. Hope to analyze whether students learned what was intended. Mr. Hope referenced the overall percentage of on-task behavior as one indication that students had met the learning goals. In addition, Mr. Hope pointed to student work completed at each center. He had already checked the papers in preparation for the post-conference. Mr. Hope pulled examples of student work from each center that provided a good representation of the majority of students. While he was a little disappointed that some of the work was done poorly and not to the capability of particular students, Mr. Hope felt that most students understood the concepts that were taught. This provided some insightful feedback about his students who were performing above grade level. By combining the work samples with the on/off task data, Mr. Hope realized that he will need to provide some more challenging tasks for these students.

Table 2 Collaborative Interpretation of the Data

Students	Percentage of Students Observed Time On/Off Task Behavior		Total Percentage for Observed Center On/Off Task Behavior	
Group 1	**On**	**Off Task**	**Center 1: Language Arts & Math Worksheets**	
Annie	100	0	**On**	**Off**
David	100	0	69	31
Maria	100	0		
Steve	75	5		
Group 2	**On**	**Off Task**	**Center 2: Reading Groups**	
Miguel	75	5	**On**	**Off**
Angie	50	50	81	19
James	75	5		
Rachel	75	5		
Group 3	**On**	**Off Task**	**Center 3: Math Manipulatives**	
Jack	100	0	**On**	**Off**
Lamont	100	0	87	12
Michelle	75	5		
Mark	100	0		
Group 4	**On**	**Off Task**	**Center 4: Interdisciplinary**	
Jenny	75	5	**On**	**Off**
Tia	100	0	100	0
Keisha	75	5		
Austin	100	0		

Kathy referred to her open-ended notes to ask Mr. Hope if he could recall where the instructional goals were altered as the lesson was taught. Mr. Hope immediately centered on the reading lesson, in particular on one group that was struggling. Kathy commented on how Mr. Hope had altered the goals of the lesson by having the students read together rather than individually. Mr. Hope's method of discussing the story with them before they drew their pictures further facilitated comprehension and helped to keep them on task. On further reflection about how the lesson could be taught differently, Mr. Hope had an idea. He could have each student concentrate on one page of the story. At the end of the lesson, the students would still be learning the same goals.

As Mr. Hope was thinking about future planning for his learning centers, ability grouping was discussed. Kathy asked Mr. Hope if he thought that ability grouping could be responsible for some of the students having difficulty staying on task. A discussion ensued as to why the off-task behavior was prevalent in some groups over others. Did some students go off-task because they actually did not understand the concept or because of the grouping? Is 20 minutes per center too long a time? After a long discussion, Mr. Hope decided that he would try some grouping variations. He would see if non-ability grouping might be used to assist struggling students. Maybe having them at a learning center with students who could serve as a peer helpers could keep struggling students on task.

Issues for Further Reflection

This story details a supervisory approach that was facilitated by a building principal to assist a teacher with the implementation of a particular instructional strategy: learning centers. The principal promoted the use of peer coaching by a fellow teacher that also incorporated a cycle of clinical supervision. Peer coaching is one model of differentiated supervision described by Glatthorn (2002) that illustrates that the direct improvement of teaching and learning can be achieved through teacher collaboration, critical reflection and inquiry, and a focus on continuous improvement.

This collaborative approach is enhanced by the utilization of criteria for effective teaching in order to encourage the teacher to identify and clarify areas for professional growth. The supervisor, further, acts as a collaborator by guiding the teacher to evaluate and be critically reflective of the relationship between his teaching and student learning. This enables the teacher to identify his weaknesses and strengths and to generate his own solutions and plans for improvement.

This story also depicts a beginning point for a schoolwide peer coaching program. The principal has plans for both of these teachers to facilitate a group, with an interest in using learning centers in their daily instruction as a means to develop interdisciplinary teaching units. The next step will be to meet with teachers to discuss how a proposed peer coaching program would fit into the instructional goals of the school.

An earlier chapter expressed concern that assessment is sometimes used to drive instruction. Should assessment drive instruction, or should instruction drive assessment? Performance-based assessment is used to drive instruction. As with most educational innovations, not everyone is supportive of performance evaluation—some educators oppose such alternative ways of measuring learning. Ideally, just as all parts of the curriculum (including evaluation) should be selected to meet the class objectives, so should the evaluation instrument. The appropriate relationship between curriculum and evaluation will be ensured if both are designed to serve the course objectives.

The criticism against the practice of letting the test drive the curriculum is valid only to the extent that the tests are unrelated to the objectives. Cause for concern is warranted because the people who are selecting the standardized tests are not the teachers, and these outside reformers are designing the tests to meet their own goals, which are often different from those of the local school.

Portfolios for Assessment Purposes. Education reform has resulted in still other terms applicable to today's schools, such as self-evaluation, continuous assessment, and progress reporting. Although they are closely related, each of these terms has a different meaning and each brings contributions to the learning process, specifically in the area of portfolio assessment. *Portfolios*, or organized collections of student works, offer an excellent opportunity to use these three forms of assessment combined.

Self-evaluation means that the students are involved in their own evaluations. This type of evaluation is important because it makes students aware of what they know and of the goals of the class. This awareness is important in multiple ways. "Students who can identify what they are learning significantly outscore those who cannot" (Chappuis, 2005, p. 40). Once aware of these goals, students can map out their way to achieve them, monitoring their own progress (Bybee & Scotter, 2006/2007). Teachers can help by providing benchmarks and rubrics (Herman & Baker, 2005) so that students can see examples of portfolios that go beyond the level of their present portfolios (Shepard, 2005). *Continuous assessment* means that the teacher has in place a system that purposefully evaluates on a daily or near-daily basis. *Progress reporting* implies that as each student progresses in each subject, feedback is given on a somewhat regular basis.

Digital portfolios, multimedia collections of student work stored and reviewed in digital format, are especially important tools for student self-assessment. Like other learning tools, the digital portfolio's effectiveness requires a common vision among all members of the learning community. David Niguidula (2005) suggests that teachers and schools ask the following questions:

- *Vision:* What skills and content should students master and demonstrate in their portfolios?
- *Purpose:* Why do we collect student work?
- *Audience:* Who are the audiences for portfolios?
- *Assessment:* How do the entries in portfolios reflect the school's assessment vision, and how can we assess the quality of those entries?
- *Technology:* What hardware, software, networking, and technical support will our school need to implement a digital portfolio assessment system?
- *Logistics:* How will students enter their work into digital portfolios?
- *Culture:* Is discussing student work already part of our school culture?

A significant advantage offered by the combination of self-assessment, continuous assessment, and progress reporting is the motivational effects they have on students. Because portfolios have a variety of artifacts and provide valuable data, they can respond to the many qualitatively different samples of work (Mills, 2006).

Promoting Higher-Order Thinking. Some of the education reform reports of the early 1980s expressed concern that American students were not being challenged to think at the higher levels of the educational taxonomies. A quarter century earlier, Benjamin Bloom and his colleagues developed the first educational taxonomy, which focused on the cognitive domain (see Figure 10.2.).

Figure 10.2 Educational Taxonomy: Cognitive Domain

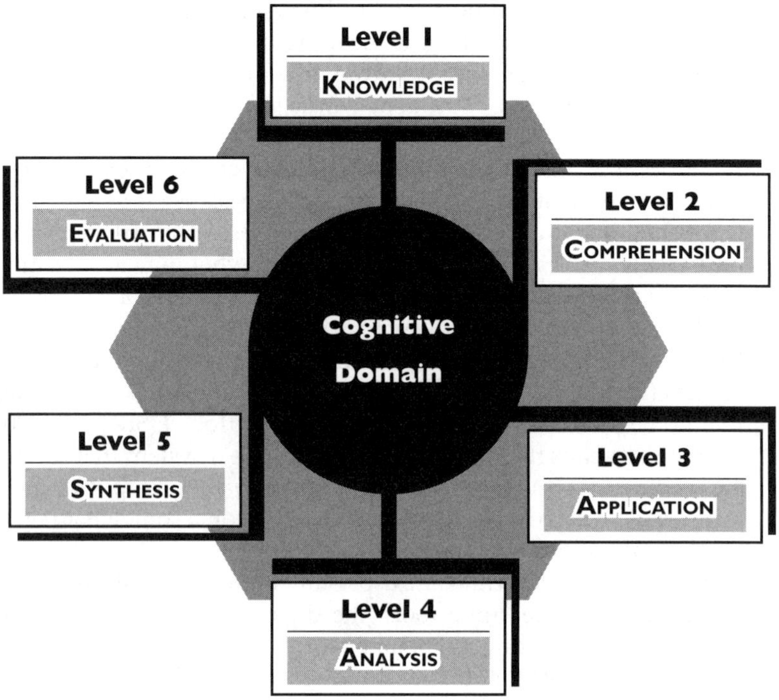

Level 1
KNOWLEDGE
Level 2
COMPREHENSION
Level 3
APPLICATION
Level 4
ANALYSIS
Level 5
SYNTHESIS
Level 6
EVALUATION
Cognitive Domain

When proceeding to higher levels of the taxonomy, the job of measuring and evaluating becomes less objective and therefore more difficult. In his education reform report, *A Place Called School*, Goodlad (1984) shared his concern over the failure of schools to require students to think above the simplest, lowest level, noting that instruction seldom moved "beyond possession of information to a level of understanding its implications and either applying it or exploring its possible applications" (p. 236). (See chapter 12 for a discussion on the use of questioning to promote higher-level thinking skills.)

Undoubtedly, the types of assessment that education reform programs are introducing in the twentieth-first century have excellent potential for raising the levels of thinking in future classrooms. But teachers will (and perhaps should) also continue using some of the traditional testing practices. For example, because teachers and students understand them, multiple-choice exams and essay exams will continue to have a place in school curricula. The next section discusses procedures for helping teachers use these types of exams to raise the levels of student thinking.

Helping Teachers Administer Classroom Tests

In order to use them effectively, teachers must be made aware of the strengths and weaknesses of essay tests and objective tests. Included in this discussion are some suggestions supervisors can make to teachers to improve their testing practices.

Essay Tests

Essay tests have been favored by many teachers because they offer important, unique advantages over traditional, objective tests. For example, they permit students to tell the teacher what they know, as opposed to objective tests that are often said to be used primarily to reveal students' lack of knowledge. More important, good essay tests cause students to internalize information and consider how the information they are studying is important to them. This quality of essay tests automatically raises learners' level of thinking above the common recall level, an occurrence that seldom happens with objective tests.

Although the terms *essay test* and *discussion test* are often used interchangeably, a distinction between these terms is necessary. Of the two types, essay tests are the more specific. Correctly written, essay test items require the reader to make certain observations about the subject being tested. From a cognitive perspective, this distinction is important; it allows teachers to test for major concepts.

Writing Essay Test Items. A common error made when writing essay test items is failure to specify exactly what is asked of students. To ensure that the expectations are clear, the first precaution that the supervisor should make to teachers is to avoid the verb "discuss," a verb that may suggest that all is expected is a sharing of opinion. In fact, the result is often a sharing of ignorance. A more specific verb such as "explain" can help avoid soliciting only opinions and unsubstantiated generalities. Further clarification can be attained by giving or asking for examples—for instance, the test item, "Explain how the Confederate States' views on economics became a major issue that eventually led to the Civil War, and give three examples of practices in the South that the Union States found objectionable." Or a home economics or family management teacher might ask students to "explain the importance of avoiding cholesterol in cooking." This teacher might follow by asking for three cooking practices that significantly reduce the amount of cholesterol.

Supervisors should remind teachers that essay items can be written to measure either convergent or divergent thinking. Since divergent questions (e.g., "What if . . ." or "Suppose . . .") raise the level of creativity, these questions deserve special consideration. A social studies teacher might ask, "Why was this location chosen for a city? What would have resulted had this town been settled at another given location?"

Essay test items should focus on important concepts and should be written to measure the depth of understanding of those concepts; therefore, most essay questions seek answers to several questions. Instead of just hoping that students will address each of several issues, the test composer should write a compound question including each issue for which a response is desired. Students should also be reminded of the need to provide evidence to support their answers to essay questions.

Scoring Essay Test Items. Because most essay items focus on major concepts, the in-depth covering of which requires compound questions, the value of each part of a question should be weighted according to the relative importance of that topic and the amount of time spent studying this content both in and outside of class. The best way for a teacher to begin scoring essay items is by taking the test before giving it to students. Critically important ideas may carry two or three points each, and less important ideas may be assigned one point each. A scale or a self-scored test with these weights assigned to each question will facilitate the scoring of the test. Often students will offer unanticipated responses that cover important ideas which are not part of the predetermined answer. To encourage independent thinking, teachers can assign one point to each of these unexpected but important and correct responses.

When assigning value to essay items, teachers may need to be reminded to consider the amount of time required answering the question. For example, a test item that requires fifteen minutes to answer should be assigned a proportional value of 25 or 30% because the time required to complete the item is 25 or 30% of the class period. Once a value has been assigned to each item, the test items should be sequenced so that the largest items (those of most value) are at the beginning of the test. This reduces the possibility of a student running out of time before attempting to answer those items with the highest value.

Bonus Items. To increase the level of motivation or to provide students with an opportunity to earn extra points to meet some other goal, some teachers choose to include a bonus essay question on their tests. Teachers who do use bonus items should structure the scoring so that both students who do not attempt to answer these questions and those who answer them incorrectly are not penalized.

Objective Tests

Opposite in many ways to essay tests items are objective test items, including multiple-choice, true-false, matching, and fill-in-the-blank. Objective test items have several advantages. Since they cover small amounts of material they are quickly completed and quickly scored, allowing for many items to be used on each test. Multiple-choice test items are particularly quick and easy to score; in recent years machine testing has expedited the scoring of multiple-choice tests. As mentioned in an earlier chapter, during times of rapid education reform teachers need more time than a typical teacher's schedule provides. Supervisors can help teachers cope with their hectic schedules by helping them improve their test construction skills.

True-False Tests

This type of test offers the same quick and easy scoring quality as multiple-choice tests. But true-false tests are less accurate because students have a 50%

It Works for Me!

Assessing Assessment

Thomas Oldenski, University of Dayton

Most teachers have never been taught how to make a good test. For the most part, they rely on their own experiences of being tested and giving tests, or they simply depend on a published test bank or use their own tests over and over again. To improve the quality of classroom assessments, the supervisor can expose teachers to principles of good test making, for example, by reading *Test Better, Teach Better, The Instructional Role of Assessment* by W. James Popham (2003, Association for Supervision and Curriculum Development), or offering a professional development program on constructing good tests.

Teachers then are asked to evaluate three to four of their own classroom tests from the perspective of these guidelines and to share these evaluations with the supervisor or within a group of teachers. Teachers are usually amazed to find out how poorly their tests are constructed and how unsuitable they are for assessing what actually was taught and learned. They can then identify ways to improve their self-constructed tests.

chance of guessing the correct answer, even when they know nothing about the content. Because of the guessing factor and because of the limited choice provided, true-false test items are significantly inferior to multiple-choice items. Supervisors should encourage the use of multiple-choice tests over true-false tests.

Matching Test Items

These items have the advantage of being quick to answer and quick and easy to score. They also have the disadvantage of being vulnerable to guessing. Like all other types of objective test items, matching test items do not provide students opportunities to express their ideas or feelings, and most matching test items measure the lowest levels of thinking. When writing matching test items, teachers should take precautions to avoid making several common mistakes. Share with your teachers some of the most common testing mistakes made by teachers, listed below.

1. Exclusive use of objective tests. Objective test items are too limited to be used exclusively on a test. Education reform has stressed the importance of students being prepared beyond the recall (memorization) level. Yet a school's or teacher's testing program usually drives its curriculum; what you test for is what you get.

Education reform stresses application, but most objective test items do not measure for application skills. Tomorrow's workers must be skilled in applying knowledge. When used exclusively, objective test items neither encourage students to apply what they learn, nor give students opportunities to express themselves. A major trait of objective test items is that they are aimed at discovering students' ignorance about the topics being tested. Although this is a valuable service, by itself it is inadequate. Tests should also provide students opportunities to explain what they understand about the topic. In other words, objective tests measure what students don't know, and they fail to provide students ample opportunities to tell what they do know. Teachers can circumvent this weakness by combining some objective items with some questions that provide these missing opportunities.

2. Failure to include higher-order questions. Because most classrooms and most textbooks are characterized by low-end cognitive questions, and because objective test items usually measure recall, teachers should be encouraged to include some higher-order questions on each test. Simple "Why?" questions usually elevate the level of thinking.

3. Using only convergent questions. Most objective test items are convergent questions that seek only one "correct" answer. That answer is usually memorized, thus requiring only simple recall and leaving no opportunities for students to use their imagination or their creativity. When measured for their levels of creativity, many contemporary classrooms are wastelands. Accordingly, tests that are composed either exclusively or predominately by objective items should also include some questions that require students to engage in divergent thinking or consider multiple alternatives (e.g., What do you think would happen if . . .? or What are some additional ways to. . . ? or In your own community, can you find examples of . . .?).

4. Improper construction of multiple-choice test items. Multiple-choice tests are so often poorly constructed that teachers need to be reminded to make a special effort to avoid some all-to-common errors:

- *Wordy questions.* Because of the pressure that students commonly feel over taking tests, care should be taken to control the levels of test anxiety. Long, wordy questions can amplify an already high level of frustration; therefore, test items should be written clearly and succinctly, using only familiar terms.
- *"None of the above."* Two advantages of multiple-choice test items are the opportunity they provide teachers to direct students to several alternatives and to ensure the credibility of each. Each response should be used to this advantage, yet the response "none of the above" does not provide a viable choice. Because it does not enable students to relate directly to the question, this response should be avoided.
- *Obvious choices.* If a multiple-choice test item is to promote maximum, high-level thinking, it must provide reasonable choices—each alternative must be a viable distracter. When teachers offer obviously correct or obviously incorrect choices, they miss the opportunity to promote evaluative thinking
- *"All of the above."* Like "none of the above," this option does little to encourage thinking or weighing of alternatives. Because "all of the above" does require a decision, its use can occasionally be justified. However, because it does not require weighting or judging each response against the

other responses, it is not as strong as items with single, correct responses; therefore, its use should be limited.

- *Negative statements.* Questions with negative verbs such as "not" (i.e., asking the student to identify the *least* correct or incorrect response) confuse and frustrate students and should be avoided.
- *Repetitive wording.* To add clarity, test questions should be written concisely. Any words that are common to all choices should be removed from all choices and placed in the question trunk. For example, consider the following question:

  All teachers:
  a. should hold at least an associate degree.
  b. should hold at least a bachelor's degree.
  c. should hold at least a master's degree.
  d. should hold at least a doctor's degree.

This question should be written:

  All teachers should hold at least a (an):
  a. associate degree.
  b. bachelor's degree.
  c. master's degree.
  d. doctor's degree.

- *Giving away the answer.* Without being aware of it, teachers often give clues and even correct answers to students. In the example above, if the last word in the trunk of the question were just *an* rather than *a(an)*, the word would be a giveaway (i.e., the answer would be the only selection that begins with a vowel).

Aligning Test Item Values with Goals and Objectives

Once values are assigned to a test, teachers should review the objectives and goals of the unit being tested to ensure that each goal and each objective are reflected. In other words, the values assigned to test items should correlate with the lesson and unit objectives and goals during the time period covered by the test.

Involving Students in Testing

Many teachers are careful to limit the types of student involvement with tests. However, constructivist teachers find several ways to involve their students with testing, such as (a) establishing testing procedures, (b) test construction, (c) test scoring, (d) test reviewing, and (e) recording scores.

- *Establishing testing procedures.* Traditionally, most teachers have made the decisions about when to test, what to test, and how to test, and they have done so without input from students. Yet, involving students in these processes can enlighten students about the testing program and empower them to take more responsibility with a part of schooling that traditionally has been off-limits to students.

It Works for Me!

Instructional Walks

Helene J. Lusa, Saginaw Valley State University

Supervisors sometimes do walkthroughs or instructional walks. Following observations, we often ask the teacher to reflect on the lesson; the supervisor's reflection is also critical. It allows observers to make connections between practices, behaviors, attitudes, and overall instruction issues across classrooms and throughout the building. Reflective practice suggests that supervisors think about their own thinking as it relates to their observations and look for trends, patterns, and connections between and among teacher practices. This gives a ready understanding of where the building is in terms of improving instruction and/or implementing new initiatives.

Select a focus for the walkthrough. Take notes on your observations, and then share those thoughts with your teachers. Don't forget to look for positive trends in instruction, use of best practices, and other indicators of growth based on your institution's school improvement plans. Positive notes or encouraging comments in a faculty meeting based on these reflections can do much to promote teacher motivation for instructional improvements.

- *Involving students with test construction*. Schools with high student achievement levels use objectives and goals that students understand. Assuming that the testing content parallels the class objectives (and it should), an effective way to make all students aware of the importance of the content being studied is to involve them with selecting the test items. Some teachers are concerned that this practice robs the testing program of rigor; however, when involved in school leadership decisions students are usually more demanding of themselves and their peers than are their teachers.
- *Test scoring*. Some teachers have always asked their students to help score objective tests. Although students' abilities to score essay test items are fairly limited, with guidance students can learn to do so. Involvement in test scoring provides opportunities to develop deeper understanding of the content. Students' ability to assist in scoring essay items can be improved by using rubrics, and supervisors should recommend that teachers invite their students to take part in their design (Easton, 2007).
- *Test reviewing*. Unfortunately, students may not appreciate the learning opportunity that is provided by reviewing tests. Teachers have recently rediscovered the power of test reviewing to clarify misunderstandings and develop concepts. Remind your teachers of the opportunity that test reviewing offers their students.
- *Recording scores*. A major value gained from the practice of students recording their own test scores is that it establishes a continuous, ongoing record of progress. Students who establish and maintain such a record are reinforced each time they can see that, indeed, they are mak-

ing progress in each subject. A secondary value is that it gives students an opportunity to work with and view testing as a positive, learning activity, not just something negative that happens to them. A major assessment role of supervisors is helping teachers and students learn to view testing as an integral part of the learning program at their school.

Testing in the Affective Domain

So far, this chapter on helping teachers test and evaluate has focused on the cognitive domain, but testing also should cover the affective domain. We have previously documented the high level of concern over behavior in contemporary society. Indeed, a look through the newspaper on any day of the week, any week of the year, will reinforce the need for attention to morality and values. In chapter 8 we discussed teachers' responsibilities for teaching values to their students, and their function as role models.

A few things should be made clear at the outset of this discussion on attitudes and values. First, the affective domain (our emotions) is inextricably tied to the cognitive domain (learning). Second, teachers have no choice but to deal with the affective domain. Since the role of schools goes beyond helping students improve their test scores, teachers need to be reminded that education is more than learning: It is about thinking, behaving, and feeling in certain ways. To illustrate the difference between the schools' cognitive and affective responsibilities to students, consider a lesson on ecology in which the students learned several ecological facts and concepts yet failed to adjust their behavior to help improve ecological conditions in their community and school.

Chapter 8 presented a discussion of the five levels of the affective domain: receiving, responding, valuing, organizing, and characterizing. The upper levels of this domain reflect more than knowledge; they reflect a willingness to permanently change behavior. Teachers may need help in discovering ways in which to change students' behavior. The restructuring that many schools are currently experiencing can be used as a major vehicle for effecting permanent changes in students' behavior. In fact, at many schools restructuring begins with the question, "In what ways do we want the program to change our students?"

Conclusion

Supervisors have an important role in changing the way teachers use tests and evaluation. Our schools have a history of using summative evaluation almost exclusively. Summative evaluation occurs following instruction for the purpose of assigning grades. Schools have made little use of formative assessment—evaluation done before, during, and sometimes even after instruction to help improve learning.

The normal curve is a model that describes the "natural" behavior (when they are left unaltered or when left to chance) of many things in nature. E. L.

Thorndike noticed that when the frequency of occurrence of tens or hundreds of thousands of intelligence tests scores is recorded, they distribute in a bell-like pattern (the bell curve). In error, this curve has been used to assign grades, forcing students to compete for a small percentage of As and Bs.

Education reform has encouraged the use of different types of evaluation, including *curriculum alignment* (aligning the evaluation system with the taught curriculum), *authentic assessment* (tests to determine students' success in reaching valued goals), *performance-based assessment* (tests that require students to use information to solve problems), *continuous assessment* (assessment that is a part of the ongoing curriculum and instructional process), and *self-assessment* (involving students in keeping records of their academic progress). Portfolios are commonly used to meet several of these goals.

Education reform also encourages the use of assessment to promote higher-order thinking. Some education reform reports have alleged that little is done in American classrooms to encourage students to think at higher levels. Reaching this goal requires helping teachers move away from traditionally used objective tests such as multiple-choice, matching, and true-false tests and toward using more essay tests.

Questions for Discussion and Reflection

1. How can teachers be encouraged to use formative assessment more effectively?
2. Education reform programs base the success of schools and teachers on students' performance on standardized tests. What effects does this have on curriculum? On instruction?
3. Education reform programs encourage the involvement of parents in the education of their children. How can teachers persuade parents to support the use of criterion-referenced evaluation?
4. One purpose of portfolios is to keep students motivated by showing them their academic accomplishments each day. Can you think of portfolio requirements that can be added to encourage the development of social skills?
5. In some states the emphasis on standardized test scores has raised the anxiety of students and teachers to levels that actually interfere with other goals, such as the development of social skills. Can you think of ways the supervisor can adjust the assessment program to lower teacher and student anxiety?

Suggested Activities

1. Interview a local school administrator. Examine the school's portfolio policy. List the three qualities of the policy that you think are the most important.
2. Make an appointment with a professor of evaluation and measurement, and ask this professor for advice on converting test scores into grades.

3. Ask a teacher in your field to let you attend a class session in which the teacher and students construct a test. Afterward, reflect on this session with the teacher and together write a statement to guide teacher–student cooperative test construction.
4. Visit the site of an outcomes-based education program. Ask the administrators to describe how they overcame objections to the development of this program. In particular, ask how the objections to values education were handled.
5. Visit a teacher who uses ongoing self-assessment. Make a set of guidelines to use to help others introduce self-assessment in their classes.

Chapter 11

Helping Teachers Manage Their Classrooms

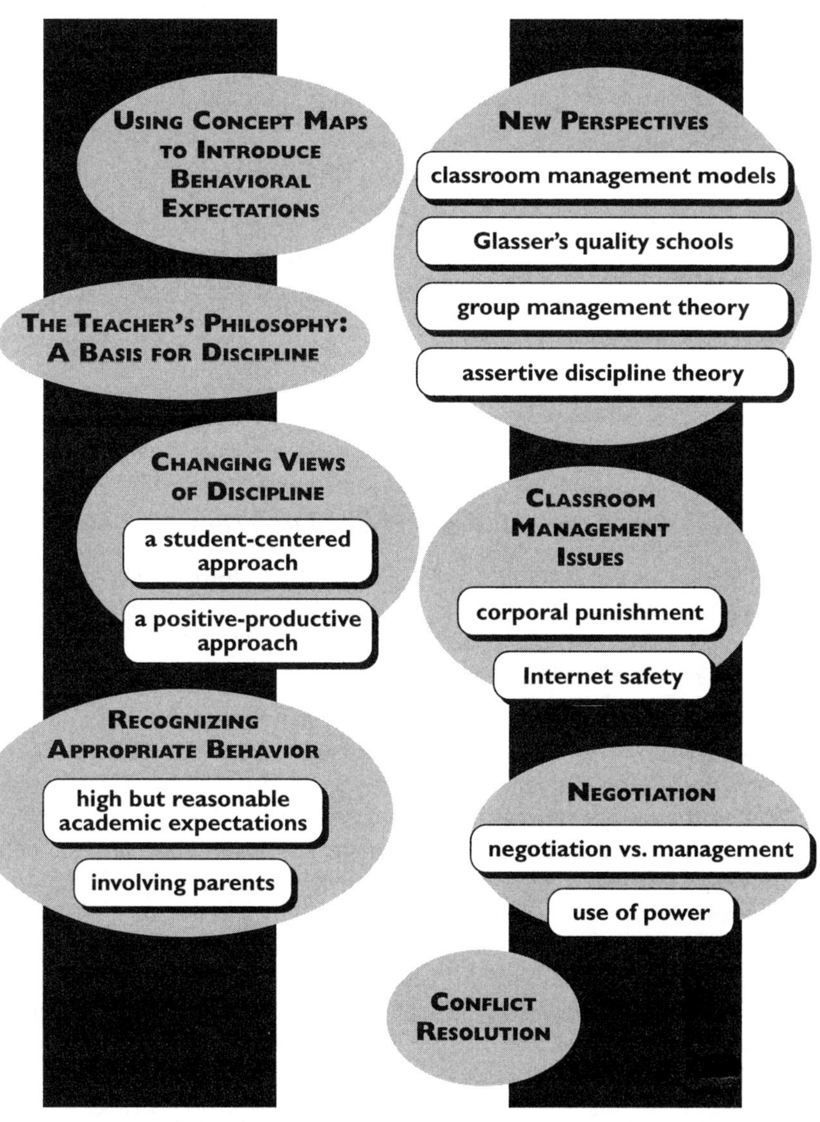

Using Concept Maps to Introduce Behavioral Expectations
The Teacher's Philosophy: A Basis for Discipline
Changing Views of Discipline
a student-centered approach
a positive-productive approach
Recognizing Appropriate Behavior
high but reasonable academic expectations
involving parents
New Perspectives
classroom management models
Glasser's quality schools
group management theory
assertive discipline theory
Classroom Management Issues
corporal punishment
Internet safety
Negotiation
negotiation vs. management
use of power
Conflict Resolution

> *When school leaders make classrooms safe, they also meet the expectations of parents who often assume when they drop off their children to school that their children will be safe.*
>
> —V. H. Gordon,
> "Administrative effectiveness in making classrooms safe"

Objectives

After completion of this chapter, you should be able to

1. Describe how disciplinary programs must change to meet the conditions of today's culture
2. Choose a discipline/management model and support its use
3. Identify some ways of involving parents in the classroom disciplinary program
4. Intelligently debate the use of corporal punishment, and present evidence to support your position

Constructivism Misunderstood

Jim Williams had looked forward to his new principal's position since his successful interview three months ago. Although it required relocating and moving his family to an unfamiliar community, Jim knew that before long his gregarious family would adjust, and the new area would seem like home.

The new position offered twelve-month employment, which Jim admits is important to a family who is making house payments. But Jim's main cause for excitement was the opportunity to expand the use of his skills. Jim's master's degree in school administration had a strong central theme: Principal as Instructional Leader. He particularly was looking forward to experimenting with some student-centered approaches. Having developed some simulation games while teaching but never seeming to have the freedom that he needed to really experiment with these new games, this position would provide him more latitude. Five years ago, during his bachelor's degree program, Jim was introduced to mastery learning. He believed in some of its methods, especially the use of formative evaluation and criterion-referenced evaluation. He also thought that the opportunity for students to remediate without penalty just made good sense.

Lately, Jim had been reading a lot of literature on some education reform programs. The feedback on several programs was encouraging. The case-study method was get-

ting some excellent reports. Jim had also become intensely interested in constructivism, and he wondered about the potential of these approaches (e.g., case study, simulation, mastery learning) to reach some of the constructivist goals. But there appeared to be one weakness in most of the education reform programs: Where was the research? Few programs even claimed to be conducting any research to measure the effectiveness of these innovations. This is where Jim thought he could make a significant contribution. His master's degree required a thesis, and he had found the research exciting.

But after being in town for only a couple of weeks, Jim had already discovered some disappointing barriers. Absenteeism plagued the district. Having moved from a small college town where the average daily attendance was over 90%, Jim was shocked to learn that the year-round average daily attendance in his new community was below 80%. Furthermore, many of the students who managed to get to school on time arrived in no condition to learn because they were staying out until the early morning hours. Evidently, many children's parents hung out in the bars until 1 or 2 a.m., and they insisted on their rights as free Americans to take their children with them.

Perhaps this general parental attitude was behind another condition that Jim also knew would be a serious threat to any programs that he might introduce to the system: an apparent total lack of discipline. One of the first classes he visited was a real eye opener. Pat Blythe, a first-year teacher, was the assigned teacher of the tenth-grade art class. In Jim's one private meeting with this teacher, he had found Pat to be bright. Pat was also enthusiastic over the role change from student to teacher. Jim quietly entered the door at the back of the classroom and quickly took an empty seat, wanting to be as unobtrusive as possible.

Jim soon realized that his efforts to avoid disrupting the class were totally unnecessary. The class was complete chaos. Some students were screaming, and others were running about at will. At one point, a student with a can of spray paint chased another student, shouting at him as both students ran and leaped across the tables and chairs. Jim thought this outburst was outrageous, but unfortunately Pat seemed to ignore the rampage, as he also ignored most of the other students, choosing to provide individual attention to one student at a time.

During Pat's planning period, a private conference was held to give feedback on this unusual observation. Pat explained that the current literature supported student-centered teaching: "Constructivist teachers not only are supposed to permit student activities but should also encourage them." Pat continued, "In a recent faculty development workshop we were told that we should not even tell our students our own opinions and perspectives about lessons until they have first told us their perspectives. The speaker told us that if we tell students what we understand then students will stop thinking for themselves. She said that the only way students will really understand is to create new knowledge for themselves."

Jim recognized truth in Pat's comments. In fact, he had read about most of these observations that Pat was making. Constructivists do, indeed, believe that students must discover and generate their own understandings. And he, too, had read that the teacher's role is to resist the temptation to tell students something that they should be discovering for themselves. But Jim was aware that there was a contradiction here. This teacher's attempt to follow constructivist theory was misguided. Learning would never occur in an environment of total chaos—at least not desirable learning.

Pat had been given an opportunity to explain and had given what seemed to be a serious explanation. Jim realized that something needed to occur before these students could benefit from constructivism, simulation games, case studies, inquiry, or any other types of lessons. Without order, there would be no learning in this class, or in any other class. Jim knew that his first job was to establish some order in this school.

Reflection

What conditions are needed to replace discipline problems with effective instruction? How much latitude do students need to make learning occur? What types of responsibilities do teachers have to misbehaving students? To the classmates of disruptive students? Do constructivist lessons need more structure or more freedom than traditional lessons? What is the principal's responsibility for discipline throughout the school? In what ways, if any, does the subject dictate discipline? Which must come first, good discipline or good instruction?

The vignette introducing this chapter reeks of negligence, and negligence leads to lawsuits. Vivian Gordon (2006) reports on a study of negligent risks in 97 school buildings. Sixty-two of the 97 school buildings in the study needed more supervision. In other words, there were times during the day in which these 62 buildings had unsupervised classrooms. Notably, the study reported instances of teachers walking to other teachers' classrooms for visits, teachers talking to other teachers in the hallways, teachers failing to supervise students in the hallways (even when those students were bullying other students), teachers arriving late at school, and students sent out of the room unsupervised. The results of this study show that teachers need help with developing an awareness of their classroom management responsibilities.

Introduction

> Interstate School Leaders Licensure Consortium (ISLLC) Educational Leadership Policy Standard No. 3 defines a school administrator as an educational leader who promotes success of all students by ensuring management of the organization, operations, and resources for a safe, efficient, and effective learning environment.

Good behavior results from good lessons that meaningfully involve students, but no lesson, however well-planned and executed, can guarantee perfect behavior. For this reason teachers must learn to take measures to prevent problems from occurring. Furthermore, teachers must know how to resolve problems once they occur. This chapter is written to help supervisors assist their teachers in meeting these two goals. Several classroom management models are discussed. The overriding goal is to help teachers establish classroom climates so that students will discipline themselves.

Clearly, the teacher's ability to establish and maintain an orderly climate in the classroom is a prerequisite for maximum learning to occur on a continuing basis; yet most teachers say that their academic preparation failed to give them an adequate classroom-management knowledge base (Garrahy et al., 2005). It is clear that establishing and maintaining an orderly classroom is challenging to today's teachers; beginning teachers especially are aware of this challenge. When new teachers are surveyed about their concerns, discipline is typically the first and sometimes the only concern on many lists. Establishing and maintaining a classroom environment conducive to learning may even be the greatest challenge that today's teachers face. Teaching school poses no more formidable challenge than managing student behavior. When teachers fail in classroom management, their teaching efforts will likely also fail. Furthermore, once a functional classroom climate has been established, the job has just begun; teachers must continuously work to maintain positive learning conditions (Garrahy et al., 2005, Chance, 2008). Many otherwise good teachers have left the profession because of their inability to manage the classroom.

Like Pat in the vignette at the beginning of this chapter, some teachers are under the misguided impression that they are not supposed to restrict stu-

It Works for Me!

The Mismatched Worldview Syndrome

Sandra S. Murray, The University of Tennessee at Martin

Statistics have shown that most classroom teachers are white, middle-class females with a white, middle-class outlook on the world. The student population, however, does not always reflect the same demographic. One way to change how teachers view the students is to engage them in a book study. Two especially insightful books are Curwin and Mendler's *Discipline with Dignity* and Payne's *A Framework for Understanding Poverty*. Both books give the teachers a different view of the lives of impoverished children and of children in general. Give each teacher a copy of the selected book during the final faculty meeting of the school year. Ask them to read the book and be prepared to discuss it at the first faculty meeting in the fall.

At the first faculty meeting, have a list of questions for the staff to discuss, first in small groups and then as a whole. Ask them to share their thoughts during that initial meeting, and then extend the discussions throughout the entire school year at faculty meetings. Provide additional reading on other topics that arise from discussions. Use some of the exercises that are found in the Payne book.

References

Curwin, R. L., & Mendler, A. N. (1999). *Discipline with dignity* (2nd ed.). Alexandria, VA: Association for Supervision & Curriculum Development.

Payne, R. K. (2005). *A framework for understanding poverty* (4th ed.). Highlands, TX: aha! Process, Inc.

dents' behavior—that somehow any such restrictions will also restrict learning. Most teachers feel powerless to change discipline at their school. Others fail to control their students because they do not believe that they have the right to discipline them. But teachers have more than a *right* to enforce discipline: They have a *responsibility* to do so. Students who want to learn have a right not to be disrupted by others. Sometimes, today's teachers forget that student rights should parallel the purpose of schools. In fact, teaching and learning without disruption are the rights of teachers and students. Teachers deserve the right to teach, and students deserve the right to learn without unnecessary disruption. Discipline problems are often a result of poor planning and poor instruction. Maintaining a well-behaved classroom is essential but should never be considered an end in itself. Perhaps the single most effective deterrent to discipline problems is a well planned lesson with clear objectives and meaningful student tasks. In diverse classrooms, clear goals can focus students' attention away from their differences and redirect their attention to the lesson. Research has found that prejudice is reduced when people have common goals (Longerbeam, 2007), but even teachers who plan and teach effective lessons occasionally see the fruits of their work destroyed by disruptions. Principals who are prepared to help teachers establish and maintain effective classroom-management programs can help increase the learning that results from good planning.

Using Concept Maps to Introduce Behavioral Expectations

This chapter, like all other chapters in this book, is preceded by a graphic organizer (or concept map) that highlights the major concepts discussed in the chapter, showing their sequence and interrelationships. A professor (or student) could use the simplified concept map in Figure 11.1 to introduce a discussion of the chapter.

Because students begin assessing the ethos of each teacher's classroom on the first day of school, you may wish to encourage teachers to use a concept map on the first day of class to guide the development of students' perceptions about the behavior expectations in each class. Begin by writing the short statement in the center of a blackboard, on an overhead projector, or in a Whiteboard or PowerPoint presentation: "Good behavior is a prerequisite for maximum learning." Emphasize this statement. On the perimeter, begin adding key concepts in classroom management. Single-word expressions are best—for example, such words as respect, safety, and discipline might be written by a teacher who considers these qualities critical to maximum learning. Next, the teacher will add a few empty satellite circles for students to identify behaviors they consider essential.

Used in this way, concept maps ensure the coverage of important content and offer an invitation for student participation and ownership in the class. Notice that the map in Figure 11.1 has some empty circles. The teacher can enter (or invite students to enter) a word in each circle as the lesson progresses. Any section in any chapter in this or any other text can be introduced using this same approach. Students can be encouraged to use this strategy to introduce class presentations.

Figure 11.1 Using Concept Mapping to Introduce Lessons and Promote Concept Development

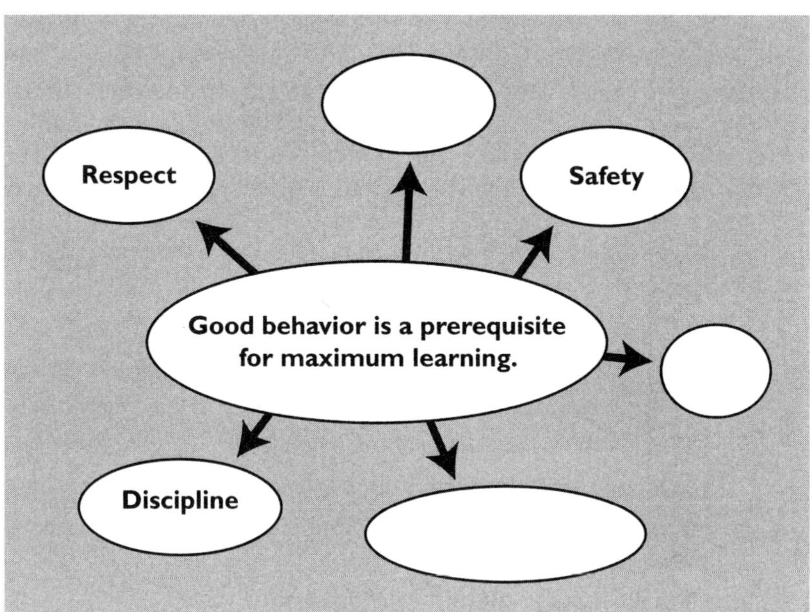

The Teacher's Philosophy: A Basis for Discipline

Effective teachers establish routines and use them to initiate and maintain a desirable pattern of student behavior (Garrahy et al., 2005). Teachers must have rules, and the consequences for breaking them must be clear. Paradoxically, as essential as rules are, those that work well for one teacher may be a total failure when used by other teachers.

Effective classroom management is *situational* or *contextual:* Individual teachers must be encouraged to craft programs that are congruent with both their school's policy and with their own individual belief systems. Teachers must find their disciplinary techniques to be congruent with both their own philosophy and their students' needs. Furthermore, discipline is a temporary condition. Once teachers discover the needs of their students and use this knowledge to craft an effective classroom management program, they must then work to maintain program effectiveness.

Changing Views of Discipline

This book stresses that teaching is a highly complex process. Chapter 4 criticizes the piecemeal quality of traditional faculty development programs for offering quick-fix tricks to resolve all types of teacher problems. Chapter 6 emphasizes the use of philosophical, psychological, historical, and social foundations to develop curricula. The same level of depth needed to design curricula is required to develop and maintain a sound, effective classroom-management program. Such a design will represent a major shift from traditional views of classroom management and discipline. Any temptation to use a loud voice, a paddle, harassment, or other forms of intimidation to maintain control must give way to a solid plan that is designed to put learning first. This new discipline must involve student–teacher relationships, teachers' skills in organizing and managing classroom activities, and teachers' instructional skills.

As you help your teachers search out and refine their own philosophy of classroom management, you might wish to begin by asking the following questions:

- Who is really responsible for discipline?
- What do you consider the ultimate purpose of classroom discipline?
- What personal characteristics do effective disciplinarians share?
- What is the relationship between constructivism and discipline?
- Why do some youngsters choose to misbehave?
- What is your expectation of students insofar as the need for quiet and stillness in the classroom?
- What behaviors should teachers model?
- How does teacher behavior affect student behavior?
- How is classroom discipline changing?
- How far can/should teachers relinquish responsibility for discipline to their students?
- Is time better spent planning to prevent problems or learning how to solve them?
- What is the relationship between self-concept and behavior?
- What special qualities enable some teachers to be powerful role models?
- What do you view as the ultimate goal of discipline?

A Student-Centered Approach

The challenge to twenty-first-century educators is to meet the state and national standards by embracing a student-centered approach to learning (Graham & Cannamore, 2006). However, traditionally—almost invariably—teachers have set rules without involving students. Some teachers exclude their students from the classroom policy-making process because they fear that their students would be far too lenient on other students who break the rules, yet such is not the case at all. In classrooms where students have been permitted to set rules for behavior and punishment for misbehavior, they have often set more severe and restrictive guidelines and far more severe punishments than their teachers would have set. The incident in Box 11.1 exemplifies student-centered discipline.

Box 11.1 A Student-Centered Discipline Program

The North Central Association for Accrediting Schools team was in the Chicago metropolitan area, evaluating a local school, when a discussion on discipline ensued. A host responded, "If you want to see a unique discipline program, I'll show you one." With that, they drove to a rough looking part of the city. As they drove up to an alternative school, they noticed streets strewn with fast-food cartons, wrappers, and cups. When they parked, a student was assigned to stay with their car. The host explained that in this neighborhood, without protection, cars lose batteries, alternators, and other vital parts.

As the team entered a two-story building, they saw a young man sitting beside the inside stairs with a gallon bucket beside him. As the team moved upstairs, they could hear a student becoming argumentative. It was obvious that he wanted a dispute with the teacher, but the teacher declined to comply. Instead, the teacher turned to the rest of the class and said, "Class, I don't believe Mr. Jones is going to let us continue our lesson in this room." With those comments, he led the group downstairs to another room, leaving the disgruntled student sitting by himself upstairs. The accreditation team followed the class back downstairs, noticing that the lone student and bucket had not moved.

As the lesson continued downstairs, the unhappy student rejoined his classmates and again began disrupting the lesson. Again the teacher turned to the class and said, "Class, I don't believe Mr. Jones will let us continue the lesson here," leading the students back to the room upstairs, followed by the accreditation team. Once again, the student followed his classmates and attempted to disrupt the lesson. But this time, a couple of students turned to the disruptive student, letting him know in no uncertain terms that they had enough of his disruptions. After that, the lesson continued without further disruption.

After the class ended, the team returned downstairs for a conference with the principal, who explained that about the only requirement for admission to this school was denial of admission by all other schools in the area. He told them that the school had a student disciplinary committee that was consistently tougher on violations than the faculty were. He also explained that the student with the bucket was being disciplined by the student disciplinary committee for a conduct violation. Specifically, he had filled a wall with graffiti, and his punishment was to paint over his vandalism. The student refused to do so and would not be allowed to return to his classes until he accomplished the task. The principal said that the offender had been sitting for three days with the bucket of paint and that sooner or later he would paint the wall and return to class.

Maintaining classroom discipline is a major, ongoing concern (Rose & Gallup, 2005). The incident depicted in Box 11.1 is a true story. The purpose of including this experience is to illustrate that students can be, and often are, firm disciplinarians. Some even think that the practices of student disciplinarians can be unduly harsh. Can you think of benefits from having students serve on disciplinary committees? Precautions that should be taken? What advice would you give to a faculty that is revising its disciplinary policy?

Teachers should ask students to identify common behavior problems in school. The simple act of involving them in shaping the discipline/management program shows a positive concern for students, and that concern will be reciprocated. In classrooms where students have had a part in shaping the rules of behavior, the power of peer pressure will work to ensure student compliance with these rules.

Involving students in planned learning activities also lowers the number of discipline problems. Effective classroom managers keep their students involved at all times with tasks that students find meaningful. Less effective teachers sometimes use photocopied in-class assignments that students often do not understand and that involve little physical movement. Such assignments can actually provoke misbehavior rather than prevent it.

A Positive/Productive Approach

Sometimes teachers need a reminder to emphasize learning, not misbehavior. While it's true that effective classroom managers establish and maintain procedures for dealing with behavioral problems, it's important to note that they also accentuate instruction and de-emphasize misbehavior. The best way to deal with disruptive behavior at any level is to teach well. As Paul Chance playfully puts it, "Developing your craft as a teacher will reduce the number of disruptions more than anything else you can do, short of coming to class wearing a karate outfit with a black belt and carrying a police officer's nightstick" (p. 129). Making a major crisis out of every disciplinary situation serves no purpose and will likely be counterproductive.

Nonverbal communication can be used to curtail disruptions. For example, *proximity control* is an effective strategy for curtailing misbehavior. It simply means walking over to where disruptive behavior occurs and remaining in the area until the disruptions subside. A slight stare of disapproval can discourage disruptions. The instructional setting and the teacher's nonverbal (body) language give students extremely strong impressions about a teacher's management and disciplinary intentions, tolerances, strengths, and weaknesses.

An excellent way to begin establishing a positive/productive program is with the teacher's own behavior. Teachers who exhibit a passion for their lessons can ignite the interests of students.

Recognizing Appropriate Behavior

It's important that your teachers realize that they can be a powerful force in their students' lives. When students are asked to identify important teacher characteristics, invariably they focus on the affective dimension of their teachers. Specifically, students point to the relationship between teachers and their students. A term frequently cited is "respect for students." Teachers often show this respect by placing confidence in their students. Rather than using excessive reprimand for inappropriate conduct, good classroom managers take every opportunity possible to recognize *appropriate behavior* (for example, "At this weekend's Special Olympics, I know everyone will show good sportsmanship, as you always do"). Conversely, if teachers do not think their students are capable, they tend to set low expectations for them.

High but Reasonable Academic Expectations

Problems are far less likely to occur in classrooms where students are continuously challenged, yet, a survey of 170,000 high school students found that only about half of today's high school students feel adequately challenged (McCarthy & Kuh, 2006). See Figure 11.2.

Teachers tend to hold low expectations for students whom they consider limited in their capacity to learn (Good & Brophy, 2007). The reverse of these statements is also true: Teachers who believe their students are especially capable set high expectations for them. In turn, in classes with high-expectation, students work hard to earn this reputation. Consequently, discipline problems are diminished (Johnson & Busch, 2006). Unfortunately, according to McCarthy and Kuh (2006), only one-third of high school students are excited about their classes. Another contributing factor to these attitudes may concern the lack of feedback students are given on their performance. When asked how often they receive feedback on their work, half of the students in this study said that they either seldom or never get prompt feedback. This teacher behavior could, and probably does, affect both student performance and grades.

Figure 11.2 Percentage of Responding High School Students Who Agree or Strongly Agree They Are Challenged to Do Their Best Work at School (by Grade)

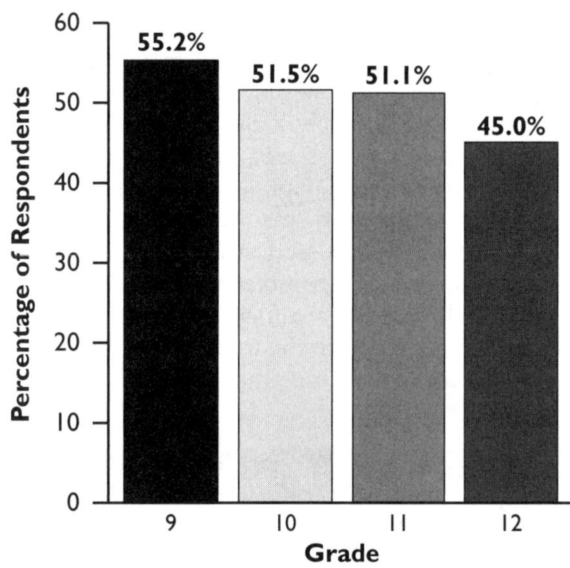

From *High School Survey of Student Engagement*. Copyright © 2005. Used with permission of the Center for Evaluation and Education Policy.

New Perspectives

Decreasing the amount of attention that the teacher gives to misbehavior is an unobtrusive means of sending a message to students—the message that in this classroom, learning is far more important than disruptions. The purpose, of course, is to place instruction and learning first. But de-emphasizing strategies should not be construed to mean that misbehavior is unimportant. The big difference here is that misbehavior is symbolic of underlying causes and that teachers should seek the causes while addressing the misbehavior. Two necessary changes in perceptions are essential.

First, in traditional classrooms, when student behavior was out of sync with school expectations, teachers believed that the students should adjust their behavior to fit the demands of the teacher. Although many teachers still have this perception, other teachers are not so quick to find the students at fault. These teachers are aware that misbehavior is often the result of inappropriate rules, so they seek ways to adjust the rules to comply with student expectations. When students misbehave it may be the result of many factors, such as boring lessons, unclear expectations, or personal problems or needs. Recent inclusion laws magnify the already major challenges to well-disciplined classrooms (Weishaar, 2007). To remain effective, classroom managers, teachers, parents, and administrators must adjust their daily behavior. Classroom management strategies should be based on a solid understanding of students' personal, psychological, and learning needs.

Teachers should also know that student behavior is often a reaction to the teacher's behavior. Make sure that faculty members who say they experience behavior problems aren't unwittingly causing the problems themselves. The incident discussed in Box 11.2 depicts this reactive behavior of students. The supervisor's responsibility is to make teachers aware of any inappropriate behavior toward their students. Video recording a lesson and cocritiquing the recording with the teacher is an effective strategy for pointing out counterproductive teaching practices.

Box 11.2 A Student Leaves His Reading Group

The telephone rang three times before Jim Sears could answer it. The voice on the other end had an unmistakable tone of irritation. It was Jim's son's teacher, Ruth Dobbins, a veteran elementary teacher. She made no effort to suppress her feelings.

> Mr. Sears, you must come and discuss Tommy's behavior. It gets worse every day. In my thirty years of teaching, I've never had a student leave one of my reading groups. Today, Tommy left his group, not once, but twice. It has become clear that something must be done. Can you come over, say, tomorrow?

Jim thought the request was a bit abrupt and a little unnecessary, but he certainly wanted to be supportive of his son's education. "OK," he told Mrs. Dobbins, "I think I can get away from work long enough to drop by for a visit."

Having established the best time for the visit, Jim and Mrs. Dobbins said goodbye. That evening, Jim sat down with Tommy to ask him what the problem was. Looking a little sheepish, Tommy told his father:

> Aw, Dad, I'm just so *bored* with that reading group! The other kids don't read well enough or fast enough. I've already read the whole story, and they're still at the beginning. Mrs. Dobbins never pays any attention to me. What's the use of trying, if all I get out of it is being ignored? I just don't see the point of wasting my time.

Jim told Tommy that although it sounded as if he might have some valid points, Jim still needed to hear Mrs. Dobbins' side of the story before deciding what to do.

The next day, Jim arrived at the school a few minutes early. As he peered thorough the single glass pane in the center of the door, he noticed that the class was in session. Mrs. Dobbins asked a question. Although Jim was unable to hear the complete question, he did make out the first words, which were enough to tell the nature of the question: "Can anyone tell me . . . ?" With these words, hands shot up all over the room. Throughout the room, students were literally stretching so hard that they were coming out of their chairs. Obviously, each student wanted to be selected to answer the question. But instead of letting anyone respond, Mrs. Dobbins continued talking.

With increasing interest, Jim continued to watch through the small glass pane in the door. A student's hand slowly lowered, then another and another. Eventually, all of the hands were lowered and the frantic waving had been replaced by a once-again passive group of students. The student who had raised his hand first and who was so eager to answer Mrs. Dobbins' question had lowered his arm and now was using it as a pillow. Jim got the feeling that this wasn't the first time such a situation had occurred in this classroom. He thought, "No wonder Tommy leaves his reading group. This teacher is forcing students to be passive, and even when she asks them to respond, she won't let them." As he continued to wait for his session with Mrs. Dobbins, Jim thought, "At least my session will soon be over and I won't have to face this teacher day after day. Unfortunately, Tommy and his classmates aren't so lucky."

Involving Parents 

As Barrera and Warner (2006) have reminded educators, many of the classroom problems that teachers must cope with may actually develop outside the school. Sometimes it might be necessary to go there for answers. Often parents are accomplices in their child's problem behavior (Garrahy et al., 2005). Current education reform programs seek to remedy this situation by increasing the levels of parent involvement with schools.

> Interstate Leaders Licensure Consortium Standards (ILLC) Standard No. 4 for School Leaders requires "collaborating with families and community members."

Supervisors should make it clear to their faculty that involving parents means more than tattling on students who have misbehaved. Tom Good and Jere Brophy (2007) suggest that before contacting parents the teacher should be  prepared to give them some suggestions on actions they can take to help their child—in ways that leave misbehaving students feeling that the parents and teacher are on their side.

A team of teachers in an urban elementary school in Pittsburgh learned that an effective way to reach difficult students was by involving them in problem solving. These teachers also learned that as students became involved in this activity, the

level of involvement of their parents increased accordingly. In general, as students become more engaged with their school, their families also become more involved.

Help your faculty to persuade parents to foster good study habits in the home. Teachers should encourage parents to set a definite time for study each day, with a beginning and ending time and no interruptions; provide the proper environment; and provide support and guidance when their children become frustrated. These guidelines are consistent with earlier comments supporting positive and proactive classroom management programs, because the guidelines focus on instruction and homework—not on misbehavior or punishment. Continuous, positive involvement of parents on homework assignments significantly improves student behavior (Kyriakides, 2005). There is also evidence that parent involvement with classroom and homework assignments improves retention (Barrera & Warner, 2006).

Using Technology to Connect with Parents

In prior chapters we have discussed some ways that technology can be used to involve parents in their children's education. The Internet offers teachers an opportunity to stay connected with parents through e-mail, blogs, and listservs. Rather than using these technological tools to communicate negative messages about bad behavior, perhaps a far better approach to encourage positive student behavior over the long term is to engage parents with their children's academics. Newsletters focused on homework assignments, classroom projects, and announcements of special classroom events can keep parents apprised of many of their children's activities. These same tools can be used to announce the successes of students. Most parents will welcome positive news about their children and their school.

It Works for Me!

Project-Centered Parent Involvement

Jack G. Blendinger, Mississippi State University

Common sense, backed by research, indicates that when parents are involved in their children's education, students achieve more and behave better, regardless of the family's socioeconomic status, ethnic-racial background, or educational level. Acknowledging the importance of parent involvement is easy, but making it happen is another matter.

For over a quarter of a century, I have helped educators develop successful school–home partnerships through project-centered action. Before taking action, the principal and teachers assess the quality of the school's parent involvement in each of three dimensions: (1) communication with parents, (2) parents helping in their children's learning at home, and (3) parent participation at school. After completing the assessment, they set goals and develop schoolwide projects (e.g., encouraging students to read at home through read-aloud programs intended to bridge the gap between the classroom and the home) designed for the purpose of achieving the goals. Once implemented, project activity is regularly evaluated and results discussed at faculty meetings.

Electronic or digital portfolios, as mentioned earlier, offer a unique and contemporary approach to help inform parents of children's efforts, progress, and achievement over time. For a particularly helpful and informative example about enhancing parent–teacher communication by using a Web-based system that features specific artifacts to document academic progress, see Markley, Schmidt, Dirksen, and Fulher (2006).

Classroom Management Models

Chapter 13, geared toward helping the reader understand the use of theory, introduces some theories that undergird educational practices. Although none of these theories directly concerns behavior management, the same motivation theory that helps us understand why some students put forth effort to succeed academically should also help us understand why some students are more willing than others to comply with the school's behavioral rules. For example, theories such as stimulus-response psychology, behavioral psychology, and phenomenology contribute to understanding human behavior in general. Other theories are aimed specifically at understanding and controlling student conduct. Following is a discussion of some of these theories, which supervisors can share with their teachers.

Glasser's Quality Schools

Psychiatrist William Glasser (2006) believes that teachers have the right to teach in an environment that permits learning to occur without a lot of disruptions. He encourages the development of classrooms that involve all students. He further believes that such environments can be created without the use of punishment.

Unlike traditional schools that are forever looking for ways to control students, Glasser's schools are based on the premise that much of the undesirable classroom behavior that characterizes many contemporary schools is the product of our traditional ABCDF grading system. Glasser maintains that Cs and Ds have become socially acceptable so long as students graduate. While Glasser admits that abolishing the ABCDF grading system is unlikely to happen anytime soon, he believes that the new standardized tests are actually creating an opportunity for teachers to get away from issuing a lot of Ds and Fs.

Glasser's Quality School model replaces external control with *choice theory.* This is achieved by creating a "connecting" environment. Students are permitted (actually encouraged) to help each other succeed, to the point of helping each other on their tests. According to Glasser, when students misbehave, it is usually because they feel hopeless. By early elementary-school age, many students have already become convinced that they are incapable of succeeding at a high level, and they keep their goals low to avoid failure. As a result, these students become bored and may act out their frustrations in the classroom. However, by providing encouragement and assistance, if the school shows them that they can succeed at a high level, soon they will begin working to protect their good student image.

Glasser's Quality Schools have six characteristics (see Box 11.3). These schools have no room for failure, which is not an option for either the teachers or the students. The teacher energy that is typically wasted on getting the upper hand on the student is channeled toward learning.

Box 11.3 Glasser's Quality Schools

In order to become a Quality School, students and teachers are taught *choice theory** (that people are empowered when given opportunities to choose their behaviors) to reach a common ground in establishing a supportive, caring environment and in building healthy relationships that contribute to school success. As stated on Glasser's Web site,

> All of us know quality when we see it; in school it is the difference between success and failure. In order to achieve quality in the classroom, students have to be managed more effectively by their teachers. Furthermore, they must be asked to do work that is worth their while and not seen as "boring." . . . School is boring because the institution is based upon myths and incorrect presumptions regarding human nature. In the dictionary the word "boring" is defined as "uninteresting, unsatisfying." . . . [Students are] bored because they are not satisfied with uninteresting material.

In terms of behavior management, Dr. Glasser suggests that teachers move away from control and coercion. He recommends engaging the students in a quality learning experience, modeled through a method known as *lead-management.* In Quality Schools, the staff, parents, and students all become involved in the quality learning process. Administrators and teachers create a more need-satisfying curricula to help students gain confidence and move through a process of self-evaluation and co-verification of student work. Schools are encouraged to maintain programs such as cooperative learning that are consistent with the Glasser philosophy. Glasser's criteria for a Quality School appear below.

1. Relationships are based on trust and respect, and all discipline problems (not incidents) have been eliminated.
2. *Total learning competence* is stressed, and an evaluation that is below competence (or what is now a "B") has been eliminated. All schooling is replaced by useful education.
3. All students do some *quality work* each year that is significantly beyond competence. All such work receives an "A" or "A+" grade.
4. Students and staff use *choice theory* in their lives and in their work at school. Parents are encouraged to participate in study groups to become familiar with choice-theory ideas.
5. Students do better on state proficiency tests and college entrance examinations. The importance of these tests is emphasized in the school.
6. Staff, students, parents, and administrators view school as a joyful place.

*To learn more about choice theory, visit Dr. Glasser's Web site (http://www.wglasser.com).

Group Management Theory

When Plato wrote his *Republic,* he expressed concern that as the populations throughout the world would continue to grow, some negative consequences would result from forcing people to live in congested communities (see Davis & Burgess, 1901). Interestingly, over two thousand years later the major cities, each with its ghettos, give testimony to Plato's concerns. Plato warned that if people chose to live too close to each other, it would bring out the worst in human behavior.

Group management theory is concerned with the forces that interact among groups when in close quarters, specifically (for our purposes) in the classroom. This theory is not concerned with fault finding, or in blaming groups or individuals. In fact, the underlying assumption of group management theory is that neither groups nor individuals intentionally misbehave. Rather, the assumption is that when groups are given clear goals, unless they face obstructions, they will pursue those goals. The teacher's first role is to make sure that the group goals are clear and that they are understood by all students. Then the teacher must monitor the classroom to ensure that any elements that might interfere with goal attainment do not develop.

Using punishment to keep students working toward the goals should never be a first resort, and, if it is used, teachers must make sure that students understand why. Teachers should never use punishment when they are angry or overly excited. Rather, the punishment should be a natural reaction to rule breaking.

Assertive Discipline Theory

Assertive discipline is based on the premise that the teacher has both the right and responsibility to maintain order in the classroom, including the right to use punishment to achieve this goal. The role of the teacher who uses this method is to communicate the classroom requirements to students, clearly and firmly. The teacher then follows through with the appropriate actions required to ensure that the rules are followed. Assertive discipline theory also espouses the use of rewards to reinforce appropriate behavior. According to MacNaughton and Johns (1991, p. 53), teachers should:

1. Make clear that they will not tolerate anyone preventing them from teaching, stopping learning, or doing anything else that is not in the best interest of the class, the individual, or the teacher.
2. Instruct students clearly and in specific terms about what behaviors are desired and what behaviors are not tolerated.
3. Plan positive and negative consequences for predetermined acceptable or unacceptable behaviors.
4. Plan positive reinforcement for compliance, including verbal acknowledgment, notes, free time for talking, and tokens that can be exchanged for appropriate rewards.

5. Plan a sequence of steps to punish noncompliance (e.g., ranging from writing a youngster's name on the board to sending the student to the principal's office).

Some teachers find the assertive discipline model a little too assertive and a little too punitive.

* * *

This chapter gives advice taken from the research and practices of others as found in the professional literature. All of this information is aimed at helping prepare teachers to be proactive and prevent unnecessary disruptions. Much emphasis is on making connections. The case study below is not written to help teachers become master problem solvers of day-to-day disruptions. Rather, it encourages teachers to think about management in a different way, not as problem solving so much as developing a climate that channels students' energy toward learning.

Problem Solving in Classroom Management

Stephen D. Lapan, Pamela J. Powell, Linda K. Shadiow, and Patricia A. Hays • *Northern Arizona University*

Early in our careers we try to emulate effective teachers. We also try to remember what worked from our teacher preparation, but somehow this doesn't add up to a set of guiding principles that can be applied and reapplied as similar circumstances arise.

Once on the job, most instructional supervision occurs only when we are having serious problems. If we seem to be running classes without discipline problems or parents' complaints, the supervisor/mentor is off in other directions where obvious problems are in need of attention. Left on our own, most of us somehow manage to learn how to respond to the unpredictable and to operate an acceptable if not ideal classroom, no matter how haphazard or intuitive this process may be. This management story reflects three assumptions about teachers and their supervision:

1. Teaching is best learned through direct experience and participation, not by applying known principles or strategies.
2. Instructional supervision can be proactive and supportive of professional growth, not just reactive only when there are problems.
3. The role of the supervisor can be to guide and facilitate rather than being a rule giver.

The Scene and the Players

The story takes place at Dempster, an urban middle school with approximately 1,100 students. Due to recent district policy changes, a large turnover at Dempster produced a staff of mostly first-, second-, and third-year teachers. The instructional supervisor, Assistant Principal Maria Chavez, considered this an opportunity to implement some ideas she learned about mentoring and professional development.

After some background reading and initial discussions, the teachers agreed to work in study-action teams of two to three members each, grouped around interests and particular issues. The objective was that each team would identify issues they would like to reflect and act on during the school year. Ms. Chavez would then meet with each team as the teachers begin to study their teaching and practice new strategies.

One team of two, Lisa Carlson and Tony Romero, chose classroom management as their focus. Both were language arts teachers who expressed a strong interest in examining areas for potential improvement. Supervisor Chavez met with these two teachers, explaining that improvement could be developed through each practitioner's direct experience and practice, followed by reflection and subsequent planning for trying out new strategies.

The Team Plans

As the meeting opened, Tony shared that while he understood that they did not have to focus on "problems" in classroom management, he had two students who posed a real concern for him. Lisa and Maria listened as Tony painted the picture.

> *Tony Romero (TR):* It's like this. Seems to me most of the students are pitching in. They like the story we're reading and are keeping up pretty well. But Logan and Terry don't. I don't know, they just don't seem to care. They sit in the back and talk and pass notes during class discussion, and they can't answer any questions about the story. If they're getting anything, I don't know what.
>
> *Lisa Carlson (LC):* Well, have you tried. . . .
>
> *Supervisor Marie Chavez (SC):* Excuse me, Lisa, but I want to try something here, maybe another tack. How about instead of giving Tony possible solutions, we help him make a plan?
>
> *TR:* Well, I'm not sure what to do.
>
> *LC:* I remember one thing we talked about in last week's meeting. I think it was to start planning by making a list of words we associate with the issue.
>
> *SC:* Yes, brainstorming. When you said, "They don't care," we could put "care" on our list. What are all the other words you can think of?

As Lisa and Tony talked, Marie made this list:

- care
- notes
- talking
- lazy
- attention
- interest
- understand
- distract
- focus
- need
- learn
- playing

> *SC:* Let's see if we can make a plan that looks at positive change.
>
> *TR:* I'm not very positive about these two. I guess that maybe if they aren't *interested* in the short story we are reading, they could read another one.
>
> *SC:* Let's back up a bit, if you don't mind. What is your objective for reading this story?
>
> *TR:* The story is *Two Soldiers.* It's to show how some authors write stories to emphasize character development over plot.
>
> *LC:* That story's such a good example of that. It would be hard to find another one as good for seventh graders.
>
> *SC:* Could they do something else to meet the objective?
>
> *TR:* You know what I'm missing here? I haven't even talked with them about this. Maybe my plan should include finding out what's going on and maybe what *interests* them.
>
> *LC:* OK, but they can't just do what they want, right?
>
> *SC:* If it achieves the objective?
>
> *TR:* Well, this is actually a good start for my plan. I didn't want to hog the time, Lisa.
>
> *LC:* Sure, but what is your plan at this point?
>
> *TR:* I'll develop some questions to ask Terry and Logan. Maybe run them by both of you first. I also think that they could have other choices, like writing a story or a play, or even creating something with the character-versus-plot idea.
>
> *SC:* Remember, we want to collect some information too as we try out our plans. Tony, what do you think about recording your talk with the boys so we can discuss how it worked later?
>
> *TR:* I'll think about that. I could audiotape it. Then maybe I should plan to get their comments later about how this worked.
>
> *SC:* Good idea. We don't have to be too formal about this, but write this plan out, would you? (Tony nods in agreement.) What about you, Lisa?
>
> *LC:* Well, I do think about management in a good way too, not just something that's a problem. My classroom discussions are working okay, but I just think things could be better somehow. . . .

Issues for Further Reflection

The processes of *issue identification* and *action planning* are sometimes called *action research*—when teachers take ownership for deciding what to study, as well as how to go about it, with some facilitation from someone trained in this kind of improvement activity. The supervisor guides more than directs while also offering reminders about how to make the process work effectively. This approach is characterized by teacher collaboration for improvement. The emphasis on situational problem solving follows the idea once explained by Schon (1983) as *move testing*, the kind of behavior certain professionals such as architects, therapists, and teachers must engage in to solve real-life problems.

Classroom Management Issues

All supervisors should be familiar with the latest research findings on issues such as corporal punishment, violence prevention, Internet safety, the power of negotiation, and conflict resolution and should ensure that their faculty members are well informed.

Corporal Punishment

During the nation's first 300 years, the most frequently used method to enforce discipline was corporal punishment. Although it is now outlawed in most states, corporal punishment nevertheless remains alive and well in many school districts throughout the country. If you work in a state that allows the use of corporal punishment, you may wish to share with your teachers the observations of supporters (MacNaughton & Johns, 1991, pp. 390–391). Some arguments supporting the use of corporal punishment include the following observations:

1. It is one procedure among many. As a consequence of rule infraction, it works with some students in some circumstances.
2. It is supported by many parents. In such cases, use of corporal punishment is consistent with support of home problems.
3. It is a considerably less severe form of punishment than many other kinds. Administered judiciously and without rancor, it is far less harmful than suspension.
4. It is immediate, which is a relief to the student.

Other educators have reservations about the use of corporal punishment in the classroom, and some strongly object to it. Paul Chance (2008) offers some observations in criticism of corporal punishment.

> What are the costs of corporate punishment? An obvious one is the risk of physical injury. . . . A natural consequence of corporal punishment is fear of those who administer the punishment. This can result in "ditching" school or dropping out. And a fearful climate is unlikely to inculcate a love of learning. Another consequence is retaliation. Students get even by stealing, committing acts of vandalism, and sometimes through violence. Finally, there is the risk of psychological damage. Children are remarkably resilient, but physical punishment in school of a child who is being abused at home may increase the risk of depression or other psychological disorders. Even children who are not abused at home might develop problems such as chronic anxiety. (pp. 135–136)

Internet Safety

Internet safety continues to be a major classroom-management issue. Today's teachers are challenged with the responsibility of protecting their students from the harm that can result from using mediated technology—specifically, online technology. Unlike students of the past, twenty-first-century students are continuously in peril as they make contact with a world of misinformation—much of which is designed to take advantage of them. We know that today's students are better informed than ever before, but this is not always a good thing. Not only is some of the information they encounter incorrect, but some is often designed to do them harm. The gateway to their vulnerability is ignorance. Our schools must make them aware of the areas of their vulnerability. Supervisors can help teachers become proactive and take some precautions to protect their students from potentially dangerous online situations. You can help your teachers build an Internet protection program by sharing the following Web sites:

- *The SafeKids.com Web site* (www.safekids.com)
  This Web site offers a wealth of Internet safety information and tools for teachers, including video and audio slide shows, timely articles and blog entries, safe socializing tips for teens, guidelines for parents, and a free e-mail newsletter
- *The iSafe (Internet Safety Program) Web site* (http:www.isafe.org)
  The iLearn online program allows users to access e-Safety education modules, including:
  - iLearn—for educators, about online safety school
  - iParent—for online safety in the home
  - iMentor—for students, so they can educate their peers, family, neighbors, and community
- *NetSmartz Internet Safety Presentations* (http://www.netsmartz.org/Presentations/)
  Free, multimedia Internet safety presentations tailored for specific audiences, parents and communities, tweens, teens, and younger children include the latest statistics, online resource, videos, and expert tips to educate, engage, and empower children and adults to be safer online and offline

A particularly effective example of an Internet protection program is that of Johanna Mustacchi (2008), a communications and media literacy teacher in upstate New York. She developed a program to help school leaders and their faculty, using an Internet-based method to shield students that takes advantage of the same online system that is the source of potentially harmful online technology. The strategy is to make students aware of the dangers of technology and other media, and to enlighten students about the strategies media experts use to take advantage of them. For example, although music videos can deliver harmful misinformation, by choosing safe videos teachers can use this medium to motivate and enlighten their students. Mustacchi uses carefully selected YouTube videos to capture her students' attention. She engages students in an in-depth analysis of Wikipedia, one of the top sources of online misinformation.

Safe Online Social Networking. Recent research has found that about half (52%) of teenage social networking messages contain potentially harmful information (Techtree News Staff, 2009). The SafeKids.com Web site discussed above features safe socializing tips for teens. In Mustacchi's (2008) Internet safety program, she spends two weeks teaching social networking, with total attention on the media (e.g., the importance of such sites as MySpace and Facebook, how they work, and their dangers). Using two subjects that are natural motivators for young people—sports and art—she leads her students in assessing their own strengths and affinities and shapes her program accordingly.

Negotiation

Some educators find the idea of management objectionable because the term connotes manipulation and top-down control by the teacher. Likewise, many instructional supervisors—particularly those who endorse participatory management and student empowerment—may find the management concept objectionable. Although they may accept the assertion that the teacher is responsible for managing such items as space, time, instruction, and materials, they may reject the idea of managing students. An alternative that these supervisors might accept more readily is negotiation.

Negotiation vs. Management

Negotiation has some qualities that closely parallel the constructivist theme that runs through this book. For example, a well-respected social scientist, Lev Vygotsky, often spoke of *negotiating meaning* (see chapter 14). For our purposes we can interpret his discussion to apply to two or more students making sense of a situation or solving a problem by talking through a given situation. Such student empowerment can be a key to minimizing classroom behavior problems. Negotiation does not mean that the teacher is no longer responsible for ensuring a climate conducive to learning, nor does it mean that the teacher relinquishes the responsibility for ensuring the safety and learning of all students. These goals are nonnegotiable. Rather, negotiation is built on the belief that, when given the power, students can regulate their own behavior. This is the same shift that is reflected in the overall goal set for this chapter, to help teachers move from imposed discipline to student-driven self-discipline.

Use of Power

When allowing for negotiation, teachers must relinquish the use of certain types of power and improve their understanding and use of other types. Types of power that most teachers have at their disposal include: (1) legitimate power, (2) coercive power, (3) expert power, (4) referent power, and (5) reward power. *Legitimate power* is derived through the position one holds. For example, teachers may have the power to force students to comply with their demands "because I am the teacher." Teachers who choose to negotiate must relinquish their legitimate power. *Coercive power* comes from the ability to administer punishment. Obviously, teachers who negotiate cannot rely on the use of coercion.

Teachers who choose to negotiate classroom discipline are left with the remaining types of power: expert, reward, and referent. *Expert power* results from having expertise. This type of power becomes a useful tool when negotiating. Teachers who are perceived as having considerable expertise in their fields, which includes both their content disciplines and pedagogy, are likely to find this expertise useful in garnering student agreement on various parts of the negotiation process. Expert power is a useful type of power for negotiating classroom discipline. *Reward power* comes from the ability of a person to give others things that they prize. These can be either tangible or intangible items. Teachers who choose to negotiate classroom discipline use reward power; however, they may learn that intangible reward power such as praise and approval are preferable to tangible rewards. Reserved for discussing last because of its degree of appropriateness and usefulness to the negotiation process, *referent power* results from a positive relationship with others. For example, a warm, caring boss is often able to persuade others to work hard because they value this person's commitment to their own well-being. Because a major purpose behind negotiating classroom discipline is the desire to involve students and get their opinions, the act of negotiation itself reflects a lot of care for students. Teachers who use negotiation must rely heavily on the use of referent power.

Conflict Resolution

Even those teachers who devise and implement effective programs to prevent discipline problems will occasionally face situations involving misbehavior and therefore should have a predetermined approach for resolving problems. The first step is to diagnose the cause of the misbehavior. This does not imply that teachers should, or could, ever have a cookbook set of steps or algorithm that will always work. There is no quick, easy, or fail-proof formula for diagnosing the cause of pupils' behavior problems (Good & Brophy, 2007).

The point is that students choose either to behave or to misbehave, and for either choice they have reasons. Most behavior has a cause. Teachers need to understand *why* students sometimes choose to misbehave. (See Pawlas & Oliva, 2007, pp. 167–179, for an excellent discussion of causes of behavior problems.) Although for many infractions a definite single cause may never be determined, the teacher always needs to collect all the information possible on students who habitually cause problems. Because teachers are often forced to make decisions without all of the information they desire, it's important to consult as many sources as possible. Some preliminary sources from which teachers can seek information on students include attendance records, cumulative records, other teachers, parents, peers, siblings, social workers, and the student causing the trouble. The student who is causing the problem is listed last; however, that student is the most important information source.

To ensure that they are taking precautions to prevent the occurrence of avoidable discipline problems, teachers can use the self-evaluation instrument shown in Box 11.4 to take inventory of their beliefs and behaviors that shape the climate in their classrooms.

Box 11.4 Classroom Management Self-Evaluation Inventory

- ☐ 1. An established written behavior code is in place.
- ☐ 2. A behavior code is communicated clearly to all students.
- ☐ 3. Students are involved in setting or revising the classroom behavior code.
- ☐ 4. Emphasis is on instruction and learning rather than on misbehavior.
- ☐ 5. High academic expectations are held for each class.
- ☐ 6. Academic expectations for each class are clearly understood and referred to on a daily basis.
- ☐ 7. Unobtrusive strategies are used to curtail discipline problems.
- ☐ 8. Parents are involved positively and continuously.
- ☐ 9. Efforts are made to emphasize students' feelings of self-worth.
- ☐ 10. A plan is in place to help students in crisis is in effect.

Notice the close relationship between instruction and discipline reflected in this inventory. Notice also the involvement of students and the role of communication in maintaining a well-disciplined class.

Conclusion

At times all teachers' lessons are threatened by disruptive students. In the history of the Gallup Polls of the Public's Attitudes toward Public Schools, discipline has consistently been found to be a continuous and growing problem in American schools. Supervisors must, therefore, help teachers and administrators establish and maintain a classroom environment conducive to learning by emphasizing exciting learning opportunities, not by restricting misbehavior. Teachers may need to be reminded that because an orderly classroom is a prerequisite for maximum learning, they have both the right and responsibility to establish and maintain a program to ensure order and control.

Today, successful discipline/management programs use positive approaches that require teachers to examine their historical, philosophical, social, and psychological beliefs. Positive discipline/management programs emphasize instruction and learning, and in doing so they de-emphasize discipline and problems. Good lessons minimize disruptive behavior. Glasser's quality schools, for example, have been designed to reverse the negativism in schools and replace it with positive attitudes, making students feel capable and good about themselves, virtually eliminating failure.

Traditionally, many teachers have not involved students in setting discipline/management rules; however, when students are involved in rule setting, they are more supportive of those rules. Similarly, many students have not been told the reasons for rules; but when they understand the reasons behind discipline/management rules, students are more compliant with those rules.

Group management theory sees disciplinary problems as consequences of forces that exert pressure on social groups. The teacher's role is to clearly specify class goals and then monitor the class to eliminate elements that would work against the rules. These theorists endorse the use of punishment, but do so with care to ensure that students understand the reason for the rules.

Assertive discipline theory says that teachers have the right to use both rewards and punishments to maintain classroom discipline. Assertive discipline teachers are serious; they brook no nonsense, no foolishness. Students are told the exact outcomes that will result from appropriate behavior and the results for inappropriate behavior.

In the past, force has been used to impose discipline on students, but this approach is known to be ineffective. Corporal punishment has both pros and cons; the cons far outweigh the pros. Some educators object to the terms *discipline* or *management* because they view these as "top-down" control by the teacher. Because of these views, and because of the current reform emphasis on participatory management and student empowerment, collaboration might be a better approach for contemporary classrooms because it relies on internal forces, encouraging students to manage their own behavior. Ultimately, each teacher must develop a management program that is consistent with the teacher's own philosophy of the nature of young people and the nature and purpose of discipline. Supervisors can assist teachers by helping them identify their own beliefs about the nature of youth and the purpose of discipline and by helping them select or design strategies that reflect their most basic beliefs.

Supervisors can help by encouraging teachers to set up a plan for dealing with infractions. Further assistance can be given by helping teachers identify several sources of information on troubled students and learning to resolve problems in the absence of some desirable yet unavailable information.

Questions for Discussion and Reflection

1. How has the view of discipline changed over the years?
2. Why is positive discipline better than negative discipline?
3. What are some qualities of discipline/management models that you consider undesirable?
4. To what limits should teachers go to control student behavior in the classroom?
5. What relationship, if any, exists between creativity and classroom management?

6. What advantages does self-discipline have over imposed discipline?
7. What is the parent's role in classroom discipline?
8. How can schools encourage stronger parental involvement?
9. What are the most attractive factors included in the theories discussed in this chapter?
10. Discuss some ways that supervisors can help their teachers keep their students safe on the Internet, at school and at home.
11. What implication does Plato's warning about urbanization have for classroom management?

Suggested Activities

1. Talk to the president of a local school's parent-teacher association. Ask the president to work with you to coplan a meeting to increase parental involvement in the school's discipline program. Examine the current policy and practices and discuss (a) changes that would improve the current policy and (b) strategies for presenting each in a way to obtain the parents' support.
2. The first few days of the year set the climate for discipline. Interview three teachers, asking each how the topic of discipline is introduced and discussed. Make a list of those practices that you like. Using the list, design a written set of guidelines to introduce your discipline rules to your students.
3. Ask three teachers for examples of instructional strategies that have positive effects on their students' behavior.
4. Ask a local principal to help you identify an area of disagreement over classroom discipline. Arrange a teacher panel to discuss both sides of this topic.
5. Arrange a student panel debate over the use of homework (or another controversial practice) as part of a school's discipline program. Include students who support this practice and students who object to it.

Chapter 12

Conducting Observations

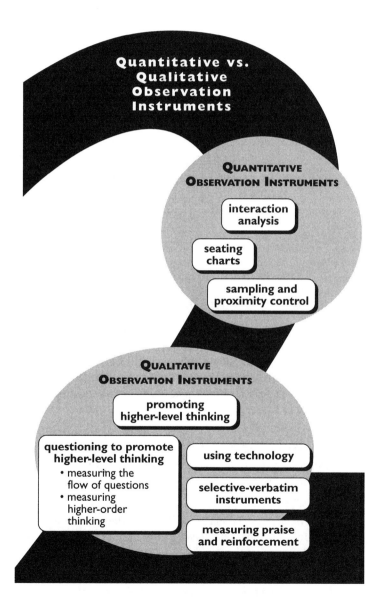

Quantitative vs. Qualitative Observation Instruments

QUANTITATIVE OBSERVATION INSTRUMENTS

- interaction analysis
- seating charts
- sampling and proximity control

QUALITATIVE OBSERVATION INSTRUMENTS

- promoting higher-level thinking
- questioning to promote higher-level thinking
  - measuring the flow of questions
  - measuring higher-order thinking
- using technology
- selective-verbatim instruments
- measuring praise and reinforcement

> *Observation is difficult and complicated because it requires the supervisor to make use of many different skills, which we can cluster into two basic categories: determining what to observe, and determining how to observe.*
>
> —J. Daresh, *Supervision as proactive leadership*

Objectives

After completion of this chapter, you should be able to

1. Select observation instruments that can help teachers meet their objectives
2. Alter observation instruments to meet teachers' special needs
3. Help teachers design observation instruments to enhance learning and classroom management
4. Help teachers use observation instruments to meet the needs of diverse classes
5. Combine technology and observation instruments to meet teacher objectives

The Importance of Being Honest

Ken Sorensen had just accepted a new job as department head at a flagship research institution. The large program had several satellite campus centers, both stateside and abroad. Part of Ken's responsibility was to ensure quality instruction and continuing accreditation on all of these campuses. One of the first assignments he gave himself was to accompany some of the faculty members in his department to a satellite site to advise students.

The team arrived at the satellite campus before any of the students arrived. It was early evening and, being teachers, most of the clients, like themselves, had worked all day, rushed through a drive-through restaurant for a burger-to-go, and hurried on their way. Soon the students began to arrive. The evening promised to be fun.

One of the accompanying faculty members was an affable middle-aged man named Bob Wallace. Dr. Wallace's smile and enthusiasm created immediate warmth in any setting. Everyone who knew him liked him, but as Ken would soon discover, this didn't mean that they would completely trust him.

Ken's randomly selected advising station was adjacent to Bob's station. The session was just beginning when Ken noticed that Bob lit up the room with his enthusiastic welcome to his first client. "Well, hello Angel! Take a seat right here and tell me how you have been doing." Clearly, Bob was greeting a student whom he had come to know very well and with whom he had obviously developed a strong rapport. The moment she walked through the door, he called her by her first name. The tone of his voice was positive and uplifting. As Bob's newly appointed superior, Ken was totally impressed with this new colleague. This, he thought to himself, is how all teachers ought to treat their students.

Shortly after, Ken's own first advisee arrived, and he began poring over the student's schedule and giving advice. In the corner of his eye, he could see that Bob's session with Angel was going well. Ken was hoping that he could be just as helpful this evening as he advised his first students at this school.

Bob had taken his time and obviously had enjoyed giving thorough advice to his first student. As she left, he gave her a goodbye with kind and flattering words that let her know that she was very special to him. Ken began to become a little suspicious. Something seemed a little off-base here, but he didn't know just what. Had Bob gone over the line with his attempts to be friendly? Maybe all was well and Ken had just had a long day.

Then, he heard Bob greet a second student. "Hello, Angel! How have you been doing?" Bob's enthusiasm hadn't changed at all, but neither had his greeting. By the end of the evening, Bob's salutations had become a permanent fixture in Ken's mind. Bob greeted every female student as though she were a long-lost friend, and he used the same greeting, "Hello, Angel!" That night, as he retired for the evening, Ken thought about the importance of a teacher's friendliness and pleasantness, but he also thought about the importance of teacher integrity. Was Bob being too pretentious—or worse, patronizing of his female students?

Reflection

This vignette is a reminder that all teachers should always be completely respectful and honest with students. As important as they are, even enthusiasm and friendliness are no substitutes for the need to be completely honest. The vignette is also a reminder that teachers need to see themselves as they are seen by their students. This is more difficult than it might seem, because the teacher doesn't always see the classroom as the students see it. Fortunately, over several decades educators have designed instruments that enable teachers to get a more objective view of the many events that occur daily in their classes. The purpose of this chapter is to help you familiarize your teachers with and become competent using instruments designed to let them see their classrooms as their students, supervisor, and others see them.

Introduction

Arguably, the most important of all supervisory roles is that of observing teachers' classrooms, helping teachers get a more complete and accurate view of their classrooms by introducing observation instruments, and helping teachers use these tools to improve the quality of learning in their classes. A few principles are basic to this process. First, improvement in any classroom must begin with the teacher's philosophy. Before teachers can begin improving their classrooms, they must first look inward and identify their individual beliefs about the purposes of teaching (see chapter 6). For example, teachers who embrace diversity will need in their observational toolboxes some special tools designed to identify the widely diversified needs of a body of students. Teachers who embrace constructivism will want some instruments that have the potential to help them improve the levels of engagement in hands-on learning.

One of the best features of becoming a teacher is the opportunity the profession provides to improve from day to day and year to year. But improvement doesn't come automatically—the only way to have continuous improvement is by reflecting on each lesson.

The Reflective Practitioner

The Interstate New Teacher Assessment and Support Consortium recognizes the absolute necessity for teachers to reflect on their lessons.

> INTASC Principle No. 9 sees teachers as reflective practitioners who continually evaluate the effects of their choices and actions on others.

Teaching is a highly complex behavior set in an even more complex environment. Teachers often have as many as 1,000 interactions a day with their students (Good & Brophy, 2007). Each interaction may carry responsibilities for immediate decisions. Furthermore, every single communication means something—even the acts of refusing to respond, withdrawing, or otherwise being passive (Woolfolk Hoy & Hoy, 2009). In addition to the many interactions that occur daily *between* teachers and their students, many interactions can occur *among* the students—interactions that the teacher must monitor, channel, and regulate.

Trying to implement a planned lesson while orchestrating all the classroom activities can be challenging, to say the least, and can leave teachers exhausted by the end of the day, often without the ability to reconstruct the day's many sequences of events. Yet to be effective, teachers must continuously improve their instructional and management skills, and to do so requires the ability to notice the many simultaneous classroom events and the role that the teacher's own behavior plays in shaping these events. To do so, teachers must have systems and tools for collecting the data needed to analyze the multitude of events that occur daily in their classrooms. Furthermore, they may need the assistance of a supervisor or their peers to ensure that they continuously improve their practices. One of the most effective tools for this purpose is the *evaluation instrument*.

Most behavior problems result from poor instruction. Although teachers should view observation instruments first as tools to improve instruction, fortunately these same tools can be used to gain a better view of the students' general behaviors. The remainder of this chapter is written to help supervisors work with faculty members, either individually or in groups, to help them examine and improve their classroom learning climates.

On the Internet, and in books and professional journals, the knowledge base in today's educational literature offers a variety of observational instruments that can be classified into two types: quantitative and qualitative. Together, these tools provide teachers with a lens that enables them to capture and focus on the many interactions in their classrooms. Remembering that qualitative instruments and quantitative instruments are different and that each offers teachers opportunities that the other cannot offer, let's examine the features and uses of each type of instrument.

Quantitative vs. Qualitative Observation Instruments

When teachers are put in charge of their first classroom and given total responsibility for its success, most are shocked by the number and variety of events that can occur within a class period. At this point in their career, most teachers have focused their attention on the lesson, with the idea that if they have a good lesson plan and have the ability to explain it clearly, success will be forthcoming. But now they realize that while they are attempting to communicate the lesson, they need a wide-angle lens that will allow them to observe all

It Works for Me!

Applying Models and Metaphors to the Real World

Cynthia Reed, Auburn University

The mental models we use in our day-to-day interactions with others can either limit or enhance our ability to address key issues. I like to use this activity within the first few weeks of my supervision course to develop our class community and gain insights into the types of experiences my students have had with supervision conferences. I find the activity especially helpful in terms of students developing a deeper understanding of how others view supervision conferences, so they can consider these multiple viewpoints when conducting their own conferences as supervisors.

For this activity, I begin the class by reminding students that the mental models or images we have about experiences are often brought to bear on our day-to-day interactions with others. These mental models or images are like metaphors; they are visual and emotional representations of a situation. For example, a metaphor for peer coaching might be yin and yang . . . opposites joined together to create a whole. I ask students to think about and then create a visual representation of a metaphor they might use to describe some aspect of the supervision conference with a building-level supervisor, based on their own prior experiences. Depending on class size, we either break into discussion groups of 8 to 10 or share the metaphors and brief explanations as a whole group. We use these metaphors as a vehicle to discuss the purposes for supervision and how the supervisory process is viewed by others. We identify issues for my future supervisors to remember when they are conducting supervisory conferences with staff.

the other events occurring throughout the classroom. *Quantitative observation instruments* provide this need, giving the teacher a comprehensive, wide-angle view of all or most of the events that occur throughout a lesson.

But sometimes teachers need to focus more closely on a specific student. A student may be experiencing a learning hiatus, for example. Teachers are unlikely to be able to offer special help without being able to single out this student and get a close-up view of the student's interactions with the teacher and with classmates. To get a better (in-depth) understanding of the behavior of an individual student, teachers need another type of instrument, one that will let the teacher follow the student over some period of time, from a few days to several weeks or even months. Fortunately, teachers have at their disposal several such instruments called *qualitative observational instruments*, which enable teachers to get a close-up view. For instance, a teaching assistant or supervisor could conduct a case study of the student, noting behaviors that distract the student or behaviors that stimulate learning. Such a study can provide insight into the behavior of a disruptive student. Both quantitative and qualitative instruments are discussed in greater detail later in the chapter.

Before making any type of classroom study, the teacher should decide what information is needed most and then choose an instrument designed for that purpose. Will the instrument be designed to meet the needs of a particular student? To better understand a particular teaching strategy? Based on the information needed, an instrument should be chosen that best enables the collection of data that will give teachers the information they seek. When making the observations, the researcher should focus on just one thing: collecting the data accurately. This requires postponing all judgments about the events. After the data are gathered and processed (tallied, averaged, etc.), there will be ample time to analyze them.

Novice teachers should begin by getting a more general, overall picture of their classrooms before attempting to meet the specific needs of individual students. Make sure your faculty is aware that local school districts offer observation tools. It is important that new teachers discover these tools early and learn to become good observers. (See Glickman et al., 2007, chapter 14, for a comprehensive discussion of observation tools and skills.) Unfortunately, many teachers do not take time to become good observers until it is too late and they find themselves in desperate situations. As a result, these teachers are prone to have one and only one purpose in mind: the need to gain control of a situation gone bad. This puts teachers in a negative situation as they constantly struggle to resolve a conflict, unable to be proactive and experience continuous improvement. Supervisors can help teachers avoid such undesirable situations by encouraging them to be proactive.

Quantitative Observation Instruments

Following is an introduction of several quantitative observation instruments, including interaction analysis, seating charts, sampling instruments, and selective verbatim instruments. You will see how these tools can be altered to meet the special needs of teachers.

Interaction Analysis

One of the first quantitative observation instruments, *interaction analysis*, was developed during the mid-twentieth century by Ned Flanders, a professor at the University of Michigan. Like other quantitative observation systems, interaction analysis give teachers two options: (1) They can invite a supervisor, administrator, or coteacher to visit their classes to use the instrument to record classroom interactions; or (2) teachers can make a video recording of their own lessons to view later as a way of analyzing the lesson in its entirety (reviewing and analyzing parts of the lesson that need special attention).

It Works for Me!

Using LiveText to Help Teachers Improve Their Observation Skills

Charlotte King Eady, Jacksonville State University

To give aspiring instructional leaders practice in focused teacher observation, live, real-time video streams of teachers (skilled and unskilled) in action can be used. The mentor sets up video equipment in the classroom to "stream" the video to off-site locations. LiveText (www.LiveText.com) is a platform that can be used for this purpose. The instructional leader accesses the video via LiveText, completes an online observation form, and shares or submits the final observation feedback via LiveText. This is very useful for both online and traditional classes. Most universities use particular instructional platforms that can be used for this purpose. Video streams can be archived for future use as well.

Unfortunately, video recordings are not as popular as they were a few decades ago. The author considers this a mistake and highly recommends extensive use of this tool, both in the preparation of new teachers and in providing help to in-service teachers. The need for quantitative instruments is often acute among beginning teachers, and the value of video recordings is greatest among this group.

When the necessary equipment is available, teachers should be encouraged to make video recordings of their classes. Most classrooms have so many activities occurring simultaneously that it is difficult, if not impossible, to see everything that is happening. By making recordings, teachers can revisit their lessons at their leisure. They can even stop the recording and replay parts of the lesson that they find confusing or disturbing. In one of his most famous poems, Robert Burns expressed the wish that some power would give us the gift "to see ourselves as others see us." He could have spent a lot of time in public school classrooms! In fact, although most teachers believe they see themselves as others see them, when they actually see themselves teaching they often discover some great discrepancies between how they think they teach and how they really teach. The author has witnessed, firsthand, astounded teachers who play back recordings of themselves teaching and actually argue with the recording: "This is not me. I wouldn't say that," or "I can't believe I use the word 'like' so often, or that I constantly say 'and uh.'"

Seating Charts

One of the oldest and simplest observation systems involves the use of *seating charts*, visual diagrams of the classroom layout. Seating charts have endured because they are easy and fast to make, easy to understand, and highly versatile. Depending on its intended use, a seating chart can show as little as the teacher's desk and the students' desks. Even in their simplest form, seating charts can be used to improve the quality of both instruction and classroom management.

The sample seating chart shown in Figure 12.1 was designed to gather data that could be used to improve communication in the classroom. It is imperative

Figure 12.1 Communication Seating Chart

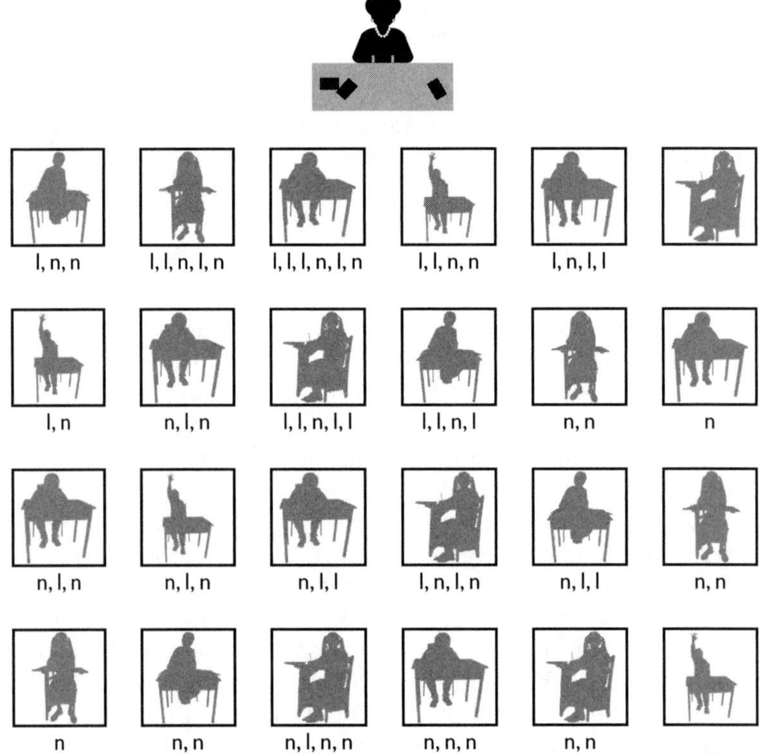

that all students be involved in discussions of the major concepts being covered in each lesson. Yet, by quickly glancing over this seating chart, the teacher can see that several students in this class are being left out of discussions. By looking a little closer, the teacher can see not only that individuals are being ignored, but also that entire areas of the room are being neglected. Without realizing it, many teachers fail to involve the students who sit in the back rows and those who sit on the teacher's extreme left and right. The teacher who uses this chart (or a supervisor or concerned fellow teachers who use the chart to help this teacher) would discover that a significant part of the conversation taking place in this room does not focus on the day's lesson. Having been made conscious of this shortcoming, this teacher can alter his or her behavior so that all students are involved in daily discussions of each lesson and its major concepts.

Sampling and Proximity Control

In classrooms with twenty or more students, hundreds of verbal and nonverbal interactions occur within the span of a single lesson. Because of the complexity of classroom interactions, supervisors who try to record all of these events learn quickly that the task is impossible. Two techniques, time sampling and event sampling, can reduce this complexity and render it manageable. In *time sampling*, the recorder selects an interval (say, every two minutes) and records whatever events may be occurring at each time. In *event sampling*, the recorder begins by selecting a particular event or action that occurs within a selected time frame.

One way teachers can increase the positive impact they have on the quality of both learning and student behavior in the classroom is by moving about and getting closer to students (Armstrong et al., 2009). Use of the teacher's position to deter or control misbehavior is known as *proximity control*. In addition to deterring misbehavior, the teacher's nearness invites clarification-related questions by students who do not fully understand assignments. The seating chart in Figure 12.2 (on the following page) can help teachers gain a perspective on how effectively they are using proximity control. This chart is divided into six equal segments. By recording the teacher's position every two minutes, the observer can show the teacher how often and how frequently each part of the room is visited. The goal is not to encourage the teacher to spend equal amounts of time among the classroom sections, for some students may require more help than others. Indeed, some students may require more attention to deter behavior problems. At other times, such as the beginning of each period, a teacher who uses direct teaching may require the use of the chalkboard. Rather than striving for an equal balance of time in each part of the classroom, the goal is to help the teacher get a view of her general movement about the classroom. In some classes the teacher might discover that individual students and groups of students (areas in the classroom) are being completely ignored.

Figure 12.2 Proximity Control Chart

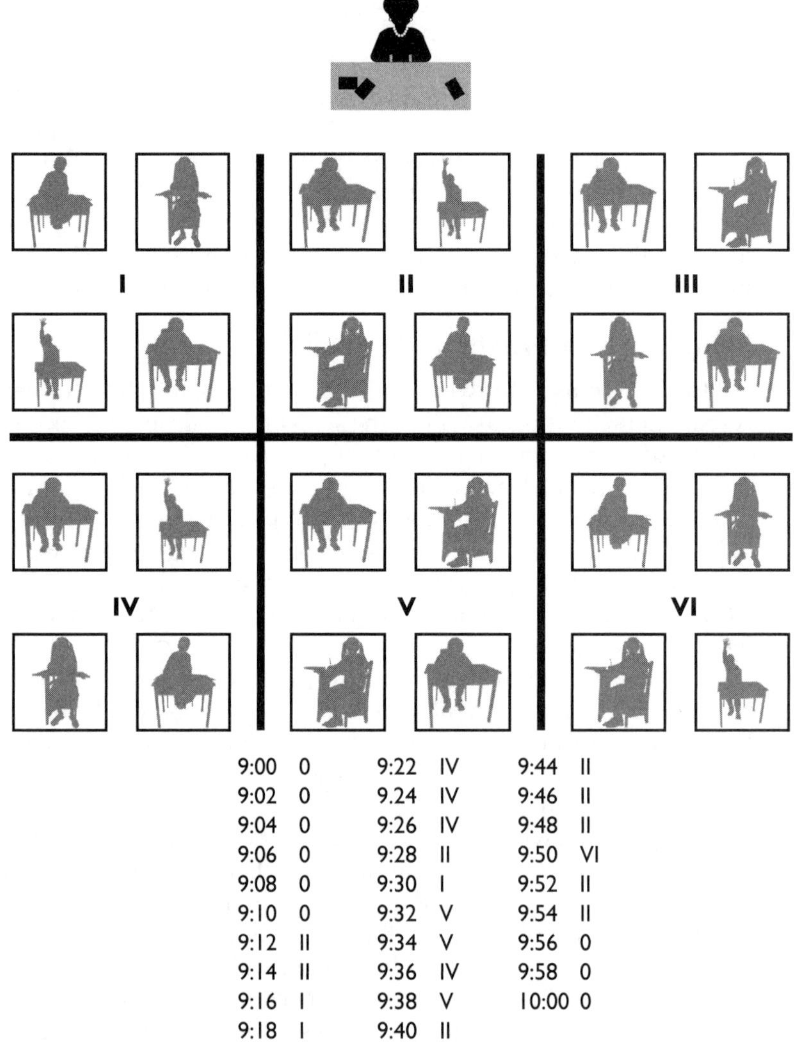

Time	Zone	Time	Zone	Time	Zone
9:00	0	9:22	IV	9:44	II
9:02	0	9.24	IV	9:46	II
9:04	0	9:26	IV	9:48	II
9:06	0	9:28	II	9:50	VI
9:08	0	9:30	I	9:52	II
9:10	0	9:32	V	9:54	II
9:12	II	9:34	V	9:56	0
9:14	II	9:36	IV	9:58	0
9:16	I	9:38	V	10:00	0
9:18	I	9:40	II		

0 = Teacher is at the desk or the blackboard and is not circulating among students.

Selective-Verbatim Instruments

The *selective-verbatim instrument* is a quantitative method that enables the teacher to capture the exact words used by the teacher and students. Because most classrooms are characterized by rapid verbal interactions, any attempt to capture all comments would likely fail; therefore, selective-verbatim instruments are designed to capture comments at selected intervals. According to Pawlas and Oliva (2008),

> The supervisor may selectively sample a variety of verbal events during the observation period, may choose to record specific behaviors that he or she feels are significant, or may limit recording to specific behaviors previously agreed on by the supervisor and teacher. The supervisor may wish to use a combination of verbatim recording and note taking. Recording of observation data can be a very personal undertaking and, like handwriting, may not be decipherable from one supervisor to the other. (p. 380)

Qualitative Observation Instruments

Sooner or later, all teachers will need the ability to gather in-depth information to raise the level of thinking in their classrooms, or to meet the widely divergent needs of students within a classroom (or to better use technology to meet these needs). They may wish to meet the needs of a particular student, or to better understand a particular teaching strategy. Such goals require qualitative observation instruments because they can extend beyond the gathering of data—these goals call for instruments that can help teachers make *value judgments*. Sometimes the best results are attained by combining the use of both quantitative instruments and qualitative instruments.

Promoting Higher-Level Thinking

Higher-level thinking is a worthy goal in any classroom, a goal embraced by teachers and parents. Even the general public recognizes the importance of the need for citizens to be able to engage in higher-level thinking. A recent national poll (Rose & Gallup, 2007) found that over three-fourths (81%) of the nation's citizens believe that all public school teachers should be required to spend part of each day learning how to help their students perform or achieve at higher academic levels. Yet this is not a goal that all teachers can reach without special training. Preparing students to use higher-level thinking requires special staff development. Today's teachers have the dual goals of increasing their students' learning and teaching them to think at higher levels. Increased academic attainment requires raising the levels of thinking in the classroom. Teachers have several viable approaches available to lead their students to higher-level thinking. One of these approaches is through the use of questions.

* * *

Left unaddressed, an individual's bad behavior can and usually does escalate, infecting the behavior of the entire class. But, as seen in the following case study, a well-developed strategy under the guidance of an experienced teacher can bring control to a deteriorating situation.

Why Me?

Janet Finch and Trinetia Respress • Tennessee State University

E.D. Hallow Elementary School is nestled in the beautiful mountains of eastern Tennessee. With a teacher-to-student ratio of 1:20, its 800 students are about 40% African American, 30% Hispanic American, 20% Caucasian American, and 10% other. The pre-K through fifth-grade school is noted for excellence. Moreover, the school received the prestigious National Blue Ribbon School title for the past two academic school years. Parents are very involved, and they really enjoy it!

Dr. Garrett, the principal, was acutely aware of a very bright and energetic first-year teacher (Mrs. Barry) who needed an assignment. Mrs. Barry had a lifelong dream of teaching elementary school and, in fact, changed careers just to fulfill that dream. Coming from a family of second-grade teachers, she wanted to make a difference in the lives of children. What a beautiful and warm-hearted person!

Mrs. Barry was assigned a class of 20 students, including seven with Attention Deficient Hyperactivity Disorder (ADHD); however, these students had not yet been classified as special education students. With an average IQ of 175, these students consistently outscored their counterparts on all standardized examinations. The remaining students had a range of abilities.

Within a few weeks, Mrs. Barry became concerned over the behavior of some of the ADHD students and worried that it might limit the academic achievement of other students. She e-mailed several of the parents about her concerns, appealing to them for their help. Anticipating that the parents largely would work together to solve this issue, she was awestruck when not one parent seemed to care. One parent actually responded that it was Mrs. Barry's job to use classroom-management skills to control the classroom. Oh gosh, she thought, *Why me?* What am I going to do?

Wondering if she might be overreacting, Mrs. Barry decided to first touch base with a couple of the more experienced teachers. Mr. Harold, a ten-year tenured teacher, offered to help. He asked her for a detailed account of what had been happening with the students. Mrs. Barry explained that several of her ADHD students were unable to sit still and frequently fidgeted with their hands or feet. They popped in and out of their seats in class and at lunch. Sometimes they would even squat down in their chairs like lions ready to leap out at their victims. They were constantly running and climbing in inappropriate places such as their desks, chairs, and tables. Quite frankly, said Mrs. Barry, they were simply all over the classroom and it was disruptive to the other students. They were talking too much and just blurting out answers without regard for classroom rules. She also told Mr. Harold that although their own grades were excellent, other students' grades were declining.

Perplexed by this story, Mr. Harold said he needed time to reflect on it and that he would get back with her in a couple of days. Relieved at his response, Mrs. Barry was a bit more optimistic. After a couple of weeks, they set up a time that he could stop by to observe the class.

On Mondays, Mr. Harold observed the classroom during his planning time from 10:00 a.m. to 10:45 a.m. (The observation instruments he used appear on the opposite page.) He determined on-task behavior by noting the number of students who were actively engaged in listening and appropriately responding to the teacher, how many were completing in-class assignments on time, how many were actively engaged in ancillary academic activities, and how many were reading. Also, he determined off-task behavior by noting how many students were engaged in disruptive behavior or play during instructional time; how many students were engaged in peripheral conversations; how many were not engaged in substantive student–teacher interaction; how many seemed to be daydreaming; and how many were generally violating class rules.

At the end of three classroom observations, Mr. Harold had witnessed some of the same behaviors that Mrs. Barry observed, such as climbing; excessive talking; unnecessary trips to the pencil sharpener; blurting out answers; standing on desks, chairs, and tables; and other severe disruptions to the learning process. To his dismay, not only were the students with ADHD behaving in this manner, but students without ADHD had also begun to copy their behavior. Mr. Harold concluded that Mrs. Barry's observations

Mr. Harold's Classroom Observation Forms

Student	10:00	10:05	10:10	10:15	10:20	10:25	10:30	10:35	10:40	10:45
ADHD #1	ON-T	ON-T	OFF-T	OFF-T	ON-T	OFF-T	OFF-T	OFF-T	ON-T	OFF-T
ADHD #2	ON-T	ON-T	ON-T	ON-T	OFF-T	OFF-T	OFF-T	OFF-T	OFF-T	OFF-T
ADHD #3	ON-T	ON-T	OFF-T	ON-T	ON-T	OFF-T	ON-T	OFF-T	OFF-T	ON-T
ADHD #4	ON-T	ON-T	ON-T	OFF-T	OFF-T	ON-T	OFF-T	OFF-T	ON-T	ON-T
ADHD #5	ON-T	ON-T	OFF-T	ON-T	OFF-T	ON-T	OFF-T	OFF-T	OFF-T	OFF-T
ADHD #6	OFF-T	ON-T	ON-T	OFF-T	OFF-T	OFF-T	OFF-T	ON-T	OFF-T	OFF-T
ADHD #7	ON-T	ON-T	ON-T	OFF-T	OFF-T	OFF-T	OFF-T	OFF-T	ON-T	ON-T
Total ON-T										
Total OFF-T										

Activity # 1

Directions: Tally the number of On-Task (ON-T) and Off-Task (OFF-T) behaviors of the seven students with ADHD identified during Mrs. Barry's classroom observation. Indicate the time periods these students are most frequently on task and off task. Provide Mrs. Barry with recommendations on how she can improve the behaviors of students during these time periods.

Classroom Observation Checklist	How many students are actively engaged in listening and appropriately responding to the teacher?	Are classroom assignments completed on time?	Are a variety of instructional strategies used? (peer-to-peer teaching, group activities, discussion, etc.)	How many students are engaged in on-task behavior? (reading, completing assignments, writing, hands-on activities, etc.)	How many students are engaged in off-task behavior? (talking, disturbing others, playing, daydreaming, out of seat, etc.)	How effective are the teacher's classroom management strategies? (Praise, consistency, follow-up, proximity, one-on-one assistance, etc.)
Student #1						
Student #2						
Student #3						
Student #4						
Total						
Percent						

Activity # 2

Directions: Use the instrument above to observe a class at your local elementary school. Tally the number of times you observe the behaviors indicated in the table. Once you have completed your observation, total the frequency and percent in which each behavior occurred for each student. Upon completion, provide a description of what occurred during this classroom observation.

and concerns were valid and the situation was in dire need of intervention. Accordingly, he decided to meet with her to brainstorm comprehensive behavior-management strategies for high-quality resolutions, not only for the students with ADHD but also for their counterparts.

The next week they met and decided to use the following components of the newly founded behavior management plan. Although the school district permitted corporal punishment, Mrs. Barry considered it punitive and detrimental to development. Additionally, she concluded that praise and encouragement would be fundamental and integral components on which the plan would be built. The components to the behavior management plan are as follows:

- Review daily classroom behavior expectations and consequences.
- Establish the need for active parent partnership in the behavior-management process.
- Engage lessons that require high student participation.
- Employ proximity control.
- Provide one-on-one assistance.
- Prohibit students with ADHD from sitting next to one another.
- Increase student motivation through the use of praise.
- Integrate social-skills instruction as an integral part of the curriculum.
- Engage students in small-group work and peer-to-peer teaching.
- Encourage students to self-monitor their behavior, with rewards for appropriate behavior.

Mrs. Barry used this behavior-management plan throughout the remainder of the year. Consequently, her students became increasingly more responsible. She noticed an increase in their attention spans and their ability to work with each other. Finally, Mrs. Barry's students scored the highest in the school district in every category on the SAT-10.

Issues for Further Reflection and Application

1. Did Mrs. Barry react in a timely manner to the onset of the inappropriate behaviors?
2. Were there environmental factors that may have contributed to the context of the scenario?
3. Was the response of the parents appropriate?
4. Do you think that the parents' lack of concern reflected a deeper societal problem?
5. What could Mrs. Barry have done differently in regard to shaping the presenting behaviors?
6. Was creating a behavior-management plan the best initiating response?
7. What would you have done differently in terms of developing a behavior management plan?
8. Was the plan inclusive enough to shape the behavior of non-ADHD students?
9. Applying developmental supervision, which approach would you use with Mrs. Barry in working through her classroom management issues?

Questioning to Promote Higher-Level Thinking

Although Socrates wasn't a writer, he clearly had something special going on with his teaching style, and his unique approach was built around questions. Twenty-five hundred years later it is difficult to even talk about raising thinking levels without the use of questions. John Dewey's preferred *problem-solving approach* to teaching (a reflective thinking process consisting of a structured, organized series of questions) has endured for over a century. Questioning and problem solving have become key platforms for building contemporary, constructivist classrooms. According to Mike Schmoker (2007, p. 67), "High-quality, common curriculum is the most powerful factor that affects levels of learning. Virtually all courses can become catalysts for inquiry—and a means to teach the skills that the future demands this ability of all students—when we build the curriculum around good questions."

Questions are the rungs on the higher-level thinking ladder, and supervisors should help their faculty recognize that some questions are better than others. A review of the educational taxonomies can point teachers in the right direction. Questions that work best to raise the level of thinking require students to compare and contrast, defend a position, rank, and justify. Questions can also be great motivators. Landsman and Gorski (2007) remind us that some students "yearn to participate and tackle provocative questions" (p. 43).

Some observation instruments are more suited than others for helping teachers improve their use of this teaching strategy. Prior to examining some of these tools, a quick review of a few preliminary steps can serve as advance organizers for both supervisor and teachers.

You might encourage teachers to write at least some of their questions while they are planning their lessons. According to Bond (2007), this can help avoid asking vague questions. Putting key questions on PowerPoint slides can ensure that all students follow them. Bond also suggested that teachers establish their expectations before they begin asking the questions, letting students know if they are to always raise their hands before responding. This is also a good time to remind students not to ridicule their peers, and to ensure students that so long as they are serious, there is no such thing as a bad response to a question.

To avoid embarrassing students, a teacher may choose to begin by calling a student's name *before* addressing that student with a question. Teachers should also remember to give each student ample time to answer. If, after waiting a reasonable time, an answer still isn't forthcoming, *scaffolding* can be used to help the student. For example, the teacher can give part of the answer, wait, give another part and wait, continuing this sequence until the question is answered.

It Works for Me!

Know Your Instruments

Kathleen Jenkins, Delta State University

Early in the semester students are introduced to several instruments used to collect data in the classroom as part of the supervision process. These instruments measure one area to be addressed in supervision based on teacher need and the agreement of the teacher and the supervisor prior to the observation. The instruments used include time on task, teacher verbal and nonverbal behavior, teacher interactions with students, and depth of knowledge levels of questions asked by the teacher.

Each graduate student uses the assigned instrument to assess a role-played lesson presented by students who had the course the previous year. The students who are observing use only one instrument each, but several different instruments are used during the process. After the role playing is complete and students have completed the instrument, they gather in groups according to the instrument used. They discuss their findings and the problems encountered in the process. Each group reports its findings to the large group. After this activity, the students begin using the instruments in actual classrooms the following week.

Teachers should listen carefully to each answer and then respond to each student's remark. The author has witnessed many teachers' failure to correct student answers, even when those answers were dead wrong! Wrong answers should always be noted and corrected. This can and should be done tactfully by helping the student reach the correct answer. Once a question is answered, it can be followed by other questions that focus on the same topic, raising the level of thinking. After a student responds, the teacher can verify the correctness of that answer by saying, "That's right," and then asking the class how she knows whether the question is right or wrong.

Having made teachers aware of these preliminary steps, let's now examine some observation instruments that can be used to help teachers improve their use of questions.

Measuring the Flow of Questions

We've already seen that seating charts can be designed for many specific uses. For qualitative observation purposes, the seating chart in Figure 12.3 was designed to measure the flow of the questions a teacher asked these students. This seating chart accomplishes this objective, and more. On closer inspection, we can see that this chart has a key that indicates each student's gender. This chart would enable the supervisor to point out this teacher's proclivity to aim most questions at males at the expense of slighting females. A similar chart could be made to ensure an adequate flow of questions directed to minority students. With slight alterations, a seating chart can take on a completely different use, as is the case with the seating chart in Figure 12.4. This is basically the same chart that is shown in Figure 12.1, except for a small alteration: An area has been *shaded* to show the teacher's *target zone*—the area of the room to which teachers direct most of their comments and questions. Most teacher–student eye contact is made with students sitting within this zone. Awareness of this can encourage the teacher to purposefully expand the target zone to include students in the back rows and those who sit on the extreme sides of the room.

Figure 12.3 Questioning Seating Chart

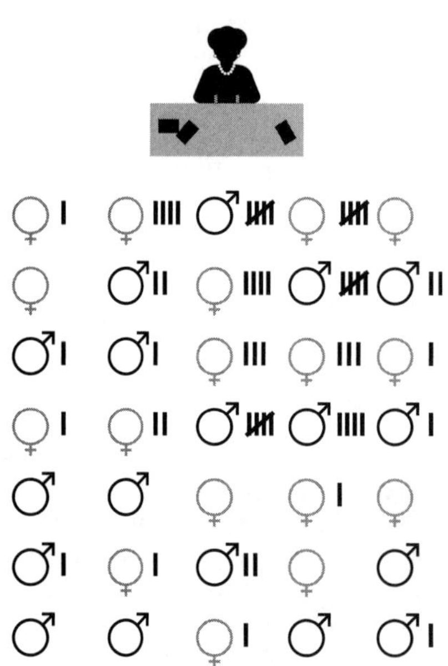

Measuring Higher-Order Thinking

By once again altering the seating chart shown in Figure 12.1, this instrument can be used to gather information on teachers' attempts to raise the level of thinking in their classrooms. As shown in Figure 12.5 (on p. 350), the only

Figure 12.4 Defining the Teacher's Target Zone

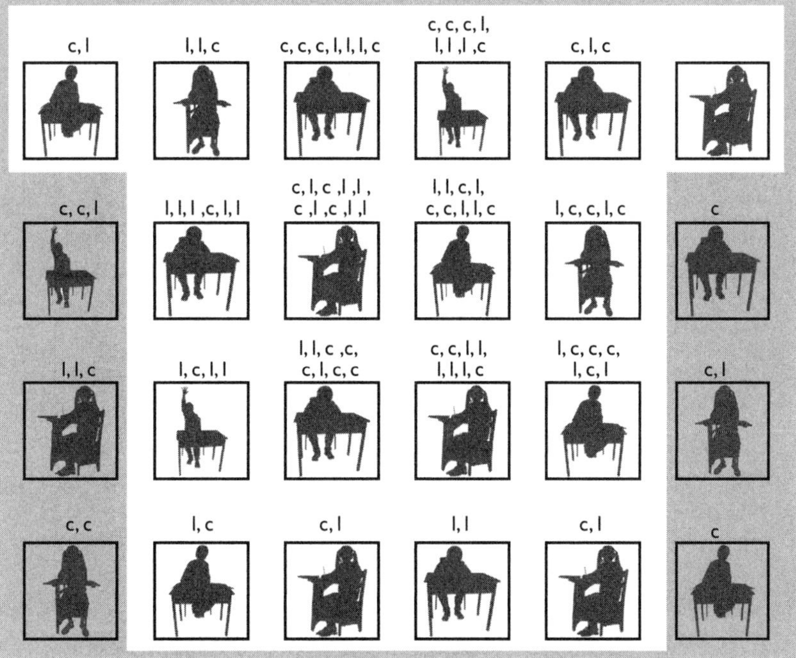

c = teacher-initiated questions to clarify a student's comment
l = teacher initiated questions to raise the level of thinking

difference in this chart is that the key has been changed, using an *h* to indicate whether the teacher's questions prompt higher-level thinking or whether the teacher's questions only ask students to recall *(r)* without raising the thinking level. The additional follow-up questions may come immediately after a student's comment, or the teacher may return to the topic later during the lesson and direct further questions to this student as the investigation resumes.

Using Technology

Michael and Paul Colombo (2007) reported on a seventh-grade science teacher, Ms. Daniels, whose 20- to 24-student classes range from struggling English-language learners to fast-paced gifted and talented students. To address their diverse needs, Ms. Daniels uses differentiated instruction, building units around enduring understandings. Her main avenue for raising the

Figure 12.5 Higher-Order Thinking Chart

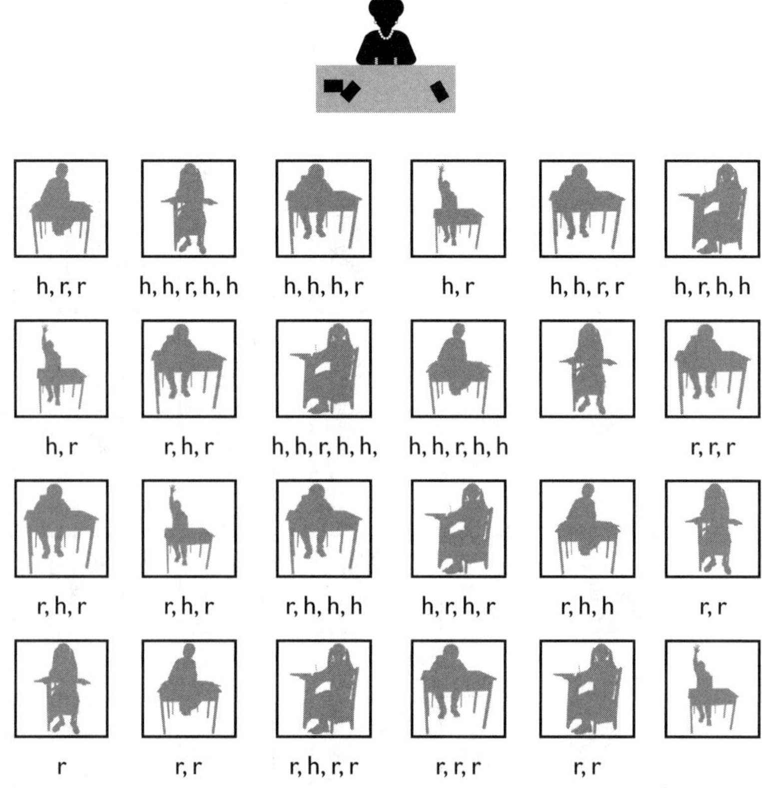

thinking levels of her students is through the use of questions. She explains, "Helping students focus on the essential questions provides context for learning and keeps students focused. It also allows students to demonstrate their level of understanding in various ways" (Colombo & Colombo, 2007, p. 61). Using PowerPoint, Ms. Daniels shows projections of pages from their science text to demonstrate to her students how and where they can find concepts, new vocabulary, and important explanations.

To extend class time, Ms. Daniels uses blogs to reinforce strategies. The blogs contain text, audio, and video files archived on a Web page. These blogs allow students and teachers to write to each other, questioning and commenting on each other's entries. The audio files (podcasts) allow students to listen to descriptions and explanations. The video files allow them access to audio combined with video.

Teachers with access to either Macintosh or Windows can find clear and easy-to-follow help with setting up blogs. See WordPress.com and Blogger.com.

Edublogs (http://edublogs.org) bills itself as "the largest education community on the Internet" and "an ideal site for educators who want to blog with support." Teachers can sign up for a free WordPress-powered blog. For those new to blogging, the site provides information on setting up a blog, how teachers can use their blog with their students, and how to begin a blog-based conversation. Free applications include Apple iTunes, available for both Macintosh and Windows (www.apple.com/itunes); and Audacity, podcasting software available for both Macintosh and Windows (http://audacity.sourceforge.net/download). WordPress offers open-source blogging software available for Macintosh, Windows, and Linux: Users load to their own servers for full blogging capabilities (http://wordpress.org). This includes a free blog account with full text and graphic capabilities; participants need to store podcast files elsewhere and link to them (http://wordpress.com).

Measuring Praise and Reinforcement

In a way, students have always been their own worst enemies. Instead of supporting each other, as is highly encouraged by constructivist practices, many students are quick to "take down" their classmates by using ridicule and sarcasm. This practice is common in far too many contemporary classrooms, and it not only hurts the victims but also distracts from the lesson and causes discipline problems. To help curtail the use of negativism in the classroom, teachers should use a generous amount of praise and reinforcement. If video recorded for self-assessment purposes or recorded by a peer or supervisor, teacher comments in the classroom like those represented in Box 12.1 could be used to help teachers recognize the extent to which they are using (or are failing to use) praise and reinforcement, and how effectively they do so.

One might generalize and say that the more praise used in the classroom the better, but this is true only if the praise is serious and students recognize it as such. One way to make sure that students take praise seriously is to personalize it. The teacher whose classroom is being measured in Box 12.1 uses stu-

Box 12.1 Measuring Praise and Reinforcement

Time	Teacher Comments
8:10	Anita, it's obvious that you read our assignment.
8:15	Julio, you nailed this problem!
8:23	Arnie, that's a good question. Did you hear it, Steve?
8:35	Earlier, Jesus, you said that . . . and you were right. How does Jesus's point apply here?
8:41	Patricia, I hope your enthusiasm for math continues. It can open a lot of doors if you keep it up.
8:47	Lashanda, your decimal is off by one point but your process is perfect.
8:52	Wally, if we gave stars for the most improvement, you'd look like the Milky Way.
8:55	I'm proud of every one of you for your continuous hard work.
9:00	You should find these homework problems easy because you have already worked one of each type in today's lesson.

dents' names, a practice that has a personalizing effect. A common but worst-case scenario is the teacher who, wittingly or not, adopts an expression and uses it over and over again. (Recall Bob Wallace's approach in this chapter's opening vignette.) For example, some teachers follow all of their students' comments with "Right" or "That's good," using these responses until they become meaningless. The practice of the teacher in Box 12.1 is far better, because each of this teacher's comments is individualized so that the student knows the teacher is engaging in his or her own thought processes. The comment to Jesus is especially powerful: It tells him and the rest of his classmates that the teacher focuses on individuals' comments to the extent that what the students said is remembered throughout the lesson.

Occasionally directing words of encouragement and praise to the entire class is a good practice, so long as these are balanced with a lot of individualized comments. For example, notice the comment about homework at the end of this lesson. We have already noted that homework should be given to reinforce skills and should not require skills that students have not developed. Many students are threatened by homework assignments, because they reason that if they had trouble working problems with a teacher present to help them, their chances of figuring them out without a teacher's help are greatly diminished.

The simple observation instruments discussed in this chapter are only a sample of the available tools that supervisors can recommend to teachers for gathering a better understanding of the daily classroom events. Many are available on the Internet; others can easily be designed by supervisors and their faculty. Most such instruments benefit from peer collaboration in the observation and analysis process. It's important to remember that the instruments themselves cannot advise teachers or tell them what they should do. However, effective teachers will use the knowledge they gain by using these and other instruments to improve the climate and, therefore, the learning in their classrooms.

It Works for Me!

Using Praise

Ralph Lindahl, Alabama State University

When writing up observations of teachers' behaviors, do not forget to discuss the positive behaviors you observed. After all, what is complimented is often repeated. However, it is essential to discuss these positive behaviors in the context in which they were successful. Praise the teacher for the behavior and discuss how it was particularly appropriate to the specific context. That way, the teacher will not be encouraged to repeat the behavior indiscriminately but rather will repeat it in situations when it is most likely to be effective again.

Conclusion

Paramount among the supervisor's responsibilities is the job of helping teachers more fully and accurately "see" their classrooms. A clear vision of the interplay between the teacher and students and among students is essential for both successful instruction and effective classroom management.

A variety of simple instruments can help teachers gain a clearer picture of their classrooms in action. Supervisors are encouraged to introduce general observation instruments, showing teachers how to use them to get an overall picture of their classrooms. Teachers can modify any of these instruments to answer specific questions about their classrooms.

Supervisors are advised to delay selecting an observation instrument until after they have decided the type of information they need most, and they are advised to delay making any value judgments until observations are completed and the data are recorded.

Questions for Discussion and Reflection

1. What is the relationship between instruction and classroom behavior?
2. How can teachers increase the probability that students will answer their questions correctly?
3. What category of observation instruments is best for getting a close-up look at a particular behavior?
4. How can teachers let students know that they are really listening to their students' comments?
5. What are some guidelines for using praise and reinforcement?
6. What are two methods for using questions to raise the level of thinking in classrooms?
7. How can a teacher use technology to improve classroom questioning?

Suggested Activities

1. The sample observation instruments shown in this chapter were chosen because they provide a way to gain insight into some important goals, such as improving diverse students' needs. Review this book's table of contents and index for other major goals, choose one that you consider especially important, and design an observation instrument to gather information on that goal.
2. Interview a supervisor, ask that supervisor to identify some ways that Generation X teachers (those born between 1965 and 1980) are different than other teachers and, with this supervisor's help, make a list of the unique ways in which this supervisor interacts with these teachers.

3. Review the seating charts discussed in this chapter, choose one, and alter it to gather data on two additional categories of information that you consider important to teachers.
4. Extend the use of observation beyond the classroom by holding a discussion with classmates. Begin by reviewing the discussion of technology in this chapter and explore different ways that you might use higher-order thinking.

Chapter 13

Helping Teachers Use Research

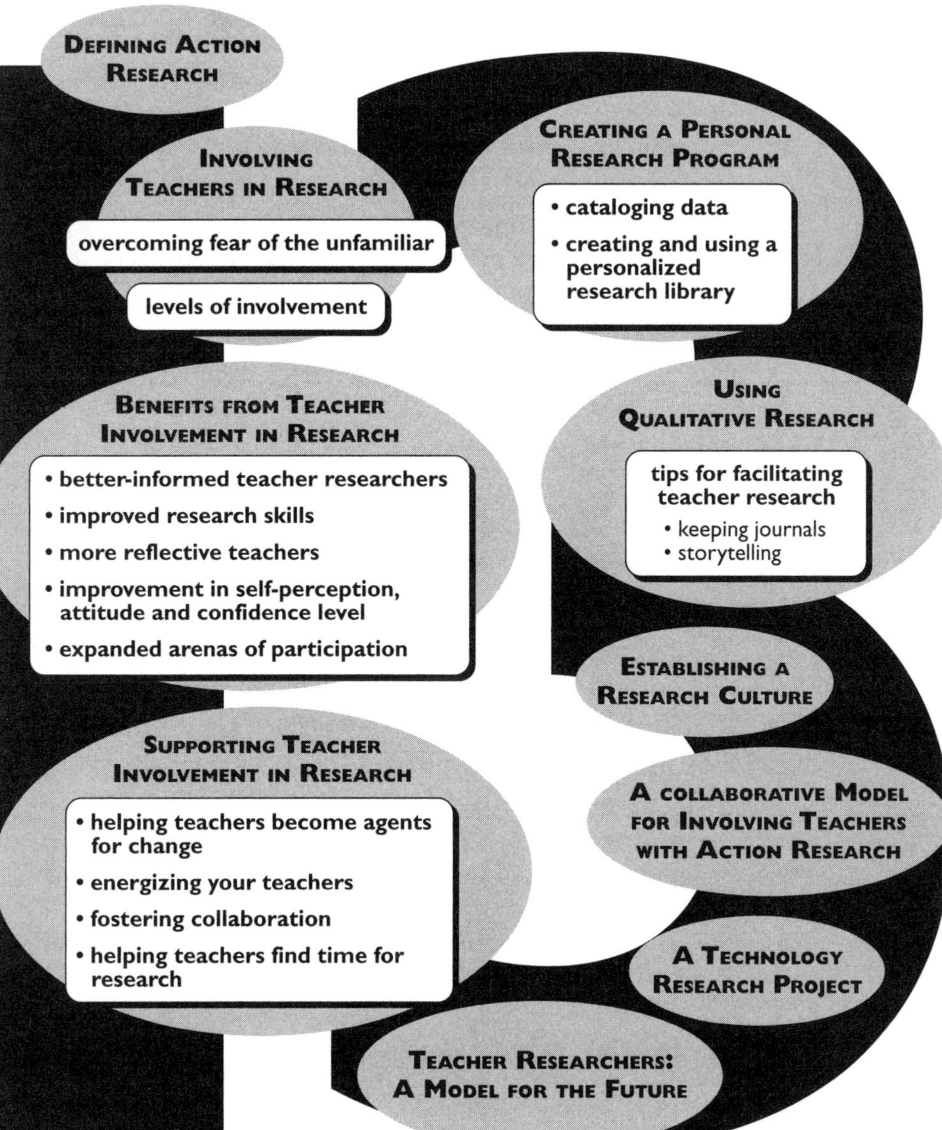

DEFINING ACTION RESEARCH
INVOLVING TEACHERS IN RESEARCH
overcoming fear of the unfamiliar
levels of involvement
CREATING A PERSONAL RESEARCH PROGRAM
• cataloging data
• creating and using a personalized research library
BENEFITS FROM TEACHER INVOLVEMENT IN RESEARCH
• better-informed teacher researchers
• improved research skills
• more reflective teachers
• improvement in self-perception, attitude and confidence level
• expanded arenas of participation
USING QUALITATIVE RESEARCH
tips for facilitating teacher research
• keeping journals
• storytelling
ESTABLISHING A RESEARCH CULTURE
SUPPORTING TEACHER INVOLVEMENT IN RESEARCH
• helping teachers become agents for change
• energizing your teachers
• fostering collaboration
• helping teachers find time for research
A COLLABORATIVE MODEL FOR INVOLVING TEACHERS WITH ACTION RESEARCH
A TECHNOLOGY RESEARCH PROJECT
TEACHER RESEARCHERS: A MODEL FOR THE FUTURE

> *It is hoped that an ever-evolving research base will help all institutions of school leadership preparation and professional development to learn from each other.*
>
> —R. Harchar, K. Campbell, & B. Smith, "Reality check: Designing a new leadership program for the 21st century"

Objectives

After completion of this chapter, you should be able to

1. Identify several characteristics of action research and cite journal references to support this response.
2. Explain some ways of breaking down common barriers to teacher involvement in research.
3. Give some reasons why teachers often avoid research.
4. List and discuss some results of teacher involvement in research.

Pine Grove School

Southern Hills Elementary School is recognized as a leader in the state because, throughout the years, its teachers have given faculty development workshops to faculties of other schools throughout the state. Their leader image is reinforced each year when the Southern Hills students score at or near the top on the state's standardized test. But not everybody is in awe over Southern Hills' performance record. On the contrary, negative, critical comments are often heard, comments such as, "Sure! They are located adjacent to Southern University's campus. Most of their parents teach at the university, and they have all the advantages of being located in a university town." Or "Sure, that's the test-tube babies again. They get the first shot at testing all the new curriculum and instructional programs." Or, "Did you know that the state hires one or more of these teachers every year? They are given leave to work in the state department of education; so they're there to get first choice of all the new programs and grants. I'll bet half of the requests for proposals are written specifically for them."

Everyone was shocked when Southern University's teacher education program selected another school to use as a professional practice school. They had assumed that Southern Hills would be the first choice. But, instead of choosing this premiere school, Southern University chose to team up with Pine Grove Elementary, a small, rural school located in an adjacent county.

At first, the Pine Grove teachers were shocked at this decision; later they were honored to be chosen. But their enthusiasm waned after a visit by a Southern University professor who made a proposal that left many Pine Grove teachers feeling threatened. Dr. Adams told the teachers that he had come to establish some research teams. Each team would consist of a Southern professor, a Pine Grove teacher, and a graduate student.

Dr. Adams explained that this idea was part of the university's plans to restructure its teacher education program. Several education reform reports had said that nothing short of complete restructuring would work, that all teachers would have to get into the business of generating knowledge, and that the only way to do this was by conducting research. This, he said, was what had brought him to Pine Grove.

Most teachers sat quietly while their guests talked. A few mumbled to their closest neighbors. Someone said that he suspected that the "publish or perish" rule was behind all this "research talk." A few others shared the suspicion, but most just sat and listened.

Following the meeting, a Pine Grove department chair, Ann Wallace, asked for a meeting with the principal, Ben Ellis, who had taught for ten years on the Pine Grove faculty before becoming the principal just three years ago. A few preliminary courtesies were exchanged. Then Ann said, "Mr. Ellis, I called you because I need your advice. When Dr. Adams from the university was recently over here to speak to our faculty about a restructuring program that's underway in the Department of Education, he said the program would require several of the university faculty members to work on a daily basis with our faculty. The university wants their Department of Education faculty to join our faculty in some research projects. You know that our teachers have never had time to conduct research."

Ann was interrupted for a moment when Ben asked her whether the faculty had the skills needed to do research. "Well, to be frank, I doubt that many of our teachers have ever conducted a research project. That's one of the problems. Although I doubt that they would admit it, I suspect that most of our teachers find the idea of conducting research a little scary. The other problem is that they don't see any need for it. They are saying that they became teachers because they enjoy teaching, and had they been interested in research they would have become researchers or professors. They also make another good point: University professors are given released time to conduct research. They teach from six to twelve hours a week, and our teachers teach thirty to thirty-five hours a week."

Mr. Ellis replied to Ms. Wallace, "You know that some of our state's most vocal critics have been saying that our colleges have failed to work with our elementary and secondary schools, and vice versa. I don't think we have any alternative but to try to cooperate with the university's request. So, I need you to talk to our teachers and help them see the advantages in collaboration and research, and help them develop the skills that they will need to succeed in this program. You can use some of the faculty development budget and even a few in-service days if you need to. I will help you get whatever else may be required to succeed. And, oh yes, I wanted to tell you that our next scheduled in-service is Monday. Could you please arrange to meet with our faculty at that time? I could spare a half-day on Monday for you to get the project underway."

Mr. Ellis knew that he had a lot of work to do to prepare for this first meeting. As he promised Ann to give the project his best effort, he thought, Why do these "opportunities to help" always come without proper time to prepare? "Oh well," he concluded, "such is the nature of the life of a principal."

Reflection

The situation at Pine Grove Elementary reflects several often overlooked elements of teacher involvement with research. This vignette points to a less-than-desirable relationship between research and practice. Unfortunately, this conclusion is supported in current literature. Stephen Davis (2007) says, "Feedback from the field suggests that a gap between research and practice persists while bridges between them remain tenuous and unsteady" (p. 569). But, now that teachers are required by NCLB law to use research-proven practices, scholars and practitioners must redouble their efforts to bridge the research–practice gap. If teachers are to take on this additional responsibility, they must be shown the need for their involvement, they must see how they and their students will benefit from it, and the school's priorities must be aligned with those of the district office. Ideally, teachers should be led to initiate research projects, ensuring they have ownership in each project. As you read this chapter, think about the challenge of getting teachers to recognize the importance of conducting their own research.

Introduction

> Interstate New Teacher Assessment and Support Consortium (INTASC) Principle No. 9 sees the teacher as a reflective practitioner who constantly evaluates the effects of his or her choices and actions on others.

This chapter is about action research and how supervisors can encourage teachers to conduct some action research studies in their classrooms. It is based on the widely accepted premise that "research should drive practice and practice should fuel research" (Bush, 2006, p. 511). The term *action research* has several definitions, as you will see.

Education reform reports of the 1980s and 1990s, and later the No Child Left Behind legislation, have made demands on schools and teachers that require total restructuring of schools and radical changes in teacher behavior (Mills, 2006). Throughout this book, we have said that teachers must change their practices. Instead of clinging to the safe haven of their classrooms, where they use tried but unproven methods, teachers must transcend this boundary and get involved with restructuring their schools. Instead of teaching in the same old ways that they were taught, teachers must become risk takers and experiment with new methodology. Instead of being dispensers of information, teachers must be creators of knowledge so that, in turn, they can lead their students in their own creation of knowledge.

Action research is a viable vehicle to help teachers develop into empowered, self-confident, risk-taking leaders (Pinnick, 2006; Marshall, 2005; Steel & Craig, 2006). As you read this chapter, consider the advantages that action research offers teachers who are bold enough to use it.

Defining Action Research

> Think of action research as a huge meteor falling into the middle of the supervision ocean. As it hits, it causes a rippling of water that activates the four seas of direct assistance, professional development, curriculum development, and group development. The rippling of water continues to increase in force until a giant wave gathers and crashes onto all instructional shores, sweeping away the old sand of past instructional failures and replacing it with the new sand of instructional improvement. (Glickman et al., 2007, p. 412)

The literature is replete with definitions of action research. But before examining someone else's definition, perhaps you could benefit more by forming your own definition. Consider this an invitation to create some knowledge before asking your teachers to do the same. While there is no single correct definition of action research, this does not imply that one person's definition is as good as another's. Action research has some common qualities, and good definitions reflect most of the qualities or characteristics that educators say describe action research.

One characteristic that many, perhaps most, educators associate with action research is its levels of formality/informality. Unlike other scholarly research, some action research is rather informal. Teachers who are repelled by research (perhaps because they associate it with their highly structured brush with research in a graduate program) may welcome the opportunity to conduct this less formal type of research.

Whether formal or informal, action research must be conducted with a purpose, and that purpose is to solve a problem (Mikovich & Evans, 2006). As a lawyer might say, it is *premeditated*. The problem should be one that the investigators (school administrators or classroom teachers) view as important. By investigating the existing program, action research enables investigators to self-examine or reflect on their situation. Reflection plays an important role in improving teaching and, of course, the intent is usually to self-improve. Put another way, the goal is self-improvement through investigation.

Geoffrey Mills (2006) offers the following definition: "Action research is any systematic inquiry conducted by teacher-researchers, principals, counselors, or other stakeholders in the teaching/learning environment to gather information about how their particular schools operate, how they teach, and how well their students learn" (p. 5). Some salient characteristics of action research are shown in Figure 13.1.

Figure 13.1 Characteristics of Action Research

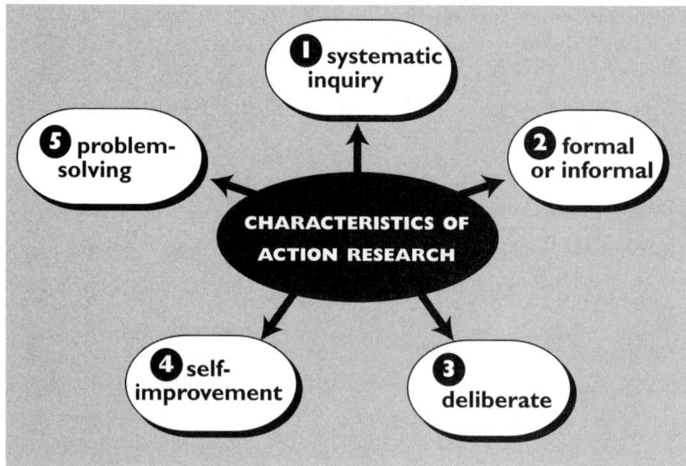

Unlike traditional research, which requires months or even years to get feedback, action research is more immediate. It can have an impact on the learning in classrooms during its course rather than having to wait until research results are translated into practical classroom models.

Many teachers have discovered that action research provides answers for questions that are relevant to their professional lives and classrooms and, in particular, to their instructional responsibilities. The idea that by conducting some simple investigations teachers can solve many of the problems that plague their classrooms makes action research seem like a natural practice for all dedicated teachers. One might conclude that all serious teachers would want to conduct some studies in their classrooms, but such has not been the case. On the contrary; through the years teachers have been reluctant to conduct research.

Elsewhere in this book we have expressed concern that most teachers do not conduct research or make use of research findings. Although teachers' reasons for isolating themselves from research vary from teacher to teacher, a few common concerns are shared by most teachers. Teachers' tendency to shun research can be attributed, at least in part, to some enduring perceptions that teachers hold about action research. For example, teachers have always tended to view research as an abstract activity rather than a concrete activity, like teaching. Similarly, teachers are said to view research as being too theoretical and superficial.

Study the characteristics of action research shown in Figure 13.1 and the definitions given in Box 13.1. Using the information in the figure and the box, you should be able to present an image of action research that teachers will find nonthreatening and, indeed, inviting.

Box 13.1 Some Definitions of Action Research

Action research is

- a possible collaborative reflection between teacher and scholar
- teachers becoming more acutely aware of what is happening in their classrooms and beyond
- a form of self-reflective inquiry that can be utilized by teachers in order to improve the rationality and justice of (a) their own practices, (b) their understanding of these practices, and (c) the situations in which these practices are carried out
- any systematic inquiry, large or small, conducted by professionals and focusing on some aspects of their practice in order to find out more about it, and eventually to act in ways they see as better or more effective
- practitioner-led research implemented in the practitioner's own practice

Involving Teachers in Research

You may wish to help teachers develop some simple questionnaires for gathering data about their classes or about the students' perceptions. If so, you should follow up to ensure that some change(s), however simple, are being made by using the feedback to improve classroom practices. Various levels of involvement with action research will be explored later in this chapter.

Overcoming Fear of the Unfamiliar

Many teachers feel threatened by research. This is understandable because many—perhaps most—teacher education programs have failed to prepare teachers with the understandings and skills needed to be competent researchers and, equally important, to feel comfortable with research (Bingham et al., 2006). Many teachers shun research because they perceive it as a very difficult, rigorous process requiring many skills that they fear they do not possess. They have a mental image of rigid designs that are fully understood only by full-time university researchers. This type of research, "Capital R-Research" (Bingham et al., 2006), has been etched in many teachers' memories: "Many were intimidated and could not see how this type of research could apply to their own situations" (p 682). Supervisors can help by letting teachers know that action research can be as simple as an inventory given to a class of students to gather information for improving the classroom conditions. If they have used even the simplest of observation instruments discussed in chapter 12, the most research-phobic of your teachers may be surprised to realize that they have already been practicing action research.

Although many teachers traditionally have not been involved with research, the number of teachers who have conducted classroom investigations has increased as result of the No Child Left Behind legislation. Those teachers have engaged in classroom research in a variety of ways and at different levels.

Levels of Involvement

The ways in which teachers have been involved with research, and more specifically, teachers' levels of involvement with research, have affected the results of their involvement. In other words, the types and levels of involvement have affected the benefits derived from doing research. See Table 13.1.

Table 13.1 Levels of Teacher Involvement with Research

Level	Teacher's Role
Level I: Teachers as helpers	Have no input into the selection of the problem to be studied. Offer their classrooms and students to be studied. Help gather data. May or may not see the results.
Level II: Teachers as junior researchers/partners	Have minimal input into the selection of the problem being studied. May make suggestions, but the final decisions are made by the researcher. Seldom have access to the results.
Level III: Teachers as full researchers	Select the problem, design and conduct the study, and decide how to use the results. Full partners (collaborators) have an equal say in choosing the problem and in interpreting and using the results. Often coauthor professional journal articles.

Level I. At this level, the lowest level of involvement in research, teachers have been delegated roles as helpers. Having no input, either into the decision to conduct the research or the selection of the problem, these teachers may not even be aware that an investigation is being conducted. In the past, the problem to be studied has often been selected by a university professor, and the problem selected has been based on the criteria for promotion or tenure. As a result, the chosen problem has often had little interest to the teacher. At this level the teacher is merely a helper whose role is to offer the classroom and furnish the subjects (students) to an outside researcher. At Level I, the teacher may be asked to collect data and, once collected, submit these data to the researcher. The Level I teacher-researcher may never learn the results of the study.

It should not be surprising to learn that teachers engaged in Level I research are often less than enthusiastic. In fact, for many this is an understatement: Being kept in the dark about the purpose of the study, and often even uninformed of the findings, has led many Level I teacher-researchers to develop a strong resentment toward research. Without the courtesy of being given a reason for the study, and certainly without any awareness of the benefits to the involved teachers or to their students, teachers at this level know only that involvement in action research takes up a portion of their valuable time and energy.

Unfortunately, a study of the history of teacher involvement with research shows that most teacher involvement has traditionally been at Level I. Teaching has always been a demanding role (Marshall, 2005); few other professions place such relentless tension on their members, denying them regularly scheduled breaks, giving them no opportunity for a relaxing lunch hour, and giving them nightly home assignments. With such a workload, it is little wonder that most teachers are less than enthusiastic when asked to commit a substantial amount of their time and energy just to assist someone else whose schedule may be less demanding than theirs.

Asking teachers to gather data for a study that belongs to someone else demonstrates a lack of appreciation of teachers, reflecting the all-too-familiar misconception that teaching doesn't require much planning. Ironically, teachers have been denied adequate planning time because they have been perceived by others as relatively unimportant; and yet, as pointed out in chapter 1, ample research and literature have shown how important the teacher is to the learning process (Phelps, 2006; Shechtman et al., 2005).

Level II. At the second level in Table 13.1, the teacher may be informed of the problem being studied but may have had no input in the selection of the problem. At this level, the teacher may make suggestions about the procedures used to gather data, but the final decisions belong to the researcher. At level II, the teacher seldom has access to the findings of the study. It is not surprising that, as with Level I, teachers at this level feel less than enthusiastic over the "opportunity" to "participate."

Level III. At the highest level of involvement, the teacher is a researcher. In fact, the teacher may be a lone researcher who selects the problem, designs the study, collects the data, interprets the data, and draws conclusions and implications—and as a result makes changes in classroom practices. Level III teacher-researchers often write articles and publish their findings in professional journals.

Not all research at this level is conducted by a lone teacher. Some Level III research is conducted collaboratively by teams of teachers, university professors, and doctoral students. When Level III teacher-researchers are part of a team, the teacher is an equal partner in all respects. Thus, the problem chosen is usually one that focuses on a current classroom problem. At this level, teachers also have access to the findings. When articles are written for and published in professional journals, the teachers are full coauthors and receive equal credit as such.

In recent years, largely as a result of the No Child Left Behind legislation, yet another alternative way has developed in which Level III collaborative research can occur. In K–12 classrooms all over the country, teachers are collaborating with fellow teachers without the involvement of a university professor. Obviously, this arrangement gives the teachers total control of the process, from the point of identifying a problem to be studied to announcing and using the findings.

Conducting research and writing about the findings empowers teachers. Supervisors can help by encouraging teachers to form research/writing teams and by arranging in-service education to prepare teachers for these activities. Continuous dialogue among team members is essential. Reporting on a national

It Works for Me!

Using Observation Data to Improve Instruction

Dianne L. Taylor, Louisiana State University

The purpose of supervision is to improve instruction, which is best done in a supportive, collegial atmosphere. A technique I've used when supervising student teachers is also one I use when teaching instructional supervision—that is, to ask the teacher to choose the topic for feedback (*not* criticism). By making it clear for the first couple of observations that the teacher can choose the focus, whether it is a single problematic student, use of instructional time, or some other instruction-related issue, control has been given to the teacher, helping to establish a supportive atmosphere. Sometimes data are collected by scripting; at other times we create a measure specific to the focus identified. Having chosen the area of focus, the teacher is interested in the feedback. After the observation, the teacher gets a copy of the data, I have a copy, and we both analyze the data independently. Then, we meet to discuss the *data,* not our opinions, regarding the identified focus and next steps the teacher might take. Both student teachers and in-service teachers have reported that this approach is very helpful.

study, Barnett Berry (2005), president of the Center for Teacher Quality at Chapel Hill, North Carolina, found that a major factor retarding progress is too little time in general for teachers to work with and observe one another.

Benefits of Teacher Involvement in Research

At the lower levels, most advantages of teacher involvement in research are very limited or nonexistent. However, all variations of Level III teacher involvement in research produce important benefits for those involved. Some of these benefits are listed below.

Better-Informed Teacher-Researchers

Teachers need new knowledge to cope with the complex issues they face, and they are continually seeking information on how they can use their instructional time more efficiently, how students can learn more, how children can teach other children, and how students' educational progress can best be evaluated. Teachers who are involved with research are better informed on these and other issues. The additional information gained from being involved with research is not limited to content information; teachers involved in research also become more knowledgeable about teaching methods.

Improved Research Skills

Involvement with research also gives teachers an improved understanding of the research process. This increased understanding, coupled with the experience of working directly with research, prepares teachers to be better researchers and also better consumers of research. Recall from chapter 1 that teachers seldom base their choice of teaching behaviors on those factors that improve learning. Variety is essential, because each learner's needs are different (Lovelace, 2005). Through involvement with research, teachers increase both their knowledge of teaching methods and their repertoire of methods.

More Reflective Teachers

Effective teachers are decision makers, both proactive and reactive. It bears repeating that teachers make as many as 1,000 decisions each day. Effective teachers think about or reflect on their behaviors and the effects they have had. Reflection on practice is essential to learning and to improving teaching on a daily basis (Rallis et al., 2006). Action researchers share this quality of reflection. Through reflection, involvement in research causes teachers to become better observers, and to question their own beliefs and the assertions of others. This critical analyzing behavior extends beyond their own classrooms, as teacher-researchers question university-based research and standard school practices.

Some school environments demand a high level of teacher compliance. At many of these schools, questions about school policies and procedures are not welcome because the administrators consider them an unnecessary nuisance. This makes the supervisor's role in shaping the school ethos critical. The supervisor must convince administrators that questions are healthy, and that they should be encouraged and used to improve the learning environment. The case studies throughout this book are good examples of supervisors and faculty reflecting on and challenging the practices followed in their schools.

Supervisors can give their faculty good advice on being reflective researchers. Teachers need to reflect on their daily behaviors, the results of each, and the reasons for the results (although this list may be no more than speculation disguised as logical deduction). Weekly tests should be analyzed and the results shared among teachers, and teachers should collaboratively reflect on the implications of these results on a weekly basis (Guskey, 2007/2008). Teachers also need to reflect on long-term matters. Keeping a journal or a daily log is one method of reflecting on both immediate and long-term matters. Ironically, most teacher time is focused on the immediate tasks, yet most improvements come from long-term planning. A log will allow your faculty to reflect on teaching, both immediately *and* over time.

Improvement in Self-Perception, Attitude, and Confidence Level

Teachers involved with research become lifelong learners (Bingham et al., 2006). Such teachers experience changes in their self-concepts. Self-actualization (see chapter 4) occurs through the increased sense of professionalism, expertise, and empowerment that results from becoming a teacher-researcher.

At a time when most teachers are burdened with heavy workloads, teacher burnout is common. Involvement in research is a rich, much-needed source of energy for teachers. In fact, involvement with research leads to a more positive attitude in general. When people have the confidence to face problems or challenges, they display a positive attitude. Involvement with research keeps teachers willing to take on new challenges. Bingham and colleagues (2006) reported that teacher involvement in research led to a sense of pride in helping to create a body of *craft knowledge*—the insight gained from their work-related knowledge about such issues as curriculum and instruction, discipline, collaboration, and parent involvement. An additional benefit of this positive change in disposition is that teachers interact more with others. Involvement with research allows teachers to grow.

Expanded Arenas of Participation

As mentioned earlier, education demands the restructuring of the whole school, necessitating the participation of all teachers and other professionals at the school and within the entire community. Community-based action research projects (Fitzgerald & Brain, 2008; Shepherd et al., 2008) can give teachers a new appreciation of the positive support offered by families and other community members. See the case study in chapter 15 for an example of the good things that come of such partnerships.

Some of the more important advantages of teacher involvement with research are:

- improved self-image
- better-informed teachers, both in their fields and in their chosen practices
- more reflective teachers
- overall improvement in teaching
- increased repertoire of classroom-management behaviors
- increased variety of instructional methods
- better problem-solving skills
- increased awareness of student needs
- becoming less prescriptive and more proactive
- becoming lifelong learners
- becoming critical readers and users of literature
- becoming more collaborative

Supporting Teacher Involvement in Research

Good supervisors have a compelling need to learn all that is possible about their profession. Understandably, they often are surprised to learn that their greatest challenge is not to possess all the latest knowledge about content and pedagogy. Rather, the greatest challenge that supervisors face is helping teachers change their attitudes.

It Works for Me!

Journal Logs and USB Drives

JoAnn Susko, Rider University

As a supervisor you will be required to observe teachers on a daily basis. Consequently, you will be afforded a tremendous opportunity to observe some truly talented teachers who can provide you with an extensive repertoire of effective teaching strategies. The key to your success as a supervisor in making specific recommendations regarding instruction to novice and developing teachers will lie in your ability to quickly retrieve some of these strategies so that they can be conveniently shared during conversations following your observations/classroom visits. Whether you are a relatively new or veteran supervisor, I suggest that you begin to record these effective instructional strategies in a manner that makes them instantly accessible, by saving them on your computer and keeping them on your person in a USB drive.

It is equally important that you categorize these effective strategies in a manner that makes them easily retrievable, according to the area of instruction that they specifically address. For example, possible categories for effective instructional strategies might include planning, class climate, motivation, and classroom management. A folder for each of these effective instructional strategies could be created to house the great ideas you accumulate.

Implementing the process of journaling outstanding instructional strategies will not only contribute to your effectiveness in supervising instruction, but it is also quite likely that you will increase your credibility with the teachers that you supervise. Have this valuable information at your fingertips, ready to share at a moment's notice. Being able to make specific suggestions/recommendations to teachers is a clear indication that you possess a strong knowledge base in the area of effective instruction—a quality in a supervisor that is both admired and respected by teachers.

Helping Teachers Become Agents for Change

Most supervisors have discovered that schools are self-preserving institutions; the culture of many schools discourages change, forcing teachers into the trenches to seek safety. The fact that teachers have a proclivity to teach like their own former teachers taught adds to their resistance to change. The result of these combined forces is a cadre of unjustifiably complacent teachers who are content to remain unchanged and determined to uphold the status quo. Ironically, often such teachers are not even pleased with the status quo; it is just the lesser of two evils (change being perceived as the greater of the two). When teachers have become so comfortable and secure with the way things are that they are afraid to try something new, involvement with research can reverse this condition because it has the power to pull teachers out of their ruts, replacing complacency with a sense of mission and taking their professional growth to a new level.

Of all the knowledge and skills required of instructional supervisors, perhaps most often needed is the ability to energize teachers. Involvement with research, like involvement with any innovation, can stimulate teachers' interests and give them a reason to feel good about their schools. Research can cause teachers to grow in wisdom and confidence, teach them to be eloquent speakers and group leaders, and help them become assertive and knowledgeable advocates for change.

Fostering Collaboration

According to Bingham and colleagues (2006), "Professional isolation is a debilitating factor in teacher development in general, and it may be even more detrimental to the development of teacher researchers" (p. 688). The Professional Development Center in Palo Alto, California, encourages teacher-researchers to reflect on their practices and share their experiences with other teachers. Teachers who engage in research should be given more encouragement and opportunities to talk with other teachers. Just sitting around and discussing their research projects with their colleagues can provide teacher-researchers many needed insights into teaching. Teachers' stories are a powerful means of helping them reflect on their practices. Whether it's a formal conference or an energizing discussion in the teachers' lounge, perhaps one of the best ways for a teacher to grow is to get together with colleagues, simply to talk about teaching.

Supervisors can capitalize on the advantages of collaboration and discussion by holding seminars—regularly scheduled meetings to explore specific research topics or experiences. Teachers should realize that the discussions alone are not the equivalent of research, nor should they be substituted for research. But such seminars and support groups are indispensable for many teachers who need reinforcement and support from their peers. Open discussion enables the participants to create a safe environment for learning.

When teachers choose to collaborate on research, the most important basis on which to select partners is work habits. Teachers with Type A personalities are self-motivated, whereas Type B personalities are "laid back" and easygoing. When the two join, Type A frustrates Type B by rushing the process, and Type B frustrates Type A by dragging his or her heels. Supervisors can help by encouraging the teaming of like personalities.

Table 13.2 shows some common barriers to teacher involvement with research and some suggested bridges for overcoming these barriers. Supervisors can help teachers identify problems they want to research, clarify the research role of each teacher, and initiate support groups.

Table 13.2 Barriers and Bridges to Successful Teacher Involvement with Research

Barriers	Bridges
Failure to commit fully to research	An initial awareness of the commitment required for success
Lack of commitment	Involvement in selection of the problem to be studied
Inadequate planning time	Consideration of flexible schedules, such as block scheduling
Isolation from their peers	Participation in meetings and seminars on specific research topics or experiences

* * *

Unlike the scholarly basic research conducted by expert statisticians and researchers and written up in pedantic articles in scholarly journals, action research is a practical tool that many teachers use to solve local problems. The following case study shows how a principal leads his faculty to use action research to solve some of the problems that plague their school. This model can be used to identify and remove problems of all types, leading to teacher ownership of continuous improvement in their school.

Using Research for Change: The Case of the Aspiring Principal

Luana Zellner • Sam Houston State University

The reassignment of the campus principal at Martin Luther King Jr. (MLK) Elementary School on the first day of school came on the heels of a year of discontent over low student achievement scores, high teacher turnover, and parents' complaints. These factors contributed to the negative feelings and the cloud of depression that seemed to hang over the faculty and staff at MLK. Instead of a learning community, the campus was just a place where you picked up your paycheck. With its cloud of gloom and doom, MLK Elementary obviously didn't live up to the dream of its namesake.

In November, the campus got its first real break with the appointment of a new principal, "Superman Gary," who was handed a list of tasks to be accomplished by May. Most importantly, he was assigned the task of bringing the faculty together into a supportive team as soon as possible. Having Linda as his assigned "principal intern" gave Gary needed support while figuring out his role in leading the campus. He was excited to have Linda on board as his assistant during these stressful times. Gary was instrumental in Linda's decision to focus her principal internship project on changing campus climate and campus morale.

Gary and Linda decided to make it their first mission to change the harmful, negative atmosphere. Day after day, Linda greeted her classroom teachers with a smile and encouraging words. When she saw them laugh and say something positive to each other, she would say, "Gotcha!" Her frequent recognition and supportive comments from teacher to teacher were greatly appreciated. The faculty loved and respected her "cheerleader" efforts to boost campus morale every day. However, Linda's positive approach wasn't adopted among the recipients. Responsibility for campus climate and morale was not addressed by the staff. Instead, climate and morale were viewed as something to be fixed by someone else. The question became, "Who was going to fix the morale problem?"

Taking *Action*

As an aspiring principal, Linda was required during her principal internship to identify a campus issue that would help her develop leadership skills and more importantly would benefit the school. She was sure that her faculty needed something that would make them feel good about themselves and restore confidence in their administration and in their work environment. Her informal praise strategy among the faculty was only a starting point—what would it take to change climate and morale?

Grounded Theory—Action Research

Linda's first step was to show evidence that there was a widespread morale problem among the faculty. She did this by using a grounded theoretical approach to researching this problem. With the support of her principal, Linda was to become an action researcher. In addressing the issues of climate and morale, with the help of her principal Linda laid out a strategic action-research plan. Together they planned a change strategy that required Linda to collect and analyze data from a variety of sources. The *action research* approach (often referred to as *grounded theory*) is a popular strategy used when performing inquiry in school settings. Grounded action research develops specialized skill and knowledge to enhance the ability to find common ground, and to get to a place where all points of view are relevant, valuable, and valid in an increasingly diverse society (Strauss & Corbin, 1990). For this reason, Linda and Gary selected this qualitative research paradigm to investigate and analyze any data Linda was going to collect and use. Her research would lead to information on teachers' perception of the school, their role in changing the climate, and their willingness to participate in strategies that might positively improve climate and morale.

The Action Research Plan

Steps in Linda's action research plan were as follows:

1. ***Investigate how teachers perceived their working relationship with each other and how they perceived their work environment.*** Linda did this by having teachers anonymously complete and return a questionnaire. Questionnaires were passed out during a faculty meeting to ensure a 100% rate of return.

2. ***Get the faculty to dialogue about their concerns during a faculty meeting.*** Teachers and staff were given ample time to openly discuss their views and concerns. They were then asked to identify the five most important issues that might affect student achievement. The list of issues was posted on large chart paper and hung in the faculty lounge for all to view and discuss until the next faculty meeting. In this open forum the faculty had listed 130 issues. The top issue listed was teacher turnover. A second prominent issue was the knowledge that the community didn't think they (the teachers and staff) were doing a good job. A third important issue was lack of support and collaboration among the teachers. With the information gathered at the faculty meeting, Gary and Linda created "Operation Gotcha," a program designed with the objective of improving campus climate and morale.

3. ***Use the collected data in planning an intervention strategy.*** Gary and Linda agreed that for the "Gotcha" program to be successful, faculty members needed to move from followers *needing direction* for implementation to followers *taking responsibility* for direction and implementation. The relationship of the leader and followers (the team) are the locus of the Hersey-Blanchard situational leadership model (Hersey & Blanchard, 1993). In this model (see Figure 1) the leader not only directs and controls but also receives feedback and communication from subordinates in this theoretical construct. This approach entails more listening, providing support, giving feedback, and communicating among participants. Gary and Linda used this model as a guide in working with the staff and faculty.

Figure 1 Hersey-Blanchard Situational Leadership Model

Supportive Behavior (A Lot ↑ Little)		
A Lot	**Participating/ Supporting S3** For people with high competence but variable commitment	**Selling/ Coaching S2** For people with some competence and some commitment
Little	**Delegating S4** For people with high competence and high commitment	**Telling/ Directing S1** For people with low competence and high commitment
	Little → A Lot	
	Directive Behavior	

Following are the appropriate leadership styles as defined by Paul Hersey and Kenneth Blanchard.

Telling/Directing (S1). Defined as a high-task/low-relationship behavior, telling involves leaders giving ample direction to subordinates. Decisions are made by the leaders. Leaders define the roles and tasks of the followers and supervise them closely.

Selling/Coaching (S2). Selling is considered a high-task/high-relationship behavior. It is also referred to as a "coaching" approach, as subordinates are given some direction by the leader but are also encouraged to "buy into" tasks. In the selling situation, members are generally willing but not necessarily able. Decisions are still made by the leader, but there is some explanation of decisions with subordinates. This is a great strategy for people who have some competence but lack commitment.

Participating/Supporting (S3). Participating is a high-relationship/low-task behavior, thus involving a greater deal of support and communication and less directing and controlling. Members in this situation are considered able but, for whatever reason, are unwilling. Decisions are made cooperatively between the leader and subordinates. For people who have competence but lack confidence and motivation, this strategy works best.

Delegating (S4). In a delegating situation, behavior is described as low-relationship/low-task. The leaders are still involved in the decisions and problem solving, but control is with the followers, who decide when and how the leader will be involved. For people who have both competence and commitment, this strategy works best. They are able and willing to work on a project themselves, with little supervision or support. Responsibility for decisions and responses is left with subordinates.

4. ***Implement the plan.*** Gary and Linda introduced the intervention plan for the "Gotcha" program to the faculty for further input prior to its implementation. The plan included celebrations during monthly faculty meetings to honor those teacher actions that earned a "Gotcha" (a paper ticket) from anyone on the faculty and staff. The Gotchas were awarded for positive verbal or physical acts of kindness and support to fellow workers. Once a month, all faculty and staff would place their Gotchas into a fishbowl for a drawing. Linda had arranged for the Gotchas to be exchangeable for gift certificates, books for professional development, or an extra planning period during the month. The program became so popular that grade-level teams solicited local businesses to donate free services and gift certificates. Even bus drivers and cafeteria workers were included in the plan. After the first month, everyone was handing out as many tickets as they could. The more tickets received, the more chances one had to earn a great prize at the monthly drawing.

5. ***Check the plan periodically and assess its impact at the end of the year.*** For the first four months Linda and Gary met with team leaders and with grade-level teams every two to three weeks to gain information about the effect of the Gotcha program. These meetings gave them information regarding how teachers and staff accepted the program as well as the opportunity to further assess teacher and staff buy-in of the program. Linda administered a modification of the Concerns Based Adoption Model (CBAM) by Gene Hall and Shirley Hord (2000). This particular model was used because it helps identify the stages of concern that subjects (teachers and staff) have with a new innovation—in this case, the Gotcha program. The following table is an example of what might be typical expressions of concern about the new innovation.

Stage of Concern	Expression of Concern
Refocusing	I have some ideas that might work even better.
Collaboration	I would like to know how I can relate what I am doing to what others are doing to improve campus climate and campus morale.
Consequence	I would like to know how my use of the Gotcha program is affecting learners as well as teacher retention. How can I refine this program so it has more impact?
Management	I spend much of my time passing out "Gotcha" slips to people and thinking of what I need to do to be more positive.
Personal	I don't know how passing out Gotcha slips will affect me.
Informational	I want to know more about the Gotcha program.
Awareness	I am not interested or concerned.

Through the use of the CBAM model survey, teachers and staff anonymously expressed their understanding as well as their acceptance of the Gotcha program. The assessment stages ranged from 0 (no buy-in and no knowledge of the program benefits) to 6 (complete buy-in and complete understanding of the Gotcha program, with a desire to further improve and refine its use in the future).

What Does a Positive Campus Climate Look Like?

After two years, the Gotcha project had evolved into the following campus model:

1. *Development of Teachers and Staff.* Monthly faculty meetings became monthly celebrations. Teachers celebrated the positive way they related to each other, and how often they worked together to achieve common goals.

2. *Development of Teacher Leadership.* Each grade level selected a teacher leader to facilitate their grade-level meetings and to represent them at monthly campus improvement meetings. Depending on the confidence and experience of the grade-level team, the principal (Gary) or assistant principal (Linda) would take on the role of director or supporter during team meetings. This approach was consistent with the Hersey-Blanchard theory of leadership model.

3. *Development of Teachers as Action Researchers.* Each grade level addressed issues as a team and planned strategies for how classroom or grade-level issues would be approached. Emphasis was on each teacher becoming a data-driven decision maker. Weekly grade-level meetings looked like this: (a) celebration of teacher accomplishments during the week, (b) celebration of academic benchmarks, (c) addressing issues on chart paper, (d) selecting the three most important issues to be addressed that month, (e) developing an action research plan for tackling the issues, (f) reviewing the data, (g) designing and implementing an action plan for change, (h) reviewing the plan by the next grade-level meeting, and (i) adjusting the plan. Develop, implement, review, and adjust was the action research plan for each grade level.

In the following two years, the Gotcha program served as a first-of-the-year kickoff for the campus. Gotcha tickets were used as a way of reinforcing collaboration among teachers, staff, and administrators. The program was also used to help novice and veteran teachers get acquainted. Linda became the official assistant principal of the school, and Gary stayed on as its principal. Teacher turnover and student achievement were still major issues at MLK, but improvement was taking place. Linda and Gary both agreed that they needed more time for the innovation to work. Both agreed that change takes more then one school year and that leadership theory does help address the challenges teachers and administrators face in addressing school issues. Utilizing research strategies for addressing real-life issues in school settings became an essential administrative tool for both administrators and teachers at MLK. The mentor relationship between Gary (the principal) and Linda (the teacher and administrator-in-training) helped both of them to accomplish their goals. Even though the mentor aspect isn't addressed in this case study, it played a key part in Linda's professional development. Knowing that her principal supported her in her efforts to initiate improvement was a huge part in the success of her project.

Issues for Further Reflection

Perhaps this type of case study was not what some would expect for a chapter on research. However, it is actually a reminder of the versatility of action research. Action research studies can be designed by a single administrator or teacher, a department, or an entire school, and such studies can be quantitative or qualitative.

Helping Teachers Find Time for Research

If today's teachers were asked why they do not conduct research, many would quickly say they are too busy—they haven't the time to conduct research. Indeed, when a cohort of teachers was asked this question, 100% gave this reason (Bingham et al., 2006). Although it may sound like an excuse, a look at the schedules of some contemporary teachers definitely gives the claim some credibility. Education reform has exacerbated this problem, with teachers' schedules being too heavy to permit them time to engage in much, if any, research.

Teacher-researchers need time for conducting research and time for questioning, discussing, and pondering. The problem of already overcrowded schedules that so accurately characterizes contemporary teaching has already been addressed as a major deterrent that dissuades teachers from conducting research. Supervisors can help. A good place to begin is by guiding teachers to select problems to study that do not demand excessive time. Once a problem is identified, many teachers need help organizing the work. Without good organization skills much time can be wasted, an even greater problem when collaboration is involved. The supervisor can help by seeing that each team member's specific role is clearly delineated.

In chapter 1 we discussed ways in which collaborative planning could be accomplished, despite teachers' crowded calendars and busy schedules. Much like the process involving distance learning, asynchronous communication makes it possible for teachers to collaborate at their own convenience rather than at the same time. Discussion boards, blogs, e-mail, listservs, shared electronic calendars and other technological tools (see the AirSet example on p. 15) can help to make collaborative research a much less time-intensive process.

Focusing on Learning

When encouraging teachers to become involved with research, supervisors should keep in mind that the main incentive that lures teachers to research is different than the attraction that pulls professors toward research. Although there are many reasons that professors conduct research, the most common reason is to get published—a requirement for promotion, tenure, and merit pay. In contrast, teachers conduct research to discover practices that will improve their teaching. While it's true that teachers' roles in curriculum planning are now extending beyond their classroom walls, and hopefully teachers will be involved in schoolwide and districtwide research, there is motivational value in limiting teachers' first research project to their own classrooms. It is not enough that classrooms be researched; they need to be researched *by teachers*.

Setting the Stage

By far, the most practical and effective approach to motivating and helping teachers use research is to make it a seamless part of each teacher's professional life. Perhaps the fastest and easiest access to a life of research is through the professional journals. A prerequisite to helping teachers find time for research is to make research an important part of the school ethos; and the first step in doing so is to ensure that teachers see other teachers reading a certain type of professional literature. Place journals so that teachers will come into contact with them on a daily basis. Schools that do not do so unwittingly support a hidden curriculum with the message that research is "unimportant here in the real world, where our business is to deal with practical issues."

The teachers' lounge is an excellent area to house a few practical journals that address pedagogy. Department chairs may wish to have at least one content journal displayed in the immediate area. After teachers become accustomed to reading practical journals, eventually more research-based journals can be added. But in the meantime, the principal and department chairs should find time in meeting agendas to develop the idea that research occurs on many levels, including reading professional articles, and that involvement at all levels is important. By making journals easily accessible, a time-saving strategy is already underway. From here, teachers will need help in creating a personal research program, an expedient data retrieval system, and a personal research library.

Creating a Personal Research Program

Combat your teachers' perception that becoming a researcher is yet another role that they are being told they must adopt and fit into their busy schedules. The key is in helping them to perceive research as something that they do *for themselves*. Because this means that research must serve each teacher's goals, each teacher needs a personal research program. Once teachers have discovered that they can make time for research, supervisors can assist them in creating a personal program. Following are some time-saving tips that supervisors can share with teachers who are conducting research. Steps to make this process successful include developing an expedient system for cataloging data and creating a personal research library.

The good news is that the process of developing a personal program is easy and fast. Begin by providing each teacher with an inexpensive 8 ½ × 11-inch ring binder to use as a research journal. Label the spine *Research,* and include a dozen sheets of lined paper. The remainder of the research binder can be used to store intriguing articles from current journals or newspapers, but be highly selective because clutter can slow things down.

When perusing journals, teachers should look for two things: data and quotable quotes. Data in the form of percentages are powerful. For example, one teacher who read an article in *The Physics Teacher* noticed that over 85% of all U.S. high school physics classes are being taught by teachers who are teaching out of field. Realizing that fewer than 15% of physics classes are being taught by qualified teachers, the teacher used this statistic to write a grant pro-

It Works for Me!

Using Authentic Data

Greg Gibbs, St. Bonaventure University

In our educational leadership classes, project work and case studies are a big part of the curriculum. Rather than inventing data to create a case study, collaborate with local districts and work on real data and real problems. Students in educational leadership classes do not always have real data available for their projects. Help them out by contacting local districts and using their data for such projects as developing school improvement plans, budget scenarios, and instructional improvement. We have seen this process serve the local districts as well as the students' needs, with a much greater focus on reality.

Through this process, our classes often help districts find answers to nagging problems. Solutions often can be elusive to those close to the problem, and our students have a level of objectivity that can be a real plus. They can see the impact their work has on local education while developing their own leadership skills.

posal that funded several summer physics institutes for teachers who regularly taught physics but were uncertified to teach it, enabling them to complete their physics degrees.

Quotable quotes can be almost as powerful as percentages. A quotable quote is a brief statement that clearly communicates an important message. For example, a teacher read in the local newspaper that an adjacent congressional district had the highest high school dropout rate in the country. The teacher was so shocked by the statement that he used it to write an article for a national journal, and later a grant that funded a successful partnership program between that school district and a local university. The program enabled graduates of the local high school who pursued college degrees to return each year to encourage students to stay in school and go to college. These research binders can serve as a key tool for teachers to use in writing grant proposals (see chapter 15).

Cataloging Data. Data and other potentially valuable information are worthless unless they are readily accessible. To ensure the accessibility of their research information, ask your faculty to turn to those lined pages in the front of their research binders. On each page, ask them to draw a line one-third of the way down, and a second line two-thirds of the way down the page, separating the page into three equal parts. For a topic on which teachers wish to gather more understanding, they should take their binders to the reference section of the library. Using a reference catalog such as the *Education Index* (or using the computer), teachers can locate some articles whose titles suggest they will be enlightening about this topic. Using the American Psychological Association (APA) reference system, teachers can enter the information for each article in one of the sections on the lined pages. (APA was chosen because most education journals use this reference system.) For a simplified example, see Figure 13.2.

Figure 13.2 Cataloging Data

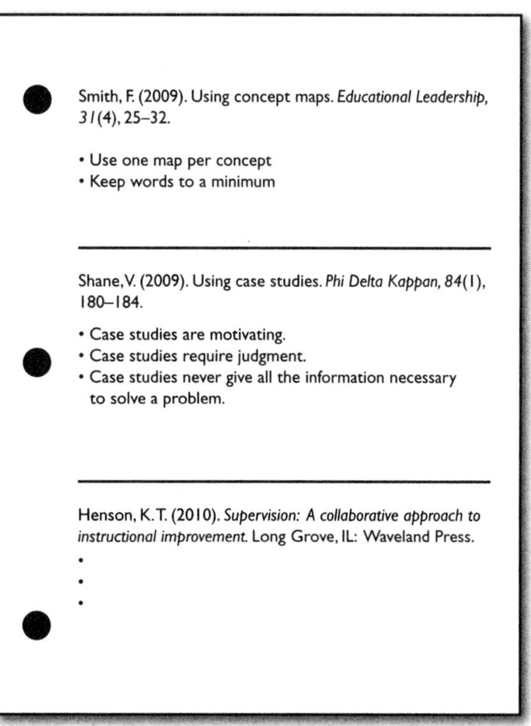
Smith, F. (2009). Using concept maps. *Educational Leadership, 31*(4), 25–32.

- Use one map per concept
- Keep words to a minimum

Shane, V. (2009). Using case studies. *Phi Delta Kappan, 84*(1), 180–184.

- Case studies are motivating.
- Case studies require judgment.
- Case studies never give all the information necessary to solve a problem.

Henson, K. T. (2010). *Supervision: A collaborative approach to instructional improvement.* Long Grove, IL: Waveland Press.

-
-
-

With a few of these entries recorded, and the research binder and a stack of Post-it notes handy, teachers can retrieve the journals containing the articles they select and open each journal to one of the articles. Using a Post-it, they should flag the first page of each article. Be aware that this is where many people waste the most time! Tell your teachers not to attempt to read all of the articles. Rather, they should peruse each, noting importance percentages, data, and quotable quotes. Call your teachers' attention to the fact that their binders have room for recording at least four or five entries from each article. Obviously, some of the articles won't contain any information that they consider important enough to record, but other articles may provide several entries. The net results will be that having spent no more than an hour or two in the library, they will have collected a good amount of rich data and quotes that they can use to launch their own research study or write an article synthesizing data from these journals.

This system is so simple and effective that it can be used equally well by a lone researcher or by a team of researchers. In fact, a middle-level or high school department or an elementary grade-level faculty can use this system to investigate any topic that draws their interest.

Creating and Using a Personalized Research Library. The system just described is a streamlined method for collecting a wealth of research and other important information in a very short time. The next step is to use these data and any resources that teachers have available in their classrooms (or at home) to write a professional article or grant proposal. The supervisor can reassure teachers that this is an easy and enjoyable process: All that is required to accomplish this quickly is to establish a personalized research library and learn how to use it efficiently. All your teachers need is an inexpensive set of bookshelves.

Teachers can start by collecting all the recent journals they can find. They can begin with any periodical journals that they receive at regular intervals. They might also ask a local college librarian to give them any education journals that it discards each year. Because of space, many libraries destroy their periodicals after having shelved them for only a few months! Your teachers may actually be providing them a service by taking these journals.

Next, each time they receive a journal, teachers should take a few minutes to peruse its table of contents for topics they may wish to research. Using Post-its, they should write one word on the note and form an index on the journal. When shelving a new journal, it should be shelved with the spine inward, leaving the Post-it note side exposed, with the most recent journal in front. This provides ready access to the latest articles on the topics that are of most interest.

When a teacher is ready to write an article or grant, or to initiate an individual research study, he or she can pull from the shelves only those issues with one or more articles on the chosen topic. This enables teachers to bypass about 95% of all the articles in their library and saves them all the time that would have been needed to sift through all the journals before beginning to write.

Advise your teachers to assemble all the quotes they have accumulated on a given topic so that they tell a short story. Now, keeping these quotes in this order, they should write a paragraph or two about each quote. The results will be an interesting, well-organized article or the foundation for a good research project or grant proposal.

Using Qualitative Research

The field of education has traditionally used empirical research studies, because most research conducted by educators is steeped in rigor (e.g., careful selection of research design, careful selection of the population and sample, and careful selection of statistics for the study). Because at many institutions in-depth study of research methodology occurs mainly at the doctoral level, many teachers find the term *research* a little foreign, a little intimidating. Also, because empirical, quantitative research studies usually deal with large numbers of subjects located throughout the country, these studies seem more than a little inappropriate to a teacher who usually works with no more than 30 or 40 students at a time.

Teachers who find quantitative research either threatening or inappropriate may wish to consider using an entirely different type of research. *Qualitative research* was introduced in chapter 12, in the form of observation instruments. If teachers have become comfortable using such observation instruments and realize that they are a form of qualitative research, they will be much less intimidated by the concept. This type of research uses an inductive approach and therefore is a little less exacting than the quantitative approach. Unlike quantitative researchers, who emphasize the need to be exact, qualitative researchers' main priority is to gather broad information about a particular problem. Box 13.2 contrasts the characteristics of qualitative and quantitative researchers.

As you can see, quantitative research is based on the belief that science involves making hypotheses and theories and then testing them. Throughout the first part of a study, the deductive method is used. Indeed, the most common (and, for many, an insurmountable) challenge to the quantitative researcher is the task of narrowing down the topic and project size to render the project manageable. The last part of quantitative studies involves inductive thinking: To render the findings useful the researcher must be able to generalize them to a larger audience.

Box 13.2 Quantitative vs. Qualitative Researchers

Quantitative Researchers	Qualitative Researchers
• Use a prescribed research process for gathering data	• Use a relaxed, informal process for gathering data
• Use statistics to record data exactly	• Use general dialogue, as in stories or journals, to record data
• Make hypotheses and then gather data	• Begin gathering data before making a hypothesis
• The researcher purposefully remains detached from the study	• The researcher often becomes part of the study

In contrast, qualitative researchers enter the field and begin collecting data before making hypotheses. A stark difference in qualitative and quantitative research studies is in the way they are written up. While quantitative research is reported in a very rigid sequence of prescribed steps set down by Sir Francis Bacon in the sixteenth century, qualitative researchers report their studies in a narrative style. To be rigorous, qualitative research must have credibility, transferability, confirmability, and authenticity (Applequest, 2007; Krathwohl, 2009). The report often reads almost like a journal or a piece of fiction—an easy, comfortable, and enjoyable style enabling the readers to feel almost as if they are part of the study. Although rejected by educators for decades, qualitative research is beginning to receive some respect, and it may serve practitioners better than quantitative research (Davis, 2007).

Tips for Facilitating Teacher Research

In addition to the observation instruments discussed in chapter 12, there are many ways for teachers to practice qualitative research, both inside and outside their classrooms. Some qualitative research techniques that supervisors can share with their faculty include journal keeping, storytelling, ethnography, and case study (for an in-depth discussion of the case-study method, see chapter 14.

Keeping Journals. We have established that an important product of involvement with research is the reflection that occurs as a natural consequence. Teachers who conduct research reflect more on their practices, causing them to seek out their reason(s) for using each practice. This reflection can be enhanced by using a journal to record each experience. In the absence of an ongoing record, teachers who are not involved in research accumulate practices without reason.

Preventing mindless accumulation of teaching practices is just one advantage of teachers keeping journals. Another is the feedback that journals can provide on the progress teachers make, especially when they work on action research projects over a period of time. We need a human-resource system to ensure that developing teachers work on a sustained problem rather than isolated problems (Rallis et al., 2006). We need a way to record and measure this continuous growth, and teacher-researchers need to feel gratified, to have some way to have their progress recognized. Often progress occurs slowly, and by keeping their own daily or weekly journal they can see the gradual pattern of growth and can profit by further reflection on their work, as they mature as professionals.

Storytelling. Telling stories is natural in all professions, mostly as a form of entertainment. Often, however, it serves a deeper purpose. When our country was being settled, storytelling was a national pastime. The types of stories told and written during this early period of our history partially reveal their function. Such stories not only served to entertain, but also to take the spellbound audiences' attention off the harsh realities of their often difficult and tragic lives. For example, out of the northern Midwest came the story about Paul Bunyon, the mighty lumberjack and his companion, Babe, a blue ox that was so big his footsteps formed the Great Lakes. Further west, Pecos Bill was known for his ability to lasso a tornado. Like these great exaggerations, ghost stories also served an escapist function.

Similarly, teachers' stories about their classrooms serve a purpose beyond entertainment. Storytelling plays an important part in fostering collaboration among teachers. The stories they share about their classroom experiences provide opportunities for reflective dialogue. It is primary through story, one student at a time, that teachers organize their thinking and tap into the collective, accumulated wisdom of their profession.

This use of storytelling as a vehicle for reflection requires looking beyond the facts in the story. A good story stirs the imagination, invites multiple and varied interpretations, and provokes the listener to question: What did that mean? Why did it happen this way? What might have happened if . . .? Like any art, both storytelling and story listening (interpretation) require the skill and the ability to interpret and vicariously experience the event. Teachers use stories to make sense out of their experiences. By writing them down, purposefully and systematically reflecting on them, and sharing them with others, teachers can improve their understanding of current experiences.

A good story has ethnographic value in that it provides seemingly insignificant details which, collectively, enable the reader or listener to better understand the culture. Stories can be related to the readers' or listeners' own circumstances, enabling them to better understand their own circumstances and cultures. Understanding their school's culture is vital for your teachers, and storytelling can contribute greatly to that understanding.

Establishing a Research Culture

Ethos refers to the shared attitudes, beliefs, and values of a community. It is the spirit of a group of people. Unfortunately, the ethos of many schools does not support the conducting of research.

The school's culture can be a powerful force. You'll recall that we first discuss school culture in chapter 4, in relation to staff development. *Culture* is an invisible framework of standards representing beliefs and values that are perceived as having worked well in the past. While some view it simply as "the way we do things around here," culture has tremendous power over individuals. Even the idea of a school having an ethos—of being distinct from other schools—is powerful. Although at some schools teachers tend to view research as too theoretical and abstract for their "real" world, participation in research actually has the ability to cross cultural boundaries.

Regrettably, the culture and ethos at many schools can make teachers ashamed of their involvement with research; and teachers who do conduct research studies may almost feel a need to apologize for being involved in a behavior that runs outside or perhaps even counter to the established school norm or culture. As a result, at a time when many universities are stressing teaching and are de-emphasizing research, teachers or supervisors are not likely to get much support for research from higher-education institutions.

At schools where research is viewed as a less-than-positive feature, the supervisor can help to alter the school's research image. Effective schools research has found that lasting, positive changes at schools require the support of the administration. Testifying to the importance of leadership of the local school administration, Bell (1993, p. 597) said, "It is futile to even try to improve a school if the leadership is lackluster." The principal can reshape a negative image by periodically giving status reports to the faculty, showing research progress, and by expecting and accepting mistakes along the way. According to Glickman (2006, p. 690), "The answer may lie in learning from one another, looking at research, and sharing our successes and failures, so we can learn to move more directly toward success." Faculty newsletters and faculty meetings can be used to achieve this goal.

The supervisor may consider creating a Research Reporting Form, such as the one shown in Box 13.3, to give to the principal and request that it be distributed monthly to department chairs so that faculty members can report their research progress on a regular basis. The supervisor may also wish to

Box 13.3 Research Reporting Form

Name: ______________________________

During the month of __________, 20___, my role in research has included:

Writing an article. Article title: ______________________________

Will this article be, or has it been, submitted for publication? If so, name of journal(s), newsletter(s) or periodical(s): ______________________________

____

Completing a grant proposal. Coauthors' names include:

____

____

Title of proposal: ______________________________

Amount of funds requested: ______________________________

Submitting a proposal. Coauthors' names include:

____

____

Title of proposal: ______________________________

Name and address of potential funding agent to which this proposal was submitted:

____

Submitted by: ______________________________

Date: ______________________________

contact some national or state professional association's executive offices to learn of annual research awards and then nominate faculty members as candidates for these awards. Should a faculty member or a team win a research award, this would create an opportunity to give recognition to the researchers and send a positive general message about the importance of research to the local school district.

Kim Marshall (2005) suggests that supervisors use *rubrics* to create a culture around learning, "a culture in which nondefensive analysis of student learning is 'the way we do things around here'" (p. 734). Closed quantitative evaluations can lead to superficial accolades that paint an unearned superteacher environment where all teachers get high marks, or they can lead to low scores that may damage teachers without suggesting ways to improve. Both oral and written dialogue can have these undesirable results, unless the dialogue is accompanied by rubrics. Rubrics pinpoint specific reasons for good or poor evaluations by giving descriptions of behaviors that exemplify the level (usually from 1 to 4) that the teacher receives.

A Collaborative Model for Involving Teachers with Action Research

Research offers teachers a way to empower themselves. By getting involved in research, teachers can move from a reactive mode to a proactive mode. Proactive teachers are not satisfied to let their environment totally determine their behavior. While the environment is shaping some of their behavior, proactive teachers are also reshaping their environment.

As shown in Figure 13.3 (on the following page), proactive decision-making teachers are unwilling to sit back and react all the time. Instead, they take charge of their world and, indeed, help shape and determine what their classrooms and schools will become. Proactive teachers make concentrated efforts to anticipate problems. This requires the ability to live partially in the future. A calendar can be used to help foresee future problems if the calendar is previewed regularly. In the absence of a formally issued school calendar, proactive teachers create their own calendar of events.

Staying current in their teaching fields and in pedagogy is another essential part of being a proactive teacher. This feat is usually accomplished by attending professional meetings and reading professional books and journals. Teachers can benefit from both research and nonresearch-type journals, especially those that feature abstracts. Because teachers' schedules are so crowded, and because today's teachers have access to so many journals through the Internet, attempting to keep up with them can be daunting. Encouraging teachers to select journals that have abstracts is one time-saving solution (Miech et al., 2005).

Proactive teachers use their mission statements and state and national standards to solve existing problems and to prevent new problems from developing. When they think they have identified potential oncoming problems, they check their standards to determine whether the potential problem is unrelated

Figure 13.3 A Proactive Decision-Making Model

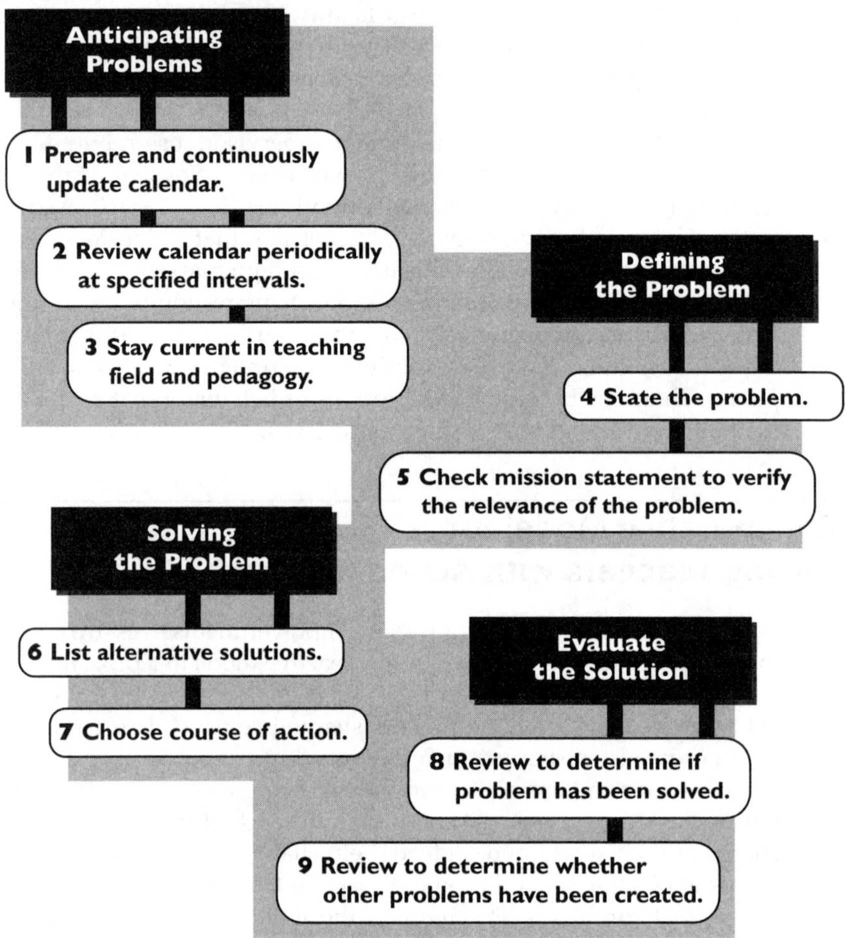

to the school's mission and to the standards. If so, there may be no "real" problem that is significant enough to merit further attention.

Proactive problem-solving teachers list possible solutions to each problem, a process that gives them alternatives or choices in ways of handling the problem. The next step is equally important: Proactive teachers must be decisive and unafraid to act. Once the choice is made or the solution applied, these teachers evaluate the results to determine whether the problem has truly been solved and whether the process has uncovered further problems.

Schools that are located near colleges or universities have opportunities to plan cooperative partnerships (see chapters 1 and 4) with these institutions. Collaborative partnership programs that use action research to learn more about the disciplines and teaching are rewarding to all parties, including junior- to senior-level teachers. Since 2005, the Association of Teacher Educators has conducted academies to pursue the design of better partnerships aimed at helping teachers learn their role as researchers. Reporting on the work of the first academy, Ed Pultorak and his colleagues (2006) offer some practical advice that supervisors can use to initiate and sustain a cooperative action research program that emphasizes the role of teacher as researcher. They caution against building a partnership program around just one or two individuals. Should these individuals move, get promoted, or take different job assignments, the program would likely die. Supervisors can prevent such a situation by encouraging interested parties to adopt a theme for which all members share a passion. The theme can be based on one or more disciplines, on a part of the school's mission that these teachers embrace, or it can cover several related standards that the school must find ways to meet.

Pultorak and colleagues (2006) stress a concern expressed earlier in this book: protecting the status of the participants. All partners, including novice teachers, must have equal status. You can help by making sure that the playing field is level for all members. For example, if the professors can hold meetings during the workday, you might work with the principal to obtain this privilege for the teachers. The professors will have complete freedom to pursue scientific inquiry into the group goals, yet the teachers probably will have to balance their time between working to attain these goals and a different set of goals set by the standards and test makers. You may be able to help your teachers align these two sets of goals.

It's also important to be sensitive to the difference in the two parties' reward systems. Try to help the principal find a way to reward the partnership teachers for their successes as they pursue this mission. Special recognition can improve self-concepts and serve as an incentive for further research.

A Technology Research Project

Collaborative learning requires teacher involvement in research with an eye on the state standards, including those that deal with technology. Since 2005, NCLB has required the U.S. Department of Education to develop, update, and publish a national long-range technology plan. Encourage your teachers to become familiar with these national technology objectives and your own state's technology plan by directing them to the National Educational Technology Plan (NETP) Web site (http://www.nationaledtechplan.org), where they can download the plan in its entirety. Here, too, they can read the success stories of several states and districts.

Teacher-Researchers: A Model for the Future

When examining the effects that involvement in research has on teachers, it becomes apparent that participation in action research produces teachers who will be successful in their twenty-first-century classrooms. The world is becoming more complex, more information rich, and more demanding of fresh thinking (Martinez, 2006). In many ways, the new world will reflect the paradoxical qualities that Charles Dickens so vividly described in *A Tale of Two Cities:*

> It was the best of times, it was the worst of times, it was the age of wisdom, it was the age of foolishness, it was the epoch of incredulity, it was the season of light, it was the season of darkness, it was the spring of hope, it was the winter of despair, we had everything before us, we had nothing before us, we were all going direct to Heaven, we were all going the other way.

Like the rapidly changing world of the French Revolution, the new world of education reform will challenge teachers with paradoxes. It will demand teachers who are self-confident but aren't afraid to reflect on their teaching and question their own methods, teachers who are ready to change when a change is needed, teachers who have become experts yet are dedicated to lifelong learning.

Conclusion

All states are responding to the demands of the No Child Left Behind legislation and in doing so are making demands that will require teachers to become lifelong researchers—to become skilled in action research techniques and dedicated to conducting research, and to become risk takers—not because they are careless or foolhardy but because they know that this is the only way they can be educational leaders.

By conducting research, teachers accrue many benefits. They solve problems that they face daily. They empower themselves to be leaders by establishing knowledge bases in pedagogy and in their content fields, and they continually add to these bases. In addition to being better informed, teachers who conduct research become more analytical and reflective of their own behavior, becoming more flexible and less defensive (Bingham et al., 2006). Involvement with research helps teachers become change agents or catalysts for change throughout their schools.

Through collaboration with others as equal partners in research, teacher-researchers will learn to ask questions and base decisions on sound data. Their involvement in research will be a prerequisite to the development of the attitudes needed to successfully restructure twenty-first-century schools.

The ethos or climate in many schools dissuades teachers from conducting research. Supervisors can help their schools make the transition into the new century by sharing with their teachers the advantages that accrue when they become involved with research addressing particular problems experienced by the teachers in their classrooms.

Questions for Discussion and Reflection

1. Why should teachers be encouraged to conduct research?
2. How do proactive teachers use standards?
3. What is asynchronous communication, and how can it give teachers more time for research?
4. How can supervisors create research-friendly cultures?

5. Why do teachers find qualitative research less threatening than quantitative (empirical) research?
6. Examine teachers' reasons for shunning research. How would you respond to each of these reasons?

SUGGESTED ACTIVITIES

1. Through a local school principal, contact a teacher who is a competent researcher. Ask this teacher for help in designing a study to address a current concern in the teacher's school.
2. Start a journal. Reflect on the successful strategies you have used to help teachers become involved with research. Near the end of this course, ask your professor if you may share this journal with your classmates.
3. As a supervisor, you should model the directions you recommend for your teachers. For a seven-day week, record all your activities and list the amount of time spent in each. Block all of your uncommitted time. Next, choose a daily time that you can designate for conducting research.
4. Use the information from this chapter on the benefits of research to teachers to help a school faculty improve its general attitude toward research.
5. Working with a local principal, help a teacher to improve learning in the classroom. Hold a meeting with several innovative teachers, and ask them to share ideas for improving the school's research culture.

Chapter 14

Helping Teachers Use Theories and Models

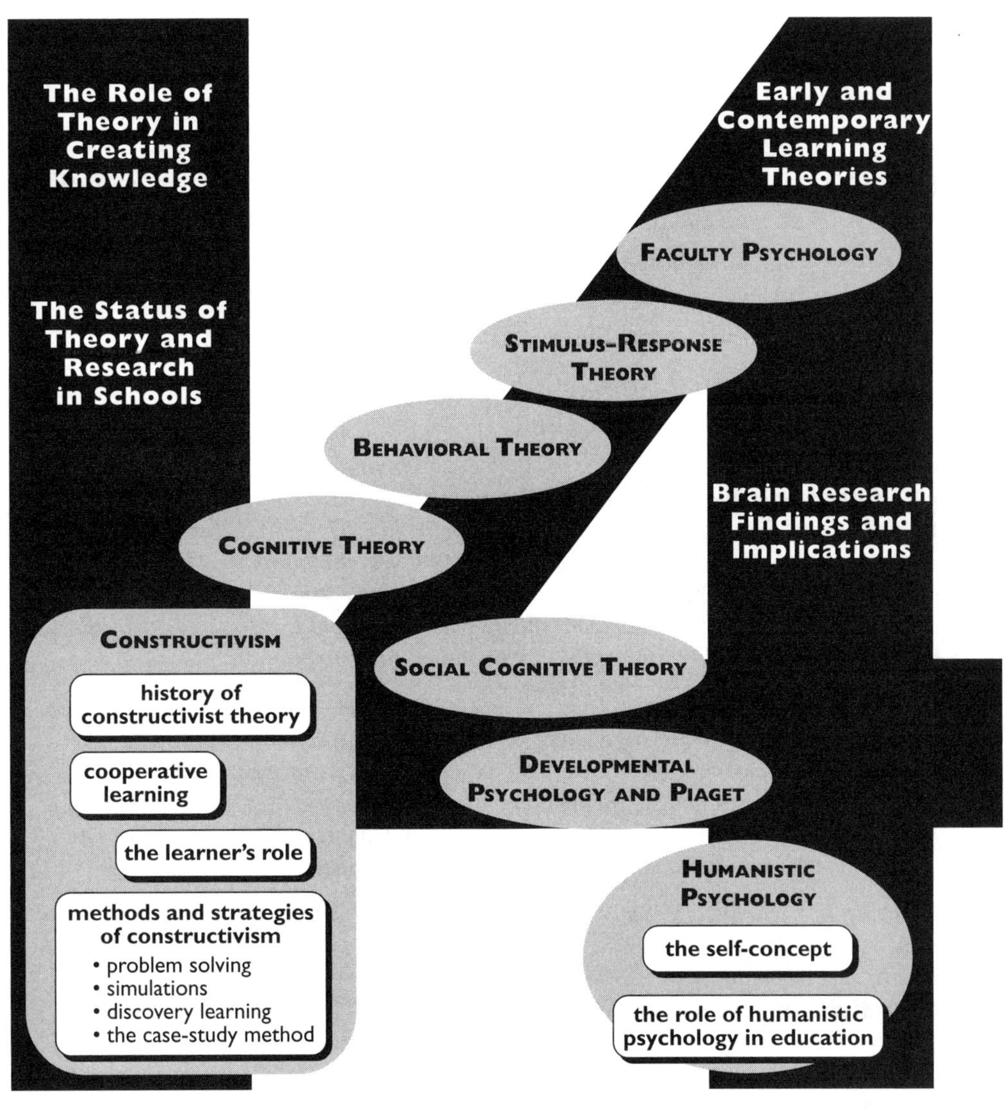

The Role of Theory in Creating Knowledge
The Status of Theory and Research in Schools
Early and Contemporary Learning Theories
Faculty Psychology
Stimulus-Response Theory
Behavioral Theory
Cognitive Theory
Brain Research Findings and Implications
Constructivism
history of constructivist theory
cooperative learning
the learner's role
methods and strategies of constructivism
• problem solving
• simulations
• discovery learning
• the case-study method
Social Cognitive Theory
Developmental Psychology and Piaget
Humanistic Psychology
the self-concept
the role of humanistic psychology in education

To make sense, theory needs context.

—J. Pacha & L. Curry, "The p–12 educational administration best practices improvement spiral models"

Objectives

After completion of this chapter, you should be able to

1. Understand the role that concepts play in learning
2. Help teachers promote the understanding of the major concepts in their disciplines
3. Convince teachers to use theory to improve learning in their classes
4. Help teachers use constructivism to improve their teaching

Fred Kramer's Learning Theories

By the time Fred Kramer received his first principalship, he had studied several theories of learning, including faculty psychology, stimulus-response theory, behaviorism, Gestaltism, and developmental theory. In the last required course in his master's degree leadership program, which he is taking through a distance-learning compressed two-way video program during his first year on the job, Fred is studying only constructivism. Prior to this semester, Fred was a self-proclaimed eclectic educator who believed that all educators should embrace several theories and adopt the best of each. But in this final class, his professor admonished all students to use exclusively the constructivist approach to learning.

Fred appreciated the convincing studies that support constructivism, yet he also saw features in other theories that he believed to be accurate and which he considered good practice. He wondered how he should approach his own teachers regarding the use of theories in their classrooms. Should he encourage individual teachers to use the theories they considered best, or should he endorse the use of constructivism by all teachers?

Believing in participatory leadership, Fred ultimately decided to design a development program to educate these teachers about all *these theories and then permit the faculty as a whole to choose between letting each teacher make an individual selection and selecting one theory which all could use.*

Reflection

Although Fred Kramer may appear to be taking the easy way out, his decision to let the faculty choose reflects a level of understanding that is necessary for administra-

tors who are thinking about building a learning community. Fred has reflected on his previous knowledge about theories. What learning theories are you familiar with? Which theories do you think offer promise for improving classroom learning? What are the features about each of these theories that you would encourage teachers to use? As you read about the various theories discussed in this chapter, consider the research that supports each theory and any research that refutes it, and continue to explore ways to familiarize teachers with these theories and help them apply the ones that will work best, both in their individual classrooms and throughout the school.

Introduction

> Interstate new Teacher Assessment and Support Consortium (INTASC) Principle No. 9 views the teacher as a reflective practitioner who constantly evaluates the results of his or her behavior.

Teachers can use theories and models to improve their practice. This chapter discusses the role and status of theory in elementary and secondary schools. Several theories are reviewed, with special emphasis given to the constructivist theory that undergirds this text. Supervisors need to know how various theories can be used to enhance learning in the classroom, and they should encourage their faculty to take an eclectic approach and borrow from a combination of theories to improve classroom learning. "Teachers often focus instruction on the formulas and processes needed to solve different types of problems but neglect to teach the concepts on which these tools are based" (Marshall, 2006, p. 356).

In many classrooms throughout the country students are sitting passively, completely unaware of the events designed to stimulate learning. Other students are involved in activities designed to cause learning to happen, activities such as completing photocopied handouts and laboratory assignments. Yet, when questioned, many of these students don't know *why* they are involved in these exercises. They don't even wonder about any connection between the daily activities and the objectives of the day's lessons. Nor do they see a connection between the way they spend their class time and the structures of the disciplines they are studying.

Other more serious-minded students memorize isolated facts. These students will exit school with nothing more than diplomas and a head full of disconnected facts. They may know that amoeba and paramecia are microscopic, one-celled animals. They may even know their modes of reproduction and their modes of transportation, but they will never know or wonder *why* they have studied these subjects. Most will never wonder how the majority of topics they have studied relate to their own lives—if, in fact, they do relate at all.

If asked, most American students could not identify the major concepts they are studying, nor could they develop models or theories to express the concepts and conceptual themes that permeate their curricula. There are many reasons why today's students are so unaware. It all begins with teachers' attitudes.

Many teachers set their targets too low, merely striving for a quiet classroom where students are busy (Bartholomew, 2007). In such classrooms students are unaware of any connections between the content they are studying and their daily activities, because they were not involved in the development of their curricula or the selection of those activities. Instead, those who are serious are busy memorizing knowledge that belongs to others.

The difference in these traditional patterns of education and the goals for today's schools is *depth of understanding*. For example, suppose students learn that the Magna Carta was signed in the year 1215. This is good information; it lets all students know that the document wasn't signed last week. However, it would be more meaningful if students knew of other thirteenth-century events that would give them a contextual frame of reference. But even then, the worth of this information is of little consequence unless these students understand that this document was the forerunner of our own democratic way of life.

The goal of today's learning is that all subjects must have this level of depth, this higher-order level of thinking. From here, students can extend their understanding by holding discussions with the teacher and with each other. Michael Martinez (2006) says that collaborative forms of learning are recognized as having great potential to benefit students: "It is probably because of a vaguely realized sense that the capacity of higher-order thought is often cultivated by first engaging in a social setting, just as Vygotsky claimed" (p. 698). Theory can and must play an important role in extending the depth of students' knowledge and in developing an awareness of their current levels of understanding.

The Role of Theory in Creating Knowledge

This chapter endeavors to assist instructional supervisors in helping teachers lead their students in deeper thinking by using theories to generate knowledge. It is designed to help supervisors acquaint teachers with the role that concepts, models, and theories should play in all classrooms in schools throughout the country.

In chapter 3 the word *concept* was defined as a content generalization, which means that it is an idea having implications that go beyond the immediate events. Concepts can take the form of sentences, such as "to forgive is divine" and "cleanliness is next to Godliness"; or they can be words or things such as studying, triangle, vacuum cleaner, honesty, or H_2O. Concepts can be hooked together to form theories, increasing their generalizability and meaning. Some sample theories are listed below.

- Hard work can lead to success.
- Ignorance produces prejudice.
- Practice makes perfect.
- Freedom is a state of mind.

- No country or individual can be ignorant and free.
- Heat causes objects to expand.
- Smoking causes cancer.
- Moving objects follow a straight path unless acted on by an outside force.
- Speed kills.

It Works for Me!

Using Exit Cards to Teach Concepts

JoAnn Susko, Rider University

The use of *exit cards* is an excellent strategy for teachers to consider as a part of their regular instructional practice. Exit cards are normally used at the end of a lesson to assess whether the students have grasped the concepts presented during the lesson, can apply the newly learned concepts to a problem situation, and provide additional feedback regarding the concepts introduced and discussed. Therefore, exit cards usually involve having the students respond to the following questions:

1. What have you learned today?
2. What questions do you still have about what we have discussed? Is there anything that you still don't understand?
3. Can you think of any ways in which you can apply what you have learned today to real-life situations?

The use of exit cards satisfies the need for closure at the end of a lesson and is reflective of effective teaching.

Theories are statements that tie together related concepts. According to Kerlinger (1973, p. 9), "A theory is a set of interrelated constructs (concepts), definitions, and propositions that present a systematic view of phenomena by specifying relations among variables, with the purpose of explaining and predicting the phenomena." Initially, this definition may just sound like a bunch of words with obscure meanings. But on closer look, we see words like *systematic* and *interrelated*. By identifying relationships, theories help both scientists and practitioners understand why things behave as they do, enabling them to predict future behavior. Teachers—not just science teachers and mathematics teachers, but *all* teachers—can use theories to help students understand the content of their studies and make predictions about topics they are studying.

Theories, like knowledge, are never absolute. Sometimes relationships are so complex, so abstract, or so large (or small) that students need help to fully comprehend them. *Models* are used to help us understand the realities they represent. The purposes of a model are to help us organize what we already know, to help us see new relationships, and to keep us from being dazzled by the full-blown complexity of the subject. A model is not intended to be a picture of reality, but rather a tool for thinking.

Philosopher Immanuel Kant (1793/2006) explained the significance of theory: "No man claiming to be practically versed in a science can disdain its theory without exposing himself as an ignoramus in his field." Littky and Grabelle (2004) say that all significant improvements require a model. Successful application of a new model has two requirements. First, the model itself must be understood. Then, it must always be adapted to the local site (Davis, 2007).

The Status of Theory and Research in Schools

In the past, as with practitioners in any discipline, many teachers have held the same disdain for theory as they have for research. For example, some can be heard saying, "It may work in theory, but out here in the real world where I work, that's another thing." Other common comments evidence an opinion that theory and practice are opposites: "Theory may be useful up in the ivory towers, but I know what works down here in the trenches."

Some people tend to separate both research and theory from common sense, choosing the latter on the basis that it is more practical. For example, for decades teachers have used corporal punishment because common sense told them that corporal punishment works. Now, during the twenty-first century, most teachers doubt this "commonsense" conclusion; at best, corporal punishment may only postpone misbehavior because it addresses only the *symptom* of an underlying problem.

When properly understood, theory helps the scientist or practitioner to avoid common mistakes. For example, when common sense is in charge, laypeople unwittingly choose incidents that support their beliefs. In contrast, when they use theories and concepts they do so loosely, often selecting evidence simply because it is consistent with their hypothesis.

Another pitfall for nonscientists is concluding or assuming a cause–effect relationship just because two events correlate. The research scientist systematically tests under controlled conditions and often concludes that correlated events are coincidental or are caused by a third variable. Ozmon and Craver (2008) summarize these concerns over teachers' failure to use theory:

> Teachers constantly call for practical solutions to education problems. But this concern with "practicality" is itself open to analytic inquiries: just what is the meaning of "practical" in this instance? Often, the "practical" teacher wants a technique, a gimmick, to apply to and solve his dilemma. It is reasonable, however, to observe that such "practical" solutions are often theoretical in the worse sense. Techniques are sometimes used indiscriminately. They are applied generally and universally in situations for which they were not designed; however, they are deemed "practical" because their mechanics are known and they are capable of being acted upon. (pp. 269–270)

Research scholars contribute their part to the theory/practice divide. Many researchers have lost touch with the day-to-day complexity of human interactions in school; many educational researchers publish their research in scholarly (read aloof) research journals rather than in practical journals; many use erudite language that prohibits nonresearchers from understanding the research; and many choose research topics that are of little use or concern to teachers (Davis, 2007). With NCLB's demand for research-based practices, the need to bridge this gap has never been greater.

A major cause for teachers' estrangement with theory and research is their world of isolation. Teachers seldom have opportunities to discuss theories and research with their peers, nor do they have time to scour the journals regularly (Jensen, 2008b). Effective use of research requires skills in seeing the relationship between the findings and the local landscape. In other words, applying research requires adaptive skills. One way in which supervisors can help is by creating *networking* opportunities for teachers. For example, *school-based learning committees* by their very nature encourage adaptive thinking (Duffy & Kear, 2007). Just the act of belonging to a group gives individuals an identity, and the effect is magnified when members express their ideas and help to shape the group's mission. Such engagement gives teachers new experiences, language, and resources (Niesz, 2007).

Networking and the vast benefits it offers can be raised to another level by adding research. Supervisors can best serve teachers by helping them identify common areas of interest and helping them initiate action research projects that address those areas. As in the case study in the previous chapter, theory and research can complement each other in these projects. To become a contrib-

It Works for Me!

Using Theory in the Real World

Cynthia Reed, Auburn University

I have used the following activity in an advanced graduate-level course on curriculum and instructional leadership to teach students about the importance of understanding student learning needs, local context, and how to evaluate curriculum.

Conduct an interview with a building principal or teacher leader involved in decision making about the recent purchase of a curriculum product related to the design or delivery of instruction. During the interview focus on: (a) the theoretical frameworks involved when making the decision; (b) the process used; (c) who was involved and why they were selected; and (d) the barriers and facilitating factors hindering or supporting the change once the product was purchased. Write a one- to four-page report about your findings to be turned in to the professor, and prepare an informal presentation for the class about what you learned and how you will use this information as a teacher leader or building principal.

Following the informal presentations, have the class identify the frequency of each theoretical framework used, key aspects of the selection process, who was involved, and the barriers and facilitating factors related to the curriculum change using the new product. Develop a class list of key lessons learned and how this information could be used in future product adoption situations. If appropriate, share the class-developed list with those interviewed for the class project.

uting member, teachers should be encouraged to join the groups that they find most interesting.

The teaching strategies and curricula that educators adopt implicitly reflect the learning theories which they advocate (Jaramillo, 1996). Keeping in mind some of the reservations that teachers have about theory, and the realization that all can benefit from understanding theory, let's examine some of the psychological theories that underpin education programs.

Early and Contemporary Learning Theories

In a way, the cumulative process called *learning* is a mystery. Because we cannot see it happen (we can only see the results), perhaps we will never understand exactly how it occurs. However, this does not mean that your faculty cannot benefit from exploring and reflecting on the work of others who investigate learning. Several theories about how learning occurs have added to our understanding of the process. The more thoroughly your teachers understand these theories, the better they will be equipped to design and execute curricula and lessons.

Learning theories, like all types of theories, are never perfect or permanent. As more is learned about the ways our brains operate, what factors promote understanding, and what factors deter our understanding, old theories are modified or discarded. For example, for many decades educators embraced decay theory to explain why we forget, but now that theory has given way to interference theory—the belief that things get in our way and prevent us from recalling what we once knew. A review of some of the more widely accepted learning theories will show just how much our perceptions of learning have changed, even in the brief span of a century.

Faculty Psychology

At the turn of the twentieth century, the dominant learning theory was faculty psychology. Faculty psychologists believed that the brain was similar to a large muscle. They believed that, like other muscles, in order to grow, the brain required exercise; and, like other muscles, maximum growth required rigorous exercise. Furthermore, faculty psychologists thought that the brain had faculties (capacities) of which reason was just one. The brain was also believed to have the capacity of will. The development of willpower required unpleasant exercise because it seemed obvious that individuals could not develop willpower while enjoying themselves. This idea led to the general belief that to be effective, schools had to be unpleasant.

A century later, residue can still be found from this theory; several education reform reports call for "increased rigor." But a major difference can be seen in how educators have changed their perceptions of the need for rigor. Certainly, many contemporary educators share their predecessors' belief in the importance of rigor in all disciplines; however, unlike their predecessors many contemporary educators believe that teachers can make their classes both rigorous *and* enjoyable.

Stimulus-Response Theory

In the early twentieth century, Russian psychologist Ivan Pavlov's stimulus work with dogs had begun to affect Americans' perceptions of learning. Pavlov received a Nobel Prize in 1904 for the discovery that he could condition the dogs to behave in certain ways. American psychologists had begun testing the effects of various types of stimuli on the behavior of small animals, such as pigeons and guinea pigs. E. L. Thorndike's work solidified this theory involving stimuli and the resulting responses. The overall belief of this theory is that most human behavior is a series of responses to a variety of stimuli. Taken to its extreme, stimulus-response theory says that since all behaviors are responses to stimuli, all that is needed to control individuals' behavior is to use the particular stimulus that matches the desired behavior.

Of course, stimulus-response theory had its opponents. Critics insisted that some behavior is self-initiated or intentional as opposed to responsive. The symbol for stimulus-response theory (S–R) was changed to S–O–R to allow for that behavior that is initiated by the organism.

Behavioral Theory

As the twentieth century progressed, an increasing number of critics of stimulus-response theory began to shape an opposing theory that eventually replaced S–O–R as the most widely accepted theory of human behavior. This theory is known as *behavioral psychology,* often called *behaviorism.*

Behavioral psychologists (or behaviorists) believe that most human behavior is not in response to stimuli but instead is overt or intentional and self-initiated. Most college students attend college, not as a natural reflex to a stimulus but rather because they choose to do so and because they have purposes to fulfill. Behavioral psychologists make full use of reinforcement.

It Works for Me!

Critical Thinking for Supervisors

Kenneth E. Lane, Southeastern Louisiana University

It is not enough to believe that learning occurs through exposure to information on supervision. The learner must be able to demonstrate critical thinking in order for supervision to be conducted effectively. When students engage in any new learning, they bring with them their existing mental models that may enhance or hinder their learning. Supervision should design and embed learning processes that facilitate positive transfer from existing to accurate mental models. This process will require the creation of a learning process that addresses the structure of the task initially learned and its relationship to the transfer task, the supervision processes involved and their relationship to meaningful learning, the conditions necessary to retrieve knowledge gained, and the background knowledge of the learner. Critical thinking is a trait that must be taught and learned in order for the supervision methodology to be understood and applied. If not taught, supervision will be ineffective.

While previous learning theories (called transmission models) implied that teaching is a matter of *transmitting* a fixed body of content to learners, newer programs were different; they were based on a model that implied that teaching is a *process* of helping students develop knowledge.

Cognitive Theory

Behaviorism remained the dominant model until about 1960, when the "space race" and related educational concerns resulted in the Woods Hole Conference that spun off a series of new programs designed to fix America's "dysfunctional" schools. Behaviorists were criticized for being too dependent on overt behavior to explain learning. Cognitive theorists look beyond behavior to explain brain-based learning and proposed looking at learning *patterns* as opposed to isolated *events* (see the section below). Whereas in behaviorism, the locus of control over learning activities lies with the environment, with cognitive theorists it lies with the individual learner.

Constructivism

A new approach to teaching and learning was named *constructivism*, because it held that learning required constructing new knowledge from the learner's own experiences. The teacher's role in constructivist teaching/learning is to give students problems that let them discover relationships between new information and prior understanding.

Constructivism evolved from *Gestalt psychology* or gestaltism, which views learning as the process of recognizing patterns. Gestaltists believe that learning occurs when individuals see patterns and that the patterns formed by associating concepts with one another create new knowledge. A common statement seen in Gestalt psychology literature is, "The whole is more than the sum of its individual parts." Another important Gestalt term is *insight*, which occurs when new patterns suddenly emerge. Gestalt psychologists would say that important scientific discoveries are less a product of methodically following the scientific process and more a product of insight, which often follows long periods of observing or investigating a phenomenon and then stepping back to view the problem from a different perspective.

History of Constructivist Theory

Constructivist learning theory has its roots in a broader genre of theory called *sociocultural theory*, developed in the 1930s by a Russian social scientist and teacher named Lev Semyonovich Vygotsky. To understand Vygotsky's view of learning, one must first understand his view of social and cultural development. He believed that youths become integrated into their society by interacting with their peers and with adults, especially their parents and teachers. Both their peers and their adult leaders use *language* to help them develop socially. Vygotsky believed that learning occurs in much the same way that social development happens—through interaction with peers, adults, and the physical environment. By interacting with the physical or concrete world in a social context, youths learn to solve problems; furthermore, their peers and teachers help them understand the mental processes they use to do so. "As adults, teachers use their abstract knowledge of the language they learned from others throughout their lives to direct lessons that will facilitate their students' understanding of new concepts" (Jaramillo, 1996).

According to Vygotsky, the learner brings an actual level of problem-solving skills to each problem-solving assignment. Of course, individuals have limits to the level of complication or difficulty of problems they can solve. Vygotsky called this distance between a student's level of problem solving skills and that student's immediate potential for development through problem solving the *zone of proximal development*. Supervisors should stress the importance of this concept to their faculty, because it is critical in guiding children's learning development. The teacher's role is to *model* problem solving and use a process which is called *scaffolding*—introducing problems that are progressively more challenging but still within students' zones of proximal development. In this manner, teachers help students develop increasingly complex concepts and problem-solving skills.

Cooperative Learning

Vygotsky's work over half a century ago led to the development of another contemporary teaching strategy—*cooperative learning*—that is prevalent in today's schools. Cooperative learning involves assigning students to small groups and giving them authentic or lifelike problems to solve. Contemporary cooperative learning theorists believe that each group member should be held responsible for the other members' understanding of how to solve the problems at hand.

As students collaborate in small groups to solve a common problem, Vygotsky proposed that each student talk to other group members about the problem and explain to the other group members the process he or she used in attempting to solve the problem. Vygotsky believed that having students explain their mental processes when solving problems can help them improve their understanding of the problem and can also help them heighten their own level of problem-solving skills. Vygotsky called this process of peers arriving at a common understanding by social interaction via problem-solving concepts *negotiating meaning.*

The Learner's Role

An interpretation of Vygotsky's view of the learner's role as contrasted with traditional views is shown in Table 14.1 (on the following page). As shown in the table, Vygotsky's view of the role that students should play in the classroom differed sharply from traditional views. Rather than being passive receivers of facts, he thought that students should be actively involved in solving problems. Rather than working quietly alone, he believed that students should work in small groups, helping others learn how to solve problems *and* helping them understand how their minds work. Rather than demanding that

Table 14.1 Contrasting Views of the Learner's Role

Beliefs about:	Traditional Views	Vygotsky's View
The individual nature of learning	Learning is an individual activity.	Learning is an interactive activity.
The source of knowledge	The learner is a receiver of knowledge.	Learners create knowledge.
The direction of learning	Learning is a top-down activity (teachers direct what students learn).	Learning is a bottom-up activity (teachers facilitate rather than direct student learning).
The nature of knowledge	Understanding is based on facts.	Understanding is based on major concepts and themes.

students remember facts, he thought the purpose of school should be to help students understand major concepts and themes. (This last idea is the foundation for *concept development* learning theory, a theme of this book.)

As one might suspect, this shift in student role necessitated a major shift in the instructional role of teachers, shown in Table 14.2. Vygotsky's view of how youths learn separates his view of the teacher's role from the view held by traditional educators. It bears repeating that instead of feeding facts to students, Vygotsky thought that teachers should (1) actively engage students with problems, (2) challenge them to solve increasingly more difficult problems, and (3) encourage them to discuss their problem-solving strategies with their fellow group members (in other words, collaborative problem solving).

Vygotsky's work is so much a foundation to the development of constructivist learning theory that any attempt to separate him from the constructivist programs that are currently reforming our schools would be, at best, superficial.

Table 14.2 Contrasting Views of the Teacher's Role

Beliefs about:	Traditional Views	Vygotsky's View
The appropriate level of complexity	Teachers should make all information as simple as possible.	Teachers should set information just above students' current level of competence (scaffolding).
Required teacher knowledge	Teachers need mastery of their disciplines.	In addition to mastery of their discipline, teachers need an understanding of how students negotiate learning.
Interpretation	Teachers must interpret information.	Teachers must interpret the social settings in the classroom.
Curriculum and instruction	Teachers attend to instruction.	Teachers attend to instruction *and* curriculum.

Methods and Strategies of Constructivism

Traditional teaching methods that place students in a passive, receiving role and the teacher in an information-delivering role do not work well for constructivist lessons. Some methods that do work well for constructivists include problem solving, simulations, discovery lessons, and the case-study method, all of which provide opportunities for students to construct knowledge. (Techniques for planning and executing these methods are discussed in chapters 8 and 9, respectively.)

Problem Solving. An essential part of constructivism is problem solving. By facing and solving problems, students learn to apply previously acquired knowledge to existing problems. The curriculum programs that resulted from the Woods Hole Conference required students to use specific materials to solve problems. These were three-dimensional, hands-on instruments (such as weighing scales, testing kits, and compounds) that often arrived at the schools in large boxes, complete with step-by-step directions. The programs effectively turned each classroom into a laboratory, where each activity was student-centered to the point that the teacher was often considered unnecessary. Even though the programs were "teacher-proof," they were highly stimulating because they involved hands-on, problem-solving activities.

Simulations. An excellent vehicle for constructivist lessons because it places students in active roles, simulation provides problems for students to solve using both convergent and divergent thinking (see chapters 8 and 10). Students find simulations highly motivating, and because this method actively involves students in discovery learning, knowledge learned through this method is retained longer than knowledge acquired through more traditional methods.

Discovery Learning. As a learning/teaching method, discovery learning received tremendous support from Jerome Bruner, secretary/recorder for the Woods Hole Conference. Discovery learning generates new knowledge by providing opportunities to develop insights. For example, a science teacher might ask students to identify a mineral by performing acid tests, color tests, and hardness tests.

The Case-Study Method. This method, which presents students with either a real-life or a fictional situation, is a student-centered, problem-centered approach. Good cases always conclude with a problem to be solved by students and require them to sift through irrelevant and relevant information to make judicious decisions. Once the relevant information is identified, students must organize it to give it new meaning. Students at all levels, including graduate students, enjoy using the case-study method because it permits them to be involved and because it involves discussions with other students. Unlike statistical analysis and numerical data, which students and teachers may find detached and unengaging, case studies can paint a picture of how schools work and therefore are more likely to be embraced by practitioners (Davis, 2007). Students also enjoy discussing the cases with their peers. The case-study method has been a trademark of the Harvard Business School for almost a century, and cases and vignettes are being used at an unprecedented rate in textbooks.

* * *

As administrators, supervisors, teachers, and students prepare to improve their schools, each faculty must discover its own preferred ways to reach this goal. But one quality is constant among all schools that make substantial improvement: The individual faculty members have learned how to work together to set and reach common goals. The case study below describes how one faculty has turned to the field of business to learn how to collaborate. Here, a principal uses Tuckman's theory of small-group development to bring together a new campus and turn it into a success.

Helping Teachers Use Theories

Julie P. Combs and Stacey L. Edmonson • Sam Houston State University

Schools contain many subgroups of teachers, such as those functioning as academic departments, grade-level teams, special programs coordinators, school decision-making teams, and ad hoc committees. High-performing groups within a school support a positive overall culture and are thus an indicator of effective schools. In fact, if school culture does not allow for the effective interaction of teachers, then not even the best instructional practices will be very successful in achieving positive student and campus outcomes (Watson, 2001).

Schein (1992) claimed that "the only thing of real importance that leaders do is to create and manage culture, and the unique talent of leaders is their ability to work with culture" (p. 2). The ability to establish a strong culture focused on teaching and learning is one of the primary responsibilities of today's principals (Fink & Resnick, 2001; Taylor & Williams, 2001). With this in mind, school administrators who understand culture, including small-group dynamics, can offer leadership interventions to develop groups at their schools. As principals work to improve conditions that support student learning, application of the following theory may prove helpful.

Tuckman (1965) proposed the following stages of group development after analyzing the results of 50 studies: (a) forming, or the orientation stage; (b) storming, or the dissatisfaction stage; (c) norming, or the resolution stage; and (d) performing, or the production stage. Later, Tuckman and Jensen (1977) reviewed 22 studies and added a fifth stage—the termination or adjourning stage.

Tuckman's (1965) model is sequential, developmental, and thematic. Groups move through the stages in a prescribed sequence, and the length of time for each stage varies according to the characteristics of the group members and the effectiveness of group leadership. The model has a developmental nature as groups must resolve the challenges presented in the current stage in order to progress to the next stage. As a result, groups can be detained in any one stage until specific leadership actions move the group forward. The model is also thematic in that each stage is characterized by two themes, one relating to the group's task functions and one connected to its relationship dimension.

The Community

The school district was located in a predominantly affluent suburban setting near a major city in the southern United States. During the principal's eleven-year tenure as a school administrator the school district was experiencing rapid growth, with annual rates ranging from 6 to 10%. A majority of students lived with college-educated parents who held high expectations for the school system.

The School

The superintendent named the new principal of a newly built neighborhood school. The student population of this campus represented greater diversity than the rest of the district, with 60% White, 20% Asian, 15% Hispanic, and 5% African American. Approximately 14% of the students at this campus qualified for the National School Lunch Program, again higher than the district average. Over 17% of the students had limited English proficiency. Responsibilities for opening the school included selecting team leaders and teachers, purchasing equipment, initiating a parent organization, meeting with students, and establishing schoolwide procedures.

Small groups, or teams, were organized by grade levels or special programs and included eight teams: one for each grade from kindergarten through fifth grade, and two for the elective and support areas. Team-leader applicants were interviewed and selected seven months prior to the opening of school. Responsibilities included the development of performing teams, the oversight of curriculum issues, and the management of purchasing functions. Each team ranged in size from 4 to 12 members. The principal provided the team leaders with monthly training for the purposes of developing a positive school climate and accomplishing instructional goals.

The Principal

The principal had worked in another district for several years as a teacher and administrator and in her current district for just a short time as an assistant principal. She was nervous about the task of opening a new campus, although she felt prepared for the task. The high expectations of both the district and its constituents made the job of principal, particularly of a new campus, a very high-stress position. The principal's self-imposed standards for excellence added to this pressure. However, this principal was also well versed in educational theory and felt strongly about using research-based techniques for school improvement.

The Theory

Tuckman's (1965) model provides educators with information that can be used to improve group performance. By understanding the stages, members can form realistic expectations relating to the challenges faced by groups. When members accept that dissatisfaction and conflict are normal processes in team development, and when effective leadership is applied, then groups can become high-functioning teams.

Stage 1: Forming. In this stage, personal relationships are based on a sense of dependence, particularly toward the group leader. Group members tend to practice safe and patterned behavior, relying on the group leader for direction. Group members want to be accepted by the group and actively seek to understand how they are alike and different as compared to other group members. Members avoid controversy, and many will keep their feelings to themselves. Members may experience feelings of discomfort, anxiety, confusion, or impatience. The major focus during this stage is one of orientation, or becoming aware of the group's tasks and the members. Discussion supports task definition. In order to move from Stage 1 to Stage 2, members must address orientation and dependency issues and be willing to risk conflict.

Stage 2: Storming. This next stage is characterized by competition and conflict, both in relationships and in the tasks of the group. As group members attempt to complete tasks, conflict occurs in areas involving leadership, structure, and authority. Some individuals choose to conform to group ideas; others may react with aggression or assertion. Still others may be silent and harbor negative feelings that surface at later times. Members want to know guidelines, responsibilities, rules, rewards, and criteria related to the assigned tasks. Groups must manage conflict and begin to embrace collaborative problem solving in order to move to the next stage.

Stage 3: Norming. In this stage, cooperation characterizes the group's interpersonal relationships. Group members acknowledge all members' contributions as the group successfully solves group issues. Openness to change, respectful listening, and shared leadership characterize the behavior of group members. Trust increases as members understand and identify with one another, and members experience a sense of belonging and a feeling of relief from having solved previous group conflicts. Related to the task, group members openly share information and give feedback, often producing creative solutions. Because members enjoy the group collaboration, they may begin to fear the inevitable future breakup of the group, resulting in resistance to change.

Stage 4: Performing. This stage is reached by few groups. Groups in the performing stage experience true interdependence and productive problem solving. Members can work equally well independently, in smaller subgroups, or as a larger unit. Member roles dynamically change to meet needs of the group and individuals. Members are attentive to both tasks and relationships. Members support experimentation and strive for high achievement goals. The group experiences unity, high morale, and loyalty.

Stage 5: Adjourning. Tuckman's final stage involves the termination of task behaviors and group relationships. Groups can experience either planned or abrupt endings. Concluding a group can create some apprehension—in effect, a minor crisis. Leaders can provide support to members by facilitating task termination and the disengagement of relationships, such as offering a recognition ceremony or reception to provide members with an opportunity for closure.

The Story

In this scenario, the principal decided to apply Tuckman's model in the development of effective teams on her new campus. She shared Tuckman's theory with team leaders at an initial meeting. She wanted the leaders to form realistic expectations for their teams and to assess and support the teams' development. Following the initial introduction, team leaders revisited the model in individual conferences with the principal. She facilitated each leader's development with additional training and dialogue. She modeled the application of Tuckman's theory with the group of team leaders, assessing their progress (and the principal's own progress) through the stages and sharing strategies for change.

The theory was applied year after year, and teams cycled through the stages. As group membership changed, teams reentered the forming stage. At times, teams remained in the storming stage. When interventions were not successful in moving the team forward, changes in group membership or group leadership sometimes occurred. Teacher leaders were able to build high-functioning teams that resulted in student success. During each year of the principal's ten-year tenure as principal, the school received an exemplary rating by the state's education department. Five years after opening, the school applied and won the National Blue Ribbon School of Excellence award.

Issues for Further Reflection

The ability to build culture through the effective use of groups is critical to the success of both schools and their leaders. Research has shown that such use has a direct impact on student performance (Fink & Resnick, 2001; Taylor & Williams, 2001). Equally important, however, is a leader's ability to recognize the importance of theory and its application in practical educational settings. The bridge from theory to practice provides a vital component to moving schools forward. Practice that is not based in theoretical, research-grounded ideas is typically a hit-and-miss process, with students' achievement at risk; likewise, theory that is never put into practice is as useless as a book that is never taken from the shelf. Knowing how to take appropriate theory and put it into effective practice can make the difference between average campuses, teachers, leaders, and students and those that are exemplary. The principal's application of Tuckman's model at this highly successful school confirmed the potential of theory as a guide to practice.

Social Cognitive Theory

We have already established that people's experiences, environments, and behaviors affect how they learn. Social cognitive theory provides the groundwork for interactive learning, a key component in both constructivism and cooperative learning. Social cognitivists believe that learning occurs best in a social setting (where two or more students learn together), because people learn by watching what others do (*modeling*). Discussions are an important element of teaching from a constructivist perspective because they capitalize on the social nature of learning and promote deeper understanding.

Developmental Psychology and Piaget

Developmental psychology originated in the eighteenth century with Jean Jacques Rousseau, who outlined stages of development in his book, *Émile.* But the person most often identified as the father of developmental psychology is the twentieth-century psychologist Jean Piaget. Perhaps the one single theory that is being used most widely today to help teachers understand learning and other behaviors of young people is Piaget's cognitive development theory. He studied children's thought processes at varying ages. Prior to his theory, educators had thought that the minds of children developed in an even process paralleling their chronological aging. As a *stage theorist* (who postulates that development progresses through a series of qualitatively different phases), Piaget rejected the thinking of his predecessors.

He also believed in *cognitive readiness,* that concept that children's ability to learn depends on a combination of their biological maturation and their prior experiences. Piaget considered mental growth as the acquisition of new mental abilities not previously present. He was considered a constructivist in the sense that he perceived learning not as just the accumulation of knowledge but as the creation of knowledge. He believed that individuals have schemes, or systems that are internal frameworks for organizing learning and guiding behavior. According to him, learning occurs as a result of an individual constructing new schemes and as a result of the individual's differentiating and integrating existing schemes.

Piaget believed that as children confront information that is congruent with their existing belief system, they rather easily *assimilate* the new information. But when confronted with information that conflicts with their existing belief system, individuals must alter the existing belief system to *accommodate* the conflicting information. As shown in Figure 14.1, learners progress smoothly as long as the new information they confront agrees with their belief system. Incidentally, little learning is occurring at such times. However, when

Figure 14.1 The Learning Pattern

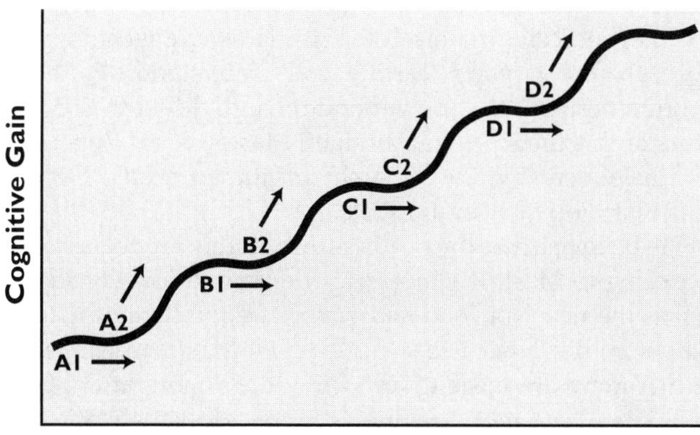

the learner confronts information that conflicts with prior understandings (points A_2, B_2, C_2, and D_2), individuals experience maximum learning in the process of accommodating for the difference.

This work has significant implications for the instructional supervisor. Most teachers work hard to make information seem reasonable to learners—that is, to make learning easy. Piaget did not believe that such teacher behavior was fruitful. Although he did not believe in making schoolwork difficult or boring, he thought that teachers should purposefully introduce conflicting information or information that would cause discomfort in the learner. Piaget believed that learners will work to reconcile the difference and thereby escape this *state of disequilibrium*. The environment must be challenging enough to contain situations that students fail to immediately fit their established patterns of thought structures (Longerbeam, 2007). Paradoxically, he believed that individuals seek out and enjoy experiences that bring on disequilibrium.

Effective supervisors know that teaching depends on cognitive abilities. Piaget believed that at different developmental stages learners deal with information in different ways. Of all his work, he was best known for his developmental stages, which he developed to describe how children process information at different stages of their development. These *cognitive development stages* were as (1) sensorimotor (birth to about two years of age); (2) preoperational (approximately age two to seven); (3) concrete (approximately age seven to eleven); and (4) formal (approximately age eleven through adulthood). It's important that supervisors understand each of the development stages as they relate to the students in their schools. Although detailed information about each stage is not reprinted here, it is readily available online from multiple sources. Encourage your teachers to become familiar with these stages as they share information with their students, and to look for signs that information is understood.

Humanistic Psychology

Humanistic psychology (also called perceptual psychology) is a motivational theory that grew out of a clinical setting. Humanistic psychologists believe that the behavior of individuals is heavily affected or shaped by the way they perceive themselves. Humanistic psychology endorses a personal approach. By showing warmth and understanding, helpers often strengthen the bond between themselves and the individual they are helping. Three originators of this theory were Abraham Maslow, Carl Rogers, and Arthur Combs.

Maslow created the hierarchy of human needs (Figure 14.2) to explain the focus that motivates individuals.

He believed that the needs shown in this model are common to all humans. According to Maslow's hierarchy, the lowest-level needs (physiological needs, such as the need for food and water) are the strongest, and they must be satisfied before the other needs can be met. Maslow believed that all the needs in the hierarchy are basic to an individual's motivation. Only when these basic needs have been met does the need for self-actualization come into focus. *Self-actualization* refers to a drive to develop capabilities in order to grow as a per-

Figure 14.2 Maslow's Hierarchy of Human Needs

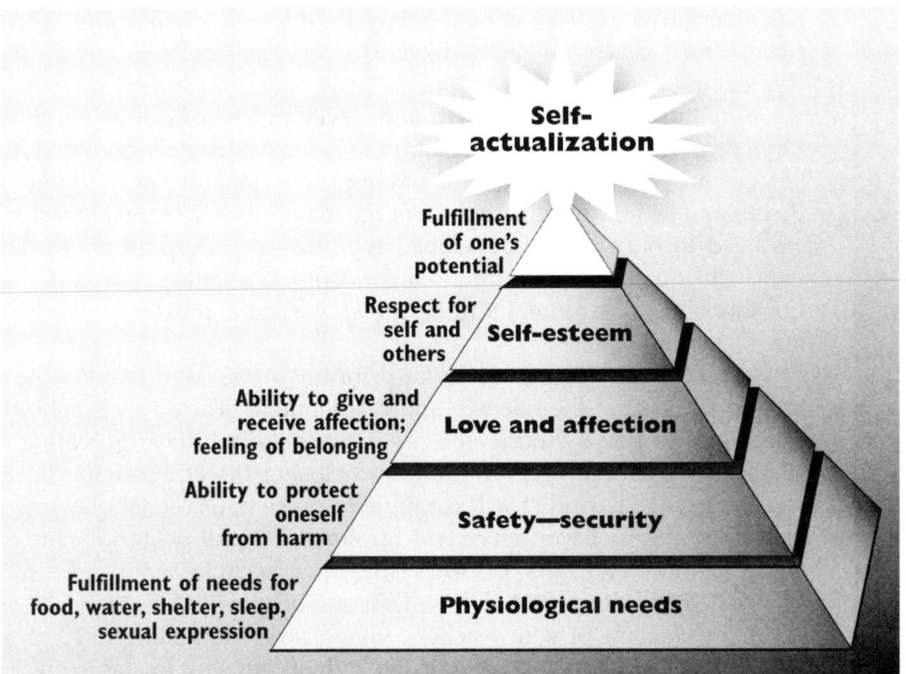

son. For one person, this drive may manifest itself in a need to stay in top physical shape, while another person may feel a need to improve a hobby-type skill, such as playing the guitar or piano. Still another person may feel a need to develop computer expertise. Some people's self-actualization may take a more abstract form, such as philosophical, emotional, or intellectual growth that involves more than one particular skill.

Maslow's list is dominated by feelings; he saw individuals' cognitive behavior as being inextricably connected to their emotions. His views can best be understood through the following words, which he wrote just weeks before his death.

> As I go back in my own life, I find my greatest education experiences, the ones I value most in retrospect, were highly personal, highly subjective, very poignant combinations of the emotional and the cognitive. Some insight was accompanied by all sorts of autonomic nervous system fireworks that felt very good at the time and which left as a residue the insight that has remained with me forever. (Maslow, 1973, p. 159)

Another leader in the development of humanistic psychology was Carl Rogers. As a psychologist, Rogers used a technique called the *sounding board*. His was a facilitating approach—to listen, care, or empathize to help clients solve their own problems. *Empathic understanding*, another technique conceptualized by Rogers, involves understanding another person's feelings. "When a teacher has the ability to understand a student's reactions from the inside and has a sensitive awareness of the way the process of education and learning seems *to the student*, then the likelihood of significant learning is increased" (Rogers, 1967, p. 304).

Facilitating the total growth and development of pupils requires at least three primary conditions. In addition to being adequately prepared in the subject or course to be taught, and having some general knowledge or learning theory and technical skills to present the materials in a learnable fashion, teachers need to have a well-developed repertory of interpersonal skills through which they can establish, maintain, and promote effective interpersonal relationships in a classroom. Of these skills, one of the most important is *empathic listening* and response.

Our educational and curricular priorities are skewed to favor the development of an elite in the sciences and mathematics. They are also skewed in the opposite direction by those who say that we should make educating impoverished and disadvantaged children and closing the ethnic achievement gap a top priority. This conflict will continue to make educational planning difficult, because we cannot well serve two masters who pull us in opposite directions (Hess & Rotherham, 2007). Supervisors must learn to listen and communicate with teachers who reflect this wide range of views. Although you may take exception to some of your teachers' views, your influence and support will be strengthened if you can learn to listen with an open mind and express contrary views in a way that will not draw resentfulness from your teachers.

Another important figure in the field of humanistic psychology is Arthur Combs, who posited that perhaps the most important single cause of a person's success or failure educationally has to do with *what he believes about himself.* Combs and his coresearcher, Donald Snygg (1959), concluded that as long as teachers insist on forcing material that, from the student's perspective, has no relevance to them or their lives, education will be an arduous process. Teachers must get to know their students, because the motivation to learn is inside of them (in what Combs called the *phenomenal self*—a term related very closely to *self-concept*).

The Self-Concept. Humanistic psychologists emphasize the importance that the self-concept plays in an individual's behavior. They believe that positive self-concepts are essential for successful behavior and that individuals have a need for self-actualization in order to succeed. Individuals who believe themselves capable of success succeed more than those who feel inadequate. There is no better way to improve your own self-concept than by realizing the progress you and your teachers make and by recognizing your faculty's successes. JoAnn Susko's tip in chapter 13, "Journal Logs and USB Drives," is a good place to begin. Several variables that affect success are shown in Figure 14.3.

In their theory of the phenomenal field, Combs and Snygg (1959) contend that individuals have boundaries that define the way they see themselves and their worlds. The total space encompassed in Figure 14.3 (the *perceptual field*) shows everything of which the individual is aware. Within this outer ring, some

Figure 14.3 Factors that Affect Self-Concept

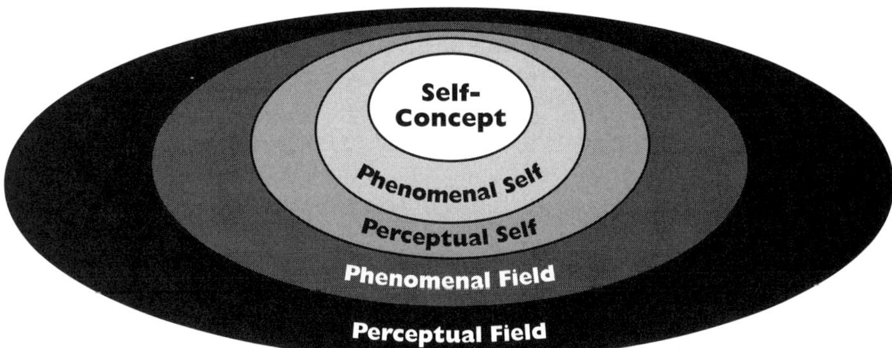

figures in our worlds remain "out there," remote and unable to influence our behavior very much. These things aren't important to us; if we hear others mention them we will probably ignore the discussion. Their effect on us is minimal.

Just inside this ring is a more concentrated area known as the *phenomenal field*, representing things that we do care about because they effect us in some way (e.g., the weather forecast calls for rain, so I'd best take my umbrella). Although our behavior is affected, things inside the phenomenal field are not life-changing events.

The three remaining fields (perceptual self, phenomenal self, and self-concept) involve the self, and to a degree all of us are self-centered. Even those things that we just "know about" ourselves (the *perceptual self*) have some importance to us—for example, my hair is brown; although I may not think that matters, it affects my choice of clothes. The next ring (*phenomenal self*) represents ways of seeing oneself that *do* matter—for example, I am a demanding teacher; I am a hard worker.

The center of Figure 14.3 is reserved for those ways in which we see ourselves that are most important to us—for example, I am honest, fair, and reliable; this is my *self-concept*. Those images that we hold dearest are the ones that can affect our behavior most. A positive view of self contributes to self-actualization.

The importance of models and theories is readily apparent in this concentric-ringed example. Chapter 1 discussed the importance of leading teachers to be collaborative, lifelong learners dedicated to improving the quality of learning in their schools. Chapter 13 mentioned the importance of teachers sharing feedback on the rate of progress in their classrooms. Once teachers prioritize these objectives, they will form a learning community whose members learn to put community goals near the center of this model—in effect, these goals become part of their self-concepts.

The Role of Humanistic Psychology in Education

Humanistic psychologists believe that individuals are basically good, basically trustworthy, and naturally motivated to achieve. They believe that the school, and in particular the classroom, should nurture this growth. The role of the teacher should be to arrange experiences within their students' reach, encourage them until they succeed, and then recognize their success.

Humanistic psychologists are quick to point out that historically our schools have not worked this way. Students have been treated as the enemy. Punishment has been used to force students to behave. Students have been set in rows, taught to be quiet and still, and forced to behave in a like manner. According to the 1962 Association for Supervision and Curriculum Development Yearbook Committee, instead of nurturing student growth, over time schools rob children of their desire to become self-actualized. Although these words were written almost fifty years ago, they describe many contemporary schools.

> The natural thrust of motivation can be clearly seen in beginning first grade students. There is an almost limitless desire to "know," to find out about things. . . . Something happens however, as students move through school. Teachers tend to assume more and more responsibility for deciding what is to be learned, how the child shall be motivated, and the way he shall learn. Less attention is given to what children think and feel and believe, and increasing emphasis is placed on factual content. . . . Succeeding school years, instead of increasing opportunities for choice, prescribe more and more the children's learning experiences. (pp. 87–88)

Humanistic psychologists object to such treatment because it fails to recognize the nature of the individual. Help your teachers realize that each student is unique, and if children are to become more creative they must be allowed and encouraged to be different.

Brain Research Findings and Implications

For several decades scientists have hypothesized that individuals use only a small percentage of their mental capacity. During the 1970s and 1980s substantial research was conducted to learn more about how the brain works. These studies have yielded new and fascinating information about the brain that can be used in schools to make the learning environment more nurturing.

Since the nineteenth century, scientists have known that various sections of the brain exert major control over specific activities (e.g., for more than a century scientists have known that the left hemisphere of the brain controls speech). Since the late 1960s brain research has shown that most school curricula focus on the types of learning that occur in the left hemisphere (i.e., logical, familiar knowledge). Of significant importance to educators is the rather recent discovery that the right hemisphere, once called the minor hemisphere, is not minor at all. Here is where a variety of creative behaviors is determined, for the right hemisphere is the part of the brain where patterns are recognized.

The implications of this research for school curricula are great. Although our schools have done a relatively good job providing left-hemisphere learning opportunities, they have done a poor job helping students use the creative right hemisphere of their brains. Schools are required to teach subjects that require left-hemisphere activities, but few schools require subjects that engage the right hemisphere. For example, as we discussed earlier, although many elementary schools require art to be taught, few have well-planned art programs with a constructivist basis that would enable students to indulge in creativity. The instructional supervisory implication is clear: Efforts should be made to ensure that students are given opportunities to engage in right-hemisphere activities, and such activities should be part of every class.

Conclusion

Concepts are generalizations based on recurring patterns; they are the basis of all thinking and learning. Understanding any discipline requires recognizing and understanding the major concepts that undergird that discipline. Models, or simplified representations of reality, help us understand extremely complex relationships and events. Scientists use theories to predict and explain, whereas laypeople use "common sense" that is often misleading. Teachers can profitably use theories to plan curriculum and instruction, especially learning theories.

Developmental psychology can be used to design lessons that match the developmental level of the learners. The work of Swiss psychologist Jean Piaget can help educators realize students' limitations. His cognitive development theory states that students learn most when they discover discrepancies between new and previously learned knowledge (disequilibrium). His experiments with young children are recognized extensively by educators worldwide. This, and the related work of other developmental psychologists, led to the development of another theory called constructivism. Constructivists believe that the only way that learning occurs is by linking newly learned information to previously acquired understandings.

Another psychological field that has contributed heavily to the development of sound education programs is humanistic psychology. Humanistic psychologists are concerned with each learner's perception of self, especially insofar as an individual's self-confidence as a learner. They believe that successful education requires the learner to perceive learning as important, that human product is determined by perceptions and needs, and that the emotions play an important role in learning. The works of Abraham Maslow, Carl Rogers, and Arthur Combs are the basis for humanistic theory.

By understanding the basis of behavior and mastering empathic skills, supervisors can improve their ability to influence teachers' behavior. By sharing this knowledge with teachers, supervisors give them the opportunity to reap the benefits of this knowledge in the classroom.

Questions for Discussion and Reflection

1. How can teachers develop models to guide their instructional practices at their school?

2. What are some theories that guide contemporary teaching practices?
3. How can supervisors use knowledge of the self-concept to design lessons?
4. Have most of today's schools moved beyond the mere teaching of facts? On what is your answer based?
5. Is instruction generally better in elementary schools or in secondary schools? Explain your answer.
6. In which subjects is instruction superior? Inferior?
7. How can instructional supervisors teach an appreciation for theory?
8. How should supervisors respond when teachers contrast the world of theory and the "real" world?
9. Should teachers attempt to require all students to apply all information that is covered in their classes? Why or why not?
10. Should teachers set "mental traps" for students? Why or why not?
11. Which is more detrimental: providing instruction above the students' present growth levels, or below? Explain your answer.
12. How can instructional supervisors help teachers and administrators create a more humanistic environment?
13. Which of your school experiences have made you feel most adequate, and which experiences have left you feeling inadequate?

Suggested Activities

1. Ask an outstanding teacher to share a concept for which she or he has found an effective teaching strategy. Discuss the reasons that this strategy works.
2. Choose a textbook (either this book or another book in your content area) and identify the major concepts in a chapter that you wish to know more about. Check each concept against the qualities listed in the definitions given for "concept" in this chapter.
3. Choose any important concept or idea. Develop a strategy for teaching this generalization to high school seniors. Now, using Piaget's developmental theory, develop a strategy to teach the same concept to fourth-grade students. Contrast the two strategies.
4. Research the topic *humanistic education*. Write a brief paper relating humanistic education and constructivism.
5. In the curriculum center in the local district office, find three current textbooks in your field. Choose a particular chapter common to all three texts. Make a chart showing the major content generalizations or concepts in each text. Identify those concepts that are common to: (a) all three texts, (b) only two texts, and (c) only one text. Compute the percentage of concepts that are (a) common to all three texts, (b) common to only two texts, and (c) unique to one text. Using this chart, give a presentation on concepts to your teachers.

Chapter 15

Helping Teachers Acquire Resources

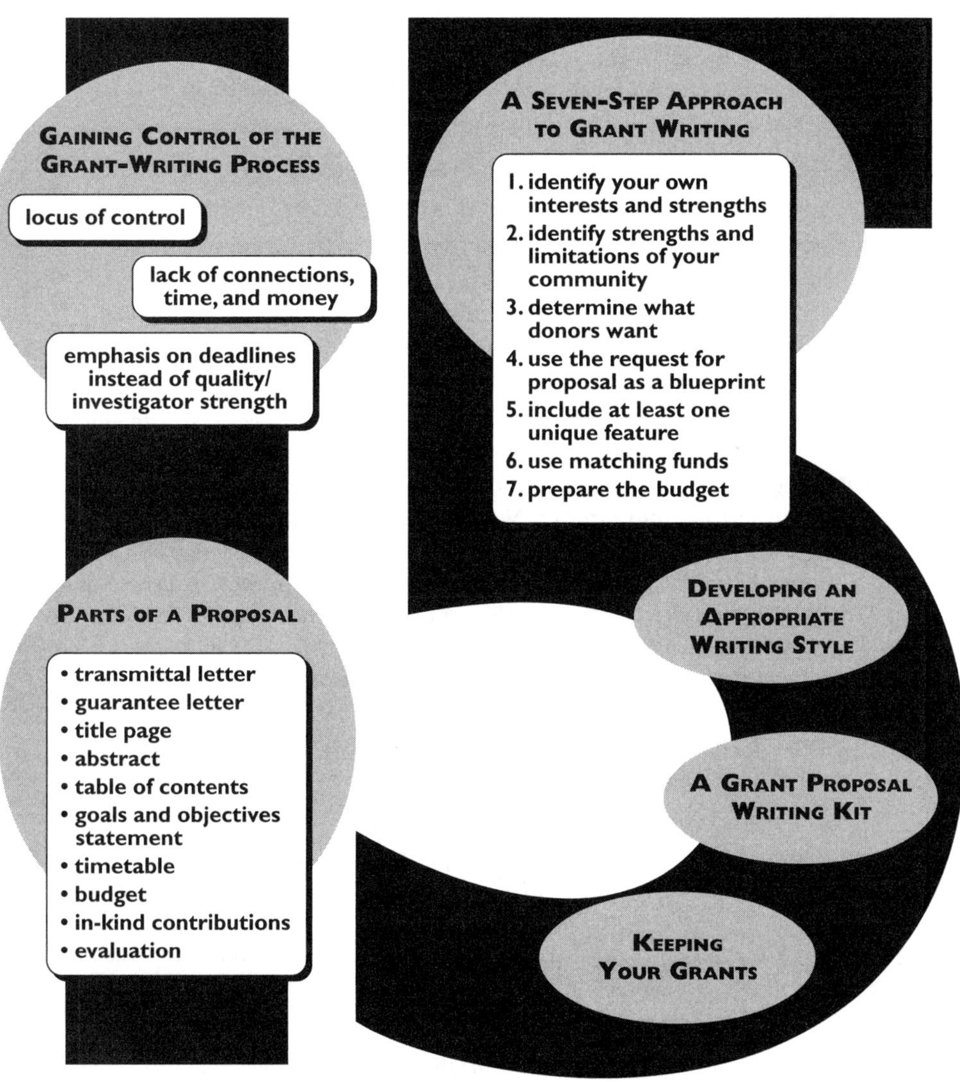

GAINING CONTROL OF THE GRANT-WRITING PROCESS
locus of control
lack of connections, time, and money
emphasis on deadlines instead of quality/ investigator strength
PARTS OF A PROPOSAL
• transmittal letter
• guarantee letter
• title page
• abstract
• table of contents
• goals and objectives statement
• timetable
• budget
• in-kind contributions
• evaluation
A SEVEN-STEP APPROACH TO GRANT WRITING
1. identify your own interests and strengths
2. identify strengths and limitations of your community
3. determine what donors want
4. use the request for proposal as a blueprint
5. include at least one unique feature
6. use matching funds
7. prepare the budget
DEVELOPING AN APPROPRIATE WRITING STYLE
A GRANT PROPOSAL WRITING KIT
KEEPING YOUR GRANTS

> *You can succeed at grant writing at the level at which you are willing to work.*
>
> —K. T. Henson, "Writing for publication: Steps to excellence"

Objectives

This chapter prepares you to help teachers

1. Use the triangular model to develop competitive proposals
2. Systematically search out probable funding sources
3. Match funding sources with grant proposals
4. Use strategies to get their grants re-funded

A Summer Institute for Physics Teachers

Three years after his National Science Foundation Academic-Year Institute proposal was accepted, providing him with a free master's degree and preparing him for a doctoral program, science teacher Chris Camp held his terminal degree in hand and realized the power of grant writing. Now he had accepted a position at a local university, where he encountered two things that would further shape his life. On the news, he learned that 85% of the nation's high school physics teachers were teaching out of field. The fact that fewer than 15% of our high school physics teachers were fully prepared to teach physics bothered him. Later, when seeing a request for proposals for block grants in science and mathematics, Chris knew this was his opportunity to improve science teaching in his state. His next step was to contact the physics department at his university and invite the department chair to join him in writing a proposal for a physics institute.

Chris knew that block grants are national allocations blocked to each state and that in each category only one grant would be approved. He carefully studied the RFP, using it as though it were a blueprint. Seeing that it repeatedly used the word rigor, *he knew that the winning proposal would have to be perceived as rigorous. He also knew that to do a good job, his institute would have to do more than "talk the talk": It would also have to "walk the walk." So he required his participants to take twelve hours of physics each summer.*

Chris knew at least two other things about grant evaluators: Many of them are bean counters. They like data, percentages, and numbers. So, right up front—in the introduction—he used the statement, "Eighty-five percent of all high school physics teachers are unprepared to teach physics." The other thing Chris knew about grant evaluators was that most are overwhelmed with a huge supply of similar, poorly written proposals. This meant that they would welcome any proposal that stood out from the group. So his proposal would be made different by containing several unique qualities.

The first unique quality in this proposal was a special course taught by a master teacher—a master high-school science teacher who, using the state-adopted physics textbook, would work the problems at the end of each chapter. For a teacher who lacks a degree in physics and yet is assigned to teach physics, nothing could be more helpful than watching a "master" demonstrate how to work physics problems! In addition to being a unique experience, this would help the many teachers who struggled to stay ahead of their students.

A second unique quality in this institute was the weekly seminars that would use the varied expertise among the physics professors to dazzle the teachers with their insights. A robotics specialist would bring his robot to the class and have it perform to the teachers' verbal commands. A quasar specialist would give an evening lecture in the observatory, where the institute cohort of teachers would visit galaxies and quasars. Even a retired physics professor with a career pastime of studying the lives of physicists would regale the cohort with fascinating facts about the personal lives of these people.

Knowing that many participating teachers in the institute would be coming from poor schools, a weekly free and inexpensive lab section was included. Each week, throughout the summer, institute participants would perform hands-on experiments and demonstrations that they could later perform for their students.

Chris kept in mind that his first grant was the result of completing not just one application to a university but 22 applications to different institutions (only one of which was funded), and consequently he added one additional quality to tempt the evaluators: He offered his services and that of the chair of the physics department as codirectors of the institute. This amounted to a large in-kind contribution.

The proposal won over all the competition, and the first summer was a huge success. To ensure that the grant would be re-funded, the following fall Chris drove throughout the state to visit each participant. During his first visit he realized that these trips could hold the key to having the funding extended. On each visit he asked the teacher two questions: "From last summer's institute, what have you found most useful?" and "How might the institute have been adjusted to better serve you?" Each fall, these questions were repeated. The results were used to rewrite the proposal, letting Chris stay one step ahead of the competition. During his five years at this institution, the faculty members at all of the other state universities submitted proposals but were never able to take the grant from Chris's university.

Reflection

With their heavy teaching loads, today's teachers are likely to see grant writing as "the straw that could break the camel's back." Grant writing is time consuming, and teachers are strapped for time. Although supervisors cannot lengthen their teachers' days and weeks, they can help by providing encouragement and by assisting their teachers in expediting the grant-writing process. This chapter is based on twenty-five years of surveys, workshops, and grant writing. The strategies described have proved to be effective over thirty times, earning millions of dollars. Better yet, this is a simple, straightforward, and practical approach that supervisors can use to encourage and help teachers develop the skills required to produce highly competitive proposals.

Often, grant writers place all of their emphasis on need. Although establishing need is important, convincing the funders that you will do the best job at meeting their goals is far more important. Chris used the 85% data to establish need, but he didn't belabor it. Instead, he immediately got busy crafting a proposal that was clear and strong enough to convince the evaluators that, indeed, he was the best person for the job.

Introduction

> Interstate New Teacher Assessment and Support Consortium (ISLLC) Educational Leadership Policy Standard No. 3 holds leaders accountable for ensuring management of the organization, operations, and resources.

Lack of resources has always been and continues to be a major barrier to teacher effectiveness. Eric Gleibermann (2007), a former California teacher, says that this need goes beyond the common sources for funding. "Federal, state, and local funding combined provide urban public schools with nothing close to the level of resources they need to educate all children well" (p. 459).

The common lack of financial support for teaching is widely recognized. The 38th Annual Phi Delta Kappa/Gallup Poll of the Public's Attitudes toward the Public Schools reported lack of financial support/funding/money to be the biggest problem facing the public schools (Rose & Gallup, 2006).

> In the United States, only 52% of education dollars reach the classroom, and only about 43% of education staff members are classroom teachers. In other industrialized nations, about three-fourths of education resources are spent directly on instruction, and classroom teachers represent from 60% to 80% of all staff members. (Darling-Hammond, 2005, p. 240)

The result of this low percentage of funds reaching the classroom is a continuous, serious shortage of resources, both fiscal and human. Often, teachers are in such need of school supplies and materials that they use money from their own pockets to purchase them (Mikovich & Evans, 2006.)

When attempting to meet the No Child Left Behind legislative requirements, the need for human resources is the greatest, most handicapping need that teachers face (Everhart, 2006). In Japan, the local government designates one full-time teacher for every two beginning teachers in a school to support

It Works for Me!

Using Human Resources

Beverly Findley, Eastern Illinois University

Engage your local human resources in staff development. Have local physicians, mental-health personnel, or law-enforcement personnel provide short presentations (under 30 minutes) on topics that staff could use in addressing the needs of the whole child. Examples of appropriate topics include signs of depression and signs of eating disorders. Law-enforcement personnel can address problems they encounter with adolescents and teens within the community and help redirect these at-risk students. This provides a partnership between the school and the community while providing valuable information to staff.

Of course, another way to acquire support for increased human resources is through stipulating the necessary additional human resources in a grant proposal and including the cost for them in the proposal's budget.

teacher induction. Compared to U.S. teachers, who have almost no in-school time for professional learning or collegial work, Japanese teachers are given 20 or more hours a week for planning, visitations to other classrooms and schools, and demonstrations of teaching strategies. This absence of support in the United States leaves many of its teachers desperate for more support.

The acquisition of resources—particularly resources needed to improve teaching—is an essential responsibility of today's supervisors (Daresh, 2008). In this chapter you will find practical information for supervisors to help their schools in their struggle for more resources. Few teachers have been taught how to write successful proposals. Supervisors can help teachers and administrators prepare for writing competitive grant proposals by involving them in grant-proposal writing workshops. Supervisors who have large budgets have the option of sending several teachers to such workshops to develop the skills they need to prepare competitive proposals, or they can bring the workshop to their teachers. The second choice is the better option, because it is less costly and because the supervisor can conduct the workshop, ensuring that the teachers will develop the necessary skills.

A word of caution is due. Because education reform programs can be found in all states, the demand for more money to operate the schools has significantly increased. As a result, the competition for the monies that are available through grants has sharply increased. But the grant-funding well is not dry. On the contrary, it has more money than ever before, not thousands or millions but billions of dollars that the funders are eager to give to your teachers. All that is required is to prepare a proposal that will convince the funders that your teachers will meet the funders' needs better than anyone else. The rest of this chapter will show you exactly this can be done.

Gaining Control of the Grant-Writing Process

Success begins in the mind. No golfer ever won a tournament without self-confidence. Likewise, your teachers are unlikely to win a grant until they start believing in themselves. You can help by correcting some misperceptions that stand between them and the finish line. An excellent place to begin is by identifying some negative attitudes and inaccurate perceptions that defeat novice grant writers.

Many novice grant writers become unduly concerned over what they perceive to be their status. Most of your teachers probably do not consider themselves grant writers. They worry because they feel they lack the time and connections that others (their competitors) have, and they become discouraged. Indeed, many teachers conclude that the best way to handle what they see as a less-than-level playing field is to completely ignore grant writing. Help them realize that these disadvantages are only temporary barriers that can be overcome with a good shot of self-confidence and determination.

Perhaps due to the anticipated reward, many grant writers become obsessed with (and blinded by) the need to meet the deadlines with their proposals. To be sure, deadlines are important, but this awareness need not become a distraction that diminishes the quality of proposals. In his own grant-writing workshops over the past 30 years, the author has repeatedly witnessed this compulsion in the participants. This urgency to meet the deadline can often result in crafting less-than-excellent proposals. Remind your teachers that because grant writing is highly competitive, the best way to succeed is to emphasize quality above all else—and that includes meeting deadlines. Being consistently successful requires writing the very best proposals possible.

Other necessary shifts in attitudes involve moving emphasis from the grant writer's goals to the funding agency's goals and shifting the focus from emphasizing the grant writer's needs to emphasizing the grant writer's strengths.

Table 15.1 lists some of the faulty ideas and attitudes that defeat novice grant writers. The counterproductive practices and perceptions in the left column guarantee grant-writing failure and must be replaced by the corresponding effective ones in the right column.

Table 15.1 Ideas and Attitudes Affecting Grant Writing

Faulty Practices and Perceptions	Effective Practices and Perceptions
external locus of control	internal locus of control
lack of money, time, and connections	sense of efficacy
emphasis on deadlines and investigator's needs	emphasis on quality and investigator's strengths

Locus of Control

Grant writing is like bowling, and there are essentially two ways to bowl. You can join a friend or two whose sole purpose is to talk about their bowling skills or, perhaps, who use bowling as an excuse to drink beer and have a good time. These players aren't bad people; there's nothing wrong with having a good time. But if they think this system will result in their becoming great bowlers, they are misguided. Watch them approach the lane in a nonchalant manner, lobbing the ball down the alley, and waiting for Lady Luck to deliver a strike. But she seldom does. Many grant writers are the same. When they see a request for proposals (RFP), their only goal is to meet the deadline. Only too soon, they too, will know the fickle nature of Lady Luck.

Other bowlers study their form, carefully polishing it and gradually gaining more and more control. Eventually, some bowlers gain so much control that the moment they release the ball, they see the path it will take before it makes its trek down the alley. In their minds, they watch the ball go about three-fourths of the way down and then begin breaking quickly to the left. With their eyes closed, they can envision the ball raking the pins off as though they were a solid triangle—no loose pin bouncing around and hitting other pins, because none are left standing. When these expert bowlers throw a perfect ball, they may not even stay to watch the pins go down because they know they will. This state of affairs is called *control.* These players have gained control. They don't believe that any external force has power over their bowling skills. They know that not every ball they throw will be a strike, but they also know that most of their balls will be right on target and that the power to accomplish this lies within themselves.

Expert grant writers are no different. They become experts by practicing and polishing their craft, gradually getting better and better until they can feel the forthcoming success. Some expert bowlers throw straight balls; others throw curves. It doesn't matter; the point is that they learn what's right for them and that they practice and perfect their skills. Expert grant writers must also learn what works best for them. But just as the laws of physics control bowling balls, principles of grant writing guide those who succeed at this game. Supervisors should foster self-confidence in their teachers and stress the need to believe in themselves, replacing any external loci of control (that fabled "Lady Luck") with internal control (self-confidence).

Lack of Connections, Time, and Money

A faulty perception that can defeat would-be proposal writers before they begin is the belief that the big, prestigious institutions will get all the available money. The reality is that most funding agencies don't base their decision on the size or reputation of the institution; instead, they fund the proposal that they think will do the best job. You can be from a small, unknown institution and still get funded by developing the most convincing proposal. A related misconception is that successful grant writing requires connections. While connections can definitely help, if you have none you can make some connections by visiting or phoning the funding agency. If you decide to phone, know what you are going to say in advance, and keep your conversation brief. Use your call to inform the agency about your forthcoming proposal and to discover some of the agency's preferences beyond those that are stated in the RFP.

The Right Emphasis

People write grants with the hope of fulfilling their needs and desires. Ironically, this focus does not serve them well. On the contrary, *by focusing entirely on their needs and desires, many grant writers ignore the fact the most funding agencies have their own needs*. These agencies are looking for people who will help them fill these needs. In a highly competitive grant-writing world, the grant writers most likely to be given the grant are those who convince the readers that they will do the best job meeting the agency's needs. When a grant proposal fails, many grant writers assume the cause of failure to be that they haven't convinced the agents that they have the greatest needs. So they rewrite the proposal, increasing the emphasis on their own needs—the results often being a desperate proposal. While such proposals may win the sympathies of the agents, they seldom win the grants.

A far more effective approach would be to gain a better understanding of the agency's needs, and to design the proposal to make it meet *all of them*. There are two ways supervisors can help. First, since few grant writers are aware of these two conflicting perspectives of need (and the impact they have on getting funded), you should call your teachers' attention to this common error. Second, you can help your teachers ferret out their prospective funding agencies' needs. A good place to begin is with the RFP itself. Most RFPs are written by a committee of agents. Each member contributes by identifying one or more of a particular agency's needs and by ensuring that these needs are addressed in the RFP.

Examine an RFP that your faculty members are considering. Very carefully underscore each desire expressed in the RFP. Then examine your teacher's proposal draft and make certain that every agency need expressed (either stated forthrightly or even hinted at) is covered in the proposal. Finally, a winning proposal must be convincing. Just mentioning each agency need won't suffice; the proposal must convince the readers that if given the grant, your teachers will do a superb job (better than all the competition) meeting these needs.

* * *

In the 1980s, a research team led by John Goodlad discovered that every school has some highly dedicated and competent teachers. Many of these teachers remember the imperfect elementary, middle-level, and high schools they attended, and they are driven by these memories to "make things better." In the following case study you will find that grant writing is an invaluable tool available to all teachers for use in improving their schools.

Reconnecting with Your Roots: Maria's Dream Realized

Patricia Williams and Beverly Irby • Sam Houston State University

Violence permeated this largely Hispanic, urban community—street gangs fighting over turf, graffiti splattering buildings, shootings occurring all too frequently. Amid this chaos there was a huge elementary school with some very caring, devoted teachers. One such teacher was Maria, a fourth-grade teacher who had begun her education and learned English in that same school as a child. Now she had returned as an adult, to "make a difference."

While taking a districtwide grant seminar, Maria had mentioned that she wanted to help her community and her students, and to do that she needed a plan and dollars. Therefore, she telephoned me, since I was the elementary district supervisor, to see if I had any suggestions. In an exasperated voice, she exclaimed, "It's getting worse, and I have to keep my kids off these streets before something happens. They need adult supervision rather than running wild after school. And they need to recognize their ability to succeed rather than becoming dropouts as soon as they're old enough."

As we talked, she stated that most of her students lived in the neglected apartment complex across the street from the school. When they came home after school, no one was there to meet them with milk and cookies. Life, said Maria, is different today than when she grew up with a stay-at-home mom who met her at the bus every afternoon and had a snack waiting when she arrived at home. The community had changed over the years. Her school children usually parked themselves in front of the TV, chatted endlessly on the phone, babysat their younger siblings, or roamed the streets.

We agreed to meet the following week to plan a strategy, and I said that in the meantime I would contact Maria's principal, the area superintendent, and other teachers to see if they would be interested in working on a grant. She had talked to Principal Savedra previously about wanting to do something, but she did not have a real plan of action. The principal assured her that if she could come up with a plan, he would help. Right now, he was so busy analyzing test scores, developing budgets, and handling teacher transfers that he didn't have time to think about any extra project. He barely had time to keep abreast of what was happening daily on the campus.

When we met on Friday afternoon, Maria came with a list of goals. Her main goal was to find a way of keeping her kids off the streets and doing their homework. She needed resources, both in terms of funding and people, and she had found one—me. We began by thinking about Maria's students and their needs. What could we do so that the students had fun-filled learning activities and a place to go after school? Maria asked me if I could help her search for funding sources and write a grant. She also needed other district staff members who had actually been through the process previously, so we agreed to commit to this project if the school district administrators were on board. With a resounding "yes," the area superintendent, the principal, and two other elementary teachers, Rachel and Juan, said that they wanted to participate.

At our meeting, we discussed successful grants that the district had received. I explained that Julia Burciago, the math specialist, had developed a grant two years ago with a local university professor to assist students in improving mathematics and science scores. In that collaboration they had received a $180,000 grant from a philanthropic organization. I scheduled a meeting between Julia and Maria to help Maria familiarize herself with the steps to take in designing the grant, and also with the evaluation procedures needed. Maria next checked with other teachers in her elementary school. Even though they agreed it was a good idea, most said that they were too busy to take on another project.

Over the next two months, Maria, Rachel, Juan, and I met once a week to put together a rough draft. Rachel had been taking counseling courses at the local university, and she recalled that Dr. Wilson, a counselor educator, had worked with the district previously on gang-related issues. She requested his assistance, and he agreed to review the draft proposal, make suggestions, and determine how he and his graduate counseling students might become involved in this project.

In developing the grant, our team decided to concentrate on the five W's and H—who, what, when, where, why, and how, but not necessarily in that order. The *why*, the most important W, was stated in Maria's initial goals—helping elementary kids to stay off the streets and complete their school assignments. To meet this goal, we needed an after-school program (*what*) for all the elementary students who lived in the complex (*who*).

Next, we discussed *where*. Maria remembered our grant seminar discussion about in-kind gifts, such as donated facilities, that often help get a grant funded. We agreed that the best place for an after-school program would definitely be the apartment complex, where three-fourths of the elementary students lived. We talked about contacting the apartment manager and complex owner to find out more about the facilities. Maria had visited her students' parents at times, so she knew that there was a large game room, but she didn't know if it was being used frequently. To aid us, we brainstormed questions we might ask the manager. Was there a charge for using the room? *When* would the room be available—afternoons and early evenings? Could it be used year round? Was it available Monday through Friday? Would the owners possibly donate the room to keep the students active in worthwhile endeavors rather than painting graffiti on the brick walls?

How to make her dream come alive for her students, as well as all the others who lived there, was the dilemma. We needed a substantial grant that would continue for several years, not a one-shot funded program that put the students on the streets after a brief hiatus. With counselors-in-training involved, we even thought of short-term and long-term community problem-solving projects that the elementary students themselves would solve and correct some of the poor conditions in which they lived.

If we secured the place, who would direct the after-school program, and how would they be paid? We needed individuals who would do more than simply play games with kids; we needed adults or peer tutors who could help with math, science, and English homework. Many of the students were English language learners with Spanish as their native language. Could we find tutors to help the children learn English? Would the elementary school be able to help staff the program in some way? If we asked teachers to help, we needed to pay them rather than expect them to work all day and for free in the evenings.

What furniture, equipment, and technology would be needed? It would be great to have several computers, and I read that one of the universities near us was having an auction to get rid of outdated equipment and furnishings. We thought we might be able to find bargains there. Also, the owner of a furniture store only two blocks from the school had previously donated items to the school. He might help with the funding, especially if he received publicity for his store. As you can tell, our minds were racing with both questions and ideas.

Our next step was to begin searching the Internet and books, such as the *Catalog of Federal Domestic Assistance* and the *National Data Book of Foundations*, for possible granting sources at the federal, state, and local levels. I brought materials from my office, and as a team we located both government grants, such as those connected to No Child Left Behind, and private funding sources. To narrow our search, we thought of key words, such as after-school programs, English language learners, and literacy. Eventually, we narrowed the search to twelve possible sources and looked at grants they had previously funded.

In addition, we brainstormed community sources that might be willing to provide grant funding for a portion, if not all, of the money required. As we carefully scrutinized their missions, we narrowed our field to six that closely matched our needs. As we read their requests for proposal (RFPs), we considered ways to make our program stand out from the zillion other proposals that they typically receive each year.

What could be our hook that attracted potential funders? At one of our weekly meetings, Rachel informed the team that she had the perfect plan. Dr. Wilson had mentioned to her that the government was really interested in learning "what works." To do that, he had indicated that much of what was being funded was research to determine "what works" and what could be replicated in other districts across the country. Light bulbs flashed in Rachel's head. That's what the team needed—a program that could be used in various locales, including other states. Dr. Wilson thought perhaps that they could get a research grant that capitalized on (a) a university–school partnership, (b) a randomized trial study that compared an experimental group to a control group of students, and (c) services to low-income, English-language-learning students.

To determine how much this program would cost, we planned a budget showing the proposed expenditures each year for the next five years and guesstimated how many students would participate. Not only did we list the expenses, but we also gave a detailed description of precisely how the money would be used. We knew we needed to contact parents about the plans, get their input, get some of them to serve on an advisory council, develop the plan of research, complete the human-subjects approval process in the district and at the university, and see if anyone would be willing to serve as volunteers for the project. By having an advisory council composed of school officials, parents living in the complex, community business leaders, the program director, and Dr. Wilson and Maria (the coprincipal investigators), we felt that we would be receiving input from all the major stakeholders.

Maria said that she hadn't realized how many details were involved. Yes, we had talked about them in the grant seminar, but it was "quite different when you're actually writing a grant proposal," and this grant was "a big one." Now that we had many of the particulars on paper, it was time to meet with others to discuss the feasibility of this plan and get additional input. How could we divide the responsibilities? We needed to meet with the apartment owners and manager, and Juan said that he would be responsible for contacting them. He lived at the complex, so he already knew the manager well. Mr. Savedra said he would go with him. Rachel agreed to compose a seven-item questionnaire for parents, written in both English and Spanish, to find out if they wanted such a program. She felt that the obvious answer was "yes," but we needed data to back up our claims. As elementary supervisor, I agreed to finalize the grant proposal draft along with Dr. Wilson and Maria, including the budget, and e-mail it to everyone. Dr. Wilson agreed to do this work voluntarily as a service to the district and community. Maria would present our plan at the next faculty meeting, since she was the one who got everyone excited about it initially. Mr. Savedra exclaimed, "Maria's enthusiasm will be contagious!" The entire team planned to meet again in two weeks to finalize the plans. Maria's dream was about to become reality—or was it?

Issues for Further Reflection

1. Suppose that Maria's grant was funded through the federal government: What next steps would you take as the elementary supervisor? Would you meet with all principals about the grant? Would you meet with the school board via the superintendent? How would the funding be monitored? Who will clean the location and prepare it for the program? Since this after-school work is being done off campus, should you as the supervisor discuss liability with the school attorney? Why or why not? (Such concerns are resource considerations by the supervisor.)
2. Suppose that Maria's grant was *not* funded through the federal government and that the funding agent sent back comments about the grant: What are the next steps you would take as the supervisor?
3. How did the elementary supervisor use resources in a collaborative process to assist a teacher to attempt to improve the achievement of students?

Getting Started

Teachers must realize that plenty of money is waiting for the taking. Second, they must accept the fact that they can become incredibly successful if they are willing to take the time to learn how to do things right. Then, all it takes is crafting a proposal that convinces the funder that their proposal will do the best job of meeting the funder's goals.

Two approaches can be used to write successful grant proposals: (1) Your teachers can choose a topic, write a proposal, and then search for a funder; or

(2) they can start by exploring funding opportunities and then let those opportunities guide their topic selection. Neither of these approaches is superior to the other, although some may argue that the latter is more economical. The choice should be determined by the needs of the local schools. Suppose a school has a particular goal that requires funds. For example, perhaps the school lacks resources needed to meet a state standard or a graduation requirement. In this case, writing the proposal and then searching for support seems logical. In the absence of a specific goal, searching the sources to locate topics that agencies wish to support and crafting proposals to meet these funders' specified goals seems more prudent.

By now, hopefully your teachers understand the priorities of successful grant writers. You can further ensure that they do by sharing the information shown in Figure 15.1. Because the funders' goals must take precedence over all others, these are listed at the top of the triangle. These questions will help your teachers investigate each potential funder.

The grant writer is represented in the left base angle because successful grant writers, like successful bowlers, must know themselves, as Socrates wisely advised us to do. Know your strengths and use them; know your limitations and respect them. Know your favorite topics, and match these with the funders' goals. This will generate the passion and enthusiasm required for continuous success. The right base angle represents the strengths of your community, city, school district, and region. Serious grant writers are familiar with

Figure 15.1 The Triangular Model for Grant Writing

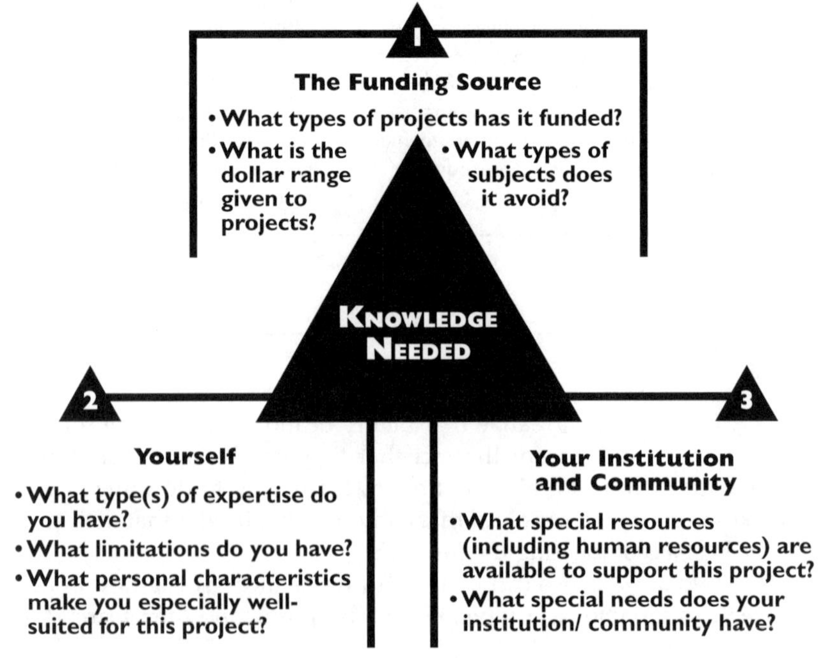
1
The Funding Source
• What types of projects has it funded?
• What is the dollar range given to projects?
• What types of subjects does it avoid?
KNOWLEDGE NEEDED
2
Yourself
• What type(s) of expertise do you have?
• What limitations do you have?
• What personal characteristics make you especially well-suited for this project?
3
Your Institution and Community
• What special resources (including human resources) are available to support this project?
• What special needs does your institution/ community have?

these and they use them, along with those of their school district and their own personal qualities, to convince the funders that they can do the best job meeting the funders' needs.

Parts of a Proposal*

Although the parts of a proposal are likely to vary from one proposal to the next, most proposals follow the general format shown in Figure 15.2. Some of your teachers may be familiar with this format, but many others will benefit from your sharing this figure.

Figure 15.2 Parts of a Proposal

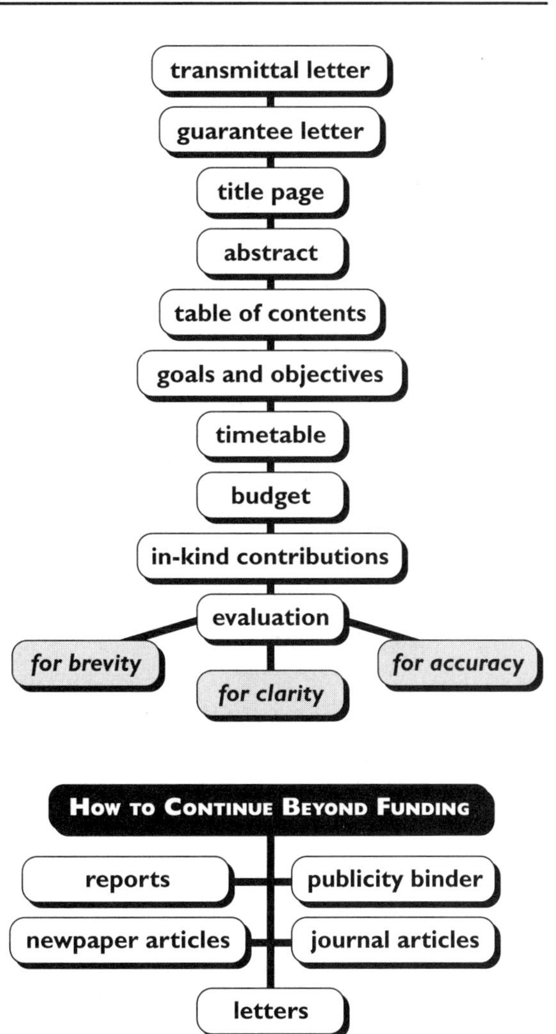

The Transmittal Letter. For our purposes, a transmittal letter is a short, one- or two-page letter signed by someone who represents the people or organization seeking funds (for our purposes, a school) to the entity that has generated the RFP. This letter is the first thing your potential funder will read, so it should effectively present the goals of the proposal, stating why your teachers believe it can fulfill the funder's needs, and why they are capable of accomplishing what they've proposed. A sample transmittal letter written by university president is shown in Box 15.1 (on the following page). Note the effective "attention grabber" sentence that makes up the first paragraph—a good example of a quotable quote (discussed in chapter 13).

*The sample guarantee letter, abstract, project calendar, and goals/objectives statement appearing in this section were taken from a proposal to the National Science Foundation authored by André Green, Andrea M. Kent, and Phillip Feldman, College of Education, University of South Alabama, and are reprinted with permission of the authors.

Box 15.1 Sample Transmittal Letter

Mr. Robert P. Anderson
Executive Director
Southwest Foundations, Inc.
108 Holly Hill Drive
P.O. Box 55
Lubbock, TX 79493

Dear Mr. Anderson:

A recent study released by the U.S. Department of Health has reported obesity as the number one health problem of America's youth.

The Nurse Practitioner Program in the School of Allied Health and Nursing at Southwest University seeks support for the enclosed proposal, titled the Ashley Obesity Reduction Program for America's Youths. We have taken a holistic approach to this problem because we believe that most of today's weight problems result from a change in lifestyle. Our proposed program begins at the pre-elementary school level because this same report says that poor eating habits and sedentary lifestyle begin at this early age.

We have chosen to send this proposal to you because we know that your organization is committed to improving the health of individuals of all ages, especially teenagers and children.

Because our state has the highest rate of obesity in the nation, we believe that our need for addressing this issue is acute; however, our decision to attack this problem is based on an even greater factor: Our organization has studied health practices among youths and has experimented with developing health foods for over one hundred years. We have accumulated a knowledge base to build upon.

Please let us know if further information or explanation is needed. Thank you for considering this proposal.

Sincerely,

Jania K. Worley, President
Southwest University
301 University Avenue
Lubbock, TX 79493
Phone: (999) 999-9999
Fax: (111) 111-1111

The Guarantee Letter. This is a short, one- or two-page letter signed by the superintendent or a designated administrator to guarantee that the school district will live up to its agreement. Because superintendents are so busy and the deadline for submission may be near, you can help your teachers by advising them to draft a short transmittal letter and submit it online (or on paper, with an accompanying disk) so the superintendent can make the necessary changes. If the letter is well written, often the superintendent will immediately sign it. This expedites the process and helps toward meeting the deadline. A sample guarantee letter is shown in Box 15.2.

Box 15.2 Sample Guarantee Letter

Dr. Alan Johnson
Department of Chemistry
College of Arts and Science
University of South Alabama
Mobile, AL 36688

Dear Dr. Johnson:

I am pleased that you are leading an effort to develop and submit a math and science targeted-partnership proposal to the National Science Foundation to enhance student achievement in Alabama and to create Teacher Leaders for future generations of scientists and mathematicians. We are particularly glad that the Alabama State Department is involved as a full partner in this initiative.

Building on our current investment of $33M in the Alabama Math Science and Technology Initiative (AMSTI) and the Governors Commission on Quality Teaching, we will support your efforts through the proposed AMSTI-MSP Math Science Partnership to institutionalize increased math and science content for teachers.

We see your work as vital in helping to shape our newly proposed certification Standards for Teacher Leaders. We will work with you to incorporate these principles into the new Teacher Leader Standards so that all teachers in holding an elementary teaching certificate can surpass the current minimum requirements of 12 semester hours of math and 12 semester hours of science.

The work of AMSTI in Mobile at the University of South Alabama has been an example for the entire state. You have established a strong track record, and we are delighted to extend to you our full support in this most important initiative.

Please keep me informed about the proposal review and next steps.

Sincerely,

Dr. Joseph V. Smith
Superintendent, District 111

The Title Page. Most proposals have a title page, which gives the potential funder an easy way to recognize the proposal and contact the author. By keeping the title page simple and clear, the author can use it to make a favorable impression on the proposal evaluators and the potential funders. The information on the title page should include the title of the proposal, the foundation to which it's being submitted, the institution that is submitting it, and the date of submission.

The Abstract. By now your teachers should have the idea that all parts of every proposal can and should be carefully designed to *sell* the proposal to the targeted funder. Many proposals are never read. Proposals are culled because they are poorly written and because they fail to capture the interest of the readers. So much time is spent preparing proposals, and teachers are so busy with NCLB and preparing students for standardized tests, that it seems especially tragic that a busy teacher would invest time preparing a proposal and then have it tossed aside, never to be read. But an astute grant writer can prevent this from happening.

As a tool for selling the proposal, perhaps the most valuable of all parts is the abstract, since it is the only part that the writer can be sure will be read. Even though some RFPs do not ask for an abstract, including a short, well-designed abstract as part of each proposal can make the difference in whether the proposal is seriously considered. A sample abstract is shown in Box 15.3.

Box 15.3 Sample Abstract

The University of South Alabama seeks NSF funding to develop the AMSTI-MSP (AMSTI—Math Science Partnership) under program solicitation 08-525 which supports the creation of Targeted Partnerships. The goal of the current proposal is to build upon Alabama's already existing Alabama Math Science and Technology Initiative (AMSTI), a $33M state-funded program that provides teachers with (1) 100% of the inquiry-based instructional materials and (2) the continuing professional development support needed by elementary and middle school mathematics and science teachers to meet the objectives of their respective courses of study. Teachers who participate in the proposed AMSTI-MSP will earn a master's degree with concentrations in mathematics and/or science and will receive certification as a Teacher Leader. The already existing AMSTI program at the University of South Alabama offers a $5M inventory of mathematics and science instructional materials and seven math and science specialists for classroom support.

The sample abstract shown in Box 15.3 was effective. Notice that in just a few words it clearly describes the purpose of the proposal. It also shows that the proposal author makes a strong commitment to the project. Successful grant writers know how to get inside each funder's head. Your teachers can, too, if you advise them to add a short sentence or two telling how their project will be sustained once the funding stops.

The Table of Contents. Another tool that your teachers can use to sell their proposal is a table of contents. Although, like the abstract, a table of contents is not always called for in some RFPs, it is far too important to omit. Box 15.4 shows the table of contents that accompanied the Summer Physics Institute Proposal. Remember that this proposal competed against proposals written by all other colleges and universities in the state and, year after year, it outperformed all the other proposals. Share it with your teachers, and ask them to notice how quickly this one sheet of paper allows anyone to locate any part of the proposal. Even readers of proposals that don't ask for the abstract and table of contents will appreciate having them, if they are kept short and clear.

Statement of Project Goals, Objectives, and Anticipated Outcomes. Some RFPs require this information (see an example from an actual proposal in Table 15.2 on p. 428). The purposes and outcomes are major expectations for the project, and the descriptions specify the conditions under which you expect your subjects to achieve them and the degree to which you expect each participant to perform. This statement must clearly tell the readers exactly what your teachers want their program to achieve.

Box 15.4 Sample Table of Contents

I. PROJECT SUMMARY

II. PROJECT DESCRIPTION

- **A. Objectives**
- **B. Participant Selection**
  1. Number of participants
  2. Policy for submission
  3. Selection procedure
- **C. Program Content**
  1. Physics 110
  2. Physics electives
  3. Integrated laboratory
  4. Seminar
- **D. Additional Components**
  1. Follow-up activities
  2. Evaluation

III. STAFF

IV. FACILITIES

- **A. Instructional facilities**
- **B. Housing facilities**

V. INSTITUTIONAL SUPPORT

VI. BUDGET

The Timetable. If the funders are interested in the proposal, they will want to know when the initiative will start. When will each step get underway? When will it be complete? The best way to communicate this information is to create a visual chart, a flow chart (usually called a timetable) with arrows that show the major steps and the sequence of events. A timetable can be as simple as the sample shown in Figure 15.3A, or it can be as detailed as the project calendar in Figure 15.3B (both on p. 429).

The Budget. When people think about grants, they think of money. A clear budget simplifies the proposal. People who evaluate proposals are careful to approve only those that show hope of delivering the best services, and at a reasonable rate. While it's true that funders want quality work, they also want it to be reasonable. This does not mean that they expect it to be inexpensive. If the budget is too small, the proposal will be unrealistic. If it is too large, the readers will suspect that your teachers' main purpose is to serve themselves, not the funder. Accordingly, advise them to plan to spend the amount needed to do an excellent job, but no more. Advise your teachers to proceed as outlined below.

Begin by listing tangible items. Rank them, putting the most costly at the top. Repeat this process with intangible items. Considering that most funded proposals are funded for less than the proposed budget requests, your teachers will need a way to prepare to negotiate without making their proposal suffer. A technique that has worked very well for the author is including a nice secondary feature that enriches the program, but one that can be deleted without diminishing the quality of the program's main purposes. This technique is tantamount to preparing an excellent meal and adding an expensive wine: Even if

Table 15.2 Detailed Project Goals and Major Outcomes Statement

Increased Student Achievement in Math and Science		
Goals	**Major Outcomes**	**Descriptions**
Create and Implement Challenging Courses and Curricula (Research Strand 1)	Implementation of State Standards and Courses of Study in math and science	The AMSTI curriculum will be integrated into the State Courses of Study and Standards for Math and Science.
Recruit, Prepare, and Retain Teacher Leaders (Research Strand 2)	(1) Systemic development of standards for Math and Science Teacher Leaders. (2) Teacher leaders in K-8 schools will assume new roles and responsibilities.	(1) Alabama's Standards for Teacher Leaders will be developed and revised to deepen subject matter content and to require more inquiry-based instruction in the preparation and continuing education of K-8 math and science teachers. (2) Teacher Leaders will become school-based coaches who will provide coaching, demonstration, and best practices for all teachers of mathematics and science.
Raise Academic Achievement of Students in Math and Science (Research Strand 3)	(1) Increase inquiry-based instruction. (2) Align instruction with the Alabama Standards and Courses of Study in math and science; (3) Improve Critical Thinking Skills	(1) Students will move from didactic to active learning in mathematics and science. (2) Instructional materials will be better aligned with State Courses of Study and national Standards in Math and Science. (3) Students and teachers will deepen their understanding of subject-matter content.
Provide Professional Development (Research Strand 4)	(1) Professional Development (AMSTI Summer Institutes) for existing K-8 teachers, STEM faculty and College of Education faculty. (2) Teacher Leader Academy for Teacher Leaders	(1) AMSTI-NSF will build on the state-funded two-week AMSTI Summer Institutes to provide intensive professional development for math and science teachers in Grades K-8. The state-funded AMSTI institute will prepare 800 teachers. STEM faculty and College of Education faculty will collaborate in its delivery. (2) The AMSTI-NSF Teacher Leader Academy will culminate with 120 teachers completing their master's degrees in mathematics or science education and certification as a Teacher Leader.
	Standards-based Professional Development for renewal of teaching certificates	Continuing professional development for K-8 mathematics and science teachers that is standards-based ensuring that the renewal of teachers' certificates will include increased participation in curriculum-specific subject matter content and pedagogy.
	AMSTI-NSF Teacher Leader Learning Network	Participating schools will restructure school time to provide ongoing, on-site professional development experiences. One-hundred and fifty hours of professional development beyond the Summer Institute will be provided to all participants over a five-year period.

Figure 15.3A Sample Timetable

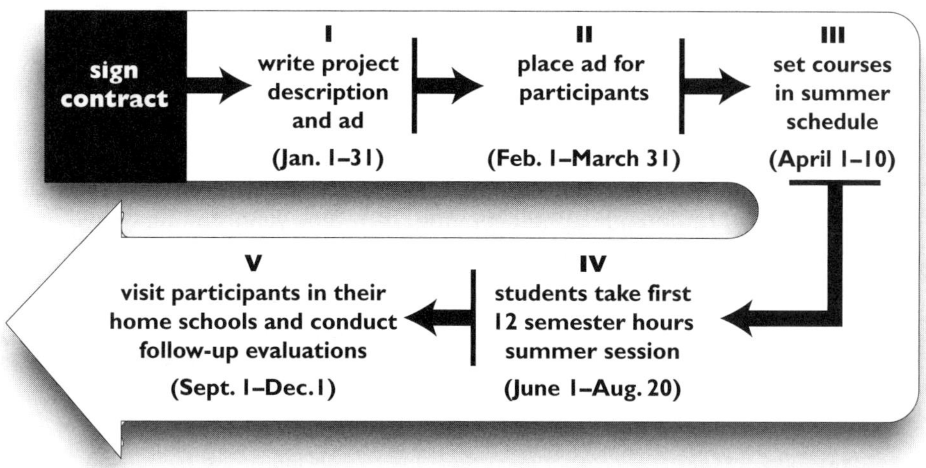
sign contract
I
write project description and ad
(Jan. 1–31)
II
place ad for participants
(Feb. 1–March 31)
III
set courses in summer schedule
(April 1–10)
IV
students take first 12 semester hours summer session
(June 1–Aug. 20)
V
visit participants in their home schools and conduct follow-up evaluations
(Sept. 1–Dec. 1)

Figure 15.3B Project Calendar

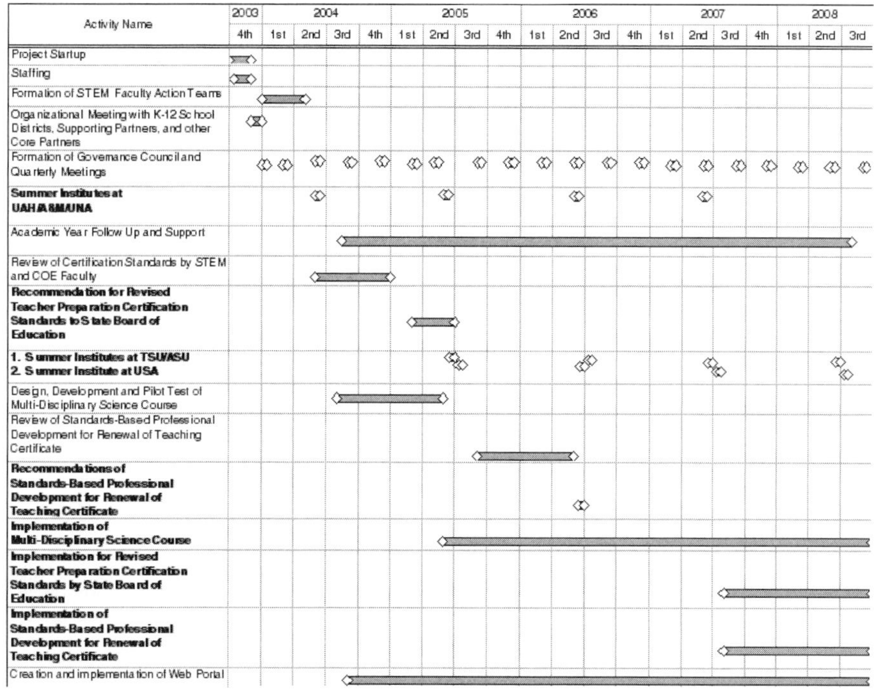
Activity Name
2003
2004
2005
2006
2007
2008
4th
1st
2nd
3rd
Project Startup
Staffing
Formation of STEM Faculty Action Teams
Organizational Meeting with K-12 School Districts, Supporting Partners, and other Core Partners
Formation of Governance Council and Quarterly Meetings
Summer Institutes at UAH/A&M/UNA
Academic Year Follow Up and Support
Review of Certification Standards by STEM and COE Faculty
Recommendation for Revised Teacher Preparation Certification Standards to State Board of Education
1. Summer Institutes at TSU/ASU
2. Summer Institute at USA
Design, Development and Pilot Test of Multi-Disciplinary Science Course
Review of Standards-Based Professional Development for Renewal of Teaching Certificate
Recommendations of Standards-Based Professional Development for Renewal of Teaching Certificate
Implementation of Multi-Disciplinary Science Course
Implementation for Revised Teacher Preparation Certification Standards by State Board of Education
Implementation of Standards-Based Professional Development for Renewal of Teaching Certificate
Creation and implementation of Web Portal

you substitute a less expensive drink, the quality of the meal is still preserved. The budget in the physics institute proposal is shown in Box 15.5.

In-Kind Contributions. In most proposals, in-kind contributions have become increasingly important. The word *in-kind* means noncash. In-kind contributions include donated expenses such as salaries. (The most common are secretaries' salaries, but if the authors of the proposal wish to contribute part of their time to codirect the program, an equal percentage of their salaries can count as in-kind contributions.) Other common in-kind items include space, utilities, library use, tuition, and photocopying. In recent years funders have expected, and usually demanded, the grant recipient's institution to contribute more and

Box 15.5 Physics Institute Budget

TUITION AND FEES			
Tuition		$552.00	
University Fees		$104.00	
Lab Fees 3 @ $25.00		$75.00	
		$731.00	
	× 15 =		$10,965.00
FIRST-TIME APPLICANTS (6@$15.00)			$90.00
PARTICIPANT SUPPORT:			
Commuters (4)			
Mileage (3000 @ $0.22)		$660.00	
Meals (40 @ 4.25)		$170.00	
Lab Kits/Materials		$40.00	
Textbooks		$25.00	
		$895.00	
	× 4 =		$3,580.00
Residents (11)			
Room (10 weeks @ $50.00)		$500.00	
Mileage		$60.00	
Meals		$467.50	
Lab Kits/Materials		$110.00	
Textbooks		$25.00	
		$1,162.50	
	× 11 =		$12,787.50
TOTAL PARTICIPANT SUPPORT		$2,788.50	
TRAVEL FOR FOLLOW-UP ACTIVITIES			$400.00
INDIRECT COST REIMBURSEMENT (16% of $11,062.50)			$1,770.00
PROJECT BUDGET TOTAL FOR 15			$29,592.50

more, often requiring a dollar-for-dollar match. In other words, to obtain a million dollars from some funders the recipient would have to show at least a million dollars worth of in-kind contributions. The case study in this chapter is a good example of resourceful grant writers' ideas for in-kind contributions.

The Evaluation. The last part of the proposal is the proposal evaluation. Encourage your teachers to include plans for both an internal evaluation and an external evaluation. The internal evaluation is conducted locally, often by the institution's research and evaluation office and sometimes by the principal investigator (the main grant writer) and his or her collaborators. The internal evaluation is a formative evaluation, aimed at providing feedback to improve the quality of services rendered. An excellent example of internal evaluation is seen in the physics teachers' summer institute proposal. Remember that each year, after the institute was over, the director drove to each participant's school to ask two simple questions. The first was, "Can you show me examples of how the institute benefited you and your students?" In other words, show instances where some of processes learned about in last summer's institute are now being implemented in classes or labs. The second question was, "Can you think of ways the institute might have served you but did not?" These two simple questions were responsible for this proposal being refunded repeatedly. Obviously, funders may suspect that any internal evaluation might be prejudiced; therefore, you should encourage your teachers to always plan (in their budget) to hire external evaluation experts to give an impartial assessment of your program.

A Seven-Step Approach to Grant Writing

Some teachers would gladly write grants but don't know how to begin. Following is a seven-step approach to developing an irresistible grant proposal. This model involves (1) identifying your own strengths and interests, (2) identifying the strengths and limitations of the community, (3) determining exactly what the donor wants, (4) using the request for proposal (RFP) as a blueprint, (5) including at least one unique feature, (6) using matching funds, and (7) preparing the budget.

1. Identify your own interests and strengths.

One of the most common reasons that grant proposals fail is because the author has little or no relationship to the proposal beyond the act of writing it. Successful authors of fiction and nonfiction commonly advise aspiring writers to write about those things that mean the most to them. Award-winning author Marjorie Rawlings, for example, tried for years to write Gothic novels. Her editor and friend Maxwell Perkins, who edited for the likes of Ernest Hemmingway and F. Scott Fitzgerald, advised her to stop trying to write Gothics and write about more familiar topics, such as her neighbors whom she frequently described in her letters to Perkins. After many Gothic failures, she finally became desperate enough to take her editor's advice. Her first novel about her neighbors, *The Yearling*, won a Pulitzer Prize. Within three years she followed with her autobiography, *Cross Creek*, which also was a best seller.

Topics with which the author is familiar—topics in which he or she has a genuine interest—should be first considerations when searching for grant proposal topics. Professionals often limit themselves unnecessarily by focusing only on their professional interests. Sometimes teachers are fortunate enough to develop hobbies that tie together their personal and professional lives. For example, a science teacher who benefited from a National Science Foundation Institute in Earth Science studied invertebrate paleontology and mineralogy and became fascinated with invertebrate fossils and rocks, which he collected whenever he traveled. While teaching middle-level science in the Appalachia, he enjoyed the mythical stories that his students' parents and grandparents told about snakes. This teacher learned to make professional use of his personal fascination with snake myths, and he devised an activity that enabled his students to test them. Through these constructivist experiments, students were allowed to personally discover flaws that disproved each myth.

When searching for grant proposal topics, this teacher should consider his interest in and knowledge of snakes and their lore, as well as his interest in trilobites and other invertebrate fossils. English teachers might consider successful authors and poets in their region. History teachers certainly have their favorite historical personalities. A retired physicist who had a lifelong hobby of studying the personal lives of renowned physicists might consider writing grants to disseminate his knowledge to teachers.

An Example of a Successful Choice of Topic. When helping a faculty (as opposed to individual teachers) write grant proposals, the faculty as a unit should agree on several common ideals that it values. For example, a faculty might prize an experiential curriculum. In fact, one high school history faculty became excited about experiential education and decided to develop an early

It Works for Me!

Cost-Free Change

Thomas Oldenski, University of Dayton

Change seems to be one of those concepts that many teachers are not enthused about. In order to help teachers appreciate the experience of and the need for change, I have teachers take the time to write two journal entries: "My Ideal Day at School" (in this scenario, students and administrators must be there) and "My Not-So-Ideal Day at School." The teachers then reflect on what they wrote, identify themes or patterns, and comment on what needs to be done in order to change the not-so-ideal days to become more like the ideal days. Then they develop ways in which this can happen and what steps are needed for this change to occur. Usually they discover that change can occur without any financial cost and by one's commitment to make it happen. This activity can be done either with a small group of teachers or with the supervisor interacting with a teacher.

American, turn-of-the-century program. Through a partnership with a local university's department of secondary education, this faculty began meeting informally to explore possibilities.

There was a very old log home within the community that had long been abandoned. At the request of a history teacher, this old house was donated to the school. A team of teachers and students carefully dismantled the small cabin-like home, log by log, and reassembled it on the school campus. Another team of students researched the lives of the families who had lived in this house. A few old photos and some very old contracts were found among a pile of debris. Each photo and document was carefully mounted and framed, later to be hung on the walls of the rebuilt house. A history of each family of dwellers was carefully researched, attractively formatted and printed, and framed for wall mounting.

When the building was complete, a celebration was held—not just any celebration but a turn-of-the-century celebration. A music teacher worked with a team of students to research the types of music that reflected the era. An authentic band was formed involving members of the community, complete with dulcimers and fiddles. The chair of the local department of secondary education agreed to call a square dance, and dance lessons were given in the gym so that by the night of the big event one of the teachers and several students were quite accomplished.

At the time this old cabin was built, sacred harp music was popular. The students who discovered this fact memorized some hymns from the time period and sang them at the closing of the event. Following the custom of the era, the students sang the words to each stanza and followed by vocalizing only the notes of the stanza. A cakewalk, a three-legged-race, and a rope-pulling contest entertained students of all ages. Carefully researched ghost stories held the attention of the students' younger brothers and sisters. Ice cream was made, using hand-cranked freezers.

The event was a complete success, whetting the appetites of students and teachers alike. They were beginning to enjoy their expertise about life at this time in history, and they wanted to expand this expertise and the related activities. A local annual crafts festival featuring such crafts as basket weaving, cane-bottomed chair making, log splitting to make roof shingles, and corn-shuck doll making fueled their enthusiasm.

This faculty and student body had taken the first step toward successful grant writing. They had looked inward and identified particular activities that they enjoyed, and they had even related their personally prized activities to their profession. (To see the results of their next step, read the following section.) Perhaps even more important, they had begun bonding as a learning community. The hands-on, constructivist, learner-centered activities were fun, and these teachers were beginning to discover ways to turn each activity into an educational experience.

2. Identify strengths and limitations of your community.

Before writing a grant proposal, writers should always pause to survey their own community, identifying any strengths and weaknesses they can use to enhance the chances that their proposal will be funded. When donors establish funds to use to support grants—whether these funds belong to a government agency, a business, or an individual—the purpose of most of these funding programs is to help society, either all or part of it, as opposed to helping an individual. Therefore, any individual or group wishing to tap into these resources can enhance the chances of getting a proposal funded by using the community as a reason for asking for the resources. For example, a school faculty wishing to restructure to meet a state or district education-reform practice can use the local community (school, city, or region) to convince the potential donors that their money will be wisely invested if entrusted to them.

The faculty with the log house (a true story as opposed to a fabricated example) was not content to end its experiential curriculum development program within the arena of the local school. Their next step was to contact a state senator in a major city nearby, who in the past had given support to the building of a life-size, three-dimensional model of a steel mill. The senator wanted to preserve the process of turning raw iron ore into steel. With this senator's help, the group managed to secure permission to build several log houses and a turn-of-the-century church and school. One log house became the site of a hand-operated paper mill; another became a candle factory.

A square cement floor was poured for square dancing. To gain a better understanding of the time, games of the day were researched and duplicated. A faculty member from the university's biology department took several classes of students to a nearby park to classify and label the native trees along a nature walk.

When the physical facilities were finished, arrangements were made for schools in the immediate and contiguous counties to bus children to the park. The senator was helpful in getting a line established in the state budget to support two doctoral students' assistantships at the university's college of education for the purpose of overseeing the operations of the experiential program, which now serves thousands of children annually.

The developers of this program found a means of financing their educational dream. Had their efforts failed, they could have written a grant proposal to one of two national steel industries that had plants operating in the city. Funders are more likely to provide support to the communities in which they are located. A common expression is often heard in grant offices that reflects this practice: "Industries favor programs that are within the shadows of their own smokestacks."

These educators had several strengths that they could have used as leverage to gain support of their proposal. They had already conceptualized it in their local school. They proved their resourcefulness and their level of commitment to their dreams by rebuilding the log house on their campus. Another asset that this team had to offer was the partnership between school and university. Today, legislators and educators alike are endorsing the effectiveness of partnerships between teacher education programs and public schools. Furthermore, education reformers are claiming that the best, longest-lasting reforms are schoolwide, collaborative efforts of entire school faculties as opposed to individual, districtwide, or statewide efforts. Today's literature is also replete with articles that support constructivist, hands-on curricula, of which experiential programs are prime exemplars. These educators could capitalize on these assets simply by citing research and literature that support these approaches.

Although we have suggested that grant-proposal writers should capitalize on both the strengths and weaknesses of their communities, so far (in the case of the turn-of-the-century project) only strengths have been identified. Upon closer inspection, we can also identify weaknesses or needs. For example, suppose the grant writers for this program could show that the many children who would benefit had no opportunities for hands-on participation in early American history. A simple survey could be conducted by sending a short questionnaire to the schools throughout this county and its bordering counties to ask how many of these students had seen a steel mill, a paper mill, or candle factory, and how many had actually helped make paper or candles. Not every community has log cabins or steel mills, but every community has a history and old buildings that can be used to ignite student interest.

3. Determine what the donors want.

One step that was passed over lightly should be emphasized. Potential funders want proof that their money will be wisely invested. Most RFPs receive far more proposals than the available resources can support, making the process highly competitive. Taking time to conduct surveys and review the literature to make sure that the proposed project is, indeed, really needed can give a proposal the winning edge.

4. Use the request for proposal as a blueprint.

Frequently heard comments in grant-proposal writing workshops suggest that many educators believe that companies and individuals fund proposals as a way to save money. Although it is true that some grants may reduce the amount of income tax owed, this doesn't mean that giving money away nets the funder a profit. Nor do funders support proposals with the sole purpose of giving away money. Rather, funders usually want something in return for their support.

Experienced grant-proposal writers know to carefully examine each request for proposal when selecting a possible funding source. Indeed, they know that the secret to unlocking the resources is often found in the RFP. Carefully responding to each part of the RFP can, and usually does, significantly increase the chances of acceptance. The writers of many RFPs often evaluate the proposals these RFPs solicit. This means that each proposal evaluator may have included a particular directive in the RFP that he or she wishes to see in each funded proposal. Knowing that the winning proposal will be the one that garners the most votes, writers should purposefully address every part of the RFP.

5. Include at least one unique feature.

Most funding agencies have a team of proposal evaluators who evaluate all proposals received in response to a request for proposal. Most RFPs receive dozens or even hundreds of proposals. Because these readers are charged with the task of reviewing all of these proposals, and because most of the proposals are made similar by the restrictions set out in the RFP, the result is a boring assignment. Furthermore, the similarities among the proposals make the task of singling out one proposal for funding extremely difficult.

Teachers can give their proposals an edge by planning into each proposal one or more unique features. As an example, consider a $1.1 million proposal written to acquire five networked microcomputer labs. The proposal writer had a unique opportunity to meet with a potential corporate funder, but he was given only 20 minutes to present his proposal. Consequently, he gave what amounted to five proposal abstracts, each lasting for only four minutes. At the end of the time limit, he asked the potential funder if he had heard anything that was interesting. The immediate reply was, "Tell me more about the laboratory school." Following this brief meeting, the potential recipient developed a full-blown written proposal that featured the laboratory school. The result was a funding in full of a requested $1.1 million budget for equipment and networking.

6. Use matching funds.

Today more than ever before, grant funders expect the recipient to commit matching funds. Since few grant writers have large amounts of money to invest in their grant proposals, most writers ask their employers to make in-kind contributions (contributions other than cash), offering instead the use of existing resources such as building space, secretarial time, and equipment.

For several years after the personal computer was introduced in the field of education, requests for the purchase of computers became so common that many proposal evaluators were (and perhaps remain) reluctant to approve requests that included them. The logical conclusion is to resist the temptation to include computers and other expensive equipment in your proposal. If unavailable costly equipment is required, a good alternative is to rent it. The funding agency will be less likely to balk on renting the computer, because it is obvious that the author is not trying to net a personal toy.

7. Prepare the budget.

The proposed budget is considered by many to be the single most important part of a grant proposal. The ability to prepare an effective budget can vastly increase the chances that a proposal will be funded.

Budget preparation is the final part of the proposal-writing process because the rest of the proposal (the narrative) is used to write the budget. Examine each major part of the proposed activity; then prepare a corresponding portion of the budget to fund each part. The amount of money requested to fund any part of the proposal should be roughly proportional to the significance of that part. For example, in the sample physics summer institute proposal, a series of three semester credit-hour course offerings was the major part of the activities; therefore, it should constitute the most expensive item. Experienced grant proposal evaluation teams check each part of the budget against the narrative to make certain that each item in the budget is necessary and reasonable.

It Works for Me!

A Cadre of Experts

Sandra S. Murray, The University of Tennessee at Martin

The constant innovations in education make it a daunting task for teachers to keep informed about their profession. Often, fiscal and time restraints make it difficult to provide staff-development and curriculum-planning time for the entire staff. One technique for increased teacher curriculum knowledge and on-site assistance for teachers is to develop a cadre of curriculum experts. Any teacher who has a desire to become an expert in a specific subject and is respected by the faculty is "supertrained" in his or her selected subject area. That person then becomes the go-to person for teachers, provides staff training, and assists with curriculum planning. As staff development and conference opportunities become available, the subject expert can train the other teachers.

Developing an Appropriate Writing Style

As mentioned earlier, many otherwise excellent grant proposals are rejected because of their inappropriate or poor writing style. George Hademenos (2005) says that for our ideas to have the best chance of getting funded they must be simple to understand and easily implemented. Perhaps the greatest mistake is an error in style. Figure 15.4 (on the following page) reveals most of the mistakes that authors make when writing. The remainder of this chapter will focus on helping teachers develop an effective grant-writing style. Here, *writing style* actually refers to editing, a process that follows the completion of a first draft. Grant writers should understand that the job ahead is to write grants, and they should forge ahead to draft their proposals without concern for grammar, spelling, punctuation, or style. Encourage your teachers to first capture their good ideas on paper. Then they should carefully craft each paragraph and each sentence, making the message crystal clear. Apart from having something worthwhile to offer, clarity and brevity are the two most important features that define an effective grant-writing style.

Over 25 years of biennial surveys to editors of professional journals (Henson, 2005) have found that a leading cause of rejection is faulty writing style. When questioned further, these editors explained that their contributors are too wordy and too pedantic, often producing manuscripts that read like dissertations. Share this information with your teachers, and persuade them to heed the advice of these editors when they are writing grant proposals. The same style that works so well for writing journal articles works equally well for writing grant proposals. It makes sense; funders will not spend their money on projects they can't understand.

Imagine that you are one of several proposal evaluators who have been reading proposals all day long. It's dinnertime, but you still have several pro-

Figure 15.4 Developing an Appropriate Writing Style

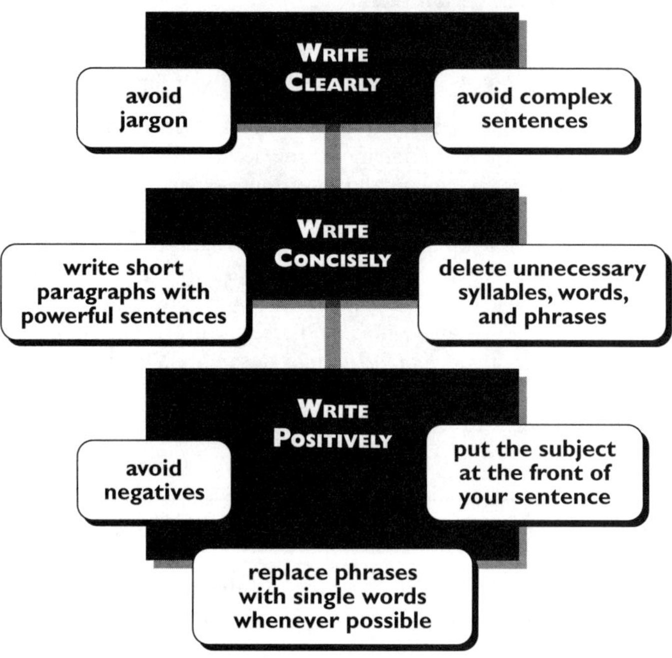

posals to read before you can call it a day. You are weary and hungry. All day long you have read one wordy, rambling, confusing proposal after another. Most of the proposals remind you of dissertations. The serious grant writer's challenge is to craft a proposal that will elicit the opposite reaction from you: "Finally, I have found one that I can understand!" Following are some tips that will help your teachers develop an effective grant-writing style.

- *Write short paragraphs.* Too often, evaluators must face paragraphs that run for a page or longer. This is a huge mistake. Each paragraph should have only one major idea. When you start another idea, start a new paragraph.
- *Write powerful sentences.* You can help your teachers to do so by making the following suggestions:
  - Keep sentences short. One extra clause, phrase, or word can kill the meaning.
  - Use concrete nouns for subjects.
  - Put the subject at the front of the sentence.
  - Use active verbs (use present tense, avoiding *ed* and *ing*)
  - Immediately follow the subject with the verb.
  - Never start sentences with indefinite words like there, it, he, or she.
  - Avoid gender-equity issues, and the awkwardness they cause, by pluralizing pronouns.

- Use common, everyday language; avoid unnecessary jargon. Replace complex words and expressions with more simple ones—for example, replace *as well as* with *and, utilize* with *use,* and *prioritize* with *rank.*
- Avoid starting sentences with pronouns and prepositions, and begin most sentences with concrete subjects. Too often, sentences begin with the word *there.* The reader must read half the sentence to discover the subject.
- Avoid ending sentences with *etc.*
- Avoid number errors such as *the data was* and *the family were.*
- Edit, edit, edit!

A Grant Proposal Writing Kit

To be effective in their efforts to help schools access money through writing grant proposals, supervisors need their own grant proposal writing kit. The kit should include a minimum of the following materials: (1) a *Catalog of Federal Domestic Assistance,* (2) a *National Data Book of Foundations,* (3) a copy of *Grant Writing in Higher Education,* (4) a copy of *Developing Successful Grant Proposals,* and (5) a set of PowerPoints or transparencies made from the lists found in this chapter. Following is a brief guide for your use of each of these resources.

1. *Catalog of Federal Domestic Assistance.* This catalog is an excellent source of information on topics that the federal government is willing to fund. This single source lists over one thousand pages of federal funding sources, giving the type of programs funded by each source, the requirements of each program, and the address of each source. For about $50 you can obtain a copy of the latest edition of the Catalog from the Superintendent of Documents, U.S. Government Printing Office, Washington, D.C., 20402. Better yet, visit the Web site (http://www.cfda.gov) and download the PDF version for free.

As with all sources, writers of proposals for these monies should pay particular attention to the specified objectives for each of these grants.

2. *The Foundation Center.* This is the number-one resource for gathering information on foundations. It has four offices and many cooperating libraries throughout the country. The Center's main publication is the *Foundation Directory,* which costs about $200. You can also subscribe to the Foundation Directory online (http://fconline.foundationcenter.org) at several plan levels, from basic to professional. An advantage to using this resource is that you omit the many foundations that fund only a few dollars worth of proposals annually. Each of the 6,600 foundations listed in the *Directory* has assets of at least a million dollars, and each awards a minimum of $100,000 a year. The Foundation Center also has computer search facilities, the Federal Assistance Programs Retrieved System (FAPRS).

3. *Grant Writing in Higher Education.* This handbook for educators at all levels addresses those questions that are asked most by novice grant writers. The book gives examples of successful grants written by professors to assist public schools and identifies the unique qualities of each proposal. The book (ISBN 0-205-38919-8) is available from Allyn & Bacon for about $30.

4. *Writing for Publication: Road to Academic Success*. This book focuses on writing style. Its intent is to help educators and others develop a simple, straightforward style with the purpose of communicating effectively. Educators often combine jargon and verbosity, resulting in less-than-clear communication. Effective grant writing requires the opposite: simple, concise, and clear writing. This book has a special chapter on grant proposal writing that describes a number of successful school-community partnership grant proposals. This book (ISBN 0-205-43319-7) is available from Allyn & Bacon for about $35.

Helpful Web Sites

The following online sources cited in Education Update (ASCD, March 2007) include a variety of types of major funding agencies:

Charity Navigator (www.charitynavigator.org) rates charities by evaluating two broad areas of financial health—organizational efficiency, and organizational capacity.

Foundation Center (www.foundationcenter.org) maintains a comprehensive database of U.S. grant makers, connecting them with nonprofits. It operates research, education, and training programs designed to advance philanthropy.

The National Association of State Charity Officials (www.nasconet.org) oversees charitable organizations in the United States.

Nonprofit Guides (www.npguides.org) offers free Web-based grant-writing tools for nonprofit organizations, charitable and educational public organizations, and other community-minded groups.

Avoiding the Scams

Because grant writing is a lucrative business, it has a way of drawing an inordinate number of scam artists. But, like all travelers on today's highways, experienced grant writers eventually learn how to maneuver around these obstacles. The following Web sites should help your teachers feel more secure when submitting proposals:

Government Grants Review
http://www.governmentgrantsreview.org
This consumer advocacy review group researches and gathers data on government grant programs.

Government Grants Online Reviewed
http://www.grants-reviewed.org
This organization vets RFPs to eliminate "make money" scams.

Grants.gov
http://www.grants.gov
This organization provides a valuable public service. It is a good source for exploring government-sponsored grants. It is a central storehouse for information on over 1,000 grant programs and provides access to approximately $500 billion in annual awards. Although it may sound too good to be true, this source is not to be confused with the plethora of "come-on" commercials that promise to give you money just because you want or need it. In fact, almost

none of the grants.gov agencies make awards to individuals, and none of them provide personal financial assistance. Instead, most of these grants are awarded to state, city, or local governments or tribal governments; public housing authorities; small businesses; and—most important for our purposes—to *education organizations including independent school districts, public and state-controlled institutions of higher education, and private institutions of higher education.*

Federal Education Agency Grants

Association for Supervision and Curriculum Development (ASCD)
http://www.ascd.org

Kappa Delta Pi
http://www.kdp.org

National Association for the Education of Young Children (NAEYC)
http://www.naeyc.org

National Association of Elementary School Principals
http://www.naesp.org

National Association of Secondary School Principals (NASSP)
http://www.nassp.org

National Council for the Social Studies
http://www.socialstudies.org

National Council of Professors of Educational Administration (NCPEA)
http://www.cnx.org/lenses/ncpea/endorsements

National Council of Teachers of English
http://www.ncte.org

National Council of Teachers of Mathematics (NCTM)
http://www.nctm.org

It Works for Me!

Rallying Support

Patricia Green-Powell, Florida A&M University

Many national religious organizations are committed to play a part in improving the educational opportunities available to children in the local communities that are served by their houses of worship. Together, national organizations, their local affiliates, schools, communities, and individuals can make a positive difference in family involvement in education, helping help children achieve high standards and improving schools.

In its efforts to provide school supplies for the children in its community, New Mt. Zion A.M.E. Church located in Tallahassee, Florida, sponsors an annual "backpack" school program, where children are given backpacks filled with the necessary supplies that they need for the new school year. It should be noted that Griffin Middle School, which is located about .2 miles south of New Mt. Zion A.M.E. Church, performed better than other schools located in disadvantaged communities.

National Education Association (NEA)
http://www.nea.org

National Middle School Association (NMSA)
http://www.nmsa.org

National Science Teachers Association (NSTA)
http://www.nsta.org

Phi Delta Kappa
www.pdkintl.org

Keeping Your Grants

Writing good grants takes time. Once funded, the grant writer can't afford to lose them. Following are a few suggestions you can give your teachers to help them remain successful.

Emphasize to your teachers that grant writing should not be considered a one-shot, piecemeal activity. Remember the bowler who just drops in off the street at the local bowling alley for an occasional game. That bowler will never become great. But, as a grant writer, your teachers can become as successful as they are willing to work to become. Teachers are professionals, so we are talking about a personal, ongoing grant-writing program for each teacher.

Developing a research library (see chapter 13), which can be housed in a three-ring binder, is an excellent beginning. Provide each teacher with a binder and suggest that each time they read a newspaper or professional journal, the teachers look for statistics. As mentioned at the beginning of the chapter, many grant evaluators are bean counters; they love statistics, numbers, and percentages because these are more exact than words. Also encourage teachers to look for quotable quotes—short, simple sentences that make a strong point clearly. For example, the sample physics institute grant discussed earlier started with, and was built upon, this simple sentence: "Over 85% of the nation's high school physics teachers teach out of field." A million-dollar technology grant began with a sentence taken from a news report, "So and So County is located in the congressional district that has the highest high school dropout rate in the nation." Both of these short statements provided powerful evidence of the acute needs of the beneficiaries of these grants. Verbal presentations can also be rich sources of quotable quotes and statistics.

Tell your teachers to write each quote exactly as they see or hear it. If it appears in writing, cite the source exactly and completely. If it is in a journal, include the article title, all authors' names and initials, the year, the exact journal title, the volume number, the issue number, the first and last page numbers of the article, and, if a quote, the exact page(s) on which the quote appeared. Most education journals use the American Psychological Association (APA) style (see Box 15.6).

When attending professional meetings, teachers should take their pens and notebooks (or laptops) and capture useful data and quotes to include in their

Box 15.6 Sample Referencing Style (APA)

For a periodical:

Author, A. A., Author, C. C., & Author, F. F. (year). Title of the article: Upper case immediately following a colon. *Title of Periodical, volume number*(issue number), xxx–xxx.

If the journal does not have a volume number, include the month it was published in the parentheses immediately preceding the year.

For a book:

Author, A. A. (year of publication). *Book title: Subtitle* (pp. xxx–xxx). City: Publisher.

For an online document:

Author, A. A. (year). *Title of work.* Retrieved month, day, year, from source.

research binders and later in their grant proposals. Copy the keynote speakers' quotes verbatim, citing the exact name of the speaker, the official conference title, the exact title and time of the speech, the city, and the date.

Another value of the research binder is its function as a storehouse for documentation. As your teachers' grants are funded, remind them to always write articles (even if it's only for the school newsletter) so they can document their programs' successes and share the results with others. Potential funders know that "it makes no sense to invest time and money in new programs if teachers are not prepared to deal with the changes. An effective and ongoing support system and staff development programs must be a major part of any effort to implement new curricular practices in schools" (Daresh, 2007, p. 278).

This documentation may be submitted to professional journals and local newspapers, and they may be turned into proposals or presentations. Copies of program announcements that include the presentations, and copies of letters from school officials or professional association officers where presentations are given, should be kept in the binder. These documents remind funding agencies that, unlike many eloquent writers who fail to efficiently use the support they receive, the money given to support your proposal continues to get results.

All of these comments suggest that such data can be used again and again to write one grant after another. Too often, educators shortchange themselves by thinking that using a fact, quote, or statistic in more than one proposal is unprofessional or unethical. Successful grant writers don't think that way. It would be tantamount to buying a carpenter's power drill, using it for one job, and throwing it away.

Conclusion

Encourage your teachers to ignore those who would tell them that grant writing is a waste of time or that there are no longer sufficient funds available to make it worth their time. This is simply not true. On the contrary, more funds are available today than in the past, but getting these funds requires the ability to write highly competitive proposals. By attending workshops, reading books on this topic, and dialoguing with successful grant writers, teachers can develop the required expertise.

Successful grant writing requires the ability to find good topics. Encourage your teachers to first determine their purpose for writing a grant proposal, identify their strengths and weaknesses and the strengths and limitations of their school, school district, and community.

The request for proposal (RFP) is the grant writer's most valuable tool. Encourage your teachers to examine every line of it for tips, and then follow up on every one. Remind them to include at least one unique feature that will make their proposal stand out from the others.

Closely following the RFP is essential. Offering substantial matching funds further enhances one's chance of acceptance. In-kind funds such as salaries, facilities, and equipment can be used instead of offering cash. A dollar-for-dollar match, or more, is often expected and is sometimes required.

Encourage your teachers to prepare a budget that is hefty enough to do a good job, but advise them against padding it. They should be as protective with grant money as they are with their own. They can do this and still prepare to negotiate by including a stand-alone feature. When told that they must reduce the budget, they can simply point out that removing this feature from the proposal will take away a desirable ancillary goal but will not damage the quality of the proposal.

Questions for Discussion and Reflection

1. Describe the development of a proposal budget relative to the development of the body of a proposal.
2. What role should the request for proposal (RFP) play in writing a proposal?
3. Describe the status of grant proposal writing. Include statements about the degree of competition and the availability of funds.
4. List and describe the major steps in grant proposal writing.
5. How can a writer determine whether it is better to begin by choosing a topic and then searching for funders, or to begin by checking the topics of available funding?
6. Name and discuss some important library resources that can become tools for grant writing.
7. How can community weaknesses be used to strengthen a grant proposal?
8. How much responsibility do instructional supervisors have for helping schools secure funding?
9. Should supervisors ever take total responsibility for writing a proposal to help a school or a school district? If so, under what conditions?
10. Describe a purpose for which you would like your teachers to write a proposal. In your description of a potential proposal topic, describe one unique feature that would gain the evaluators' attention.

11. Describe a common pitfall in proposal budgets that often discredits proposal writers, and tell how this pitfall can be overcome.
12. To what extent should proposal writers let their own individual interests and goals influence their selection of proposal topics?
13. How would you advise faculty members who ask for your help in preparing a proposal with a deadline set for next week?
14. What advantages do school–university partnerships offer to proposal writing?

Suggested Activities

1. Visit the local district superintendent's office. Interview a member of the superintendent's staff, such as the associate or assistant superintendent for curriculum. Ask this administrator to identify some serious needs in this district. Make a list of these needs.
2. Invite a local school administrator to join you in surveying the strengths and weaknesses of the school. Make a list of the strengths and a list of the weaknesses and, reflecting on both, write a brief description of ways these might be used to strengthen a proposal.
3. Interview a local school counselor. Ask the counselor to identify some special needs. At the library, examine *The Federal Register* and the *Catalog of Federal Domestic Assistance*. Identify some possible funding agencies and lead some teachers and administrators in preparing a proposal to fulfill these needs.
4. Visit a local college or university's contracts and grants office. Get a copy of a request for proposal. Share it with a few faculty members and go over each separate part of the RFP, showing how you might address each part.
5. Interview a local university's or college's foundation officer. Ask this person for advice in seeking a grant from an individual donor or for seeking a corporate gift. Take notes and file them in your portfolio.

References

Adkins, W. (n.d.). PEAK (Prevention and education through the arts for kids). Retrieved July 17, 2008, from www.peaktexas.org

Aguirre, A. (2005). Quoted in Bob Krajewski, In their own words. *Educational Leadership, 62*(6), 14–18.

Aldridge, J. & Goldman, R. (2007). Current issues and trends in education (2nd ed.). Boston: Allyn & Bacon.

Alexander, J. (1994). Multicultural literature: Overcoming the hurdles to successful study. *The Clearing House, 67*(5), 266–268.

Allen, T. (2004). No school left unscathed. *Phi Delta Kappan, 85*(5), 396–397.

Alvy, H. (2005). Preventing the loss of wisdom in our schools: Respecting and retaining successful veteran teachers. *Phi Delta Kappan, 86*(10), 764–766.

American Management Association (2006). *Secrets to making change happen.* Retrieved April 27, 2007, from http://www.AMANet.org/LeadersEdge/editorial.cfm?Ed-155

Apple, M. W. (1990). Is there a curriculum voice to reclaim? *Phi Delta Kappan, 71*(7), 526–530.

Applequest, K. L. (2007). *Parent experiences with early intervention and special education services: Narrative accounts.* Unpublished manuscript.

Armstrong, D. G., Henson, K. T., & Savage, T. V. (2009). *Teaching today: An introduction to education* (8th ed.). New York: Upper Saddle River, NJ/Columbus, OH: Pearson/Merrill/Prentice-Hall.

Association for Supervision and Curriculum Development Yearbook Committee (1962). *1962 Yearbook: Perceiving, behaving, becoming.* Alexandria, VA: Authors.

Barr, A. S., & Burton, W. H. (1926). *The Supervision of Instruction.* New York: Appleton.

Barrera, J. M., & Warner, L. (2006). Involving families in school events. *Kappa Delta Pi Record, 42*(2), 72–75.

Barth, R. S. (2006). Improving relationships within the school house. *Educational Leadership, 63*(6), 9–13.

Bartholomew, B. (2007). Why we can't always get what we want. *Phi Delta Kappan, 88*(8), 593–598.

Bassett, P. F. (2005). Reengineering schools for the 21st century. *Phi Delta Kappan, 87*(1), 76–78, 83.

Beck, C., & Kosnik, C. (2006). *Innovations in teacher education: A social constructivist approach.* Albany, NY: SUNY Press.

Belcher, R. N., Ruhl, M. L., Gates, D., & Foley, N. (2006). A model two-year residential internship program to attract highly qualified beginning teachers from rural communities to urban schools. *The Journal for the Liberal Arts and Sciences, 10*(1), 64–70.

Bell, T. H. (1993). Reflections one decade after *A Nation at Risk. Phi Delta Kappan, 74*(8), 592–600.

Berry, B. (2005). Recruiting and retaining board-certified teachers for hard-to-staff schools. *Phi Delta Kappan, 87*(4), 290–297.

Bingham, C. S., Parker, S., Finney, P., Riley, J., & Rakes, K. (2006). The Teachers as Researchers Academy: Building community, expertise, and a knowledge base for teaching. *Phi Delta Kappan, 87*(9), 681–688.

Bintz, W. P., & Dillard, J. (2007). Teachers as reflective practitioners: Examining student stories of curricular change in a fourth-grade classroom. *Reading Horizons, 47*(3), 203–227.

Bloom, B. S. (1956). *Taxonomy of educational objectives: The classification of educational goals—Handbook I: Cognitive Domain.* New York: McKay.

Bloom, B. S. (1984). The search for methods of group instruction as effective as one-to-one tutoring. *Educational Leadership, 41*, 4–17.

Bobbitt, F. (1918). *The curriculum.* Boston: Houghton-Mifflin.

Bogle, L. R., Cook, V. S., & Day, S. L. (2007). Charting the course of improvement: Using hybrid programs to enhance pedagogy for the preparation of school leaders. In L. K. Lemasters & R. Papa (Eds.), *At the tipping point: Navigating the course for the preparation of educational administrators—The 2007 yearbook of the National Council of Professors of Educational Administration* (pp. 305–309). Lancaster, PA: DEStech Publications.

Bolin, F. S., & Panaritis, P. (1992). Searching for a common purpose: A perspective on the history of supervision. In C. D. Glickman (Ed.), *Supervision in transition: 1992 ASCD Yearbook.* Alexandria, VA: Association for Supervision and Curriculum Development.

Bond, N. (2007). Questioning strategies that minimize classroom management problems. *Kappa Delta Pi Record, 44*(15), 18–21.

Boston Digital Bridge Foundation (2006). Case study: O'Donnell School SY '05–'06. Technology goes home @ school builds parental involvement. Retrieved December 12, 2008, from http:www.cityofboston.gov/bra/digitalbridge/pdf/TGHCaseStudy6.pdf

Boyer, E. (1997). *Scholarship reconsidered: Priorities of the professorate.* Princeton, NJ: Carnegie Foundation for Advancement of Teaching.

Brewster, C., & Railsback, J. (2001, May). Supporting beginning teachers: How administrators, teachers, and policymakers can help new teachers succeed. Portland, OR: Northwest Regional Educational Laboratory (NWREL).

Brinson, D., & Steiner, L. (2007). Building collective efficacy: How leaders inspire teachers to achieve. [Issue brief]. Washington, DC: Center for Comprehensive School Reform and Improvement. Retrieved January 12, 2009, from http://www.centerforcsri.org/files/CenterIssueBriefOct07.pdf

Brookhart, S. M. (2007/2008). Feedback that fits. *Educational Leadership, 65*(4), 54–59.

Brooks-Young, S. (2006). Get it done online. *Technology and Learning, 27*(3), 36.

Brophy, J., & Good, T. L. (1994). Teacher behavior and student achievement. In M. C. Whittrock (Ed.), *Handbook of research on teaching* (4th ed., p. 337). New York: Macmillan.

Brown, C. A. (2005). Computer software genres that help students think. *Kappa Delta Pi Record, 42*(1), 42–44.

Brown, C., Combs, J., & Jackson, S. (2006). Using student feedback to improve faculty effectiveness in the classroom. In F. L. Dembowski & L. K. Lemasters (Eds.), *Unbridled spirit: Best practices in educational administration—The 2006 yearbook of the National Council of Professors of Educational Administration* (p. 27). Lancaster, PA: DEStech Publications.

Brown, D. S. (1990). Middle level teachers' perceptions of action research. *Middle School Journal, 22*(2), 30–32.

Bunting, C. (2006). Getting personal about teaching. *Phi Delta Kappan, 88*(1), 76–78.

Burton, W. H. (1926). *The guidance of learning activities: A summary of the principles of teaching based on the growth of the learner* (3rd ed.). Englewood Cliffs, NJ: Prentice-Hall.

Busch, S., Johnson, S., & Robles-Pina, R. (2007). *School climate improves significantly when principals consistently address the climate over time*. Paper presented at the meeting of the Southwest Educational Research Association, San Antonio, TX.

Bush, T. (2006). The National College for School Leadership: A successful English innovation. *Phi Delta Kappan, 87*(7), 508–511.

Butler, J. D. (2010). Selecting activities to personalize the curriculum. Case study in K. T. Henson, *Curriculum planning: Integrating multiculturalism, constructivism, and education reform* (4th. ed.). Long Grove, IL: Waveland Press.

Bybee, R. W., & Scotter, P. V. (2006/2007). Reinventing the science curriculum. *Educational Leadership, 64*(4), 43–47.

Camilleri, J. (2007). *Healing the inner city child: Creative arts therapies with at-risk youth.* London: Jessica Kingsley.

Campbell, K., & Porter, B. (2006). Best practice: Instructional leadership through teacher evaluation. In F. L. Dembowski & L. K. Lemasters (Eds.), *Unbridled spirit: Best practices in educational administration—The 2006 yearbook of the National Council of Professors of Educational Administration* (ch. 5). Lancaster, PA: DEStech Publications.

Carlson, J., & Irons, J. (2006). Implementing best practices in the classroom: What do administrators need to do to change teacher behavior? In F. L. Dembowski & L. K. Lemasters (Eds.), *Unbridled spirit: Best practices in educational administration—The 2006 yearbook of the National Council of Professors of Educational Administration* (p. 293). Lancaster, PA: DEStech Publications.

Cearley, A., & Bennett, A. (2008). Parental involvement goes high-tech. *University of Southern California/USC News.* Retrieved December 13, 2008, from http://www.usc.edu/uscnews/stories/16000.html

Carroll, J. B. (1963). A model of school learning. *Teachers College Record, 64*, 723–733.

Chan, S. (2006, June 27). By the script. *The New York Times.*

Chance, P. (2008). *The teacher's craft: The 10 essential skills of effective teaching.* Long Grove, IL: Waveland Press.

Chappuis, J. (2005). Helping students understand assessment. *Educational Leadership, 63*(3), 39–43.

Check, J. (2002, Summer). National Writing Project: Reflection and Reform. *The Quarterly, 24*(3). Retrieved December 2, 2008, from http://www.nwp.org/cs/public/print/resource/406?x-print_friendly=1

Cheney, C. D. (1989). The systematic adaptation of instructional materials and techniques for problem learners. *Academic Therapy, 25*(1), 25–30.

Chimes, M., & Smith, P. (1990). What I read over my summer vacation and readings on cultural diversity. *The Clearing House, 64*(1), 44–46.

Christopher, S. (2007/2008). Homework: A few practice arrows. *Educational Leadership, 65*(4), 74–75.

Clabaugh, G. (2004). Risk management and at-risk students: Pernicious fantasies of educator omnipotence. *Educational Horizons, 82*(3), 180–183.

Clarke, G., & Harris, S. (2006). Preparing scholar-practitioner leaders: A suggested model of best practices for dimensions of change. In F. L. Dembowski & L. K. Lemasters (Eds.), *Unbridled spirit: Best practices in educational administration—The 2006 yearbook of the National Council of Professors of Educational Administration*. Lancaster, PA: DEStech Publications.

Clement, M. C. (1996). A curriculum and resources for beginning teachers programs. *Kappa Delta Pi Record, 32*(3), 87–90.

Clymer, J. B., & William, D. (2006/2007). Improving the way we grade science. *Educational Leadership, 64*(40), 36–42.

Colombo, M. W., & Colombo, P. D. (2007). Blogging to improve instruction in differentiated science classrooms. *Phi Delta Kappan, 89*(1), 60–63.

Combs, A. W., & Snygg, D. (1959). *Individual behavior* (Rev. ed.). Boston: Allyn & Bacon.

Comer, J. P. (2005). Child and adolescent development: The critical missing focus in school reform. *Phi Delta Kappan, 86*(10), 757–763.

Cooper, H. (2007). *The battle over homework* (3rd ed.). Thousand Oaks, CA: Corwin Press.

Counts, G. S. (1932). *Dare the schools build a new social order?* New York: John Day.

Cromwell, S. (2008). *Is your school's culture toxic or positive?* Retrieved December 3, 2008, from the Education World Web site: http://www.educationworld.com/a_admin/admin/admin275.shtml

Cuban, L. (1986) *Teachers and machines: The classroom use of technology since 1920.* New York: Teachers College Press, Columbia University.

Curts, J. (2004). A constructivist approach to teaching how polls work. In K. T. Henson, *Constructivist strategies for diverse middle-level classrooms*. Boston: Allyn & Bacon.

Dagenhart, D. B., O'Conner, K. A., Petty, T. M., & Day, B. D. (2005). Giving teachers a voice. *Kappa Delta Pi Record, 41*(3), 108–111.

Danielson, C. (1996). *Enhancing professional practice: A framework for teaching.* Alexandria: VA: Association for Supervision and Curriculum Development.

Daresh, J. C. (2007). *Supervision as proactive leadership* (4th ed.). Long Grove, IL: Waveland Press.

Darling-Hammond, L. (1993). Reforming the school reform agenda. *Phi Delta Kappan, 74*(10), 756–761.

Darling-Hammond, L. (2005). Teaching as a profession: Lessons in teacher preparation and professional development. *Phi Delta Kappan, 87*(3), 237–240.

Darling-Hammond, L., & Baratz-Snowden, S. (2007). A good teacher in every classroom: Preparing the highly qualified teachers our children deserve. *Educational Horizons, 85*(2), 111–132.

Davidson-Taylor, C. M. (2002). Is instruction working? *Principal Leadership, 3*(20, 30–35.

Davies, L. (2002). *Education and conflict: Complexity and chaos.* London: RoutledgeFalmer.

Davis, H., & Burgess, G. (Trans.) (1901). *The Republic: The Statesman of Plato* (pp. 209–210). New York: Dunne.

Davis, S. H. (2007). Bridging the gap between research and practice: What's good, what's bad, and how can one be sure? *Phi Delta Kappan, 88*(8), 569–578.

Dawson, C., & Rakes, G. C. (2003). The influence of principals' technology training on the integration of technology into schools. *Journal of Research on Teaching in Education, 36*(1), 29–49.

Deal, T. E., & Peterson, K. D. (2009). *Shaping school culture: The heart of leadership* (2nd ed.). Hoboken, NJ: Jossey-Bass Education.

Dembowski, F. L., & Lemasters, L. K. (Eds.) (2006). *Unbridled spirit: Best practices in educational administration—The 2006 yearbook of the National Council of Professors of Educational Administration*. Lancaster, PA: DEStech Publications.

Dewey, J. (1910). *How we think.* New York: D. C. Heath.

Dexter, R., Berube, W., Moore, A., & Klopfenstein, M. (2005). *Key components of a new teacher induction and mentoring program.* Retrieved November 21, 2008, from http://www.mentors.net/03library/keycomps.html

Doolittle, V., & Trombetta, E. (2006). Defining moments: The transformative potential of professional learning communities. In F. L. Dembowski & L. K. Lemasters (Eds.), *Unbridled spirit: Best practices in educational administration—The 2006 yearbook of the National Council of Professors of Educational Administration* (p. 175). Lancaster, PA: DEStech Publications.

Duffy, G. G., & Kear, K. (2007). Compliance or adaptation: What is the real message about research-based practice? *Phi Delta Kappan, 88*(8), 579–581.

Dufour, R., Eaker, R., & Dufour, J. (2002). *Getting started: Reculturing schools to become professional learning communities.* Bloomington, IN: Solution Tree.

Easton, L. B. (2007). *Engaging the disengaged: How schools can help struggling students succeed.* Thousand Oaks, CA: Corwin.

Ebert, E. S., & Culyer, R. C. (2008). *An introduction to education*. Belmont, CA: Thompson/Wadsworth.

Echevarria, J., & Short, D. (2001). *Selected findings from the CREDE SIOP research project.* Washington, DC: Center for Applied Linguistics.

Echevarria, J., & Short, D. (2002). *Using multiple perspectives in observations of diverse classrooms: The sheltered instruction observation protocol (SIOP).* Retrieved February 20, 2009, from http://crede.berkeley.edu/tools/policy/siop/1.3doc2.shtml

Echevarria, J., Vogt, M. E., & Short, D. (2000). *Making content comprehensible for English language learners: The SIOP model*. Boston: Allyn & Bacon.

Education Commission of the States Clearinghouse Notes (1991). *Corporal punishment: State ban or justification statute?* Denver: Education Commission of the States.

Egbert, R. L. (1984). The role of research in teacher education. In R. L. Egbert & M. M. Kluender (Eds.), *Using research to improve teacher education*. Lincoln, NE: American Association of Colleges for Teachers Education.

Einstein, A. (1951). Autobiographical notes. In P. A. Schilpp (Ed. & Trans.), *Albert Einstein: Philosopher-scientist* (p. 7). The Library of Living Philosophers. Vol. VII. New York: Tudor.

Einstein, A., & Infield, L. (1938). *The evolution of physics: The growth of ideas from early concepts to relativity and quanta.* New York: Simon and Schuster.

Eisner, E. (1994). *The educational imagination* (3rd ed.). New York: Macmillan.

Eisner, E. W. (2005). Opening a shuttered window: An introduction to a special section on the arts and the intellect. *Phi Delta Kappan, 87*(1), 8–10.

Elam, S. M., Rose, L. C., & Gallup, A. M. (1994). The 26th Annual Phi Delta Kappa/Gallup Poll of the Public's Attitudes toward the Public Schools. *Phi Delta Kappan, 76*(1), 41–56.

Escobar, D. (1995). *Report to the membership*. Washington, DC: American Association of College for Teacher Education.

Everhart, R. B. (2006). Why are schools always begging for money? *Phi Delta Kappan, 88*(1), 70–75.

Fantini, M. D. (1986). *Regaining excellence in education*. Columbus, OH: Merrill.

Ferrero, D. J. (2005). Does research-based mean value neutral? *Phi Delta Kappan, 86*(6), 433–437.

Fink, E., & Resnick, L. B. (2001). Developing principals as instructional leaders. *Phi Delta Kappan, 82*(8), 598–606.

Fitzgerald, K., & Brain, D. (2008). The community action research initiative: A pragmatic experiment in education through engaged citizenship. Paper presented at the annual meeting of the APSA teaching and learning conference online. Retrieved February 2, 2009, from http://www.allacademic.com/meta/p11523_index.html

Foster, M. (2004). An innovative professional development program for urban teachers. *Phi Delta Kappan, 85*(5), 401–406.

Francis, L. (2005). Public policy and specialized style. *Technology and Learning, 26*(4), 13.

Franklin, J. (2005). Blogging and benefiting: Spreading the word. *Educational Update, 47*(2), Alexandria, VA: Association for Supervision and Curriculum Development.

Frye, B., Bottoms, G., & O'Neil, K. (2005). The principal internship: How can we get it right?. Retrieved January 15, 2009, from the Southern Regional Education Board Web site:

http://www.sreb.org/programs/hstw/publications/pubs/05V02PrincipalInternship.asp.

Fullan, M. G., & Stiegelbaur, S. (1990). *The new meaning of educational change* (2nd ed.). New York: Columbia University, Teacher College Press.

Gardner, H. (1993). *An anatomy of creativity.* New York: Basic Books.

Gardner, H. (2003, April). *Multiple intelligences after twenty years.* Paper presented at the annual conference of the American Educational Research Association, Chicago, IL.

Garrahy, D. A., Cothran, D. J., & Kulinna, P. H. (2005). Voices from the teachers: An exploration of teachers' management knowledge. *The Journal of Educational Research, 99*(1), 56–63.

Gibran, K. (1923). *The prophet.* New York: Alfred A. Knopf.

Gilbert, M. B. (2006). Are you talking too much? Considerations for best practice. In F. L. Dembowski & L. K. Lemasters (Eds.), *Unbridled spirit: Best practices in educational administration—The 2006 yearbook of the National Council of Professors of Educational Administration* (ch. 27). Lancaster, PA: DESTech Publications.

Gilbert, S. L., & Smith, L. C. (2003). A bumpy road to action research. *Kappa Delta Pi Record, 39*(2), 80–83.

Gimbert, B. G. (2000, December). *Crescendos of voice and multiple perspectives in an intern learning community in a professional development school context.* Paper presented at the Australia Association of Educational Research, Sydney, Australia.

Glasser, W. (2006). *Every student can succeed.* Chatsworth, CA: William Glasser, Inc.

Glatthorn, A. A. (2002). *Differentiated supervision* (2nd ed.). Alexandria: VA: Association for Supervision and Curriculum Development.

Gleibermann, E. (2007). Teaching even 100 hours a week leaves children behind. *Phi Delta Kappan, 88*(6), 455–459.

Glickman, C. (2006). Educational leadership: Failure to use our imagination. *Phi Delta Kappan, 87*(9), 689–690.

Glickman, C. D., Gordon, S. P., & Ross-Gordon, J. M. (2007). *Supervision and instructional leadership: A developmental approach* (7th ed.) Boston: Pearson/Allyn & Bacon.

Goldburger, S., & Kazis, R. (1996). Revitalizing high school: What the school-to-career movement can contribute. *Phi Delta Kappan, 77*(8), 547–554.

Gonzales, P. (2009). Highlights from TIMSS 2007: Mathematics and science achievement of U.S. fourth- and eighth-grade students in an international context. Retrieved April 1, 2009, from http://nces.ed.gov/pubs2009/2009001.pdf

Good, T. L., & Brophy, J. E. (2007). *Looking in classrooms* (10th ed.). Boston: Allyn & Bacon.

Goodlad, J. I. (1984). *A place called school.* New York: McGraw-Hill.

Goodlad, J. I. (2003/2004). Teaching what we hold sacred. *Educational Leadership, 61*(4), 18–21.

Gordon, H. R. D. (2008). *The history and growth of career and technical education in America* (3rd ed.) Long Grove, IL: Waveland Press.

Gordon, S., Butters, J., Maxey, S, & Ciccarelli, J. (2001). *Improving instruction through observation and feedback.* Alexandria, VA: Association for Supervision and Curriculum Development.

Gordon, V. H. (2006). Administrative effectiveness in making classrooms safe: Observations in 97 school buildings and their implications for practice. In F. L. Dembowski & L. K. Lemasters (Eds.), *Unbridled spirit: Best practices in educational administration—The 2006 yearbook of the National Council of Professors of Educational Administration* (ch. 35). Lancaster, PA: DESTech Publications.

Graham, B. F., & Cannamore, P. C. (2006). Case pedagogy and standards-based teaching. In F. L. Dembowski & L. K. Lemasters (Eds.), *Unbridled spirit: Best practices in educa-*

tional administration—The 2006 yearbook of the National Council of Professors of Educational Administration (ch. 23). Lancaster, PA: DEStech Publications.

Gray, D. L., & Smith, A. E. (2005). No teacher left behind. *Kappa Delta Pi Record, 42*(1), 7–9.

Gross, P. A. (2005). In my view. *Kappa Delta Pi Record, 41*(3), 102–105.

Grubb, W. N. (1996). The vocationalism: What it is, what it could be? *Phi Delta Kappan, 77*(8), 535–546.

Guarino, C., Santibanez, L., Daley, G., & Brewer, D. (2004, May). *A review of the research literature on teacher recruitment and retention.* Education Commission of the States.

Guskey, T. R. (2003). How classroom assessments are improving. *Educational Leadership, 60*(50), 6–11.

Guskey, T. R. (2005a). Mapping the road to proficiency. *Educational Leadership, 63*(3), 32–38.

Guskey, T. R. (2005b, April). *Formative classroom assessment and Benjamin S. Bloom: Theory, research, and implications.* Paper presented at the Annual Meeting of the American Educational Research Association, Montreal, Canada.

Guskey, T. R. (2007/2008). Leadership in the age of accountability. *Educational Horizons, 86*(1), 29–34.

Haar, J. M., & Robicheau, J. W. (2007). Being attentive to changing student demographics: Minority school leadership and multicultural environments. In L. K. Lemasters & R. Papa (Eds.), *At the tipping point: Navigating the course for the preparation of educational administrators—The 2007 yearbook of the National Council of Professors of Educational Administration* (pp. 191–197). Lancaster, PA: DEStech Publications.

Haberman, M. (1989). More minority teachers. *Phi Delta Kappan, 70*(10), 771–776.

Hademenos, G. (2005). Grant Writing 101. *Principal, 84*(3), 33–35.

Hall, B. L. (2006). Rethinking leadership education for the real world. *Phi Delta Kappan, 87*(7), 524–525.

Hall, G. E., & Hord, S. M. (2000). *Implementing change: Patterns, principles, and potholes.* Boston: Allyn & Bacon.

Hammer, M., & Polnick, B. (2007). Preparing tomorrow's science teacher. *Educational Leadership, 64*(4), 80–83.

Hancock, R. (in press). The new digital divide. *AASA Journal of Scholarship and Practice.*

Hanson, S., & Moir, E. (2008). Beyond mentoring: Influencing the professional practice and careers of experienced teachers. *Phi Delta Kappan, 89*(6), 453–461.

Hanushek, E. A. (1994). *Making schools work.* Washington, DC: The Brookings Institution.

Harchar, R., Campbell, K., & Smith, B (2006). Reality check: Designing a new leadership program for the 21st Century. *NCPEA Education Leadership Review, 7*(2), 111–130.

Hargreaves, A., & Dawe, R. (1989). Coaching as unreflective practice. Paper presented at the Annual Meeting of the American Educational Research Association, San Francisco.

Henderson, A. T., & Mapp, K. L. (2002). *A New Wave of Evidence: The Impact of School, Family, and Community Connections on Student Achievement, Annual Synthesis 2002.* Southwest Educational Development Laboratory, National Center for Family and Community Connections with Schools. Retrieved December 12, 2008, from http://eric.ed.gov/ERICDocs/data/ericdocs2sql/content_storage_01/0000019b/80/1a/e3/85.pdf

Henson, K. T. (1986). America's public schools: A look at the recent reports. *USA Today, 114*, 75–77.

Henson, K. T. (1996). Teachers as researchers. In J. Sikula, T. Buttery, & E. Guyton (Eds.), *The Association of Teacher Educators handbook of research on teacher education* (2nd ed., ch. 4). New York: Macmillan.

Henson, K. T. (2004). *Grant writing in higher education.* Boston: Allyn & Bacon.

Henson, K. T. (2005). Writing for publication: Steps to excellence. *Phi Delta Kappan, 88*(10), 772–781.

Henson, K. T. (2010). *Curriculum planning: Integrating multiculturalism, constructivism, and education reform* (4th ed.). Long Grove, IL: Waveland Press.

Herman, J. L., & Baker, E. L. (2005). Making benchmark testing work. *Educational Leadership, 63*(3), 48–55.

Hersey, P., & Blanchard, K. H. (1993). *Management of organizational behavior: Utilizing human resources* (6th ed.). Englewood Cliffs, NJ: Prentice Hall.

Hess, F. M., & Rotherham, A. J. (2007). NCLB and the competitiveness agenda: Happy collaboration or a collision course? *Phi Delta Kappan, 88*(5), 345–352.

Hirsh, S. (2002). *Together, you can do more*. Retrieved January 15, 2009, from http://rethinkstaffdevelopment.org/library/publications/results/res10-02hirs.cfm

Hoerr, T. R. (2007). Supervising Generation X. *Educational Leadership, 65*(2), 85–86.

Holmes, J. (Ed.). (2005). *The Fourth Yearbook of the National Society for the Study of Education, Part One: The Education and Training of Secondary Teachers*. Chicago: University of Chicago Press.

Holzberg, C. S. (2006). Safe at home. *Technology and Learning, 26*(10), 34.

Hoover, J. J. (1990). Curriculum adaptation: A five step process for classroom implementation. *Academic Therapy, 25*(4), 407–416.

Hopkins, D. (1990). Integrating staff development and school improvement: A study of teacher personality and school climate. In B. Joyce (Ed.), *Changing school culture through staff development.* 1990 ASCD Yearbook. Alexandria, VA: Association for Supervision and Curriculum Development.

Hord, S. M. (1997). Professional learning communities: What are they and why are they important? *Issues about Change, 6*(1), 1–8. Austin, TX: Southwest Educational Development Laboratory.

Hoy, W. K., & Miskel, C. G. (2008). *Educational administration: Theory and practice* (8th ed.). New York: McGraw-Hill.

Huffman, J. B., & Hipp, K. K. (2003). *Reculturing schools as professional learning communities.* Lanham, MD: Rowman & Littlefield.

Huggest, A. J., & Stinnett, T. M. (1958). *Professional problems of teachers*. New York: Macmillan.

Huling-Austin, L. S., Odell, P., Ishler, R., & Edlfelt, R. (1989). *Assessing the beginning teacher.* Reston, VA: Association of Teacher Educators.

Hunt, J. W. (2007). The impact of the No Child Left Behind Act on administrative morale. In L. K. Lemasters & R. Papa (Eds.), *At the tipping point: Navigating the course for the preparation of educational administrators—The 2007 yearbook of the National Council of Professors of Educational Administration* (pp. 217–223). Lancaster, PA: DEStech Publications.

Irons, E. J., & Aller, W. (2007). Relationship building—navigating the future through practice: Implications for administrator preparation. In L. K. Lemasters & R. Papa (Eds.), *At the tipping point: Navigating the course for the preparation of educational administrators—The 2007 yearbook of the National Council of Professors of Educational Administration* (pp. 49–58). Lancaster, PA: DEStech Publications.

Jacobowitz, T., & Onore, C. (2004). Case method teaching as democratic practice. *Kappa Delta Pi Record, 41*(1), 35–57.

Jakes, D., & Brennan, J. (2006). Creating a visual classroom. *Technology and Learning, 27*(3), 30.

Jaramillo, J. A. (1996, Fall). Vygotsky's sociocultural theory and contributions to the development of constructivist curricula. *Education,* 117. Retrieved January 5, 2009, from http://findarticles.com/p/articles/mi_qa3673/is_n1_v117/ai_n28677164/pg_1?tag=artBody;col1

Jensen, E. P. (2008a). A fresh look at brain-based education. *Phi Delta Kappan, 89*(6), 409–417.

Jensen, E. P. (2008b). Exciting times call for collaboration. *Phi Delta Kappan, 89*(6), 418–423.

Johnson, E. S. (2007). Sailing through the murky waters of leadership ethics: Use of problem-based learning in an educational leadership graduate course. In L. K. Lemasters & R. Papa (Eds.), *At the tipping point: Navigating the course for the preparation of educational administrators—The 2007 yearbook of the National Council of Professors of Educational Administration* (pp. 490–497). Lancaster, PA: DEStech Publications.

Johnson, G. M. (2006). Online study groups: Reciprocal peer questioning vs. mnemonic devices. *Journal of Educational Computing Research, 35*(1), 83–96.

Johnson, R. B. (1994–1995). Qualitative research in education. *SRATE Journal, 4*(1), 3–6.

Johnson, S. A., & Busch, S. (2006). Understanding leadership behaviors of principals. In F. L. Dembowski & L. K. Lemasters (Eds.), *Unbridled spirit: Best practices in educational administration—The 2006 yearbook of the National Council of Professors of Educational Administration* (ch. 36). Lancaster, PA: DEStech Publications.

Kannapel, P. J., Moore, B. D., Coe, P., & Aagaard, L. (1995, April). Opposition to outcome-based education in Kentucky, Appendix A. Paper presented at the Annual Meeting of the American Educational Research Association, San Francisco. Retrieved December 12, 2008, from http://www.eric.ed.gov/ERICDocs/data/ericdocs2sql/content_storage_01/0000019b/80/1/4/4d/03.pdf

Kant, I. (1793/2006). *On the old saw: That may be right in theory but it won't work in practice* (E. B. Aston, Trans.). Philadelphia: University of Pennsylvania Press. (Original work published 1793)

Keefe, J. W., & Amenta, R. B. (2005). Whatever happened to the Model Schools Project? *Phi Delta Kappan, 83*(6), 400–448.

Keller, B. (2005, July 27) Teachers flocking to online sources to advance and acquire knowledge. *Education Week, 24*(43). Retrieved February 23, 2009, from http://www.edweek.org/ew/articles/2005/07/27/43online.h24.html

Keller, B. M. (1995). Accelerated schools: Hands-on learning in unified community. *Educational Leadership, 52*(5), 10–13.

Kennedy, R. (2006, July 27). The arts may aid literacy, study days. *The New York Times*, p. E1.

Kentucky Education Professional Standards Board. (2008, fall). *Kentucky Teacher Internship Program, teacher performance assessment handbook.* Retrieved January 12, 2009, from http://www.kyepsb.net/documents/EduPrep/Kentuckyteacherstandards.doc

Kerlinger, F. (1973). *Foundations of behavioral* research (3rd ed.). New York: Holt, Rinehart, & Winston.

King, M. (1991). Cooperative planning workshops: Helping teachers improve. *NASSP Bulletin, 75*(536), 42–56.

King, P. M., & Kitchener, K. S. (1994). *Developing reflective judgment: Understanding and promoting intellectual growth and critical thinking in adolescents and adults.* San Francisco: Jossey-Bass.

Kopkowski, C. (2008, May). Why they leave. *NEA Today: A review of the research literature on teacher recruitment and retention.* Denver, CO: Education Commission of the States.

Kowalski, T. J. (2006). Part-time faculty and distance education: Quandaries in educational administration's swamp. In F. L. Dembowski & L. K. Lemasters (Eds.), *Unbridled spirit: Best practices in educational administration—The 2006 yearbook of the National Council of Professors of Educational Administration* (ch. 3). Lancaster, PA: DEStech Publications.

Kowalski, T. J., & Reitzug, V. C. (1993). *Contemporary school administration.* New York: Longman.

Krathwohl, D. R. (2009). *Methods of educational and social science research* (3rd ed.). Long Grove, IL: Waveland Press.

Krathwohl, D. R., Bloom, B. S., & Masia, B. B. (1964). *Taxonomy of educational objectives: The classification of educational goals. Handbook II: The affective domain.* New York: McKay.

Kreitner, R. (2007). *Foundations of management* (pp. 394–396). Boston: Houghton-Mifflin.

Kretovics, J., Farber, K. S., & Armaline, W. D. (2004). It ain't brain surgery: Restructuring schools to improve the education of children placed at risk. *Educational Horizons, 82*(3), 213–225.

Kulick, C. C., & Kulick, J. A. (1989). Meta-analysis in education. *Review of Educational Research, 13*(20), 321–340.

Kyriakides, L. (2005). Evaluating school policy on parents working with their children in class. *Journal of Educational Research, 98*(5), 581–298.

Labbo, L., Leu, D., Kinzer, C., Teale, W., Cammack, D., & Kara-Soteriou, J. (2003). Teacher wisdom stories: Cautions and recommendations for using computer-related technologies for literary instruction. *The Reading Teacher 57*(3), 300–304.

Landsman, J., & Gorski, P. (2007). Countering Standardization. *Educational Leadership, 64*(8), 40–44.

Lapan, S. D., & Hays, P. A. (2010). Collaborating for change. Case study in K. T. Henson, *Curriculum planning: Integrating multiculturalism, constructivism, and education reform* (4th ed.) Long Grove, IL: Waveland Press.

Larson, W. K., Howley, A., & Burgess, L. (2007). Preparing school leaders to support rural communities of the future. In L. K. Lemasters & R. Papa (Eds.), *At the tipping point: Navigating the course for the preparation of educational administrators—The 2007 yearbook of the National Council of Professors of Educational Administration* (pp. 380–390). Lancaster, PA: DEStech Publications.

Lederman, L. M., & Burnstein, R. A. (2006). Alternative approaches to high-stakes testing. *Phi Delta Kappan, 87*(6), 429–439.

Lee, V., & Smith, J. B. (1994, fall). High school restructuring and student achievement: A new study finds strong links. *Issues in restructuring schools, 7*(3). Retrieved December 8, 2008, from http://www.wcer/wisc.edu/archive/cors/Issues_in_Restructuring_Schools/

Lefkowits, L., & Miller, K. (2006). Fulfilling the promise of the standards movement. *Phi Delta Kappan, 87*(5), 403–407.

Leithwood, K., Menzies, T., & Jantzi, D. (1994). Earning teachers' commitment to curriculum reform. *Peabody Journal of Education, 69*(4), 38–61.

Lengyel, L., Vernon-Dotson, L. J., & Lane, M. (2008, February). *School/university partnerships: Collaborating with an alternative program.* Paper presented at the American Association of Colleges for Teacher Education Annual Meeting & Exhibits, New Orleans, LA.

Lerner, M. (2006). *The left hand of God*. New York: HarperCollins.

Levin, D. (2005). The leadership imperative. *Technology and Learning, 26*(4), 12–13.

Lewis, A. (2006, April). Washington commentary. *Phi Delta Kappan, 87*(8), 564–565.

Lewis, C. (2000). *Lesson study: The core of Japanese professional development*. Invited address to the special interest group research in mathematics education, American Educational Research Association, New Orleans, LA.

Lewis, C., Perry, R., Hurd, J., & O'Connell, P. (2006). Lesson study comes of age in North America. *Phi Delta Kappan, 88*(4), 273–281.

Lieberman, A., & Miller, L. (1992). Professional practice schools: Linking teacher education and school reform. *Teacher College Record, 92*(1), 105–122.

Lindahl, R. A. (2007). Navigating the future through practice: A heuristic model of the role of supervision in the school improvement process. In L. K. Lemasters & R. Papa (Eds.), *At the tipping point: Navigating the course for the preparation of educational administrators—The 2007 yearbook of the National Council of Professors of Educational Administration* (pp. 391–400). Lancaster, PA: DEStech Publications.

Littky, D., & Grabelle, S. (2004). If we love our children more than we love our schools, the system must change. *Educational Horizons, 82*(4), 284–289.

Longerbeam, S. D. (2007). *Creating compelling college learning: Diverse peer interaction and intellectual development in living-learning programs.* Unpublished study. Flagstaff, AZ: Northern Arizona University.

Lounsbury, J. H. (1991). A fresh start for the middle school curriculum. *Middle School Journal, 23*(2), 3–7.

Lovelace, M. K. (2005). *Meta-analysis of experimental research on the Dunn and Dunn Model. Journal of Educational Research, 98*(3), 176–183.

Lowery, C. D. (1908). The relation of superintendents and principals to the training and professional improvement of their teachers. *Seventh Yearbook of the National Society for the study of Education: Part One*. Chicago: University of Chicago Press.

Lunenburg, F. C., & Irby, B. J. (2005). *The principalship: Vision to action.* Belmont, CA: Wadsworth/Thompson.

Lunenburg, F. C., & Ornstein, A. C. (2004). *Educational administration: Concepts and practices.* Belmont, CA: Wadsworth.

Macfarlane, E. (1995, May). Parent involvement does make a difference in student achievement. In *The ERIC Reader* (pp. 1–2). Bloomington, IL: ERIC Clearinghouse on Reading, English, and Communication.

MacNaughton, R. H., & Johns, F. A. (1991). Developing a successful school wide discipline program. *NASSP Bulletin, 75*(536), 47–57.

Maeroff, G. I. (1993). *Changing teaching: The next frontier.* Washington, DC: National Foundation for the Improvement of Education (NFIE).

Manning, M. L., & Lucking, R. (1991). The what, why, and how of cooperative learning. *The Clearing House, 64*(3), 152–156.

Marble, S. T. (2006). Learning to teach through lesson study. *Action in Teacher Education, 28*(3), 86–89.

Marcellino, P. A. (2006). A teambuilding model for the educational leadership classroom. In F. L. Dembowski & L. K. Lemasters (Eds.), *Unbridled spirit: Best practices in educational administration—The 2006 yearbook of the National Council of Professors of Educational Administration* (ch. 24). Lancaster, PA: DEStech Publications.

Marshall, K. (2005). It's time to rethink teacher supervision and evaluation. *Phi Delta Kappan, 86*(10), 727–735.

Marshall, J. (2006). Math Wars 2: It's the teaching, stupid! *Phi Delta Kappan, 87*(5), 356–363.

Martin, G. E. (2006). The challenge for systemic change: The president's message. In F. L. Dembowski & L. K. Lemasters (Eds.), *Unbridled spirit: Best practices in educational administration—The 2006 yearbook of the National Council of Professors of Educational Administration* (ch. 1). Lancaster, PA: DEStech Publications.

Martinez, M. E. (2006). What is metacognition? *Phi Delta Kappan, 87*(9), 696–699.

Marzano, R. J., & Pickering, D. J. (2007). Errors and allegations about research on homework. *Phi Delta Kappan, 88*(7), 507–513.

Maslow, A. (1973). What is a taoistic teacher? In L. J. Rubin (Ed.), *Facts and feelings in the classroom.* New York: Walker.

Massachusetts Bay Colony (1647). The Acts and resolves of the providence of Massachusetts Bay, Vol. 1, quoted in M. J. Holmes (Ed.), (2005). *The fourth yearbook of the National Society for the Study of Education, part one: The education and training of secondary teachers* (p. 470). Chicago: University of Chicago Press. ERIC Document SP 034 949.

Mathews, D. (2008). The public and the public schools: The coproduction of education. *Phi Delta Kappan, 89*(8), 560–564.

Mathews, J. (2008, November 28). Should teachers ignore poverty's impact? *The Washington Post*. Retrieved March 19, 2009, from http://www.washingtonpost.com/wp-dyn/content/article/2008/11/28/AR2008112801130_pf.html

Matthews, K., & Brown C. G. (2007). Technology leadership practices of secondary school principals. In L. K. Lemasters & R. Papa (Eds.), *At the tipping point: Navigating the course for the preparation of educational administrators—The 2007 yearbook of the National Council of Professors of Educational Administration* (pp. 157–165). Lancaster, PA: DEStech Publications,

Mayo, K. E., & Whitley, C. (2004). Professional learning communities. In K. T. Henson, *Constructivist teaching strategies for diverse, middle-level classrooms* (pp. 47–52). Boston: Pearson/Allyn & Bacon.

McCarthy, M., & Kuh, G. D. (2006). Are students ready for college: What student engagement data say. *Phi Delta Kappan, 87*(9), 664–669.

McColl, A. (2005). Tough call: Is No Child Left Behind constitutional? *Phi Delta Kappan, 86*(8), 604–610.

McLester, S. (2005). Twenty-five years down the line. *Technology and Learning, 26*(4), 4–8.

McNamee, G. D., & Chen, J. (2005). Dissolving the line between assessment and teaching. *Educational Leadership, 63*(3), 72–76.

McWhinney, T. S., & Sagan, L. (2007). The power of personal relationships. *Phi Delta Kappan, 88*(6), 460–471.

Mentoring Leadership and Resource Network (Dec./Jan. 1998–1999). "I'm out of here!" High turnover rate punctuates importance of mentoring programs. *IEA/NEA Advocate* [electronic version], p. 8. Retrieved November 21, 2008, from http://www.mentors.net/03library/outtahere.html

Merkley, D., Schmidt, D., Dirksen, C., & Fulher, C. (2006). Enhancing parent-teacher communication using technology: A reading improvement clinic example. *Contemporary Issues in Technology and Teacher Education, 6*(1), 11–42.

Meyer, C. F., & Rhodes, E. K. (2006). Multiculturalism: Beyond food, festival, folklore, and fashion. *Kappa Delta Pi Record, 42*(2), 82–87.

Michelli, N. M. (1995). Investing in schools through teacher professional development. In D. Else (Ed.), *The dynamic interaction of higher education, teacher education, and school reform: A TECSCU Dialogue*. Monograph Series, Vol. I, No. 1. Cedar Falls, IA: Teacher Education Council of State College and Universities and Institute for Educational Leadership, University of Northern Iowa.

Miech, E. J., Nave, B., & Mosteller, F. (2005). The 20,000 article problem: How a structured abstract can help practitioners sort out educational research. *Phi Delta Kappan, 86*(5), 396–400.

Mikovch, A. K., & Evans, S. (2006). The role of collaboration in curriculum decisions. Case study in K. T. Henson, *Curriculum planning: Integrating multiculturalism, constructivism, and education reform* (3rd ed.). Long Grove, IL: Waveland Press.

Mills, G. E. (2006). *Action research: A guide for the teacher researcher* (3rd ed.). Upper River, NJ: Pearson/Merrill/Prentice-Hall.

Mitchell, C., & Sackney, L. (2001). *Communities of learners: Developing leadership capacity for a learning community.* Paper presented at the annual conference of the American Educational Research Association, Seattle, WA.

Mohr, N., Dowd, J., Maicon, E., & Haag, K. (1996). *Learning Leadership for Change: Lessons from the Field.* Providence, RI: Brown University.

Morford, L. (2007). National Counsel of Professors of Educational Leadership. President's message. In L. K. Lemasters & R. Papa (Eds.), *At the tipping point: Navigating the course for the preparation of educational administrators—The 2007 yearbook of the National Council of Professors of Educational Administration* (pp. 3–6). Lancaster, PA: DEStech Publications.

Morphew, V. N. (2000). Learning and instruction: A constructivist approach. In L. Lau (Ed.), *Distance learning technologies: Issues, trends, and opportunities* (ch. 1). Hershey, PA: Idea Group.

Mullen, C. (2006). Hope replenished: Exceptional scholarship strides in educational administration. In F. L. Dembowski & L. K. Lemasters (Eds.), *Unbridled spirit: Best practices in educational administration—The 2006 yearbook of the National Council of Professors of Educational Administration* (ch. 11). Lancaster, PA: DEStech Publications.

Murata, A., Lewis, C., & Perry, R. (2004, October 21). *Teacher learning in lesson study: Developing professional capacity and resources.* Paper presented at the annual meeting of the North American Chapter of the International Group for the Psychology of Mathematics Education, Delta Chelsea Hotel, Toronto, Ontario, Canada [PDF]. Retrieved January 23, 2009, from http://www.allacademic.com/meta/p117624_index.html

Murphy, J. T. (2006). An interview with Henry Mintzberg. *Phi Delta Kappan, 87*(7), 527–528.

Mustacchi, J. (2008). What's relevant for YouTubers? *Educational Leadership, 65*(6), 67–70.

Myles, B. S., & Simpson, R. L. (1994). Understanding and preventing acts of aggression in school-age children and youth. *The Clearing House, 68*(1), 55–61.

Myrick, P., & Jones, R. (1991). How instructional leaders view staff development. *NASSP Bulletin, 75* (536), 1–6.

National Awards Program for Model Professional Development. (2002). *Building bridges: The mission & principles of professional development.* Retrieved January 21, 2009, from http://www.ed.gov/G2K/bridge.html

National Center for Education Statistics. (1995). *America's teachers ten years after* A Nation at Risk. Washington, DC: U.S. Department of Education.

National Center for Education Statistics. (2002). *Schools and staffing survey, 1999–2002.* Washington, DC: U.S. Department of Education. Retrieved March 12, 2007, from http://nces.ed.gov

National Center for Education Statistics. (2006). Indicators of school crime and safety: 2005 (NCES Report 2006-072). Washington, DC: U.S. Department of Education.

National Clearinghouse for English Language Acquisition [NCELA]. (2006). 2004–2005 poster. Retrieved March 12, 2007, from http://www.ncela.gwu.edu/stats/2_nation.htm

National Commission on Excellence in Education. (1983). *A nation at risk.* Washington, DC: Author.

National Comprehensive Center for Teacher Quality. (2007). *Lessons learned: New teachers talk about their jobs, challenges and long range plans.* Retrieved November 20, 2008, from http://www.publicagenda.org/reports/lessons-learned-new-teachers-talk-about-their-jobs-challenges-and-long-range-plans-issue-no-3

National Council for Accreditation of Teacher Education. (2008). *What is a professional development school?* Retrieved December 3, 2008, from http://www.nacate.org/public/pdswhat.asp?ch=133#top

National Policy Board for Educational Administration (NPBEA). (2008). *Major projects.* Retrieved January 22, 2009, from http://www.npbea.org/projects.php

National Science Foundation. (2008, January). *Science and engineering indicators 2008.* Chapter 1, Elementary and Secondary Education, Ongoing Professional Development, Figure 1-15, Collaborative professional development activities of public middle and high school teachers: Academic year 2003–04 (p. 34). Arlington, VA (NSB 08-01; NSB 08-01A). Retrieved December 1, 2008, from http://www.nsf.gov.statistics/seind08/pdf/co1.pdf

Nehring, J. H. (2007). Conspiracy theory: Lessons for leaders from two centuries on school reform. *Phi Delta Kappan, 88*(6), 425–432.

Newbold, B. L. (2004). The faceless mandates of NCLB. *Kappa Delta Pi Record, 41*(1), 7–10.

Newcom, R., Belcher, M. L., Gates, D., Foley, V., Henry, P., & Joyner, M. (2006). A model two-year residential internship program to attract highly qualified beginning teachers from rural communities to urban schools. *Journal for the Liberal Arts and Sciences, 10*(2), 64–70.

Niesz, T. (2007). Why teacher networks (can) work. *Phi Delta Kappan, 88*(8), 605–610.

Niguidula, D. (2005). Documenting learning with digital portfolios. *Educational Leadership, 63*(3), 46–47.

No Child Left Behind Act of 2001, PL 107-110, 115 Stat 1425. (2002).

Noddings, N. (2005, September) What does it mean to educate the whole child? *Educational Leadership*, *63*(1), 8–13.

Noddings, N. (2008). All our students thinking. *Educational Leadership, 65*(5), 8–13.

Noguera, P. A. (1998, July 9). Toward the development of school and university partnerships based upon mutual benefit and respect. *In Motion Magazine.* Retrieved January 15, 2009, from http://www.inmotionmagazine.com/pnsup1.html

Nolan, T., & Huber, T. (1989). Nurturing the reflective practitioner through instructional supervision: A review of the literature. *Journal of Curriculum and Supervision, 4*(2), 126–145.

Normore, A. H., & Floyd, A. (2005). A roller coaster ride: The twists and turns of a novice teacher's relationship with her principal. *Phi Delta Kappan, 86*(10), 767–771.

Nourie, B. L. (1995). Ten more truths about teaching. *The Clearing House, 68*(3), 177–180.

Novak, D. (1991). An exploration of computer use by beginning elementary teachers. In D. Carey, D. Willis, & J. Willis (Eds.), *Technology and teacher education annual—1991* (pp. 264–267). Charlottesville, VA: Association for the Development of Computing in Education.

O'Day, J. (2004). Gravity, innovation, and system change. *Educational Horizons, 82*(4), 306–314.

Office of English Language Acquisition. (2006). *OELA's national clearinghouse on English language acquisition and language instruction education programs.* Retrieved March 13, 2007, from http://www.ncela.gwu.edu/expert/faq/01leps.htm

Ohler, J. (2005). Ubiquitous band with customization, and digital speak. *Technology and Learning, 26*(4), 4–8.

Oliva, P. F. (2007). *Developing the curriculum* (6th ed.). New York: Addison-Wesley, Longman.

Oliva, P. F., & Pawlas, G. E. (2007). *Supervision for today's schools* (7th ed.). New York: John Wiley.

Ouzts, D. T., Taylor, K. K., & Taylor, L. A. (2004). A learner-centered curriculum based on award-winning literature. In K. T. Henson (Guest Ed.), *Education, 124*(1), 76–85.

Owens, E. (2008, November 28). Quoted in J. Mathews, Should teachers ignore poverty's impact? *The Washington Post.* Retrieved March 19, 2009, from http://www.washingtonpost.com/wp-dyn/content/article/2008/11/28/AR2008112801130_pf.html

Owens, L. (2006). Transitioning with No Child Left Behind. Case study in K. T. Henson, *Curriculum planning: Integrating multiculturalism, constructivism, and education reform* (3rd ed.). Long Grove, IL: Waveland Press.

Ozmon, H. O., & Craver, S. M. (2008). *Philosophical foundations of education* (8th ed.). Columbus, OH: Merrill.

Pacha, J., & Curry, L. (2006). The p–12 educational administration best practices improvement spiral modes. In F. L. Dembowski & L. K. Lemasters (Eds.), *Unbridled spirit: Best practices in educational administration—The 2006 yearbook of the National Council of Professors of Educational Administration* (p. 425). Lancaster, PA: DEStech Publications.

Pajak, E. (1993). *Approaches to clinical supervision: Alternatives for improving instruction.* Norwood, MA: Christopher-Gordon.

Parsons, J., & Jones, C. (1990). Not another test. *The Clearing House, 64*(1), 17–20.

Parsons, P., Heaston, A., & Nettles, S. M. (2006). A partnership approach to designing curricula to reduce the achievement gap between minority and mainstream students. Case study in K. T. Henson, *Curriculum planning: Integrating multiculturalism, constructivism, and education reform* (3rd ed.). Long Grove, IL: Waveland Press.

Pawlas, G. E., & Oliva, P. F. (2008). *Supervision for today's schools* (8th ed.). New York: John Wiley.

Payne, C., & Washington, L. (2008). *Establishing a Center for Minority Teacher Development and Training*. Paper presented at the annual meeting of the American Association of Colleges for Teacher Education. Retrieved January 16, 2009, from http://www.allacademic.com/meta/p35923_index.html

Penuel, W. R., & Riel, M. (2007). The "new" science of networks and the challenge of school change. *Phi Delta Kappan, 88*(8), 611–615.

Peterson, A. (2002, May–June). National Writing Project. Teacher stories: School reform's missing link. *The Voice, 7*(3). Retrieved November 21, 2008, from http://www.nwp.org/cs/public/print/resource/366?x-print_friendly=1

Pettiwell, J. A. (1939). *The saber-tooth curriculum*. New York: McGraw-Hill.

Phelps, P. H. (2006). The three r's of professionalism. *Kappa Delta Pi Record, 42*(2), 69–71.

Philip, L. (2005). As cited in Bob Krajewski, In their own words. *Educational Leadership, 62*(6), 14–18.

Pinnick, D. J. (2006). Characteristics of enlightened management. *Journal for the Liberal Arts and Sciences, 10*(3), 27–39.

Pitler, H. (May/June, 2006). Viewing technology through three lenses. *Principal, 85*(5), 38–42.

Popham, W. J. (2005). Squandered instructional zeal. *Educational Leadership, 62*(7), 92.

Popham, W. J. (2007). Another bite out of the apple. *Educational Leadership, 64*(6), 83–86.

Powell, J. V., & Lee, S. (2003/2004). Teaching techniques and computerized simulation in early childhood classrooms. *Journal of Educational Technology Systems, 32*(1), 71–100.

Prensky, M. (2005). Students as producers. *Technology and Learning, 26*(4), 12.

Pride, K. (2001). *Science concepts.* Retrieved January 27, 2009, from the Sheppard's Science Resources Web site: http://www.can-do.com/uci/lessons99.concepts.html

Protheroe, N. (2007). Alternatives to retention in grade. *Principal, 96*(3), 30–33.

PsycholARTSical: Psyched about the arts/Arts for at-risk students. (n.d.) Retrieved July 17, 2008, from http://en.wikibooks.org/wiki/PsycholARTSical:_Psyched_about_the_arts_for_At-Risk_Students

Public Agenda. (2008, May 21). *Diverse classrooms challenge new teachers' skills.* [press release]. Retrieved November 21, 2008, from http://www.publicagenda.org/print/16850

Pultorak, E., McCarthy, J., & Young, M. W. (2006). School and university partnerships and the role of teacher as researcher. *Action in Teacher Education, 28*(1), 99–109.

Qualifications and Curriculum Authority (n.d.). *Parent power.* Accessed January 29, 2009, from http://www.innovation-unit.co.uk/images/stories/qca-06-2723-parent-power.pdf

Rallis, S., Tedder, J., Lachman, A., & Elmore, R. (2006). Superintendents in classrooms: From collegial conversation to collaborative action. *Phi Delta Kappan, 87*(7), 537–545.

Ravitch, D. (1992). National standards and curriculum reform: A view from the Department of Education. *NASSP Bulletin, 76*(548), 24–29.

Reeves, D. (2007). Academics and the arts. *Educational Leadership, 65*(4), 80–81.

Reeves, D. B. (2008). Effective grading practices. *Educational Leadership, 65*(5), 85–87.

Resta, V., Nelson, S., & Huling, L. (2010). Reenergizing a school in a high-challenge environment. Case study in K. T. Henson, *Curriculum planning: Integrating multiculturalism, constructivism, and education reform* (4th ed.) Long Grove, IL: Waveland Press.

Richards, J. (2006). Setting the stage for student engagement. *Kappa Delta Pi Record, 42*(2), 92–94.

Ritchart, R., & Perkins, D. (2008). Making thinking visible. *Educational Leadership, 65*(5), 52–61.

Roberts, J. L. (2008). Talent development: A "must" for a promising future. *Phi Delta Kappan, 89*(7), 501–506.

Robertson, B. (2006/2007). Getting past inquiry versus content. *Educational Leadership, 64*(4), 67–70.

Rogers, C. R. (1967). Autobiography. In E. Boring & G. Lindzey (Eds.), *A history of psychology in autobiography, Vol. 5*. New York: Appleton Century Crofts.

Rogers, E. M. (1983). *Diffusion of innovations* (3rd ed.). New York: Free Press.

Rooney, J. (2007). Who owns teacher growth? *Educational Leadership, 64*(7), 87–88.

Rose, L. C,. & Gallup, A. C. (2005). The 37th Annual Gallup/Phi Delta Kappa Poll of the Public's Attitudes toward the Public Schools. *Phi Delta Kappan, 87*(1), 41–57.

Rose, L. C., & Gallup, A. M. (2004). The 36th Annual Gallup Poll of the Public's Attitudes toward the Public Schools. *Phi Delta Kappan, 86*(1), 41–48.

Rose, L. C,. & Gallup, A. M. (2006). The 38th Annual Phi Delta Kappa/Gallup Poll of the Public's Attitudes toward the Public Schools. *Phi Delta Kappan, 88*(1), 41–56.

Rose, L. C., & Gallup, A. M. (2007). The 39th annual Phi Delta Kappa/Gallup Poll of the Public's Attitudes toward the Public Schools. *Phi Delta Kappan, 89*(1), 33–45.

Roth, K., & Garnier, H. (2006/2007). What science teaching looks like: An international perspective. *Educational Leadership, 64*(4), 16–19.

Ryder, R. J., Burton, J. L., & Silberg, A. (2006). Longitudinal study of direct instruction effects from first through third grades. *The Journal of Educational Research, 99*(3), 179–191.

Saffold, F. (2003, December). *Mentoring: A win-win situation*. The Mentoring Leadership and Resource Network. Retrieved December 3, 2008, from http://www.mentors.net/03library/win_win.html

Sarason, S. B. (2004). *And what do you mean by learning?* Portsmouth, NH: Heinemann.

Sato, M., & Atkin, J. M. (2006/2007). Supporting change in classroom assessment. *Educational Leadership, 64*(4), 76–79.

Scheetz, J., Waters, F., Smeaton, P., & Lare, D. (2005). Mentoring in a PDS program: What's in it for me? *Kappa Delta Pi Record, 42*(1), 33–37.

Schein, E. H. (1992). *Organizational culture and leadership*. San Francisco: Jossey-Bass.

Schein, E. (2006). *Kurt Lewin's change theory in the field and classroom. A2z psychology.* Retrieved March 18, 2007, from http://www.a2zpsychology.com/article/kurtlewin'schangetheory.htm

Schlechty, P. C. (2008). No community left behind. *Phi Delta Kappan,89*(8), 552–559.

Schmoker, M. (2007). Reading, writing, and thinking for all. *Educational Leadership, 64*(7), 63–66.

Schon, D. (1983). *The reflective practitioner*. New York: Basic Books.

Schweiker, M., Moore, D. J., & Voltmer, D. R. (2002). *The design of an enhanced curricular evaluation + portfolio (ECE+P) software system*. Retrieved December 12, 2008, from http://fie.engrng.pitt.edu/fie2002/papers/1393.pdf

Scriven, M. (1991). Beyond formative and summative evaluation. In M. W. McLaughlin & D. C. Phillips (Eds.), *Evaluation and education: At quarter century. Nineteenth yearbook of the National Society for the Study of Education* (pp. 19–64). Chicago: University of Chicago Press.

Seay, J. (1997). *Education and simulation/gaming and computers*. Retrieved December 15, 2008, from http://www.cofc.edu/~seay/cb/simgames.html

Sevier, B. (1996, Feb.). Exploring educational diversity training for tomorrow's teachers. *Access, 4*(2), 1 & 6.

Shaffer, C. R., & Anundsen, K. (1993). *Creating community anywhere*. New York: Jeremy P. Tarcher/Putman Sons.

Shaffer, D. W., Squire, K. R., Halverson, R., & Gee, J. P. (2005). Video games and the future of learning. *Phi Delta Kappan, 87*(2), 105–111.

Shank, G., & Villella, O. (2004). Building on new foundations: Core principles and new directions for qualitative research. *The Journal of Educational Research, 98*(1), 46–55.

Shechtman, Z., Levy, M., & Leichtentritt, J. (2005). Impact of life skills training on teachers' perceived environment and self-efficacy. *Journal of Educational Research, 98*(3), 144–152.

Shelton, M., Cathers, S., & Tew, L. (2006). Higher education and school district partnerships: Creating a best practice environment for field experience. In F. L. Dembowski & L. K. Lemasters (Eds.), *Unbridled spirit: Best practices in educational administration—The 2006 yearbook of the National Council of Professors of Educational Administration*. Lancaster, PA: DEStech Publications.

Shen, J., Lu, S., & Kretovics, J. (2004). Improving the education of students placed at risk through school-university partnerships. *Educational Horizons, 83*(3), 184–193.

Shepard, L. A. (2005) Linking and scaffolding. *Educational Leadership, 63*(3), 66–67.

Shepherd, K., Hasazi, S., & Aiken, J. (2008). Preparing school leaders to build and sustain engagement with families and communities. In R. Papa, C. M. Achilles, & B. Alford (Eds.), *Leadership on the frontlines: Changes in preparation and practice—The 2008 yearbook of the National Council of Professors of Educational Administration* (pp. 145–158). Lancaster, PA: DEStech Publications.

Shih, S. (2005). Role of achievement goals in children's learning in Taiwan. *The Journal of Educational Research, 98*(5), 310–319.

Shimahara, N. K. (2002). Teacher professional development in Japan. In G. D. Coker (Ed.), *National standards and school reform in Japan and the United States* (2nd ed., pp. 107–120). New York: Teachers College Press.

Simkins, M. (2005). Great minds share alike. The top ten wish list. *Technology and Learning, 26*(4), 34.

Simmons, B. J. (1991). Ban the hickory stick. *Childhood Education, 68*, 69.

Simon, M. (2008, November 28). Quoted in J. Mathews, Should teachers ignore poverty's impact? *The Washington Post*. Retrieved March 19, 2009, from http://www.washingtonpost.com/wp-dyn/content/article/2008/11/28/AR2008112801130_pf.html

Simon, S. B., Howe, L. W., & Kirschenbaum, H. (1972). *Values clarification*. New York: Hart.

Simpson, E. J. (1972). The classification of educational objectives in the psychomotor domain. *The Psychomotor Domain* (Vol. 3). Washington, DC: Gryphon House.

Slavin, R. E. (1994). *Educational psychology: Theory and practice* (4th ed.). Needham Heights, MA: Allyn & Bacon.

Smelter, R. W., Rasch, B. W., & Yodewitz, G. J. (1994). Thinking of inclusion for all special needs? Better think again. *Phi Delta Kappan, 76*(1), 35–38.

Smyth, T. S. (2005) Respect, reciprocity, and reflection in the classroom. *Kappa Delta Pi Record, 421*, 38–39.

Sparks, D. (1994). A paradigm shift in staff development. *Journal of Staff Development, 15*(4). Retrieved February 20, 2009, from http://www.nsdc.org/news/jsd/sparks154.cfm

Sprinthall, N. A., Relman, A. J., & Thies-Sprinthall, L. (1996). Teacher professional development. In J. Sikula, T. J. Buttery, & E. Guyton (Eds.), *Association of Teacher Educators handbook of research on teacher education* (2nd ed.). New York: Macmillan.

Steel, C., & Craig, E. (2006). Reworking industrial models, exploring contemporary ideas, and fostering teacher leadership. *Phi Delta Kappan, 87*(9), 676–680.

Stefanich, G. P. (1990, November). Cycles of cognition. *Middle School Journal 22*(2), 47–52.

Stein, S. J. (2006). Transforming leadership programs: Design, pedagogy, and incentives. *Phi Delta Kappan, 87*(7), 522–523.

Sterling, D. R. (2004, May). The teacher shortage: National trends for science and mathematics teachers. *The Journal of Mathematics and Science, 7*, 85–96. Retrieved November 21, 2008, from http://www.math.vcu.edu/g1/journal/Journal7/Part%20I/Sterling.html

Stiggins, R. (2005). From Formative Assessment to assessment for learning: A path to success in standards-based schools. *Phi Delta Kappan, 87*(4), 324–328.

Stine, D. (2010). Action research as an instrument of change. Case study in K. T. Henson, *Curriculum planning: Integrating multiculturalism, constructivism, and education reform* (4th ed.) Long Grove, IL: Waveland Press.

Strauss, A., and Corbin, J. (1990). *Basics of qualitative research: Grounded theory procedures and techniques*. Thousand Oaks, CA: Sage.

Tanner, D., & Tanner, L. N. (2007). *Curriculum development: Theory into practice* (4th ed.). New York: Macmillan.

Taylor, R. T., & Williams, R. D. (2001). Accountability: Threat or target? *School Administrator, 58*(6), 30–33.

Techtree News Staff (2009). Social networking unsafe/risky for teens. Retrieved January 30, 2009, from http://www.techtree.com/India/News/Social_Networking_UnsafeRisky_for_Teens/551-97433-643.html

Teitel, L. (2006). Mapping the terrain of "alternative" leadership education: Lessons for universities. *Phi Delta Kappan, 87*(7), 500–507.

Thompson, A. D., Schmidt, D. A., & Davis, N. E. (2003). Technology collaboratives for simultaneous renewal in teacher education. *Educational Technology, Research and Development, 5*(1), 73–89.

TIMSS Video Mathematics Research Group. (2003). Understanding and improving mathematics teaching: Highlights from the TIMSS 1999 Video Study. *Phi Delta Kappan, 84*(10), 768–775.

Tips for making successful change happen. (2006). HR focus. *American Management Association, 83*(3), 7, 10–11.

Torres, J., Santos, J., Peck, N. L., & Cortes, L. (2004). *Minority Teacher Recruitment, Development, and Retention*. The Educational Alliance at Brown University. Institute of Education Sciences (IES), U.S. Dept. of Education (ED-01-CO-0010). Retrieved November 21, 2008, from http://www.alliance.brown.edu/tdl/minteachrcrt.shtml

Tripses, J. S. (2006). Best practices: Statewide collaborations to strengthen school leadership. In F. L. Dembowski & L. K. Lemasters (Eds.), *Unbridled spirit: Best practices in educational administration—The 2006 yearbook of the National Council of Professors of Educational Administration* (ch. 18). Lancaster, PA: DEStech Publications.

Trowbridge, S. (2007). Educational rituals: Questioning how we educate our children. *Phi Delta Kappan, 88*(5), 395–398.

Tubbs, J. E., Terry, D., & Chan, T. C. (2006). As the crow flies. Case study in K. T. Henson. *Curriculum planning: Integrating multiculturalism, constructivism, and education reform* (3rd. ed.). Long Grove, IL: Waveland Press.

Tuckman, B. W. (1965). Developmental sequence in small groups. *Psychological Bulletin, 63*(6), 384–399.

Tuckman, B. W., & Jensen, M. A. C. (1977). Stages of small group development revisited. *Group and Organizational Studies, 2*(4), 419–427.

Turley, S., Powers, S., & Nakai, K. (2006). Beginning teachers' confidence before and after induction. *Action in Teacher Education 28*(1), 27–39.

Tuttle, H. G. (2006). Creating a tech-infused culture. *Technology and learning, 26*(11), 12–16.

Tyack, D. (1995). Reinventing schooling. In D. Ravitch & M. A. Vinovskis (Eds.), *Learning from the past*. Baltimore, MD: The Johns Hopkins University Press.

U.S. Department of Education. (2005a). *Educational technology fact sheet.* Retrieved March 19, 2009, from http://www.ed.gov/about/offices/list/os/technology/facts.html

U.S. Department of Education. (2005b, Jan. 7). U.S. Department of Education releases national educational technology plan: Next steps lead to a new golden in American education. [press release]. Retrieved March 19, 2009, from http://www.ed.gov/news/pressreleases/2005/01/01072005.html

Unger, (1994). What teaching for understanding looks like. *Educational Leadership, 51*(5), 8–10.

Veronikas, S. W., & Shaughnessy, M. F. (2004). Teaching and learning in a hybrid world: An interview with Caroll Twigg. *EDUCAUSE Review, 39*(4), 50–52.

Warner, A. (2010). Philosophies in conflict. Case study in K. T. Henson, *Curriculum planning: Integrating multiculturalism, constructivism, and education reform* (4th ed.). Long Grove, IL: Waveland Press.

Watkins, S., & McCaw, D. (2007). The tipping point: Knowledge, failure at the vision, mission, and core values level. In L. K. Lemasters & R. Papa (Eds.), *At the tipping point: Navigating the course for the preparation of educational administrators—The 2007 yearbook of the National Council of Professors of Educational Administration* (pp. 433–442). Lancaster, PA: DEStech Publications.

Watson, N. (2001). Promising practices: What does it really take to make a difference? *Education Canada, 40*(4), 4–6.

Wayman, J. (2005). Involving teachers in data-driven decision making: Using computer data systems to support teacher inquiry and reflection. *Journal of Education for Students Placed at Risk, 10*(3), 295–308.

Weaver, R., Kowalski, T., & Pfaller, J. (1994). Case method in teaching. In K. Pritchard & R. Sawyer (Eds.), *Handbook of college teaching: Theory and applications.* New York: Greenwood.

Weishaar, M. K., Borsa, J. C., & Weishaar, P. M. (2007). *Inclusive educational administration* (2nd ed.). Long Grove, IL: Waveland Press.

Wenglinsky, H., & Silverstein, S. C. (2006/2007). The science training teachers need. *Educational Leadership, 64*(4), 24–29.

Wherry, J. H. (2007). Back to school: A fresh start for parent involvement. *Principal, 87*(1), 8–9.

Wiburg, K. M., & Brown, S. W. (2006). *Lesson study communities.* Thousand Oaks, CA: Corwin Press.

Wiggins, G. (1989). Teaching to the authentic test. *Educational Leadership, 46*(7), 41–47.

Wildman, L. (2006a). Best practice: Instructional leadership through teacher evaluation. In F. L. Dembowski & L. K. Lemasters (Eds.), *Unbridled spirit: Best practices in educational administration—The 2006 yearbook of the National Council of Professors of Educational Administration.* Lancaster, PA: DEStech Publications.

Wildman, L. (2006b). The basic antinomy. In L. K. Lemasters & R. Papa (Eds.), *Navigating the course for the preparation of educational administrators—The 2007 yearbook of the National Council of Professors of Educational Administration* (pp. 7–19). Lancaster, PA: DEStech Publications.

Wildman, L. (2007). Best practices: Instructional leadership through teacher evaluation. In F. L. Dembowski & L. K. Lemasters (Eds.), *Unbridled spirit: Best practices in educational administration—The 2006 yearbook of the National Council of Professors of Educational Administration* (ch. 4). Lancaster, PA: DEStech Publications.

Williams-Boyd, P. (2004). Abandoned adolescence and a cry for help. Case study in K. T. Henson, *Constructivist teaching strategies for diverse middle-level classrooms.* Boston: Allyn & Bacon.

Willis, J. W., & Mehlinger, H. D. (1996). Information technology and teacher education. In J. Sikula, T. J. Buttery, & E. Guyton (Eds.), *Association of Teacher Educators handbook of research on teacher education* (2nd ed.). New York: Macmillan.

Windschitl, M. (2006). Why we can't talk to one another about science education reform. *Phi Delta Kappan, 87*(5), 349–355.

Wineburg, S. (2006). A sobering big idea. *Phi Delta Kappan, 87*(5), 401–402.

Wolfe, M. P., & Smith, M. (1996). Inducting new teachers: Insights for staff developers. *Kappa Delta Pi Record, 32*(3), 82–86.

Wolk, R. (2004). Think the unthinkable. *Educational Horizons, 82*(4), 268–283.

Wood, G. H. (2002). *Schools that work: America's most innovative public education programs.* New York: Plume/Penguin.

Wood, P. (2002). *No Child Left Behind Act of 2001.* Westerville, OH: National Middle School Association.

Woods, D. (2008). Web sites to know. Teacher professional development sourcebook 2008. *Teacher Magazine, 1*(2), 10. Retrieved January 21, 2008, from http://www.teachermagazine.org/tsb/articles/2008/03/01/02websites.h01.html

Woolfolk Hoy, A., & Hoy, W. K. (2009). *Instructional leadership: A research-based guide to learning in schools* (3rd ed.). Boston: Allyn & Bacon.

Wright, R. (1995). Motivating teacher involvement in professional growth activities. *The Canadian Administrator, 5,* 1–6.

Wulf, K. M., & Schane, B. (1994). *Curriculum design.* Glenview, IL: Scott, Foresman.

Zeichner, K. (2005, December). *Professional development school partnerships: A place for teacher learning.* Retrieved December 3, 2008, from New Horizons for Learning Web site: http://www.newhorizons.org/spneeds/inclusion/staff/zeichner.htm

Zepeda, S. J., & Ponticell, J. A. (1996). Classroom climate and first-year teachers. *Kappa Delta Pi Record, 32*(3), 91–93.

Name Index

Subject Index